THE WORLD OF COMPUTERS AND DATA PROCESSING

The World of Computers and Data Processing

Marilyn A. Schnake
City College of San Francisco

West Publishing Company
St. Paul New York Los Angeles San Francisco

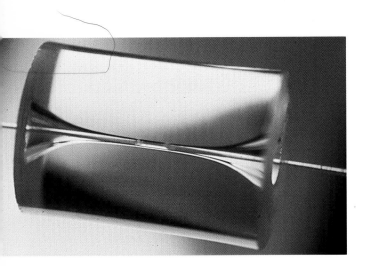

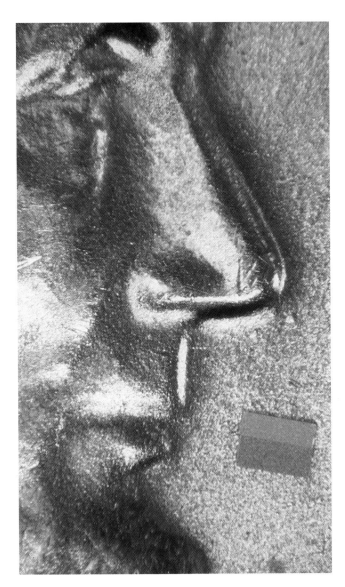

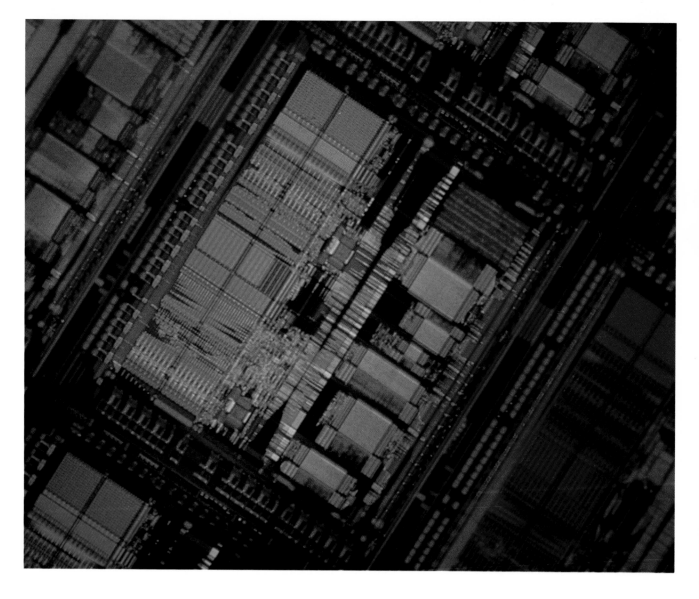

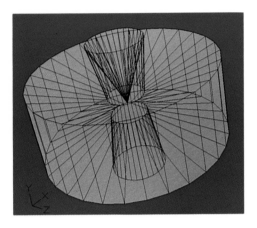

COPYRIGHT © 1985 By WEST PUBLISHING COMPANY
50 West Kellogg Boulevard
P.O. Box 64526
St. Paul, MN 55164-0526

Compositor: Parkwood
Artwork: Li Griener
Intext Design: Bruce Kortebien

Library of Congress Cataloging in Publication Data

Schnake, Marilyn.
    The world of computers

    Includes bibliographies and index.
    1. Computers. I. Title.
QA76.S3586   1985   001.64   84-29195
ISBN 0-314-85295-6

Cover Photo

A heliosiesmological view of an interior of a star. The photo shows a cut away view of the sun with one of the modes of the five minute oscillation. The right meridional plane shows the rate of energy generated in the solar core and the location of the convection zone.

Prepared by Dr. John W. Harvey of the National Solar Observatory. © 1984 NOAO.

Intext Photo Credits

xvii. *left:*—Peter Arnold. Photo by Bonnie Freer; *right:* Photo by Jerry Bushey.
xviii. Reprinted with the permission of International Business Machines Corporation.

Chapter 1 Woodfin Camp and Associates. Photographer John Blaustein. **Fig. 1.4** Optronics International. **Fig. 1.5** (*a*) and (*b*) Courtesy of Hewlett-Packard. **Fig. 1.6** Courtesy of Sperry Univac Corporation. **Fig. 1.7** Courtesy of Control Data Corporation. **Fig. 1.8** (*b*) Courtesy of NCR Corporation. **Fig. 1.12** Courtesy of Amdahl Corporation. **Fig. 1.13** Courtesy of Versatec. **Fig. 1.14** Courtesy of Zilog Corporation. **Fig. 1.15** (*a*) Courtesy of Hewlett-Packard; (*b*) Courtesy of NCR Corporation. **Fig. 1.17** (*a*) Courtesy of Wang; (*b*) Courtesy of Conrail Corporation. **Chapter 2** Courtesy of Sperry Univac Corporation. **Fig. 2.6** (*a*) and (*b*) Courtesy of Atari; (*c*) Courtesy of Apple

Credits are continued following the index.

Contents

Preface xx

PART ONE
Introduction 1

Chapter 1
General Introduction to
Computing 2

Chapter 2

Introduction To Digital Computers: Tool of the Human Mind 36

Chapter 3

Computer Systems 68

Chapter 4
Data Manipulation 98

PART TWO
Micros 129

Chapter 5
Microcomputer Hardware 130

Chapter 6

Microcomputer Software 160

PART THREE
Larger Computer Systems 193

Chapter 7

Central Processing Unit 194

Chapter 8
Input and Output Devices 226

Chapter 9
Secondary Storage 266

Chapter 10

Data Communications With Distributed Data Processing 304

PART FOUR
Software 353

Chapter 11

Beginning Programming 354

Chapter 12
Applications and Systems Programs 406

PART FIVE
Systems 447

Chapter 13
Management Information System 448

Chapter 14
Data Base
Processing   472

Chapter 15
Systems Analysis and
Design   500

Chapter 16

The Automated
Office   518

PART SIX
Today and
Tomorrow   545

Chapter 17

Computers and
Society   546

Chapter 18

The Future? 570

Appendix A

BASIC Programming A-1

Appendix B

Intermediate BASIC Programming   B-1

Appendix C

The Central Processing Unit   C-1

Appendix D

Evolution of Computers:
How It All Began   D-1

Color Galleries

Preface

When the development of this text began the question was raised: How do we make a textbook appealing enough that it will motivate, involve, and interest a student? Our answer to this question was to stress content, pedagogy, and style.

CONTENT

As the author, I tried to focus on current as well as relevant material. In order to give the student a flavor of the real world of computers and data processing, eighteen **People in Computing** essays are included. These follow every chapter.

Because of the high-interest in, and prominence of microcomputers, two complete chapters on microcomputers are included early in the text. (Chapters 5 and 6). These chapters are followed by a discussion on the availability of public domain software which stresses the use of bulletin boards, local users, and special interest groups.

To maintain an equal balance of coverage among minicomputers, mainframes, super-computers, and microcomputers, applications appear in over eighty-five high-interest boxes. These applications have been titled—WHAT'S RIGHT, WHAT'S NEW, and WHAT IF—and they have been placed in the text margins of every chapter. They focus on current uses in business, industry, education, and science. Further, a major real-life application from actual companies or institutions appear at the end of each part.

For a student to understand the detail involved in programming and problem solving, problem solving and data manipulation are stressed. Twenty projects in all are provided at the end of these chapters for reinforcement.

To provide "hands-on" experience in the BASIC language, the material is set up in Appendixes A and B so that the language, if desired, can be used in the curriculum in accordance with the professor's timing preference. Over twenty programs are included in the appendices. A *software diskette supplement* by the author is also available.

A comparative language chapter is provided stressing such languages as ALGOL, BASIC, C, COBOL, FORTH, FORTRAN, LISP, Logo, Modula-2, Pascal, PL/I, Report Program Generator, and SNOBOL. The same data was initialized in each of these languages and multiplication was performed as well. Straightforward programs of Ada, C, COBOL, and Pascal are presented because of the high-interest in them.

PEDAGOGY

To facilitate student learning the following have been incorporated in each chapter.

● A *chapter prologue* to set the stage for the material.

● *Chapter objectives* to emphasize the material to be covered.

● A *chapter outline* to organize the material.

● An *introduction* to state the need for such material.

● *Checkpoints* within the text to allow the student to test his or her comprehension of the material covered.

● An *in-text study guide* gives a terminology list, true/false questions, review questions, and discussion questions as well as projects where appropriate.

SUPPLEMENTARY MATERIALS

A *student workbook* has been prepared by the author for reinforcing concepts and terms presented in each chapter. This workbook contains short answer questions and suggestions for the solution of the projects presented in the chapter.

An *instructor's manual with testbank,* prepared by the author, outlines each chapter and provides suggestions, answers to review questions, discussion questions, and projects. The testbank includes over two thousand questions.

Transparencies are available on selected figures for adopters of this book.

ACKNOWLEDGEMENTS

It is with the deepest respect and gratitude that I write this thank you. To those dedicated professionals who provided the essays for the **People In Computing** sections at the end of the chapters, I wish to thank you for taking time from your busy schedules in order to impart to my readers your perspective on your specialized work. I am grateful to the companies who supplied company projects. A special thanks is extended to Thomas Dolan of Avon Products; Istvan Kadar and David May of Bechtel Group, Inc; Ronald Armijo of Chevron Corporation; Richard Dolan of Hewlett-Packard Company; Patricia Jent and Patricia Frey of Procter & Gamble Company; and Sergeant Moses and Sergeant Carlson of the San Francisco Crime Laboratory.

To Dave Martin at Optical Storage International, I thank him for his help and interest in this project. To Paul Hewitt, my fellow colleague who drew the cartoons in the text and in the student workbook, may I never forget him for his friendship and kindness. To Suzanne Beauregard of Sybex Computer Books goes a special thanks for her sponsoring of the Sybex Pioneer Days and for her special considerations and cooperation. Al McChristy of Executive Presentation Systems of Northern California also deserves a sincere thanks.

I am also indebted to the following reviewers who dedicated their time for the sake of creativity. Their suggestions were most helpful; their critical eye gave me a look at how they view the subject matter. I would like to mention each of these reviewers by name and school: Hossein Bidgoli, Portland State University, Oregon; Janis J. Bitely, Henry Ford Community College, Michigan; William C. Carr, Los Angeles City College, California; Marilyn J. Correa, Polk Community College, Florida; Carl W. DeWitt, College of San Mateo, California; Robert S. Fritz, American River College, California; Rod Heisterberg, Austin Community College, Texas; Lorinda L. Hite, Owens Technical College, Ohio; Jack J. Kaufman, University of Idaho; Linda Loft, Lane Community College, Oregon; Nancy Miner, California State University, Sacramento; Kathleen Ott, New Mexico Junior College; Harold Sackman, California State, Los Angeles; Sharon C. Sipe, Prince George's Community College, Maryland; Ronald Williams, Central Piedmont Community College, North Carolina.

And to the people at West Publishing who never failed to give me continual support and encouragement, may I thank you and express my gratitude. In particular I wish to mention Peter Marshall, my editor, for extending me the opportunity to publish this text. His imagination, creativity, understanding, and sense of humor are to be commended. To John Orr, whose responsibility is a mammouth one as Senior Production Editor, I cannot say enough for his continual support and encouragement, his creativity, and his dedication to excellence. And to Li Griener, the artist, I thank him for his creative and very fresh ideas on illustrations. And then there always is someone who gives that special type of extensive help and encouragement when deadlines seemed impossible and the volume of work seemed overwhelming. That special person is Judy Rowe.

Finally, I'd like to dedicate this book to that one person who is the motivating force and source of constant inspiration in my life—my mother.

Marilyn A. Schnake
San Francisco, California
January, 1985

PART ONE

Introduction

1 General Introduction to Computing

OUTLINE

PROLOGUE

"Good morning, ladies and gentlemen. Welcome to the first class session analyzing international customs and language. We will find that there are many differences; yet, there are many similarities. One word does come to mind that is pronounced the same regardless of language. I will not tell you what the word is just yet but through various reading assignments in many languages you will find that it is an amazing tool for expanding the power of our mind."

"I know the word is *computer*, Dr. Christian, but I won't tell how it is so useful to all of us."

HOW DOES IT DO THAT?

READ ON.

OBJECTIVES

After studying this chapter, you should be able to:

1. Define data processing.

2. Differentiate between data and information.

3. Differentiate among the uses for computers in various sectors: business, scientific, government, personal, medical, and educational.

4. Explain in what respects the computer's abilities are superior to human's.

5. Identify the types of computers.

6. Differentiate among the types of processing: on-line, real-time, and batch.

7. Identify some of the careers associated with using computers.

INTRODUCTION

Computers are everywhere, sometimes appearing in unexpected places and roles. Scientists, radio and television newscasters and sportscasters, auto mechanics, and secretaries all use computers in their work. Computer use in the home, in addition, is now a fact.

Computers are not newcomers to the world of business; in fact they have revolutionized the way businesses operate. Formerly, a company knew its financial status at the end of the month, but today a company can examine its net worth hourly if this is desired. Thus it can make better investments, putting its capital to work on short-term as well as long-term investments.

Nor are computers newcomers to the field of research; they have helped immeasurably in research performance and success. Would space exploration ever have been attempted without the use of computers? It would be impossible for humans to make the needed calculations for space exploration by hand-held calculator.

Computers have captured much attention; they are commonly center-stage in the world today, as shown in Figure 1.1. The computer's wide-range effect is felt both by the **user** (anyone requiring the use of some computer service, say, to have a report prepared) and by the **end-user** (a person using the computer as an adjunct to his or her regular work—for example, clerks, accountants, factory line supervisors, bank vice-presidents, and sports announcers). It is becoming essential to have a degree of computer literacy, which means having some idea of what makes up a computer, how it is used, and how it affects everyday lives.

Mystique often surrounds the world of data processing. Some people think that the person who is involved with computers is a math and electronics wizard who performs the magic of programming, depressing keys all day communicating with a computer. These images are myths.

In the 1970s, for a person to have his or her own computer was indeed a dream; today it is a reality. The home computer market in a five-year period grew from zero to $3 billion. Retailing of computers, calculators, computer games, books, programs, and supplies jumped from a $300 million market in 1978 to a $600 million market in 1979. By 1983, this figure surpassed the $12 billion figure. The total dollars involved in the entire industry, including repair of computers, exceeds $1 trillion.

There are many reasons for the tremendous use of computers. The following pages of this text look in depth at why computers are so popular as well as how the world of computers function. It concentrates on answering three major questions:

1. Why is it used?

2. How is it used?

3. Where is it used?

As we pass down the road of using computers always keep these three questions in mind. Enjoy!

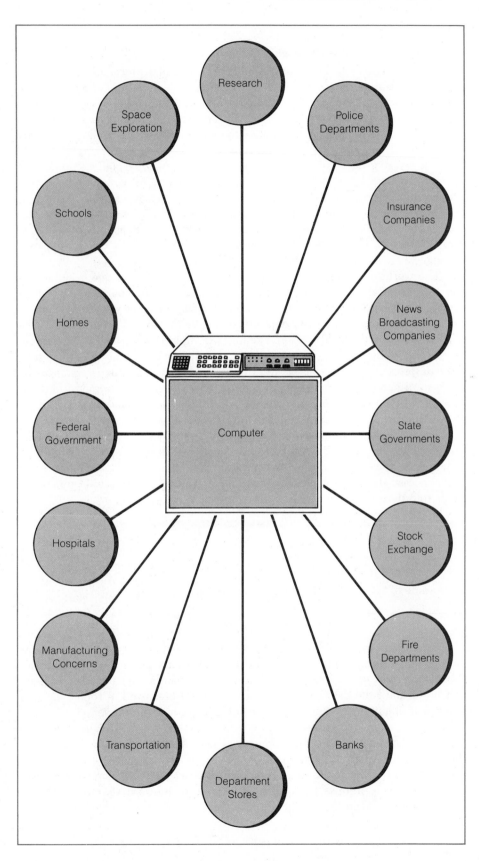

FIGURE 1.1
**The computer is the center of our
world today.**

INTRODUCTION

DATA PROCESSING

It is appropriate to begin by looking into the definition of the term *data processing*.

The word **data** means raw facts about some subject matter, which might be a person, an athletic event, a purchase, a banking account, and so on. For example, your name, address, birthplace, social security number, and major at school are data. The most important characteristics about data used with a computer are that it be accurate, complete, timely, and concise.

The word **processing** relates to how facts are handled and computed. A computer is built by people; thus its operation is based, in part, on how people process information. How does the brain use facts? Facts are stored, calculated, grouped by some common characteristic, rearranged, deleted, sorted into an order, analyzed for future use, and used for making decisions and predictions. This is how data is manipulated. All of these kinds of work are called **data processing**.

The world of data processing requires steady learning as new refinements and technological advancements continually appear on the horizon. Data processing is also a discipline of patience and accuracy. For those who enjoy change, challenge, and innovation, the data processing world holds interest; those who enjoy working with detail may find telling a computer what to do a challenge. Those who enjoy working with formulas and number crunching may fit best in the data processing world that is used in research or in scientific work. For the business-oriented, business data processing with its ever-increasing positions (for entering facts into the computer, using it to prepare letters and reports, selling computers, marketing computers, solving business problems) might be best.

The world of computers and data processing is everywhere. It is rare if anyone escapes it. Even ordering a hamburger at MacDonald's requires interaction with a computer; the cash register is a computer that adds the bill, remembers the order in case the employee needs to recall it, and even counts the number of items sold during the day.

CHECKPOINT Can you:

Identify data? Processing?

State some of the ways that data is manipulated?

It is important to differentiate between data and information. Data is raw facts, statistics, and news; **information** represents data that is in a useful form. Certainly a stack of invoices that represents a company's sales is not meaningful and useful until the data is sorted, calculated, and organized in report form. A heart beat of a patient, the selling price of gold, reduction of inventory, a set of fingerprints, a bank account balance, seat reservations for an airplane—all these represent data that is sensed, remembered, and analyzed by a computer, with the final result being information.

The level of economic indicators published by the U.S. Government is a composite which predicts the economic picture for the next six months. Many indicators are used in this prediction: the stock market, the banking institution,

WHAT IF

You and Data

Have you ever considered the number of pieces of paper that are prepared in a year from your purchases, completion of forms, and inquiries? Think of the invoice slips that are drawn up from your purchases. What about forms that you complete, for example, for magazine renewals?

What have you done today and yesterday that generated data? What experiences have you had with data that are not accurate, timely, or concise?

unemployment figures, and the money supply, to mention a few. Data is used to make this prediction; the state of the economy is the information. Information encompasses the analysis that is done on the data from the recording of it to the final report that is prepared.

Currently, the terms *data processing* and *information processing* are used almost interchangeably. The trend is slowly shifting to calling it **information processing,** however. When data processing began, the emphasis was on record-keeping—doing the payroll, inventory control, billing, and sales. Today computers still provide these services but also provide information for use in predictions for future expansion and trends and in intelligent decision making.

CHECKPOINT **Can you:**

Differentiate between information and data?

INFORMATION AGE

This is an information age. Over one-half of the U.S. work force is involved in information products or services, and the percentage is continually increasing. The information explosion has resulted in users being overwhelmed with facts. We must use only the significant ones.

Some users need information from a computer at almost the very instant information is requested by a user. To other users, however, timing is not so critical. The various needs of users must be satisfied reliably without a computer's cost being prohibitive.

Computer applications have spread into almost all types of work. An **application** refers to a type of work that is to be processed on the computer—for example, preparing a payroll, diagnosis of a disease, sales forecasting, inventory control, weather forecasting, processing of election returns, and grade point average calculation.

Even the attitude toward using computers has changed. In companies, management uses computers for intelligent decision making. In the late 1950s, management required certain applications to be run on a computer but then left a **programmer,** a person who instructs a computer what to do by the use of a language, almost totally on his or her own. Management personnel stayed far enough away in case a proposed project failed but yet close enough in case the application was a success. Today management no longer feels so threatened by computers, although having to give up some managerial decision-making power to a computer still seems threatening to some managers.

Our world today is indeed one of information. To think that a person's credit can be checked in less than 10 seconds is almost frightening. Over three million people's information is stored on the computers used by General Electric Corporation. It is for G.E.'s financial and credit authorizations, any of these people's information being available for recall.

The Data Base

Sometimes in a company, when one programmer talks to another about problems encountered with using the computer, both programmers find out to their surprise that the type of manipulation they are performing with data is much the same. Unless an exchange of problems exists in a company, there is often a duplication of effort. A communication channel must exist between departments of a company for determining the needs of users.

The use of a data base has helped greatly in alleviating some of these problems since it reduces the duplications of data manipulations that occur in different departments of a company. The data base contains the data and, hence, it separates data from the instructions that a programmer writes to tell the computer how to work with the data. Since data can be processed at very fast speeds, the use of the data base allows users to get at the desired data quickly.

With a data base, for example, using a simple example, at Peabody Brewery, Joe in the shipping department needs to know how much light and dark beer was brewed and bottled yesterday so he can fill the orders on hand. Susan in the buying department also needs to know how much beer was brewed yesterday so she can order the necessary malt and hops for future production. The needs of these two departments are rather obvious but it does illustrate that two departments can be using the same data in different ways.

The use of a data base throughout the entire company, however, rarely can be done because of the tremendous expense involved.

Think of a doctor concerned about a patient, perhaps unsure of the diagnosis; or a student preparing a report for a research paper; or a business that needs to know how a certain product has sold under certain conditions. Companies have recognized such needs and have collected much data and arranged it in a form that is usable by many people—a data base. A data base contains libraries of data that can be looked up electronically through the use of a computer. There are currently over 500 data bases that are available for a fee. The data contained in these large community-type files relate to a particular field such as law, journalism, agriculture, forestry, medicine, and the like. It takes time to collect the data for a data base, but patience and time are two very important commodities in the world of data processing.

A data base can also be set up for a particular organization or company, accumulating data stored by that group for its forecasting, planning, accounting, and general information. A user gets at the data (accesses it) in a data base by using the programs designed to find the desired data.

TYPES OF COMPUTING

There are many needs for processing data. Business data must be computed. Certainly scientific applications require extensive processing of data. Computing needs range from the monumental (government) to the modest (personal). In the field of medicine they can be most urgent. Computing needs in education are broad, encompassing all other types of processing of data. The other kinds of computing tend to be separated from each other by the type of work that each performs. All these types of computing are discussed in the following sections.

BUSINESS

Business data processing deals with the financial transactions of companies, for which there is usually a large volume of data to be processed by a computer. In business data processing, calculations are usually not terribly complex and do not require much processing time. Business data processing employs a tremendous amount of input and prepares a large amount of output. **Input** means the way of communicating with a computer in which a user supplies data that is to be processed by the computer. A user most often keys in data on hardware resembling a typewriter. Since **output** is the machine's way of communicating with users, the information that results from processing is prepared for a user, most commonly appearing in the form of a printed report. Output is only as good as the input used. There is an old saying "garbage in, garbage out," where **garbage** refers to meaningless data. Refer to Figure 1.2 for examples of the forms of input and to Figure 1.3 for examples of output.

Businesses may use a computer for graphics, generating various graphs and charts to show how much money is spent on the manufacturing of a product, on the marketing and distribution of it, and on the sale of it. These pie-shaped graphs and histograms are a common type of computer graphics.

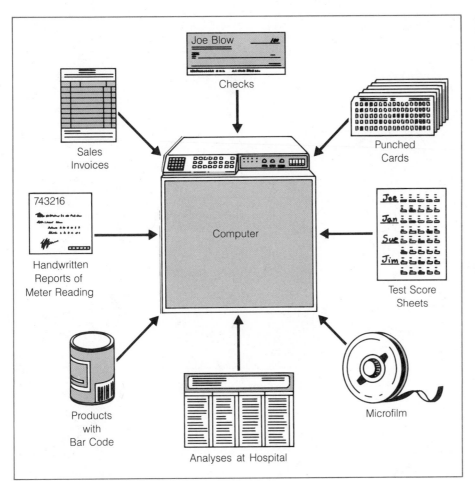

FIGURE 1.2.
The many forms of input to a computer.

SCIENTIFIC

Computing of data involves such sciences as chemistry, astrology, physics, research, space exploration, math, and statistics (also known as **scientific data processing**). Many complex calculations may be used. Just imagine all the calculations necessary to direct a satellite, to maintain or to change its orbit. Different calculations are needed to perform experiments and to transmit data back to earth. Calculations are performed in minutes by computers that would have taken years to calculate by hand.

Scientific data processing is involved in **image processing** as well, where pictures or images are generated by a series of numbers. Data can be manipulated into a picture or image or be analyzed statistically. Much of this type of work has been accomplished by the National Aeronautics and Space Administration (NASA) through its space explorations. Pictures, taken from the cameras in the satellites, are made up of a series of dots. Each dot can be coded by a number as to the intensity of the color that it represents. After the numbers are beamed back to earth from the satellite, the photographs are generated by a computer using the numerical data that color-codes the pictures. Refer to Figure 1.4.

FIGURE 1.3.
The many forms of output from a computer.

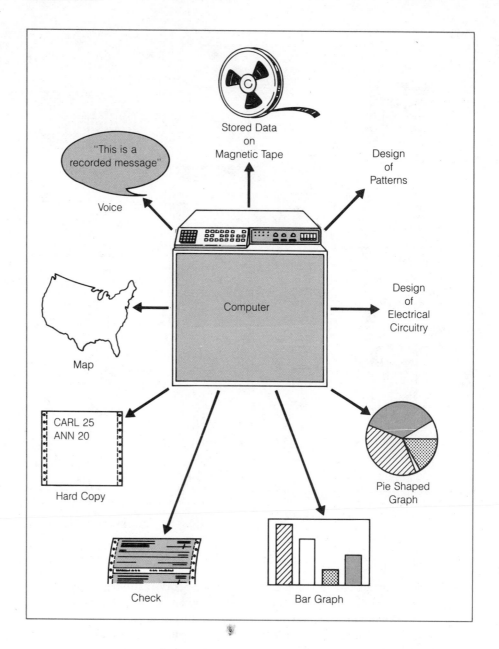

PERSONAL

Personal computing has been the focus of attention since the late 1970s. Never before have so many people had the opportunity to use computer equipment to meet personal needs. Before that time, the financial status of companies was run on computers, but the individual solved his or her financial status by the use of hand calculators or paper and pencil. Personal finance centered around the use of accounting ledgers.

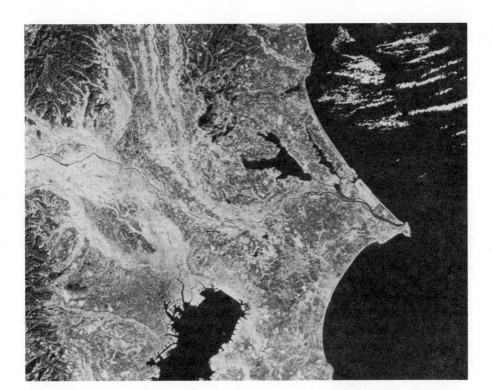

FIGURE 1.4.
Aerial photography where a computer calculates the angle with which the photo is to be taken.

People now use computers to calculate their finances; now a ledger is electronically calculated by the computer. The long columns of figures that required hand calculating are finished in a matter of seconds on a computer.

Where once correspondence was handwritten or typed, a computer can now be used for processing text, which is known as **word processing.** Formerly, when the typewriter was used, the person typed the letter as accurately as possible. Once the paper was removed from the typewriter, if errors were found the letter was retyped. With personal computers, word processing allows a letter, manuscript, report, or any text material to be typed (keyed), corrected, and neatly printed by a computer. A person can even purchase a program called a spelling checker which checks the spelling of the typed words.

Personal computing also allows anyone to use the public data bases for investigating facts about some desired subject area. Certainly the use of data bases is not limited to lawyers and doctors. A wealth of information on such subjects as the Dow Jones average, jobs available for a given type of expertise, the latest methodologies in cancer research, and campsites available for a vacation is readily available.

GOVERNMENT

Some of the biggest users of computers are the federal and state governments. An application that immediately comes to mind is the processing of income taxes.

City governments also use computers for the processing of property taxes. Even dogs cannot escape the use of computers; their required licenses are generated by computer equipment.

How often have you seen the highway patrol stop some speeder? The officer calls in the automobile license plate of the offender to check if the automobile is reported as stolen. The legitimacy of the driver's license can also be checked.

Budget figures for the data processing expenditures of government are difficult to comprehend. The federal government, for example, has over 18,000 computers and budgets over $600 billion.

MEDICAL

Computing in the field of medicine deals with investigation and research as well as calculations required for billing. More and more applications, however, deal with the retrieving (investigating) of information about illnesses of patients, with diagnoses of the illnesses, and with any relevant types of research being conducted. Years ago when a patient had a disease that was unknown or that person needed expert advice, top-rated physicians were flown in for consultation and diagnosis. Now, however, the expert system approach requires less time and effort. The expertise lies in a data base that is stored in a computer's theoretical filing cabinet (its memory). All facts about various cases are recorded and available for recall by a doctor. A doctor is then able to analyze what has happened in previous examples of such an illness, or what has resulted from certain treatments. Extensive readings from various tests are transmitted to a computer, which makes a comparison of these readings with those stored in its data base of previous histories.

EDUCATION

Computer applications centering around the educational aspect are wide open. Drill work has long been associated with computers. Computing emphasis, however, is now leaning toward the teaching of languages, writing, reading, counting, and all types of arithmetic. Preschool children are being exposed to computers as a fun tool, but the learning achieved is unbelievable.

Students in the fine arts are no longer restricted to paper for drawing, as the computer's television-like screen can be used. Students of mechanical drawing are now unlikely to use a drawing board; it has been replaced by a computer. Even students studying as choreographers use a computer for devising dance routines. Students studying music can write music on a computer, even testing it for sound.

CHECKPOINT **Can you:**

Identify some of the different types of computing in use today?

COMPUTER AS A TOOL

A computer is a combination of machines that work together. Many people talk about their **hardware** which refers to the physical pieces of equipment that make up a computer. Hardware is a very general name used to refer to all the electrical and electronic parts that make up a computer.

A computer is a tool, a tool for expanding the brain, that gives feedback (an exchange of ideas) of the thoughts and power of the mind. Like a tape recorder gives us feedback of sound, a computer gives us a feedback of the brain. Machines appear in department stores and in hospitals to give feedback of a person's blood pressure. Considering all other facets that make up the world, little wonder then that a computer can increase the user's intelligence and expand his or her breadth of understanding.

Just as the jack for a car gives the power to change a tire and binoculars give increased power to the eyes, a computer enhances the power of the mind by its accuracy, speed, and storage capability.

ACCURACY

In timing some athletic event, three judges might have three different times shown on their stop clocks just because of individual differences of response and reaction time. When contrasting a computer and a human, how many times can a human add a series of numbers and produce the same answer each time? A computer adds the same numbers two times or a million and has the correct result each time.

SPEED

The speed with which computers work is sometimes hard to imagine. Some computers do work measured in picoseconds; a **picosecond** is a trillionth of a second. Most computers operate in billionths of a second called **nanoseconds.** Other times a computer might require **microseconds** (millionths of a second) or **milliseconds** (thousandths of a second) to do some kind of processing. A computer scans through thousands of storage sites (roughly comparable to shuffling through as many manilla folders) to find one particular kind of information; this might take several milliseconds.

To get some idea of how fast a nanosecond is in the United States, imagine counting at the rate of one number per second. It would take you over thirty years to count a billion seconds. For a visual example of a billion, think of a stack of 10 million $100 bills. That equals $1 billion. The stack would be 3,700 feet high, or two-thirds of a mile. Wouldn't that catch the neighbor's eye?

Calculations are usually completed in microseconds. Comparing the speed of humans, a computer's speed is at the minimum 100,000 times faster. Not only are calculations done quickly, but some printers that prepare output can print 21,000 lines per minute while others might print 300 lines per minute. Isn't it amazing how fast the printer speeds are? What is even more amazing is that with speeds such as 21,000 lines per minute, these printers are still incredibly slow next to the computer's speed.

MEMORY

The purpose of computer memory is to hold data for later recall. As stated previously, a computer's memory enhances the power of our mind by increasing the number of facts that can be retained and manipulated. Think of memory as being like an enormous filing cabinet. The user sets up some filing technique so the data once stored there can be retrieved later. Instead of setting thoughts and notes down on paper, and then filing them away in a drawer, we can place these facts in a computer's memory by storing them. The tremendous advantages of using a computer's memory are both the speed and flexibility with which we can access (find) data.

One type of memory can hold information for as long as desired by the user unless the electrical power is lost or removed. There are other types of memory that can be used repeatedly without a computer "forgetting" or altering the facts unless the user directs it to change.

A telephone directory can be equated to a data base which can be stored in the memory of a computer. Have you ever called a large company asking for a certain employee and hear the clicking of the keys over the telephone? The telephone operator is inputting the person's name you are trying to reach. The computer memory is accessed and the telephone number is made available to you in a matter of seconds.

CHECKPOINT Can you:

Explain why a computer is a tool of the mind?

Tell how accurate a computer is?

Identify some of its operating speeds?

Explain the purpose of computer memory?

CLASSIFICATION OF COMPUTERS

There are three types of computers: analog, digital, and hybrid.

ANALOG COMPUTERS

An **analog computer,** shown in Figure 1.5, is a type of measuring equipment. It measures varying physical or electrical quantities such as pressure, temperature,

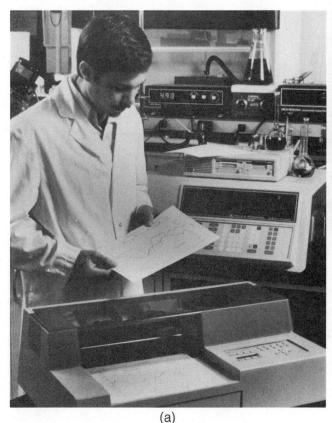

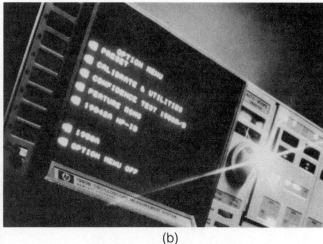

(b)

FIGURE 1.5.
Scientific world uses equipment for measuring. *(a)* UV/Visible Spectrophotometer works with a plotter which provides kinetics measurements. *(b)* Oscilloscope systems used to perform tests and adjustments on complex electronic equipment.

(a)

and voltage and is often used in scientific work. If, for example, an analysis is run to determine the amount of sugar in a person's blood, the computer is used for preparing the sample by mixing blood with proper reagents, giving a colored solution. The more intense or darker the color is, the higher the sugar content in the blood. An analog computer puts voltages and currents into a divider network to come out with different voltages that are measured to get the answer. It is like a meter that swings. In some analog computers used for blood analysis, twenty people's blood can be analyzed at once.

DIGITAL COMPUTERS

A **digital computer,** shown in Figure 1.6, is the most popular of all types of computers. A digital computer counts very carefully. It must be directed by us as to what it is to do with data. We write a step by step set of instructions that clearly specifies what the computer is to do. These instructions make up a **program.** Programs that are supplied by the manufacturer of the hardware or those programs written by a user or a programmer are known as **software.** Software is to be contrasted with hardware, the latter being the equipment.

A digital computer can do any kind of data manipulation without operator intervention and can do the manipulation in any order as long as the computer is instructed what to do. What determines when the data is to be sorted, calculated,

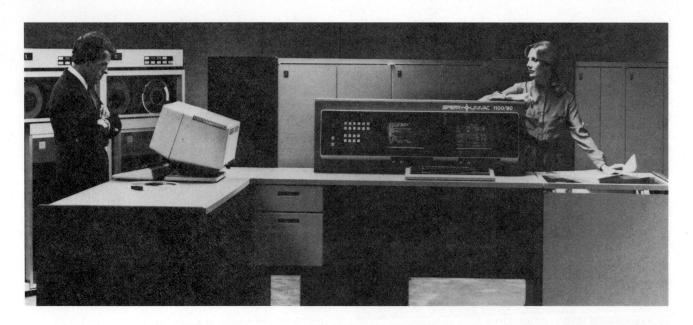

FIGURE 1.6.
Sperry 1100/90.

or printed? It is a computer program that makes the processing happen. For a payroll program, for example, a programmer had to write the details as to how the job is to be processed. A program tells a computer very precisely what it is to do. Amazing isn't it. A computer does not even know how to turn itself on or off.

HYBRID COMPUTERS

A **hybrid computer** combines both an analog and digital computer. It is used in some manufacturing and simulation, but its overall usage has declined since the 1960s and 1970s. In a steel mill, for example, there is an analog to digital conversion made in the measuring of temperatures, pressures, humidity, voltage, brightness, and other physical phenomena. An analog computer takes the measurements and transmits them to a digital computer which figures out, through a program, if any changes are needed.

Simulation is the representation of some physical phenomenon by means of operations performed by a computer. Simulation, as shown in Figure 1.7, is used for training pilots. An analogy can be made with the driver training course you might have had. An actual cockpit can be used. The pilot is put through such exercises as putting out fires, practicing crash landings, and flying through turbulence. Cartoons for crash landings begin on a television-like screen and are then projected on a movie screen. An enormous program of over 100,000 instructions has been written to make this simulation possible. To give you some idea of the extensiveness of the program, it would be like typing 1,500 single-spaced pages.

Simulation is becoming a part of the classroom in various disciplines, one of which is history. Battles of the Civil War and World War II are being recreated through simulation. This method of instruction provides meaningful and problem-

FIGURE 1.7.
Simulation.

solving situations for students. A student is given a series of criteria for making judgments. The choices are made and then the results are simulated, giving instant feedback.

CHECKPOINT **Can you:**

Explain why analog computers are used?

Explain when a digital computer is used?

Tell why a hybrid computer is used?

Explain simulation?

TYPES OF PROCESSING

Users have many processing needs requiring responses from a computer. A response from a computer refers to its looking up the desired data in its memory and returning the answer to a user. Sometimes data must be processed before the response is returned to the user. The timing of these responses is sometimes critical. Some users need a quick response, others need a response instantaneously, and others need answers or processing on the next day or in several days. To fit a user's time-frame three types of processing are available: on-line processing, real-time processing, and batch processing.

ON-LINE PROCESSING

When you shop in a grocery store, the Universal Product Code (UPC), as shown in Figure 1.8(a), identifies the product to the computer. It is from that bar code that a computer can determine the price to charge for each item. To change the price of an item, a product on the shelf need not be remarked; only the computer's memory need be changed. Refer to Figure 1.8(b). Each time someone buys an item, a computer looks up the price of that item. The price change is made once in the computer's memory. When the management of the grocery store wants to raise the price to its normal level, the computer's memory is again changed. This time, it will remember the last price instead of the sales price.

Each checkout station in this type of grocery store provides input to a computer elsewhere in the building; each requires special hardware so that it can communicate with that computer. A customer does not want to wait long for a response as to the price of the item purchased. A type of processing giving immediate feedback is called **on-line processing.** Each of the checkout stations is on-line to a computer. They are electronically connected to that computer so that each can send as well as receive data quickly—for example, in several nanoseconds (billionths of a second). Refer to Figure 1.9.

On-line processing is also often used by those companies which deal in rental cars and schools that provide computer services to students.

REAL-TIME PROCESSING

Airlines have been using a computer reservation service since the 1960s. A reservation is confirmed immediately. This capability is made possible by a network

FIGURE 1.8.

Grocery store check-out stands use computer equipment. *(a)* **Bar Codes.** *(b)* **Grocery check-out line.**

(a)

UNIVERSAL PRODUCT CODE (UPC)

100864-216736   173-559   233-353

EUROPEAN ARTICLE NUMBER CODE (EAN)

40153476   4014561780123   43214327

MSI BAR CODE

084954   493527372   274407

CODE 39

2367   BAR CODE   + %$-.+

CODABAR

12345   54321   01010   10101   99999

2 OF 5

123456   789012   010101

INTERLEAVED 2 OF 5

123456   789012   010101   666666

CODE 11

7645550   17645550   19137645550

(b)

FIGURE 1.9. **Bar code identify products.**

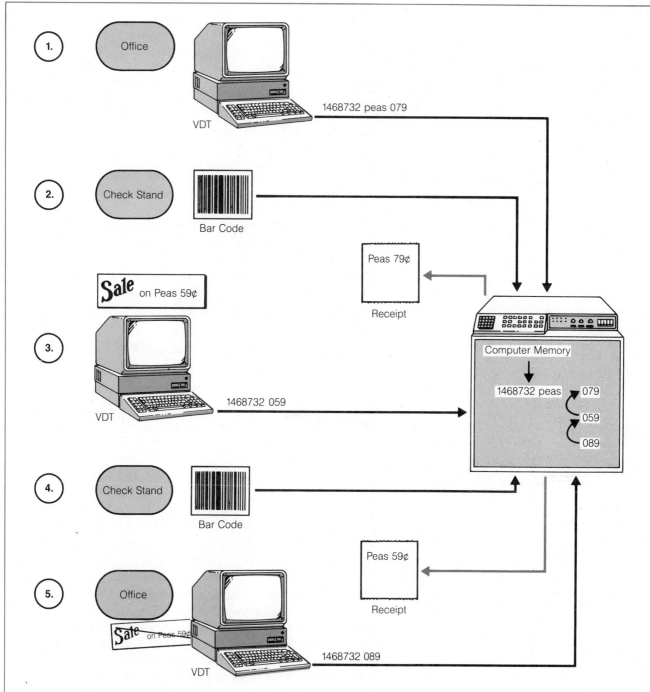

1. All pertinent stock data is keyed and stored in the computer memory.
2. When a purchase is made, the item is passed over the optical scanner which reads the bar code; this signals what stock data is to be looked up in the computer's memory.
3. Because of a sale, the price is changed by keying in the new price; the change is made in the computer's memory.
4. The sales price is correctly registered for a sale.
5. The price is changed when the sale is removed.

Key: Input ➡ Output ⬅

FIGURE 1.10.
Real-time processing.

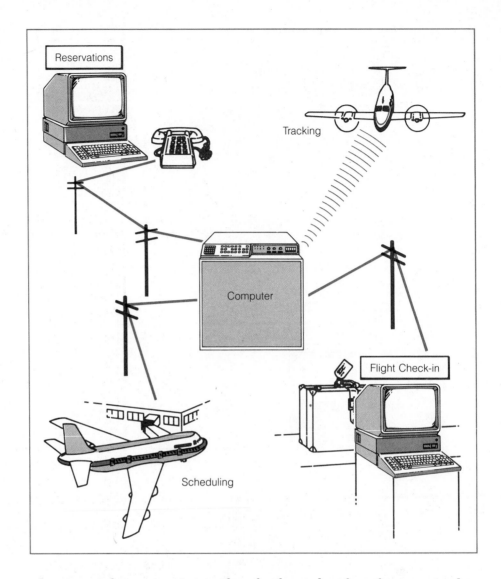

of computers that communicate with each other and perform the necessary data manipulations so a reservation can be made. This type of instantaneous processing is referred to as **real-time processing.** The major difference between real-time processing and on-line processing is the speed with which the data is handled, with real-time processing giving instantaneous responses. Refer to Figure 1.10.

Another example of real-time processing involves the space shuttle with its many computers operating in a critical timeframe. The twenty-four-hour teller banking machines have previously been associated with on-line processing. However, some checks are now being processed on a real-time basis.

BATCH PROCESSING

Assume that your college processes all student grades at one time. All instructors' grades must be turned in before any processing of student grades for a semester or quarter is begun. Student grades are processed as one group (batch), with the student numbers being previously sorted in order.

This processing example differs from the airlines reservation application since immediate responses are not given to a user. It also differs from on-line processing since a computer does not process the student records as they are received in the registrar's office, but groups them for processing during one machine run. This is an example of **batching** or **batch processing.**

Another example of batch processing could be the processing of all checks received at a bank during the day. The appropriate accounts are not updated (made current) until the batch is run. It must be pointed out that savings and loan institutions usually process savings accounts and loans, however, in real-time, so that they are instantaneously updated. Banks usually process their checking account transactions using batching. Indications are, however, that some banks have switched to the real-time processing as well. Refer to Figure 1.11. You might ask, why wouldn't all banks process in real-time? Often it is a matter of availability of a computer; it is a very busy machine. Another determining factor is how the program was originally written; it takes time to change programs.

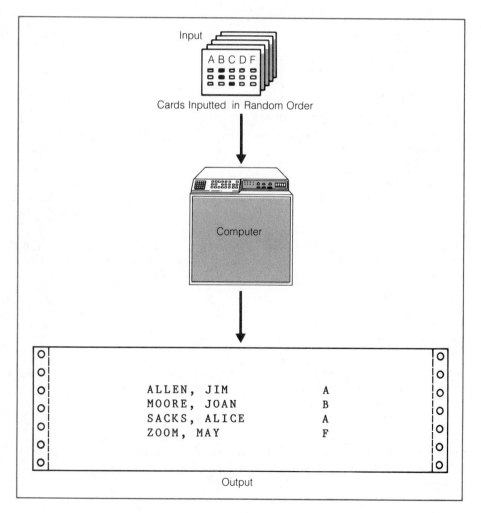

FIGURE 1.11.
Batch processing for a school application.

CHECKPOINT **Can you:**

Identify on-line processing?
Identify real-time processing?
Identify batch processing?

CAREERS IN COMPUTING

People in a great number of different careers use computers. Let us look specifically at computer use in careers that are business and scientific-oriented. It then directs attention to those people who deal directly with the computer, that is, data-processing department personnel.

BUSINESS

The accounting field is closely connected to the use of computers. There are computer-based standard cost systems. There are needs for electronic data-processing auditors who review new and existing systems to assure controls and minimize risks for a company. An accounting clerk deals with computer output continually and, through many of his or her job responsibilities, prepares data that later becomes input to the computer. The tax analyst designs input, output, processing specifications, and instruction guides to the users.

Many business people need to interact with computers in less comprehensive ways. Consider the economist who performs financial forecasts and prepares budget and financial analyses. Buyers must select saleable goods, so market surveys are used and analyzed. A claims processor in an insurance company needs information about the person's policy. All these needs can be met through computer use. Another aspect of the use of computers in the business world centers around the efforts of a time broker who brings the computing capability to many users.

SCIENTIFIC

Among fields of scientific endeavor for which computers are valuable, the work of nuclear physicists comes to mind. They use mathematical equations to do tests and to store test results.

Another scientific aspect of computer careers deals with the vast field of computer design, development, and testing. Working for a computer company provides many opportunities in engineering, sales, programming, and repair of hardware. For each opportunity there are two sides of the coin, namely hardware and software.

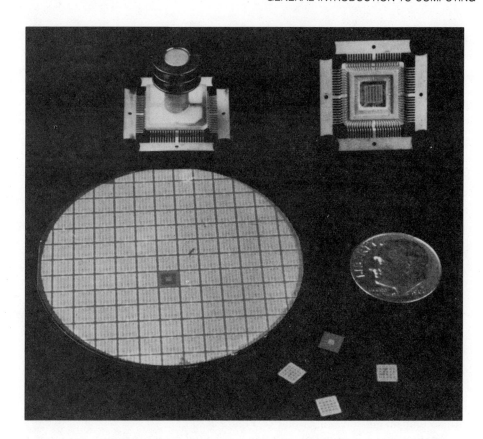

FIGURE 1.12.
An integrated circuit chip. These chips are from Wafer Stage at Production, to those being cut apart, to be mounted for use in computer equipment.

Regarding the hardware aspect, engineers design the complex circuitry on an integrated circuit chip. (See Figure 1.12). Thinking of an integrated circuit chip in layman's terms, it is a sophisticated printed circuit board (like those found in tv sets) that has been miniaturized.

Once formulated, the integrated circuit design must be tested before it is produced. A person who does drafting uses a graphics computer for testing the accuracy of the design of the integrated circuit chip to make certain that the circuitry does what is intended. The drafting person uses a **graphics computer** designed for preparing three-dimensional pictures. The pictured object can be made to turn on the television-like screen of a computer. Figure 1.13 shows the engineer holding the printed circuit board that contains many integrated circuit chips. The design of an integrated circuit appears on the television-like screen.

After the integrated circuit has been initially tested, it must be tested under operating conditions. Engineers use simulation to test, for example, if signals are being sent at the right clocking time. After the integrated circuit is produced, a program is used for probing the pins in the chip to check whether all circuits on the chip perform correctly. Think of those pins that look like little legs as being the external connection of the integrated circuit to the outside world. Refer to Figure 1.14.

People in science-oriented careers who need a graphics computer in their work are architectural designers, civil engineers, genetic scientists, and biologists. The previously mentioned business use of computer graphics in the form of pie-shaped graphs and histograms is a simple use; the testing of an oil drilling or the

FIGURE 1.13.
Engineer studies printed circuit board with integrated circuit chips assembled.

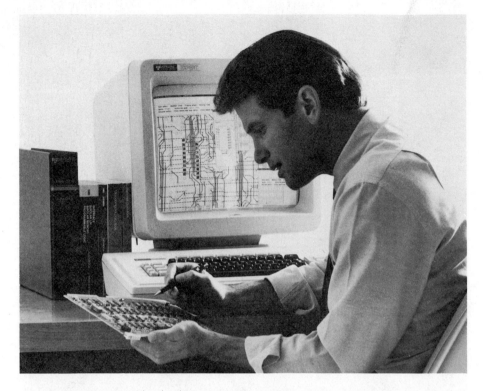

testing done by a civil engineer needs a far more sophisticated graphics computer with accompanying software. Refer to Figure 1.15.

Another example of people in science oriented careers who use a computer deals with research. A research person uses quality control by testing the data to determine if it is statistically significant or not. For example, a biochemist uses a three-dimensional atomic structure. He or she is trying to figure out how the atoms will bind, or in what configuration the binding can occur. Pharmaceutical

FIGURE 1.14.
Integrated circuit chips are mounted in carriers to be plugged into printed circuit boards.

GALLERY 1

Computers In Everyday Life

Where have computers not been part of our everyday lives? That is a difficult question to answer. Sometimes computers are visible; other times they are not. Let us investigate some of these areas that affect our entertainment, education, work, health, and scientific advancements.

1. A computer training center in Minneapolis. **2.** Colleges have used computers for registration for years, finding that the registration process is faster, more efficient, and more flexible. **3.** Automobile manufacturers and dealers proudly display the computerized dashboard.

4. Mechanics use the computerized diagnostic center for cars. State inspections, where demanded, use a computerized diagnostic center to record the results of the test of the car and to report the findings. **5.** A computer is used onboard a sailboat for communication to the outside world and for recording important memoires. **6.** Police use computers for tracking stolen automobiles, checking driver license and automobile registration, locating high crime areas and occurrences of crime, and for scheduling the officers locations and duties during the working hours.

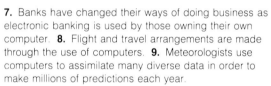

7. Banks have changed their ways of doing business as electronic banking is used by those owning their own computer. **8.** Flight and travel arrangements are made through the use of computers. **9.** Meteorologists use computers to assimilate many diverse data in order to make millions of predictions each year.

10. Gasoline companies have installed automated teller machines for customers' ease in paying bills by eliminating the need to use cash or check transactions. **11.** Computers are used in hotel lobbies for dispensing cash.

12

12. Young students are exposed to the advantages of using computers for drill work and for learning spatial concepts. **13.** Programming concepts are taught to young children so they can learn how to use the computer for their personal use.

13

14. A child enjoys the experiences of using computers for learning and for entertainment. **15.** The joys of computer games and computer arcades have challenged people of all ages. **16.** The very young are exposed early to computer-generated instruction. **17.** The very young can learn the essentials of math by making it an enjoyable challenge.

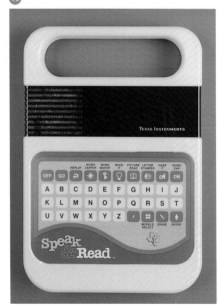

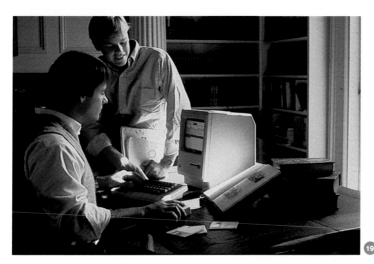

18. Although computer instruction occurs during the day, the student uses the computer for preparing homework papers in the dormitory. **19.** Two students discuss the preparing of a computer graphic project for a homework assignment. **20.** A computer is carried for use in the classroom; many colleges and universities insist upon a student owning one.

21. Each member of the family can use a computer to meet his or her processing needs.
22. A businessman takes his computer with him on business trips for recording the results of meetings and for preparing reports. **23.** A housewife enters important notes for easy reference.

(a)

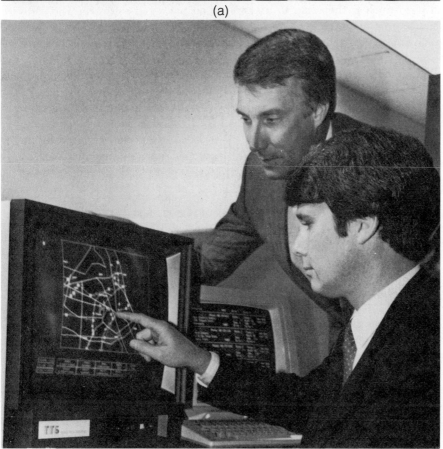

(b)

FIGURE 1.15.
Computer-aided engineering helps engineers in their work.
(a) **Graphics are used by engineers.** *(b)* **Civil engineers use computers.**

houses use this technique to find out if a drug can be produced. By using a graphics computer, the television-like screen can be viewed to determine the prospects of producing a particular drug.

The need for large computers generates some computer career opportunities. Large computers have been used for years in processing checks, insurance claims, and financial transactions. The manufacturers of these large computers must have a software staff that writes programs. Other jobs include technical writing and technical illustrating.

There are really two sides of the career coin for the manufacturers of large computers. Manufacturers of large computers sell the hardware and, separately, a software package that can be used on that computer. In the past, computer manufacturers sold the hardware and software as a package. There was one price for the combination of hardware and software which was referred to as being **bundled.** This meant that a user had to purchase the package whether the software was liked or not. Laws were enacted, however, making it mandatory, that software and hardware be sold separately (**unbundled**). This permits competition to flourish and provides a choice to a user on the software used.

As a result of these laws and ensuing competition, companies that deal just in software have come into being. They employ people whose responsibilities are to test the programs that are to be sold to the public. Any company-prepared software which is then sold to users is called **packaged software.** The software manufacturer may employ a technical writer, who uses the packaged software strictly from a user's standpoint to see if the **reference manual** that will be supplied to the user adequately details how the software or hardware is to be used. The computer manufacturer's reference manuals also provide hardware support for a user when a computer is rented, purchased, or leased by a user.

DATA-PROCESSING DEPARTMENT

Looking into the data-processing department of most installations, there are generally four groups: the operations group, the programming group, the systems group, and the technical support and repair group.

Operations Group

The **operations group** includes the computer operators, the data entry operators, the librarians, and the supervisors. The **computer operator** runs the computer. It is the operator's responsibility to make certain that the work flows through the computer in an efficient manner. Since a computer is used by many different departments of a company, the operator must be given instructions on all computer applications to be used. Figure 1.16(a) shows the operator mounting the magnetic disk (like a series of phonograph records) so the computer can use the data that is stored on it. Figure 1.16(b) shows the computer operator overseeing the operation of the computer.

The computer operator must be a reliable person who does not mind working under stress. The operator learns in detail the workings of the computer. Since

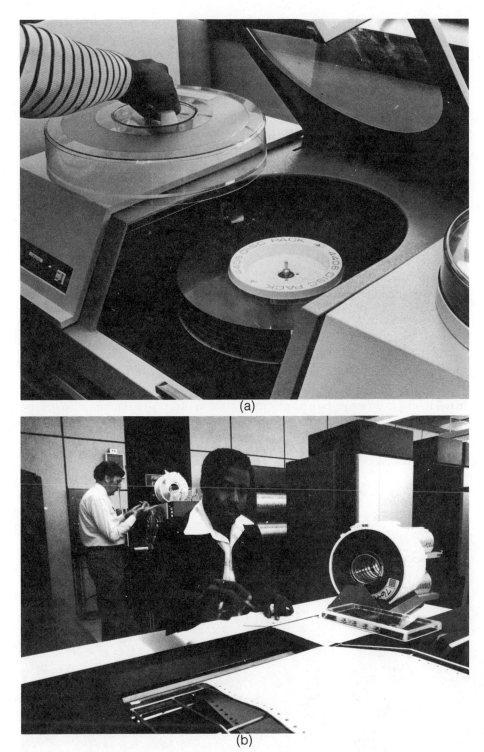

(a)

(b)

FIGURE 1.16.
Computer Operations.
(a) **Computer operator mounts magnetic disk in disk drive.**
(b) **Computer operator had previously mounted paper in printer.**

most computer centers work a twenty-four-hour day, the computer operator position is available for different shifts. Many students hold this job on the shift that works from 11 P.M. until 7 A.M., giving them the opportunity to attend school as well. The amount of training required for such a job depends upon the company. This type of job often acts as a springboard to a programming career as many companies promote from within for the programming positions. Since the turnover rate can be high for computer operators in some shops, a supervisory position is often possible in a relatively short period of time.

Data entry operator is another position available in the operations group; it entails entering data into a computer. Some possible equipment used for data entry is shown in Figure 1.17(a). Data is transferred to a computer through the use of electrical impulses that we might think of in the layman's sense as shots of electricity. This type of position requires good typing skills. The data entry operator position provides not only good exposure to the type of data that is used in a company but also gives the opportunity to become familiar with the way in which the data-processing system works.

Another position in the operations group is that of **librarian,** whose responsibility is to maintain and accurately identify all magnetic tapes used on the computer for storage of information. Librarians also manage the storage of programs that are written at a company. Figure 1.17(b) shows a librarian working with magnetic tape files for later use on the computer.

Programming Group

FIGURE 1.17.
Other aspects of computer operations. *(a)* **Data entry.** *(b)* **Tape librarian.**

The **programming group** includes jobs with different levels of programming sophistication. Programming involves the writing of instructions for the computer to tell it how to do some desired processing. Computers have their own languages, so the programmer must write the instructions in a format that the computer can understand. The program that the programmer codes must be fully tested on the computer to make certain it does the prescribed task. When the program is fully

(a)

(b)

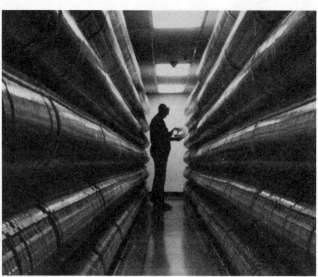

tested, the programmer prepares a written report which describes in detail what is being accomplished.

Necessary skill levels for programmers include problem-solving capability and good interpersonal communication. Important aptitudes include analytical reasoning, logical thinking, creativity, and good oral communication. The ability to communicate both orally and by written document and the ability to get along with others are important to the success of the individual. Programmers dealing with business applications are not required to be math geniuses, but a reasonable math background is expected. Programmers are basically told by the user the formulas and details needed for the application. Programmers dealing with scientific applications do need a good math background, however.

In the late 1970s and early 1980s, the job market was wide open for programmers with four-year degrees and for some with two-year degrees. The latter group began usually as **programmer trainees** who worked directly with a programmer, learning about programming and the company. After some experience, these trainees usually were promoted to programmer status.

Today's market, however, places great emphasis upon experience. The problem then becomes how you get the first programming job. There is a tremendous salary differential between experienced programmers and inexperienced ones. A sound goal for would-be programmers is to gain experience in the short run so you reap the benefits in the long run.

Systems Group

The **systems group** includes those specialized personnel who have perhaps in the past been programmers. Programming involves about one-third of the effort needed for a computer to process an application. The remaining two-thirds centers around the systems group. The **systems analyst** is someone who must continually and successfully interact with users. He or she must be able to look at a method, whether it be manual or computerized, and determine if its procedures can be improved. The systems analyst designs the entire system, including inputs, outputs, processing required, documentation (a written report), and more. Since the systems analyst's position is one of significant importance, this person usually has a good background in business and accounting. Programmers with about four years of experience can advance to this position.

Technical Support and Repair Group

The **technical support and repair group** plays an important role; its budget accounts for the most money spent after installation of the computer—approximately 30 percent of the installation costs. The group consists of the people with extensive hardware knowledge—those who concentrate on the setting of internal switches to make the machinery operate and who frequently check the computer for correct operations. The computer operator knows how to make the computer process a job, but the technical group knows what makes it operate.

This group also repairs the computer. Rather than paying for maintenance contracts or paying anywhere from $50 an hour on up to repair the computer, the major companies have their own groups, feeling that it is less expensive to pay a technician, whose salary averages about $30,000 per year.

The opportunities are there; it is up to you to take advantage of them.

CHECKPOINT **Can you:**

Identify some of the computing careers in business and science?

Identify the four groups in a data-processing department?

Distinguish among some of the jobs within each group?

Information Center

In the world of information, the user asks where can he or she get information on how you use this computer? How do you make it work? The user hears all these marvelous things that a computer can do, but, to make it work for you is quite another story.

Data processing professionals staff an **information center** that is designed to help computer users get started. Their intention is not to overwhelm a user with jargon or technical expertise, but rather to provide information on how to operate the computer. The center works on the concept that, although you are given a reference manual at purchase time, in practice you may need additional help.

The information center trains users how to use the hardware and the software that they purchased. The center's purpose is not to write programs for a user. Formerly software was developed mostly in-house by the user company. The trend, however, is changing towards the purchase of already-prepared software, for which a user only needs to know how to communicate with that software. Many users are not interested in programming. Their only purpose is to use the computer for bettering their job performance or for obtaining information that otherwise would never be available for analysis or use.

SUMMARY

- Data is facts or statistics that are in an unprocessed form. Information is data that is processed and meaningful.

- Data processing and information processing refer to the manipulation of data so that reports can be prepared and intelligent decisions made.

- Business data processing deals with the financial aspects of companies and involves large volumes of input and output.

- Scientific data processing deals with work involved in such disciplines as chemistry, astrology, physics, space exploration, and research.

• Scientific data processing concentrates on complex calculations and uses little input and output as compared to the calculations performed. Personal computing often involves word processing and financial analysis. Government computer applications are among the largest and most widely distributed; processing of taxes is one major application. Medical computing deals with billing, research, and retrieval of information. Computer applications in education are wide open, dealing with a wide range of subject matters.

• Its accuracy, speed, and storage capability make the computer an invaluable tool which has brought great change in the way that data is processed. It affects virtually every sector of society today.

• There are three types of computers: analog, digital, and hybrid. Analog computers measure varying physical or electrical quantities and are often used in scientific work. Digital computers, more frequently used by far, operate on data that are represented by separate, individual units; they are more accurate than analog computers. Hybrid computers combine both analog and digital computer functions; use of hybrid computers has declined over the past twenty years, but they are useful in simulations.

• A personal computer offers an individual opportunities for home computing that in the early 1970s seemed impossible.

• Three types of commonly used processing are batching, on-line, and real-time.

• Batching involves the collecting of all input data for an application and then processing the input as one computer run.

• On-line processing involves the use of special hardware that enables the user to get immediate responses from the computer.

• Real-time is a very sophisticated on-line system that gives instantaneous responses to the user.

• Computer-related careers abound in the fields of business and science, in addition to those careers directly associated with computing in the typical data-processing department.

• Business people such as accountants may use computers almost exclusively; other business occupations usually require at least some computer use.

• Scientists in various fields use computers to make calculations not possible if done manually. In addition, those who design, develop, test, and repair computers themselves hold scientific jobs. Engineers designing integrated circuit chips make use of graphics computers to observe the chips in three-dimensional perspective. Graphics computers have a number of other scientific research and test applications.

• Computer graphics used in business data processing are simple and do not require a graphics computer.

• Hardware and software must be sold separately, a state referred to as being unbundled.

• Opportunities for careers associated with a data-processing department are available in operations, programming, systems, and technical support and repair groups.

● The operations group usually includes data entry, librarians, and computer operators.

● Programming involves writing the program so the computer can be instructed on what to do as well as writing memos and documentation to substantiate the work.

● The systems analyst is involved in checking feasibility, designing the system, improving procedures, and documenting the system.

● The technical support and repair group have the responsibility for repairing computers and setting internal switches so that programs can be run.

● An information center provides training and helps users understand fully how a computer and program can be used.

STUDY GUIDE

REVIEW OF TERMINOLOGY

The following terminology was covered in the chapter:

analog computer
application
batching
batch processing
bundled
business data processing
computer operator
data
data base
data entry operator
data processing
digital computer
end-user
garbage
graphics computer
hardware
hybrid computer
image processing
information
information center
information processing
input
librarian
microsecond
millisecond
nanosecond
on-line processing
operations group
output
packaged software
picosecond
processing
program
programming group
programmer
programmer trainee
real-time processing
scientific data processing
simulation
software
systems analyst
systems group
technical support and
  repair group
unbundled
user
word processing

MULTIPLE CHOICE

Circle the item that completes each statement correctly.

1. All the physical components of a computer, electrical and electronic, are called:
   a. software
   b. analog computer
   c. digital computer
   d. hardware
   e. unbundled

2. Another name for meaningful facts is:
   a. data
   b. information
   c. input
   d. bundled
   e. garbage

3. This is designed for helping everyday users learn to use an already-prepared software package:
   a. help center
   b. end-user center
   c. information area
   d. information center
   e. hybrid center

4. The fastest of all computer speeds is:
   a. nanoseconds
   b. microseconds
   c. milliseconds
   d. picoseconds
   e. seconds

5. The slowest of all computer speeds is
   a. nanoseconds
   b. microseconds
   c. milliseconds
   d. picoseconds
   e. trillionths of a second

6. Information generated by a computer in report form is considered:

a. input   *d.* output
b. data   *e.* garbage
c. hardware

7. A drafting person or civil engineer needs three-dimensional pictures. They would use:
   a. a pie-shaped graph
   b. business computer graphics
   c. a graphics computer
   d. bundled hardware and software
   e. an analog computer

8. Computers usually have the capability of performing calculations in
   a. a second
   b. milliseconds
   c. nanoseconds
   d. picoseconds
   e. microseconds

9. This type of computer measures physical or electrical quantities continually:
   a. hybrid
   b. digital
   c. batch
   d. application
   e. analog

10. This type of computer is used for doing calculations, sorting, and asking questions:
    a. hybrid
    b. digital
    c. simulation
    d. batching
    e. analog

11. This type of computer is used for manufacturing products and for simulation:
    a. hybrid
    b. digital
    c. real-time
    d. analog
    e. applications

12. Which of the following is written by a human to direct a computer as to the steps it is to follow for solving a problem:
    a. hardware
    b. digital
    c. program
    d. information
    e. graphics computer

13. This type of processing gives the fastest response time to a user:
    a. picoseconds
    b. on-line
    c. batch
    d. real-time
    e. simulation

14. This type of processing collects all of its input together and then processes in one pass:
    a. applications
    b. batch
    c. on-line
    d. real-time
    e. software

15. This use of computers is for testing the accuracy with which some design functions:
    a. applications
    b. image processing
    c. simulation
    d. hybrid
    e. information processing

16. A millionth of a second is called a:
    a. microsecond
    b. millisecond
    c. picosecond
    d. nanosecond
    e. second

TRUE/FALSE QUESTIONS

Circle the T next to a true statement; the F if it is false.

1. **T/F** Your social security number, age, and birthplace are considered data.
2. **T/F** If the average age of all students in the United States taking an introductory data-processing course were to be calculated, this would be called processing.
3. **T/F** Information is exactly the same as data.
4. **T/F** The information age is soon to emerge.
5. **T/F** Personal computing always involves extensive complex calculations.
6. **T/F** Scientific data processing uses small amounts of input when compared to business data processing.
7. **T/F** Personal computing often involves word processing and personal finances.
8. **T/F** The only input a computer can use is numbers and alphabetic characters.
9. **T/F** An application refers to a job that is bundled.
10. **T/F** A computer operator's job is part of the supervisory group in the data processing department.
11. **T/F** A programmer trainee always has computer operator training.
12. **T/F** A systems analyst was a former programme in most cases.
13. **T/F** Most of the work involved in solving an application's needs is done by the programming group.

ANSWERS

REVIEW QUESTIONS

1. Define: data; data processing; garbage; hardware; software.
2. How does the computer expand the mind? How could a computer be useful to you?
3. What is a computer memory used for?
4. What are the three types of computers? How does each type differ from the others?
5. Name some applications for computing in business, in the sciences, for personal computing, in government, in medicine, and in education.
6. What is a microsecond? A millisecond? A picosecond? A nanosecond?
7. Why is ours called an information age?
8. What is word processing?
9. What does on-line processing mean? What is batching? What is real-time processing? Why are different types of processing necessary?
10. Cite some of the careers in general business that involve regular computer use.
11. Identify the four groups in a data-processing department. What positions are found in each group?
12. What job responsibilities does the computer operator have? What skills are important for this position?
13. What job responsibilities does a programmer have? What are the skills necessary for this position? What aptitudes are important for this position?

DISCUSSION QUESTIONS

1. In what types of instances would you have access to hybrid computers? To analog computers?
2. Explain in which aspects the computer is superior to humans. Give examples to support your answer.
3. The last days of December of each year, the U.S. Government sends out over 90 million tax forms. Give some examples of data that will appear on the completed forms. Contrast that data with the information that will result after the government has processed that data.

ADDITIONAL READINGS

It is important to keep abreast of the latest technological advancements that will affect computer users. The best way to keep current is to read periodicals. There are many excellent publications available; a few are listed for your convenience.

Computerworld 375 Cochituate Road, Route 30, Framingham, Maine 01701 (a weekly newspaper)

Datamation 1301 South Grove Avenue, Barrington, Illinois 60010 (a monthly magazine)

Computer Magazine P.O. Box 24008, Los Angeles, California 90024 (a monthly magazine published by IEEE Computer Society)

InfoWorld 375 Cochituate Road, Framingham, Maine 01701 (a weekly newspaper for the microcomputer industry)

Data Management 505 Busse Highway, Park Ridge, Il. 60068 (a monthly magazine published by the Data Processing Management Association)

PC World Subscription Department, P.O. Box 6700, Bergenfield, New Jersey 07621 (a monthly magazine published for those using an IBM Personal Computer)

People in Computing

David Best

COMPANY
Hambrecht & Quist, Inc., San Francisco

TITLE OF POSITION
Vice President Venture Capital

Hambrecht and Quist is a major direct venture capital firm, with its own funds as well as managed funds pooled from International and domestic sources. As an investment banking firm they provide a full range of financial and management support for high-technology companies—during start-up, with venture financing; through the developmental years with underwritings of private placements and initial public offerings; and throughout the growth and expansion phase, with debt and equity placements, merger and acquisition management, and maintenance of a market for a company's securities.

People look at venture capital as being mysterious. This is mostly due to the fact that there are no rules about how we go about our business other than those imposed by the Securities & Exchange Commission. There are no formulas. Venture capitalists make investment decisions on the basis of qualitative rather than quantitative factors. What you would think is a pretty cut-and-dried approach to making an investment decision, as you will see, is really "subjective reality".

Venture capital financing is a risk-oriented financing mechanism; a very specialized form of private equity placement. Basically, private investors are putting up money through a venture capital organization such as the one I represent. We channel that into young, high-growth companies which through their growth eventually go public, returning a profit back to the original private investors. That process has really flourished in the last few years. There is a lot more money under venture capital management today: over 9 billion dollars in fact.

A good venture capitalist is typically looking at an investment proposition with an orientation towards a long-term partnership with the company. The personal motivation of most venture capitalists is to be associated with large, on-going, and successful corporations, and so they take an immense amount of pride of authorship in helping to get firms of that stature up and running. This active investor involvement is really the "value added" from the venture capital community. It stands above and beyond the money in the measure of strength and it is a very important value added.

The availability of more money, and some tax law changes have stimulated a large number of new companies to get started with venture financing. Since 1981 over 50 percent of the investments in these new companies are in electronics-related fields. Even some of the new medical and health products are dominated by electronic related technologies.

Other investment areas include genetic engineering, industrial automation (robots), consumer, and energy. Less than twenty percent of the venture capital disbursements went into these last areas in the early years. Electronics is the dominant technology for venture investing.

The venture capitalist is looking for a unique or proprietary advantage; something that the company will have in its possession that will make it difficult for someone else to enter that same business. In general, capital intensity is not considered sufficient as a barrier to entry.

The entrepreneurial spirit is also a very important ingredient. This is a very illusive quality but it simply is the desire on the part of the starting team to build a new company and reap the financial rewards for the risks taken. This motive must be evident over others. For example, the venture capitalist will be testing if the team is more inclined to foster technology research for its own sake, or to simply draw a large salary. The entrepreneurial spirit is a very important motivator and it is a key ingredient. The amount of entrepreneurial spirit that is perceived may have a direct effect on the valuation of the company, or the type of controls that the venture capitalist would like to impose as part of the financing.

Because it is a high risk financing, a business plan (something that describes in detail the market, the product, the technology, why you will win, who the competitors are, the backgrounds of the people involved) is the essential communication vehicle with the venture world.

Be open and up front about both your accomplishments as well as short comings in your discussions with the venture community. After all, you're forming a long term alliance and partnership, not simply making a financial transaction.

2 Introduction To Digital Computers: Tools of the Human Mind

OUTLINE

PROLOGUE

Alex forgets his keys to his home, but he has no worry. All he does is walk to the front door and say "Open." He walks into the hallway and says "Close and lock." All of a sudden he realizes that his dog Rags is still in the yard, so he says "Unlock door."

Alex walks into the kitchen and finds the room unusually warm. "Cool to 73 degrees," he says. Rags barks; the door opens. Alex then says "Close and lock." Alex just can't teach Rags to bark after he comes in! The neighbors next door think something is "crazy" about Alex's house.

HOW DOES IT DO THAT?

READ ON.

OBJECTIVES

After studying this chapter, you should be able to:

1. Identify how data is set up in a hierarchical data structure.

2. Identify the functional parts of a digital computer.

3. Identify possible hardware associated with some computer systems.

4. Identify some basic hardware you could have for a personal computer.

5. Explain how data flows within a computer system.

INTRODUCTION

The digital computer is an amazing tool of our times. Consider the accuracy of space flights: the precision with which the mission is accomplished, the backup systems that are used, the way computers communicate with each other to make certain everything is going as scheduled, and the step-by-step procedures through which the mission proceeds. Consider, too, that Columbia I, the space shuttle, orbited the world thirty-six times and then touched down one minute off its predicted target touchdown time. Such impressive examples make undeniably clear the impact that digital computers have on our world. Yet, computer use does not require such a sophisticated atmosphere; in fact, computers are important to us in everyday life.

Regardless of their sophistication, computers do only three types of work. These are: calculations, logical operations, and storage and retrieval. Refer to Table 2.1.

Notice that each of these three types of work deals with data and how it is manipulated. Certainly the computer's capability to remember billions of characters of data is amazing. Its ability to do work in speeds such as picoseconds and nanoseconds can likewise seem unbelievable. To do work with few errors is also its extreme advantage. But the computer must be told what to do through the use of a series of instructions called a program. A program tells a computer when to calculate and to perform logical operations, what data to store, where to store the data in the memory, and when to retrieve data.

Data that is to be used by a computer must be accessible to users. Also, how the data is protected from misuse, its quality, and its accuracy are vital if the computer use application is to be successful.

To begin the discussion about digital computers, this chapter first looks into how data is organized for computer use so a user can access the data. Next, the parts of a digital computer are discussed. The way a computer program operates is then discussed.

HIERARCHICAL STRUCTURE OF DATA

Recalling that data means facts, all data stored in the memory of a computer is organized in a way that can be viewed as a hierarchical data structure, as shown in Figure 2.1(a). An example is shown in Figure 2.1(b).

TABLE 2.1. **Work Done by Computers.**

TYPE OF WORK	CAPABILITY
Calculations	Add, subtract, multiply, and divide
Logical Operations	Do comparisons
Storage and Retrieval	Store (remember) data in its memory
	Recall data that it stored in its memory

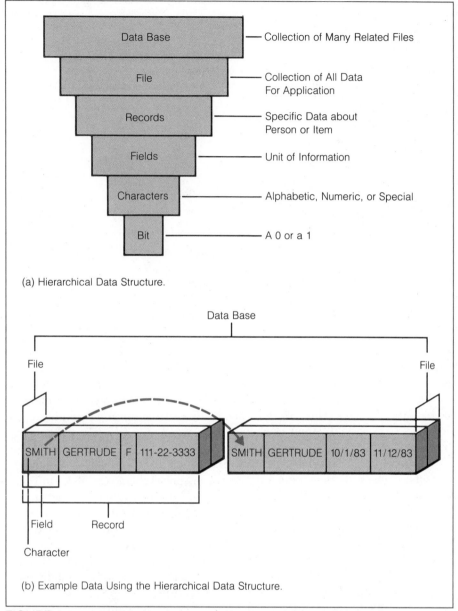

(a) Hierarchical Data Structure.

(b) Example Data Using the Hierarchical Data Structure.

FIGURE 2.1   **The structuring of data for computer use.** *(a)* **Hierarchical data structure.** *(b)* **Example data using the hierarchical data structure.**

WHAT'S RIGHT

The Need For Storing and Retrieving Data.

The Social Security Administration has data for over 150 million people whose contributions to the social security system are processed each month. The number of contributors is overwhelming, but when you consider that the social security administration must also keep records on those contributing individuals who have recently died, the volume staggers the imagination.

Millions of records must be manipulated by the computer system. Can you imagine how fast this computer system must be to be able to update all those records that need changing due to cost of living raises or the like?

Starting from the lowest level in the figure's hierarchy, the most elemental form of data stored in a computer is called a **bit** (short for **bi**nary digi**t**). As shown in Figure 2.2(a), a bit is either a 1 or a 0. Think of a bit as being like a light bulb that is either turned on (as a 1) or turned off (as a 0). A computer works with only 1s and 0s so all data is coded using these bits. Since there are just two possibilities— a 1 or a 0—the electrical circuitry and the rest of the computer hardware are less complex to design than would be the electrical circuitry for the decimal system, which requires ten possibilities in any one digit.

Bits are used in a computer to store data, to calculate, and, in fact, to do all

FIGURE 2.2
Binary digits (bits) and bytes. *(a)* A bit stores one item of data. Represented as an off (0) or on (1) electrical state. *(b)* Bytes are formed from combinations of 6, 7, or 8 bits and represent one character of data.

0	1
OFF STATE	ON STATE

(a) A Bit Stores One Item of Data, Represented as an Off (0) or On (1) Electrical State

CHARACTER	POSSIBLE BYTE CODES	COMPUTER USED FOR CODING
A	1100 0001	IBM large computers
	100 0001	Most microcomputers and large computers
	010 001	Some large computers
	1010 0001	Some very large computers

(b) Bytes Are Formed from Combinations of 6, 7, or 8 Bits and Represent One Character of Data

work. However, few programmers actually work with bits. They concentrate on the next, most elemental level, which is characters. Either 6, 7, or 8 bits—the number of which is unimportant to most users—are grouped together to form a coding for a character. This coding is called a **byte**; it allows various combinations of 0s and 1s to code different characters such as a A, G, Z, 7, 1, and so on, as shown in Figure 2.2(b).

Characters can be **numeric characters,** which are 0 through 9; **alphabetic characters,** which are the letters A through Z; or special characters. Refer to Table 2.2, noting that the **special characters** refer to those normally used as punctuation. All characters not distinguishable as to type are called **alphanumeric characters**.

Characters form **fields** of data; the combination of characters in a field collectively means something such as a person's name, address, sex, or age. The number of characters in the field depends upon how the user wishes to record the data and the possibilities of the data. For example, if the sex of an individual is to be entered, one user might key in the data using just an F or an M, while another user might spell out the word *male* or *female*. In the first case, using just an M or an F, a one-position field is used; in the second case, if the user wishes to spell out the sex of an individual, the field would use six characters since six characters appear in the word *female*. A user could even code the male sex as a 1 and the female sex as a 2; no problem exists as long as the user is consistent when the sex data is entered for each person.

If a social security number is to be entered, the field would be all numbers if it used just nine positions of data (assuming then that the hyphens were not recorded in the field). The social security number could also be entered including the hyphens, but this time the number of characters in the field would use eleven positions. Which way is preferable depends upon how the data is to be used later, necessitating then how it is stored. Including the hyphens might make the numbers

TABLE 2.2.   **Kinds of Characters and Fields**

(a) Characters

ALPHABETIC	NUMERIC	SPECIAL
A B C D E F . . . X Y Z	0 1 2 3 4 5 6 7 8 9	. , / # $ & ? : ; − + ( )

ALPHANUMERIC

A . . . Z 0 . . . 9 . , / . . . ( )

(b) Fields

ALPHABETIC	NUMERIC	ALPHANUMERIC
Alabama	00795	2A67
Ohio	10000	8-146
Bananas	00002	.68
Fruit		B&O
Apples and oranges		Hi-fi
		Geo. Smith, Sr.
		J. K. Chan

easier to read, but an additional two strokes are needed for each person's data. The more characters that you give a computer to work with, the longer it takes for the computer to do its job. Another point to remember is that the data must be entered accurately, or it is useless. Then, too, there is the problem of timeliness. Accurate data is no better than inaccurate data if the user receives requested data after he or she has no further use for it.

A group of related fields about, for example, a person or a subject matter form a **record**; Figure 2.3 shows several records, composed of various fields of data for different applications. All records for a particular application must be set up the same way, for a computer can process data accurately only if it is entered consistently.

What determines the order of the fields in a record? Before any application can be processed using computers, the **format,** which refers to the layout of the record, must be carefully designed. There are no set rules or standards followed in the industry as to the order of the fields used in a record; it is designed quite often for convenience.

Plans must be established as to which field is to be entered first in a record, how many positions each field is to take, and how the data is to be entered in the field. Other questions must be answered. Is the social security number to include hyphens? Is the telephone number to include the area code and hyphens? Is the last name to be entered first in the name field? In a business atmosphere, the way that data are entered into a field is often dictated by company standards. For

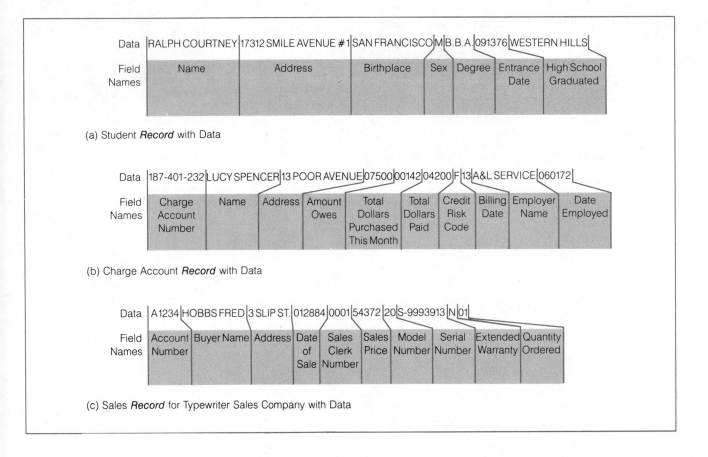

(a) Student *Record* with Data

(b) Charge Account *Record* with Data

(c) Sales *Record* for Typewriter Sales Company with Data

FIGURE 2.3

Records with possible data.
(a) **Student record with data.**
(b) **Charge account record with
data.** *(c)* **Sales record for
typewriter sales company with
data.**

personal use, however, the user makes this decision. Consistency is the key
ingredient.

The many records for a given application represent an organized collection
of data called a **file**. For example, one file could consist of all the personnel records
for the employees in a company. In a banking environment, all the checking
accounts make up a file. All the inventory items of a retail store represent a file,
with each inventory item being a record.

Consider the following example in a department store. When your application
for a charge account card is accepted, a record containing your data is inserted
into the customer file. When you purchase a clock, for example, your record is
updated (made current) to reflect the purchase of the item and the amount of
money owed to the department store. If, when you receive your bill, you question
its accuracy, your record in the file is looked up by locating your account number
in the file. The items purchased during the billing period can then be reported
to you to verify the accuracy of the statement.

In a company, say, the advertising department has its own files, the buying
department has its files, and the sales department has its files. An actual look at
these departments' data would show that much of the same data appears in each
file. Certainly data differ, but an abundance of data is repeated from file to file.

Consider also the school environment. Data about a student such as name,
telephone number, address, date of birth, social security number, high school

from which the student graduated, sex, and more, are contained in the files maintained by the registrar's office, the financial aids office, the counselor's office, and the nurse's office. Each office has its own set of files needed to process its records. Does it not seem an utter waste of storage for each office to have so much of the same data repeated over and over again? Rather, let all offices share the same common data which is needed for each department's operation.

In a **data base** the same data that is common to all users is shared in a community type of file. The amount of storage is kept to a minimum since much data repetition is eliminated. Although the concept of a data base is discussed later in the text, here it is mentioned to show how files formerly kept by different departments of an organization can be used jointly, providing the users the capability to analyze data and retrieve it in ways that were not readily available when data was arranged in separate files. (See Figure 2.4).

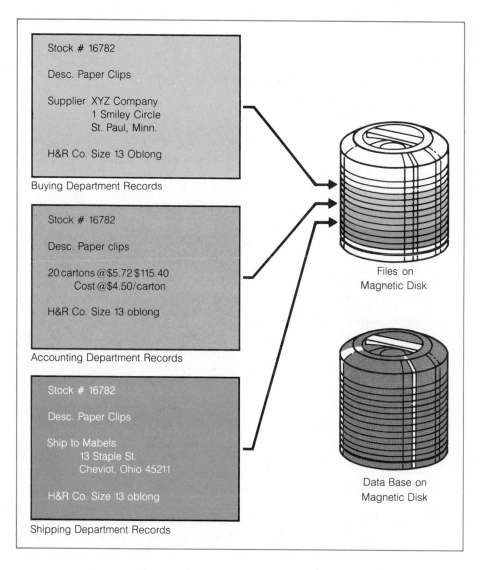

FIGURE 2.4
Data base processing versus file processing.

Stock # 16782

Desc. Paper Clips

Supplier XYZ Company
        1 Smiley Circle
        St. Paul, Minn.

H&R Co. Size 13 Oblong

Buying Department Records

Stock # 16782

Desc. Paper clips

20 cartons @$5.72 $115.40
        Cost @$4.50/carton

H&R Co. Size 13 oblong

Accounting Department Records

Stock # 16782

Desc. Paper Clips

Ship to Mabels
        13 Staple St.
        Cheviot, Ohio 45211

H&R Co. Size 13 oblong

Shipping Department Records

Files on
Magnetic Disk

Data Base on
Magnetic Disk

Equate the concept of separate files to that of data arranged in various file cabinets, which belong to the registrar's, health services, and financial aid's offices. To gather information for some desired analysis can be a monumental task. Determining how many students ever lived in the suburb of Westwood, have attended night school classes within the last year, have applied for and received more than a $300 stipend per school year from the financial aid office, and have complained of severe headaches at the nurse's office during the past three months would be time consuming. A person must physically go through each file cabinet to bring the desired data together into a meaningful form. Before data bases existed, analyses of data were often forgotten before they started or were abandoned before complete because of the time expenditure involved.

CHECKPOINT **Can you:**

Define a bit?

Define a byte?

Identify the types of characters?

Explain what is meant by a field? record? file? data base?

Explaining what makes up a computer system is appropriate at this time. The term **computer system** (as opposed to simply *computer*) refers to how the many parts of a computer are connected together to form a unity. Our hands, feet, legs, and so on, are linked together to form a complex but unified system; the computer, in similar fashion, has its computer system.

FUNCTIONAL PARTS OF A DIGITAL COMPUTER

All digital computers, regardless of size or shape, have functional parts each with a required performance or duty in the computer system. The major purpose of each functional part is listed here:

- Input device—sends data or programs to the CPU

- Output device—receives processed data from the CPU

- Central processing unit (CPU)—coordinates, calculates, and makes decisions on data

- Storage—remembers data and programs

The word **device,** as used in the above list, represents all mechanical, electronic, or electrical equipment that is used for some specific purpose. In a computer system, this takes on two forms: equipment that can be used to enter some data into the computer system and that used to show the user what a result was after the processing of data.

Peripheral device is a catchall term that refers to all hardware other than the central processing unit (CPU). Since a central processing unit is the heart of a computer system, peripheral devices are those hardware that are part of the computer system but are not the center of it. They are used to support the central processing unit. The use of peripheral devices, or peripherals, varies from company to company, as each peripheral device is selected to fit that company's processing requirements. A grocery store has different requirements for peripherals than does a bank, for example.

A computer system is many different machines that operate as though they are one. Refer to Figure 2.5 for a schematic showing the functional parts. The machines are connected by cables, channels, or buses. **Cables** is the more general term; **channels** link the various parts in larger computer systems, and **buses** are usually used in smaller computer systems, such as the personal computer. Regardless of name, they supply the communication link between the central processing unit and the peripheral devices.

INPUT DEVICES

An **input device,** a machine that communicates with a computer, is like an eye as it converts the inputs in the form of data or a program to a machine-readable form. The input device sends the data or program to the heart of a computer system which is called the central processing unit.

FIGURE 2.5 **Functional parts of a computer system.**

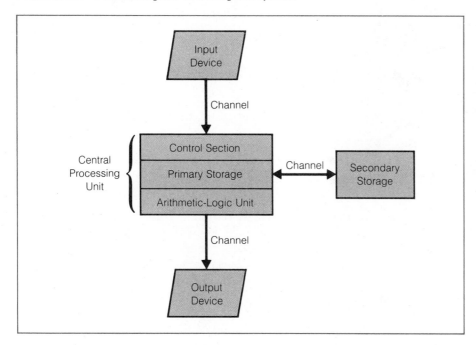

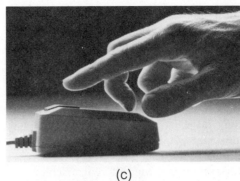

(c)

(a)   (b)   (e)

FIGURE 2.6
Input devices used with microcomputers. *(a)* **Joystick with arcade microcomputer.** *(b)* **Trackball with arcade microcomputer.** *(c)* **Mouse.** *(d)* **Touch screen.** *(e)* **Small-sized keyboard.**

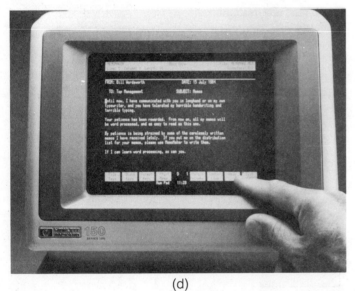

(d)

A user of a computer system selects the input devices that are best suited for the desired processing. The type of input devices can be categorized into those used for a personal computer and for a larger computer system.

Personal Computers

On a personal computer, the most commonly used input device is a keyboard that is arranged like a typewriter keyboard. Keyboards can be connected by cables to the central processing unit or can be cordless; the latter type sends its input by infra red signals to the central processing unit.

Other types of input devices used in game playing are a joystick and trackball. These devices are used to aim at a target or to avoid being attacked. A **joystick** is a lever that is pushed or pulled; a **trackball** is a ball that is rolled. A very popularly used input device on personal computers is a **mouse,** a small box that is slid. A **touch screen** is also being used where a finger is used to touch the television-like screen for instructing the computer what it is to do. Keyboard is also used for input. Refer to Figure 2.6.

But the days have gone when a person communicated with a computer strictly by the use of a keyboard, joystick, or the like. The **speech synthesizer,** as shown in Figure 2.7, now allows the user to speak to a computer. The user must give samples of selected lines so a synthesizer can recognize the pattern of speech. The speech synthesizer will, in the near future, revolutionize the way that we communicate with a computer. Although excited or irregular speech causes problems with a synthesizer at the present time, this device holds great promise for eliminating the keying process (typing) for input.

Larger Computer Systems

There are many types of devices used in a larger computer system; the text here briefly touches on some of them that eliminate the need to key in the data through a keyboard, thus assuring greater accuracy in data entry. Peripherals are discussed in more detail in Chapter 8.

FIGURE 2.7   **Speech synthesizer used in place of keyboard input.**

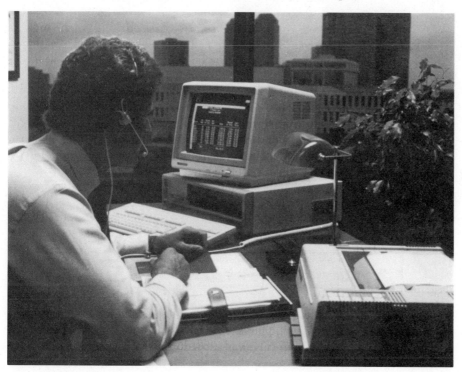

In January 1984, Digital Equipment Corporation (DEC) introduced a speech synthesizer that can revolutionize the way we work and help others. Through the use of a personal computer and a speech synthesizer, typed copy and keyboard strokes are changed into spoken words.

Children at Boston's Children's Hospital are already using the prerecorded voices of seven different people for generating a read-aloud environment. The child types messages and selects which voice is to be used for output.

MCI Corporation plans to use this synthesizer to transmit mail electronically rather than through the postal service. The user dials the 800 exchange and uses a certain identification code to gain access. The message is then read to the user. Amazing. For years synthesizers were limited to several hundred words of vocabulary.

FIGURE 2.8   **Magnetic ink characters used as input.**

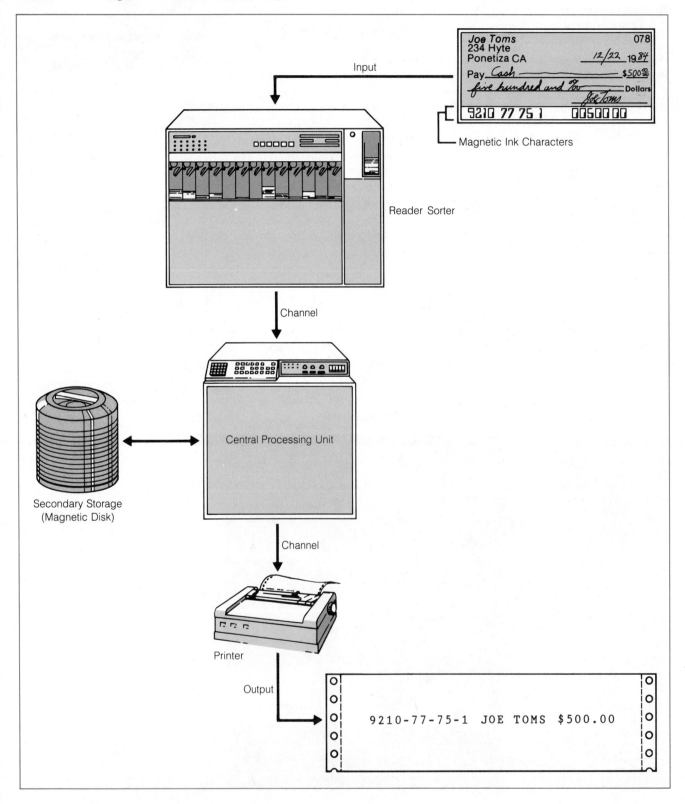

Banks with larger computer systems use a device called a **reader-sorter,** which converts the magnetic ink characters that appear on checks into a form that the computer understands, as shown in Figure 2.8. In a department store, an **optical wand** reads the labels on the clothing or other merchandise items, as shown in Figure 2.9, for inventory control purposes. A grocery store chooses an **optical scanner** to read the Universal Product Code (UPC). Bar codes are the bold lines that are marked on each product label or also appear on envelopes and inventory tags.

OUTPUT DEVICES

An **output device** is a machine that receives communication from the central processing unit. It is like the ears of the computer as they convert its electrical signals (impulses) into a form readable by humans. There are a variety of output devices, as shown in Figure 2.10. Computers usually have a **printer** as an output device. Refer to Figure 2.10(a). It can print anywhere from 16 characters per second to 21,000 lines per minute (1pm), each line of which can print from about 100 to 132 characters.

The type of communication that these devices receive can be in the form of reports, diagrams or graphs showing the data that has been processed. Refer to Figures 2.10(b) and 2.10(c). Another type can show a program that has been

FIGURE 2.9
Optical wand used in department stores.

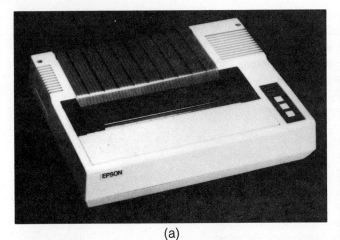

(a)

(b)

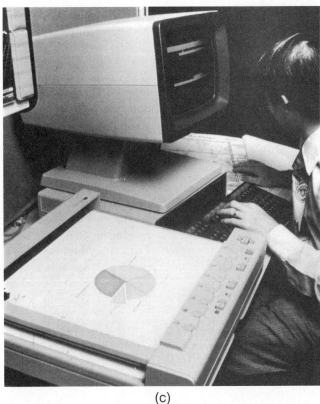

(c)

FIGURE 2.10
Printed output. *(a)* **Printer.** *(b)* **Engineer examines blueprint from drafting plotter.** *(c)* **Plotter prepares graphs.**

entered to instruct the computer as to the desired data manipulation that is to be done. The printer output is referred to as **hard copy,** or a **printout.**

Did you ever hear a recording on the telephone when you dialed a disconnected number or your call was not completed because of mechanical failure? These messages are generated by a speech synthesizer that acts as an output device from a computer system.

INPUT/OUTPUT (I/O) DEVICES

Some devices are used just for input. Others are used just for output. There are some devices, however, that handle both input and output, called **input/output (I/O) devices.** These same devices are used for inputting data or programs and for receiving processed information or messages from a computer system. Refer to Figure 2.11.

One of the most popular I/O devices is the **visual display unit (VDU),** or the **visual display terminal (VDT),** as shown in Figure 2.11(a). This device has a

(a)

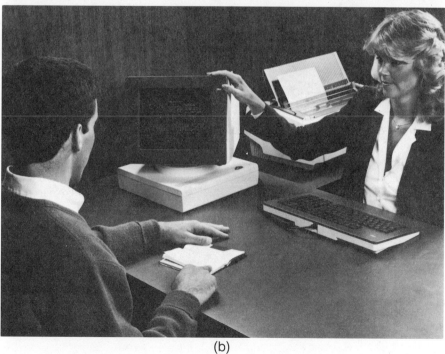

(b)

FIGURE 2.11
Visual display terminal.
(a) Engineer examines screen for results. *(b)* Teller shows bank balance.

keyboard that is used for input and a television-like screen, called a **cathode ray tube (CRT),** which is used for display purposes. The CRT shows what is keyed (entered) by a user in a form of output referred to as **soft copy,** that is, screen generated output; it lacks hard copy.

Have you ever watched people enter data on a keyboard, observe the soft copy, and then register delight, indifference, or frustration? They are using a terminal, a device which allows them to interact with a computer from almost any location. A **terminal** refers to any input, output, or I/O device; a personal computer; or a larger computer system that provides communication to a central processing unit. For that reason, the visual display unit is most often referred to as a **visual display terminal (VDT)** or **cathode ray tube (CRT) terminal.** The remainder of the text will make use of the term *visual display terminal* or *VDT*. In Figure 2.11(b) a visual display terminal is used by banks for entering a savings account number in order to find the amount in savings.

The keyboard with a visual display terminal is an input device when it is used for entering either data or a program. It can also be used for making an **inquiry,** which represents a request made for information from computer storage. A teller keys in the account number to identify which account is to be looked up by the computer. The computer carriers out this **task,** or unit of work, by looking up the account number and returning the information to the visual display terminal. Since the television-like screen shows the input at some point in time as well as the output, it is an I/O device.

CENTRAL PROCESSING UNIT

As was stated earlier, the heart of a computer is called the **central processing unit (CPU),** also known as a **central processor** or **processor.** In personal computers it was formerly referred to as a **microprocessor** but is now coming to be known as the central processing unit. In larger computer systems, the CPU is called a **mainframe.** Computers look much like boxes. Figure 2.12 shows the cover removed.

Three parts make up a CPU: the control section, arithmetic-logic unit (ALU), and primary storage. Not all computers physically contain these parts in the central processing unit. There can be a difference between logical and physical grouping. **Logical** refers to how we perceive it, **physical** to how it really is. The central processing unit is thought of as logically containing these parts but in larger computer systems primary storage may physically be a separate piece of hardware. Refer to Figure 2.13.

Control Section

A **control section** is the coordinator of an entire computer system, making all the equipment work together. The control section does not process any data but strictly directs the computer in how to carry out each instruction as written in a program.

Arithmetic-Logic Unit

An **arithmetic-logic unit (ALU)** performs the calculations and decision making as directed by a program that is stored in primary storage. When a student record is read, for example, the total of the grade points earned can be calculated, and

FIGURE 2.12
**Inside view of the Amdahl 5860
computer system.**

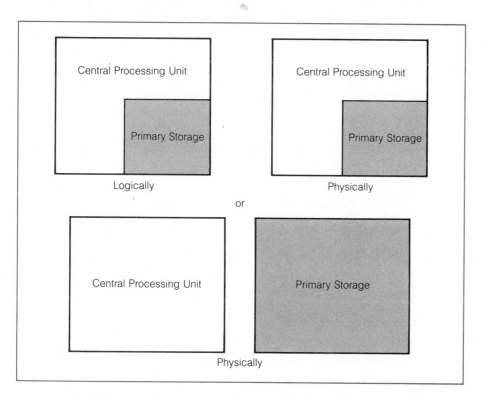

FIGURE 2.13
**Primary storage is logically part of
the central processing unit but can
be physically separated.**

WHAT'S WRONG

Can't They Make Up Their Minds What It Should Be Called?

Computer manufacturers have a way of identifying similar products by use of different names, largely because of copyright problems. Unless main memory is known to be equivalent to internal memory or to primary storage, successful communication cannot be achieved with data processors.

Sometimes computer terminology becomes mind-boggling, but, unfortunately, the basics must be learned. Concentrate on learning these similar names since any periodicals read tend to mix snynonymous terms.

the appropriate letter grade assigned. This type of processing is done by making decisions about in which grade point range the grade belongs. If, for example, the grade point range was from 50 to 75 points for an A, the program would compare the input record's total points and then determine if the grade was between 50 and 75 points so an A grade could be assigned. Each grade point range must be stated in the program so the arithmetic-logic unit can do its required calculations and decision making.

Primary Storage

Primary storage, also called **memory, internal memory,** or **main memory,** makes up the third part of the central processing unit. For ease, we will refer to this throughout the remainder of the text as primary storage. **Primary storage** is a temporary storage that is used for remembering data and programs for as long as is required to process an application, which might be seconds, minutes, or even hours. When data is remembered or looked up in primary storage, the computer operates at the speed of light.

Primary storage has a **capacity,** meaning a limit to the number of characters that can be remembered at any one time. Capacity is expressed for personal computers in terms of **kilobytes** or K, such as 32K, 64K, 512K, where **K** refers to 1,024 characters that can be stored at any one time. The capacity of mainframes is expressed in **megabytes,** which means a million bytes (characters), or technically 1,048,576 characters.

When capacity is 16K, 16,384 characters can be stored. If, on a personal computer, a user needs more primary storage, he or she can buy some chips that contain 16K or 32K for about $2. The chips can be plugged into the printed circuit board, assuming that the board can accommodate this add-on memory. This capability was unheard of in the early 1970s.

The problem with primary storage, however, is that for most types data and programs stored within it are lost when electrical power is removed. Who pulled the plug? To take care of this temporary storage problem, a long-term storage medium is available.

CHECKPOINT **Can you:**

Tell the purpose of an input device?

Tell the purpose of an output device?

Identify the work done by the ALU?

Identify the work done by a control section?

Explain why primary storage is needed?

SECONDARY STORAGE

A computer's ability to store millions of characters of data is an invaluable feature. Sometimes a user needs data to be remembered for only the length of time that the program is being executed. Other times, data must be filed away so it can be remembered for months or years—government controls dictate to businesses about the storage of some business documents. Still other data must be available for continual use by the computer.

If more storage is required than what is available in primary storage, one or more additional storage devices may be used to increase the capacity. These devices are called **secondary storage.** Examples of this type of storage are diskette and tape cassette for a personal computer. A diskette can be likened to a 45 rpm record. For the larger computer systems, magnetic disk and magnetic tape are commonly used. Magnetic disks can be likened to large phonograph records; magnetic tape reminds you of a home tape recorder. On a magnetic disk maybe 400 megabytes (million characters) can be stored. On a magnetic tape perhaps 275 megabytes are stored, sometimes even more. Refer to Figure 2.14.

Perhaps you have seen the 24-hour automated teller machines that are located outside of a bank; these machines dispense cash. Figure 2.14 shows the data center that is shared by many of the automated teller stations. The magnetic disk is in the foreground; the magnetic tape is in the background.

The name *secondary storage* is significant because all data in secondary storage must always be brought into primary storage to be manipulated. It is only in the central processing unit that questions are asked, answers are given, calculations are made, and results are sent to an output device.

Secondary storage is a long-term storage that might hold data for hours, days, or years—virtually for as long as desired. Unlike primary storage, it does not lose its data or programs when power is removed. Data stored on secondary storage

FIGURE 2.14   **Data centers for shared automated teller machines.**

WHAT'S RIGHT

An Automobile Recall

The amount of data that a computer's storage can remember is sometimes staggering to comprehend. If, for example, a car maker needs to notify each owner about a recall, automobile companies will probably use a computer service that is located in Cincinnati, Ohio. The computer storage can remember 7.8G characters where **G** means **giga,** which is 10 raised to the ninth power, or 7,800,000 characters. Not all computer storage is this large.

In order for the various car owners to be notified of a recall, each record is read. The make of a car and the year of manufacture must be checked by the arithmetic-logic unit. If the desired data is found in a record, a notice is sent to that car owner.

Can you think of some other applications at your college that use this same type of processing?

is not placed entirely in primary storage at once because of the capacity problem and the temporary memory characteristic associated with primary storage.

Examples of data stored in secondary storage could be a department store's customer file or your class notes. Since it is impossible to remember all information in your brain, you prepare notes which can be referred to at a later time. Initially, you write the notes; later you recall them by reading them. When you read them, you input the data into your brain, making the data available for processing. Like your notes, secondary storage is usually removable and is easily filed in a special filing cabinet.

At this point, having briefly discussed all the parts that make up a computer system, it is appropriate to make a comparison of the various types of hardware that can make up those parts. Table 2.3 summarizes and organizes these.

CHECKPOINT Can you:

Explain why secondary storage is used?

Determine if data is read first or written first using secondary storage?

Differentiate between reading and writing of data?

TABLE 2.3 **Comparison of Types of Hardware in a Computer System.**

HARDWARE	CENTRAL PROCESSING UNIT	INPUT DEVICE	OUTPUT DEVICE	I/O DEVICE	SECONDARY STORAGE
Central Processor	X				
Control Section	X				
Diskette					X
Joystick		X			
Magnetic Disk					X
Magnetic Tape					X
Mouse		X			
Optical Wand		X			
Optical Scanner		X			
Primary Storage	X				
Printer			X		
Reader-Sorter		X			
Speech Synthesizer		X	X	X	
Trackball		X			
Visual Display Terminal				X	

GALLERY 2

Primary Storage

This color gallery is dedicated to those people who manufacture the integrated circuit chips. The atmosphere is entirely different than one could ever imagine. Each doorway has sticky boards to clean your shoes. Employees are garbed with "bunny suits" with only their face and hands showing.

It is hoped that these photographs give you some idea of the production of the "computer on a chip" developed by Ted Hoff in 1971 at Intel Corporation.

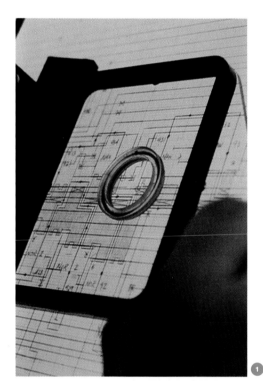

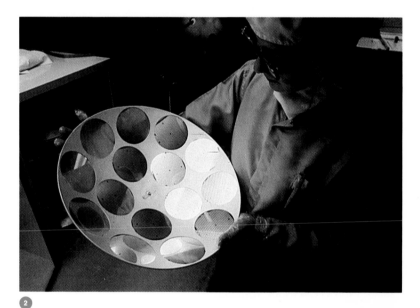

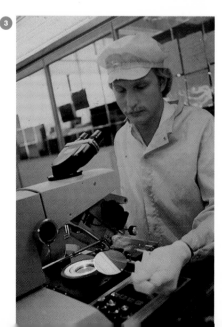

1. Designs for integrated circuits are first drawn onto large sheets of paper and checked by engineers. The circuits are the paths that the electrical impulses follow. The designs are next photolithographically miniaturized. These miniatured designs, called masks, are used to lay out the circuits on silicon wafers. **2.** Each wafer of pure crystal silicon is approximately three to five inches in diameter and can be imprinted with many individual circuits for each chip. The chips on each wafer are identical to each other. **3.** The silicon wafers are fabricated in special clean rooms. Any particle of dust would disrupt the circuitry and make the chip useless.

4. Yellow lights are used in the clean rooms because yellow does not bother the ultraviolet light that is used in the fabricating process. A photoresist, a light-sensitive chemical, is spun on the wafer in a very thin layer. The mask is then placed over the coated wafer and the wafer and mask are exposed to the ultraviolet light. After the exposure to ultraviolet light, the areas under the mask stay soft while the exposed areas harden. The mask is next removed and the wafer is etched either by an acid bath rinse or plasma technology (superhot gases).

5. The wafers are loaded into carriers, called boats. They are next to be placed in the ovens. **6.** The wafers with their integrated circuits etched upon them are loaded into high temperature (1400°C) furnaces. The sequence of photoresist, mask, ultraviolet light, etching, and baking (diffusion) is repeated for each layer. A wafer has anywhere from 3 to 15 or more layers depending upon the complexity of the design.

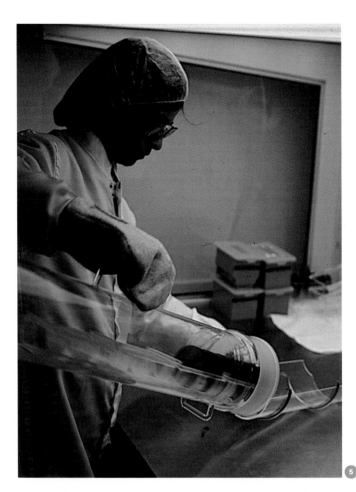

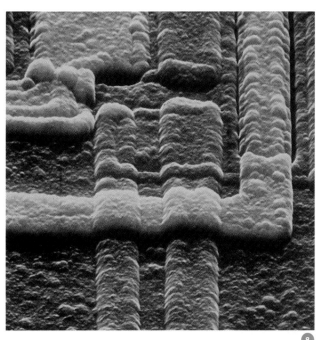

7. The wafers are periodically inspected throughout the production of the chips for any microscopic flaws. **8.** An electronmicrograph of the tiny layers on a silicon wafer form the intricate patterns of the integrated circuits. **9.** A completely processed wafer with its finished chips. **10.** A final inspection is made.

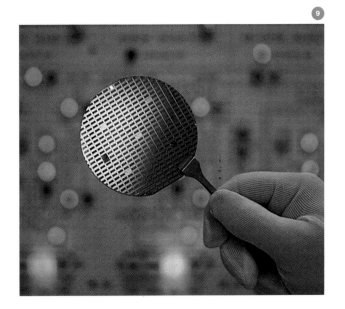

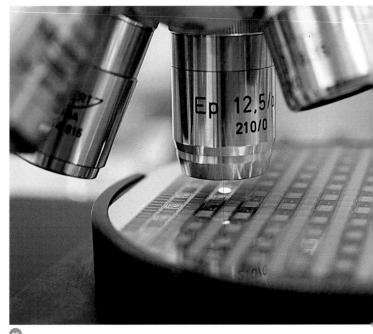

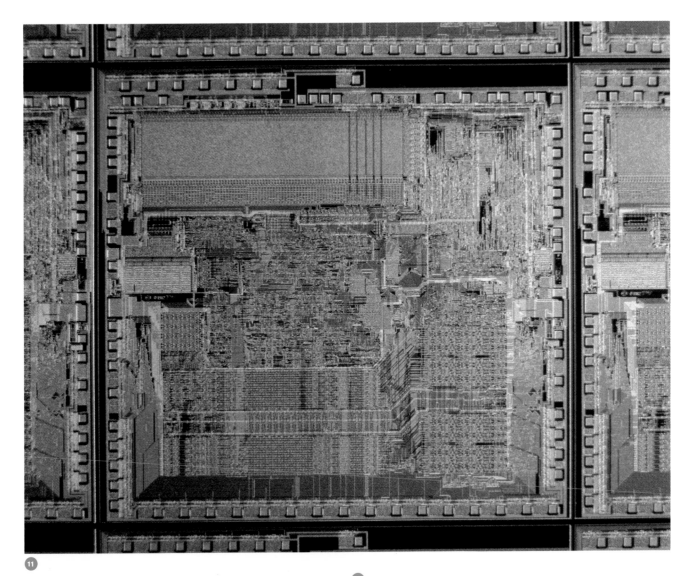

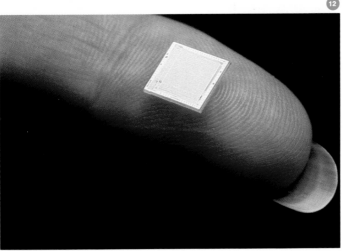

11. A 32-bit microprocessor chip with approximately 65,000 transistors and measuring about 0.3 inch per side is shown here. This chip is now ready to be "chipped off" the wafer by a diamond saw or laser. **12.** Although the chips are extremely small, they possess enormous computing power. This chip has 450,000 transistors and has as much computing power as computers that previously required an entire room to house them.

13. The completed chip next has gold wires attached to it. These wires then connect each chip to its individual carrier.

14. Automatic lead-bounding equipment such as this has helped improve productivity and increase reliability in the semiconductor industry. Before this equipment was invented, a person had to personally hand solder the tiny gold wires to the chip as shown in the previous photo.

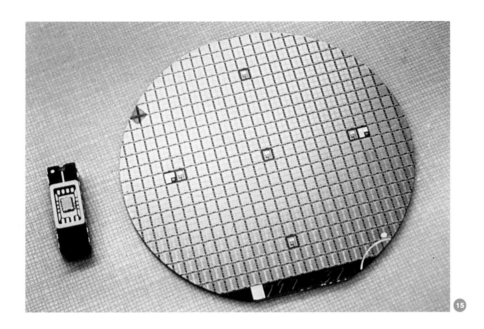

15. A chip mounted onto its carrier can be used for primary storage or as a microprocessor. The chip is ready to be mounted onto a circuit board. A complete wafer from which chips are cut is also shown. 16. NSC 800 microprocessor is an advanced CMOS (complimentary metal-oxide-silicon) device that combines high-speed and density with low power operations.

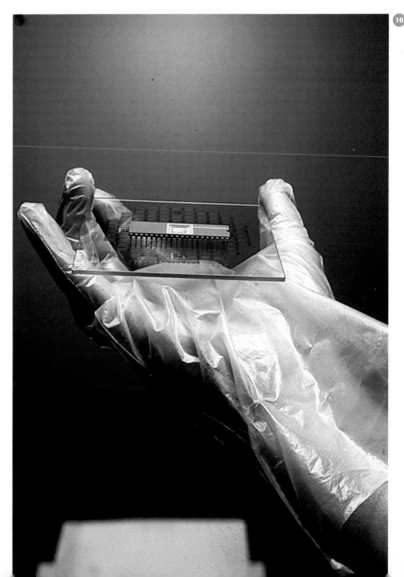

17. Assemblers inspect and load various components onto printed circuit boards. The quality of the finished product depends upon careful, continuous inspection through the manufacturing process. **18.** Finished printed circuit boards are inspected at the rate of more than 30 chips per board per second. **19.** Printed circuit boards are tested throughout the process before assembly. **20.** One of many printed circuit boards is loaded into a new computer terminal. **21.** The finished product as we know it.

A PROGRAM

Following a recipe in a cookbook is in some ways like following a program and the processing of data. In such a comparison, the ingredients listed become the data; the directions on the mixing of the ingredients and the baking time are considered the program. The combination of data and the program make the computer work.

A programmer, before writing a computer program, must determine what type of processing is needed. Next, the programmer must decide what computer language is to be used for coding a program, with the choice depending upon the type of problem being solved. Some languages work best for scientific applications; others work best for business applications; and still others work best for calculating math problems. The program written by a programmer must be translated so it can be understood by a computer. The translated program, once it is remembered in primary storage for executing the data, is then referred to as a **stored program.** It is remembered in primary storage for as long as the program executes data. Since primary storage is a temporary storage, as soon as your program is completely processed, it is replaced by a program that handles the next job. When a job is processed, data may flow back and forth between the arithmetic-logic unit and primary storage.

Refer to Figure 2.15, which illustrates the importance of the stored program and the control section as they work together. Figure 2.16 reinforces the inter-workings of the parts of a computer system by showing possible data flow within the system. Figure 2.17 follows the flow of specific data as it is inputted, calculated, and outputted.

You might feel you need a crystal ball to be able to find out what makes up a program. What does it look like? How does it work? The following example program should help you understand how a program works. It is not truly a computer program but operates like one.

Step 1 contains the rules you must follow very closely when you read the paragraph in Step 2. Be sure you understand the rules. Rereading them several times might be helpful.

● **Step 1—Rules.**

First Read a sentence in the paragraph in Step 2.

Second After you have read a sentence, keep track of the number of sentences you read in the paragraph.

Third Then ask yourself, "Is this the last sentence in the paragraph?"

Fourth Answer the question. If the answer is YES, proceed to Step 3.

Fifth If the answer is NO, refer back to the first rule, calling for you to read the next sentence. Continue reading the sentences until you eventually answer YES to the question.

● **Step 2—Paragraph Reading, Using Rules in Step 1.**

Regardless of a computer's size, a digital computer always has input, output, processing, and storage capability. The speed with which the computer operates

FIGURE 2.15   **The importance of the control section of a CPU.**

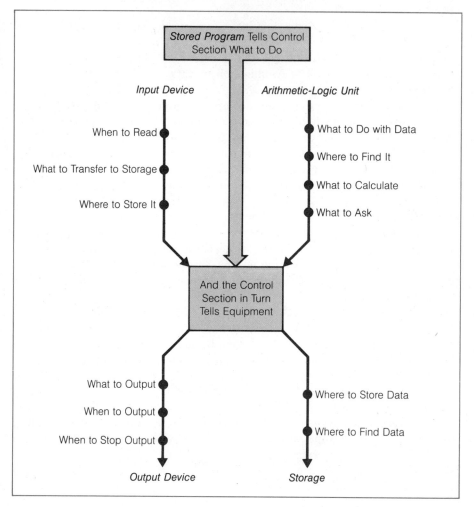

and the size of the memory are two of the most important points used for grouping computers into different size classifications.

- **Step 3—Answer Questions By Writing in the Space Provided.**

1. How many sentences did you count in the paragraph? _____

2. Do all computers have storage capability? _____

- **Step 4—Functions You Have Performed So Far.**

First   A set of rules was made up for you to follow. These rules can be thought of as orders or instructions which explicitly tell you what to do and when to do it. They make up a program.

Second You read these instructions and stored them in your brain; they then became a stored program which made the instructions accessible. Your eyes acted as input devices to your brain.

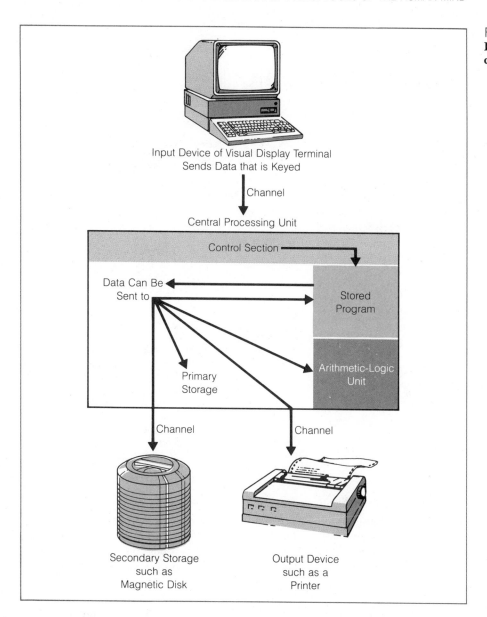

FIGURE 2.16
Possible flow of data in a computer system.

Third   You read the first sentence in the paragraph, hence inputting data to your brain. You placed the first sentence's information in a different spot in your brain than where you placed your program.

Fourth   The counting of the sentences was obviously performing arithmetic.

Fifth   When you asked the question, you had two alternatives. You made a decision; hence, you did logical work.

Sixth   When you read the second question, you began the series over again. The processing continued until finally you answered YES.

Seventh When you wrote the answers you outputted data. Without outputting data, all the facts would be kept within your brain.

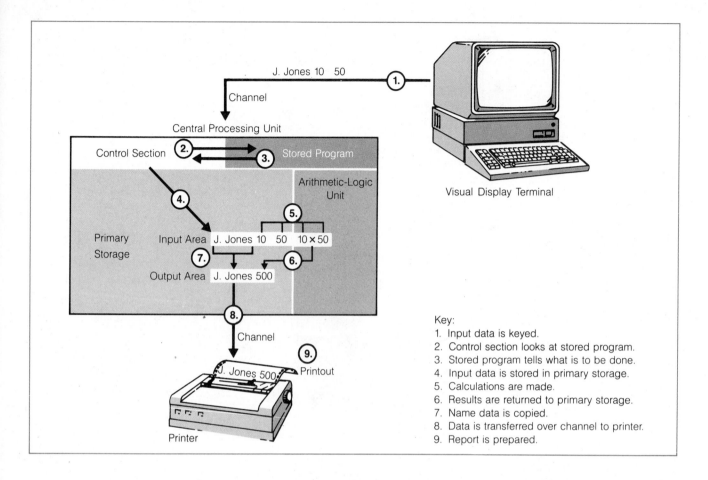

Key:
1. Input data is keyed.
2. Control section looks at stored program.
3. Stored program tells what is to be done.
4. Input data is stored in primary storage.
5. Calculations are made.
6. Results are returned to primary storage.
7. Name data is copied.
8. Data is transferred over channel to printer.
9. Report is prepared.

FIGURE 2.17
Flow of data that is inputted, calculated, and outputted.

Eighth You knew what to do by following your stored program. Each of us has some kind of coordinator that brings things into proper order and harmonizes the body so it acts as one unit. One part of the brain makes the decision on what to do; another part makes it possible for you to do what you want to do. This latter part of your brain is your control section.

A computer can be used for work that is repeated, but it does not lend itself to performing work only once. Many applications cannot be used on a computer because this type of repeat processing is not present. Other times, the use of a computer cannot be justified as it might take longer to prepare the program, test it to make certain it works correctly, and key it in than it would to do the job manually.

USE OF EDITING, RUNNING, AND STORING

The computer works no magic; users must tell it everything it is to do. When turned on, the personal computer is in **edit mode,** a type of operation in which programs or data are entered. After this is completed, the mode of operation is changed to a **run mode,** with the program being executed with the input data.

Assume that two numbers are to be added together, the sum of which is to be shown as output. To accomplish this type of processing, a program must be written and then inputted from an input device. Instructions are written by using symbols to represent a type of communication which is composed of alphabetics, numbers, and special characters, for the most part. A computer understands only 0s and 1s, however. The symbols must be changed into that form so the computer can understand, resulting in a stored program.

The edit mode has now ended. Next, a user tells the computer system that the program is to be executed (run) on the computer, with the result appearing on the output device.

Refer to Figure 2.18, which shows a personal computer system that consists of a keyboard as an input device and a central processing unit; A home television screen is used to show the results, in use in both the edit and run modes. If you

FIGURE 2.18   **Edit and run modes.** *(a)* **Edit mode.** *(b)* **Run mode.**

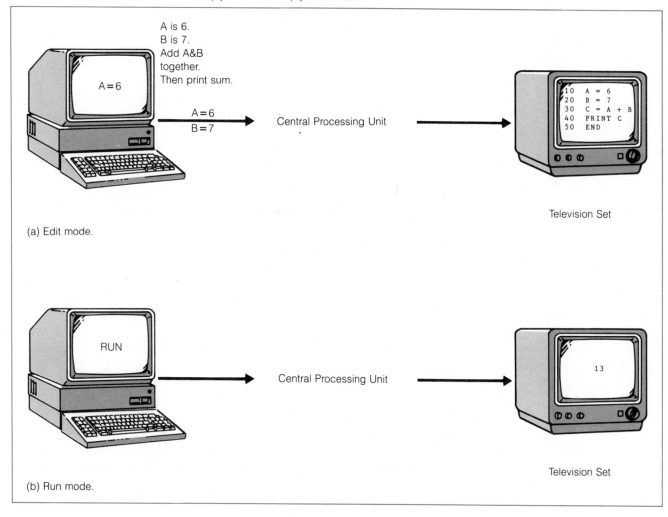

turn off the computer, the program that was inputted, the data, and the results are lost.

Assuming that the same program is to be used at different times rather than having to key it each time, let us store it in secondary storage as a file. Formerly a file was defined as holding strictly data. However, it also can hold the instructions that make up a program. The program is read (recalled) from secondary storage. In this case, the personal computer system needs a secondary storage device. A home tape recorder with tape cassette works nicely. Next time the same program is to be used, the tape is read again.

CHECKPOINT Can you:

Explain how data flows in a computer system?

SUMMARY

● Data is arranged in a hierarchy from the most important down through the least important structure, as follows: data base, files, records, fields, characters (bytes), and binary digits.

● A binary digit, or a bit, refers to the smallest unit for storing data in a computer system. A bit is either a 0 or a 1.

● A byte, the next most important unit in the hierarchical data structure, is composed of several bits used together to form the coding of a character. A character can be an alphabetic character, numeric character, or special character.

● One or more characters form a field, which represents a unit of information such as a person's name, a birthdate, a major course of study, or a grade earned for a class.

● Many fields make up the data about a person, a thing, or a happening. These fields form a record.

● The way that the fields are laid out in a record is referred to as the format.

● The many records for an application form a file. The instructions that make up a program also form a file.

● Files of data are combined into a data base. A data base refers to data that is shared by different users with the purpose of reducing repeated data and making available data that can be analyzed easily.

● Digital computers have these functional parts: input device, central processing unit, output device, and storage.

● Peripheral devices represent all devices except the central processing unit.

- The input device changes the input into a machine-readable form. There are many input devices, such as the reader sorter, optical wand, and keyboard.

- The central processing unit (CPU), or central processor, is the brain of the computer.

- The central processing unit has three parts: the control section, arithmetic-logic unit (ALU), and primary storage.

- The control section is the coordinator of the entire computer system. It does not process any data.

- The arithmetic-logic unit performs arithmetic and logical operations.

- Primary storage is also called memory, internal memory, or main memory. Primary storage has a capacity as to the number of characters that can be remembered at any one time, with capacity being expressed in kilobytes (K) for personal computers and in megabytes for mainframes.

- A program, written to instruct the computer as to the required processing, is remembered in primary storage. The stored program and the control section work hand in hand so that processing can be accomplished.

- Storage that is physically or logically part of the central processing unit is called primary storage.

- Magnetic disk and magnetic tape are very popular types of secondary storage that are used on large computer systems. Diskette and home tape cassettes are the most popular secondary storage media used on smaller computer systems.

- An output device receives communication from the central processing unit. The output device converts impulses from a computer system into a form that is readable by humans. The most widely used output device is the printer.

- Input/output (I/O) devices are used for transmitting data or programs to the CPU or receiving data from it. The most popular I/O device is the visual display terminal (VDT) which has a keyboard and a medium-sized television screen. VDTs are used for entering data or for making inquiries requesting certain data from the computer's storage.

- Secondary storage holds data or programs for a long period of time but is unable to do any data manipulation.

- Edit mode refers to the keying (inputting) process of entering programs and data into a computer system. Run mode refers to the execution of the program with the data, which produces results.

STUDY GUIDE

REVIEW OF TERMINOLOGY

The following terminology was covered in this chapter:

alphabetic characters
alphanumeric characters
arithmetic-logic unit
  (ALU)
binary digit (bit)
bus
byte
cables
capacity
cathode ray tube (CRT)
central processor
central processing unit
  (CPU)
channel
computer system
control section
data base
device
edit mode
field
file
format
giga (G)
hard copy
input device
input/output (I/O) device
inquiry
internal memory
joystick
kilobyte (K)
logical

main memory
mainframe
megabyte
memory
microprocessor
mouse
numeric characters
optical scanner
optical wand
output device
peripheral device
physical
primary storage
printer
printout
processor
reader-sorter
record
run mode
secondary storage
soft copy
special characters
speech synthesizer
stored program
task
terminal
trackball
visual display terminal
  (VDT)

MULTIPLE CHOICE

Circle the item that completes each statement correctly.

1. The many characters that are used for remembering a person's name are referred to as a:
   a. format
   b. field
   c. record
   d. file
   e. data base

2. A program or the input data that is used in the execution of a program is considered as a:
   a. format
   b. field
   c. record
   d. file
   e. data base

3. A magnetic tape, tape recorder, printer, and CRT are all examples of:
   a. input devices
   b. output devices
   c. secondary storage devices
   d. I/O devices
   e. peripheral devices

4. The connection used between peripherals and the CPU is called:
   a. a channel
   b. a cable
   c. a bus
   d. all of these
   e. none of these

5. Which device is used for reading check data:
   a. diskette
   b. optical scanner
   c. reader-sorter
   d. magnetic tape
   e. card reader

6. Calculations are performed in the:
   a. control section
   b. peripheral device
   c. ALU
   d. primary storage
   e. channel

7. A limit as to the number of characters that can be remembered is called:
   a. megabytes
   b. K
   c. logical
   d. physical
   e. capacity

8. A data base:
   a. allows data to be shared
   b. reduces the same data repeated over and over again
   c. represents data from different applications
   d. all of these
   e. none of these

9. When files are used for holding data, each department:
   a. usually has its own set of records
   b. always shares the data with other departments
   c. has a small amount of repeated data in the files.
   d. has little desire for information from other departments
   e. none of these

10. A data base is created by:
   a. using files from various departments
   b. ignoring most of the data that is already available
   c. setting up the department's records in separate files
   d. sharing data with only one other department
   e. none of these

11. Many fields of data make up a:
   a. record
   b. file
   c. capacity
   d. megabyte
   e. stored program

12. A program that is used by the computer for execution is remembered in:
   a. primary storage
   b. internal storage
   c. main memory
   d. all of these
   e. none of these

13. The coordinator of the computer system is called:
   a. primary storage
   b. ALU
   c. control section
   d. stored program
   e. peripheral device

14. The way in which the various fields are laid out in a record is called:
   a. a file
   b. logical
   c. physical
   d. a format
   e. a data base

15. Which of the following is used for originally entering the program and for entering data:
   a. output device
   b. central processing unit
   c. input device
   d. secondary storage
   e. internal storage

16. Which of the following is used for preparing a report:
   a. secondary storage
   b. printer
   c. stored program
   d. channel
   e. optical wand

17. The heart of the larger computer system is called a:
   a. CPU
   b. central processor
   c. mainframe
   d. all of these
   e. none of these

18. When you key in a program, the program will not be executed until the computer has entered:
   a. secondary storage mode
   b. control section mode
   c. primary storage mode
   d. edit mode
   e. run mode

19. What tells the control section when to input data:
   a. primary storage
   b. CPU
   c. stored program
   d. ALU
   e. input device

20. When a report is prepared by a printer, this report is called:
   a. secondary storage
   b. run mode
   c. a stored program
   d. a peripheral device
   e. hard copy

TRUE/FALSE QUESTIONS

Circle the T next to a true statement, the F if it is false.

1. **T/F** The central processing unit is composed of three parts: ALU, control section, and secondary storage.

2. **T/F** Whenever questions are asked about data, this logical work is done in secondary storage.

3. **T/F** Primary storage cannot be used unless secondary storage is also used.

4. **T/F** Secondary storage is needed since primary storage has a capacity limitation, and is temporary.

5. **T/F** A speech synthesizer will make entering of programs and data much easier for most users.

6. **T/F** All data stored in secondary storage must be brought to the central processor for any data manipulation.

7. **T/F** Internal memory is often called secondary storage.

8. **T/F** Internal storage refers to memory that is not connected to the CPU.

9. **T/F** A VDT, magnetic tape, keyboard, and printer are examples of peripheral devices.

10. **T/F** A control section gets its orders on what to do from secondary storage.

11. **T/F** A field may be made up of just one character.

12. **T/F** A file represents several fields of data, each of which pertains to the same subject matter.

13. **T/F** A file can be equated to a filing cabinet where many records are stored for later recall.

14. **T/F** Although magnetic tape is considered as secondary storage, it is used to input data.

15. **T/F** When magnetic tape is used for storing data on it, the magnetic tape is then used as output.

16. **T/F** A data base refers to many files of data that are used jointly for easy reference of facts.

17. **T/F** In a data base, none of the data which formerly appeared in many files is remembered in secondary storage.

18. **T/F** A mouse, joystick, and trackball are used as input devices for game playing.

19. **T/F** Terminal can refer to almost any input/output device.

ANSWERS

Multiple Choice: 1. **b** 2. **d** 3. **e** 4. **d** 5. **c** 6. **c** 7. **e** 8. **d** 9. **a** 10. **a** 11. **a** 12. **d** 13. **c** 14. **d** 15. **c** 16. **b** 17. **d** 18. **e** 19. **c** 20. **e** *True/False:* 1. **F** 2. **F** 3. **F** 4. **T** 5. **T** 6. **T** 7. **F** 8. **F** 9. **T** 10. **F** 11. **T** 12. **F** 13. **T** 14. **T** 15. **T** 16. **T** 17. **F** 18. **T** 19. **T**

REVIEW QUESTIONS

1. Identify each of the following: bits, characters, fields, records, files, and data bases.

2. What types of characters are there?

3. Fields of data must be entered consistently. Why is this statement true?

4. Why is format important?

5. What is the difference between files and data bases?

6. What are the functional parts of a computer? What is the purpose of each?

7. What are the three parts of the central processing unit? What is the purpose of each part?

8. Explain how the control section keeps all the hardware working together as one machine.

9. What are the differences between primary and secondary storage?

10. Do all computers have the same input devices? If not, why not?

11. What does I/O stand for? How does an I/O device differ from an output device?

12. Give an example of an I/O device. How might it be used by an insurance company? A bank?

13. What are peripheral devices? Identify eight different ones mentioned in the chapter.

14. What is a task?

DISCUSSION QUESTIONS

1. Data is organized in a hierarchical structure. Discuss how this data organization pertains, for example, to student registration data.

2. How does hardware differ from software?

3. When you registered at your college, the registrar's office processed your class schedule. Using the printout that you received from registration, discuss how the data for your class registration flowed through the computer. Draw a schematic showing the data flow.

4. A computer system represents different hardware. Explain this statement.

People in Computing

Loren D. Acord, Ph.D.

COMPANY
Mills Memorial Hospital, San Mateo, California

POSITION
Director, Neuropsychology Department

The human brain is, without question, the most complex, sophisticated, useful, and adaptable three pounds of matter on the face of the earth. It accounts in great part for all human achievement, from the most aesthetic poems and music to the most intricate and complex machinery. And yet, literally within an instant, a sensitive, creative, communicating individual can be transformed by stroke or head injury into a confused, disoriented, disabled man or woman. He or she may not be able to speak or understand speech; to concentrate on, or attend to, something of importance for longer than a second or two; and may even become lost in his or her own living room.

Brain injury is, I think, one of the most frightening and devastating tragedies that can affect any human being. At present in the United States, over 3 million people have suffered the effects of stroke or head injury—the two greatest causes of brain damage in adults. In the past, it was felt that very little, if anything, could be done to help them. Fortunately, we know better now and with appropriate rehabilitation efforts, most of those who have sustained brain injuries can look forward, with their families, to much more than being "warehoused" in a so-called resthome or the back ward of a state hospital. One of the most useful tools in the rehabilitation process is the modern microcomputer.

Because the computer is a tool it cannot replace the warmth, acceptance, and understanding of another human being. It can present stimuli—sound, color, shape, movement—in almost any predetermined fashion. The things that a computer does well are precisely those things which are essential for efficient and effective learning. And though the deficits seen in brain injury are due to damage of tissue, their amelioration is brought about by learning, the thing which the human brain is best at.

In the Acute Rehabilitation Center of Mills Memorial Hospital, Computer-Assisted Cognitive Rehabilitation (CACR) is an essential element of the rehabilitation program for brain-injured adults. Patients with cognitive deficits are evaluated by a neuropsychologist and a neuropsychology technician. The specific problems are then treated by the use of several of the current fifty or more computer programs developed for this application. In many cases, the patient works at home on his or her own computer and is seen periodically for monitoring of progress, resolution of problems which may arise, and advancement to more complex programs.

An example of one type of program is in the treatment of hemispheric neglect, one of the more frequent problems following a focal brain injury. Information enters the brain through the nerve pathways of vision, hearing, or touch and goes to what is called an "association area" where sense is made of the information and appropriate responses are coordinated. If this area is damaged, however, the brain acts as if it doesn't know what to do with the information and ignores or "neglects" it. In functional terms, the persons with a left neglect may bump into walls on the right side or eat only the right half of a meal on a plate. If they try to write something, they may use only the right half of the page. Reading is impossible because only the right half of the page is read. If they try to drive a car, anything on their left side is ignored. It is as if half the world doesn't exist, and one's ability to function is literally cut in half.

Warren C. was a fifty-six-year-old aircraft mechanic who suffered a hemorrhagic (bleeding) stroke in the right side of his brain. Among other problems, he had a relatively severe left hemispheric neglect. His medical and physical therapies were very successful, and he was able to walk, dress, and feed himself adequately. However, because of the left neglect, he could not work or drive a car. Even reading the newspaper was essentially impossible for him. Following three months of intensive work with computer programs designed to require him to attend to the left side of his world, he was able to pass his driver's license examination and return to work full time. Six months later, the president of the airline for which Mr. C. worked reported that he was "his old self" again and was being considered for promotion to a supervisory position.

This is one brief example of the usefulness of the microcomputer in an area that, before 1978, no one even considered possible. Not all cases work out as well, of course, but increasing numbers do.

3 Computer Systems

OUTLINE

PROLOGUE

Bill Beason is hired as a computer operator in a hospital. He enters the computer room to find a quiet hum of machines. As he walks into the room for his first day at work, he realizes that some computers and their various hardware in the hospital are analyzing diseases, are transmitting results from tests being conducted, are helping in the rehabilitation of patients, are preparing reports for many users, and are transmitting messages electronically throughout the hospital.

Bill says a prayer that his first day at work is one of peace and quiet and that all computers communicating with each other work successfully. He certainly doesn't need to make any telephone calls reporting malfunctions today.

HOW DOES IT DO THAT?

READ ON.

OBJECTIVES

After studying this chapter, you should be able to:

1. Differentiate among the purpose classifications of computers.

2. Differentiate among the size classifications.

3. Differentiate among the various environments under which a computer may operate.

4. Discuss how the placement of computer systems hardware has changed in the past twenty years.

INTRODUCTION

The previous chapter discussed a typical digital computer's functional parts. This chapter looks in detail at how a digital computer is classified as to purpose and size. It also examines the various environments under which a computer can operate to provide many users the greatest efficiency and flexibility possible. The chapter concludes with a look into how various computers are placed in systems in the business world.

PURPOSE CLASSIFICATIONS

Digital computers can be classified according to purpose: general-purpose, special-purpose, and dedicated general-purpose.

A **general-purpose computer** is designed to process a wide variety of applications (kinds of work or jobs) such as inventory, payroll, and calculation of some physics problem. Most digital computers fall into this classification and can be switched from one application to another by merely changing a stored program, as shown in Figure 3.1. Over 90 percent of the general-purpose computers are manufacturered by International Business Machines (IBM), Univac, Honeywell, Burroughs, Digital Equipment Corporation (DEC), National Cash Register (NCR), Control Data Corporation (CDC), and Amdahl.

A **special-purpose computer** is designed to process one specific application or problem. The program is built into the electrical circuitry, making this computer more efficient, faster, and more reliable but less flexible. If a problem no longer needs to be solved, the circuitry of the special-purpose computer can be changed by an engineer. Hospitals use special-purpose computers for monitoring patients' vital signs. They may also be used to perform calculations in submarines or in aircraft. Channels that tie the various devices with a central processing unit are special-purpose computers.

The latest type of special-purpose computers is the robots that are used in manufacturing. The most commonly used one is the one-armed robot that is used for welding. Many studies have been made; it is estimated that by 1990 much manufacturing will be done by robots. Extensive research is currently being done to perfect them. In January 1984, Zhao Ziyang of the Republic of China visited the University of California at Berkeley, where he was welcomed to the university by a two-foot-high talking robot. Oh my, what a dream to have a robot to wash the car or clean out the garage. Refer to Figure 3.2.

In a **dedicated general-purpose computer,** designed for one primary application, all or part of the instructions that manage the job for that computer are built into the electrical circuitry. Examples of use of this type of computer might be the airlines reservation system and missile and satellite tracking. A dedicated computer cannot be switched from one application to another.

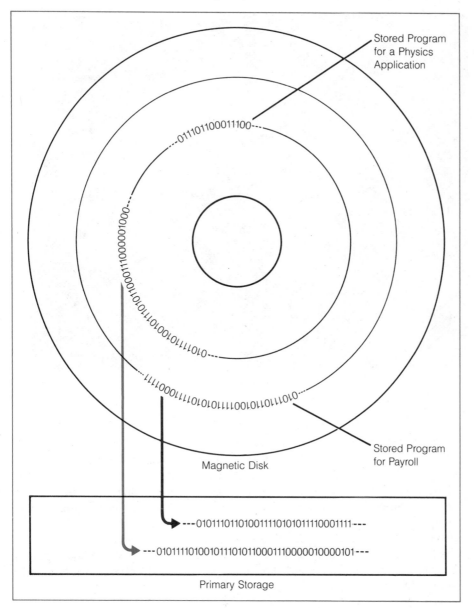

FIGURE 3.1
**General-purpose computers.
These types of computers can
easily change from one application
to another.**

Stored Program
for a Physics
Application

Magnetic Disk

Stored Program
for Payroll

---0101110110100111101010111100001111---

---0101111010010111010110001110000010000101---

Primary Storage

CHECKPOINT **Can you:**

Define general-purpose computer?

Define special-purpose computer?

Define dedicated general-purpose computer?

FIGURE 3.2
An industrial robot.

SIZE CLASSIFICATIONS

A digital computer is also classified by size. Size, in terms of processing power, has to do with the types of jobs that can be run. As a very general rule of thumb, physical size and processing power are correlated, with smaller computers having lesser capabilities. The size categories are: microcomputers, minicomputers, mainframes, and super-computers. This categorization strictly by processing capability is no longer clearcut. It used to be that the processing capability was distinguishable from one size category to another, but microcomputers and minicomputers are now overlapping the higher capability computers. Everybody is getting into everybody else's business.

MICROCOMPUTERS

The **microcomputer** or **micro** is a small, general-purpose computer which can be placed on top of a desk and so is also called a **desktop computer.** (It must be pointed out, however, that minicomputers are sometimes classified as desktop computers also.)

A home computer or personal computer belongs in the micro category. Microcomputers originally began for hobbyists in 1974 and were used for playing blackjack and tick-tack-toe. By 1977 there were 20,000 personal computers in homes. In 1982 about 1 in every 1,000 homes housed micros. By 1984 a total of

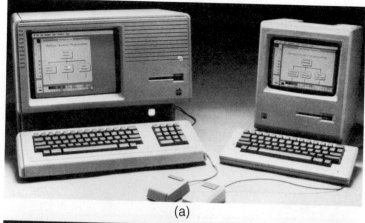

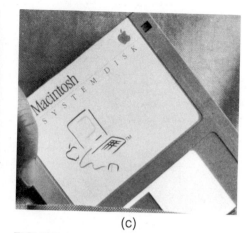

(a)

(c)

(b)

FIGURE 3.3
Personal computers with some peripherals. *(a)* **Lisa and Macintosh personal computers.** *(b)* **Peripherals. (1) Diskette. (2) Disk drive.**

over 1.5 million units had been sold for both business and home use.

Since 1977, micros have been used for such complex applications as monitoring homes for intruders, handling drill work for math and spelling proficiency, and monitoring the vital signs of patients in the intensive care units of hospitals.

A personal computer, as shown in Figure 3.3(a), is a computer system housing several chips. A chip called the microprocessor consists of an arithmetic-logic unit (ALU) and a control section. Another chip can be used for input and output, another for a stored program, and another for an operating system. Those chips that are used for memory are independent chips also. Figure 3.3(b) shows a disk drive and Figure 3.3(c) shows the diskette.

Refer to Figure 3.4 for a diagram showing data flow for a microcomputer. A keyboard is the most commonly used input. A monitor, much like a television screen, is used for output; and diskettes (similar to 45 rpm phonograph records) are used for secondary storage. A printer is frequently used for output. Notice that the hardware uses a bus as the communication channel. Also notice the placement of the control unit or controller. A **control unit** is used with peripheral devices for overseeing the transmission and formatting of the data. A **controller** is an integrated circuit chip that is used to connect the cable (bus) to the hardware. The expanded memory portion noted in the illustration allows a user to add on memory if more capacity is needed.

FIGURE 3.4
**Flow of data for a personal
computer.**

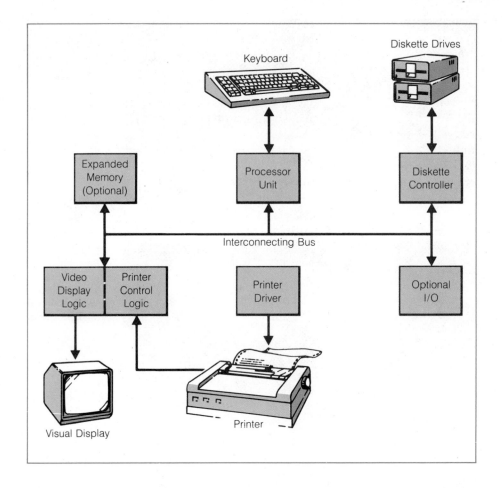

Do not confuse a control section with a control unit. A control unit works with peripherals, while a control section directs a central processing unit on how to carry out an instruction.

The cost of a microcomputer depends upon the processing power, but can range from several hundred dollars up to about $7,000. Personal computers are discussed in detail in Chapters 5 and 6.

A new line of microcomputers which is designed for serving many different users at one time has been recently introduced. This variation is called **super microcomputer** or **super-micros**; the emphasis is on business applications rather than on personal use. Refer to Figure 3.5 which shows a super-microcomputer system that can serve up to 24 users at one time.

MINICOMPUTERS

Minicomputers (minis), like micros, have made great inroads in the computer usage market. Digital Equipment Corporation's PDP-1 (programmed data processor) was developed in 1959 as the first minicomputer. Minicomputer's increased use resulted when people became accustomed to having computers located at their job site. Some minicomputers are **task-oriented;** some of the models do just one unit of work (task) or perform the solution for one application. Their stored program can be changed, however. Another reason for their popularity is that a user can purchase already-prepared programs for these minicomputers and not require the help of computer operators or programmers.

Original Equipment Manufacturers (OEMs) play a very important role in the sale of minicomputers. A mini can be sold to another manufacturer, who will add value to the original hardware. The second manufacturer will include peripherals and possibly software, adding value to the original product. A company that purchases the mini in its unfinished state is considered an OEM. OEM sales represent at least 50 percent of the minicomputer market.

Some micros and minis, called **turnkey systems,** are ready to go after being plugged in and briefly tested. Doctors and dentists use this sort of system frequently. It comes with the hardware, software, a complete set of forms, and the methods and procedures that are to be followed. From a doctor's standpoint, such applications as billing, insurance claims, listings of patient accounts, and accounts receivable are very useful programs included in the software package.

Figure 3.6 shows a minicomputer system that has two megabytes of primary storage and two gigabytes of secondary storage. Since different peripherals are usable, minis are also used in manufacturing.

In 1980, the forecasts for the minicomputer market were extremely bright; predictions projected a 30 percent increase in sales for 1983 and the years following. Historical growth rate figures that were available showed the growth rate for the years 1975 through 1979 as being between 25 and 30 percent. Companies

FIGURE 3.5 **Super-microcomputers.**

WHAT'S RIGHT

Active Minds Put to Productive Work

The microcomputer has opened doors that were firmly shut. The use of a specialized keyboard or specially designed device such as a voice synthesizer or braille terminal allows the handicapped to enter programs, test them, and even sell them for fees. The microcomputer also helps those with pacemakers by monitoring the pacemakers. Those with diabetic problems are aided by the testing of sugar levels in the blood. Deaf people can detect sound vibrations through the use of the microcomputer, opening an entirely new world to them. The working mother or father can remain at home with the children and, through the use of the microcomputer, write, test, and contract for programs right from his or her own living room.

Learn how to use the microcomputers for your own growth, job security, and general awareness.

FIGURE 3.6
Minicomputer system.

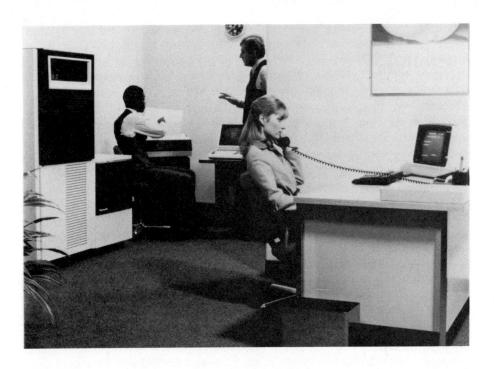

such as Digital Equipment Corporation, Hewlett-Packard, and Data General dominated the minicomputer market accounting for the majority of the $11 billion in sales.

With the recession and a drastic drop in the price of microcomputers, however, the minicomputer market grew only 20 percent in 1981 and 12.5 percent in 1982. Minis gave way to microcomputers for some processing jobs.

Minis having processing power to do a variety of jobs, like larger computer systems but usually do not have great operating speed and flexibility (although it has been proven that some minis out-perform some mainframes). However, a new group of minicomputers has arrived on the scene; these **super-minis** or **super-minicomputers** have greater processing capability than the minicomputer. Super-minis account for over 50 percent of current minicomputer market sales. Think of the super-minis as being on the high-end of the scale of the minicomputer group.

Super-minicomputers offer the advantage of a wide range of storage capabilities as well as a variety of input and output devices such as printers, magnetic tapes, and magnetic disks. Their capacity for secondary storage has an impressive upper limit of up to 512 megabytes. Their primary storage capacity (up to 32 million bytes of data) and their processing capabilities for sharing computer time among users, batch processing, and real-time processing make this computer system a powerful computer. The cost of a super-minicomputer can run as high as $400,000. Refer to Figure 3.7. Super-minicomputers are competing now with mainframes.

MAINFRAMES

The word mainframe was synonymous with central processing unit (CPU) before the tremendous growth of microcomputers. **Mainframe** is now used to refer to a large computer system that provides extensive data-processing capabilities. (These capabilities are discussed in a section later in the chapter regarding different processing environments under which computers can operate.) Mainframes provide extremely fast processing capabilities, and they are usually required to handle an enormous volume of data.

Usually, the mainframe is set apart as a large-scale computer which has faster processing speeds and faster I/O devices than minis and micros. (Until lately, mainframes were distinguishable from minis and micros because mainframes had much greater storage capability, but technological improvements have blurred this distinction.)

An example of a mainframe is the IBM 370, which represents about half of the mainframes installed in the 1970s, with a great portion of them still being used. The IBM 370 model 3033 has 12 megabytes of primary storage. An IBM 3081 has 32 megabytes of primary storage. Mainframes are used in banks, insurance companies, government agencies, department stores, research groups, and almost every company that you can think of which has had computers in its company operation for many years. Dairy operators use mainframes for maintaining 20 million records on 6.5 million cows. The records are used to determine which cows should produce the most milk for the longest period of time as well as to maintain a history on these dairy cattle.

A large-scale computer is used by companies that need a wide range of computing power as well as very fast internal computing speed, in other words, companies with great amounts of throughput. **Throughput** measures the amount of work achieved by a computer in a given day. A large-scale computer handles more jobs per day because of its speed and flexibility and represents the largest segment of the market. Banks, for example, process national credit cards using

WHAT'S RIGHT

What a Star

Would you believe that you could see the ear on the Lincoln monument from 3,000 miles away? A comparable feat is being accomplished by astronomers at the University of California's Lick Observatory, who are producing computer-generated images of stars that are 100 light-years away. Images are produced, not pictures.

X-ray analysis is used for estimating the appearance of these far-off stars. The star is divided into many thousands of parts so that each part can be accurately represented. These data readings are inputted to a minicomputer which, after many refinements of plotting, produces the image of the star.

FIGURE 3.7
VAX 11/785 Super-minicomputer System.

Minicomputers are being sold to doctors for the calculation of patients' bills and for diagnosis of diseases. This type of minicomputer system costs well over $40,000. Not all doctors are using the computer for diagnosis as yet, but many are using the minicomputer for billing. In the past, doctors paid an outside firm for the billing process but are now finding that with the capability of diagnosis, the cost of the minicomputer becomes far more reasonable.

Many doctors' offices have several visual display terminals positioned throughout the office. Formerly, there was just one visual display terminal in an office, with the person handling the accounting being the sole user. Now, however, the doctor also has a terminal in his or her office to make inquiries about research on medical cases or possible side effects from using certain medications.

Instead of the nurse waiting to see the light above the door come on, the nurse might have to learn to respond to the typed words "Come here." Unless the doctor clearly specifies the location, the trick will be to find the correct room.

one or more large-scale computers. Refer to Figure 3.8. More emphasis is now being placed, however, on using minis and micros wherever possible rather than using a large-scale computer for all kinds of work.

Mainframes are classified sometimes as a **family of computers,** when several large-scale computers belong to the same processor grouping. An example is the IBM 3081. Manufacturers introduce the large-scale computers individually or a couple of processors at a time. The family of that computer might not be totally available in the marketplace for a period of many years. Within a family of computers, there is a specific **architecture**—the design or way the different parts of the computer system relate to each other—that is common to all the processors in the family. This gives compatibility that is scaled upward or downward.

The family of computers provides the user with the opportunity to change computers with minimum problems. Perhaps a company needs more storage capacity and faster processing speed. Rather than having to change the instruction set (those instructions understood by a computer), a company will lease a computer that is upward compatible. For the leasing of a higher-level processor, the addressing of primary storage would be different, but the original programs can be run on the new system since it is compatible.

There are different levels or variations of processors in the family, but compatability exists among all. The **high-end processor,** for example, is an extension of the architecture and is usually the last processor of the family that is introduced. It contains some major improvement over the previous processors in the family. The **low-end processor** in that same family does not contain the new feature, nor does it contain many of the features in the higher-level processors. Programs run, however, on a low-end processor will run successfully on a higher-level processor in the family since most families of computers are upward compatible.

Mainframes can serve several users at basically the same time. Micros and

FIGURE 3.8 **IBM 3081 mainframe.**

minis are changing their processing capabilities, and some are able to do this. Processing rotates between programs of users, allowing two or more users to be served by a computer. It appears to users as though the computer is simultaneously processing all programs at one time. This illusion is referred to as **concurrent processing.** Since the operation of the computer is so fast, a user is unaware of its being shared.

SUPER-COMPUTERS

The top-of-the-line computers are called **super-computers.** These are the fastest, largest, and most expensive of all computers; the cost can go as high as $8 to $20 million. What do you get for all that money? You would be able to do weather forecasting, seismic studies, and nuclear research; processing not practicable for any number of humans can be handled easily by super-computers.

The super-computers represent the largest combinations of central processors that are grouped as though they are one computer system. The super-computer's processing power is so fast and its storage capacity is so large, many processors must work with the central processor for the system to work. Many of the manufacturers claim the processing speed of these computers reaches between 400 to 600 million operations per second though these high performances are never really attained. It is safe to say that the actual performance is, in most cases, closer to the 100 million instructions per second. This is extremely fast when compared to mainframes that perform in the 50 million instructions per second (mips) range.

Plans by the year 1989 for the Superspeed Project in Japan are for that super-computer to reach one billion operations a second. This super-computer system is purportedly to be compatible with IBM mainframes.

In Figure 3.9, the large vertical columns in a 90° arc are the Cray X-MP mainframe; it occupies 24 square feet of floor space. The glass doors can be opened to check any integrated circuit boards and replace them as needed in case of defective or malfunctioning hardware.

The primary storage (called by Cray as central memory) can hold up to 64 million bytes of data depending upon the model selected. A variation to its primary storage is its solid-state storage device which performs like secondary storage; no magnetic disks or magnetic tape are used with this type of storage, however. The solid state storage device uses bipolar semiconductor chips, providing 1024 million bytes of storage. The bipolar semiconductor chips are extremely fast internal storage that use the integrated circuit chip concept; these chips are used in various parts of a computer system.

The processing time of super-computers is extremely fast. Imagine humans doing 20,000 simultaneous equations accurately; large-scale computers might take a week to perform these calculations. The super-computer was designed for this type of work and completes the calculations rapid-fire.

Examples of a super-computer at Cray Research Inc.'s Cray-1 and Cray X-MP, Hitachi's S8 10/20, Fujitsu's VP2000 and Control Data Corporation's Cyber 205. There have only been about 90 super-computers sold since 1976, although 28 of that total were shipped in 1983. These computers were first used for scientific applications. In the latter part of 1982, however, the trend shifted to applications

WHAT'S RIGHT

A Shift In Emphasis

From the late 1960s, the time-share industry sold its excess computer time to those companies or individuals who wanted to rent computer time. With the tremendous decline in computer hardware costs, companies and individuals purchased their own hardware rather than rent time.

The time-share industry is a $15 billion industry and has been increasing by about 20 to 25 percent each year. The trend toward purchase rather than time rental, however, clearly shows that a shift to other means for profit is needed, as the industry's pattern is showing an uneven growth rate.

Time-share companies, to survive, have to provide special information services to customers, such as providing software allowing all the computers to successfully communicate with each other, financial services, and specialized data bases. The need is for super–service bureaus. General Electric Information Services Company (GEISCO) is channeling its efforts this way by acquiring software houses to provide needed software support to industry. Another company, Tymshare, expanded its airline reservation and billing network to meet the changing times.

FIGURE 3.9
Cray X-MP super-computer system.

that deal with aerospace, chemical, semiconductor and biomedical suppliers. Applications also dealing with big business and large companies that sell their computer time to users such as oil companies, banks, and airlines are also purchasing the super-computers.

When a company purchases a super-computer, the work done on a large-scale computer can be off-loaded (transferred) to the super-computer, thus freeing the large-scale computer for other uses. This assumes that the processing time and the transformation of the large-scale computer's code into a code the super-computer can understand are justifiable.

Table 3.1 provides a comparison of the various types of computer systems just discussed, summarizing purposes and cost range for each size classification.

CHECKPOINT **Can you:**

Identify the various size classifications of computers?
State some possible uses of each size?

TABLE 3.1. **Comparisons of Computer Systems Classified by Size.**

SIZE CLASSIFICATION	PURPOSE	COST
Microcomputer	Small, general-purpose computer; personal and business use	Up to $7,000
Super-minicomputer	Handles variety of tasks	Up to $400,000
Mainframe	Handles variety of tasks and large volume of data	Up to several million dollars
Super-computer	Handles tremendous amount of data; extremely fast processing speed	Many millions of dollars

OPERATIONAL ENVIRONMENTS

Environments under which a computer can operate vary, but usually the larger the computer system, the more types of operations can be performed. Some of these environments are briefly investigated: multiprocessing, time sharing, and multiprogramming.

MULTIPROCESSING

In 1950, some computer installations began operation as enormous **service bureaus,** essentially companies which meet a user's processing needs for a fee by providing hardware and personnel to process the jobs. They must operate on a twenty-four-hour basis, seven days a week. Western Union has been providing this computer service to companies, large and small.

A very large system such as this, which services thousands of customers, operates in a multiprocessing environment. **Multiprocessing** utilizes multiple central processing units made up of arithmetic-logic units and control sections as one computer system.

In this environment, a computer system can execute several independent programs simultaneously or one very large complex program. For an example of several independent programs, one central processor might handle all communication work with some terminals, while another performed necessary work to maintain the files of programs or data at the installation, and yet another performed work on the preparation of reports for management.

A large program demanding extensive execution time is divided into segments or modules that separate it into logical parts. For example, a central processing unit might be preparing input data into an order needed for processing, while another central processing unit is preparing necessary calculations for the next stage of a program execution; yet another is at the same time preparing output for each stage as a program is executed. As each stage or module of a program is completed, a central processing unit switches to meet the next requirements in a program.

In another example of multiprocessing, two central processing units form a mirror-like image of each other. They both do the same processing and share the same data and some peripheral devices. By running in parallel, if one of these central processing units "goes down" (becomes inoperative), the other is used for a back-up to the system. BART (Bay Area Rapid Transit) in San Francisco has two central processors do exactly the same processing as they monitor the trains that run through the subway system.

In Figure 3.10 the Cray X-MP multiprocessor system is shown. The solid-state storage device, as previously discussed, can communicate directly with the input or output subsystem. Notice how central memory (primary storage) can be bypassed, if desired, for any transferring of input or output. This is an exception to the rule. To be able to accommodate the hardware and software requirements established by other computer manufacturers, front-ends are used. These front-ends, (also called front-end processors), provide an interface which allows the super-computer to accept and understand other manufacturer's hardware and software applications. Unless the differences are communicated and understood, a computer system of one manufacturer could not use a computer system of another.

FIGURE 3.10
Cray X-MP multiprocessor system.

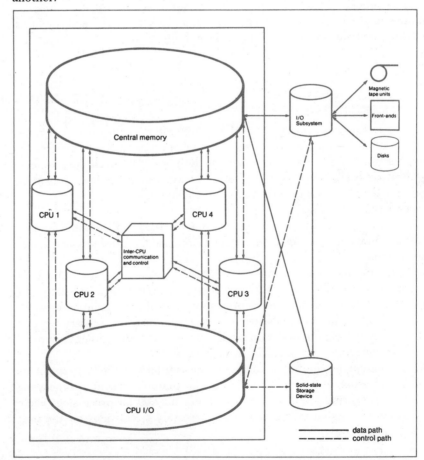

TIME SHARING

A computer installation operating in a time-sharing environment has a community-type computer that can be rented by many users, affording companies of all sizes processing capability. Users are not necessarily from one company or one organization but from many. A user pays for the service on a time-used basis plus a possible overhead cost. Although each user's files are located at a computer, these are accessible from one or more terminals at a user location as long as the user can give the appropriate account number and password. A **password** consists of some symbols that are unique to a user—such as mother's maiden name, a birth-date, a pet's name, and so on—which must be entered in the computer to gain access.

Time sharing can also be in-house, meaning that within a company various departments share the use of a computer and each pay for the cost of using that computer on the basis of time used. Refer to Figure 3.11.

A user of an in-house time-sharing system is an automobile warehouser in Michigan who carries 75 vendor lines and 25,000 part numbers. Before 1978, the entire inventory was done by manual methods, with salespeople writing the invoices, shipping records, and keeping the inventory as current as possible. The volume of data became overwhelming, and the up-to-dateness of the inventory records left much to be desired.

As is so often the case, the company turned to leasing a computer. The warehouser began the computer operation by having all its billing recorded and processed. As various other departments were changed from the manual system to the computer system, it became necessary for the computer to serve several users.

To allow this access to various users, the time of a central processing unit is divided into small portions so that the computer can switch from one job to the next without a user even realizing it is happening. Because of a computer's speed, many users can be served what appears to be simultaneously; this is referred to as **time sharing.** While a computer receives the invoice data from one of the salespeople, it might be looking up for some person in the buying department the amount of inventory on hand for a particular part number. Certainly when a computer serves many users in a given time-frame, the user does not get as quick a response time from the computer as he or she would if the user was the only one. Think of **response time** as the time that elapses from the time you asked for information until you receive it.

MULTIPROGRAMMING

The multiprocessing discussion centered around hardware. What about software? Is just one program stored and executed in primary storage? No, two or more programs work independently of each other and are not related in any way. This is referred to as **multiprogramming.** From an operating system's standpoint, two or more programs take turns for processing as the computer switches from one program to the next. Response time also is slower in this environment than if just one program was being served by the computer.

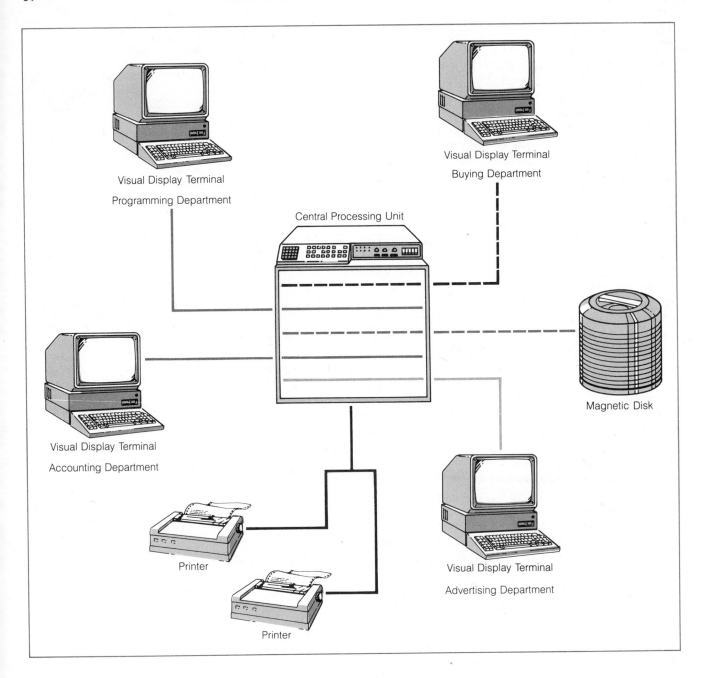

Visual Display Terminal

Programming Department

Visual Display Terminal

Buying Department

Central Processing Unit

Magnetic Disk

Visual Display Terminal

Accounting Department

Printer

Visual Display Terminal

Advertising Department

Printer

FIGURE 3.11
Time sharing.

A computer does the required processing for job 1 until that program requires some input or output time. Channels take care of the input and output functions for job 1 while a central processing unit does calculating, logical work, and primary storage fetching and storing of data for job 2. When job 2 needs input or output time, the computer is again diverted to processing job 1, or whatever other program is stored in primary storage at that time.

In a multiprogramming environment, those programs being executed differ each time. Also the number of bytes (characters) needed for each stored program differs from program to program. In addition, several programs are being executed at the same time. Larger computer systems can do several tasks at once since their operating speed is so fast; this is referred to a **multitasking.** To take advantage of a computer's speed, different programs have their input and output prepared simultaneously. There is more than one stored program being executed intermittently. Six stored programs are executed in the following multitasking example: an inquiry is being received from a terminal for job 1; a disk is being read for job 2; magnetic tape is being written for job 3; hard copy is being prepared for job 4; calculations are being done for job 5; and magnetic tape is being read for job 6. This computer is working on five jobs dealing with input and output while it does the calculation for the sixth job. Refer to Table 3.2 for a comparison of the terms multiprogramming, multiprocessing, and multitasking.

CHECKPOINT **Can you:**

Explain multiprocessing and how it is used?

Explain time sharing and why it is used?

Explain multiprogramming and why it is used?

Explain multitasking and why it is used?

TABLE 3.2.   **Comparisons of Multiprogramming, Multiprocessing, and Multitasking and Time Sharing.**

TERM	DEFINITION	PURPOSE	VIEWED FROM STANDPOINT OF
Multiprocessing	Two or more CPUs	Relieve main CPU of many tasks	Hardware
		Share primary storage between processors	
Multiprogramming	Two or more programs stored in primary storage at one time	Process one program until there is a request for input or output.	Operating system
		Makes for efficient use of computer.	
Multitasking	Two or more tasks for input and output processed at same time	Makes for efficient use of computer. Serves and satisfies many users' needs quickly.	Hardware, operating system, user
Time sharing	Two or more users being served by a central processing unit	Allows many users opportunity to use a computer's resource	User, operating system, and hardware

PLACEMENT OF COMPUTERS

The physical placement of a computer system in a company may be referred to as decentralized, centralized, or distributed. Over the past two decades, the preferred placement has changed, and each shift has brought certain advantages.

DECENTRALIZED SYSTEM

In the 1960s batch processing was the mode of operation; all the data for a particular job was collected together and run at one time through a computer. A **decentralized computer system** approach existed; this meant computers were located at individual sites, each operating independently. Duplications in data-processing staff existed, causing companies to spend many additional dollars than otherwise necessary. Management had limited control over this decentralized configuration. From the end-user's standpoint, response time—that period of time from the beginning of the inquiry to the beginning of the return of the information to the user—was good since the user had to compete for time with users at only one site. Refer to Figure 3.12.

CENTRALIZED SYSTEM

In the 1970s, **transaction processing** was a popular mode of operation; data was captured (recorded) at a local site and then transmitted to the computer over telephone lines. A **local site** refers to a location that is removed from the central site—perhaps a branch office or district office of a company. A central site might be the headquarters of a company.

A **centralized computer system** approach uses a large-scale computer accessed by remote terminals, as shown in Figure 3.13. This set-up made for less duplication in the data-processing staff, resulting in more effective management control since it set standards that users had to follow.

Another advantage that resulted was **resource sharing;** data, printers, various peripherals, programs, and telephone lines used for data transmission were shared among various sites. Refer to Figure 3.14. A failure of a telephone line or computer equipment, however, left a remote site helpless. This major problem was offset to an extent by the advantage of a user having a wider variety of peripherals and access to a variety of programs. Printers are very expensive peripherals; resource sharing permits a company to purchase a very high-quality printer since it can be shared by various users.

DISTRIBUTED SYSTEM

In the 1980s, distributed data processing is becoming more popular; it combines the strengths of centralization and decentralization. **Distributed data processing**

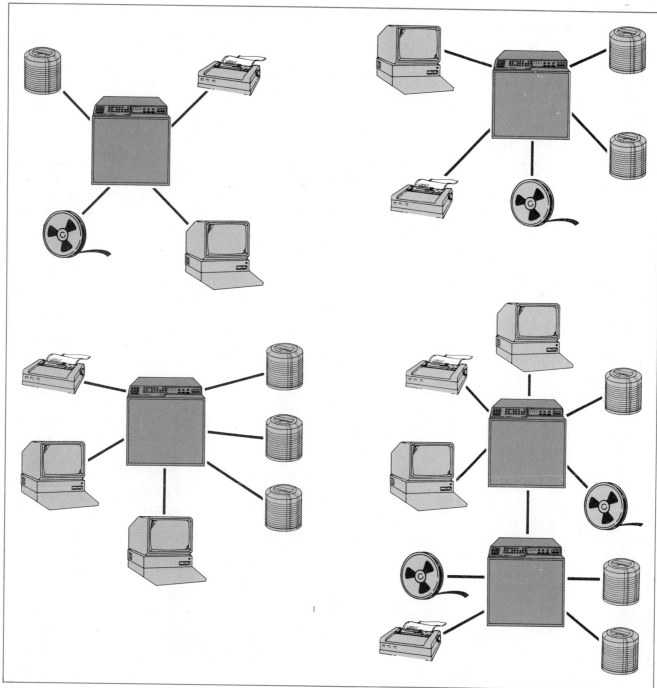

FIGURE 3.12 **A decentralized computer system for a company.**

(DDP) uses a decentralized computer system which means that many computers are doing processing at many different geographical locations. We can equate it to a sophisticated time-sharing system that has telephone lines used for connecting the computers together. Distributed data processing places computers where

FIGURE 3.13
A centralized computer system.

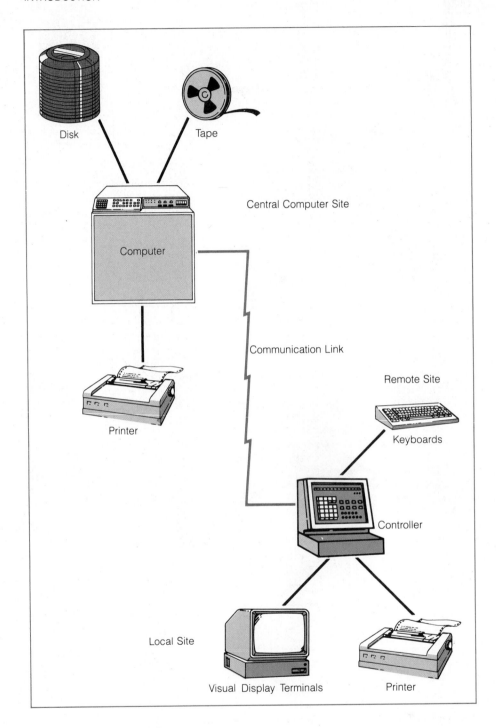

Disk

Tape

Central Computer Site

Computer

Communication Link

Remote Site

Printer

Keyboards

Controller

Local Site

Visual Display Terminals

Printer

problems and work are located, and it places data at the closest point where it is used.

Such a system, for which a company has computer centers located at different sites, has several characteristics. The entire DDP is interacting; it is not just physically scattered. Each local site is set up as a module, having the required hardware and software selected to best fit that site's processing needs. Another important characteristic is that data is shared among sites. Data must be exchanged without any problems on formatting (how data is set up within records and files), accessing (how data is retrieved), and updating. Tight controls and standards must be enforced by management so the system is efficient. When evaluating where data should be placed, every effort is made to minimize communication costs. Other considerations for placement of data involve insuring data protection from misuse and meeting needs for updating.

Some experts envision that most companies will use DDP in one form or another. The cost of housing workers in a central office site versus that in suburban office sites is much higher; the economics of this fact alone will tempt many companies to switch to DDP. Over 50 percent of the top 100 companies ranked in *Fortune* magazine have switched to DDP. Figure 3.15 shows a typical distributed data processing system.

Advantages and Disadvantages of a Distributed System

Reasons are many why companies are changing to distributed data processing or are planning to make a transition. From an end-user's standpoint, DDP is easy to use and gives flexibility since each site has its own individuality. This enables a local site to handle different applications that perhaps could not be processed on a centralized system. For example, the combining of data entry, data-base processing, inquiry, and word processing allows an automated office approach. This concept is discussed in Chapter 16.

From management's standpoint, DDP gives companies that have tremen-

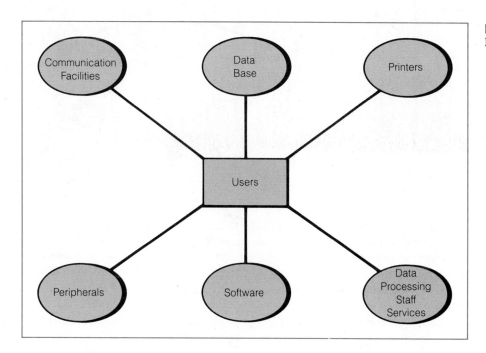

FIGURE 3.14
Resource sharing.

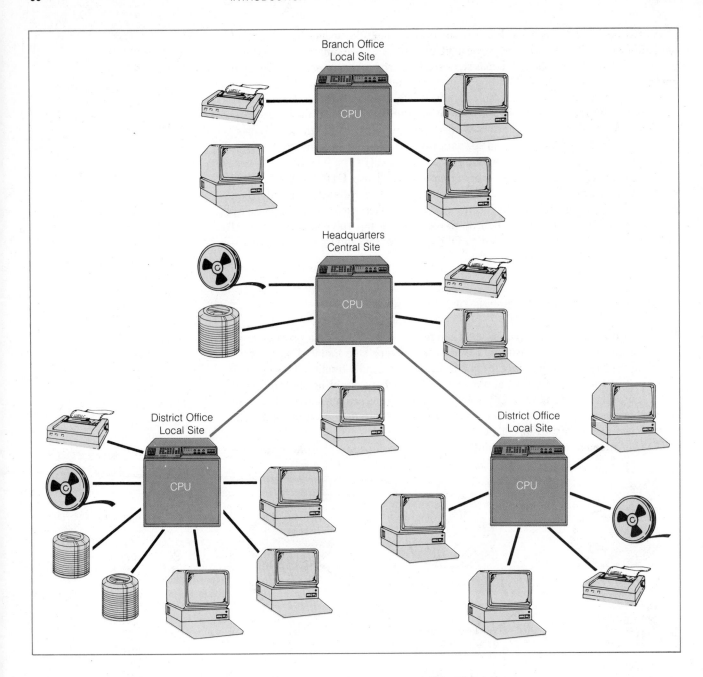

FIGURE 3.15
Distributed data processing.

dously busy mainframes an opportunity to take some of the workload off of the large mainframes and place it on the minis or micros. This avoids the need to upgrade the present central processing unit. Up-to-date equipment is used at a local site because this equipment is much cheaper than at a central site. Work is shifted to a local level along with the responsibility for a job. Response time is much quicker since a computer is located at a site requiring information.

About 80 percent of a local site's processing is strictly local, leaving only 20 percent of work needing communication to corporate headquarters. DDP then reduces communication costs since batch processing can be done at a local site. Day-end totals or data needed for corporate reports are transmitted over communication lines, eliminating a need for sending detailed records, as was formerly done in a centralized environment. Since records are concentrated at a local site, the job of auditing is made easier due to the smaller number of records being examined. The only way, however, that auditing can be a straight forward undertaking is with good, tight management controls set at the local site.

DDP is not without disadvantages, however. Many of the reasons listed why companies are not planning any DDP center around costs and staffing. A company might have difficulty justifying the costs of hardware and software to even initiate the system. Communication costs for some companies can be staggering, however, so sometimes it is a trade-off as to what costs the most over a period of years. Not only is additional hardware required, but software limitations create a high cost factor since data must be able to be shared through interconnection of computers. We shall concentrate on how this is done in Chapter 10.

Staffing needs for DDP can pose problems too. Some staff at a central site feel threatened when their work is transferred to a local site, so some lack of committment must be expected when distributed data processing is undertaken. In addition the number of highly trained professionals available is limited, so staffing local sites poses a problem. Then, too, personnel at a local site can lose sight of the system as a whole by thinking in terms of *that* site's needs and not the entire company's needs. Data may be changed in format, needed records may not be kept current and sensitive data may not be protected.

APPLICATION: DDP AND THE FBI

Before 1980 the Federal Bureau of Investigation (FBI) used a centralized system for criminal records, with a data base being maintained at the headquarters in Washington, D.C., and all the states accessing it. In 1980 the FBI discontinued its centralized approach. Had the FBI gone to a decentralized approach, each state would have maintained its own data base on criminals in that state. If this plan were followed, those criminals engaging in activities in two or more states would not be detected since each state would be maintaining its own, uncorrelated records (assuming that no composite list is prepared). Each state could maintain all the wanted lists in all states, but little communication would exist between states under a decentralized configuration.

Communication is of utmost concern to the FBI, so a mix of both centralized and decentralized approaches is appropriate. With DDP the state branches of the FBI control a system of record-keeping, with each having its own data base but also carrying on communication with other states for inquiry about criminals with records in several states. If a particular criminal has records in any other state, the communication network is used for transmitting records from one state to another.

CHECKPOINT **Can you:**

Distinguish among decentralized, centralized, and distributed computer system configurations?

Give some advantages and disadvantages for each?

SUMMARY

- Digital computers can be classified by purpose.

- A general-purpose computer can process both scientific and business problems in a wide variety of applications by switching from program to program.

- A special-purpose computer serves a particular application and has its own built-in program of instructions; its circuitry can be altered so that it can serve a new application.

- A dedicated special-purpose computer is built for a specific application and cannot be changed.

- Digital computers can also be classified by size, from smallest to largest: microcomputers, minicomputers, super-microcomputers, super-minicomputers, mainframes, and super-computers. Usually the smaller a computer system, the slower its processing speed.

- Both microcomputers and minicomputers are very popular; both can be called desktop computers. Minis are generally faster at processing data than microcomputers.

- The minicomputer market is highly concentrated with Original Equipment Manufacturer (OEM) sales. A second manufacturer will buy a stripped-down minicomputer, add value to it by possibly writing programs and adding peripherals, then sell it as a package.

- Minicomputers, also called a turnkey system, can be easily installed in offices where no professional data-processing personnel are employed. Once it is plugged in for operation, little training time is required to operate the equipment.

- The mainframe has very fast internal speed and can handle a variety of work.

- Super-computers are gradually coming into their own through their use in aerospace, chemical, semi conductor, biomedical, banking, and insurance applications. Super-computers generally execute in excess of 100 million instructions per second.

- In a multiprocessing environment, two or more central processors make up one computer system. Using parallel processing, that is, each is doing the same processing. Checking is constantly being done to make certain that the same results are obtained. Multiprocessing can also mean that two or more central processors are working on the same program or application at the same time. In multiprocessing, minicomputers can be handling the input and output processing or scheduling for a mainframe.

- Multiprogramming involves two or more programs being executed at what appears to be the same time but which are actually run independent of each other. The computer processes a job until it needs input or output. This continual switching from program to program continues in a round-robin fashion. Multiprogramming uses time sharing. Each user is not generally aware, however, of other users.

- Multitasking operates under a multiprogramming environment and refers to the simultaneous input and output of many jobs at the same time.

- Configurations used for large computer systems have varied over the past two decades, moving from an emphasis on decentralized systems to one on centralized, then distributed systems.

- Decentralized computer systems were common in the 1960s. End-users had good response time since the computer system served just one locality. A duplication in cost for staffing and storing data resulted.

- A centralized computer system was the structure most popular in the 1970s. Resources were shared, meaning fewer duplications and providing end-users with greater flexibility for problem solving since a centralized computer system was usually a large-scale computer with a variety of peripherals. In a centralized computer system, management could exercise better and tighter controls over data and resources.

- Distributed data processing, which enjoys great popularity in the 1980s, involves the dispersing of computing power at various locations within a company. Computer systems used in a DDP environment are set up separately to best fit each site's processing requirements. A distributed data processing (DDP) system combines the strengths of both centralized and decentralized computer systems although a DDP system does have some disadvantages. The advantages of using DDP are ease in use, greater flexibility for the end-users at each site, possibility of off-loading a busy mainframe, quicker response time, reduction in communication costs, and easier auditing capabilities. The disadvantages of using DDP center around staffing local sites and setting up and maintaining standards for consistency in data formatting, accessing, updating, and exchanging data.

- Placement of data depends upon where it can be most strategically located for updating, protecting, and inquiring data.

STUDY GUIDE

REVIEW OF TERMINOLOGY

The following terminology was discussed in this chapter:

architecture
centralized computer
  system
concurrent processing
control unit
controller
decentralized computer
  system
dedicated general-
  purpose computer
desktop computer
distributed data
  processing (DDP)
family of computers
general-purpose
  computer
high-end processor
local site

low-end processor
mainframe
microcomputer (micro)
minicomputer (mini)
multiprogramming
multiprocessing
multitasking
Original Equipment
  Manufacturer (OEM)
password
resource sharing
service bureaus
special-purpose computer
super-computer
super-microcomputer
  (super-micro)
super-minicomputer
  (super-mini)
task-oriented
throughput
time sharing
transaction processing
turnkey system

MULTIPLE CHOICE

Circle the item that completes each statement correctly.

1. Which computer system cannot be changed from one application to another:
   a. general-purpose only
   b. general-purpose and special-purpose
   c. special-purpose only
   d. dedicated general-purpose only
   e. special-purpose and dedicated general-purpose

2. Various computers that have the same design and are hence compatible are referred to as:
   a. its architecture
   b. low-end processors
   c. high-end processors
   d. a family of computers
   e. special-purpose computers

3. A personal computer is classified as a:
   a. microcomputer
   b. minicomputer
   c. mainframe
   d. super-computer
   e. super-microcomputer

4. OEM's are usually associated with this computer system:
   a. microcomputer
   b. mincomputer
   c. mainframe
   d. super-computer
   e. large-scale

5. The PDP-1 was associated with this computer system:
   a. microcomputer
   b. minicomputer
   c. mainframe
   d. super-computer
   e. high-end processor

6. The Cray X-MP is associated with this computer system:
   a. microcomputer
   b. minicomputer
   c. mainframe
   d. super-computer
   e. large-scale

7. Desktop computers are associated with:
   a. microcomputers only
   b. mincomputers only
   c. microcomputers and minicomputers
   d. high-end processors
   e. mainframes

8. Turnkey system refers to a computer system that:
   a. requires no professional computer operator
   b. requires no professional programmers
   c. usually needs very little testing
   d. has the methods and procedures already designed
   e. all of these

9. When two or more programs are stored in primary storage at the same time, this is called:
   a. tasking
   b. multitasking
   c. multiprogramming
   d. multiprocessing
   e. architecture

10. When multiple arithmetic-logic units and control sections are linked together to form one computer system, this is referred to as:
    a. multi-programming
    b. multitasking
    c. multiprocessing
    d. time sharing
    e. low-end processor

11. Two or more programs are taking turns in being processed on a computer, this is called:
    a. multi-programming
    b. resource sharing
    c. multiprocessing
    d. time sharing
    e. response time

12. There are many computer systems being used at different cities and each is doing its own work independent of the others with no communication existing between sites. This is called a:
    a. decentralized computer system
    b. centralized computer system
    c. distributed computer system
    d. time sharing
    e. multiprocessing

13. An expensive printer made available for all users at a company is an example of:
    a. time sharing
    b. multitasking
    c. turnkey systems
    d. resource sharing
    e. multiprogramming

14. Data is placed where it is entered and used, with each site sharing the data. This is an example of a:
    a. decentralized computer system
    b. centralized computer system
    c. distributed computer system
    d. turnkey system
    e. family of computers

15. How much work a computer turns out in a day is called its:
    a. response time
    b. family of computers
    c. multiprocessing
    d. throughput
    e. controller

TRUE/FALSE QUESTIONS

Circle T for each true statement, F for each false one.

1. **T/F** A special-purpose computer has its program already written.

2. **T/F** A desktop computer is never a large-scale computer.

3. **T/F** A normal user would never have the volume of work to own a super-computer.

4. **T/F** Microcomputers are never mainframes.

5. **T/F** A large-scale computer system is often used by companies for processing data.

6. **T/F** The most common input device for a microcomputer is a keyboard.

7. **T/F** The type of secondary storage used on the microcomputer is the diskette.

8. **T/F** A minicomputer was developed before a microcomputer.

9. **T/F** Over half of minicomputer sales is generated through EOMs.

10. **T/F** Minicomputers are often dedicated to do just one task.

11. **T/F** Company A makes a minicomputer that is lacking in programs and peripherals. It sells to Company B who adds value to the minicomputer. Company A is the OEM.

12. **T/F** A minicomputer usually costs several millions of dollars.

13. **T/F** Turnkey systems only apply to large-scale computers.

14. **T/F** A computer, although appearing that it is doing several tasks at one time, is basically doing just one job at a time.

15. **T/F** Time sharing allows a computer to service a smaller number of users.

16. **T/F** When a user needs to have very fast processing capability, he or she will order a microcomputer.

17. **T/F** Response time refers to the time used for sharing peripherals.

18. **T/F** A decentralized computer system is composed of units operating independently of each other.

19. **T/F** A centralized computer system has less duplication of staff.

20. **T/F** Management has better control over a centralized computer system than in a decentralized computer system.

21. **T/F** A distributed data processing system provides an easy way for users to satisfy their processing needs at their individual sites.

22. **T/F** A distributed data processing system is like a large time-sharing system.

REVIEW QUESTIONS

1. What is a general-purpose computer? a special-purpose computer? a dedicated general-purpose computer?

2. Where is a microcomputer used? What is it used for?

3. How does a super-minicomputer differ from a microcomputer with regard to purpose, input capabilities, and cost?

4. What is meant by a task-oriented minicomputer?

5. Are super-minicomputers and minicomputers the same hardware?

6. What is a mainframe? Where are they used?

7. What is a super-computer?

8. What is meant by throughput? Which type of computer has the greatest throughput?

9. What is multiprocessing? Give different examples of when it might be used.

10. What is time sharing?

11. What is multiprogramming? How does it differ from multiprocessing?

12. What is response time?

13. What is resource sharing?

14. In distributed data processing, where is the data located? Where can a computer be located?

15. Which computer placement system requires the most rigid setting up and enforcing of standards? Why are standards necessary?

DISCUSSION QUESTIONS

1. What are the size classifications of computer systems? What is an important characteristic about each that sets it apart from the others?

2. Are the concepts of time sharing and multiprogramming related in any way? Explain your answer.

3. Can a general purpose computer perform many tasks? If so, under which environment or environments can it operate? Is the user generally aware of other users?

4. A computer system has simultaneous input and output. Explain how this can be true.

5. What are the differences between a centralized versus a decentralized computer system with regards to management? to duplication in costs? to staffing?

6. Discuss the various advantages and disadvantages of using DDP.

PROJECTS

1. Assume you have just purchased some property in *your home state* and a title insurance company's service is used for recording that transaction. This title company has headquarters in Birmingham and has three regional offices in New Orleans, St. Louis, and Montgomery. The Montgomery, Alabama, office has four district offices under its jurisdiction. Each state has different laws on the information that is to be recorded as well as different forms that must be completed. The title insurance company must present these completed forms for your signature in order to finalize the sale. You are billed a fee varying according to the selling cost of a property plus license fees that a state requires.

    a. Why is this application a good one for DDP?
    b. Set up your proposed distributed data processing system, keeping in mind that the headquarters wants daily accounting of fees collected at all offices. Draw a schematic showing your proposed DDP system.
    c. What types of processing can be handled at the local sites versus the central site?
    d. Where is the data located? Give reasons to support your answer.

2. Using your field of interest, investigate how some large company related to that field has set up its organizational structure for computing power. Find out if the company plans any changes in the near future or has made such changes recently.

People in Computing

Sandra L. Kurtzig

COMPANY
ASK Computer Systems, Inc.

TITLE OF POSITION
Chairman

EDUCATIONAL BACKGROUND
A B.S. in math and chemistry from the University of California at Los Angeles. An M.S. in aeronautical engineering from Stanford University.

"You will never make it—a woman has no chance of succeeding in a business world dominated by men."

"You just don't have the experience in developing software for manufacturing companies."

"A manufacturing system on a minicomputer will never work."

These are some of the helpful hints people offered me when I started ASK Computer Systems in 1974. Of course, I appreciated all this encouragement, but I must admit it scared me a bit since I couldn't change the fact that I was a woman and the products I wanted to develop were a family of minicomputer-based manufacturing and financial management software products for manufacturing companies. But it was from this advice that I learned my first lesson in becoming an entrepreneur: don't believe everything people say to you or about you. Take half of what is said and analyze that for whatever useful ideas may lie hidden within. Throw the other half away because, regardless of the good intentions behind the advice, an essential factor is missing. Nobody knows you—your capabilities, your flaws, your strengths—the way that you know yourself. Therefore, there are no pat answers, no standard advice, no specific guidelines to steer you to a path of success. It varies from individual to individual, depending on your abilities and shortcomings and how you use both to attain your goals.

Prior to founding ASK, I held both technical and marketing positions with General Electric Company, Information Business Systems Division. Previous to that, I was with TRW Systems, an aerospace company.

The point is that how to succeed is an individual thing. Anyone can become a successful entrepreneur. Everyone who does follows a different path. But there are some ways to increase your chances in starting a successful venture. Remember that I said ignore half the advice people give you—here's the advice I hope you heard. First, believe in yourself. Know your weaknesses; know your strengths. You need a lot of self-confidence to tolerate the uncertainty in starting a business. Second, and most important, surround yourself with good people, the best you can find—people who are better than yourself. It's these people who make a company. Create an atmosphere or a culture that encourages team playing. Third, focus. Choose a product in a particular market segment and stick to it. Set realistic, hence achievable, goals. Fourth, expect to work long hours and make personal sacrifices. And I'm afraid the hours and sacrifices don't get any less as the company grows. And, last, if you should by chance become relatively successful, don't get too wrapped up in your own press or what people are saying to you or about you. Remember, you're still the same person who people said would never make it a few years ago.

4

Data Manipulation

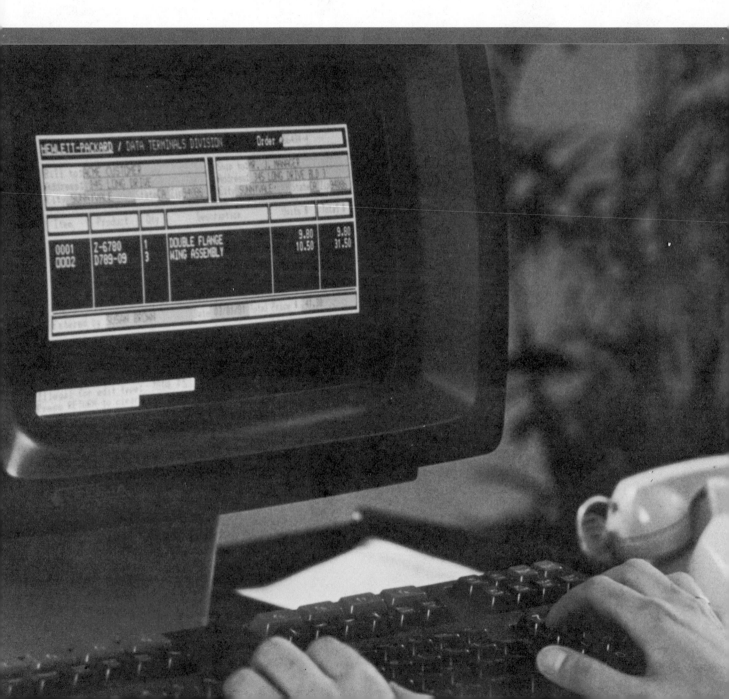

OUTLINE

PROLOGUE

Tom wishes to go to the ballet, the art show, and a professional basketball game. How can he get from one ticket agency to another with his car barely functioning? His friend tells him to go to the department store down the street since they have a ticket agency that can sell him tickets for various performances.

The man behind the counter asks which event Tom wishes to attend for the ballet. He asks Tom if he is familiar with the seating arrangement and the ticket prices. Tom tells the agent no, but he doesn't want the most expensive seats. Will these do, the agent asks, as he points to the television-like screen on his microcomputer, showing all the seat arrangements, printed in color code. Those are perfect, Tom answers.

In less than a minute, the ticket to the ballet is printed and given to Tom. Tom scratches his head and wonders.

HOW DOES IT DO THAT?

READ ON.

OBJECTIVES

After studying this chapter, you should be able to:

1. Identify data as to its type of field.

2. Differentiate among the methods of printing.

3. Explain how data is classified.

4. Explain how storage retrieval of records is done and why it is important in today's data-processing world.

5. Identify some ways that data can be associated (related) in the real world.

INTRODUCTION

The need for usable data—both accurate and complete—becomes greater each year; likewise, the uses to which that data is put multiply rapidly. If we looked into history, we would see facts being recorded by the Romans, the Greeks, and even as far back as prehistoric man. Although the means of recording data have differed with time and cultural groups, the purpose remains the same: to manipulate it into the form of useful information.

This chapter deals with manipulating data, with emphasis on microcomputer use. The various hardware of the microcomputer is used for illustration purposes. For processing on mainframes, the concepts are the same, with the exception that a magnetic disk or magnetic tape is used in place of a diskette.

ORGANIZATION OF DATA

Recalling that data means facts and that all data stored in a computer's memory is organized for use in a hierarchical structure of data bases, files, records, fields, characters, and bits.

The most elemental form of character data can be numeric characters (0 through 9), alphabetic characters (the letters A through Z), or special characters (those normally used as punctuation). Refer to Figure 4.1. Alphanumeric characters are those that are not classified as to type.

Characters form fields of data; each field is a combination of characters that collectively means something, such as an amount paid to a bank savings account or a product description. Fields are classified into three types: numeric, alphabetic, and alphanumeric (see Table 4.1).

A field that records just numbers 0 through 9 is called a **numeric field.** An example of a numeric field is an age field. Normally a person's age is reported as 18, 32, 64, not eighteen, thirty-two, sixty-four.

An **alphabetic field** contains alphabetic data, but blanks are also allowed in this type of field. An example of an alphabetic field is the name of a state or a month (only if the state name and month are spelled out).

An **alphanumeric field** contains a combination of numeric data, alphabetic data, and special characters. An alphanumeric field is composed of at least two such kinds of data—for example, numbers and alphabetics, or numbers and special characters, or alphabetics and special characters. An address is an alphanumeric field containing all three kinds of data. A person's name with a title and the desired punctuation or hyphens is an alphanumeric field. Since a person's name frequently contains special characters, the name field is usually designated as an alphanumeric field. If the user identifies the field as being alphabetic and the computer finds alphanumeric data, the job can be dropped from the computer. In such a case, the computer is unable to determine which data type is to be used.

The many fields about a person or a subject matter form a record. The many records for an application represent an organized collection of data called a file. Many logically related files form a data base.

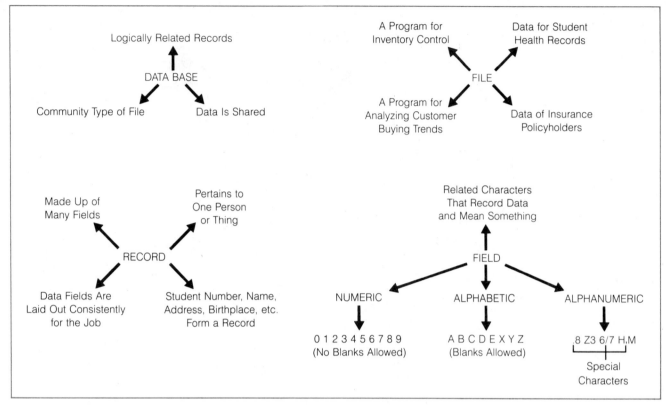

FIGURE 4.1 **Differences of data base, file, record, field.**

CHECKPOINT **Can you:**

Identify the type of data found in a numeric field? In an alphabetic field? In an alphanumeric field?

TABLE 4.1. **Examples of Data in the Three Types of Fields.**

NUMERIC DATA	ALPHABETIC DATA	ALPHANUMERIC DATA
000678	JOHN JONES	A-990
000000	TOM SAWYER	JOHN JONES, SR.
100099	HUCKLEBERRY FINN	.098
	SNOOPY Q PUBLIC	$10,000.78
		SAM & JOE

FIGURE 4.2
The many types of input.

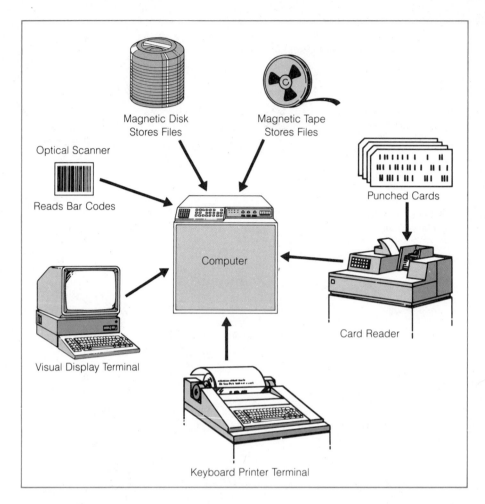

WORKING WITH DATA

When we think of processing data, the preparation of the input initially comes to mind; the only way that any processing can happen is through the inputting of data to the central processing unit. After input is fed to the computer system for processing, our attention then turns to the output; what results were generated. But we know that a computer must be carefully told how to process the input and prepare the output.

First, the following discussion centers on the importance of accurately inputting data to produce meaningful output. Next, the ways that data is processed are examined. Then, the ways that data is stored in secondary storage are discussed.

INPUT AND OUTPUT

When we work with data, the greatest amount of time is spent in preparing the input for manipulation by the computer. Input, our way of communicating with the computer, can be accomplished by depressing keys to specify the input data that is to be processed. Input can take the form of a voice that is used for sending the data to the central processing unit. Perhaps the input data is to be fed to the computer system by using a bar code or a reel of magnetic tape. Whatever means are used for transmitting the input data to the central processing unit, the purpose is the same—to have the computer manipulate the data. Refer to Figure 4.2.

It is rather unfortunate but most users direct their attention to the output. Unless the input data is accurate and timely, the output will be meaningless. Output is the end result of inputting and processing. The printed data (the results from processing) is called hard copy and can take the form of printed reports, listings, or documents. Examining the output can be time-consuming because some reports generated from data manipulations produce sizable stacks of **continuous forms** (the paper usually used for printing the hard copy). Refer to Figure 4.3.

Consider the following application. When attending a computer exposition in your city, you might complete a form like the one shown in Figure 4.4(a). When you fill in the lined areas with your data, this form becomes a **source document,** since it is the first recording of that data. Data entry operators use the source document for reference when keying the data.

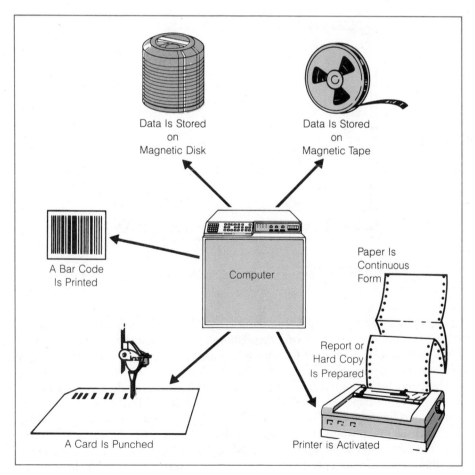

FIGURE 4.3
Some of the many forms of output.

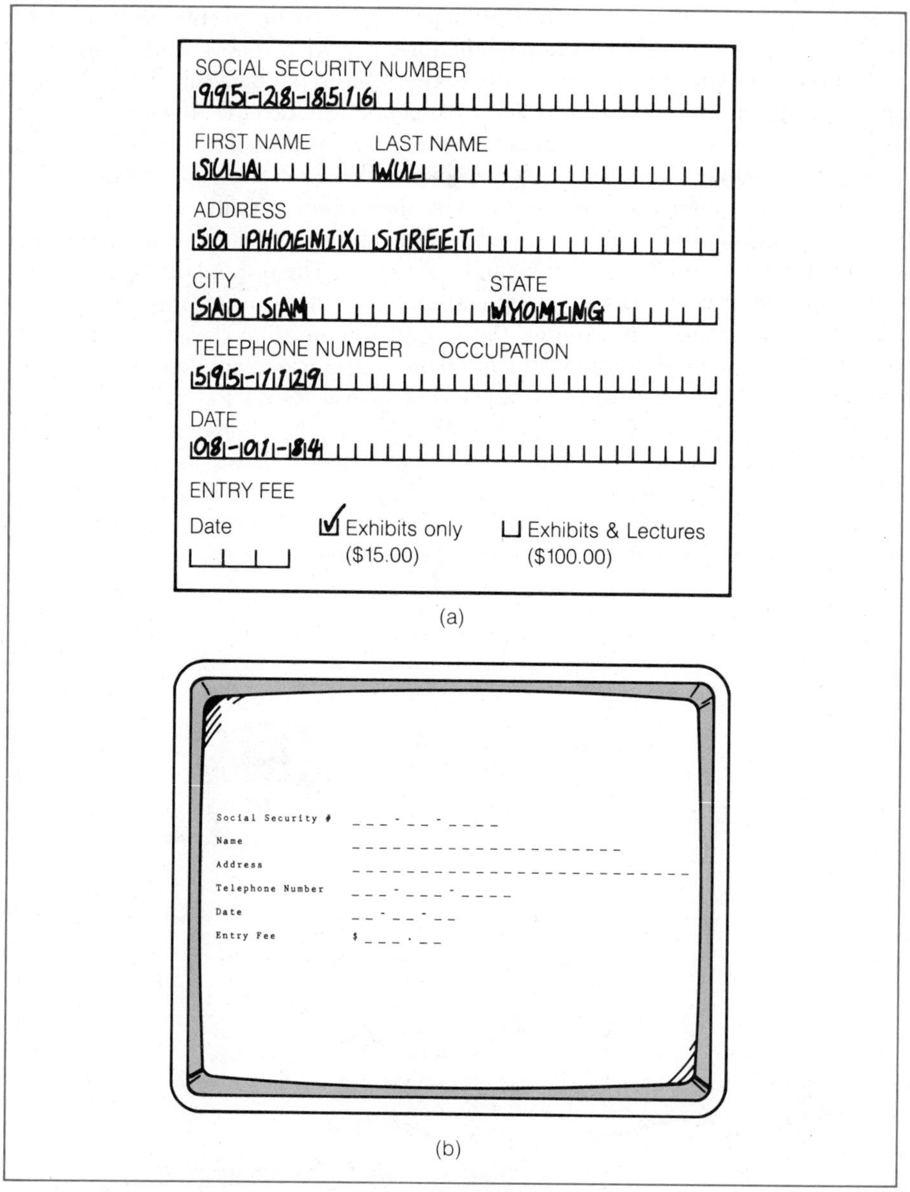

FIGURE 4.4
Source document is used for keying data (a) Facsimile of a source document. (b) An example of how this information may be formatted on a VDT.

FIGURE 4.4
Source document is used for keying data (a) Facsimile of a source document. (b) An example of how this information may be formatted on a VDT.

A keyboard on the personal computer is used for entering the data. A program written to aid a user when keying this data is stored on a diskette. Figure 4.4(b) shows an example of a screen format for this application. Notice how the dashed lines determine the maximum width of each field of data. The social security number, telephone number, date, and entry fee fields are preformatted for ease in recording the data. No blanks are allowed in these fields. The social security number and the telephone number automatically use all positions in those fields. Care must be taken when the date is recorded, however. For a date of August 4, 1983, the data could be entered as AG0483 or 080483 or 830804, depending upon how the owner of data specifies the date to be entered. Recording the date as

8483, however, would certainly be wrong; it would mean month 84 and day 83 if the month was to be recorded first in the field.

Data must be aligned properly within a field, which is called **justification;** otherwise, incorrect data results. **Right justification** is used for numeric fields, and **left justification** is used for alphanumeric or alphabetic fields. In the example date, right justification was used. The single-digit month was lined up (a zero was placed in front of the 8) on the right. The day also used right justification since the 3 was lined up at the right for that part of the field by inserting a zero in front of the 3. Refer to Figure 4.5(a), noting that all unused positions in numeric fields are filled with leading zeros. Left justification, used for alphanumeric or alphabetic data, has its data lined up at the extreme left position in the field; unused positions are left blank. Refer to Figure 4.5(b).

For our computer exposition example, the admission charge of $15.00 covers

FIGURE 4.5 **Justification of data. (a) Right Justification of numeric data. (b) Left justificiation of alphabetic and alphanumeric data.**

Assumed
Maximum Width Is 5 Positions
With 3 Whole Numbers

$100.01	is entered as	10001
$14.25		01425
$5.20		00520
$1.00		00100
.10¢		00010

(a)　Right　Justification of Numeric Data

Assumed
Maximum Width Is
6 Positions

Right Justification for
Month, Day, Year

08　03　84

Month
Day
Year

Right Justification for a Date

Assumed
Maximum Width Is
10 Positions

ONE　　　　ANOTHER　　ANOTHER　　　ANOTHER
EXAMPLE　　EXAMPLE　　EXAMPLE　　　EXAMPLE

YOUNGKEN	KYOUNG	KLYOUNG	KEN　　YOUNG
SMITHSALLY	SSMITH	SWSMITH	SALLYSMITH
DOE　　JOHN	JDOE	J　DOE	JOHN　　DOE

(b)　Left　Justification of Alphabetic and Alphanumeric Data

Assumed
Maximum Width Is
5 Positions

A-123

K-9

Left Justification for an Invoice Number

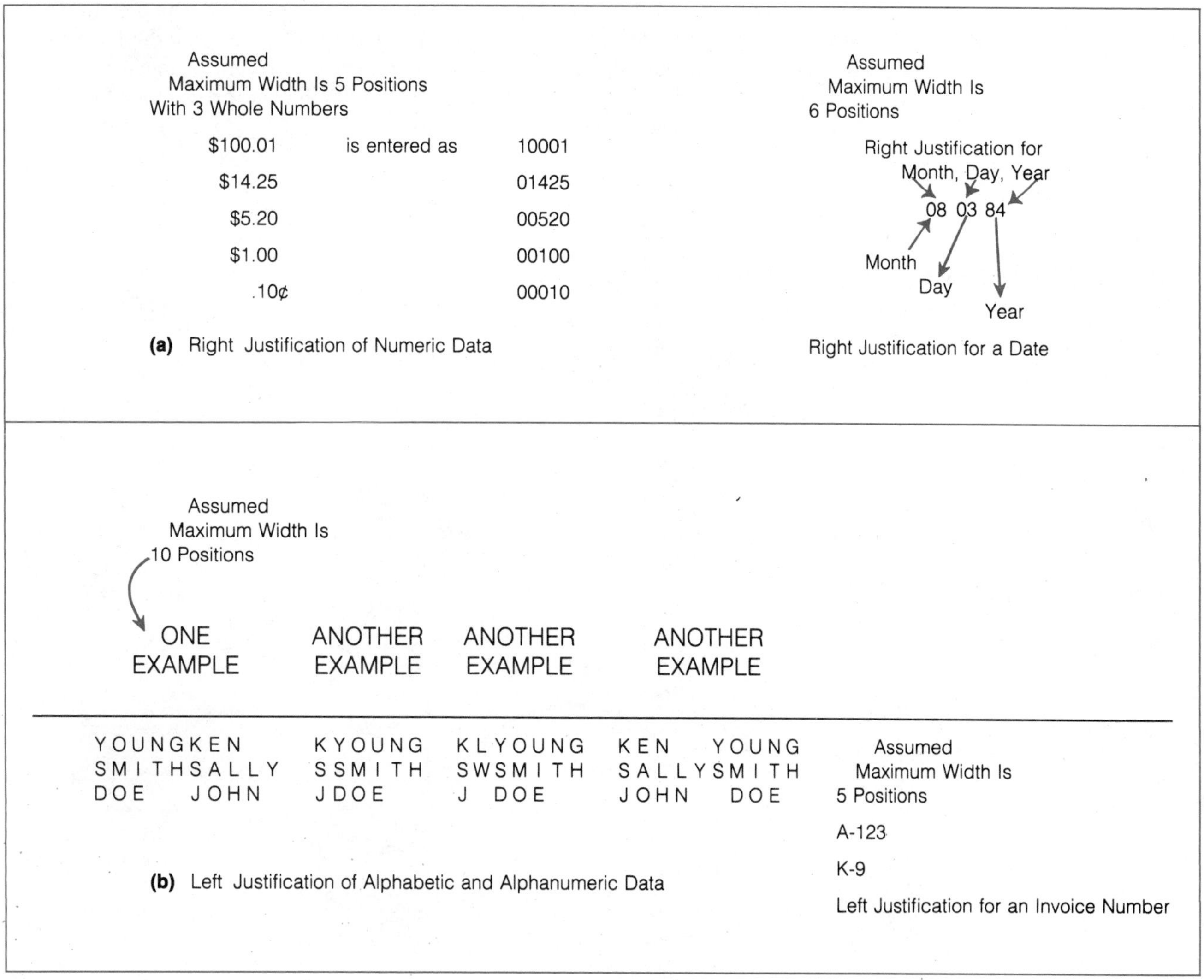

attendance at only the exhibits; $100.00 is charged for attendance at exhibits and lectures. The entrance fee of $15.00 would be entered as 01500 (no decimal point is included). The entrance fee of $100.00 would be entered as 10000. Although the dollar sign and period show on the screen for ease in entering the data, the user includes neither when entering the data. In business data-processing calculations cannot be made on fields that contain any blanks or special characters. Scientific data, however, differs; decimal points and signs are often used in the field since there is such diversity in the data.

After the data is keyed, the input data, through programmer specifications, is copied from the input area to the output area in primary storage so the printer can prepare the printing—in the case of this example, on the badge. On output, the entry fee is edited by programmer's instructions and includes the dollar sign and decimal point in the correct positions, as shown in Figure 4.6.

Each time a person's data is keyed, the input data is stored on a diskette for later use. Assume that the committee managing the exposition wishes to prepare a mailing list for announcing next year's exposition. The file of all persons attending the exposition is recorded on a diskette. A record is read from the file and transferred to primary storage, and the data is printed on labels. This method of printing is called **detail printing** or **listing** since each record is printed. A major difference between a listing and a detail printing is that a detail printing can include editing of data, like punctuation, and show totals.

FIGURE 4.6
Data is edited on output.

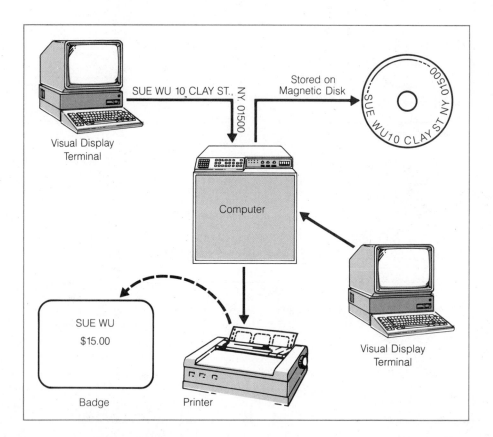

PROCESSING OF DATA

The processing of data takes several forms. The reading of a record, the moving of data in primary storage from one work area to another, and the printing of data as discussed in our computer exposition example are a few of the types used. Processing also involves logical operations and arithmetic.

Logical Operations

As was discussed in Chapter 2, the arithmetic-logic unit is used for decision making. It does this by using logical operations which deal with comparisons of data.

Logical operations deal with comparisons of data. Questions asked of a computer can be answered by it, via data-comparisons, in the following ways:

- Equal to   When two fields are the same data. ($A = B$)

- Less than   When the field being compared to another field is smaller by comparison ($A < B$, or A is less than B)

- Greater than When the field being compared to another field is larger. ($A > B$, or A is greater than B)

Classifying Data. Data is arranged in one of three forms when logical operations are performed. Sorting, grouping, and extracting are ways of **classifying data.**

- *Sorting.*   **Sorting** is the placing of alphabetical or numerical data into some sequence (order). There are two kinds of numerical order: **ascending order** (the smallest number is first) and **descending order** (the largest number is first). In Figure 4.7, the three types of sorting are shown. To make hard copy meaningful, printing is usually prepared in alphabetical or numerical order.

If the committee for the computer exposition wants to generate hard copy of all attending the computer fair, sorting by name must be done before printing. If an analysis, however, is to be performed to determine which area of the city had representation at the exposition, sorting of zip codes in numerical ascending order is required. The programmer gives instructions for sorting, either by writing a sorting routine into his or her program or by filling in missing instructions in a program that is provided to the users at the installation (company) as part of the operating system. A diskette is used for holding the sorted file.

- *Grouping.*   **Grouping** means arranging data into different categories. Since each category has a common characteristic, this type of manipulation involves the comparison of data to locate all data with the distinguishing characteristic.

Suppose you wish to enter a long-distance running contest. The day before the contest you pay your entrance fee and complete a form giving personal data and telling whether you have entered any Olympic tryouts or games. All runners in the race are classified, or grouped, as to ability. On the day of the race you report to the official booth to check the listing which indicates in which race you are entered.

WHAT IF

You and Data

Assume you are a candidate for public office in your home town. You must carefully analyze your opponent's viewpoints on many of the important issues; you must be adequately prepared for your debate.

How could grouping of data be accomplished for this type of application? Give many examples.

FIGURE 4.7
Three types of sorting.

ADAMS	JOHN	$1400
BROWN	SALLY	$1800
HERMAN	GERRY	$10
HERMAN	SAM	$2900
YACHS	TOM	$1400

Data Was Sorted in *Alphabetical* Order
Who Are the Sales Representatives?

HERMAN	GERRY	$10
ADAMS	JOHN	$1400
YACHS	TOM	$1400
BROWN	SALLY	$1800
HERMAN	SAM	$2900

Data Was Sorted in *Numerical Ascending* Order
Who Sold the Least?

HERMAN	SAM	$2900
BROWN	SALLY	$1800
YACHS	TOM	$1400
ADAMS	JOHN	$1400
HERMAN	GERRY	$10

Data Was Sorted in *Numerical Descending* Order
Who Sold the Most?

In this example, the following processing was performed to create the listing:
(1) Each source document's data is first entered on a diskette. All the data collectively is considered a file; each contestant's data is a record.
(2) When registration is closed, the data recorded on the diskette is read record by record, sorted, and stored on another diskette.
(3) The data is classified by grouping runners of the same skill level and experience into the appropriate race.
(4) A printout is generated which shows the classified data. Refer to Figure 4.8.

● *Extracting*. **Extracting,** or **selecting,** is performed via a programmer's instructions when certain data is chosen from the file for a specific purpose. Data are compared to determine if they meet some predescribed conditions.

In our running contest example, the committee rules that no contestant under the age of 10 is allowed to run in the race. The entire file is read, with each record being checked for the age specification. A printout is prepared to show which data met the specifications (which contestants are under 10 years of age). The printout, as shown in Figure 4.9, is an **exception report** since it shows data that represent unusual circumstances. An exception report condenses unusual and important data for a user into a report; it is the exception to the rule. A listing presents a

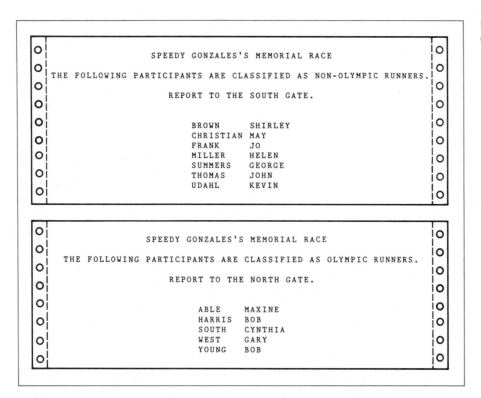

FIGURE 4.8
Grouping data.

report of all records read as input regardless of the content of data (see Figure 4.8).

An exception report is extremely useful in business. Management by exception is much in evidence; because time is such an important consideration, managers want to know the exceptions rather than the common occurrences. A savings and loan company is not interested in which of its mortgagees paid their real estate taxes on time, but rather in those who failed to pay on time. Computerized reporting allows more flexibility than ever in such a management style.

CHECKPOINT **Can you:**

Identify and differentiate among the ways that data can be classified?

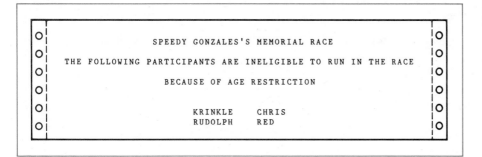

FIGURE 4.9
Exception report.

Arithmetic Operations

The arithmetic-logic unit (ALU) performs calculations by multiplying, dividing, adding, and subtracting according to the programmer's instructions. The programmer instructs the computer as to the order in which calculations are to be performed. Taking square roots, raising a number to a power, doing exponential work, and solving an equation that contains parentheses are all performed easily on a computer.

Summarized Data. Calculations are performed quickly and easily using a computer, but many calculations can also be easily done on a hand-held calculator. How often have we ever wondered, however, how much money we have spent on certain items, such as food, clothing, transportation, and housing, in a given period. For such calculations, a computer's program comes in handy for **summarizing data,** or condensing it into some meaningful form or groups.

Each grouping that is to be summarized can be set up with a unique code so the dollar costs can be added to that specific group to which the item belongs. For example, purchased shoes, hats, and jeans would all be assigned to the clothing group, perhaps coded as C. The same principle is followed for each of the other groups that are to be condensed.

Weekly hours worked by employees provide another example of summarized data (see Figure 4.10(a)). Let us investigate how these weekly hours were calculated. Each day an employee punches a time clock. The data from the time cards is keyed by a data entry operator and stored on a diskette in the order in which the operator collects the time cards. So that the data can be summarized for each employee, the data is first sorted by employee number. The data is summarized by comparing the employee number of the first record with the employee number of the next record. Refer to Figure 4.10(b). As long as the records being read have the same employee number, the desired calculations are performed. When the field being compared changes (the employee number differs from one record to the next), the line is printed with the respective totals for that employee's data just processed. The next employee's data is then processed with the comparison of employee numbers and calculations being used. This type of processing continues until all records are read and processed. This type of printing is called **summary printing.**

The union contract specifies hourly rates which are coded from 1 through 7 as shown in Figure 4.10(c). Notice how the hourly rate is coded on the daily record but the actual rate is printed on the summary printing.

CHECKPOINT **Can you:**

Define summarized data?

Tell when it can be used?

Differentiate among the various types of printouts?

FIGURE 4.10
**Reports showing summarized
data. (a) Detail printing of daily
hours. (b) Summary printing of
weekly records. (c) Table of rates
stored in primary storage within
the program.**

	EMPLOYEE NUMBER	DEPART- MENT	DAILY HOURS WORKED	WORK DAY	HOURLY RATE CODE
Equal Employee Numbers	12345	BUY	10	MON	4
	12345	BUY	10	TUE	4
Add	12345	BUY	10	WED	4
Unequal — Print	12345	BUY	10	THR	4
Equal	54321	ACT	11	MON	6
	54321	ACT	11	TUE	6
Add	54321	ACT	10	WED	6
	54321	ACT	10	THR	6
	62123	SHP	12	MON	2

(a) Summary Printing of Weekly Records

EMPLOYEE NUMBER	DEPART- MENT	WEEKLY HOURS WORKED	HOURLY BASE SALARY	TOTAL SALARY
12345	BUY	40	$5.60	$224.00
54321	ACT	42	$5.99	$257.60
62123	SHP	12	$5.20	$62.40
			TOTAL	$544.00

(b) Detail Printing of Daily Hours

CODE	HOURLY RATE
1	$5.00
2	$5.20
3	$5.45
4	$5.60
5	$5.75
6	$5.99
7	$6.45

(c) Table of Rates Stored in Primary

SECONDARY STORAGE

As was discussed earlier, a diskette is used for storing data for smaller computer systems; a magnetic disk is used for large systems. Any company or person who wants to capture data must decide upon its format and how data is to be accessed from secondary storage (looked up). Let us not be concerned at this time as to how a user sets up files in secondary storage and communicates with a program that manages the organization of a file, but rather, let us concentrate on how data can be used from secondary storage.

Usually records within a file are sorted into a prescribed order by using a **key,** a unique code that identifies each record and sets it apart from all others. For example, a student number and name could be keys used for processing student data. A company might use an employee's social security number as a key. A state department of motor vehicles that handles driver's licenses might use driver's license numbers and birthdates as keys. A file is then written in that order, for example, by license number in ascending order. One or more keys can be used to identify a record depending upon how the record is to be accessed and the concern for guaranteeing that the correct record is selected from the file (one key alone may be duplicated, as for example, in the case of people having the same birthdate).

The current prevalance of much of today's processing centers on on-line processing—allowing users to get at data now rather than having to wait hours as is done in batch processing—makes the use of a key valuable; the key provides a user the means to access just the desired record from the file. How a file is created through the use of keys and how a programmer instructs the program what to do is of no concern to us at this time. Our concentration is on data and its manipulations. We must assume, however, data can be accessed through the use of keys.

Storage Retrieval and Update

The retrieval of records from secondary storage plays a major role in processing. There are three purposes for retrieving records from an already created file: (1) to allow data in that record to be viewed; (2) to update (change) a record so it reflects the most current data; and (3) to delete from a file a record that is no longer active.

The question becomes, how can we find data that is stored in secondary storage? Since secondary storage is like an enormous filing cabinet, we must provide some means of identifying data or a record. The technique used is called **searching.** Searching involves looking for a particular property or type of data by matching data (comparing whether they are equal). An entire file might be searched to determine if, for example, a person qualifies by virtue of a certain skill as a candidate for a new position in the company. Or, searching for a particular employee number can tell who that employee is, and the data associated with that key.

When any project or problem is to be solved using computer equipment, processes should be thought out and careful planning done before the undertaking is started. An example will help show why careful planning is necessary as well as various uses for data retrieval.

Joe and Amy start a service, matching car buyers and sellers; they will process information using the personal computer they own. They run an advertisement in a newspaper to attract prospective buyers and sellers of exotic cars (see Figure 4.11). Aunt Flossie Smith no longer needs her Porsche to go to the flea market on Saturdays, so she completes the form and submits it to Joe and Amy. Her data needs to be entered as a record. To be able to identify each record, the pair must make up a key for each, thus enabling them to distinguish it from another later. Thinking the situation through, they feel they need two keys, one to identify the car and the second to identify the owner.

A car's identity could be coded easily using three alphabetic characters for the car and two digits for the year. You certainly don't want to make the key difficult to work with, yet it should be meaningful. Numbers could be used in a key rather than alphabetics—for example, 1 could be a Porsche, a 2 might mean Mercedes, and so on—but alphabetics are generally easier to use. It is possible to change alphabetics that are used in a key into strictly numeric data. This gives a programmer more flexibility in processing a program and yields maximum speed in processing.

A key used for an owner is composed of an owner's last name. Most of the time this key will point to the desired record. In a case involving several people with the same last name, however, the program may have to display more than one record.

Capturing Data

When they receive the data for today's advertisements, Joe and Amy must then make the data usable on the computer; they key (type) the data, a process called **capturing data.** There has to be some plan as to how a user names the file that records each day's data. They decide that calling the file TODAY is fine and after

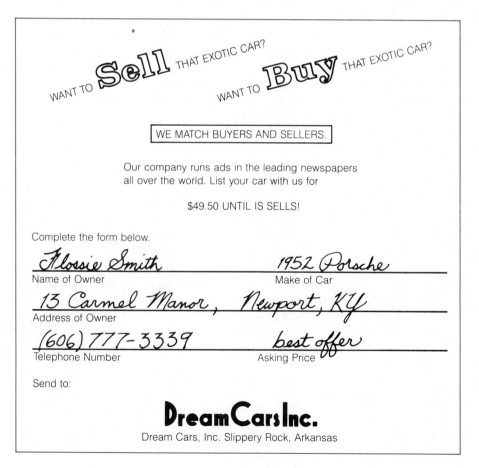

FIGURE 4.11
Newspaper advertisement.

the word TODAY they will record the date—for example, TODAY05.01 for May 1. A diskette is reserved for recording the ads received during a month.

Merging Files

The second day of their operation they realize they have a problem. The second day's data is captured into the file called TODAY05.02. A subscriber calls Joe for some information. Looking through the two separate daily files of subscribers takes too long; he realizes that something must be done. There is a definite need for one file that represents all active subscribers.

To be able to answer questions accurately and to keep an up-to-date inventory of the cars for sale, they must combine yesterday's listings with those received today. The same diskette is used for each daily recording, with the file named for each day, as previously discussed. Combining today's advertisements with yesterday's will produce an active master file. The only efficient way to combine two files together is to make certain that records in both files are in the same sequence. The easiest of all sequencing by key is that of ascending order, probably resulting in how we normally place items in order in everyday life.

At the end of the day, they sort the data in today's file by using a program that Amy wrote while in college. Files having the same record key sequence can be combined, forming one consecutively ordered file for output. This is referred to as **merging.** To merge the two files, a comparison of keys is done, with the lesser valued key (a 1930 Mercedes is lesser in value than a 1930 Rolls Royce since M comes before R in the alphabet) placed at the beginning of the newly created file. Refer to Figure 4.12, noting how the key of the first record in the active file is compared with the key of the first record in today's file. The process continues until both input files' data are fed into a newly created file. They decide to call it ACTIVE.

Making an Inquiry

The next day, a prospective buyer calls the office, requesting information about a 1952 Porsche. Two diskettes are used on the computer; one holds the ACTIVE file, and the other holds the program. An inquiry is made to the ACTIVE file by giving instructions to the computer that all 1952 Porsche's are to be displayed on the monitor, using the key of POR52. Amy enters the information, as shown in Figure 4.13, notes the response from the computer, and gives Aunt Flossie Smith's name and address to the prospective buyer. If no data for 1952 Porsches were included in the file, the computer, through programmed instructions, would respond with the word *none* on the monitor.

Updating

A week later, Aunt Flossie Smith calls to say that her car is sold. To retrieve just that record from storage, both keys are used (a person could have more than one exotic car listed for sale). The car key gives the car's identity and the owner's key assures that just Aunt Flossie Smith's record is retrieved. This record is updated (made current) by storing the word *sold* in the status field. The record is then returned to the ACTIVE file.

FIGURE 4.12 **Files are merged by comparison of keys.**

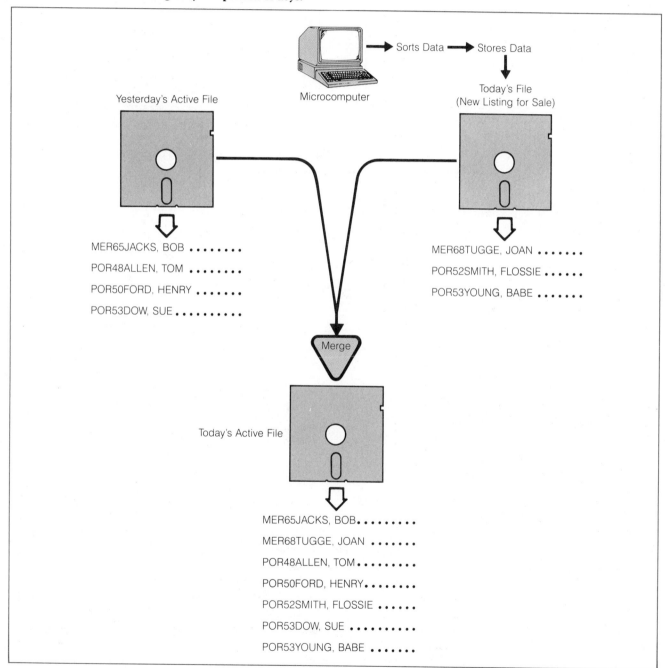

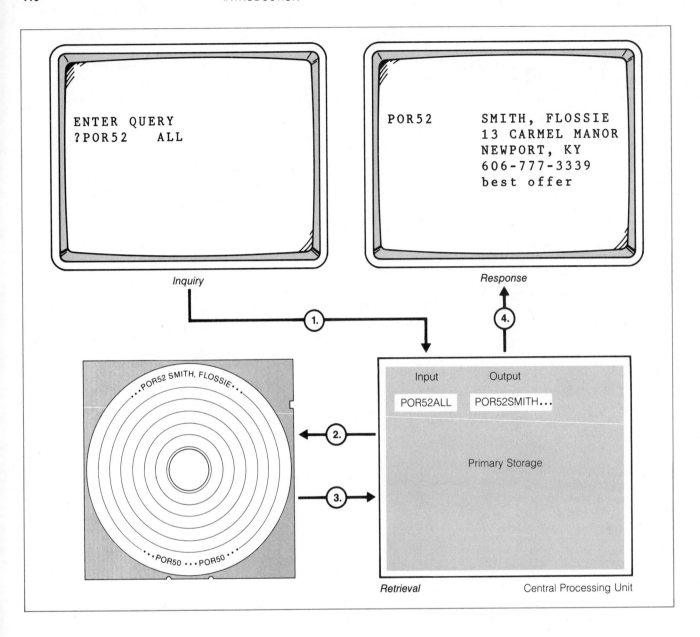

ENTER QUERY
?POR52   ALL

Inquiry

POR52   SMITH, FLOSSIE
             13 CARMEL MANOR
             NEWPORT, KY
             606-777-3339
             best offer

Response

1.

4.

...POR52 SMITH, FLOSSIE...

...POR50 ... POR50 ...

Input	Output
POR52ALL	POR52SMITH...

Primary Storage

2.

3.

Retrieval   Central Processing Unit

FIGURE 4.13
The inquiry, the retrieval of the record, and the response.

Deleting

Joe and Amy operate a thriving business, making many entries to the diskette. Then without warning, the capacity of the diskette is reached—in other words, there is no more room to store data. What is to be done?

One way to make room on the diskette is to delete the records from the ACTIVE file that are no longer needed. All records for cars that have been sold are removed from the ACTIVE file and stored in a SOLD file. The SOLD file is to be a file representing all cars sold since the operation began. Cars sold next month will be merged with those records already in the SOLD file. (It is wise to avoid quick discarding of data. Always make a backup copy of any data that is deleted from a file.) An exception report of the deleted data could be prepared.

Assume that it is the last day of June. For end-of-the-month processing, Joe and Amy will be dealing with three files: the ACTIVE file for the month of June, the SOLD file from the beginning of the operation through May, and the new ACTIVE file to be created and used for July.

In the example of end-of-the-month processing a specific key is not being looked at, but rather each record in the ACTIVE file is read and the status field examined. To accomplish the writing of an up-to-date SOLD file, processing must begin at the first record in June's ACTIVE file. Is the status field marked *sold?* If it is, write the record to a merged SOLD file. If it is not marked *sold*, write that record on a new ACTIVE file (July's file). Continue the processing until the entire ACTIVE file for June is read. The newly written ACTIVE file becomes the ACTIVE (master) file for the next month's processing. The old ACTIVE file is kept for recovery of any data and for any future analyses of data that may be necessary.

Since Joe and Amy like the personal touch, they use their word-processing program for sending a form letter. The personalized letter generated from that program and sent to Aunt Flossie Smith is shown in Figure 4.14.

FIGURE 4.14
Word processing.

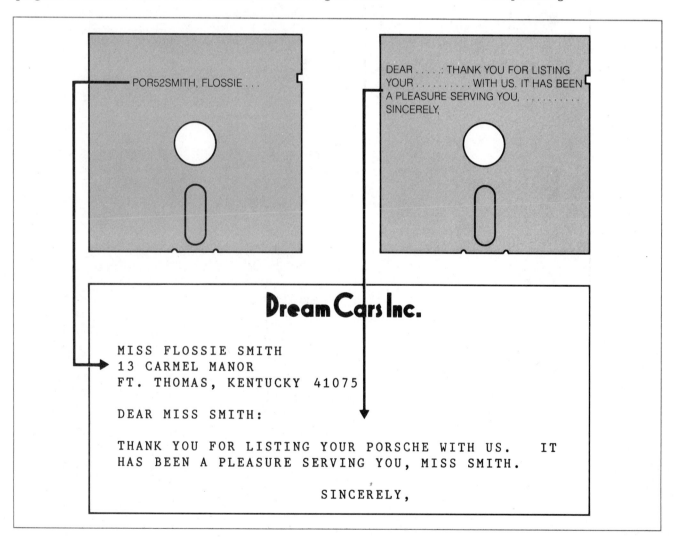

Joe and Amy's operation becomes so successful, a large automobile leasing company named Good Times buys the company and its services. Table 4.2 summarizes the terms presented in this chapter.

TABLE 4.2. **Comparisons of Data Manipulations.**

MANIPULATION	TYPE	PURPOSE
Arithmetic	Summarize data	Condense data into a meaningful form
	Calculate batch totals	Accumulate totals associated with everyday life totals
Classify	Sort numerically	Place data in numerical ascending or descending order
	Sort alphabetically	Place data in alphabetical order
	Group data	Place data with common characteristics into categories or groups
	Extract data	Compare if data meets prescribed conditions
	Search data	Match data by comparing a key to find a desired record
File Manipulation	Search through records	Look through a file, comparing for a desired condition
	Merge records	Bring together various records that have a common application
	Update records	Make the file current
	Delete records	Remove undesired record or inactive record from current file
	Add records	Include (add) new records to an already existing file
	Inquiry on a record	Look up data in a record that is stored in secondary storage
Print	Detail printing	Print one line for each record read; also print possible totals
	Exception report	Print unusual circumstances
	Listing	Print one line for each record read
	Summary print	Print one line for each category read

CHECKPOINT **Can you:**

Define capturing data? Updating? Inquiry? Deleting? Merging? Searching? Explain when sorting is used?

Need for Information Today Goes Beyond Record-Keeping

The preceding example shows how data can be stored in and retrieved from a file. If the data processing of this example were performed in a department of a large company, the files would be considered application-oriented (organized and maintained for a certain application). The data would be owned by the department, with no other departments in the company sharing it.

Information is indeed a corporation's important resource. Formerly, record-keeping was the major thrust of data processing but that has changed. As an example, at Good Times, a new vice-president of the company, Bill Goodrich, is appointed to oversee the operation of many departments, with the newspaper ads being one of his responsibilities. He begins asking questions:

● How much more successful can this operation become?

● Can this newspaper advertising help us in leasing cars?

● What type of newspaper advertising is most successful for the exotic cars and for leased cars?

● In which area do we get more responses from the ads?

● How many days does an ad run in the newspaper until the car in question actually sells? Until the car is leased, is there any particular make that requires shorter advertising time than other makes?

To be able to answer these questions, the historical records must be analyzed. There is definitely a need for information, rather than just for record-keeping.

The need for information, however, is not confined to the use of just one department's records. Rather the information needed is scattered over most of the company and various departments must duplicate it. Why not have many departments of a company or members of an organization share the same data, using it for record-keeping and for decision making? If this concept is followed, the data is stored in a data base.

The need for information never ceases, and the different ways that data are associated (related) is ever changing to fit interests and happenings. So, too, it is in the use of computers; individuals wish to make associations or analyses of data that may never before have been made. The use of a file in retrieving such data is much too cumbersome; too much time would be involved sorting the file each time a new relationship were to be analyzed.

The data in a data base is set up in a way that facilitates its analysis in many different ways, allowing a user to determine which relationships of data are to

WHAT IF

You Are A Winner!

Congratulations! You have just been employed at the Guaranteed Results Dating Bureau. On the first day, you are told of the company's need to set up a data base about its clientele to provide better service to the members.

You must design the source document so the various data relationships can be established. What type of data associations could be used for finding an ideal partner or friend?

exist. The data base, recall from Chapter 2, is a community-type file that is arranged by how data is related (associated). The data must be carefully analyzed and set up so a user can reference data from the data base from many and varied viewpoints.

Take, for example, the case of Hiram Scarem, sports announcer for a major league baseball team. Hiram has a record book that contains all the historical facts about each player who has played or is currently playing the game. All this data is made available to all the sports announcers through the use of a record book.

In the middle of a game, a fan calls in and wants to know which pitcher in the history of major league baseball has, at the end of the season, the most wild pitches in a game and has the highest earned run average. If the record book does not categorize the data by such a breakdown, the sports announcer must page through it to find the pitcher who has the most wild pitches and then look up the pitcher with the highest earned run average, comparing the names until the answer is found. Another fan calls in later and wishes to find out the player's name who has a batting average over .300, has thrown (as a pitcher) more than 50 wild pitches, and has issued only 200 bases on balls in his career.

Hiram could use a personal computer and a data base with the desired data, and tell it to prepare soft copy of the pitcher's name who has a batting average over .300, has thrown over 50 wild pitches, and has issued 200 or fewer bases on balls. In this example, batting average for pitchers, wild pitches, and bases on balls become the means of relating data.

The data base is created, updated, and maintained by a program that manages it, so the different associations can be easily referenced by a user. The data base is discussed in detail much later in the text; it is mentioned here to make you aware that data can be set up other than in files.

Let us illustrate how files are used for conversion to a data base. When a company changes from a file organization to a data base, the changeover is usually done by application, using the files of that application to place the data in the data base by characteristics. The next department's files are then inserted in the data base, and so on.

Certainly a user could find use for many associations of data using a personal computer. You could, for example, set up all the names and addresses of your relatives, friends, and colleagues in a data base. At Christmas time you could then have your personal computer print name and address labels of all those people listed in your data base, choosing to ignore certain lists of names and addresses if you so desired. You could also arrange your data base so that it would print out the various names and addresses of people to whom you should send birthday cards each month.

CHECKPOINT **Can you:**

If data were to be related in files as it is in data bases, what processing would be required? Describe why this is impractical.

SUMMARY

- Data is organized by fields within records, which are in turn within files. Files can be organized to form a data base.

    A file is an organized collection of related data about some subject matter, for example all data on participants in a contest. A record contains a unit of information within the file—for example, about the individual participant. Each record can be broken down into fields, which store a particular type of data, such as a birthdate or skill level for the individual contestant.

- There are three broad classifications of fields: numeric, alphabetic, and alphanumeric. Numeric fields contain numbers 0 through 9. Alphabetic fields contain characters A through Z. Alphanumeric fields can contain a mix of numbers, alphabetics, and special characters. There are at least two kinds of data in such fields.

    Examples of numeric fields are quantities, ages, measurements, and dollars and cents. Examples of alphabetic fields are the names of the states, months of the year, and zodiac signs. Examples of alphanumeric data are names that contain titles with punctuation, addresses, product descriptions, and standard automobile license numbers.

- Punctuation is usually not included on the input data for business applications. For scientific applications and personal computing punctuation is usually included. It is still recognized as a numeric field, however.

- Punctuation is included on output in all cases, if appropriate.

- The source document is the form on which data are originally recorded.

- Hard copy refers to printed reports, listings, or documents. Most often, hard copy is printed on paper called a continuous form.

- A listing shows a printed line for each input record that is read.

- Exception reports show unusual circumstances; pulling out data that show the few exceptions is especially helpful to management.

- Classifying data takes three forms: sorting, grouping, and extracting, or selecting. Sorting of data can be done by alphabetical order, numerical ascending order, or numerical descending order. Grouping data is the arranging of data into different categories according to the needs of the user. Selecting data is the choosing of some specific data from the file.

- Summarized data is the result of condensing much data into some form that the user needs.

- Data in secondary storage can be retrieved for recall to determine what data is contained in a specific record in a file. A key can be used to find the desired record, which can then be updated or deleted from the file.

- To have data shared among individuals or departments, a data base is created. All the user is concerned about is to specify the various ways that data is to be associated when using the data base.

- The data stored in a file that is owned by a department is converted to a data base.

- A program creates, updates, and maintains the data base.

STUDY GUIDE

REVIEW OF TERMINOLOGY

The following terminology was discussed in this chapter:

alphabetic field
alphanumeric field
ascending order
capturing data
classifying data
continuous form
descending order
detail printing
exception report
extracting
grouping
justification
key
left justification
listing
logical operations

merging
numeric field
record
right justification
searching
selecting
sorting
source document
summarizing data
summary printing

MULTIPLE CHOICE

Circle the letter of the correct answer for each question.

1. Which of the following is not true:
   a. A special character is used for punctuation.
   b. An alphabetic field contains alphabetics and possibly some blanks.
   c. A field that contains the data HEB/4 is an example of a special character field.
   d. A numeric field cannot contain blanks.
   e. A record has a key.

2. Data to be placed in order can be arranged by:
   a. ascending order only
   b. searching data
   c. using only numerical data
   d. grouping data
   e. either ascending or descending order

3. When data is aligned so the unit's position in a number always lines up, this is referred to as:
   a. numerical justification
   b. alphabetical justification
   c. alphanumerical justification
   d. right justification
   e. left justification

4. You present your driver's license to the manager of a supermarket for identity. The manager writes down your driver's license. The license becomes the:
   a. summarized data
   b. key
   c. source document
   d. exception report
   e. extracted data

5. On a diskette, you have keyed thirty records, each of which represents a different student in one of your classes. If you wanted each record to be printed, you would want a:
   a. hard copy
   b. listing
   c. list printing
   d. summary printing
   e. printout

6. If, using the records described in question 5, you wished to find out total credits each student was attempting to gain this semester, you would want:
   a. a detailed printing   c. a listing

b. a summary   d. an exception
   printing   report
                e. a hard copy

7. If, using those same thirty records, you wished to print out the names of those students who had been or currently are on the dean's list, you would want:
   a. a detail printing   d. an exception
   b. a listing   report
   c. a summary   e. a hard copy
      printing

8. Printed reports, listings, or documents are referred to as:
   a. a detail printing   d. an exception
   b. a listing   report
   c. a group printing   e. hard copy

9. The paper most often used for printing is called:
   a. listing paper   d. hard copy
   b. continuous paper   e. hard copy form
   c. continuous form

10. The process of bringing together two or more files to create a current file is called:
    a. selecting   d. sorting
    b. grouping   e. merging
    c. classifying

11. When a record is retrieved from secondary storage, assuming that more current information is to be stored in it, we want to:
    a. make an inquiry   d. sort data
    b. select data   e. merge data
    c. update data

12. A method for locating a record in secondary storage can be done by having each record contain:
    a. a search   d. classified data
    b. a key or keys   e. extracted data
    c. logical operations

13. How data is associated refers to how a user:
    a. wants to use the   c. wants to analyze
       data   certain data
    b. wants to join   d. all of these
       certain data   e. none of these
       together

14. In order for files to be merged, the files to be combined must:
    a. be in the same   d. not contain any

     order   special characters
b. have the same   e. not have data
   number of   already extracted
   records   from them
c. be in ascending
   order by key

TRUE/FALSE QUESTIONS

Circle T if a statement is true; F if it is false.

1. **T/F** Data such as an address is called an alphabetic field.
2. **T/F** Logical operations deal with the comparison of data.
3. **T/F** Sorting of data can be by ascending or descending order.
4. **T/F** Ascending numerical order means that the largest number appears first.
5. **T/F** Grouping of data is first done so that data can be sorted.
6. **T/F** Summarized data represents data that has been condensed into some meaningful form.
7. **T/F** Assume that student names and weights were recorded for an entire class. To find out who weighed the most, the file can only be sorted by descending order.
8. **T/F** If a printed report was to be made of all students who weighed more than 200 pounds, this report would be an example of detail printing.
9. **T/F** A printed report made of all students' records contained in a file would be an example of a listing.
10. **T/F** If all those students who weighed under 150 pounds, between 150 and 185, and more than 185 pounds were counted, and the totals printed, this would be an example of an exception report.
11. **T/F** Records are retrieved from secondary storage so that data can be recalled and updated.
12. **T/F** Records are often identified by the use of a key that points to an employee, a stock item or an accomplishment.
13. **T/F** Two or more files of data can be merged, or joined as one file.
14. **T/F** For files to be merged, sorting is done if the files are not in the same sequence.

15. **T/F** When data is extracted from the file, a comparison of data is performed to determine if the data is equal to, less than, or greater than some predescribed condition.

16. **T/F** If student records were grouped by major course of study, the count of the number of students enrolled in a major would represent summarized data.

17. **T/F** Many files could be analyzed for different data associations.

18. **T/F** The only trouble with the analysis mentioned in question 17 in practice would be the excessive time involved in processing the request for information.

19. **T/F** A data base is usually created from the existing files of departments.

20. **T/F** The data stored on secondary storage is always called a data base.

21. **T/F** Student data could be set up in a data base in such relationships that a user could easily obtain a listing of students who have a GPA over 3.2, have a hobby of playing softball, and dislike the cartoon character Snoopy.

22. **T/F** File organizations are not used for continually changing relationships of data because of cost and time factors.

ANSWERS

Multiple Choice: 1. **c** 2. **e** 3. **d** 4. **c** 5. **b** 6. **b** 7. **d** 8. **e** 9. **c** 10. **e** 11. **c** 12. **b** 13. **d** 14. **a** *True/False:* 1. **F** 2. **T** 3. **T** 4. **F** 5. **F** 6. **T** 7. **T** 8. **F** 9. **T** 10. **F** 11. **T** 12. **T** 13. **T** 14. **T** 15. **T** 16. **T** 17. **T** 18. **T** 19. **T** 20. **F** 21. **T** 22. **T**

REVIEW QUESTIONS

1. Give five examples of keys that are used in everyday business activities. Why are they used?
2. What is hard copy? What is a continuous form?
3. What are the three ways of classifying data?
4. What are the three possible ways of sorting data?
5. When is selecting, or extracting, used?
6. What types of manipulations are used when data is summarized?
7. Give three examples of summarized data.

8. How does a record differ from a file?
9. Identify the types of printouts: listing, exception reports, and summary printing.
10. How does left justification differ from right justification? When is each type of justification used? Give five example situations in which each type of justification would be used.
11. Why is *storage* retrieval of records important? How might it be used? Give an example of the *various* ways it is used.

DISCUSSION QUESTIONS

1. Consider the data that is recorded by the registrar's office at your college. What possible files could be maintained in the registrar's office?
2. Consider your personal data on record at your college. Identify some of the data that makes up your record.
3. Is sorting a necessary manipulation before data is merged? If so, why? Explain how files are merged.
4. Again considering your college environment, what types of summarizing of data could be performed by the registrar's office?
5. Explain how the use of a data base generally differs in concept from use of various files.

PROJECTS

1. A newspaper company has all subscription records stored on a diskette. When a person is hired for delivering papers, the company prepares a list of all subscribers' names and addresses that the deliverer is to service. Consider the following circumstances:
   a. When the subscribers go on vacation, they call the newspaper company to stop delivery for that period of time. How could this vacation processing be handled?
   b. How could the newspaper company inform the newspaper deliverer of the vacationing subscribers?
   c. When the company gives the deliverer a list of all the subscribers, what type of printing is used?
   d. How could the newspaper company handle complaints about service, making the subscribers feel that the company really cares?

2. A mailing house supplies you with a list of all the farmers in your state. Each record contains the farmer's name, address, telephone number, type of crop (fruit, vegetable, or grain), years of farming experience, and number of acres reported to the nearest tenth.

   a. Set up some data for each of the above fields. Determine the width of each field and the type of field that each represents. Correctly justify the data in the field.

   b. Is any punctuation included in the number of acres per field? Why or why not?

   c. You wish to send your company's catalogue to all farmers who have more than twenty-five acres, farm vegetables, and have at least ten years of farming experience. What types of data manipulation are necessary to accomplish this processing?

3. You work for a company that uses a mailing list compiled from the department in your state that handles registration of passenger cars. This list includes all registered drivers in your state. Your company has purchased a listing of all the real estate owners in your state. What data manipulations are necessary to create from the two listings a single list that has no duplicate names?

4. You own a record store that sells all the tapes and albums by major singers of your favorite type of music (for example, blues, rock, or country and western).

   a. Prepare a key for identifying your stock. Examine several records and determine what common type of data exists. Also consider what type of information is needed for reordering.

   b. Set up a format for the records, determining which data fields are needed for inventory control. Make up some appropriate data.

   c. How could summarized data be used in this application? Prepare some example of possible output, using the input data prepared in b above.

People in Computing

Elizabeth (Bets) Strohl

EDUCATION BACKGROUND:
B.A., Social Science

TITLE OF POSITION:
Senior Vice President

COMPANY:
Bank of America

Current Position
I am responsible for a unit called Personnel Systems and Administration at Bank of America. Within this unit, there are a number of different functions. We provide systems development support for the Personnel Department. We handle all manual processing of payroll and personnel data before and after the data is processed by the various computer systems, and we have a unit that makes and services loans to our employees.

I joined the bank in the Systems Department and spent many years there first as a programmer/analyst and then as a manager. In the last few years, I have taken responsibility in other fields such as operations and product management. On a day-to-day basis, having challenges presented from different fields keeps the job exciting. And being able to integrate my knowledge of these areas and come up with solutions to problems is really rewarding.

One of the things I like best about the job is working with people. It's truly rewarding watching people grow as they gain experience in the job. As a high level general manager now, I could not succeed without the detailed training and knowledge gained in my early career in systems. Actually, the process rather than the knowledge was the important aspect. By learning the process in one field I have been able to apply it much more quickly in others.

Future
Technological improvements will facilitate problem solving and thus be supportive of the role of a general manager. On the other hand, the problems will become more complex and the pace will quicken.

Students desiring to enter the field of data processing should first and foremost understand that data processing is a means to an end—that is, it provides solutions to business requirements. Thus, their success as programmer/analysts, computer operators, and so on, will be dependent upon their willingness to study and learn the aspects of the business they are providing data processing support for. Openings for people skilled in data processing will continue to grow over the next five years.

Application

BECHTEL

The Computer Specialty Group of Bechtel's Hydro and Community Facilities uses structural computer programs for analysis on every phase of engineering. Structural, architectural and engineering design processes are advanced through the intelligent use of the computer. The slide rule was the tool used for this type of work prior to the early 1960's; studies involving possible two-story frame structures could take days or weeks to complete all necessary equations. Today, after all appropriate data is collected, which is indeed time-consuming, it is a matter of minutes before the computer generates the plan.

Computer structural analysis, although complex, can be done cheaply when compared to the entire project cost. A concrete arch dam, for example, was analyzed for a cost of $600; a stadium cover for $1,100 was also analyzed by the structural analysis programs.

A design of a temple was made and approved by the reigning royalty. The throne hall is 652 feet long by 179 feet. Its roof height is 190 feet. The roofline is curved; its ends are cantilevered, measuring 90 feet long. When Bechtel engineers were called in to prepare a structural analysis of the design made by another company, Bechtel engineers used a three-dimensional structural test program and found the roof could not adequately pass wind and earthquake tests. The problem was solved by redesigning the building. More than 1,200 tons of steel were removed from the plan as a result of the calculation, resulting in a saving of $2.5 million in steel costs alone. Four models were used for projecting the correct design. There were 1,882 connecting points, 4,683 elements of data, and 13 different loadings used in this structural test. The structural analysis test cost $13,300.

The final proposed model, as shown in Figure A-1 was prepared by the computer using Bechtel's structural computer analysis program. Figure A-2 shows the temple under construction.

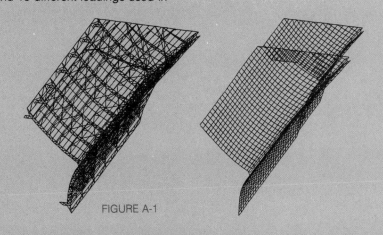

FIGURE A-1

FIGURE A-2

PART TWO

Micros

5 Microcomputer Hardware

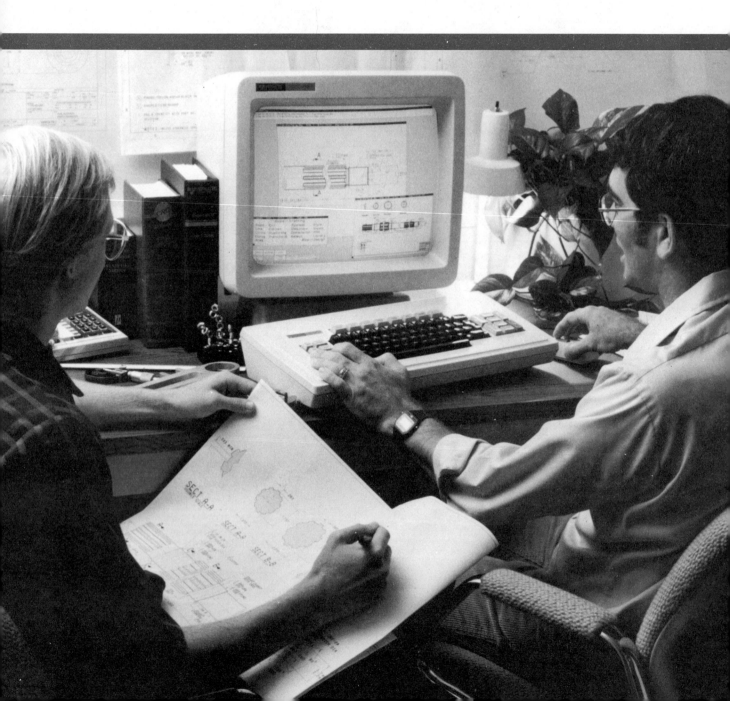

OUTLINE

PROLOGUE

On July 4, 1983, at 3 A.M., the *New York Times's* first edition lost its complete data for printing. The 90,000 copies of the first edition were blank, as the computer lost everything it was to print from memory.

HOW DOES IT DO THAT?

READ ON.

OBJECTIVES

After studying this chapter, you should be able to:

1. Identify events and progress associated with hardware development in the microcomputer industry.

2. Explain why the use of microcomputers has been so successful.

3. Explain how a user uses a keyboard and a monitor.

4. Identify some of the components used in a microcomputer system, excluding secondary storage.

5. Differentiate between writing of data and reading of data on secondary storage devices.

6. Identify some of the hardware needed for storing data on a diskette.

7. Identify the different types of memory used.

8. Describe when compatability exists between microcomputers.

INTRODUCTION

Where else in the world could an industry begin in 1974 to serve hobbyists and in seven short years become a several billion dollar industry? Where else could there be five manufacturing firms in 1975 and fifty-five firms by 1979? In 1975, Atari shipped 4,000 microcomputers used for game playing. By 1979, fifty-five manufacturing firms shipped 255,000 microcomputers, many of which were capable of both playing games and doing some word processing (the manipulation of text material such as letters, manuscripts, poetry, and the like). At the end of 1982, 1.6 million microcomputers were installed, many having a primary emphasis on word processing and calculation capability. By 1985, it is estimated that there will be 19 million in use.

The cost of microcomputers has been declining. Some home computers that were priced about $1,000 in 1979 were selling in 1983 for about $100. Other home computers dropped as much as $600 in price. Even the cost of more expensive personal computers has drastically declined, making them far more affordable.

The words *personal computer, home computer,* and *microcomputer* are often used interchangeably in discussion. For clarity, let us think of microcomputers as being those computers that originated for game playing, elementary types of calculations, and for the entire microcomputer computing industry as a whole. Refer to Figure 5.1(a). This definition will separate microcomputers from minicomputers, mainframes, and super-computers. Let us refer to personal computers as those found in the home and office, as shown in Figure 5.1(b), for processing letters, calculating financial affairs, and preparing schedules. Some games, such as chess, can be played on personal computers, but their emphasis is not for game playing.

HISTORICAL DEVELOPMENT OF MICROCOMPUTERS

Continual efforts were made to make computing power into a very concise package but at the same time to yield extremely accurate results. Much work was being done at various locations in the United States. Then in 1971 engineers at Intel Corporation designed the integrated circuit, creating the concept of a **"computer on a chip"**. This first microprocessor chip, the Intel 4004, was really not intended to be a general-purpose computer as we know it today. Rather it was designed for a small Japanese company which wanted an integrated circuit chip designed so they could customize it for the various calculators they manufactured. This concept revolutionized the architecture (the building block) of computers allowing microcomputers to emerge.

The person who conceptualized the idea that someday every person would own his or her own personal computer, and who also coined the phrase "personal computer" was Ed Roberts, founder and president of MITS, a company located in Albuquerque, New Mexico. Hobbyists' kits of Altair microcomputers were sold

FIGURE 5.1
Microcomputers. (a) Game playing. (b) Personal computer.

by MITS beginning in the early part of 1975, allowing a hobbyist to build his or her own microcomputer at home. The Altair, the first personal computer, was shown on the cover of *Popular Electronics* in the January, 1975, issue. In the early part of 1976, Steve Jobs and Steve Wozniak were designing the prototype and later began building the printed circuit boards for microcomputers for their friends. It was impossible to keep up with demand, so in 1977, these two young men founded Apple Computer.

When the microcomputer industry began in 1974 with the Altair microcomputer, the purpose was to provide hobbyists with a chance to tinker with boards that were composed of only a panel of lights and switches. Users had to pay for defective parts. They even paid for them in advance, and sometimes they never received them in satisfactory condition. As the industry grew, it became more business-like and professionally operated. The hobbyists were patient people because they felt part of the revolution that would soon emerge.

The revolution continued, with improvements being made so rapidly that the next generation of microcomputers resulted in 1977. The Apple II computer was a far more sophisticated personal computer than the Apple I computer, which sold only about 50 computers. Such companies as Vector Graphics, Altos, Cromemco, Tandy Corporation, and North Star emerged with their products. These companies provided a complete package for a user by incorporating hardware and software. The leading microcomputer firms are shown in Table 5.1. Although IBM

TABLE 5.1.   **Popular Brands of Microcomputers.**

COMPUTER NAME	MANUFACTURER NAME	RAM CAPACITY	NO. OF DISK DRIVES	CAPACITY OF DISKETTE	OTHER OPTIONS	APPROX. PRICE
Apple IIe	Apple Computer, Inc.	64K	0	0		$1400
Apple IIe	Apple Computer, Inc.	64K	1	140K		$1900
Apple III	Apple Computer, Inc.	256K	1	140K		$2700
AT&T	AT&T	128K	2	360K	7 usable expansion slots	$2700
Atari 600XL	Atari, Corp.	16K	0	0		$ 164
Atari 800XL	Atari, Corp.	48K	0	0		$ 200
Compaq	Compaq Computer Co.	128K	1	360K		$2195
Compaq	Compaq Computer Co.	128K	2	360K		$2995
IBM PC	IBM Corporation	64K	1	320K		$2100
IBM XT	IBM Corporation	128K	1	360K	megabyte hard disk	$5000
ITT	International Telephone and Telegraph	128K	2	360K		$1600
Morrow Micro Decision	Morrow Designs	64K	2	360K		$1900

entered the microcomputer market only in 1981, this company has captured a significant portion of the market.

CHECKPOINT Can you:

Identify some of the events associated with hardware development of microcomputers?

SUCCESS OF MICROCOMPUTERS

The success of microcomputers can be attributed to the fact that they place computing power in the hands of millions of people at reasonable cost. Opportunities for computing are now available that were never thought possible. Data communication systems are designed for strictly a personal computer use. These systems, called **videotex systems,** provide the facilities for transmitting electronic messages and data over a communication network. At the time of this writing, there are two main suppliers: The Source and CompuServe. **The Source** is owned by a subsidiary of Reader's Digest, while **CompuServe** is owned by the tax firm H&R Block. Both companies supply the capability of accessing large data bases and communicating with members of the videotex system. An initiation fee and an hourly charge are required of members using the service. Can you imagine how these videotex systems will grow in popularity and usage?

A personal computer can be used as a **stand-alone** (working independently) or as a terminal. Jobs are now being executed on personal computers that were formerly scheduled for busy mainframes and minicomputers. The processing power of a personal computer cannot equal that of a larger computer system's; however, the intent is not to compete with mainframe speed or memory capacities but only to provide processing capability to millions who would otherwise not be able to use a computer. The microcomputer industry, however, is achieving processing power that years before was only associated with mainframes. Minis, mainframes, and microcomputers have their unique roles in data processing. Individual computing needs normally do not necessitate the nanosecond speed or many megabytes of memory available on mainframes.

Why are newspapers or magazines needed? If each household had a personal computer and these were tied together in a network, you could use your personal computer for reading the latest news developments, perhaps saving trees now cut down for newsprint. Or an international communications network might make it possible for anyone to talk to anyone else in the world through the use of his or her own computer. This does not sound too far-fetched when you think that microcomputers did not even exist until 1975, and in 1982 there were over 200,000 in use in large corporations alone.

CB users have brought the personal computer into their world by using a nationwide electronic information service based in McLean, Virginia, called The Source. These CBers tune into various channels and type conversations to each other, with the messages quickly passing up the **monitor,** the television-like screen used for visual display of input and output on a personal computer. For this type of entertainment, they are charged $6 an hour.

Can you imagine the day will come when you, sitting at your personal computer in your home, take tests and transmit them electronically via telephone lines? Currently, Carnegie-Mellon University is working with IBM to build a data base accessible by all students, professors, and eventually all alumni. Tests can be taken by computer, scored by computer, and transmitted to the professor by computer. Papers can be processed by word processors and stored in the data base; the professor could then access the stored text, print it out at home, and grade a typed paper at his or her leisure.

The day has arrived when banking is being done with the use of a personal computer and the bank's computer equipment for the purpose of handling inquiries about checking or savings accounts, completing credit applications, paying bills, and performing other routine banking transactions.

Consider the impact that will result when voice is used as usual input rather than the keying of data or programs. Voice recognition is being used to a limited extent at the time of writing. Can you imagine that, once voice recognition is improved so its hardware is cheap, there will be talking coffee pots, watches, and personal computers?

CHECKPOINT **Can you:**

Explain why the use of personal computers has become so widespread?

Give some examples of their usage?

WHAT'S NEW

Windows In Computers?

That is right, there are windows in computers. **Windows** provide a two-dimensional, split screen type of viewing that is shown on the television-like screen called a monitor. You can view those program instructions you are coding, what is happening to the price of gold on the commodity exchange, and what scheduling plans are set up for you at this hour simultaneously through various windows on the monitor.

To be able to use concurrent processing, you must have 256K and have a 16-bit microprocessor. Your microcomputer can be printing a report, retrieving the latest airline schedules for your trip to New York, and calculating how much money you have remaining for the month on which to exist. You need windows to peek in and monitor what is going on. Windows come with a software package that you can purchase.

PHYSICAL COMPONENTS

Without becoming too technical in describing components of the typical microcomputer system, let us briefly examine some of the hardware that is currently being used. The focus shall be on the microprocessor, keyboard, monitor, printer, various types of secondary storage, and the types of semiconductor memory.

MICROPROCESSOR

The heart of the microcomputer is the microprocessor (MPU), which contains the arithmetic-logic unit and the control section. In the infancy of microprocessors, the little chip dealt with 4 bits and then progressed to 8 bits. The microcomputers built before 1983 were generally 8-bit processors. Today, 32-bit and 16-bit microprocessors are being sold along with 8-bit microprocessors. An 8-bit microprocessor takes a little longer to do work, and its storage capacity is more limited than that of the 16-bit and 32-bit microprocessor. A company that does independent research on products, Datapro Research Corporation, in May 1983 reported that 8-bit microcomputers still dominate sales, although there is a challenge by the 16-bit and 32-bit microcomputers. One reason is that 8-bit microcomputers have fully proven programs and operating systems that have been tested and used for several years. Another reason is most users do not demand or need such speed. And now comes the real reason; they are cheaper.

You might ask, will the 32-bit microprocessor be the largest size microprocessor? Control Data Corporation (CDC) has a 64-bit microprocessor. It is possible to "tie" integrated circuit chips together; that is the reason that the bit size is increasing. There is a limit, however, to everything.

The 16-bit microprocessor has the advantage of being able to hold two or three application programs at once and still accommodate the user's file. In January 1983, Commodore computers announced it will use the Zilog Z8000 16-bit microprocessor in its next generation of computers. Examples of the 16-bit microprocessor are the Z8000 and the Intel 8088. Other 16-bit microprocessors used are the Intel 8086/8088 microprocessor or the MC68000 microprocessor from Motorola, Inc. Currently, the IBM Personal Computer uses the Intel 16-bit microprocessor. IBM Corporation invested $250 million in cash payments to Intel for the use of their microprocessor.

A 16-bit or a 32-bit microprocessor is more appropriate for the business world than for most individuals. Users of 8-bit microprocessors work on only one file at a time. If your system is to have multi-users and concurrent processing (simultaneous processing of many programs at one time), you need a 16-bit or 32-bit microprocessor.

KEYBOARD

Input for microcomputers is usually accomplished via a keyboard, which may be cordless on some models. A keyboard, as shown in Figure 5.2, uses the same

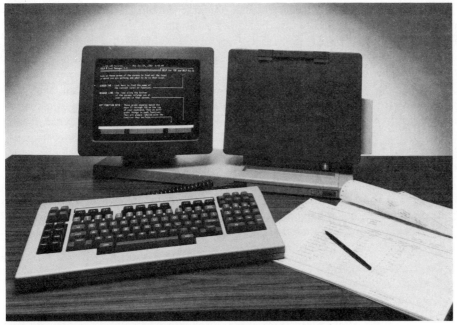

FIGURE 5.2 **Close-up of keyboard.**

Toggle Switches Can Pose Problems For New Users.

Some of the personal computers such as the IBM Personal Computer have a numeric keypad to the right of the standard keyboard. Most of the cursor movement keys are positioned in this right keypad. When the personal computer is turned on, the toggle switches are off. Think of a toggle switch as being like a light bulb that is turned on or off. For example, a key has printed on it an 8 and an arrow that points upward. As long as the number lock key (NUM LOCK) has not been depressed by the user, this key will move the cursor up a line at a time. Depress the NUM LOCK key once and the toggle switch is set to on. Depression of the 8 key now codes an 8. Depress the NUM LOCK key again, and the 8 key returns to cursor movement.

Also notice on the IBM Personal Computer that a key that has two lines forming 90° angles with an arrowhead (⏎) is used for the RETURN KEY. For shifting as used on a regular typewriter, for upper and lower case use, depress the key that has an arrow pointing upward; these keys are located in the standard keyboard location.

alphabetic keyboard layout as on typewriters. The keys take on various forms for different manufacturers. Some use a membrane-type of key, much like that on microwave ovens, which generally prevents any speed typing. Another type uses keys like those on calculators but these too are not as good for keying as those using keys that appear on electric typewriters.

Some keyboards are limited to uppercase alphabetics only. This poses a problem if the keyboard is ever to be used for word processing. It is possible, however, on some microcomputers to add a plug-in circuit board that allows for lowercase letters as well.

Numbers are positioned on many keyboards in the same position as is used on electric typewriters. Some of the more expensive personal computers that are used in business as well have numeric keypads set to the side for easy entering of numeric data.

A space bar is used on a keyboard just as it is used on any typewriter. The RETURN (or ENTER) key is used for programming when you wish to end an instruction, but it is not used when you are keying text, except when spacing is needed between paragraphs or for ending a paragraph. The word processing program that manages the text manipulation provides for words to wrap around to the next line when a line is filled with characters.

The more expensive personal computers have special keys used for ease in programming or keying, called **function keys** or **user-defined keys.** These keys are often marked with the letter F and a number or some special marking. These keys can be programmed to make keying of data or programs easier. By depressing a function key one time, you might save many other key strokes.

With a typewriter, to position the desired line of typing you merely roll the paper to that line. With terminals or microcomputers, you must move a cursor.

In 1978, Apple introduced its Apple II, an 8-bit microprocessor using the 6502 microprocessor chip. Most people thought that the Apple II would, just like a soldier, fade away when the 16- and 32-bit microprocessors became available. The 8-bit microprocessors are slower and are limited to a single-user environment.

Through the wonders of technological advancement and money, a company announced that in November 1983 that it would provide an 8086 16-bit microprocessor that could be added on to the current 8-bit Apple II.

Still another firm worked fervishly to provide a hardware and software compatibility with the old 6502 chip. This company has designed the 65816 microprocessor, a 16-bit chip that merely replaces the old 6502 chip. Can this 65816 chip need new software? Yes, but it is far cheaper than replacing the entire hardware.

Almost anything can be done as long as someone is willing to spend the time, energy, and money!

A **cursor** is a little flashing bar or dot that points to the next location to be entered on a monitor. The trick is to get the cursor positioned at the correct spot on the monitor. On the keyboard, there is a set of keys with arrows printed on them. A user can depress a key on the keyboard with the appropriate arrow for positioning the cursor by either moving it up, down, or to either side. Some computer systems allow a user to position a cursor by the use of a ball, called a trackball, that can be rotated to move a cursor to any position on the monitor. A joystick, also mentioned in Chapter 2, is used for movement of a cursor in game playing. Even a head band can be used for game playing. The mouse, ever increasing in popularity, is a little box that is slid to move the cursor. Some computers allow a user to touch the screen for cursor movement.

Some personal computers have a HOME key that can be used for positioning the cursor at the left top corner of the screen. A table appears in Table 5.2 for your convenience in aiding you with the cursor movement. Even brief experience should bring awareness that the name *cursor* was very appropriately chosen; *cursor* is the Latin word for "runner."

MONITOR

A keyboard is commonly attached to a monitor, or television-like screen. Not all microcomputers have a monitor, however, as some people save the cost of a monitor by using their home television screen instead. Refer to Figure 5.3.

A user looks at the monitor to see what has been keyed or what message or messages have been sent from the microprocessor. Most monitors measure about 11 or 12 inches diagonally, although some are much smaller. The large ones have about 24 vertical rows. The number of characters that can appear on a horizontal line varies. Some monitors only show 40 to 80 characters. Monitors that have fewer characters than 80 are not as easy to use for word processing simply because the text is compact.

You might ask, what happens when you are typing a letter that is more than twenty-four lines long? How can you see the entire letter? Lines can be moved up and down on the monitor through the use of **scrolling**. Scrolling gets its name from the way that a person would read a scroll or a rolled up paper. To scroll, you give commands to the editor program that controls how the cursor is to move forward or backward, either many lines or just one line. A **control key** and some other key designated in the editor program are depressed by a user to communicate the desired scrolling.

CHECKPOINT **Can you:**

Explain how a user uses a keyboard and monitor?
Tell why a cursor is used?
Explain what is scrolling?

TABLE 5.2. **Comparisons for Moving Cursor.**

TO MOVE CURSOR	TIMEX 1000	PET COMMODORE 64	ATARi 400 OR 800	IBM PC	TRS 80	APPLE*
One Position to Right	[SHIFT] [8→]	[←CRSR→]	[CTRL] [↑]	Press space bar or num lock off [↑]	Depress space bar once or [↑]	Press [ESC] and press [K] key
One Position to Left	[SHIFT] [5←]	[SHIFT] [←CRSR→]	Depress [DELETE/BACKSPACE] (erases data) [CTRL] [←]	Set num lock off [↓]	[↓]	Depress [ESC] key and press [J] key
One Position Down One Line	[SHIFT] [6↓]	[CRSR] [↑][↓]	[CTRL] [→]	Set num lock off [↓]	[→]	Depress [ESC] key and press [M] key
One Position Up One Line	[SHIFT] [7↑]	[SHIFT] [↑CRSR↓]	[CTRL] [←]	Set num lock off [←]	[←]	Press [ESC] key and then press [I] key
Delete a Character	[SHIFT] [DELETE 0]	Press [INS/DEL] once	Press [DELETE/BACKSPACE]	Press [BACKSPACE] once	[CTRL] [↓]	press [↓] key
Insert a Character	[SHIFT] [EDIT 1]	[SHIFT] [INS/DEL] Inserts spaces now type in character	[CTRL] [INSERT]	Press [INS] once	[CTRL] [↑]	Position cursor, Press [→] key, and cursor advances
Change a Character	Delete it first, go back, type in new character	Change character to space first, then type in new character	Move cursor, type over character	Move cursor, restrike new character	Overstrike it	Position cursor press [←] key and strike new character

*Press any key to escape after using ESC key and desired key

FIGURE 5.3
Monitor, keyboard and disk drive.

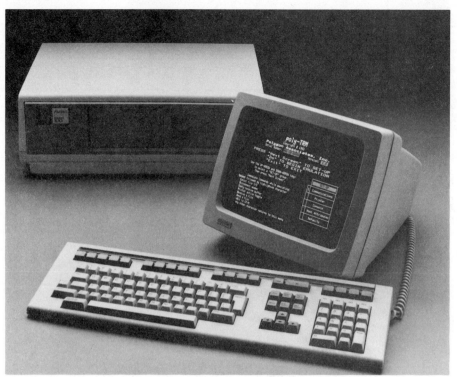

PRINTERS

How printers are classified as to quality of the printing, the printing mechanism, and so on, is discussed in Chapter 8. The costs of printers vary from several hundred dollars up to several thousand. The speed with which printing is accomplished varies also, with approximately sixty characters per second being considered a slow speed printer. Two popular types of printers are frequently used, namely the dot-matrix and the daisywheel printer. The dot-matrix printer prints with a series of dots, resembling the lights used on scoreboards. A daisywheel printer prepares quality output resembling that of an electric typewriter. Refer to Figure 5.4.

BUFFER STORAGE

A computer can execute instructions faster than we can blink our eyes, but a printer can print only about 80 or 100 characters per second. That might seem fast, but certainly it is not when compared to microsecond speed. **Buffer storage** or a **buffer,** a high-speed internal temporary storage area, is used to compensate for the speed differentials and different flow rates of data that exist between the central processing unit and the peripherals. The purpose of a buffer is to speed up throughput on the central processing unit, to keep the central processing unit busy by efficiently using its time. The buffer sends or receives data from the

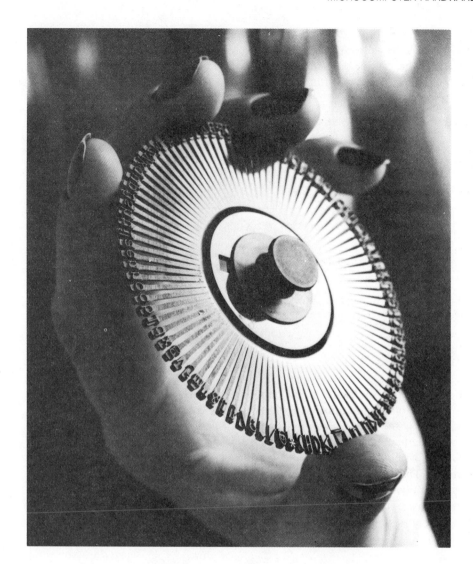

FIGURE 5.4
Daisywheel.

central processing unit at high speed transfer rates, not some rate determined by the input or output device's speed capability. A buffer is included on a printed circuit board as an integrated circuit chip.

An example of a buffer storage can be shown by the use of a microcomputer and a printer. Let us assume that you keyed in some text and wished to prepare hard copy. Instructions are given to the microcomputer to print the text contained on a certain diskette. The microcomputer and the printer communicate with each other through the operating system. A portion of the text is transferred from the diskette to the primary storage called random access memory, (RAM), and the printer begins printing the text. Part way through the text you decide to discontinue any further printing since you notice some errors. You depress keys on the keyboard to stop printing. If the printer contains a buffer storage, it will continue printing what is contained in the buffer. If the buffer storage is 1K, about one-half page will be printed before the buffer storage runs out of text. If the buffer storage is 2K, it will print about one page of text, even though you instructed it to stop. If the printer does not contain a buffer, almost the instant you instruct the printer to stop, it will stop printing.

 **Can you:**

Identify some of the components used in a microcomputer system other than secondary storage?

SECONDARY STORAGE

Let us now look at some of the secondary storage used on microcomputers: tape cassettes, tape cartridges, and diskettes. Refer to Figure 5.5.

Tape Cassettes

Tape cassettes were discussed in Chapter 2; a home tape recorder and a regular tape used for voice and music is a viable alternative, although better performance is achieved with tape designed for computer usage. Refer to Figure 5.5(a). As you know if you have recorded two recordings on the same tape, locating the second recording without sequentially playing the tape through the first recording is a problem. That same problem exists when using a tape cassette, but its low cost certainly outweighs some of its inconvenience. In addition, because of the reasonable cost of tape cassettes, it is possible to use a tape cassette for just one or two programs, and thus reduce the problem in locating many programs or data stored on it.

Tape Cartridges

Tape cartridges are those media that are inserted in a slot in a computer (commonly used for game playing). The problem with this type of storage is that it stores only programs and cannot store data as tape cassettes or diskettes can. They store the program, but once the computer is turned off, the calculations and data that were inputted are lost and must be rekeyed if tape cartridges are to be used again. If your data will change each time, this is a good medium for you. They can be purchased for $40, including the cartridge as well as the program. Refer to Figure 5.5(b).

Disks

Tape cartridges and tape cassettes offer very reasonable storage costs, but they are inconvenient. Much secondary storage for personal computers centers around

(a)

FIGURE 5.5
Storage media. (a) Cassette. (b) Disk drive positioned under monitor. (c) Diskette.

(b)

(c)

the use of disk drives and diskettes, as shown in Figures 5.5(c) and 5.5(d) respectively. The disk drive is the hardware that operates much like a record player; the diskette is what is used for storing data, programs, or text. The diskette resembles a 45 rpm record that is enclosed in a plastic jacket that stores programs or data.

The cost of a disk drive is about $400 or $500, but if time is critical to you, the cost can be justified by the speed with which disks operate. Two or three minutes might be required to store a letter on a tape cassette, whereas the disk drive using a diskette can do it in about one or two seconds.

Some personal computers have one disk drive, while others have two. If two are used, one disk drive, called **disk drive A,** holds a diskette that contains the programs which make up part of an operating system. **Disk drive B** is used for holding a diskette that will contain a user's program, data, or results from processing. Some manufacturers, however, refer to the disk drives as drives 0 and 1, or as drives 1 and 2.

A disk drive contains an arm and an arm motor which position a read-write head on a diskette as the diskette is rotated. A **read-write head** is the hardware used for writing (storing or remembering) bits and for reading (playing back) the contents that are already stored there from a magnetic storage medium like a disk. Let us think of whatever is written on a diskette—a letter, a manuscript, or a program—as the **contents.** All contents are coded using binary digits (bits) which take the form of a 1 or a 0. A read-write head writes a 1 differently than a 0. As was discussed in Chapter 2, bits are the most elemental form of data; usually 6 to 8 bits are used together to represent a character. These bits are written in a string, like a string of beads, on an area of the diskette.

Latest developed hardware is including a hard disk, as shown in Figure 5.6,

FIGURE 5.6
Microcomputer system with hard disk drive.

which is permanently mounted and operates much like a series of phonograph records. A hard disk does not have the handling problems like those involving the use of a diskette but costs from $3,000 and up. Users who need hard disks are those working with large volumes of data, such as accounting records.

Diskettes

For those who wish to use their personal computer for calculations or word processing, diskettes are by far the easiest and least expensive secondary storage medium to use, costing about $4 each.

Many personal computers use diskettes, or **floppy disks** so named because they are flexible. Refer to Figure 5.5(c). They are shaped much like a record enclosed in a plastic jacket. The diskette rotates about 300 or more revolutions per second inside a plastic jacket when it is inserted in a disk drive as shown in Figure 5.7(a). Some diskettes use varying speeds, so they can store more data on the larger sized tracks.

A read-write head makes physical contact with a diskette for coding bits in a designated area [see Figure 5.7(b)]. Since a read-write head physically touches a diskette, any dust, hair, or smoke particles seem like mountainous terrain for a read-write head, and can cause it to **crash** into a diskette, making some or all of the diskette inoperative.

A user might use a fresh diskette for each application. When disk drive A is being used for reading the contents of a diskette, a small red light on that disk drive door lights up and remains on until disk drive B is used for writing or reading. When the contents are being copied from one diskette to another, the red lights on the disk drive doors are continually switching on and off.

FIGURE 5.7(a)
Diskette being placed into disk drive.

FIGURE 5.7(b)
Illustration of a diskette.

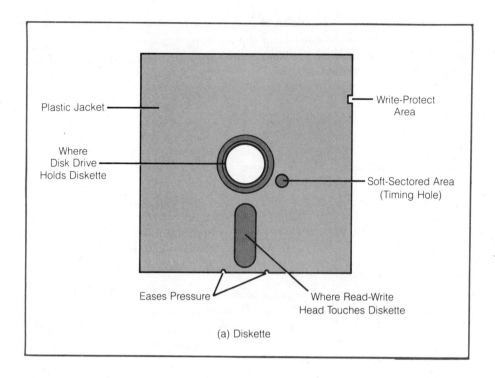

Plastic Jacket

Write-Protect
Area

Where
Disk Drive
Holds Diskette

Soft-Sectored Area
(Timing Hole)

Eases Pressure

Where Read-Write
Head Touches Diskette

(a) Diskette

The same type of operation occurs for reading and writing if just one disk drive is available but a user keeps changing diskettes in the one drive to accomplish the correct sequencing for the reading or writing of data or programs.

CHECKPOINT **Can you:**

State the advantages of using tape cartridges? Tape cassettes? Diskettes? Hard disk?

Differentiate between reading and writing on a diskette?

Tell how disk drives are identified?

Size of Diskettes. Most diskettes have basically the same physical appearance. Some systems use a 3½-inch, a 5¼-inch, or an 8-inch diskette (the latter was originally designed by IBM for trouble-shooting in mainframes). A problem exists in how data is formatted on a diskette, for each microcomputer manufacturer has its way of storing and coding the data. A **formatter** is part of a controller which appears as an integrated circuit chip on the printed circuit board. It is used to code the contents stored on diskettes. A **controller,** an integrated circuit chip, provides the interface (a common type of connection) for attaching the disk to the hardware. There is a lack of compatability (not being able to understand and communicate) in most computer systems, as is discussed shortly. The formatter and controller are designed by a computer manufacturer so that diskettes used for one personal computer brand are not understood by another. This poses no problem for a user as long as a user keeps the same personal computer. If your personal computer is beyond repair, you must either find one that is of the same brand and the same vintage or find someone who has a program to translate one personal computer's code into another's.

Tracks and Sectors. Data or programs found on diskettes are stored on **tracks,** which form concentric circles (see Figure 5.8). Each track is self-contained, unlike the spiral grooves on phonograph records. The number of tracks used on a diskette depends upon its physical size and the specifications of a manufacturer. On most systems using a 5¼-inch diskette, there are 48 tracks to the inch, with 40 tracks in all available for use. On most 8-inch diskettes, there are 96 tracks stored in one inch, but only 80 tracks are used. The number of tracks per inch is noted as **tpi.**

How often have you erased something and later regretted it? The notch that appears near the right top edge of the plastic cover is used for **write protection.** A user covers this notched area with a piece of aluminum-like foil that prevents any changing of the contents stored on a diskette. When you no longer wish to protect the contents of the diskette, you simply remove the aluminum foil and store new data on the diskette. A program in the operating system always checks

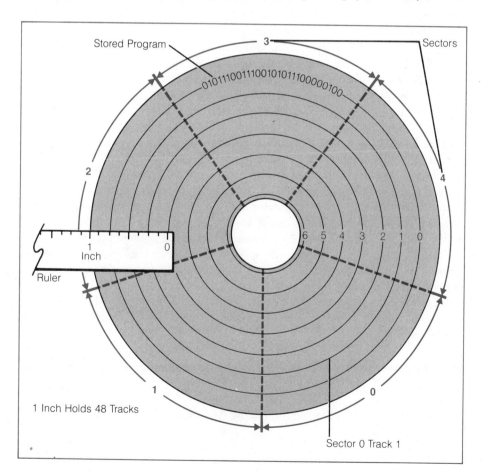

FIGURE 5.8
Sectoring.

this write-protect area in case a user accidentally tries to alter the contents of a diskette that is write protected. If this is the case, the operating system generates a message on the monitor telling of such an error.

There is a small circle area shown on the jacket with a matching hole on a diskette that a user occasionally sees. A diskette is subdivided electronically into wedges like pieces of pie, with each piece referred to as a **sector.** When a diskette contains the one hole, software electronically subdivides the diskette into sectors, referred to as **soft-sectored.** When a diskette is **hard-sectored,** the sectoring is done by the hardware. The hard-sectored disks have one hole for each sector, unlike the soft-sectored disks that have just one timing hole. Refer to Figure 5.7(b).

Each track has a number; each sector has a number. Many diskettes have data stored on the top and the bottom side and are referred to as **double-sided,** but others can store data on only one side and are referred to as **single-sided.** The combination of a track number, a sector number, and the side of the diskette used constitute an address to a computer. It is through the use of an address that a record can be located without having to read an entire file to find a desired record. The meaning of an address here is much like that of an address of an apartment complex on a street, with each apartment also having its own number. How a computer finds the desired record in a file is covered in Chapter 9, on secondary storage.

The capacity of a diskette is stated in **density,** which refers to the maximum number of bits it can store. **Double density** means that approximately 500,000 characters can be stored on a diskette. **Quad-density** means about a million characters can be stored at any one time. Some computer systems, however, may only store about 100,000 characters per diskette. To give you some idea of that amount of storage, many of the chapters in this text use about 50K of storage, where K stands for a *kilobyte*, consisting of 1,024 characters.

Diskettes represent the weakest link in the chain of microcomputer hardware. Although they are a great breakthrough in inexpensive secondary storage—an average $4 or $5 for about 300,000 characters—there are moments of total frustration. If you happen to bend a floppy disk or get cat hair or dust inside the plastic jacket, some or all of the contents of a sector may be lost. Part or most of the diskette contents may be saved if you have a program that can read all of the contents other than on that bad sector and then write the contents onto another diskette. If you happen to scratch the area where the read-write head reads and writes data, you stand the chance of losing most of the contents of the diskette.

Users must be like those at the space center—have back-ups, and back-ups for back-ups. This means making a copy of the original and having it available just in case something happens to the original. If the contents on the diskette are very difficult to re-create, you might want to make a back-up (copy) for a back-up. There is no difference between the original and a copy when dealing with magnetic reproduction.

CHECKPOINT **Can you:**

List the various hardware used for getting data stored on a diskette?
Tell why each is used?

FIGURE 5.9
Printed circuit board.

SEMICONDUCTOR MEMORY

Looking closely at a printed circuit board as shown in Figure 5.9, note that there are various types of semiconductor memories used in a microcomputer. These same types are also used in the minicomputers, mainframes, and super-computers.

There are four classifications of semiconductor memory used for storing data and programs. These are known (by their acronyms) as RAM, ROM, PROM, EPROM, and EEPROM.

Random access memory (RAM) accounts for the volatile memory used in primary storage. A **volatile memory** is one that loses its storage contents when electrical power is removed. Pull the plug and there goes the data! Data or programs stored (written) in secondary storage are brought from secondary storage to RAM. The programs or data stored in RAM can be read (played back) as many times as needed. When you no longer need a program or data, a new program or data is written in RAM, replacing the former one. Because of the volatility of RAM, some businesses use a battery for back-up electrical power.

The cost of RAM memory has steadily decreased. In 1978, for example, some RAM cost 36 cents per character. In 1979, the cost had decreased to 32 cents per character. By 1985, the projected cost figure is .0048 cents per character. Because of denser packing of data and lower costs, the industry standard RAM has changed from a low of 1K and 4K to 64K and, now, to 256K.

The 256K RAM chip was originally manufactured in September, 1983. It is estimated that the world market for this chip is about $3.7 billion in a seven year period. To give you some idea of the amount of information stored in a 256K chip, all of the information found on a single newspaper page can be successfully stored there. The presence of the 256K chip in the computer world will affect the computing power by making it faster and cheaper.

Read only memory (ROM) is a non-volatile memory. A **non-volatile memory** retains its stored contents when electric power supply is removed. Since this memory is permanently written into the circuitry by the manufacturer of a chip, the program cannot be changed by a user. A user's program only reads from it. Programs or data stored in ROM are referred to as **firmware** rather than hardware or software (since they are neither, but rather a combination of the two; i.e., "harder" than software but not as "hard" as equipment).

An application for this type of memory might be a program that prints bar codes. A computer uses this ROM memory chip for its instructions on how to print the bar code. If ROM were not used for this application, the instructions that print the bar code would have to be loaded into primary storage (RAM) each time a user wanted the desired printing.

Another example of the usage of ROM memory occurs when a user turns on a personal computer and some prompts (messages) appear on the monitor. These prompts are stored in ROM. For example, prompts might tell a user to mount a certain diskette so the computer can be used.

A variation of ROM memory is called **programmable read only memory (PROM)**. PROM is also a non-volatile memory. A user can have his or her program written into this type of memory just once. Let us assume that you own brand X computer. You won some programs that are written for brand Y's computer. Brand X computer cannot communicate with brand Y since each computer understands only its own language. To solve this problem, you purchase software that emulates (imitates) brand Y's language so your brand X computer knows what processing it is to do. This emulator program is written and stored in PROM in your brand X computer used for processing the job. Now the job can be run successfully.

A second programmable ROM memory is called **erasable programmable read only memory (EPROM)**. It is a non-volatile memory. The memory is erased by an ultraviolet light, which then permits another program to be stored there. An application might be a user who wants his or her own program to be stored in a read only memory. When this chip is manufactured, a very small window appears on the top of the chip so ultraviolet light can penetrate. If you look inside a microcomputer, however, the window on the EPROM chip is usually covered with a label so you do not see the window. Currently, a 256K chip is available, while a 512K chip remains in testing.

Electrically erasable programmable read only memory (EEPROM) is the newest of the semiconductor memories. It is also called **E-square PROM.** It is non-volatile memory but can be erased easily and is not as sensitive as EPROM to heat when operating. The EEPROM is slower than a RAM but faster than an EPROM in program speed. Because it can be erased electrically in just some part or all parts of the memory, the EEPROM is more expensive to process and use but cheaper to package. Currently, 64K EEPROM is the maximum memory size.

Consider the situation of a company that makes video games. If the game is stored in ROM or PROM and the game does not sell very well, the company has a lot of money tied up in these integrated circuit chips that cannot be changed. How can the company have greater flexibility but at the same time meet the needs of customers? Although EPROM is erasable by ultraviolet light, the carrier (the holder) must be opened up and have ultraviolet light applied to erase the contents. The cost of EPROM is certainly more than PROM and ROM. The trick is to develop an EEPROM which allows the game to be changed electrically without the expense of opening up the carrier (the holder).

The types of semiconductor memory just discussed are presented in table format, along with their characteristics, in Table 5.3.

One last comment about hardware. When using some microcomputers, you might hear a fan or fans working. These are designed for carrying away the heat that builds up as electricity passes through the integrated circuits. The microcomputer is air-cooled. Mainframes are often cooled by helium or water, however.

CHECKPOINT **Can you:**

Identify the various types of semiconductor memory?

Give an example of each one's use?

TABLE 5.3.
Types of Semiconductor Memory

TYPE		SIZE OF CHIP	PURPOSE	PROGRAMMABLE BY USER	VOLATILE OR NON-VOLATILE*
RAM or	Random access memory	4K to 256K	Primary storage	Yes	volatile
ROM or	Read only memory	1K to 128K	Stores programs and prompts	No	non-volatile
PROM or	Programmable read only memory	4K to 128K	Stores programs	No	non-volatile
EPROM or	Erasable programmable read only memory	4K to 128K; 256K soon	Stores programs	Yes	non-volatile
EEPROM or	Electrically erasable programmable read only memory	Up to 256K	Stores programs	Yes	non-volatile

*Volatile memory is lost when power is turned off; non-volatile means that stored contents are not lost when power is removed.

COMPATIBILITY OF PERSONAL COMPUTERS

Can you use your friend's personal computer and then later use your aunt's? The amazing thing is that your friend's personal computer will not understand your aunt's computer code unless they are identical or **compatible.** Compatibility can be grouped into different classifications:

1. Reading and writing code on diskettes.

2. Using the same microprocessor.

3. Using the same operating system.

4. Having the same entire system architecture, which refers to the internal hardware logic (the microprocessor, RAM, ROM, controller, formatter, bus, and so on).

Looking at the list causes concern that any two brands are compatible on all points. Since the IBM PC was introduced, some twenty manufacturers advertise that they have created products that are compatible with it. Certainly some of these products are compatible with some of the above listed points, but not all of them.

You might ask, why would another manufacturer try to be compatible? It is a matter of marketability, supply and demand, and being able to offer a product at a substantial savings. With the compatibility feature incorporated, purchasers can then avail themselves of the very large supply of software available for the IBM PC, assuming that the software works satisfactorily.

CHECKPOINT **Can you:**

Explain how personal computers can be compatible?

SUMMARY

● Many applications run today on personal computers were formerly run on mainframes and minicomputers.

● The processing power of a microcomputer is not intended to compete with that of the mainframes.

● The purpose underlying the use of microcomputers is to give computing power to a tremendous number of people.

● Nanosecond speed is not as critical on microcomputers as it is on mainframes.

● Microprocessors are 8-bit, 16-bit, or 32-bit. The 8-bit are cheaper, slower, and do not have the capability of serving two or more users. The 16-bit and 32-bit microprocessors can serve several users at basically the same time. A 64-bit microprocessor was announced in 1984.

● A keyboard is attached to a monitor. The latest developed equipment is cordless.

● Keys can be membrane-like, calculator-like, or electric typewriter-like, with the latter permitting fast keying.

● Not all keyboards have both upper- and lower-case.

● Some keyboards have a numeric keypad set to the side for easy keying of numbers.

● A control key is used for signalling to the editor program how the cursor is to be moved. A control key also is used for scrolling, by which a user can view other parts of the data or program in use by moving lines up or down on the monitor.

● A cursor is that blinking or flashing bar or dot that shows the next available position to be keyed.

● A monitor, a television-like screen, is used as the visual display for showing the keyed input and any output.

● Voice recognition will someday replace the keyed input.

● A cursor can be moved by using various keys that are marked with arrows that position the cursor up, down, or to either side.

● A trackball, joystick, head band, touch-screen or mouse can also be used in some systems for positioning the cursor.

● The Source and CompuServe are nationwide electronic information systems that are commonly used by personal computer owners to send electronic messages from one point to another.

● A buffer compensates for different rates with which data flows between primary storage and the peripherals.

● Microcomputers can use a tape cartridge, tape cassette, hard disk, or diskette for secondary storage.

● A tape cartridge stores only a program. All data and calculations performed are lost as soon as the computer is turned off.

● A tape cassette provides storage for programs, data, text, or images. A disadvantage is the difficulty of locating a specific portion of the contents on the cassette when several programs are stored.

● A hard disk system does not use diskettes but has permanently affixed platters (which look much like phonograph records) for storage of data.

● A disk drive is that hardware used for holding the diskette.

● A read-write head is used on removable or hard disk drives for writing (storing) data or reading (playing the data back).

● A crash may occur if dust, hair, or any other foreign particles come in contact with a read-write head.

- Floppy disks or diskettes are used for secondary storage.

- A diskette can rotate about 300 revolutions per second inside the plastic jacket. Some drives use a variable speed.

- An aluminum foil tab can be placed over the edge of diskette for write protection, ensuring that no writing occurs which destroys the contents.

- Tracks on a diskette are used for storing data, programs, images, or text. Some diskettes use 40 tracks while others use 80.

- Sectoring is used for providing an area of a track that can be addressed by a computer. It electronically subdivides a track, as though into pieces of a pie.

- Sectoring can be done by software (this is called soft-sectoring) or by hardware (hard-sectoring).

- Semiconductor memory, the greatest majority of which is RAM, is usually volatile memory. This means memory contents are lost when the power is removed. A back-up power source such as a battery is used to counteract this disadvantage.

- RAM, ROM, PROM, EPROM, and EEPROM are the types of semiconductor memory that are available in primary storage.

- RAM (random access memory) is volatile memory. It is used for storing data and programs for as long as needed for processing a job. When the job is finished, the contents in RAM are replaced with the new job that is to be processed.

- ROM (read only memory) holds data or programs that can only be read by the user. Other variations of ROM are PROM, EPROM, and EEPROM; special equipment is required for storing instructions in these types of memory. ROM, PROM, EPROM, and EEPROM are non-volatile memory.

- Firmware refers to the programs stored in ROM.

- Compatibility of personal computers is evaluated in some of these areas: reading and writing on diskettes, the uses of the microprocessor, operating system, and the remaining architecture.

STUDY GUIDE

REVIEW OF TERMINOLOGY

The following terminology was discussed in this chapter:

buffer	firmware
buffer storage	floppy disk (diskette)
clones	formatter
compatible	function keys
CompuServe	hard-sectored
computer on a chip	monitor
contents	non-volatile memory
control key	programmable read only
controller	memory (PROM)
crash	quad-density
cursor	random access memory
density	(RAM)
disk drive	read only memory (ROM)
disk drive A	read-write head
disk drive B	scrolling
double-density	sector
double-sided	single-sided
electrically erasable	soft-sectored
programmable read	stand-alone
only memory or E-	tape cartridges
square PROM	The Source
(EEPROM)	tracks
erasable programmable	videotex systems
read only memory	volatile memory
(EPROM)	windows
	write protection

MULTIPLE CHOICE

Circle the item that completes each statement correctly.

1. A television-like screen that is used on a microcomputer is called a:
   - *a.* monitor
   - *b.* cursor
   - *c.* track
   - *d.* control key
   - *e.* buffer

2. A user knows which position is next to be entered on the monitor by the flashing bar or dot called:
   - *a.* a monitor dot
   - *d.* a cursor

   - *b.* a function key
   - *c.* an arrow key
   - *e.* a floppy disk

3. A disk drive is:
   - *a.* software
   - *b.* hardware
   - *c.* an operating system
   - *d.* The Source
   - *e.* never a hard disk

4. Data, programs, or text can be stored on a floppy disk, also referred to as a:
   - *a.* hard disk
   - *b.* disk drive A
   - *c.* diskette
   - *d.* formatter
   - *e.* sector

5. You wish your program to be stored on a diskette. The diskette is to be:
   - *a.* tracked
   - *b.* read
   - *c.* formatted
   - *d.* sectored
   - *e.* written

6. A diskette always has:
   - *a.* sides, tracks, and a formatter
   - *b.* 80 tracks
   - *c.* double-density and sectors
   - *d.* one or two sides, tracks, and sectors
   - *e.* a read-write head

7. The number of bits stored per inch of track is referred to as:
   - *a.* capacity
   - *b.* density
   - *c.* formatter
   - *d.* sectored
   - *e.* write protected

8. Assuming that the manufacturers have called the disk drives A and B, disk drive A refers to the disk drive normally used for:
   - *a.* writing data
   - *b.* formatting data
   - *c.* write protecting
   - *d.* reading from the operating system
   - *e.* sectoring data

9. The number of tracks on a diskette is always equal to:
   - *a.* 40
   - *b.* 48
   - *c.* 80
   - *d.* 96
   - *e.* none of these

10. If any hair or dust appears on the diskette, the read-write head:
    - *a.* turns on the red light on the disk door
    - *b.* will always store the data accurately
    - *c.* may crash
    - *d.* will require sectoring
    - *e.* may require write protection

11. To be able to find a desired record without having to read the entire file is achieved through:
    a. an address
    b. tracks
    c. a sector
    d. double-density
    e. a formatter

12. Data or programs stored on a diskette is referred to as the diskette's:
    a. address
    b. tracks
    c. sectors
    d. contents
    e. formatter

13. When memory does not lose its contents even though electrical power is removed, the memory is:
    a. semiconductor memory
    b. RAM, ROM, PROM, EPROM
    c. volatile
    d. non-volatile
    e. a formatter

14. Primary storage is which of the following:
    a. buffer storage
    b. RAM
    c. ROM
    d. PROM
    e. EPROM

15. This memory cannot be changed once the program is stored in it:
    a. semiconductor memory
    b. RAM
    c. ROM
    d. volatile
    e. non-volatile

16. You have a personal computer that is brand X. You get programs from a friend that are for brand Y. You need an emulator that allows brand Y's program to be executed on your personal computer. The emulator program would never be stored in:
    a. EEPROM
    b. ROM
    c. PROM
    d. volatile memory
    e. non-volatile memory

17. You wish to have a program stored in memory so you do not always have to bring it from secondary storage to primary storage for execution. This program is to be used for a year or so, and then you need to replace it with a different program. You would use:
    a. RAM
    b. ROM
    c. PROM
    d. EEPROM
    e. semiconductor memory

18. The industry standard for RAM began with:
    a. 1K
    b. 4K
    c. 32K
    d. 128K
    e. 256K

19. What type of semiconductor memory chip has a window on the chip for reprogrammability?
    a. RAM
    b. ROM
    c. PROM
    d. EPROM
    e. all volatile memory

20. The cheapest type of storage found on a printed circuit board is:
    a. RAM
    b. ROM
    c. PROM
    d. EPROM
    e. firmware

TRUE/FALSE QUESTIONS

Circle T if a statement is true; F if it is false.

1. **T/F** Because of the volatility of semiconductor memory some businesses use a battery for back-up electrical power.
2. **T/F** The marketplace for microcomputers is almost unlimited.
3. **T/F** At first, microcomputers were hand wired by the hobbyists.
4. **T/F** Although the Apple computer is very popular today, the first model of Apple computers sold about 200 computers.
5. **T/F** Some of the large microcomputer manufacturers are IBM, Tandy, Apple, North Star, and Honeywell.
6. **T/F** A keyboard is always physically attached to a monitor.
7. **T/F** To be able to identify a position that is keyed, a user moves a cursor.
8. **T/F** Hard disk is an expensive disk storage that does not use diskettes.
9. **T/F** Users of hard disks need a large volume of data to justify their use.
10. **T/F** Tape cartridge is not the only type of secondary storage media used with personal computers.
11. **T/F** When a red light comes on on the disk door, you know that the disk is malfunctioning.
12. **T/F** Data is stored on tracks that are like separate rings, called concentric circles.
13. **T/F** If an advertisement in a newspaper says that

a diskette is double-density double-sided, you know that it can store about one million characters in all.

14. **T/F** Density is always stated in the number of bits that can be stored in 40 tracks of a diskette.

15. **T/F** Any bending of a diskette may lead to your losing the contents.

16. **T/F** RAM is primary storage.

17. **T/F** A computer needs to have PROM and EPROM; otherwise, it cannot operate.

18. **T/F** The industry standard for RAM's maximum number of characters stored has gone from 1K up to 256K.

19. **T/F** All microcomputers have monitors, upper-case and lower-case keyboards, and ROM.

20. **T/F** Tape cartridges, tape cassettes, RAM, and diskettes are used for storing data and programs.

21. **T/F** A crash refers to the losing of electrical power when data is being stored on a diskette.

22. **T/F** More efficient computer systems use buffers.

23. **T/F** A hard-sectored diskette has many small circular holes in the jacket and the diskette.

ANSWERS

Multiple Choice: 1. **a** 2. **d** 3. **b** 4. **c** 5. **e** 6. **d** 7. **b** 8. **d** 9. **e** 10. **c** 11. **a** 12. **d** 13. **d** 14. **b** 15. **c** 16. **d** 17. **d** 18. **a** 19. **d** 20. **a** *True/False:* 1. **T** 2. **T** 3. **T** 4. **T** 5. **F** 6. **F** 7. **T** 8. **T** 9. **T** 10. **T** 11. **F** 12. **T** 13. **F** 14. **F** 15. **T** 16. **T** 17. **F** 18. **T** 19. **F** 20. **F** 21. **F** 22. **T** 23. **T**

REVIEW QUESTIONS

1. Do all microcomputer keyboards have upper and lower case keys? What other type of keys appear other than those used on an electric typewriter?

2. What is a monitor? What is it used for? How do you know which position is to be entered next on it?

3. What is the purpose of a read-write head? What does it write?

4. What is the purpose of using a diskette? What other name is it known by?

5. You see the following label on a diskette:
   double-sided double-density
   soft-sectored 48 tpi
   What does this label mean?

6. Why does each track on a diskette have a number?

7. What is a sector? Why does each sector have a number?

8. A diskette is single-sided. What does this mean?

9. What does RAM mean? Why is it used?

10. What does ROM mean? Why is it used?

11. How does PROM differ from EPROM? When is each used?

12. What is volatile memory? Non-volatile memory?

DISCUSSION QUESTIONS

1. In your opinion, will the demand for microcomputers keep increasing? Explain your answer.

2. Explain both volatile and non-volatile memory. Give an example of a possible application for each.

3. What hardware is involved in getting data stored on a diskette?

People In Computing

David Bunnell

POSITION
Chairman

COMPANY
PC World Communications, Inc.

EDUCATIONAL BACKGROUND
B.A. from University of Nebraska, Major in History.

Often when I meet people, they ask me how I got started in personal computing. Even though I've retold the story many times it is sometimes hard to get people to believe how the personal computer got started, much less how I became a part of it.

In 1974 through circumstances that had nothing to do with technology or computers. I found myself working as a technical writer at a little company in Albuquerque called MITS. We made kits; we made kit calculators and other kinds of electronic devices that people would patiently put together with their soldering irons.

The founder of MITS, Ed Roberts, who I consider the father of the personal computer industry, had this idea that the salvation of the company which nearly went bankrupt in 1974 would be to build

Courtesy of Sybex Pioneer Days.

a computer that you could put together from a kit. I originally had very little understanding of what Ed Roberts was talking about. Maybe that is symptomatic of visionary creative people. Often times they see something in the future: their various associates around them fail to see what they see. They are ahead of their times. Fortunately, Ed Roberts had the charisma to keep a team of very creative people together through a very difficult time to pull us through the design and the introduction of the Altair computer.

The technical editor of *Popular Electronics*, Les Solomon, who is one of the founding creative forces of this whole business, was a friend of Ed Roberts. I think the original idea of the Altair came about in a conversation in a cafe in Albuquerque over a napkin between Les Solomon and Ed Roberts. Les Solomon had faith in Ed Roberts and took a great gamble and declared that he was going to put the Altair on the cover of *Popular Electronics* magazine. The name Altair came from Les Solomon's daughter who was watching the TV show Star Trek. The space ship Enterprise was going to a star system called Altair. Les Solomon asked his daughter if she had any ideas of what a computer could be called. She said it should be called the Altair.

The very first Altair was lost when it was sent air freight to *Popular Electronics* where it was to be photographed for the cover. At the time, it was the only Altair in existence and so the very first physical personal computer is still lost somewhere. If somebody finds it, I think it would be worth a fortune.

Actually the Altair on the cover of the January, 1975 issue was a mock-up. In desperation they built a phony computer and plugged in the front panel lights to make it look like it was real. Actually there was

nothing in the box. *Popular Electronics* was brave enough to take this gamble that it was real; it would actually work.

When the Altair came out in January, 1975, apparently there were a lot of electronic hobbyists who dreamed that someday they would own their own computer. This turned out to be a very common dream. The result was that we got over 5,000 mail orders for the Altair, cash in advance, based on the magazine article. A company that was deeply in debt and on a very tight rope with the bank, was suddenly the bank's best customer.

But we still had a lot of problems; we had to build these things and deliver them.

The initial trouble with the Altair was that although it was a very interesting device once built, you could not do anything with it except program it through toggle switches on the front panel and see little lights flash off and on. It could not be interfaced with a terminal or to a video tube. Furthermore, it only had 1K of memory. Fortunately, there was a very brilliant programmer named Steven Dompier who discovered that if you put a radio on top of the Altair and turned the radio to a neutral channel, the low radio waves produced by the Altair would produce sound which would come out of the radio speakers. You could actually program the Altair to make tunes come out of the radio.

Besides having no interface to a terminal or video tube, there was also no software. Fortunately for the personal computer revolution, Paul Allen was walking across Harvard Square when he saw the January issue of *Popular Electronics*. He took the magazine to his friend Bill Gates and declared "It started; we are going to be left out of it!" It just so happened that Paul Allen and Bill Gates had been dreaming about the day when they could have their very own computer. They decided to write a BASIC language to run on the Altair. They called up Ed Roberts and asked if he would like to have BASIC on the Altair. Ed Roberts told them if, "you can show me that it works I would love to have it."

Bill and Paul simulated the Altair on their large computer at Harvard and flew out to show Ed Roberts that it would work. On the way to MITS, Paul Allen had the misconception that MITS was a gigantic computer company since he himself had been previously associated with a very large computer company. He discovered instead that MITS was located between a laundromat and a massage parlor in a shopping center. Ed Roberts offered Paul Allen the job of being the Software Director at MITS, and Paul Allen discovered he *was* the software department.

BASIC worked. Having BASIC with the Altair was what made using the computer exciting. People were now connecting teletype machines to the Altair.

A lot of things got started in the personal computer industry because of the tremendous energy and excitement that the pioneers had for the concept of the personal computer. From the beginning days of the Altair computer, we knew it was important. We knew that the personal computer could have an enormous impact on society. It was not something we created without realizing the ramifications of it.

6 Microcomputer Software

OUTLINE

PROLOGUE

Al McChristy sells to a vertical market which can be defined as a group of people or an organization with more things in common than their differences. If the software developer identified a sizeable vertical market, understood the market and its requirements and focused his marketing efforts at that market, he or she would sell successfully. With one success, a vertical market would mean modifying the program to suit another vertical market and try to repeat his or her success.

On the other side of the coin are those individuals who write software for either the joy of it and make it available to the public for free, or sell it for a profit.

HOW DOES IT DO THAT?

READ ON.

OBJECTIVES

After studying this chapter, you should be able to:

1. Explain why applications software is necessary.

2. Explain why systems software is needed.

3. Identify the types of operating systems available.

4. List the steps taken for preparation and execution of a program, stating why each step is important.

5. Explain why systems programs help manage application programs.

6. List some important considerations when selecting a personal computer.

INTRODUCTION

In Chapter 4 the way that data is manipulated by a computer was discussed. In chapter 5 the hardware of a microcomputer was stressed. In this chapter note how a user combines hardware and data manipulation through the use of programs to make the microcomputer work.

If we were to use a blender to prepare some favorite recipe, we follow two different types of directions. One set of directions pertains to the use of the blender; the second, to the ingredients called for in the recipe. To make the desired recipe requires concentrating on both sets of directions. Think of the recipe as being like a program, with the ingredients analogous to the input, the mixing and baking instructions analogous to the processing, and the baked goods analogous to output.

To make a computer process data, we need to use two different types of software: applications software and systems software. Applications software can be equated to the recipe; systems software acts like the blender in the example.

TYPES OF SOFTWARE

Since we have an overview, let us look at each type of software. Later in the chapter, we will show how these two types of software work together.

APPLICATIONS SOFTWARE

Applications software refers to those programs that are written to solve everyday problems, such as inventory control, math problems, and billing. An application program is written by a user or by a software company which charges a fee for the service. If a certain type of application is needed, packaged software (an already-prepared program) provides the easiest solution, assuming that what you want is available. Other programs, noted as public domain, are available for public use without any copyright problems. Specialized programs must be written for a user or by a user.

Since problems to be solved differ greatly (some being business-oriented, some scientific-oriented, and others math-oriented), a variety of computer languages, referred to as **high-level languages,** have been developed, each suited best to a particular type of problem. High-level languages are easier to write, can be understood on most computers without re-programming, but require longer processing time on a computer when compared to the computer's assembly language. These languages are discussed in Chapter 12.

Some applications are solved by writing in a language that is closest to machine language, called **assembly language.** This type of applications software is most efficient for processing data but has drawbacks; it is designed for one particular type of computer (brand X computer does not understand brand Y's assembly language) and deals with great hardware detail. The type of assembly language understood by your microcomputer depends upon the chip used for the logic of the microcomputer. If the microprocessor is by Zilog, then the machine language understood is Z-80. If, however, the microprocessor—which is equivalent to the central processing unit—is manufactured by Intel, for example, the Z-80 assembly language cannot be understood by that microcomputer. Intel's machine language and assembly language are designed for the 8080, 8085, or 8086 chip. Apple II and IIe computers use the 6502 microprocessor chip. This means any software that you wish to use on an Apple computer must be written for that specific microprocessor. If, for example, you purchase a personal computer, the programs sold in a package work for that computer. These programs cannot be used, however, on another microcomputer unless the same logic chip (microprocessor), is used or you purchase a program for making the conversion from one machine language to another.

Making the Microcomputer Work for You

When the National Computer Conference (NCC), sponsored by American Federation of Information Processing Societies (AFIPS), a professional computer organization, is held at various times during the year, 80,000 to 100,000 people attend each conference. These turnouts are evidence of the high interest nationwide in investigating the usefulness and fun of owning a computer.

You might ask, how can you make the microcomputer work for you? If you are interested in certain applications such as financial analysis, graphing and plotting, or preparing letters or papers on a computer, you can purchase programs that are already written and tested, enabling the microcomputer to process your data or your text. You, the user, must learn how to communicate with the packaged software—a task which might require half an hour to several hours of learning.

An example of software that significantly increased use of microcomputers involved the efforts of Daniel Bricklin, who in 1978 developed **VisiCalc**—a general-purpose program for financial analysis which provides an electronic spreadsheet allowing analysis of the different options available. VisiCalc was developed primarily for Apple computers; it led to the development of numerous such programs available today.

Through the use of **electronic spreadsheets,** an accountant no longer need maintain ledgers manually. Everything done on ledgers can be done with spreadsheets. An electronic spreadsheet displays on the television-like screen perhaps twenty columns of data across and fifty rows down, resembling a matrix. A user assigns each row of a spreadsheet a particular representation, such as the sums spent on gas and electric bills. Another row could represent the total expenditures for rent, another for food, and so on. Different time frames can be represented in columns. A user can then use all this data to answer "what if" questions. What if my salary is increased by 10 percent? How much will my savings be at the end of the month? If my salary is decreased by 1 percent and my rent is increased by 3 percent, what will happen to my savings at the end of the month? Refer to Figure 6.1.

There are more programs already written for your use than you can imagine or will probably ever need. The price in most cases is nominal when you consider

CP/M.

Another example of software development involving microcomputers centers around Gary Kildall at Intel Corporation, who became interested in microcomputers in 1972. The following year Kildall began to write a systems program called **Control Program for Microcomputers (CP/M),** which, after many improvements, has become the most widely used operating system for a user to interface with a microcomputer. CP/M was the operating system developed for 8-bit microprocessors. Now, the microcomputer industry had the software necessary for a user to run programs.

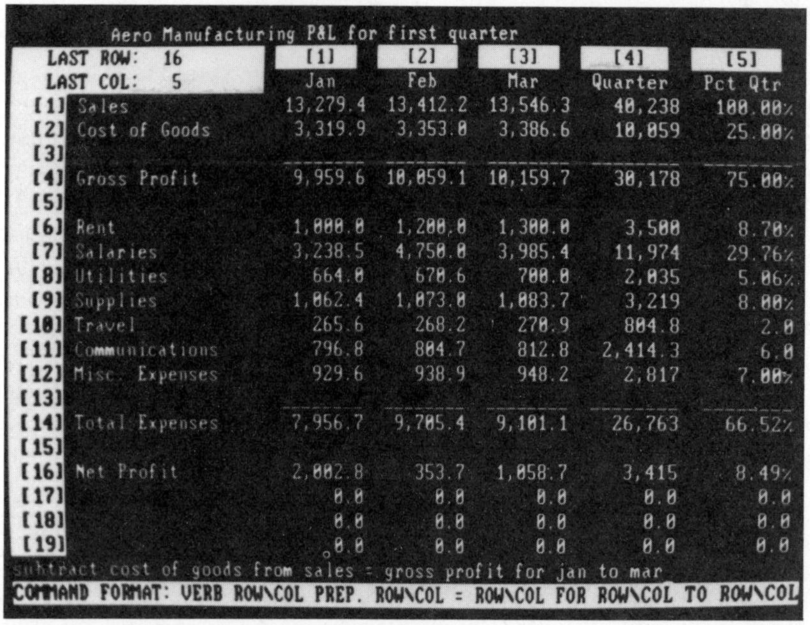

```
          Aero Manufacturing P&L for first quarter
   LAST ROW:   16        [1]      [2]       [3]      [4]       [5]
   LAST COL:    5         Jan      Feb       Mar   Quarter   Pct Qtr
   [1]  Sales         13,279.4 13,412.2  13,546.3  40,238   100.00%
   [2]  Cost of Goods  3,319.9  3,353.0   3,386.6  10,059    25.00%
   [3]
   [4]  Gross Profit   9,959.6 10,059.1  10,159.7  30,178    75.00%
   [5]
   [6]  Rent           1,000.0  1,200.0   1,300.0   3,500     8.70%
   [7]  Salaries       3,238.5  4,750.0   3,985.4  11,974    29.76%
   [8]  Utilities        664.0    670.6     700.0   2,035     5.06%
   [9]  Supplies       1,062.4  1,073.0   1,083.7   3,219     8.00%
  [10]  Travel           265.6    268.2     270.9   804.8      2.0
  [11]  Communications   796.8    804.7     812.8   2,414.3     6.0
  [12]  Misc. Expenses   929.6    938.9     948.2   2,817     7.00%
  [13]
  [14]  Total Expenses 7,956.7  9,705.4   9,101.1  26,763    66.52%
  [15]
  [16]  Net Profit     2,002.8    353.7   1,058.7   3,415     8.49%
  [17]                     0.0      0.0       0.0     0.0       0.0
  [18]                     0.0      0.0       0.0     0.0       0.0
  [19]                     0.0      0.0       0.0     0.0       0.0
 subtract cost of goods from sales = gross profit for jan to mar
COMMAND FORMAT: VERB ROW\COL PREP. ROW\COL = ROW\COL FOR ROW\COL TO ROW\COL
```

FIGURE 6.1 **An electronic spreadsheet.**

that the programs will work and require little of your time in learning. The utility programs mentioned previously can cost anywhere from $25 to $1,000, with the greatest majority falling in the $80 or less range.

Financial analysis programs, such as a spreadsheet program, cost about $250. If balancing a checkbook is a problem for you, you can purchase a program to do the task for about $120. Programs dealing with accounting packages for small businesses (to handle accounts receivable, accounts payable, inventory, and so on) cost on an average $700. Programs can also be purchased for about $200 that assist you in preparing your income tax returns.

Programs dealing with education are also available. A recent Gallup poll showed 46 percent of personal computer owners use their computers for teaching their children how to spell and do mathematics. The cost of the software for such educational programs is about $65 each. Rhymes and riddles cost about $30. An already-prepared program teaching you how to use your personal computer (how to turn it on, use certain keys, mount the diskettes, and work with files, etc.) can be purchased for about $70. A self-teaching program on how to use VisiCalc costs about $80.

For plotting or graphing a program called **VisiPoint** (known by other names, depending upon the microprocessor chip used in your microcomputer) is available for purchase. The cost of graphics varies, reflecting the degree of sophistication. Some graphic programs cost as much as $1,200. A statistics graphics program giving the minimum, maximum, sum, mean, variance, and standard deviation costs about $350.

If you wish to prepare school papers, write letters, prepare a manuscript, or do other work with text on a computer, you need a word processing program, which can be purchased for anywhere from $100 to about $450. The personal

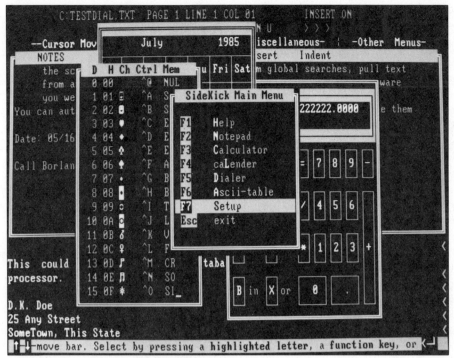

FIGURE 6.2   **Several menus in windows.**

UNIX: Operating System For Minis And Micros.

In 1969 Kenneth Thompson was involved with the development of a program called Space Travel at the Murray Hill Computer Center, which is now a part of Bell Laboratories. The program was being tested on a General Electric 645 mainframe. Although the operating system of this mainframe allowed work to be done in other than batch processing, the programmer might have to wait hours for a response from an inquiry. Mr. Thompson realized that the Digital Equipment Corporation's (DEC's) PDP-7 minicomputer was available most of the time for processing. After many refinements, Thompson wrote an operating system for the DEC PDP-7 minicomputer, composed of several programs. The Space Travel program could then be run on this minicomputer.

Because it was designed for a unified team-programming environment, the operating system was named **UNIX.** This operating system was geared for running programs in universities, government, and programs at the Bell Laboratories. By 1978, 800 such users were using UNIX as their operating system. This operating system, although designed originally for minicomputers, is in the 1980s being used for minicomputers and microcomputers.

computer you purchase might have its own word processing program bundled (included). Some word processing programs have different versions suited to many different brands of personal computers. They use a **menu,** or listing that appears on a monitor, showing the different programs or functions that can be run. The control key and the depression of one or two more keys brings in that small program for your use and executes those instructions. Refer for Figure 6.2. You can even purchase a program to check your spelling. Some spelling checkers containing 125,000 words cost only about $60.

Microcomputers are also used for solving math problems. If the programs deal with standardized problems such as calculating annuities, regular deposits or withdrawals from savings accounts, effective interest rates on investments and the mean, variance, and standard deviation of some sampled data, these programs are already written and published in books. You would use your microcomputer to key in the desired program and fill in the data that is to be used in the required calculations.

CHECKPOINT Can you:

Tell why applications software is needed?

Give some examples of this software?

If you buy packaged software to solve a problem, the cost is usually about one-seventh of what would be needed to program the application from scratch. On the other hand, however, a company may be required to change procedures that are rigidly dictated by the software company; inflexibility becomes a problem. If the users wish to change the software, they must seek directions from the software company or possibly risk losing support from that company.

When purchasing software, be careful about the licensing stipulations in the contract of sale. Copying of a program for someone else's use or the sharing of the programs within a network of computers can become a legal headache unless the program grants such usage.

SYSTEMS SOFTWARE

All computers need **systems software,** an operating system. A set of many programs that are supplied by the computer manufacturer or by a software company, the systems software manages and controls the applications software. An applications software package alone will not work on the computer. The purpose of the systems software is to bridge the gap that exists between the applications software and the hardware. Some of the needed software support includes translating, debugging, and file handling. (A more detailed discussion on the systems software for large computer systems is found in Chapter 12.) For now, however, we will concentrate on just those facts that are pertinent to microcomputers.

Returning to the recipe example discussed previously, suppose that two ingredients are 1 teaspoon of cinnamon and 2 cups of milk. To the reader of the recipe, these ingredients are precisely stated because he or she knows what cinnamon, milk, a teaspoon, and a cup are.

When we write application programs, the computer must understand what we mean. The language a computer understands is called **machine language** and consists of 0s and 1s ("on"/"off" states which are easily related to computer hardware). But when we communicate with a computer, we write an English-type of instruction, using symbols composed of alphabetics, numbers, and special characters. These symbols form a language which must be converted to 0s and 1s so a computer can understand what we wish it to perform. Systems software include the necessary translator program which accomplishes this conversion.

Misuse of the symbols in a computer language, so that, for example, an instruction is not formed correctly, causes errors called **syntax errors.** Returning to our recipe example for an analogy, suppose that a predetermined rule states that the quantity, measurement, and ingredient must appear in that order. Syntax errors would then appear if the ingredients were listed as

cinnamon 1 teaspoon

milk 2 cups

Another syntax error would be generated as a diagnostic (error message) if the listing read:

1 teaspoon cinnamon

2 milk

A computer will, after translation, show us what it considers syntax errors. We then use these messages, called **diagnostics,** and make necessary corrections enabling our program to process according to specifications. In other words, we **debug** a program. To debug our last ingredient list, we would rewrite the instruction to be 2 cups milk.

Another type of systems software, **utility programs,** or **utilities,** supply the necessary file-handling routines dealing with input and output. These are standard, routine programs that work on any kind of data. It is rare when a user wants to write these programs. Utility programs are purchased when a definite need exists for some processing capability not normally included in the systems software.

One utility program that is useful allows the copying of one diskette to another in order to make certain a backup exists. Should something happen to the original diskette, we would still have a copy to use. There is no need to write this type of program since it costs about $40 and, depending upon the program, it might even monitor the disk drive speed. Another useful program handles damaged disk records, salvaging all sectors that are still usable; such a program costs $100. Perhaps your personal computer runs under one operating system, and you wish it to use another. A utility program that permits this conversion can be purchased for $95.

Maybe you need color graphics or a program to draw circles, triangles, lines, or ellipses with a joystick; one is available for about $120. You might need to format a screen for your monitor for data entry (an example of which was shown in the previous chapter); such a utility program costs $80. It is even possible to get different type faces for your dot-matrix printer generated through a utility program costing about $125.

A sort-merge-copy program is helpful if you will be using many records for processing; for $150, you can purchase one. Perhaps sorting of data is useful to you; one sort program sorts about 5,000 records in twenty-two seconds for $25. If juggling papers is not your first love, for about $200 you can purchase a program for filing, updating, deleting, printing, and checking fields for errors. Mailing lists can be created and sorted on various keys, costing $50.

A key term to apply in selection from the lengthy list of available programs is **user-friendly;** programs that are easy to learn and use are user-friendly. This means a user does not have to be a data-processing professional to be able to use the software. The term can also apply to hardware.

CHECKPOINT **Can you:**

Explain why systems software is needed?
Tell what general purposes it serves?

Types of Operating Systems

The operating system is indeed the most critical of all programs. A variety of operating systems is available for purchase depending on how the microcomputer is to be used. Presently, most microcomputers are single-user systems; that is, the user has his or her own data that is strictly owned by that person and the user has one microprocessor (one arithmetic-logic unit and control section). The microcomputer then is serving just one user. Since microcomputers are being used in industry more and more each day, the same data needs to be shared. How this is done will be discussed in Chapter 10 (Data Communications) and Chapter 16 (The Automated Office).

When a single user is using a microcomputer, the data is not shared and the operating system's functions are then directed to getting data on and off of diskettes. Since an operating system is working with these diskettes, it is then commonly referred to as a **disk operating system.** Most manufacturers of microcomputers will mention under which operating system the microcomputer runs. Quite a variety of disk operating systems are available, with CP/M being very popular. Apple's operating system is called Sophisticated Operating System or APDOS. Tandy Corporation's Radio Shack is called TRS-DOS (Tandy Radio Shack Disk Operating System), and the IBM Personal Computer uses MS-DOS (from Microsoft Disk Operating System).

An operating system is tied to hardware by the microprocessor chip that is used. CP/M is used on the Z80 8-bit microprocessor by Zilog and the 8080 8-bit microprocessor by Intel, while the MS-DOS is used on the 8088 16-bit microprocessor by Intel.

Digital Research, Inc. (DRI) of Monterey, California, and Microsoft of Bellevue, Washington, are constantly in competition for the lead in operating systems for microcomputers. For the single-user microcomputer environment, Digital Research's CP/M has come closest to being the standard operating system for 8-bit microcomputers. In a 16-bit microprocessor, however, MS-DOS is the most popular operating system, largely due to the popularity of the IBM Personal Computer. Digital Research's 16-bit operating system is called CP/M-86 operating system.

In a multi-user environment more befitting of an industrial atmosphere, Microsoft is touting its XENIX operating system as the standard for the 16-bit microprocessor. The XENIX is the commercial version of the UNIX, an operating system developed by Bell Laboratories for Digital Equipment Corporation's (DEC's) computers. Digital Research has a UNIX version available.

Microsoft, Inc., by a license agreement with Western Electric (which owns Bell Laboratories), agreed to alter the UNIX operating system programs for non-DEC computers, since the UNIX operating system is licensed for Digital Equipment Computers. XENIX will run on those microcomputers that use a 16-bit microprocessor of Zilog Z8000, Motorola MC68000, and Intel 8086.

Another operating system that has had its influence on the microcomputer industry is Xerox's **Smalltalk.** The operating system was designed at Xerox's Palo Alto Research Center (PARC) to be independent of hardware; it can be used on an 8-bit, 16-bit, or 32-bit microprocessor. If someone wants to use this operating system, they study the implementation that has been set up and then write the code for their machine.

Smalltalk uses a mouse for an input device and generates computer graphics as its output. The computer graphics uses windows, as mentioned in Chapter 5; the screen of the monitor is sectioned so multiple tasks can be viewed. A user can then look at each of the respective windows to see what is being processed in each program. This concurrent processing is a form of multitasking, in which two or more programs are executing in a given time period of a computer. It must also be pointed out that Smalltalk can also be used for writing applications software as well.

An important point should be made here. People at Xerox PARC, Inc. were developing software for almost ten years to meet today's needs. Smalltalk was tested and improved by its designers, Alan Kay among them, over a period of ten years. Twelve- and fifteen-year-old children actually expanded and developed some of the computer graphics programs now available. For example, one program using Smalltalk showed a race horse galloping across the monitor. A jockey was super-imposed on the race horse by one of these children. Things that we take for granted today are made possible by the ingenuity and creativeness of others.

Another computer language called FORTH by Forth, Inc., is also capable of being used for systems software and applications software on all microcomputers. It includes the ability to translate applications used on one computer system for another computer system. The very pleasant surprise about this language is that it has been placed in the public domain. This means anyone can use it without danger of copyright problems. Basically, the cost of a Forth operating system is the cost of the diskette.

Another operating system, called **UCSD Pascal,** uses Pascal as its language, giving extensive programming capability. This operating system is hardware independent like Smalltalk, being able to be implemented on different microprocessors. Pascal, FORTH, and other languages are discussed in Chapter 12.

The latest developed operating systems are Intel's 80186 and 80286 systems, which provide multitasking and multiprocessing capability. These operating systems have been called **silicon operating systems** because they incorporate the hardware and operating system on integrated circuit chips, unlike the disk operating systems previously mentioned.

The discussion about operating systems for microcomputers has centered mostly on the single-user, as that represents the greatest segment of usage at the present time. In Chapter 16, on office automation, however, the need for additional processing capability is discussed as are the different environments under which microcomputers are being used and will be used in the future.

See Table 6.1 for a comparison on the various operating systems for microcomputers.

CHECKPOINT **Can you:**

Identify the various operating systems?
Tell when each one is used?

USE OF A MICROCOMPUTER

Using a microcomputer for data processing does not necessarily require a professional's orientation, but it does require patience and understanding of nine steps. They are the same steps that are done to solve business problems or to create and execute programs that are available for sale. All these programs pass through

TABLE 6.1. **Comparisons of Various Operating Systems for Microcomputers.**

NAME OF OPERATING SYSTEM	ORIGINATOR	8-BIT MICROPROCESSOR	16-BIT and 32-BIT MICROPROCESSORS	PRIMARY USE
CP/M	Digital Research, Inc.	Intel 8080, Zilog Z80	Intel 8086	Single-user environment
Concurrent CP/M 86 CP/M 86	Digital Research, Inc.		Intel 8086 and 8088	Multitasking environment
MS-DOS (PC-DOS)	Microsoft		Intel 8086 and 8088	Single-user at this time
UCSD Pascal	University of California at San Diego		Hardware independent	Extensive Pascal programming capability
UNIX	Bell Laboratories		Motorola 68000*	Mutlitasking/ multiuser environment
XENIX	Microsoft		Zilog Z8000, Motorola 68000,* Intel 8086	Multitasking/ multiuser environment
Smalltalk	Xerox		Hardware independent	Output generated uses computer graphics
FORTH	FORTH, Inc.	All	All	Ability to translate applications from one computer system to another

*32-bit microprocessor

a series of steps. Let us first of all list these steps and then expand upon each. They are:

1. Setting up objectives that are to be accomplished in the program.

2. Specifying the input and output formats that are to be used.

3. Developing first the overview of how the program is to be solved and then working out the details.

4. Choosing a specific computer language in which the program is to be written.

5. Writing the program according to specifications of the language and following the detailed logic previously set up.

6. Keying in the program on the microcomputer.

7. Translating the program into language the computer can understand.

8. Debugging a program by executing it to test if the program processes the data correctly.

9. Saving the program so it can be used later when the need arises.

SETTING UP OBJECTIVES

Before you ever use computer equipment, you must carefully plan what is to be accomplished in your program. Programmers in industry prepare objectives which become part of the documentation that is kept. Often, programmers change jobs, leaving a project incomplete. Some other programmer must be aware of the plans and reasons for this program development so the job can be completed. Also, these detailed objectives are used when the company wishes to make modifications to an already existing program.

SPECIFYING INPUT AND OUTPUT FORMATS

The user in industry communicates with the programmer or the systems analyst in the business organization as to what data is to be used and how the final report is to be presented. You as a user of the microcomputer need to plan with these same criteria in mind. If, for example, data is inputted with decimal points, calculations are done in the same format, but on the final report you may only wish whole numbers to appear. Because of the confidentiality of some data you may wish only, say, two fields of data, to appear on the report, although there might have been six fields of data used in your calculations.

The format of the input and output is shown on record form layouts (see Figure 6.3). In business systems the printers that are normally used for preparing reports generate a 132-character line. Microcomputer systems commonly have printers that print 80 characters per line. The x's shown in Figure 6.3 refer to the positions where data is to be printed. If you wish data to be printed on a form, that data must be either keyed in, manipulated, or be included in the program. If it is in neither place, the data cannot be outputted.

Perhaps you have seen pictures and calendars generated from computer programs. Many of these programs are quite straightforward, requiring only imagination and creativity. The printer spacing chart is used for laying out a design, with any character used to create the design. The design on the printer spacing chart is then converted to a series of statements to tell a computer to print (output data). The way one person pictures herself is shown in Figure 6.4(a); her printer spacing chart is shown in Figure 6.4(b).

DEVELOPING THE LOGIC

The main components of how a problem is to be solved must be thought through first. After that, the details are worked out. How the problem is to be solved must be planned, with the series of instructions that are developed being referred to as an **algorithm.** The logic is developed in modules, each module having its particular type of processing. For example, when data is inputted, this is done in a module. When data is calculated, it is done in a different module of the program. The same concept is used for printing; a program specifies how the output should appear and generates it accordingly.

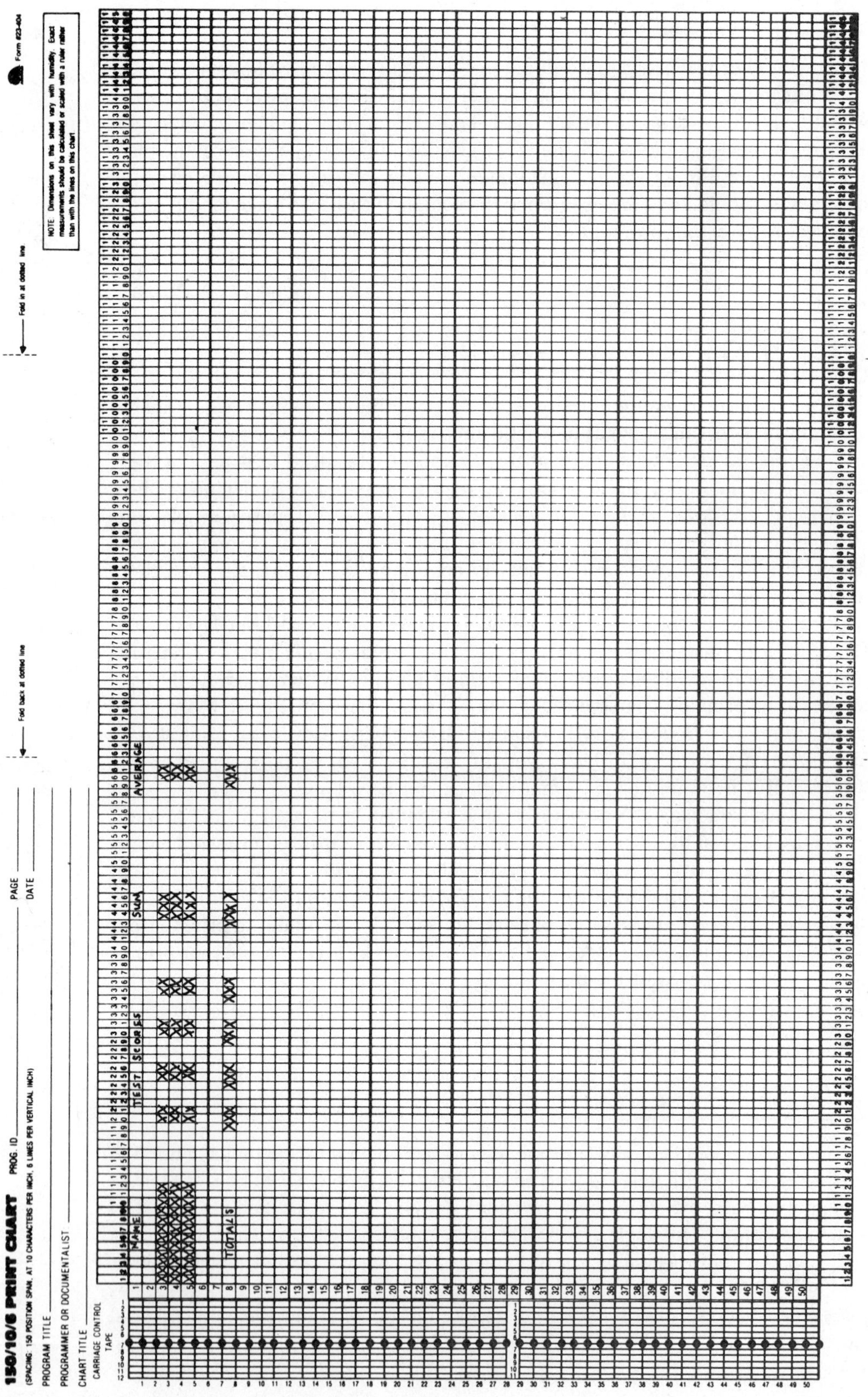

FIGURE 6.3   Printer spacing chart.

FIGURE 6.4 (a) Printer spacing chart. (b) Computer generated output from a program.

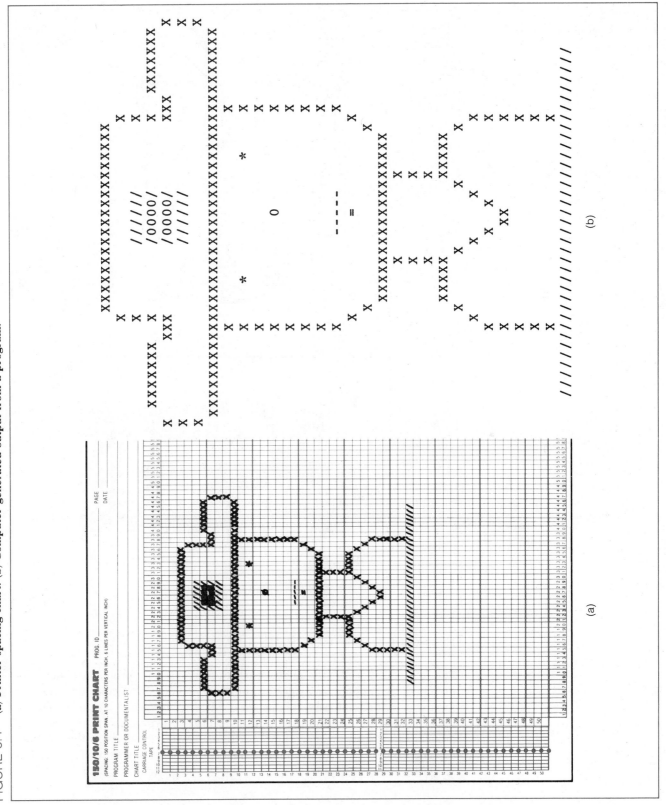

FIGURE 6.5
**Interworkings of a computer
to process an instruction.**

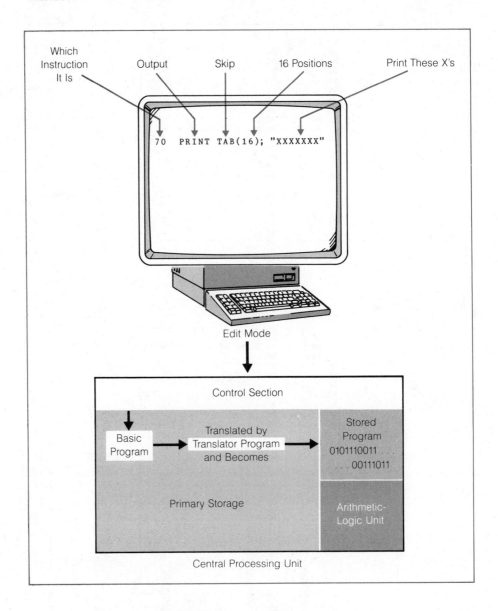

SELECTING THE COMPUTER LANGUAGE

There are many computer languages that can be used for problem solving. Formerly, the computer languages for problem solving on microcomputers were limited to BASIC and assembly language. As was mentioned, the only language understood by the computer is machine language. Programs written in a language other than machine language must be translated by a program so the computer can understand what we wish to have done. Rarely does anyone write in machine language. Refer to Figure 6.5.

WRITING THE LANGUAGE

All computer languages other than machine language must be translated, as was mentioned previously. So that accurate translation can be made, a user must precisely follow the rules that govern the language. A user cannot make up instructions in different formats. If an instruction requires a comma or a semicolon, for example, you must use that punctuation; otherwise, the computer cannot execute your program or process your data. There are times when you want to throw a microcomputer out the window because it utterly refuses to recognize an instruction that you think is just great. Almost 100 percent of the time, the microcomputer is right!

KEYING IN THE PROGRAM

Let us take a look at the keyboard. Refer to Figure 6.6. It uses many keys that we have used on a typewriter, but there are some which we have never seen before. Some keyboards have a key marked RETURN or ENTER, or have an arrow that is bent; these are used for ending a line just as the return key is used on an electric typewriter. There are keys with arrows that point upward, downward, to the left, and to the right. These keys are used for positioning the cursor, blinking bar, or dot that tells which position you are next to key in on the monitor. The keys with the arrows then determine the direction that the cursor is moved when the key is depressed. Table 5.2 on page 139 shows the ways that the cursor is moved on various computers.

Before any program can be keyed on a keyboard of a microcomputer (assuming the microcomputer is turned on), the diskettes must be inserted in the appropriate

FIGURE 6.6 **A typical keyboard.**

FIGURE 6.7
An example of two disk drives shown to the right of the monitor.

disk drives. Assuming a microcomputer has two disk drives, arbitrarily called disk drive A and B, a diskette containing the systems software is mounted in disk drive A. A diskette used for holding your applications program and data is mounted in drive B. Refer to Figure 6.7. After closing the disk drive doors, the operating system needs some instructions from you.

The operating system provides **prompts** on the screen which are questions and statements that aid you in the use of your microcomputer. When messages are generated from the operating system which you cannot understand or do not know how to correct, you use a reference manual that is supplied with your microcomputer. An example of a prompt could be one that says

INSERT DISKETTE INTO DRIVE A AND DEPRESS RETURN

TRANSLATING THE LANGUAGE

The program you write, called the **source program,** cannot be understood by the microcomputer unless it is translated into machine language. A very popular source program used on microcomputers is called **BASIC,** which is an acronym for **B**eginner's **A**ll-purpose **S**ymbolic **I**nstruction **C**ode. The translation is usually done by a program called a **BASIC interpreter,** a line-by-line translator which is furnished with the software package that accompanies your microcomputer. You enter the entire program, correcting errors as you enter the instructions. When all instructions are keyed, you tell the computer to execute the instuctions.

An interpreter checks an instruction that you entered to make certain it follows the rules for forming each instruction. If it finds the instruction unacceptable, it gives you a message telling what might be wrong. You correct the instruction and see if the interpreter will accept it this time. When acceptable, the instruction is executed. The interpreter translates and executes one instruction at a time.

DEBUGGING THE PROGRAM

After a source instruction is changed to machine language, the microcomputer tries to execute the instruction. You may find that your answer is incorrect because you failed to prepare the logic in the correct order or simply forgot to do some processing. This means that your program has bugs. You make adjustments and try executing again until the program is debugged, which means it tests out correctly. The number of times needed to try to debug the program depends upon how carefully you design the logic and write the program. Generally, the more time spent in creating the program, the faster is the debugging time.

SAVING THE PROGRAM

A program you have created can be saved on a diskette for later reference. To later execute a program, all you must remember is the name that you gave the file which is holding your program. When the diskette is inserted into the disk drive, the operating system provides a table of contents that lists the different file names stored on that diskette. You tell the computer to bring that file into primary storage so you can either edit it (change it) and execute it or execute it in the form in which it resides on the diskette. We shall expand on these concepts shortly.

CHECKPOINT **Can you:**

List the nine steps needed for preparing and executing a program?

Tell why each step is important?

USING SYSTEMS SOFTWARE WITH AN APPLICATIONS PROGRAM

A microcomputer user incorporates the systems software with his or her own program. To demonstrate the interaction, two lines of instructions will be written using the BASIC language. Like all other computer programming languages, BASIC has its rules on how an instruction is to be formed. Refer to Figure 6.8. The first part of the instruction gives a **line number** that is unique for each line of code. The line numbers are often numbered in increments of ten—10, 20, 30,

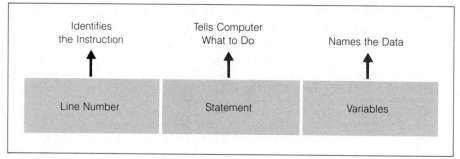

FIGURE 6.8   **The parts of a BASIC instruction.**

and so on. The purpose of the line numbers is to determine the order of each instruction in the source program. In the following illustration, only the line number and the statement portion of the instruction are used. (Details about BASIC are found in Appendix A.) In Figure 6.8 the statement tells the computer what to do, which, in our example, is to prepare output (PRINT is the statement) and to stop processing (END is the statement).

Let's assume all we wish to do is to print a message. We need a line number, say 10, the word PRINT, and the message enclosed within quotation marks. In line 20, we tell the computer that this is the last instruction in the source program, which requires that it stop processing. The BASIC program can be written with many spaces between the parts of an instruction. It might appear as follows:

```
10   PRINT "YOU HAVE TO START SOMEWHERE"
20   END
```

Having decided what is to be accomplished in the BASIC program, the next task is to instruct the computer what it is to do. A **systems diskette** is placed into one disk drive, arbitrarily called A. Disk drive A holds the systems programs, while disk drive B holds the diskette storing our programs or data. A prompt appears on the monitor (A> is used with CP/M). Since we wish to work with BASIC, the word BASIC is entered after the A> prompt; the RETURN or ENTER key is then depressed since the line ends. When using a hand-held calculator, a common practice is to set the calculator to zeros; the contents are initialized to zero. The same concept is used with primary storage and the monitor as both are initialized to blanks. Performing this type of initialization requires the use of a systems command. A **systems command** consists of a word that the operating system understands which identifies a task it is to perform. (Check your reference manual for exact details.)

Table 6.2 shows various systems commands, their purposes, and some variations on different microcomputers. Referring to Table 6.2, the systems commands of NEW and CLS accomplish the primary storage and monitor initializations. The systems command NEW is entered; the RETURN or ENTER key is depressed. The systems command of CLS is entered; the RETURN or ENTER key is depressed. Two lines of the BASIC program follow. The following has been keyed to this point:

TABLE 6.2. **Systems Commands Used on Several Microcomputers for Use with BASIC.**

SYSTEMS COMMANDS	PURPOSE	COMPAQ IBM PC	PET COMMODORE	TRS 80	APPLE
NEW	Clears primary storage	NEW	NEW	NEW	NEW
CLS	Clears the monitor	CLS	CLS	CLS	HOME
RUN	Executes the program stored in primary storage	RUN	RUN	RUN	RUN
LIST	Shows instructions in a program stored in primary storage on the monitor	LIST	LIST	LIST	LIST
SAVE	Stores a program currently in primary storage on a diskette*	SAVE "FILE"	SAVE "FILE",8	SAVE "FILE"	SAVE FILE
LOAD	Brings the file named FILE into primary storage*	LOAD "FILE"	LOAD "FILE",8	LOAD "FILE"	LOAD FILE
RUN	Brings the program called FILE from diskette into primary storage and then executes the program	RUN "FILE"	—	RUN "FILE"	RUN FILE
	Prints instructions in program stored in primary storage on the printer	Prt Sc	OPEN4 PRINT#4	LLIST	PR#1 LIST
	Shows the diskette's table of contents on the monitor	DIR	LOAD"$",8 LIST	DIR 1	CATALOG
	Erases the file from the diskette	DEL "FILE"	OPEN15,8,15 "S0:FILE: CLOSE15	KILL "FILE"	DELETE FILE

*Makes assumption that file is called FILE.

```
A>BASIC
NEW
CLS
10   PRINT "YOU HAVE TO START SOMEWHERE"
20   END
RUN
```

After the above instructions of the BASIC program are keyed and the RUN systems command is given, the instruction on line 10 is now translated by the BASIC interpreter; it changes the PRINT statement to machine language. Assume that the next instruction is keyed incorrectly—say, a line number was not included. A diagnostic follows the incorrect statement. Refer to Figure 6.9.

The advantage of an interpreter giving an immediate response as to how an instruction is formed should be very encouraging to a new user of a microcomputer. This type of interactive capability is not available on all computer languages, however. In addition, if the translator program is a compiler, syntax errors are not noted until the entire program is entered. This concept is discussed in depth in Chapter 12.

To correct the INVALID STATEMENT diagnostic, the line is rekeyed with a line number followed by END. After the RETURN key is depressed, no di-

```
10 PRINT "YOU HAVE TO START SOMEWHERE"
END ◄──────────────────────────────────── Forgot Line Number

INVALID STATEMENT ◄────────────────────── Generated by System
```

agnostic appears. The interpreter has accepted the syntax and has changed the source instruction to machine language; the instruction is executed.

Recall that the computer is in the edit mode when instructions are entered; the systems command of RUN is entered so that execution can occur. Pay particular attention that line numbers are never used with systems commands.

The output appears on the monitor, followed by the word READY on the next line. READY, Ok,], or an equivalent message, is the computer's signal that processing is completed. The complete screen would appear as follows, with the output following the systems command of RUN:

```
A>BASIC
NEW
CLS
10  PRINT "YOU HAVE TO START SOMEWHERE"
20  END
RUN
YOU HAVE TO START SOMEWHERE
Ok
```

Any time a user wishes to view on the monitor the program that is stored in primary storage, the systems command of LIST is used. Refer to Table 6.2, noting that the systems command does not use line numbers. The two lines of the program would appear on the monitor as:

```
LIST
10   PRINT "YOU HAVE TO START SOMEWHERE"
20   END
```

Recalling that random access memory (RAM) loses its contents when the power is removed, let us assume we now turned off the computer. If the computer is now turned on again and the systems command LIST is entered, nothing can be listed, for the program is gone. The program must be saved for future use.

Think of the diskette as being like a filing cabinet that contains many blank manilla folders. A manilla folder is labelled in a manual filing system for ease in locating the folder. When using a computer, the same concept is followed; a file name is given to the BASIC program. The name of the file cannot exceed eight characters on most operating systems. Table 6.2 shows that SAVE is a systems command; it is followed by the name of the file created by the user. To accomplish this processing, the following lines are entered as:

```
10   PRINT "YOU HAVE TO START SOMEWHERE"
20   END
SAVE "MESSAGE1"
```

SAVE is the systems command; hence, no line number is used. MESSAGE1 is a file name created by the user; notice the file name is enclosed within quotation marks. Assume that the microcomputer is now turned off. What happens when it is turned back on again? After typing in A>BASIC and then LIST, again nothing is shown on the monitor. Referring to Table 6.1, the LOAD systems command brings a program stored on secondary storage to primary storage. Keying in the systems command, LOAD "MESSAGE1" and depressing the RETURN or EN-TER key will make things happen. The red lights on the disk drive door flicker on and off; the program has been transferred from secondary storage to primary storage. The program does not appear on the monitor. Try the LIST command again; the program appears on the monitor. The BASIC program was in primary storage, but it had to be listed to appear on the monitor.

Examining Table 6.2 again, note that two systems commands for executing a program are shown: RUN and RUN "filename". Since the program that is to be executed is already in primary storage, the systems command RUN is used. There is a shortcut. The systems command RUN "MESSAGE1" could be used rather than the LOAD "MESSAGE1", LIST, and RUN systems commands just discussed. The RUN "MESSAGE1" systems command loads the file into primary storage and executes the program in one step. Which RUN systems command should be used? Ask yourself, is the program that is to be executed in primary storage? If it is, use RUN; otherwise, use the alternative.

Let us try one more exercise. This time the program is to print two lines: YOU HAVE TO START SOMEWHERE and THIS IS NOT SO BAD. Each program is to be kept intact for later use. Rather than rekey lines 10 and 20 and then prepare the print statement for the second printed line, a shortcut is taken for the creation of the file named MESSAGE2. As long as the contents of the file MESSAGE1 are in primary storage, any additional instruction or instructions can be entered, the contents of which can then be saved on the diskette under the file named MESSAGE2. Assuming that the printed line THIS IS NOT SO BAD is to print as the second line, the second print instruction is numbered any line number between 11 and 19. Selection of any of these line numbers accurately positions the instruction in the source program. If, however, the line was to print as the first printed line, the print instruction's line number would be between 1 and 9. Refer to Figure 6.10.

If the SAVE systems command in Figure 6.10 was rewritten to say SAVE

FIGURE 6.10
Creating a second file.

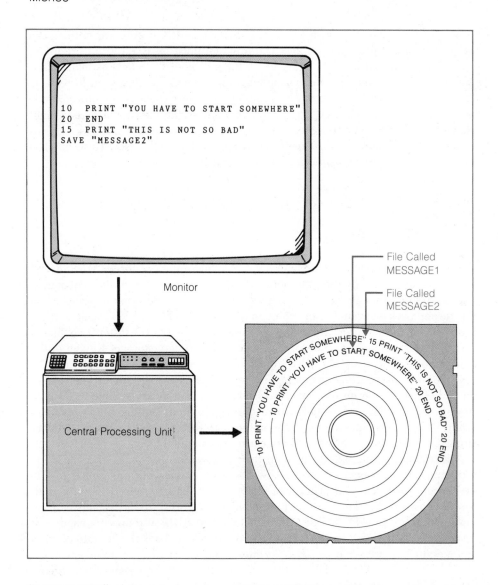

```
10  PRINT "YOU HAVE TO START SOMEWHERE"
20  END
15  PRINT "THIS IS NOT SO BAD"
SAVE "MESSAGE2"
```

Monitor

File Called
MESSAGE1

File Called
MESSAGE2

Central Processing Unit

"MESSAGE1", the original contents of MESSAGE1 would be lost and would be replaced with the new instructions.

For a manual filing system, we would never bother to keep an index of all the files in storage. It would be too time-consuming. But the systems software obliges nicely by keeping a list of the various files stored on a diskette. By using the systems command DIR or the like, the file names appear on the monitor. Can you see now why systems software is needed to manage the applications programs?

CHECKPOINT Can you:

State how systems software and applications software work together for use on a computer?

SELECTING A MICROCOMPUTER

It is unfortunate, but many of the people selecting a microcomputer are going about it in the wrong way. A logical sequence of steps is presented next. First, select your software, determining your needs as to the type of application for which you wish to use a microcomputer. Determine how easy that software is to use by having it demonstrated to you. Does the company that you are purchasing it from offer some type of instruction or will they give you a reference manual and say, "here is all you need to know"? A several-hundred-page manual is certainly not the only type of instruction you need. There are dealers who will teach you how to use the software as long as you buy it from them. This is a tremendous service and worth the nominal cost. You should also look for a technical support phone number (preferably an 800 number) which is available to the buyer or an agreement with local vendors dealing with support of the software.

Next, shop for the hardware.

1. Carefully select the type of keyboard that you wish, paying attention to the type of keys used.

2. When determining storage capabilities, you must determine how much you will use secondary storage and how much you can afford. If you spend the money for disk, two disk drives are recommended; primary storage with a minimum 64K of RAM is also recommended. Take a look at the software that you will be using the most. How much capacity does it require? Realize that some programs that provide integrated software packages can use up to 192K. An integrated software package includes a spreadsheet, word processing, data base, and the communications necessary that all programs work together.

3. If you select a monitor, make certain it is easy to read. Some monitors emit a glare which is extremely bothersome to some people's eyes. You might be staring at the monitor for hours, so choose carefully. Select a printer according to the quality of print needed. A slow printer can be bothersome, but one that is cheaply made and does not perform accurately is even worse.

4. Consider the software that is to be run. If your work centers on word processing, you will find the eighty-column screen of great benefit. An 8-bit microprocessor is sufficient.

5. Above all, before you walk out of the door with your microcomputer, make certain everything works. Make the sales person show you it works. Check the printer to make certain that the cables that are supplied do provide the necessary communication link between the console and the printer. Some hardware has limitations as to the types of printers that can be used with it.

6. Last but not least, expect to spend more money than you had planned. Selecting a microcomputer is an unbelievable experience. Beware of sales pitches. Carefully evaluate what processing capabilities are needed. You might find, if you are not careful, that the world is promised but not delivered.

State what is the most important decision as to selecting a microcomputer?

List some of the hardware considerations that are important?

SUMMARY

● Systems programs are supplied by a manufacturer or software company. Their main purpose is to manage applications programs.

● Translator programs are included in systems programs since the language symbols used to key in data differ from the machine language a computer understands.

● Applications software includes those programs written to solve a problem. High-level languages and assembly languages are types of applications program languages.

● High-level languages are easier to write, can be understood on most computers since they do not need to be re-programmed, use English-like statements, but require longer processing time for execution.

● Assembly language is the closest to machine language that humans write. A programmer must know the hardware specifics about the computer, for assembly language is more difficult to write; it is, however, much faster at processing in executing a program.

● Daniel Bricklin developed a financial analysis program called VisiCalc, which is a very popular electronic spreadsheet.

● Operating systems are the most critical of all software, as they supply the interface between the hardware and applications programs.

● Utility programs are standard, routine programs that a user needs for some particular work such as copying diskettes, formatting a screen for data entry, and recovering data lost on damaged diskettes.

● The operating system is tied to the hardware by the microprocessor chip that is used. A disk operating system is so named since its primary function is to manage the movement of the data and programs to and from the disk. CP/M is used on Z80 and Intel 8080. MS-DOS is used on Intel 8088. There are other versions, such as TRS-DOS and APDOS for Radio Shack and Apple, respectively. Silicon operating systems represent those operating systems that are included as firmware.

● Gary Kildall at Intel Corporation wrote one of the most popularly used control programs, called CP/M.

● Smalltalk, an operating system, was developed at Xerox PARC through efforts of Alan Kay and others. This operating system uses graphics for input and output. Windows are used for dividing the monitor in different sections.

GALLERY 3

Public Domain Software

Chapter 6 discussed the need for having some utility programs to meet special processing needs. There are always commercially available software. Let's look into, however, how anyone with a microcomputer can access public domain software—software free. The whole spirit behind the public domain software is one of sharing. When you begin your exposure to public domain software, you will be taking from the system. However, when you later become more sophisticated in your use, or when you need to develop software for your own needs, or wish to patch an already existing package with a modification, the time will have come to pass your software on to other people for their use. If the spirit of give-and-take does not continue, public domain software could become nonexistent. To those many users who have devoted time and energy to their programs and then passed them on to others, this salute is to you!

The only other problem that exists with use of public domain software is the failure of some to be mature in its use. If programs have copyright privileges, please honor the author's name; these are noted within the program as such. After using the various services of public domain software, a small token of appreciation such as a "thank you" might go a long way for the generous people who spend their off-work hours in serving others. It is very unfortunate that some few users ruin the services for so many by immature behavior causing some of the services to be withdrawn.

Public domain software can be available through three different sources: the user groups, bulletin board services (BBS), and the commercial versions.

With each of these sources, except the user groups, you need hardware so the communication can take place over your telephone line. You also need software to make communications possible between your microcomputer's site and the sending site.

The public domain software is distributed through the local user groups or special interest groups, called (SIGs), at a fee. Perhaps the fee is $6 per diskette which might contain fifteen or twenty programs. The fee helps to defray costs for maintenance of the disk drives and computer. Look for advertisements that appear in microcomputer magazines and local newspapers about the local user groups and SIGs. If you use one of these suppliers, you save on the telephone line costs which can become high if you become intrigued with the experience of transmitting the programs electronically.

Another way of contacting the special interest groups or local user groups is to ask the store where you purchased your microcomputer. Sometimes these stores will direct you to your local chamber of commerce or to a special interest group (SIG) that operates. Many special interest groups have been formed by the manufacturer of the computer or by interested individuals who form a group to swap software. Sometimes these users groups supply the

Public domain software can help defray costs.

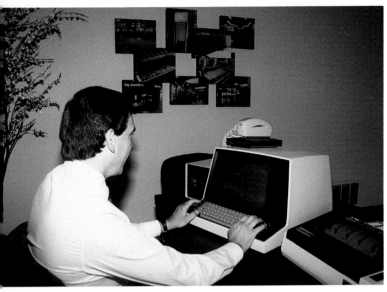

To transmit programs electronically you will need a modem.

monetary backing for the operators of the bulletin boards, called **SYSOPs** (pronounced sis-ops). Sometimes the SYSOPs supply the SIGs telephone numbers, announcing the local meeting date and place. A local computer fair also is an excellent source for the bulletin board service locations, the SIGs and the local interest groups. Publications such as *PC WORLD* that can be found in bookstores supply IBM PC SIGs and *The Computer Shopper* at P.O. Box F, Titusville, FL 32780, (305) 269-3211 supplies public domain software and lists of SIGs for most computers.

One of the distinct advantages of contacting these groups first is they often supply, at a nominal fee, the communications software which you will need to access either bulletin boards or the commercial sources. With this available, the cash outlay for the additional hardware may be $150 or less.

The details of how data communications (the transmitting of messages or programs from one site to another) is discussed in Chapter 10. All we wish to discuss here, however, is the bare necessities, as that is all you need for obtaining public domain software. Since a telephone was designed for voice transmission and what a computer sends is digital transmission, a modem is used at your microcomputer to allow the digital signals to be transmitted over the telephone line. (The modem costs about $150 or less.) If the telephone and the modem are hooked up with the microcomputer, nothing happens until the necessary communications software is used. As previously mentioned, the communications software can be obtained from the user groups.

There are two locations (sites) involved. There is the SYSOP's computer facility which is known as a host computer; it contains the public domain software that will be transferred to you. The transferring of software from the host computer to a user is called **downloading.** The host computer is usually a microcomputer that contains a hard disk as secondary storage. At your site, in order to access public domain software, you need a microcomputer, a modem, a telephone line, and the communications software that allows you to copy the programs from the host computer to your computer.

The bulletin board services began in 1978 when Ward Christensen and Randy Suess, who lived in the Chicago area, formed **Computerized bulletin board service (CBBS)** to provide users with an opportunity to leave messages for others and to later pick up responses to these messages. CBBS is still in operation; Randy Suess is still involved with the service which is located at 5219 West Warwick, Chicago, Illinois 60641. CBBS was designed for providing free software for CP/M users.

A group, called **Remote CP/M (RCPM),** which was dedicated to become more user-friendly, emerged later. The SYSOPs (pronounced sis-ops) are those dedicated people who maintain a bulletin board to distribute public domain software at no charge. Since the SYSOPs' intention is to supply a user-friendly system, they supply menus and HELP files for those needing assistance in accessing public domain software. Notes are also allowed to be left for the SYSOP; a "thank you" is a nice gesture. The RCPM operates as though you are operating your microcomputer using CP/M. Instead, however, you are operating the host computer which is instructed by you to download designated files of your choice. As soon as the desired programs are transferred, the host computer takes the next call and serves its requests. You basically are operating the SYSOP's microcomputer.

From your local interest group you receive the complete data communications software needed to connect your microcomputer to another microcomputer or your microcomputer to a mainframe. The name of this software is called MODEM or MODEM7, developed by Ward Christensen. If, however, you receive from your local interest groups, only a partial communications software package called BOOT3.ASM, you can use this to get MODEM or MODEM7. If you get the elemental communications software called MBOOT3.ASM, you may have to key in this software. MBOOT3.ASM supplies you with the capability to download the complete communications software called MODEM or MODEM7.

For your first session, make certain your diskette, to be used for capturing the public domain software, is formatted so the operating system can reference the respective tracks of the diskette. Turn your microcomputer on, with the diskette in place in the disk drive. After you dial your bulletin board telephone number, you will hear a high pitched sound. Your modem then communicates with the modem at the host computer. Your microcomputer will be sending 30 characters (300 baud) per second, using a regular telephone line (called full duplex) and using 8-bit ASCII characters with no parity and one stop bit. The ASCII code and parity are discussed in Chapter 7; the baud, modem, and the stop bit are discussed in Chapter 10. The ASCII code is used for coding a character with 0s and 1s, the parity is used for making certain characters are transmitted correctly, the baud refers to the transmittal of 0s and 1s, and the stop bit is used for telling where a byte ends.

Let's assume that when you contacted your local user group you received only the bare necessities of the data communications software. With the BOOT3.ASM program in RAM, you must tell the bulletin board service that you want the complete communications software called MODEM or MODEM7. To accomplish this transferring, enter the word TYPE. The BBS will download the full MODEM software package for you. For this first session, download the DISKMENU.DOC file and the WHATSNEW file. The DISKMENU.DOC gives you a listing of all the programs at the bulletin board service (BBS). The WHATSNEW file gives an announcement of the new software that has just been added to the system. The programs will be transmitted to your diskette. After transmission stops, type BYE. Print out the contents of the diskette and see what is available on that BBS. Now you will be in position to make a good selection of the desired software on your next call.

The commercial versions represent CompuServe and The Source. The advantages of using these services is the

Ask the store where you purchased your microcomputer about local user groups.

easy access to locating the services, the vast quantity of public domain software available, and the wide spectrum of subjects from which to choose. These services provide many special interest groups (SIGs) which are devoted to a certain computer or topic. These SIGs are usually separate from the ones previously mentioned.

If you wish to use a commercial CompuServe services, you can pay a fee of about $20. When you purchase a CompuServe Starter Kit for about $50 from the Radio Shack computer stores, you are given five free hours on the system to begin your subscription. If you call to use the service at 8 am to 6 pm, the charge is 21 cents a minute or $12.50 per hour; other hours available for use are 10 cents a minute or $6.00 an hour. If you are interested in this service, call CompuServe, 5000 Arlington Centre Blvd., P.O. Box 20212, Columbus, OH 43220 at (800) 848-8990 or (614) 457-8600. The Source can be reached at 1616 Anderson Road, McLean, VA 22102 at (800) 336-3330 or (703) 734-7540. The rates per hour are $20.75 for 7 am to 6 pm transmission and $7.75 per hour for other hour transmission.

A list of some RCPMs is provided for your convenience. These, like SYSOPs, however, change frequently so telephone numbers can become out-dated.

AREA	RCPM NAME
201-272-1874	RIBBS of Cranford
201-584-9227	Flanders
205-895-6749	NACS/UAH RBBS/RCPM
206-458-3086	Yelm RBBS & CP/M
207-839-2337	Programmer's Anonymous
213-296-5927	Los Angeles RCP/M
213-577-9947	Pasadena RBBS
214-931-8274	Dallas RCP/M CBBS

AREA	RCPM NAME
215-398-3937	Allentown RBBS/RCPM System
301-661-4447	BHEC RBBS/RCPM
303-499-9169	Boulder RCPM
303-781-4937	Denver CUG-NODE
312-359-8080	Palatine RCPM
313-559-5326	Southfield RBBS/RCPM

AREA	RCPM NAME
401-751-5025	Providence
403-454-6093	Edmonton RCPM
406-443-2768	Helena Valley RBBS/RCPM
408-730-8733	RCP/M Sunnyvale
414-647-0903	Mike's RCP/M System
415-461-7726	Larkspur RBBS/RCPM
416-231-9538	Toronto Ontario Systems One
503-758-8408	Dr. Dobb's CP/M Exchange RCPM

The following is a list of the special interest groups (SIGs).

Name	Address
Trevor Marshall	3423 Hill Canyon Avenue, Thousand Oaks, CA 91360
A. J. Lundquist	Denver Amateur Computer Society, Box 633, Broomfield, CO 80020
John Irwin	Miami Amateur Computer Group, 9159 S.W. 77th Avenue, Miami, FL
Charlie Wells	Atlanta Computer Society, 465 Northgate Pass, Atlanta, GA
Jim Mills	CACHE/CPMUG, 824 Jordan Place, Rockford, IL 61108
Dave Mitton	New England Computer Society, 13 Swan Street, Arlington, MA 02174
Keith Peterson	Box 309, Clawson, MI 48017
Secor/Thomas	CPMUG of Minnesota, 854 120th Lane NW, Coon Rapids, MN 55434
SIG/M Main Office	Box 97, Iselin, NJ 08830
Henry Kee	SIG/M Editor/Librarian, NYACC 42-24 Colden Street, Flushing, NY 11355
Fred Pfafman	2320 Heather Hill Lane, Plano, TX 75075
Al Whitney	SIG/M South Central Coordinator, 2003 Hammerwood, Missouri City, TX 77489

- UCSD Pascal is an operating system that is hardware independent like Small-talk.

- Nine steps are involved for a user to process and execute a program.

- The first of these steps involves setting up objectives as to what is to be accomplished in the program.

- The second step involves specifying input and output formats.

- The third step involves developing the logic. How the problem is to be processed is set up step by step in what is referred to as an algorithm.

- The fourth step involves selecting the computer language that is to be used. This depends upon the availability of translator programs and the application to be solved. BASIC is the most popularly used program for microcomputers. It was developed in 1963 by Professors John Kemeny and Tom Kurtz at Dartmouth College.

- The fifth step of nine in processing and executing a program involves writing the language, making it as accurate as possible. When the user fails to write the program according to the specifications or fails to use proper logic or coding, the program will not execute the data correctly. Corrections must be made (debugging), and the program is again translated.

- The sixth step in the nine-step programming operation involves keying in the program. A user is aided by the use of prompts, menus, and editor programs.

- The seventh step involves translating the language to machine language. The language must be written according to instruction specifications, since the source program must be translated to machine language. The translator program for BASIC is called a BASIC interpreter. Sometimes a user writes symbols incorrectly, producing syntax errors.

- The eighth step involves executing the program, examining the output for correctness and completeness, and debugging it, if necessary. Removing all syntax errors and incorrect logic from the program is referred to as debugging a program.

- The ninth and final step involves saving the program so it can be used at a later time.

STUDY GUIDE

REVIEW OF TERMINOLOGY

The following terminology was discussed in this chapter:

algorithm
applications software
assembly language
BASIC (Beginner's All-
  Purpose Symbolic
  Instruction Code)
BASIC interpreter
clones
concurrent processing
Control Program for
  Microcomputers
  (CP/M)
debug
diagnostics
disk operating system
electronic spreadsheet
high-level language

line number
machine language
menu
prompts
silicon operating systems
Smalltalk
source program
syntax errors
systems command
systems diskette
systems software
UCSD Pascal
UNIX
user-friendly
utility program
VisiCalc
VisiPoint

MULTIPLE CHOICE

Circle the letter of the item that correctly answers each question.

1. A program designed to calculate a grade point average is an example of:
   a. a systems software
   b. a utility program
   c. an applications program
   d. an interpreter
   e. a spreadsheet

2. A program designed to provide translation to machine language is an example of:
   a. a utility
   b. an applications program
   c. a spreadsheet
   d. a systems program
   e. a program that uses systems commands

3. When a programmer writes a computer language and fails to follow the rules of that language, he or she generates errors called:
   a. an algorithm
   b. a diagnostic
   c. a high-level language
   d. syntax errors
   e. an interpreter

4. When a computer generates messages to help a user in the operation of the computer, these messages are called:
   a. an algorithm
   b. a diagnostic
   c. a translator
   d. a menu
   e. a prompt

5. The program to solve a GPA is called:
   a. an interpreter
   b. systems software
   c. a source program
   d. a prompt
   e. a menu

6. When a programmer tries to locate errors in his or her program, that programmer is:
   a. translating a program
   b. debugging a program
   c. answering a prompt
   d. writing high-level languages
   e. using a menu

7. The language a computer understands is:
   a. high-level language
   b. BASIC
   c. prompts
   d. machine language
   e. menus

8. The way that a problem is to be solved is laid out as:
   a. an algorithm
   b. prompts
   c. a menu
   d. a utility program
   e. an operating system

9. Programs that are generally easier to write but require more processing time for execution are called:
   a. interpreter programs
   b. assembly language programs
   c. high-level language programs
   d. utility programs
   e. systems programs

10. The language closest to machine language is called:
    a. interpreter
    b. assembly language
    c. high-level languages
    d. utility programs
    e. systems programs

11. A program that can be executed on all types of data and that copies data onto diskettes is:
   a. an interpreter
   b. an assembly language
   c. a source program
   d. a systems command
   e. a utility program

12. If a user tells the operating system to LIST, RUN, and CLS, these are examples of:
   a. source instructions
   b. prompts
   c. systems commands
   d. statements
   e. menus

13. A type of program that replaces an accountant's ledgers is called a:
   a. spreadsheet
   b. machine language
   c. word processing program
   d. utility program
   e. systems program

14. The systems command used for storing a program on a diskette is:
   a. LOAD
   b. RUN
   c. SAVE
   d. LIST
   e. CLS

15. An operating system designed for running programs in universities, government, and at the Bell System, is called:
   a. CP/M
   b. MS-DOS
   c. TRS-DOS
   d. UNIX
   e. silicon operating systems

16. If you wanted to find out which files were contained on a diskette, you need to use the systems command of:
   a. LOAD
   b. SAVE
   c. RUN
   d. DIR or its equivalent
   e. NEW

17. Which operating system will run on a Z80 8-bit microprocessor:
   a. CP/M
   b. MS-DOS
   c. UNIX
   d. XENIX
   e. APDOS

18. The translator program used for BASIC language is called:
   a. CP/M
   b. a utility program
   c. a high-level language program
   d. an interpreter program
   e. machine language

TRUE/FALSE QUESTIONS

Circle T if a statement is true; F if it is false.

1. **T/F** A possible use of an electronic spreadsheet could be for keeping track of a person's stocks and bonds.
2. **T/F** When a problem is to be solved, the major ideas involved are considered last.
3. **T/F** When planning the logic as to how a program is to be solved, the programmer sets up modules, each generally performing one type of work.
4. **T/F** The operating system never helps a user in debugging a program.
5. **T/F** A programmer can never change a program once it has been executed by the computer.
6. **T/F** The saving of files is only accomplished through the use of a utility program.
7. **T/F** Utilities refer to those programs that can be used with any data.
8. **T/F** Prompts and menus are basically the same.
9. **T/F** BASIC is a source program that is classified as a high-level language.
10. **T/F** Any program written on a microcomputer can be executed on any other microcomputer.
11. **T/F** Already-prepared programs must be debugged by a user.
12. **T/F** There are quite a few disk operating systems available.
13. **T/F** Digital Research, Inc., and Microsoft are two companies in competition for operating systems for microcomputers.
14. **T/F** The average cost of utilities is about $1,000.
15. **T/F** If there is a demand for certain types of software, you can feel fairly certain that someday it will be written as a prepared program.
16. **T/F** The most recent operating systems are called silicon operating systems because the systems software is contained on silicon.

ANSWERS

Multiple Choice: 1. **c** 2. **d** 3. **d** 4. **e** 5. **c** 6. **b** 7. **d** 8. **a** 9. **c** 10. **b** 11. **e** 12. **c** 13. **a** 14. **c** 15. **d** 16. **d** 17. **a** 18. **d** *True/False:* 1. **T** 2. **F** 3. **T** 4. **F** 5. **F** 6. **F** 7. **T** 8. **F** 9. **T** 10. **F** 11. **F** 12. **T** 13. **T** 14. **F** 15. **T** 16. **T**

REVIEW QUESTIONS

1. What is systems software? What is applications software?
2. Which is the most popular language used for problem solving on microcomputers? Where was this language developed? Who were the authors?
3. What programs are combined with your source program so the microcomputer can be used?
4. Define an algorithm.
5. Why is a translator program needed? What is it called?
6. When is the translator program used?
7. When do you select the computer language you are going to use?
8. Do you write the program as you key it?
9. What is a source program?
10. Once you debug your program, can you ever re-use it? Explain your answer.
11. Must you write all programs yourself if you wish to process data? Explain your answer.
12. What is VisiCalc? UNIX? XENIX? VisiPoint?
13. Why is an operating system needed?
14. What are some of the most popular operating systems? Why are there different ones?
15. What is a word processing program used for?
16. What are systems commands? Why are they used?

DISCUSSION QUESTIONS

1. Explain why microcomputer software includes more than just application programs.
2. Identify some of the people involved in the software development for microcomputers. Why were their contributions so important?
3. What are some of the operating systems available for use? Why was the development of CP/M important?
4. Not all computer languages can be used on a given computer. Explain this statement.
5. What are clones in the microcomputer industry? What benefit does a user derive?
6. What might, in your opinion, be some of the future uses for microcomputers?
7. Explain how you go about selecting a microcomputer.
8. Give fifteen examples of already-prepared programs mentioned in this chapter. Why are they needed?
9. List the steps involved in developing an algorithm. Why is each step needed for problem solving?
10. Explain why use of microcomputers for spreadsheet (financial) analysis and word processing has become so widespread.
11. Explain how systems software must work with applications software so processing can occur.
12. The term "not invented here" has been used in the past. Explain what this means.

People in Computing

Edward Tang

COMPANY
Hewlett-Packard Company

POSITION
Project Manager

EDUCATIONAL BACKGROUND
Bachelor of Electrical Engineering
and Computer Science, University of
California at Berkeley

In one's training as a computer programmer many technical skills are developed. While these techniques lead to good technical solutions, they do not necessarily produce usable programs. There are other factors to be considered if one is to develop usable programs.

As a computer programming student, one's success is generally determined by one's technical ability. Those who show the greatest technical skills are the ones who receive the higher grades. However, in the "real" world the users will generally not be well versed in the intricacies of computer programming. They are not interested in the cleverness of the algorithms but with how well the program helps them do their jobs. All too often, the programmer has solved the technical problem, but the solution is unusable.

Such is the fate shared by many of the users of programs written today. In using a program, it appears that the programmer never tried it in a real life situation. A program may require the computer

operator to perform many extra steps, or the data must be entered in a strange order or, worse, with codes. Every programmer's first assignment should be as a computer operator or they should work in the department that he/she will be developing programs for.

In the past, the state of the computing industry dictated that people think like computers. This is exemplified by the admonition to not "bend, staple, fold or mutilate" and the ubiquitous requirement to use a #2 pencil. With the current and developing technology, there are fewer excuses for not humanizing one's programs.

I recall a programmer describing a system he designed to expedite the processing of telephone orders. Most orders were made by repeat customers who usually placed the same order each time. So, the program would automatically display the order history of a customer when the customer's identification was entered. The object was to give the customer a positive feeling for the business since it took the trouble to learn his/her habits. The flaw in the system was that the customer identification was a code number. Each customer was given a code number on his or her first call. On subsequent calls, the customer gave his/her code number to be identified by the system. The programmer was a bit puzzled by the limited success his program had. What he didn't consider was that people don't want to be known by a number, they would rather be known by their name. Certainly, using a name instead of an identification number presents additional problems, but usability is dramatically improved when you do.

Many times, a programmer will complain about having to spend extra time coding in order to handle some user quirk. What these programmers forget is that he/she deals with the problem once, but the user will encounter the problem every time the program is used.

Too often, programmers think they know what the user wants or what the user should want. The system is then designed to conform to the programmer's perception of the user's needs. When the system is put into use, the users expend much effort trying to circumvent these "features". For example, a program automatically clears out a form after each order is entered. However, what really happens is orders are received in batches from individual salesmen for the city they work in. What the data entry clerk wants is to have the salesman and city data to be the same from one order to the next. So, the clerk enters the first order, the screen clears; the clerk recalls the first order to the screen and modifies the appropriate fields for the next order, then the modified screen is entered as another order. Recalling the previous order avoids having to re-enter the salesman and city data.

The term "user friendly" is used frequently to describe a program that is easy to use. Techniques include the use of many prompts, help and information messages, and to be generally forgiving of human errors. However, programs can be *too* friendly. All the prompts and messages become irritating; they can get in the way of getting the work done. After a while, even non-technical users can learn and want to use short cuts to speed up their work.

Programs should be written to allow for at least two modes of operation: novice and expert. Ideally, the program should allow for varying degrees of expertness. A program should also allow users to tailor the programs for their particular use of the program. For example, the program could allow the user to assign new meanings to some keys. A key could be defined to fill in common default data, or to perform a series of operations. This will reduce the number of data entry errors and the time to get the work done.

Application

PROCTER & GAMBLE COMPANY

A glimpse of the computer applications being used in Procter & Gamble's research organizations reveals a kaleidoscope of technology and innovation.

Some of these applications are probably used by competitors. Others, to the best of our knowledge, are unique. But nothing in the picture is static. "Each year new projects and processes utilizing emerging computer technologies surpass those that came before," says Duane Wait, associate director, MSD.

Aiding Lab Operations

In analytical laboratories, such as those in Bar Soap & Household Cleaning Products at Sharon Woods Technical Center (SWTC), personal computers have become invaluable tools in collecting, storing and analyzing data. "With 17,000 standard analyses to do annually, we figured a 17 percent time savings last year," says Analytical Section Head Ray D'Alonzo. "As recently as two years ago, lab technicians did all enzyme computations with hand calculators. Now information on an analysis, such as measuring the enzyme level of a Biz sample, is fed directly into a personal computer."

Likewise, complex mathematical models, available with the use of spreadsheet software, are expanding scientists' predictive capabilities. Before the widespread use of personal computers, the research scientist, using only a hand calculator, was forced to keep equations as simple as possible.

"Computerization allows us to solve far more complicated problems, and the number of analyses and quality is going way up," says Mike Jensen, associate director, Tissues & Disposables Technology Division, Miami Valley Laboratories (MVL). "Now, just by pushing a button we can evaluate a new set of variables."

New computer technology is also expanding the capabilities of the research instruments used in 31 P&G analytical labs worldwide. One instrument that has become faster and more versatile through computerization is the nuclear magnetic resonance spectrometer (NMR). The NMR has been used to determine chemical composition since the '50s. Yet with earlier models, scientists were able to test only a limited array of chemicals, and then only in liquid form. Now NMRs can perform a multitude of experiments on a wide variety of chemicals—solids as well as liquids.

Robots Are Here

Within the last few years, another new type of instrument has begun appearing in analytical and products research labs at P&G. Robots, flexible mechanical arms with computers as their driving force, are increasingly being used to perform repetitive tests that must be conducted with percise, controlled conditions.

A typical example of how the robot is utilized can be found in PS&D's light-duty liquids lab at the ITC Annex. "The robot," says Technician Nancy Casper, "does 12 consecutive sudsing runs without operator intervention. It

runs right through lunchtime and never takes a break." The mechanical arm, which is hooked up to a microcomputer, dispenses soil, measures initial suds height and washes up to 30 plates per test, measuring the suds level after each five plates.

"Some generics and other competing brands' suds decrease rapidly—say after washing 20 plates," says Casper. In that case, she explains, the robot detects the end point after two suds readings and ends that particular test. Then the dishpan is automatically dumped, rinsed with hot water, and another test is begun.

Previously the tests were conducted by technicians who stood in the lab, washing dishes to the monotonous beat of a metronome and calculating the data with a hand calculator. Free of this tedious task, the technicians perform other duties, and Casper and her supervisor, Charlie Ries, are trained to program and maintain the robotic equipment.

"The application of robotics technology is having a favorable impact on laboratory operations," says Grover Owens, Corporate Technology Division, MVL.

"High on the list of benefits are productivity increases, cost savings and safe handling of hazardous materials. In most cases these benefits are not because the robot performs the work faster than its human counterpart. On the contrary, the robot is usually slower. The productivity gains are made because the robot will run longer and make fewer mistakes once properly programmed."

Faster Access To Consumer Data

New computer programs and systems recently developed in the Beauty Care Division also are winning acceptance throughout P&G. The Consumer Analysis System (CAS) allows employees in product development to instantly analyze research data from Home Performance Testing and other studies.

Dwayne Ball, Consumer Research, Beauty Care, says, "An analysis can be run in a few minutes, and this helps us to get closer to the consumer by getting a real understanding of unmet needs or reactions to products."

"Instant analyses" of consumer safety-related comments are also possible with the Consumer Safety System, a newly designed data storage/retrieval system. "With our instant retrieval capabilities," says Bob Sturm, associate director, Beauty Care PDD, "we are able to work more effectively with consumers in solving their problems and clearly demonstrate that we have a real commitment to product safety."

Also, government reports, as well as numerous special reports, are now generated in a fraction of the time it previously took to pour over computer printouts and manually put together the information.

Image Processing

More and more, scientists and engineers are developing new applications for new technologies. Image processing is one example of a new technology that has just recently been applied in consumer product research.

"Image processing," says MSD's Roland Johnson, SWTC, "is almost making the invisible visible." The technology combines the computer and the video camera to capture a picture of a sample by digitizing it—or quantifying it by computer. The digitized scene then can be enhanced to bring out obscure details.

This technique has been used to determine characteristics such as dryness or redness in the skin or to visually measure abstract properties of hair, such as how clean or shiny it is. Image processing has also been used to study paper structure and cellulosic fibers.

PART THREE

Larger Computer Systems

OUTLINE

PROLOGUE

Amy says "Grandma, that's the way things are nowadays. Gallons are converted to liters, degrees in fahrenheit are converted to centigrade, display characters are translated to ASCII, and ASCII is converted to hexadecimal. It's the sign of the times."

HOW DOES IT DO THAT?

READ ON.

OBJECTIVES

After studying this chapter, you should be able to:

1. Identify some of the characteristics associated with mainframes.

2. Differentiate among the different types of primary storage.

3. Differentiate between character-addressable and word-addressable computers.

4. Explain how bits are used in an internal code.

5. Explain when binary is used.

6. Explain why the control section is needed.

7. Explain how registers play an important role in executing a program.

INTRODUCTION

The central processing unit, as discussed in Chapter 2, is composed of primary storage, an arithmetic-logic unit, and a control section. A bus or channel connects the central processing unit with secondary storage and any peripherals used in the computer system.

A central processing unit's operating speed is measured in millions of instructions per second (mips). Mainframes have a range of from 5 to over 50 mips; the wide disparity is accounted for by the widely varied speed and processing capabilities that exist. Recall from Chapter 3 that, among the family of computers, low-end processors do not have the speed and processing capabilities of those processors on the high end of the scale. Super-computers can perform a 100 million operations per second and more.

Another characteristic associated with the central processing unit is **cycle time,** which refers to the length of time that is needed to perform an operation. Mainframes' cycle time can vary from about 26 nanoseconds up to about 400 nanoseconds, depending (again) upon the classification as high-end processor or low-end processor.

Figure 7.1 shows National Cash Register's NCR 9300 mainframe. It weighs fifty pounds, uses four square feet of floor space, has a cycle time of 150 nanoseconds, its primary storage capacity is 2 million bytes, and its cost is about $23,000.

IBM has long led all competition in the mainframe computer marketplace. Some companies have produced mainframes that are in direct competition with IBM mainframes. These mainframes can run programs on their hardware that are run on IBM computers. These computers are referred to as having **plug compatibility.** Amdahl Corporation has been a successful challenger in the marketplace by making a computer compatible with the IBM mainframes which offers considerably faster processing time at substantially lower cost to users.

In this chapter, the discussion centers on how a computer is able to store

FIGURE 7.1(a)
A mainframe computer, the NCR 9300.

FIGURE 7.1(b)   **Cover removed on mainframe.**

and find data in its primary storage, how characters are differentiated by different combinations of "on" and "off" states, how a shorthand is used for the coding of 0s and 1s, and how addition is accomplished.

CHECKPOINT **Can you:**

Identify some of the characteristics associated with mainframes?

PRIMARY STORAGE

All computer systems center around the use of primary storage. All information goes to the primary storage, making it then the prime system resource. The processing power of a computer depends upon the size of primary storage, the internal speed, and how fast the input and output can be fed to and from primary storage.

Primary storage remembers the facts for us, enabling data to be read and used many times; this ability is paramount to computer effectiveness. In the following discussion, let us concentrate on how the computer stores data, accesses (gets at) data, and differentiates data.

TYPES OF PRIMARY STORAGE

A general concept about the types of storage that are used internally in a central processing unit is really all that is needed. The discussion begins with magnetic cores, proceeds to bubble memory, and then relates and contrasts magnetic cores with semiconductor memory.

Magnetic Cores

Magnetic cores, shaped like small doughnuts, vary in outside dimensions. Some measure as small as a pin head or a grain of salt. On the outside of the magnetic core, there is a ferromagnetic substance whose molecules can be lined up (magnetized) to go in either one of two directions as shown in Figure 7.2. The molecules' direction when they are not magnetized is random; when magnetized, they travel around the outside of the magnetic core in either a clockwise or a counterclockwise direction, as shown in Figure 7.3.

In primary storage, as long as magnetic cores are magnetized, they can exist in only one of two states—magnetized clockwise or counterclockwise. There are only two possible states used in primary storage, an "on" state (a 1) or an "off" state (a 0). These two electrical states are then represented as binary digits (bits). All codings in primary storage are made up of bits. A bit is always either a 1 or a 0. When molecules line up in a clockwise direction on the outside of the core, they represent a 1 in storage. When molecules line up in a counterclockwise direction, they represent a 0 in storage. One magnetic core can hold a single binary digit at any one time. Note that the magnetic cores do not move; it is the molecules that move. Magnetic cores are magnetized by the use of wires that pass through their centers, as shown in Figure 7.3. The wires also restore data that was temporarily lost when the data is read. Previously it was noted that if the electrical power was removed, the contents of primary storage were lost. Magnetic cores, however, retain their magnetism even when the electrical power is shut off; magnetic cores are non-volatile memory.

FIGURE 7.2
Nonmagnetized versus magnetized states.

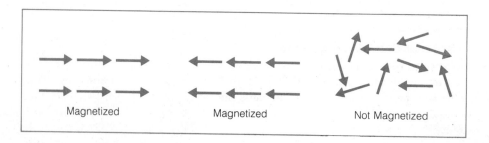

Magnetized   Magnetized   Not Magnetized

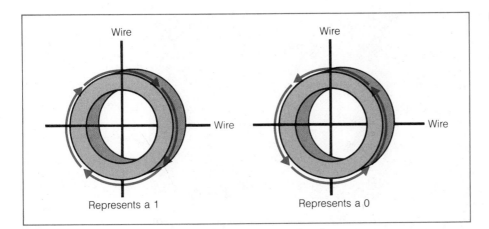

FIGURE 7.3
Magnetic core storage can be magnetized clockwise or counterclockwise.

Magnetic core was introduced in the 1950s and is still being used but only in those computers that were manufactured in the 1960s. Because of the reliability of the magnetic core, companies that have computers with magnetic cores will continue to use them for many years.

Bubble Memory

Another type of primary storage that is being used sparingly is the **bubble memory.** This, like magnetic cores, is a non-volatile memory but in addition it is a non-destructive read-out type of memory, which means that the data is not temporarily lost when the contents are read as is the case with magnetic cores. Bubble memory is assembled in an integrated circuit chip that is plugged into a printed circuit board. A very thin crystal is used in the manufacture of the bubble memory. The molecules of this crystal can then be used as very small magnets which make up magnetic domains or bubbles. The direction that the molecules travel can be changed, much as was described for magnetic cores. No physical wires are used in bubble memory for applying the electrical impulse to change the direction with which the bubble or domain floats; this is accomplished in the integrated circuit chip. Refer to Figure 7.4.

Bubble memory can be packed very dense, with 5 million bits per square inch. Bubble memory is generally faster than disk but slower than RAM. It is ideal, however, for use in microcomputers that are portable (weighing about 8 pounds or less) and for terminals that are used by salespeople. Say, for example, your parents wanted to save energy and called a consultant from the local utility company for advice on the needed insulation for proper heat conservation. As is currently done, the consultant takes measurements, turns on the terminal, keys in the data, transmits the data to a computer located elsewhere, receives the answers, and writes the answers on paper. For a computer using some types of primary storage, turning off the machine causes all calculations and data to be lost. With bubble memory, however, the transmission of the energy data to the office could be done at a later time, since the data once keyed would be retained as long as needed.

As stated previously, all primary storage uses the concept of 0s and 1s. It is

FIGURE 7.4
Bubble memory.

FIGURE 7.5
Possible ways of representing binary digits.

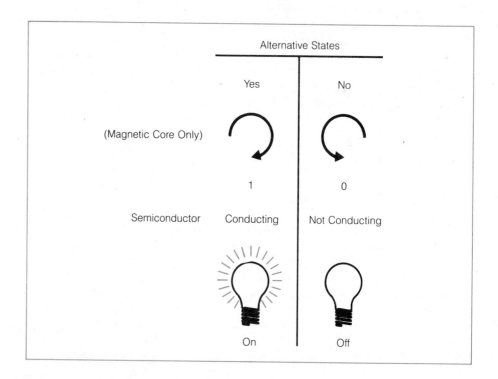

really not a 1 or a 0 that is stored but rather the electrical states of "on" or "off". From the layman's viewpoint, the 0s and 1s are the easiest to reference. Many like to think of the states represented by a 1-bit as a turned-on light bulb, while the 0-bit means the figurative light bulb is turned off. Refer to Figure 7.5 for some of the possible ways of relating to the binary digits coding system. The usual industry practice is to relate the bits to 0s and 1s.

Semiconductor Memory

All computers manufactured since the 1970s use semiconductor memory as primary storage. This type of memory revolutionized the computer industry in terms of speed, reliability, and reduction in costs. The semiconductor memory is in the form of chips, as illustrated in Appendix D and discussed in Chapter 5. Figure 7.1(b) shows the integrated circuit chips mounted on a printed circuit board.

What makes computers electronic rather than electrical in operation is the concept of the two states—"on" or "off"—with which computers operate. The concept of using two discrete states goes back to 1847 when George Boole, an English mathematician, used a shorthand for a system of logic that was originated by Aristotle. The states were either true or false or, as we think of them today, 1 or 0. These two values can be considered as being open (0) or closed (1). Refer to Figure 7.6(a).

When two switches are connected in parallel, they form a gate. Refer to Figure 7.6(b). The integrated circuits use switches that turn off and on. A **gate** is a logic device that allows two or more inputs to interact together to give one output. Think of gates as being able to open and close by using electronic switches which can be transistors.

In Figure 7.6(b) two switches (A and B) are used in parallel, producing one output possibility. The only time that the gate can transmit information is when switch A or B or both are closed. In other words, the only time any electrical impulse is emitted on the output side of the gate is when one or more switches are closed (1). Consider the following table that shows four possibilities:

A	B	OUTPUT	RESULT
off	off	off	no output (no impulse)
on	off	on	output
off	on	on	output
on	on	on	output

Gates are inside the integrated circuits and are never of concern to most users. It is through the gates, however, that the different processing possibilities exist.

FIGURE 7.6
Switches and gates. (a) A switch has two values. (b) Two switches can form a gate.

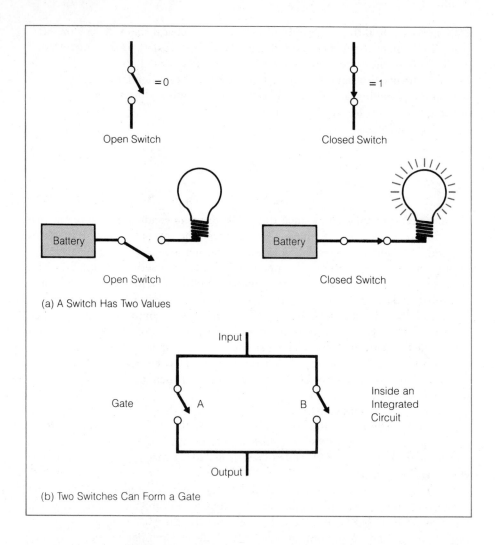

= 0

Open Switch

= 1

Closed Switch

Battery

Open Switch

Battery

Closed Switch

(a) A Switch Has Two Values

Input

Gate

A

B

Inside an
Integrated
Circuit

Output

(b) Two Switches Can Form a Gate

CHECKPOINT **Can you:**

Identify the types of primary storage used?

Differentiate among them?

Tell which type is the oldest?

Tell which type is the most dense?

CHARACTER-ADDRESSABLE AND WORD-ADDRESSABLE COMPUTERS

Digital computers read and store data in two different ways, either as character-addressable or word-addressable computers. What determines the addressability of the computer? The manufacturer determines this by selecting the appropriate software for accessing data. The **character-addressable computer** reads and stores (writes) one character in its memory at a time.

A **word-addressable computer** can look up or store many characters at a time. In a word-addressable computer, the number of characters that are treated as a word (unit) varies according to the computer being used. A **word** means the smallest number of characters that are read or stored at one time; four or six characters can be a word on a mainframe and as many as 64 characters on a supercomputer. Since word machines generally use less computer time, storage retrieval is faster.

A character-addressable computer stores one character at a storage address with the exception that numeric data can be packed (made compact) so that two numeric characters are stored at one storage address by programmer's instructions.

A **storage address** or **address** is an area in memory that has a number much like a house number on a street. Each address has a number that identifies it and differentiates it from all other addresses. A programmer's instructions determine how many positions are to be reserved for a certain field of data. Whenever that data field is to be worked with in the program (assuming one character per storage address), a computer will then read that many storage addresses. For example, a five-positions long data field with the data CIS48 would require that the C be stored in a storage address, the I in the next storage address, and so on. In Figure 7.7(a) the storage addresses used to store the data CIS48 are in storage addresses 400 through 404 for a character-addressable computer (these addresses are randomly chosen for illustration purposes). Assuming a word-addressable computer that uses six characters per word, only one storage address is used for the same data, as shown in Figure 7.7(b). Notice in Figure 7.7(a) that the storage addresses began in address 000. Where a program is stored is of no concern to a user.

How data is retrieved from a character-addressable and a word-addressable computer is shown in the accompanying cartoon. A word-addressable computer is faster at looking up and storing data. Its disadvantage, however, is in its inefficient use of primary storage since data is not generally as compactly stored as in a character-addressable computer.

DATA REPRESENTATION

Data used in most computers is one of two types: display or computational. When data is used for display purposes, it is used for any data manipulation other than calculation—inputting, outputting, selecting, deleting, rearranging, editing, and

FIGURE 7.7
Comparison of storage in character- and word-addressable computers. (a) Character-addressable computers. (b) Word-addressable computers.

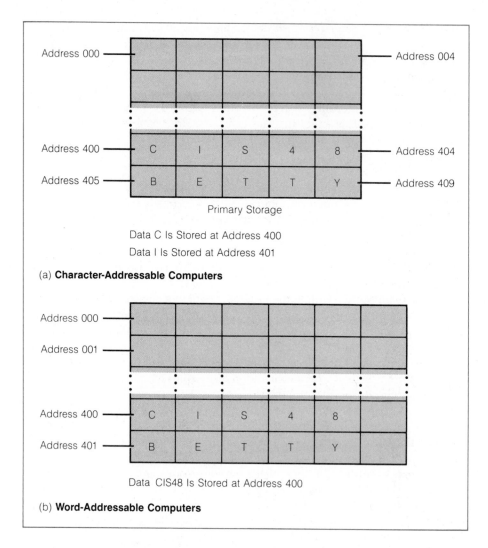

Data C Is Stored at Address 400
Data I Is Stored at Address 401

(a) **Character-Addressable Computers**

Data CIS48 Is Stored at Address 400

(b) **Word-Addressable Computers**

comparing. Most all input is considered as display characters; calculations cannot be performed on the numeric characters in the form in which they are inputted. The computer stores all display characters using an internal code, made up of 0s and 1s in a systematic way to represent each possible character that is used for display. When data is to be used for computation, display characters must be converted from an internal code to binary.

The following discussion centers on two internal codes—ASCII and EBCDIC, showing how each identifies a character. Next, binary is discussed, showing how addition can be performed. Refer to Figure 7.8 for an overview.

Internal Codes

When data is inputted or outputted, it must be stored in primary storage. The central processing unit uses an **internal code** that is dictated by the systems software.

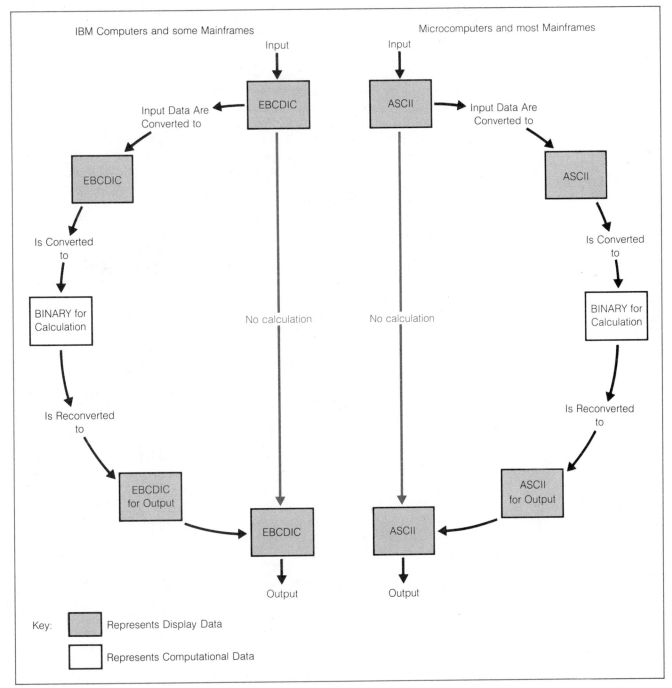

FIGURE 7.8   **The purposes of the different coding systems.**

When a character is read by an input device, the data must be translated into an internal code. Most computers use **American National Standard Code for Information Interchange (ASCII)**, pronounced "askee." IBM computers and some other mainframes use **Extended Binary Coded Decimal Interchange Code**

(**EBCDIC**), pronounced "eb-sa-dick." Other computers might use the six-bit binary Coded Decimal Interchange Code (BCDIC). BCDIC is shown in Appendix C.

ASCII and EBCDIC Codes. ASCII and EBCDIC are the most popular internal codes, with ASCII being used on most terminals, mainframes, and microcomputers. Let's begin the discussion with ASCII.

ASCII code originated in the days of the teletype, the 1920s, when data was transmitted by code. Today ASCII is used in microcomputers and in data communications. A character is coded using just 0s and 1s in various combinations. Each character has its own coding of bits, referred to as the **bit configuration.** Each bit configuration uses 7 bits to code a character or **byte.** A byte has two parts, as shown in Figure 7.9, namely a zone and a digit. Three bits record a zone, while the other four bits record a digit of the same byte. Whenever a computer uses ASCII code, it looks up the contents (data or program) at the specific address. It looks up seven bits that belong to a byte. A computer using ASCII code cannot look up less than 7 bits; hence a byte is the smallest addressable portion of storage. A character-addressable computer is then **byte-addressable.**

Refer again to Figure 7.7(a) for the character-addressable computers; a C was stored in address 400. Seven bits are used to code the character C. The same principle is used for address 401, where 7 bits are used for coding the character I, and so on.

Figure 7.10 shows the complete ASCII code. A hexadecimal shorthand is noted in this figure, but let us just ignore that for a moment.

With the numerous 0s and 1s, you might be concerned that the computer might lose a 1-bit in its data transmission. Losing a 1-bit in data transmission for the amount of a paycheck could be a disaster. To make certain that the computer transmissions do not contain errors, a checking system is built into the hardware; this system is called a **parity** check. If a 1 is changed to a 0 in data transmission, the computer points out the error to the computer operator. Parity is discussed in detail in Appendix C.

EBCDIC code is an internal code developed by IBM. Eight bits are used in the EBCDIC coding system for coding a character, or a byte. EBCDIC code is also divided into two parts: zone bits and digit bits. Four bits code the zone; four bits (called a **nibble**) code the digit. Figure 7.11(a) shows the EBCDIC code; the

FIGURE 7.9   **The two parts of an ASCII code.**

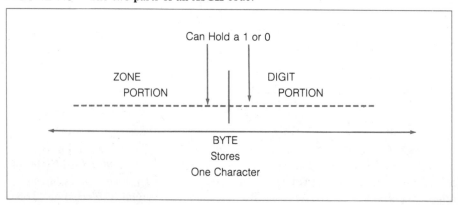

	ASCII				ASCII				ASCII				ASCII		
CHAR.	ZONE	DIGIT	HEX	CHAR.	ZONE	DIGIT	HEX	CHAR.	ZONE	DIGIT	HEX	CHAR.	ZONE	DIGIT	HEX
A	100	0001	41	J	100	1010	4A					0	011	0000	30
B	100	0010	42	K	100	1011	4B	S	101	0011	53	1	011	0001	31
C	100	0011	43	L	100	1100	4C	T	101	0100	54	2	011	0010	32
D	100	0100	44	M	100	1101	4D	U	101	0101	55	3	011	0011	33
E	100	0101	45	N	100	1110	4E	V	101	0110	56	4	011	0100	34
F	100	0110	46	O	100	1111	4F	W	101	0111	57	5	011	0101	35
G	100	0111	47	P	101	0000	50	X	101	1000	58	6	011	0110	36
H	100	1000	48	Q	101	0001	51	Y	101	1001	59	7	011	0111	37
I	100	1001	49	R	101	0010	52	Z	101	1010	5A	8	011	1000	38
												9	011	1001	39

Data

(7 Bits Code a Character)

	Zone	Digit	Hexadecimal (Hex)
	3 Bits	4 Bits	Shorthand Is
Character C Coded as	100	0011	43

Byte

FIGURE 7.10 **ASCII code.**

hexadecimal shorthand is covered shortly. Figure 7.11(b) shows how the same CIS48 data is coded in EBCDIC rather than ASCII, as previously illustrated.

To summarize:

One byte is stored at one storage address.

One byte uses 7 bits for ASCII and 8 bits for EBCDIC.

One byte has a zone portion and a digit portion.

One character is coded in one byte using ASCII or EBCDIC.

CHECKPOINT **Can you:**

Differentiate between character-addressable and word-addressable computers?

Explain the difference between a bit, a byte, and a nibble?

Explain how EBCDIC and ASCII codes differ in purpose?

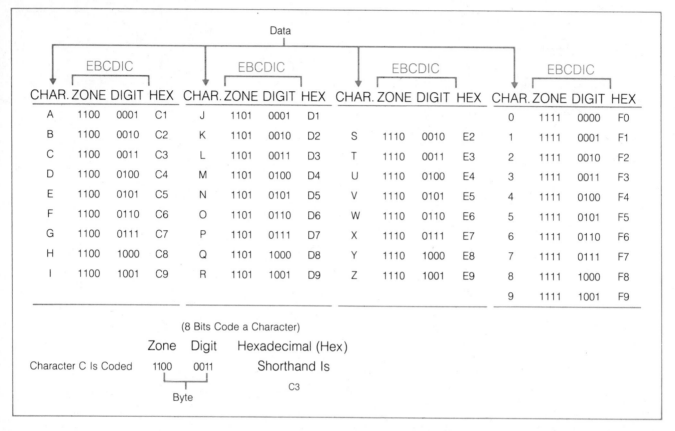

CHAR.	ZONE	DIGIT	HEX	CHAR.	ZONE	DIGIT	HEX	CHAR.	ZONE	DIGIT	HEX	CHAR.	ZONE	DIGIT	HEX
A	1100	0001	C1	J	1101	0001	D1					0	1111	0000	F0
B	1100	0010	C2	K	1101	0010	D2	S	1110	0010	E2	1	1111	0001	F1
C	1100	0011	C3	L	1101	0011	D3	T	1110	0011	E3	2	1111	0010	F2
D	1100	0100	C4	M	1101	0100	D4	U	1110	0100	E4	3	1111	0011	F3
E	1100	0101	C5	N	1101	0101	D5	V	1110	0101	E5	4	1111	0100	F4
F	1100	0110	C6	O	1101	0110	D6	W	1110	0110	E6	5	1111	0101	F5
G	1100	0111	C7	P	1101	0111	D7	X	1110	0111	E7	6	1111	0110	F6
H	1100	1000	C8	Q	1101	1000	D8	Y	1110	1000	E8	7	1111	0111	F7
I	1100	1001	C9	R	1101	1001	D9	Z	1110	1001	E9	8	1111	1000	F8
												9	1111	1001	F9

(8 Bits Code a Character)

	Zone	Digit	Hexadecimal (Hex)
Character C Is Coded	1100	0011	Shorthand Is
			C3

Byte

FIGURE 7.11

EBCDIC and hexadecimal (HEX) coding. Hexadecimal (HEX) is used as a shorthand for EBCDIC. (a) EBCDIC and Hexadecimal table. (b) Example coding.

Memory Dumps. When a programmer has made a severe error in coding a program, he or she receives a **memory dump**—a display or listing of the contents of the computer's memory. A memory dump, as shown in Figure 7.12, becomes an aid to a programmer in debugging a program. A memory dump shows the addresses, the contents stored at each address used by a programmer, and the registers. Registers are used by the control section; they are discussed later in the chapter. It takes many hours of training to become proficient in using a memory dump to debug a program. For now concentrate on the contents of data stored at an address.

Hexadecimal (Hex) Code. Although a computer stores its data in 0s and 1s, you certainly could not expect programmers to keep their sanity if a memory dump was prepared in bits. If it were, there would be a combination of eight 0s and 1s (if EBCBIC were used) for each address. Instead, a **hexadecimal** coding system is used for shorthanding the contents stored in EBCDIC and ASCII codes. We work better with alphabetics and numbers than with 0s and 1s, so alphabetics and numbers are used in the shorthand. Again, it is only a shorthand; it has not changed the value of the contents.

Let us think about our decimal system. The base is 10 which means there are 10 possibilities in any one position. These possibilities are 0 through 9. The highest that ever can be recorded in any one digit is always one less than the base. In our decimal system, one less than the base is 9. One digit higher uses two digits.

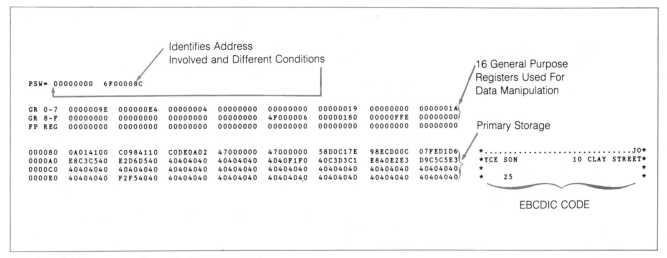

FIGURE 7.12 **Memory dump for EBCDIC code.**

The same rules apply to the hexadecimal shorthand for EBCDIC, but they are just a little more involved. Since *hex* means six and *decimal* means ten, *hexadecimal* means there are 16 possible characters in any one position. Remember, we are after a shorthand for ASCII and EBCDIC code. One hexadecimal character is used for each grouping of 4 bits used in an internal code. (See Appendix C for a discussion of various bases and why four bits are used.)

Figures 7.10 and 7.11(a) show the ASCII and EBCDIC codes respectively as well as the hexadecimal characters used for shorthanding the ASCII or EBCDIC codes. Figure 7.13 shows the hexadecimal character with its appropriate bits. Notice that the hexadecimal character begins with 0 and goes through 9, creating 10 possibilities. Since there must be sixteen possibilities in any one position, A through F are randomly chosen for the remaining six possibilities. The alphabetics replace the values of 10 through 15 because there must be just one character to represent a value in one hexadecimal position. The hexadecimal character B represents the value of 11.

Referring to the EBCDIC code in Figure 7.11(a) and the conversion chart for the bits in Figure 7.13, match the bits in EBCDIC with the conversion chart, and you will "break" the hexadecimal code that is noted for each character of data as shown in the Figure 7.11(a). If you are still confused, an example of conversion may help. Note that for an A the EBCDIC code is 1100 0001 in Figure 7.11(a); the hex shorthand for this character is C1. Using the first four bits, 1100, look in Figure 7.13 for the bits 1100. You will find that the hex character is a C. For the digits in the byte for a character A (0001), the hex character shown in Figure 7.13 is a 1. Hence, C1 is the hex shorthand for the EBCDIC code for the character A. Looking at this another way, Figure 7.14 shows just the hex shorthand for the EBCDIC code, where the data A's hexadecimal shorthand is C1.

Return to the memory dump previously shown (in Figure 7.12) but this time with a close-up of only a portion. In the extreme right portion of the memory dump, notice how JOYCE SON's data is translated. This translation occurs since these are display characters. Refer to Figure 7.15 and notice how three characters of the data have been converted from hexadecimal code to the display characters.

A Blank Is Different In Internal Codes

A friend of yours is also studying internal codes. He tells you that the space (a blank) uses a hexadecimal shorthand of 20 for ASCII code. The next day you see your friend again; this time he tells you that a space in EBCDIC code is represented as 40. You wonder what this discussion is leading to. Then he pulls out a paper that says: COMPUTERS 84

He asks your help in changing those display characters to the hexadecimal shorthand represented by ASCII code. Can you help him?

If he would ask you to show the ASCII code for those same display characters, could you do it?

Hexadecimal Possibilities		Means		Bits or		Hexadecimal Character
	0	Means	0000	Bits or	0	Hexadecimal Character
	1		0001		1	
	2		0010		2	
	3		0011		3	
T	4		0100		4	
E	5		0101		5	
N	6		0110		6	
	7		0111		7	
	8		1000		8	
	9		1001		9	
	10		1010		A	
	11		1011		B	
S	12		1100		C	
I	13		1101		D	
X	14		1110		E	
	15		1111		F	

FIGURE 7.13   **Hexadecimal conversion.**

How can this be done? Use Figure 7.13 and Figure 7.11(a) for the conversion, noting the display character shown in Figure 7.11(a). Figure 7.14 shows the same hexadecimal shorthand as shown in Figure 7.11(a), but it makes it easier to see the pattern used for hexadecimal. Notice in Figure 7.14 that the display character (the data) for an A is a C1, the same as on Figure 7.11(a).

Trying the same approach for ASCII, when data was inputted in display characters, the data was coded in ASCII. However, if ever a memory dump is taken, the characters are not shown in ASCII code but in hexadecimal. In Figure 7.10, the hexadecimal shorthand is noted along with the ASCII code. Referring to Figure 7.16, the same hexadecimal shorthands are shown.

There is a variation to the ASCII code called **ASCII-8**. It uses 8 bits rather than 7 bits in a byte. The Cray X-MP (the supercomputer discussed in Chapter 3) uses ASCII-8. Figure 7.17 shows this coding system. Since 8 bits are used in a byte, more display characters can be coded (an additional bit position allows for more combinations of 0s and 1s).

Binary

Data that is computational is stored and manipulated in a code called **binary**. Binary, like an internal code, also uses a string of 0 and 1 bits to represent a value,

	HEX ZONE			HEX DIGIT
C	D	E	F	
A	J		1	1
B	K	S	2	2
C	L	T	3	3
D	M	U	4	4
E	N	V	5	5
F	O	W	6	6
G	P	X	7	7
H	Q	Y	8	8
I	R	Z	9	9
			0	0

Data

A Character of:

0 Coded in EBCDIC Code would be a Hexadecimal of F0.

E Coded in EBCDIC Code would be a Hexadecimal of C5.

K Coded in EBCDIC Code would be a Hexadecimal of D2.

FIGURE 7.14   **Hexadecimal conversion for characters coded in EBCDIC code.**

but this string is usually 16 or 32 bits long and its format is different. For example, a microcomputer uses 16 bits or 32 bits of 0s and 1s strung together to represent a binary value. Most minicomputers and mainframes commonly use a combination of 32 bits of 0s and 1s to represent a value. As an example, a 75 is shown in binary representation and internal code representation, so you can see how the two differ:

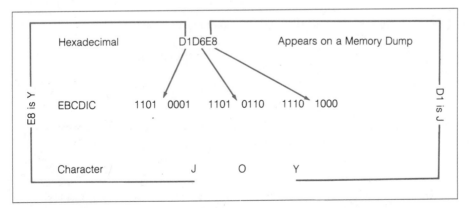

FIGURE 7.15
Use of memory dump shown in Figure 7.12.

FIGURE 7.16

Hexadecimal conversion chart for characters coded in ASCII code.

	HEX ZONE		HEX DIGIT
3	4	5	
1	A	Q	1
2	B	R	2
3	C	S	3
4	D	T	4
5	E	U	5
6	F	V	6
7	G	W	7
8	H	X	8
9	I	Y	9
	J	Z	A
	K		B
	L		C
	M		D
	N		E
	O		F

Data

To Use the Conversion Chart:
Locate the Character (Data) on the chart.
Find the Zone in the chart above the Character.
Find the Hex Digit in the chart at the right.

A Character of 0 Is a Hexadecimal of 30 (Zone and Digit)

E Is a Hexadecimal of 45

K Is a Hexadecimal of 4B

- ASCII code for 75 is   011 0111   011 0101

- Binary value for 75   00000000000000000000000001001011

    A binary representations for numbers might look this
    00000000000000000000000000000110
or any combination of 1s and 0s in any of those 32 positions.

CHECKPOINT **Can you:**

Tell when binary is used?

CHAR	ZONE	DIGIT	HEX	CHAR	ZONE	DIGIT	HEX	CHAR	ZONE	DIGIT	HEX	CHAR	ZONE	DIGIT	HEX
A	1010	0001	A1	J	1010	1010	AA					0	0101	0000	50
B	1010	0010	A2	K	1010	1011	AB	S	1011	0011	B3	1	0101	0001	51
C	1010	0011	A3	L	1010	1100	AC	T	1011	0100	B4	2	0101	0010	52
D	1010	0100	A4	M	1010	1101	AD	U	1011	0101	B5	3	0101	0011	53
E	1010	0101	A5	N	1010	1110	AE	V	1011	0110	B6	4	0101	0100	54
F	1010	0110	A6	O	1010	1111	AF	W	1011	0111	B7	5	0101	0101	55
G	1010	0111	A7	P	1011	0000	B0	X	1011	1000	B8	6	0101	0110	56
H	1010	1000	A8	Q	1011	0001	B1	Y	1011	1001	B9	7	0101	0111	57
I	1010	1001	A9	R	1011	0010	B2	Z	1011	1010	BA	8	0101	1000	58
												9	0101	1001	59

FIGURE 7.17.   **ASCII-8 code.**

CONTROL SECTION

The control section must be able to communicate with the various functional parts of the computer. To do this, it too needs instructions; these instructions are in the most elemental form of a program called **microcode.** The microcode instructions direct the control section as to what it is to do. All computer operations are synchronized by a **clock** that emits pulses at a fixed rate. To a normal user the use of microcode and a clock are unimportant; the user's concern is that the equipment works. The control section uses **registers**—temporary high-speed storage areas, not part of primary storage, that serve as the intermediary between the control section and primary storage; their work deals with accepting, transferring, and holding instructions or data that are involved in the execution of a program. Registers can also be used for calculation. The number of registers found in a central processing unit varies, but some mainframes have upwards of sixteen registers that can be programmed by a programmer writing assembly language. There are other registers that are used for timing the job; for handling exponential work; for indicating if a comparison of data was equal, less than, or greater than; for indicating when a calculation has changed to a negative answer; and more. Without all of these registers working together, the control section could not manage and coordinate the processing of programs. Refer to Figure 7.18.

CHECKPOINT **Can you:**

Tell why the control section is needed in a computer system?

REGISTERS

The types of registers used by a computer vary. Some of the major registers that are used are the following:

● **Instruction register**   This points to the next instruction's address that is to be executed. It is like a memory aide that points to what the computer is to do next.

● **Storage register**   This holds the instruction that is to be executed. The storage register supplies the means for the data to enter the arithmetic-logic unit and to be returned to primary storage.

● **Address register**   This holds the address of the data that is called for by the instruction.

In a BASIC program that was introduced in Chapter 6, we used a PRINT statement along with a message that was to be outputted. The message was enclosed within quotation marks.

Let us use the following program to illustrate how the registers are used by the control section. The computer changes the BASIC program into machine language whose 0s and 1s the computer understands. The BASIC program we write is as follows:

```
10  PRINT "THERE ARE ONLY 0S AND 1S:
20  END
```

The operating system stores the message that we wish to print into a series of storage addresses, the locations of which are unimportant to a user. Let us suppose that the storage address that will hold the message to be printed begins at storage address 400.

The computer has to know which instruction to execute, where that instruction is stored, what that instruction tells it to do, and where that instruction's data is stored. To point to which instruction is to be executed, the control section uses the instruction register. Once that instruction is fetched (read) from primary storage, it must be **decoded** (broken down into what is to be done, and where the data is stored which requires manipulation). The operation that is to be done is placed in the storage register and the address of the data to be manipulated placed in the address register. Figure 7.19 shows the way registers sort out and hold such information for the BASIC program mentioned above.

The number of bits used in a register varies. Most mainframes use 32 bits. Super-computers use 64-bit registers. Eight-bit microprocessors use 16-bit registers which allow them to have roughly 64K, or 65,536 different addresses (two raised to the 16th power is 65,536). The 16-bit microprocessor using the Intel 8088 chip can address up to 1 megabyte (million bytes). Those microprocessors using the Motorola 68000 chip can address up to 16 megabytes.

Whether the programmer deals with the actual registers depends upon the computer language that is used. The high-level languages do not require any knowledge of registers or their uses. Languages such as COBOL (written for solving business problems), FORTRAN (for solving scientific problems), or BASIC (written to solve business and math problems) require no programming knowledge of registers and their uses. Use of assembly languages, however, requires programmers to manipulate data in registers.

Figure 7.20 shows the various registers used in the Cray X-MP super-computer. The central memory (primary storage) is composed of 1 to 8 million 64-bit words. Since the internal code is ASCII-8, each display character uses 8 bits; 8 bytes are grouped together to form one word. Notice in the extreme right portion there are four sections. The address section, for example, uses two types of registers, called B and A, to accomplish addressing capabilities. The scalar section deals with work done sequentially, one step after the other. The vector section is used for work done in parallel (all at one time). In layman's terms, consider the situation of people boarding a bus. When this is done serially, only one person can board the bus and pay his or her fare. When, however, the capability exists to do this in parallel, eight people could board the same bus and pay their fare at the same time.

CHECKPOINT **Can you:**

Explain how registers play an important role in executing a program?

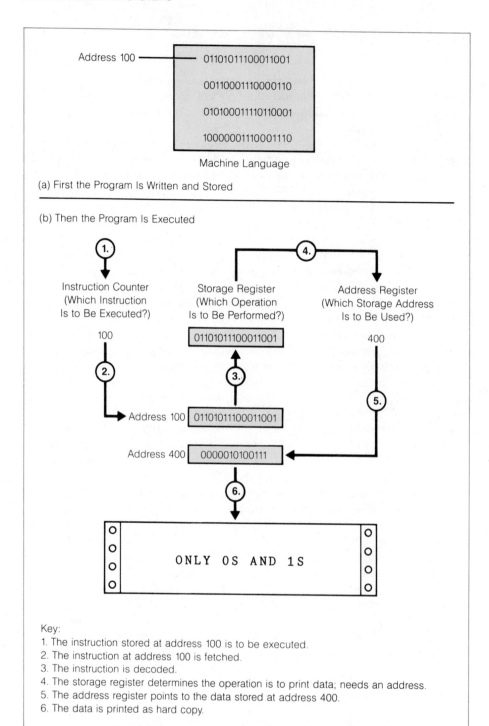

Address 100 ——— 01101011100011001

00110001110000110

010100011110110001

10000001110001110

Machine Language

(a) First the Program Is Written and Stored

(b) Then the Program Is Executed

1.

Instruction Counter
(Which Instruction
Is to Be Executed?)

Storage Register
(Which Operation
Is to Be Performed?)

Address Register
(Which Storage Address
Is to Be Used?)

4.

100

01101011100011001

400

2.

3.

5.

Address 100 01101011100011001

Address 400   0000010100111

6.

ONLY 0S AND 1S

Key:
1. The instruction stored at address 100 is to be executed.
2. The instruction at address 100 is fetched.
3. The instruction is decoded.
4. The storage register determines the operation is to print data; needs an address.
5. The address register points to the data stored at address 400.
6. The data is printed as hard copy.

FIGURE 7.19   **The control section uses registers. (a) First the program is written and stored. (b) then the program is executed.**

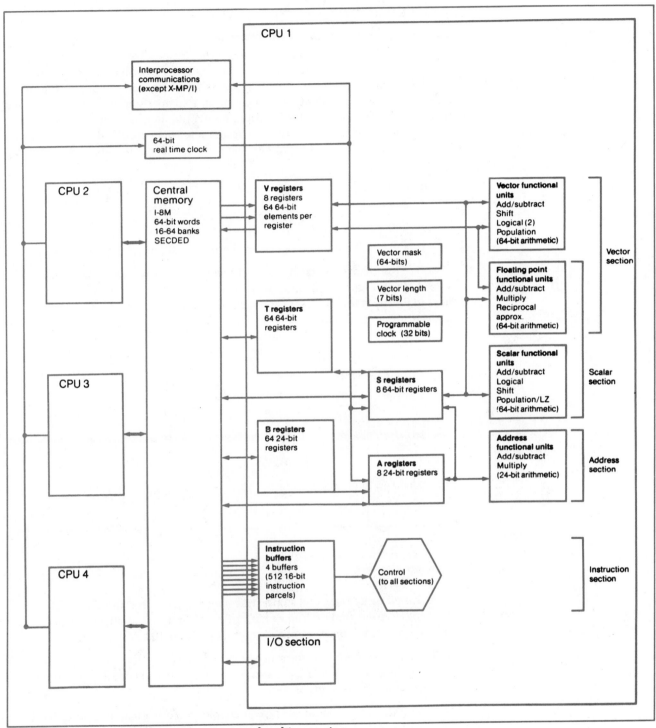

FIGURE 7.20   **Cray X-MP use of registers and multiprocessing.**

ARITHMETIC-LOGIC UNIT

The arithmetic-logic unit carries out the processing called for in the stored program. The arithmetic-logic unit uses the registers according to the instruction written by the programmer. All computers have registers used for performing arithmetic functions; counting; evaluating if a comparison of data is equal, less than, or greater than; and for determining if a number has a negative value.

Let us introduce you to the way a computer does its calculations. Basically, all calculations are done by adding. The computer adds the bits in the following way:

$$0 + 0 = 0$$
$$0 + 1 = 1$$
$$1 + 0 = 1$$
$$1 + 1 = 0 \text{ with a carry of 1 to the next position on the left.}$$

Use the binary digits shown in the conversion chart for hexadecimal code; refer back to Figure 7.13. Let's add a 4 and a 5 together. We will use just 4 bits here to illustrate the process of adding (rather than the actual 32 bits representing a given number). Figure 7.13 shows that the bits for a 4 are 0100, and for a 5, 0101. Let's add them. Check our answer with that in Figure 7.13.

```
      carry 1
4 in binary is 0100
5 in binary is 0101
               ────
               1001
```

CHECKPOINT   Can you:

Tell what registers are?

Tell why they are used?

SUMMARY

● A central processing unit's operating speed is measured in millions of instructions per second (mips). The range can be from a low of about 5 mips to over 50 mips for mainframes. Super-computers perform 100 mips and more.

● The time required to perform an operation is the cycle time. A central processing unit's cycle time for mainframes can be anywhere from about 26 nanoseconds up to about 400 nanoseconds.

● A central processing unit can be compatible with other manufacturer's hardware (usually with IBM). These central processing units are then called compatible or plug compatible.

- Two possible states are used in primary storage, an "on" state (a 1) or an "off" state (a 0).

- Magnetic core, the oldest type of reliable primary storage, was introduced in the 1950s and is still being used in some mainframes.

- Magnetic core is non-volatile memory which means that the magnetism is retained even though the power is removed.

- Binary digits called bits are used for coding data in storage.

- A bit can be a 1 or a 0. When using magnetic core, the 1-bit state means the core is magnetized clockwise, while the 0-bit state represents counterclockwise magnetization. It is the molecules on the outside of the core that are magnetized.

- Bubble memory is a non-volatile memory; the bubble floats in a looped pattern on a piece of crystal. Absence of a bubble represents a 0 bit; presence of a bubble represents a 1 bit.

- Semiconductor memory is the most widely used memory as all recently manufactured computers use this type of primary storage.

- Computers can be character-addressable or word-addressable.

- Character-addressable computers are byte-addressable; that is, eight or seven bits make up one byte, and all eight (or seven) bits are referenced when data is either read or stored in storage.

- Word-addressable computers can look up or store many characters at one time. Many mainframes use four or six characters to represent a word.

- Primary storage stores all data as various combinations of 1s and 0s, whose states can be thought of as being equated to a lightbulb which is either "on" (a 1) or "off" (a 0).

- Internal code, used to store all input and output data that are in the form of display characters, uses only 0s and 1s.

- The internal codings of EBCDIC, ASCII, and BCDIC are used for only input and output. They are never used for calculations.

- A storage address is an area that has a number that identifies it from all other addresses in primary storage.

- Data is represented either as display characters or as computational data. Display characters are used for inputting, outputting, editing, and comparing data; these characters use the internal code dictated by the systems software.

- Data used for calculation must be computational data, which means the data must be represented as binary. All display characters that are inputted which require calculations must be changed to binary for calculations.

- ASCII code is used on microcomputers and most mainframes. It uses 7 bits to code each display character. The first three bits represent the zone, the last four bits represent the digit.

● EBCDIC code is used on IBM computers and some other mainframes. It uses eight bits to code a byte. The first four bits represent the zone, the last four bits represent the digit.

● Since the smallest number of bits that can be looked up or stored by a character-addressable computer is 7 or 8 bits, depending upon whether ASCII or EBCDIC is used, this computer is then byte-addressable.

● Each character has its own coding of bits, referred to as a bit configuration.

● To assure that data has not been changed because, say, a 1-bit was lost in the transmission of data, a checking system called parity is used.

● A memory dump, a display or listing of the contents of the computer's memory, is used by programmers in debugging a program that contains severe errors.

● Memory dumps contain a shorthand for the internal code, addresses, and registers, to name a few elements.

● Hexadecimal code is used as a shorthand for ASCII and EBCDIC code. This shorthand uses one hexadecimal character (ranging from 0 to 9 and from A through F) to represent 16 different possibilities. One hexadecimal character is used for each zone and digit portion in the internal code of EBCDIC or ASCII.

● Binary uses 16 or 32 bits to code a number to be used for calculation.

● The control section must be able to communicate with the various functional parts of the central processing unit. The communication is accomplished through the use of temporary high-speed storage areas called registers.

● Registers accept, transfer, and hold instructions or data that are involved in the execution of a program.

● Many registers are used in a computer system, with the number varying depending upon the computer being used.

● Some of the major registers used are the instruction register, storage register, and address register.

● The instruction register holds the address of the next instruction that is to be executed.

● The storage register holds the instruction that is to be executed. This register supplies the means for the data to enter the arithmetic-logic unit and to be returned to primary storage.

● Most programmers (other than those who write in assembly language) are not concerned with registers when writing source programs.

STUDY GUIDE

REVIEW OF TERMINOLOGY

The following terminology was discussed in this chapter:

address
address register
American National
   Standard Code for
   Information
   Interchange (ASCII)
binary
bit configuration
bubble memory
byte
byte-addressable
character-addressable
   computer
clock
cycle time
decoded
Extended Binary Coded
   Decimal Interchange

Code (EBCDIC)
gate
hexadecimal
instruction register
internal code
magnetic cores
memory dump
microcode
nibble
parity
plug compatibility
register
storage address (address)
storage register
word
word-addressable
   computer

MULTIPLE CHOICE

Circle the letter of the item that correctly completes each question.

1. The oldest form of primary storage is:
   a. magnetic core
   b. semiconductor
      memory
   c. bubble memory
   d. binary
   e. none of these

2. Bit is shortened from the words:
   a. binary numbering
      system
   b. binary
   c. binary coding
   d. binary digit
   e. byte

3. The type of memory that contains the most bits in the smallest area is called:
   a. magnetic core
   b. binary digits
   c. bubble memory
   d. semiconductor
      memory
   e. none of these

4. A computer retrieves data by:
   a. using character or
      word
      addressability
   b. only closing gates
   c. only using
      magnetic cores
      or bubble
      memory
   d. storing everything
      in binary
   e. mips

5. Each byte in primary storage has:
   a. a magnetic core
   b. one zone and two
      digits
   c. two binary digits
   d. one storage
      address
   e. one hexadecimal
      character

6. Six characters can make up one:
   a. internal code
   b. word
   c. bit configuration
   d. memory dump
   e. hexadecimal
      character

7. The purpose of this is to represent (using various combinations of bits) the various display characters stored in primary storage:
   a. word-
      addressability
   b. character-
      addressability
   c. internal code
   d. binary
   e. memory dump

8. If the data ACES was stored in primary storage and four storage addresses were used, the computer would be classified as being:
   a. word-addressable
   b. character-
      addressable
   c. byte-and-bit
      addressable
   d. storage
      addressable
   e. digit addressable

9. If the data 49'ers was stored in primary storage and only one storage address was used, the computer would be classified as:
   a. word-addressable
   b. character-
      addressable
   c. byte-addressable
   d. storage
      addressable
   e. none of these

10. 1100 0010 is referred to as a character's:
    a. byte configuration
    b. binary
    c. byte-
       addressability
    d. bit configuration
    e. mips

11. The series 0000000001010100111111100000001 is an example of:

a. a byte   *c.* ASCII code
b. a bit configuration   *d.* EBCDIC code
                         e. a binary value

12. How many characters are there in a hexadecimal coding system:
    a. 2   *d.* 16
    b. 10   *e.* F
    c. 15

13. In EBCDIC, how many bits make up a byte:
    a. 1   *d.* 8
    b. 2   *e.* 16
    c. 4

14. In EBCDIC or ASCII, the byte is divided into:
    a. bits and bytes   *d.* one hexadecimal
    b. zone and digit   character
    c. digit and zone   *e.* 4 bits

15. When data is keyed, that input data is stored in primary storage in:
    a. the same   *c.* internal code
        character format   *d.* microcode
        as it was keyed   *e.* two hexadecimal
    b. binary   characters

16. When data is keyed, that input data must later be converted to:
    a. clock pulses   *d.* binary if
    b. binary for hard   calculations are
        copy   to be done
    c. binary for all   *e.* hexadecimal
        manipulations   characters for
                             calculations to be
                             done

17. A display of addresses and their contents and the registers used by a computer, which a programmer can use for debugging, is called a:
    a. byte hard copy   *d.* storage address
    b. word-addressable   hard copy
        hard copy   *e.* register
    c. memory dump

TRUE/FALSE QUESTIONS

Circle T if the statement is true; F if it is false.

1. **T/F** Binary digits represent two possible states.
2. **T/F** The user really does not care if magnetic cores or semiconductor memory is used for primary storage.
3. **T/F** There really are no 0s or 1s in primary storage.
4. **T/F** A character-addressable computer is faster than a word-addressable computer at looking up data in primary storage.
5. **T/F** A character-addressable computer can look up just a nibble, if the programmer so desires.
6. **T/F** If a character-addressable computer is being used, five storage addresses are set aside to hold the data HELLO.
7. **T/F** If a word-addressable computer is being used, there would be one storage address used for holding the data FINE.
8. **T/F** The number of characters in a word depends upon the specifications of an applications program.
9. **T/F** Display characters represent data that is inputted or calculated.
10. **T/F** Examples of internal codes are EBCDIC, BCDIC, or ASCII.
11. **T/F** When data is keyed on a terminal, the highest number in any one position in a numeric field is a 9.
12. **T/F** When the keyed data is stored internally, the data is stored in the internal code.
13. **T/F** If any calculations are to be done, the input data must first be changed to the internal code, and then is translated to binary.
14. **T/F** If the programmer gets a printout of everything stored in primary storage that pertains to his or her program, this is referred to as a problem dump.
15. **T/F** EBCDIC or ASCII code appears on a memory dump.
16. **T/F** If a character is used for display purposes, it means that the data will only be calculated.
17. **T/F** There are always 8 bits that make up a byte.
18. **T/F** The control section uses registers to know what data is to be transferred to primary storage.
19. **T/F** Registers can hold data, an instruction, or an address for an instruction.
20. **T/F** If an instruction register is holding a 704, the next instruction is stored at address 704.
21. **T/F** The address register holds the instruction that is to be executed by the computer.

ANSWERS

REVIEW QUESTIONS

1. Why is primary storage used?
2. Identify the types of primary storage used.
3. What is a bit? What are its possible states?
4. What is meant by a storage address? What can be stored in a storage address?
5. When is EBCDIC used? ASCII?
6. In EBCDIC, each character representation is divided into two parts. What are they?
7. When is binary used?
8. If the initials in your name were stored in primary storage, which EBCDIC code would appear?
9. If the initials in your name were stored in primary storage, which ASCII code would appear?
10. Using data from question 9 above, what hexadecimal characters would appear on a memory dump? How many hexadecimal characters would appear for each input character?
11. What are registers? Why are they used?
12. What is a memory dump?

DISCUSSION QUESTIONS

1. Assume that primary storage holds the following data:

    19 OAK STREET

    a. How many bytes are needed to hold this data?
    b. How many bits to store the data in EBCDIC? In ASCII?
    c. How many storage addresses are used?
    d. If the above data were to be inputted and later printed, which coding system could be used?
    e. How would the above data be represented in EBCDIC code? in ASCII code?

2. Are there really 0s and 1s stored in primary storage? Explain your answer.

3. Use your instructor's name for this computer class to answer the following questions. Assume that his or her title and last name are the only data. Answer the following questions:
    a. How many bytes are used for coding the data?
    b. How many bits are used for coding the data?
    c. How many storage addresses are used, assuming a character-addressable computer?

4. Explain why registers are essential to a computer.

People in Computing

Gene M. Amdahl

COMPANY
Trilogy Systems, Inc.

POSITION
President

EDUCATIONAL BACKGROUND
B.S. in Engineering Physics, South
Dakota State University
Ph.D. in Theoretical Physics,
University of Wisconsin

The initial strategy that we elected to exploit at Trilogy was the opportunity to produce an IBM compatible computer. The reason for doing this was an opportunity to make a very high performance computer. If you sell a high performance computer with a large price tag, you have to find a market that's ready to exploit it; the largest such market is the IBM-dominated market today. It is over 7 billion dollars, in terms of mainframe and memory, and it's growing at the rate of approximately fifty to sixty percent per year, in terms of computing power requirements. Financially, it's growing faster than the personal computer market. Even though everybody seems to view this as a dying market place, it happens to be the most vital and alive one today. Also, we expect to have an advantage in that marketplace; it's

very important for some of the large users to have a very large computer, because that reduces the number of ways in which they have to fractionate the work load in order to distribute it amongst a great many computers. It means a great deal economically to them and so we expect to have a very positive position in that marketplace.

It also is helpful from the standpoint of starting a company that we don't have to have a large field force in order to have a large market. Not only is the product itself a high price tag product, but the customers are all prepared to use it. They will use it in the same way as before; they are very sophisticated users, and so they are all prepared to utilize it without much support from us. In terms of selling it against IBM, we did all that missionary work at the time we had the Amdahl Corporation. It was a tough job to develop that market or open it to other manufacturers, but we successfully did. We expect immediate acceptance if products warrant it. And finally, the major reason for doing this is that it really provides an unparalleled opportunity for high gross margin, which will help pay back the development costs very, very rapidly.

If we look at the beginning of this market (1976 is chosen because that was the first full year of shipments of the Amdahl Corporation), during that year some 300 machines were sold at the high end of the market. We expect by 1986 the market will be ten times as large.

If you look at the history or evolution of the computing power, the year 1965 was the year of introduction of IBM's largest commercial processor, IBM 360 model 65, that was the forerunner of today's. They improved that in 1970 by about a factor of two by introducing the Model 165. They

improved that again in 1972 with the Model 168. Then in 1977 IBM offered the IBM 370 Model 3033; in 1981 they introduced the 3081J, then the 3081K. Amdahl Corporation came out in 1975 with its 470 equipment. At the time of the IBM 3033 announcement, Amdahl Corporation improved their 470 offering to be the 470V8, then after the IBM 3081 offering, Amdahl Corporation introduced the 580 or the 5860. We expect that the 5860 will be improved in 1984 to provide a performance higher than we expect will come from IBM.

This has been the way the market has improved equipment introduced into it. IBM was very sluggish during the period during which they had no competition. And it put on its racing stripes after Amdahl Corporation established its position very firmly in that marketplace. And both companies, since that time, have raced forward at about the same rate of about 17 percent per year. This percentage is essentially the rate at which technology can normally expect to be advanced.

Let's look at what's happened in pricing since IBM brought out its 3033 and elected to put on its racing shoes. IBM had before that time been offering their products at about $2,000,000 per million instructions per second. Now after seeing competition, they suddenly readjusted their frame of reference and dropped the price down to $750,000 per million instructions per second. Since the time of the 3033 announcement, IBM has reduced the price of computing, whereas before it had always been increasing the price. So, competition you can see, has really been good for the customers and that cost performance has been dropping at the rate of about 17 percent per year. Extrapolating through to 1986, we expect the price will drop down to about $200,000 per million in instructions per second. If we look at the other compatible manufacturers, they have traditionally offered about a 30 percent price performance advantage. We expect that they would be offering in 1986, approximately $140,000 per million instructions per second.

8 Input and Output Devices

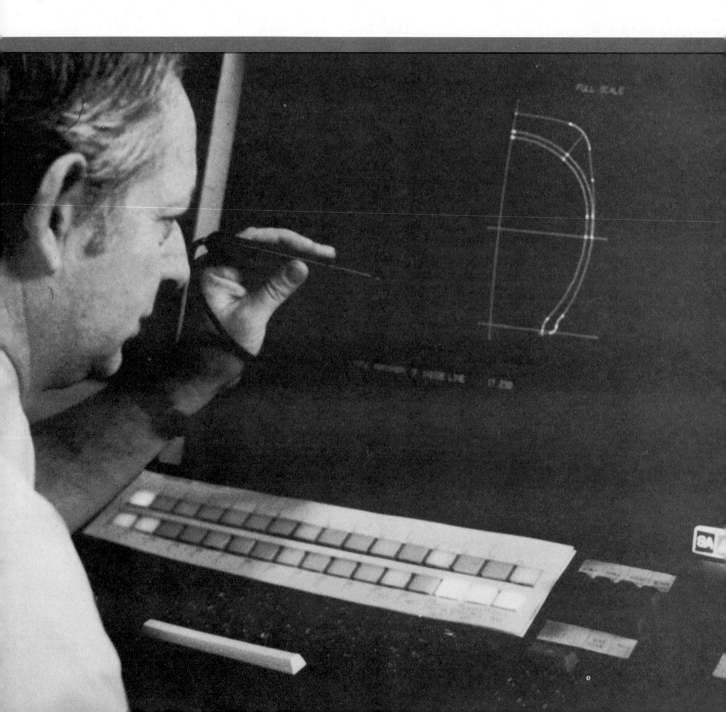

OUTLINE

PROLOGUE

The Internal Revenue Service (IRS) is finally coming of age in the use of computers. Can you imagine the problems that exist on April 15 when the ten regional offices handle more than 1.5 billion returns and other documents? Does it not seem rather impossible that IRS hand sorts and retrieves documents? Under the manual system, it sometimes takes six weeks to retrieve a desired form.

The plan is for a conversion to computerized handling to begin in 1984 for the so-called "short forms" and those forms sent by banks to the IRS specifying the interest paid to individuals.

How can such volume of data ever be handled conveniently? How can hard copy be easily attained from records?

HOW DOES IT DO THAT?

READ ON.

OBJECTIVES

After studying this chapter, you should be able to:

1. Differentiate between on-line and off-line devices.

2. Identify the key entry devices and how they are used.

3. Explain why banking installations need hardware designed specifically for them.

4. Briefly describe how the electronic funds transfer (EFT) has the potential for making a cashless society.

5. Identify the various types of printers used.

6. Explain why Computer Output Microfilm (COM) is used.

7. Briefly describe how the point of sale (POS) terminal operates.

8. Identify the purposes for the use of a portable terminal, a digitizer, Computer-Aided Design, and various printer plotters.

INTRODUCTION

Most installations have some basic input and output devices, among them the printer and the visual display terminal. In this chapter, we visit various companies to investigate why other input and output devices are chosen. The mention of a device's use in a particular company in the following discussion in no way implies that the device cannot be used at other sites as well.

Since the late 1960s, the trend has been away from punched cards, although before that period the punched card was the primary source of input. A variety of input and output devices are used, with that variety increasing more each day, for the following reasons:

1. An installation chooses input and output devices that best fit its processing needs. For example, an invoice a salesperson prepares or the checks you write are used as input. The use of a source document (original recording of data) saves recording time, improves accuracy of data, eliminates need for verification of data by an operator, and saves filing space.

2. A programmer is able to use some input/output devices for active communication with a computer. Referred to as interactive mode, this communication aids in debugging (testing) a program and also allows for fast response from the computer (as opposed to waiting for a job to be run in the batched jobs).

3. Results from processing or answers to inquiries can be sent to several terminals, if desired. A terminal refers to an input or output station that is usually removed from the computer site but can be used to send or receive data from the computer. Some terminals are portable, making them usable by those who travel in their jobs.

CHECKPOINT Can you:

Tell why different input and output devices are used rather than punched cards?

ON-LINE AND OFF-LINE DEVICES

A computer system has many peripheral devices (hardware other than the central processing unit), which can be input or output devices. Those peripheral devices that transmit data to a central processing unit or receive data from it are said to be on-line. In other words, **on-line** means that a device is under the control of a central processing unit—physically, as well as electronically connected. When a device is **off-line,** it cannot receive data from a central processing unit (if it is an output device) or transmit data to a central processing unit (if an input device).

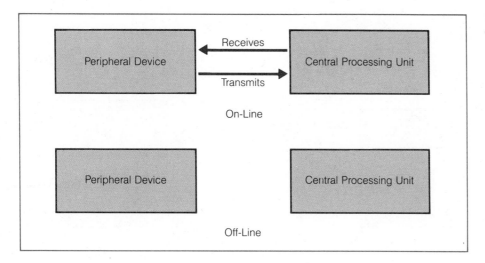

FIGURE 8.1
On-line or off-line processing

Sometimes a user determines if a device is to be on-line or not by depressing a button or raising a lever. This feature will be discussed with the respective equipment in this chapter. Refer to Figure 8.1.

The more commonly used input and output devices are discussed below. To give you some idea of the increase in use of on-line devices, in 1979 there were about 3 million devices installed. In 1984 it is projected that 7.5 million will be sold.

CHECKPOINT **Can you:**

Differentiate between on-line and off-line devices?

VISIT TO A SERVICE BUREAU

The first company on our tour is a service bureau, a company that provides data entry service and all other processing needs for many smaller companies. A company sends its source documents to a service bureau, which captures the data, processes it, and sends the results to the user. The service bureau must meet a variety of needs for its customers. For that reason, it offers different types of devices for keying data, requiring that the data entry person be trained for each method of data entry. Let us visit the data entry department where these key-entry devices are located and see why each is used.

In a data entry department, **key-entry devices,** used by an operator, as the name implies, to key in data, can take several forms: key-to-tape, key-to-cartridge,

FIGURE 8.2
Key-entry devices.

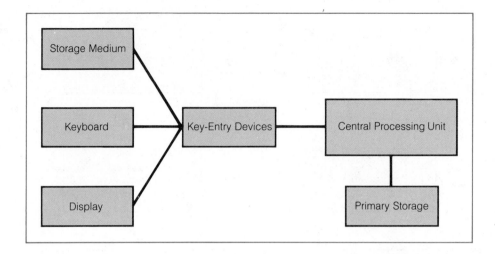

and key-to-disk. These devices have a display, a keyboard, and a medium for storing data, as illustrated in Figure 8.2.

These devices serve three purposes. First of all, they reduce the time that would otherwise be required to record data on punched cards since they provide a faster data entry. Second, they reduce the size of storage needed for physically storing data. Since punched cards are bulky and can be dropped easily, the sequence of the data often is mixed. Lastly, they position the recording of the data at the site where the data is generated. When the shift in usage came about in the early 1970s from punched cards to key-entry devices, the key-entry devices were positioned where the data was collected. For example, an insurance office that collects policy payments usually had a key-entry device. The transmission of the collection data to the main office of the company was accomplished at a later time in the day or night. This was a common practice when batch processing was popularly used.

When, however, on-line processing increased in usage, many of the key-entry devices in large corporations were changed to terminals, providing an interactive capability with the computer at the main office. There still is a need, however, for the key-entry devices; some applications are processed efficiently using batch processing.

Looking over the shoulders of some of the data entry personnel, we notice that some of the source documents are payroll records. Other data entry personnel are keying data regarding new personnel records. Others are keying records regarding shipments received from various suppliers. Another person is keying inventory figures that were taken last night at some small company. This same company's sales data is also being recorded.

KEY-TO-TAPE

A device that contains a large magnetic tape reel catches our eye. Who would use such a device, we ask the tour guide? An installation that requires fast input and uses magnetic tape for its secondary storage might choose a **key-to-tape** device to key data directly onto magnetic tape, which is later usable by a computer.

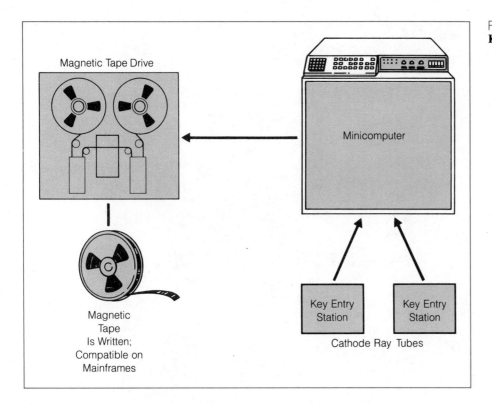

FIGURE 8.3
Key-to-tape.

Once the tape is written, it can be used on tape drives because it is compatible with tape equipment. Our tour guide tells us that the key-to-tape device is being used for keying data for a small company's inventory control. Other times the data entry person works with recording contributions made to humane societies and nonprofit organizations. Refer to Figure 8.3.

KEY-TO-CARTRIDGE

Another variation of a key-to-tape device is a **key-to-cartridge** that uses a small sized magnetic tape for its recording. The tape is ¼-inch wide and is about 450 feet long and is commonly used with minicomputers. Figure 8.4 shows a variation— a tape cassette. This media is familiar to microcomputer users. Of all things, tape cassettes are found in an electronic calculator. Refer to Figure 8.5.

VISIT TO A MEDICAL GROUP

The next company to be visited is a medical group. As we enter the door, we notice there are six doctors's names listed on the door, each of whom has a different

FIGURE 8.4
Cassette in electronic cash register.

specialty. Until two months ago, this medical group always had its billing done by an outside firm. Just recently, the medical group purchased the necessary in-house terminals along with the right to use a computer system that is located 500 miles away. The new computer system is to be used to aid in diagnosis as well as for billing. As we pass down the hallway, we notice that each doctor has his own terminal. The staff also have terminals. At the end of the hallway we find the data entry persons busy capturing data for the new computer system. All historical data about each patient must be included in the system. The data must be keyed using a prescribed format, so the programs used for billing can work with the data. After the initial data is keyed, the service bureau will send a data entry operator on a daily basis to key in all new data that results during the day. The doctors chose a key-to-disk system for their storage medium.

KEY-TO-DISK

A **key-to-disk** system uses a diskette or magnetic disk for its data recording. A key-to-disk system has many key stations, one of which is shown in Figure 8.6. Data that is recorded by an operator is then stored on a magnetic disk, allowing

FIGURE 8.5 (a)
**Electronic cash register. (a) Outside view.
(b) Inside view.**

(b)

FIGURE 8.6
Key-to-disk.

up to 64 different key stations to use the same minicomputer system.

Figure 8.7 shows a variation with a **key-to-diskette** system being used. The tower-shaped processor as shown in Figure 8.7, is an example of an OEM (Original Equipment Manufacturer) product where a software company has added value by the inclusion of software to allow many key-to-diskette stations to operate successfully in the data entry system.

CHECKPOINT **Can you:**

Identify the various types of key entry devices?

Tell how each differs in theory?

VISIT TO A COLLEGE COMPUTER LABORATORY

The next stop on our tour takes us to a busy college computer laboratory. Students hurry to pick up their hard copy; others are pondering over the various devices.

FIGURE 8.7
Key-to-diskette.

In the laboratory we find several different types of terminals that are used for transmission to a mainframe: teleprinters, visual display units (called cathode ray tube terminals), and a remote job entry.

TELEPRINTERS

We find students entering programs and data on teleprinters, as shown in Figure 8.8. In addition to being a terminal, the **teleprinter** also includes a printer for preparing hard copy—an advantage to a person whose typing skills leave room for improvement—and for receiving messages in hard copy from the central processing unit. Company executives, sales people, newspaper reporters, and others who are mobile in their work use these teleprinters as portable terminals for recording data and then transmit it to the home office. The hard copy feature assures them a copy of the transmitted data.

Western Union has used this type of hardware for years, although they are being phased out. These older devices are called **teletypewriters.** Teletypewriters, like teleprinters, also give hard copy. Paper tape, however, was frequently used for recording the data that was transmitted to or received from the central processing unit. The paper tape is much like ticker tape. Refer to Figure 8.9.

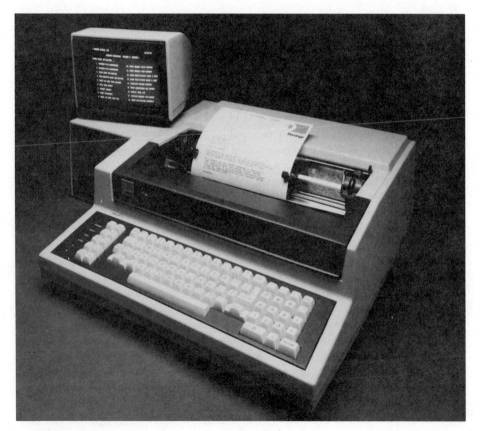

FIGURE 8.8
Teleprinter.

FIGURE 8.9
Teletypewriter.

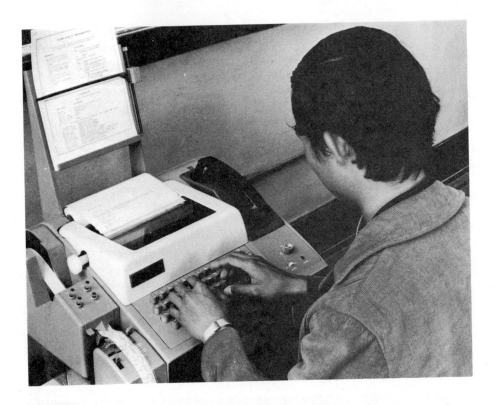

VISUAL DISPLAY TERMINALS (VDTs)

We now visit the most popularly used of all the devices in the laboratory. The **visual display terminal (VDT)**, the most commonly used input device, contains a keyboard that is used for inputting data and a cathode ray tube that provides output on its screen, referred to as a soft copy. The information shown on the cathode ray tube is that of the transmitted data sent to or received from a central processing unit.

We notice that the visual display terminals are being used in three different ways by students in the laboratory. Upon close examination of the cathode ray tube, we notice that some use it for an alphanumeric display. These students are preparing term papers; they are using a word processing program to enter, change, delete, and rearrange the text. How the program is used is discussed in Chapter 16, on office automation. We notice that business majors have graphic displays on the cathode ray tube, being used for plotting marketing trends. Some students are doing their statistical homework on the terminal. Others are using an interactive graphic display commonly used by scientists to display criteria. One engineering student is using the cathode ray tube for displaying how the binary digits are being turned on and off in his stored program. He is following the inner workings of the computer circuitry as the program is executed. Because visual display terminals are usable by many for various purposes, they are frequently called **workstations.**

It is fascinating to see the cathode ray tube show graphs and drawings. There are two ways for generating computer graphics, one of which is by a line drawing that uses the x and y coordinates and the other by the use of dots. Each **pixel** (an abbreviation for picture element), or dot, identifies a location on the screen and has an identifying number. Think of the cathode ray tube as being a large matrix which is made up of a number of dots, or pixels. The number varies, but many cathode ray tubes have 256 dots across and 192 dots down. Others can have a 512 by 512 (square) dot screen.

As we walk around the room, we notice that some cathode ray tubes even have color. Used sparingly in the 1970s, color graphics have become more popular today. Each dot can be red, blue, green, or a mix of these, with a programmer determining the color that is to be used.

Applications using a visual display terminal are numerous. Some examples are: the Internal Revenue Service monitors tax returns; the military monitors the launching of rockets; a hospital examines a patient's history files and determines the medication to prescribe; television networks analyze the status of bills in Congress; and lobbyists determine the elected official's voting record.

A visual display terminal, in addition to its keyboard, can also have a light pen that is used on the cathode ray tube. Refer to Figure 8.10. An architecture student asks for a copy of the blueprints for a certain automobile. After the blueprint copy is displayed on the cathode ray tube, the student can point to certain lines that are to be erased from the drawing. Other lines can be inserted on the screen by the use of the light pen. Additions or deletions work since there is a stored program to direct these activities. Also notice how the graphics tablet is used with the light pen for making changes on the monitor.

REMOTE JOB ENTRY

There is one more device to view on our tour in the computer laboratory. It is a card reader, but where is the central processing unit? The card reader's location

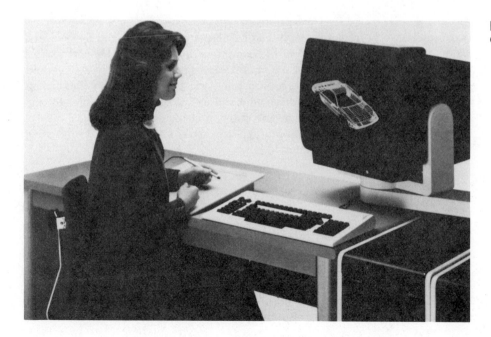

FIGURE 8.10
Geometry processing terminal.

FIGURE 8.11
**Card reader, one part of remote
job entry (RJE).**

is considered to be remote since it can be placed several thousand feet, several miles, or thousands of miles from the computer. If a printer and a card reader, which normally are contained at the same location as the central processing unit, are located at a remote site, they are classified as a **remote job entry (RJE).** This type of device is used by only those who still use punched cards. Refer to Figure 8.11. The terminology, remote job entry, is changing to mean visual display terminals that are used for keying data at a site distant from the central processing unit. This is discussed in Chapter 10.

VISIT TO A BANK

The next company on our tour is a national bank, where we will view a special type of equipment used for check processing, savings processing, and Christmas club collections. Our tour guide stops us in the hallway to remind us that we will see some of the activities that also take place in our branch bank.

CHARACTER RECOGNITION DEVICES

Banks need several devices that read characters encoded in magnetic ink, printed copy, and typed copy, or handwritten copy.

Magnetic Ink Character Recognition (MICR) Devices

Magnetic ink character recognition (MICR) devices are used for reading magnetic ink characters. Rather than enter all check account numbers and dollar amounts, an installation uses a magnetized ink to print the account number and the amount of a check, as shown in Figure 8.12.

Every branch in a national bank receives many checks during a working day and prepares **batch totals,** totals calculated on meaningful data such as total deposits in savings accounts, total withdrawals, amount paid by checks, and the number of checks received at that branch. The checks and batch totals are sent to the data processing center. The checks are taken to a **proof inscriber** (pictured as shown in Figure 8.13), which calculates the batch total and encodes the amount of the check on the lower right-hand corner of the check, as shown in Figure 8.12.

After the batch totals calculated in the proof inscriber (proof machine) agree with the batch totals supplied by the branch, the checks are placed in the reader-sorter, as shown in Figure 8.14. The tour guide walks our group into a room, where we see nothing but a mass of reader-sorters.

Since checks are used as source documents, a bank needs a **reader-sorter** to read the magnetic ink characters that are coded on the checks, to send the data over the channels to the central processing unit for processing, and to sort the

FIGURE 8.12 **Check uses magnetic ink characters.**

IDENTIFIES THE BANK THAT CHECK IS DRAWN ON (TRANSIT OR FRABA FIELD)	ACCOUNT NUMBER AND TRANSACTION CODE (ON US FIELD)	AMOUNT OF CHECK (AMOUNT FIELD)

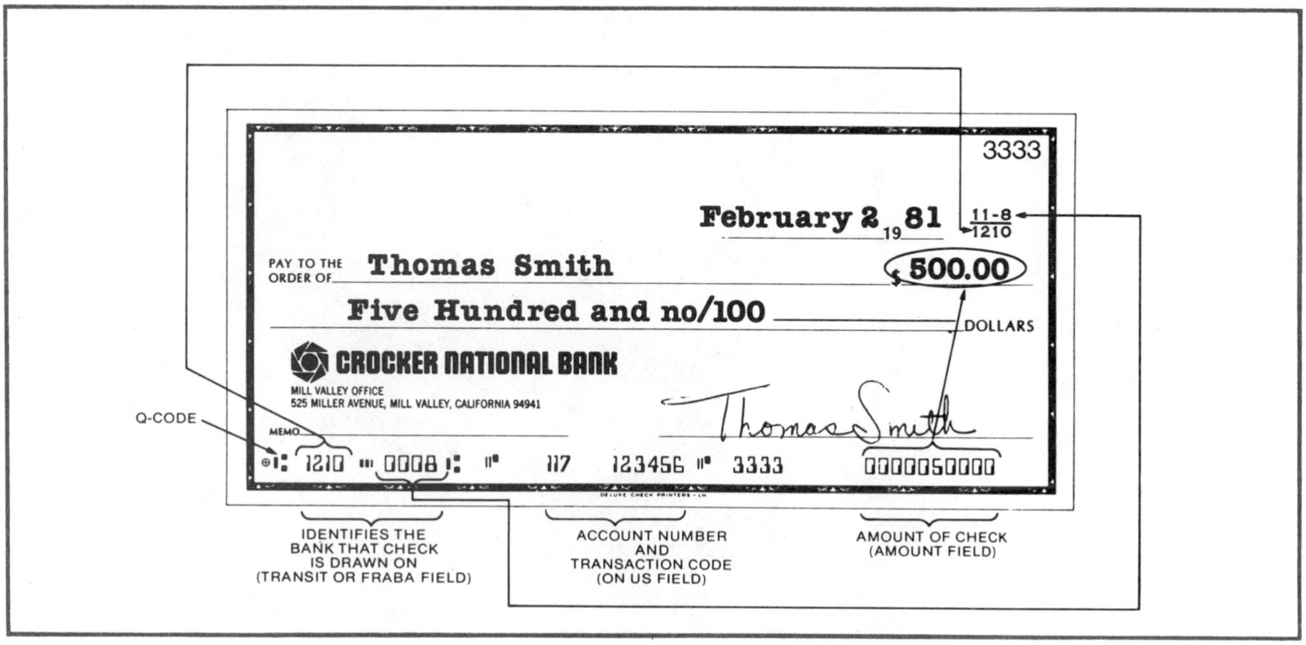

FIGURE 8.13
Proof inscriber.

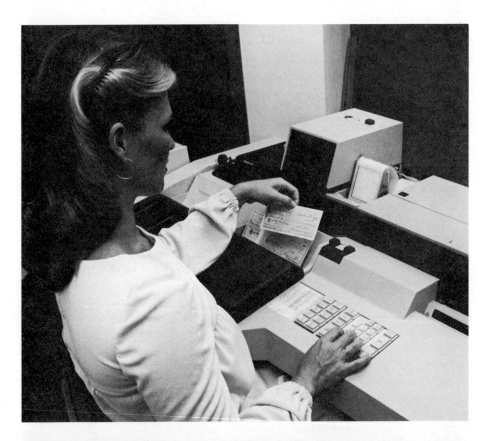

FIGURE 8.14
Reader-sorter.

checks by branch, city code, and account number. Magnetic ink characters are read by a reader-sorter, and all data is transmitted from a central processing unit to a tape drive and to a disk drive, as shown in Figure 8.15. Magnetic tape is used only as a backup, in case the disk drive is damaged. Should a check jam occur at the reader-sorter, a computer operator can backspace the tape to see which was the last check data read and transmitted. Many times a visual display terminal is used for detecting the last transmitted check data.

Where are the central processing unit, magnetic disk, magnetic tape, and printers? The tour guide tells us that the magnetic tape drives and magnetic disk drives are on the floor above us; the printers and central processing unit are two floors up. Our tour continues.

Storage becomes a problem if the installation is required by law to keep an account of all check data for several years. Magnetic tape data can be microfilmed and stored indefinitely in a very compact storage. This is an application of computer output microfilm (COM), which is discussed shortly.

FIGURE 8.15 **Reader-sorter reads data, transmits data to central processing unit, and data is stored on magnetic disk and tape.**

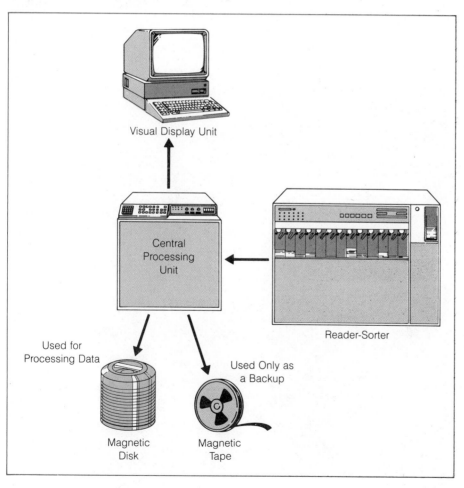

Optical Readers

If an installation has large volumes of input data, it might choose optical scanning equipment to reduce key entry time. Optical readers permit a source document to be used as input.

There are three types of optical readers. One type is called an **optical mark sense reader.** It reads test score sheets on which a user has filled in a small dotted line area; an example is Scantron score sheets. Another type is called a **bar code reader,** which reads the bar code printed on grocery items; these devices are discussed later in the chapter.

A third type is the equipment that reads handwritten, printed, or typed data and is called an **optical character reader.** This equipment has a scanning device that can read the light and dark spots of a character and determine the data. When handwriting is used as input, there are, however, very specific ways for forming a character. A user usually must be formally trained how to prepare a document. Once the data is read by an optical character reader, it is coded into the internal code of the computer and processing continues in its usual way. Banks use such equipment for Christmas club collections. A person promises to pay a specific amount each week or month to the Christmas club. With each payment, the person uses one of the preprinted tickets for identifying the account with its appropriate payment.

FIGURE 8.16 **Automated-teller machines used for lobby environment.**

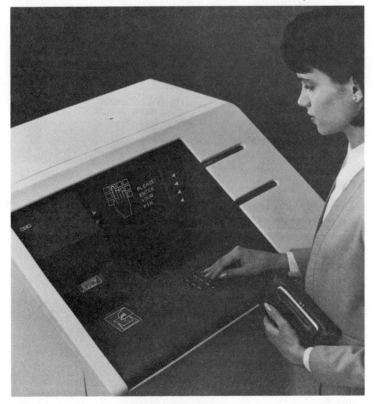

AUTOMATED TELLER MACHINES (ATMs)

Automated teller machines (ATMs), as shown in Figure 8.16, are those twenty-four-hour teller machines positioned outside of a bank or in a grocery store. At the time the account is set up with the bank or grocery store, the user determines his or her password (a secret code), and this password is stored in secondary storage. When a user wishes to withdraw money, a plastic card is inserted into the machine, the password is keyed, and the requested money is released from the automatic teller machine.

The automated teller machines are used in bank locations, usually located on the outside wall of the bank. New equipment is now being used in lobbies of hotels and office buildings. A user inserts a plastic card into the ATM and then must key into the machine his or her **personal identification number** called **PIN.** Not only can these machines be used to disperse cash but they can also be used for transferring funds from a savings account to a checking account. The balance of the account or accounts is electronically handled. Regular deposits such as monthly paychecks and regular payment of bills such as mortgage payments and automobile payments can be handled through the electronic funds transfer.

CHECKPOINT **Can you:**

List and explain the operation of some of the hardware needed in banks for processing checks?

The automated teller machines are part of a developing system called the **electronic funds transfer (EFT),** which has the capability of transferring funds electronically throughout the world. The Electronic Funds Transfer Act that was passed by the 95th Congress went into effect in May 1980. Using EFT, no actual check or money order is drawn; the system works strictly electronically. Many citizens have their social security checks directly deposited in their checking accounts. This protects the recipient from possibly having the check stolen and also provides faster service for the deposit.

The master plan for the EFT is to couple the automated teller machine and the point-of-sale devices (the electronic cash registers that are discussed shortly) together so that funds are transferred electronically; in theory, such a system would eventually produce a cashless society. To accomplish this, large department stores and supermarkets that have point-of-sale terminals would have communication lines running from the store to the bank. Some movement has begun in this direction, but the EFT has met with some consumer resistance and has not been as successful as originally hoped.

Our tour continues in the bank. The printers are found on different floors. If the computer system is a mainframe, it will use different printers than those used for a microcomputer or minicomputer. These differences are noted as the tour proceeds.

CHECKPOINT **Can you:**

Explain the goals of electronic funds transfer?

PRINTERS

A printer is and always has been the busiest of all peripherals since most applications have printed reports. Technological advancements are continually being made, with the printing speed doubling about every six years. Some printers can print in Spanish, Italian, French, German, and Russian as long as the required fonts are used. Even the Japanese language, with over 1,000 characters, can be printed. Frequently a forty-eight-character set is used; it is made up of twenty-six alphabetics, ten numbers, and twelve special characters. Other printers might use upper and lower case characters as well and use a wider variety of special characters.

Our tour guide explains that a little background information about printers is necessary before we continue the tour. Three different categories are applied in the classification of printers. They print by impact or nonimpact methods; they prepare output by character, line, or page; and the characters they form are either solid or dot matrix.

Impact and Nonimpact Printers

The oldest type of printers is the **impact printer,** which uses a mechanical unit such as a hammer to strike a ribbon against paper. Sometimes a print hammer that hits the character against the paper fails to fire so that a particular character does not print. Carbon copies can be made when impact printers are used.

The **nonimpact printer** uses heat, chemical, electrical, or optical techniques to print output, resulting in quieter operation and better printing quality. A nonimpact printer can also print a company logo at the top of a page, along with the printed material.

Character, Line, and Page Printers

A **character printer,** or **serial printer,** prints one character at a time. A **line printer,** or **parallel printer,** can print one line at a time.

A **daisywheel printer** prepares letter quality printed output much like that generated on a typewriter. Perhaps you have seen an electric typewriter that has a ball which turns as it selects the desired character for printing. The movement of the ball must be in synchronization with the typewriter mechanism so the correct character prints. The same concept is used with various printers that use a hammer to make the imprint on the paper. The printing mechanism, whether it is a wheel, chain, belt, or drum uses the same concept as each moves for selecting the desired character and has a hammer strike it as the character goes by.

The daisywheel printer, as shown in Figure 8.17(a), has a wheel that rotates. The end of the spokes on the wheel makes the character impression against the ribbon. Wheels are interchangeable, if you need to change printing fonts.

One type of line printer is the **wheel printer;** each of its 120 wheels contains 48 characters. The wheel turns to any of these 48 characters. A character is printed when the selected character on the wheel strikes against the ribbon. Another type of line printer, the **chain printer,** uses a horizontal chain for holding the five sections of 48 characters. Refer to Figure 8.17(b). Another type is a **band printer,** which moves a band continuously in front of the print hammers. Refer to Figure 8.17(d). Yet another type of line printer, the **drum printer,** has characters engraved around the surface of a drum. The number of sets of characters depends

FIGURE 8.17   **Printers. (a) Daisywheel printing mechanism. (b) Chain printer. (c) Drum printer. (d) Band printer.**

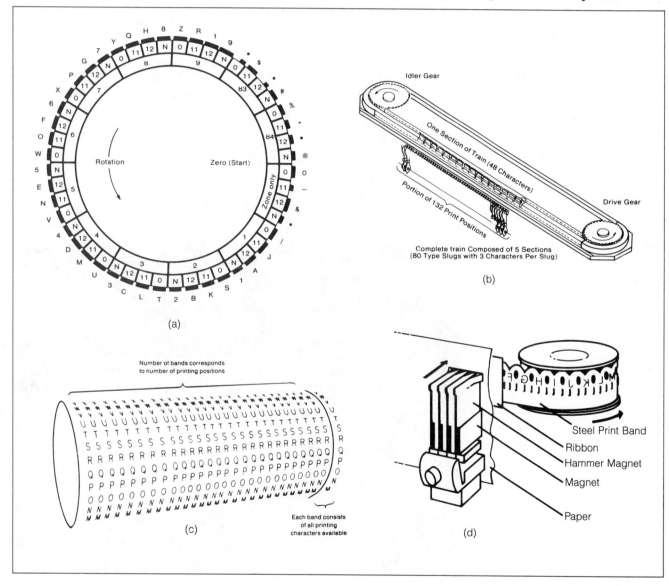

upon how many characters are to print on one line. The drum rotates so the desired characters can print. Refer to Figure 8.17(c).

A **page printer** appears to print an entire page at a time. The printing is done so quickly (up to 21,000 lines per minute for some laser printers) that the entire page seems to appear instantaneously. Sometimes the speed of a page printer is stated in pages per minute (ppm) rather than lines per minute (lpm). Page printers are often called *laser printers* or *electronic printers*. These printers use a rotating disk that contains the full complement of characters that can be printed. A light source is passed through the rotating disk which reflects the selected characters onto photographic paper. The paper is then developed which is used for making copies. The quality of the print is extremely high. Laser printers are being used today for printing books. In the future, use will increase in the office where very large amounts of output is generated from word processing used on microcomputers and minicomputers. Refer to Figure 8.18.

Solid-Character Versus Dot Matrix

A **solid-character printer** prints characters much like those a typewriter produces. A **dot matrix printer** produces characters consisting of little dots, much like the numbers on an electronic scoreboard. The actual matrix, or grid, is often a rectangle measuring 5 by 7 dots. Selected dots within the grid are pressed against a ribbon, forming a character. A dot matrix serial impact printer, commonly used for data processing and output on personal computers, works in this fashion. Refer to Figure 8.19(a).

A dot matrix can print serially or by line, using impact or nonimpact technology. Refer to Figure 8.19(b). Those applications frequently using the dot matrix

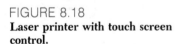

FIGURE 8.18
Laser printer with touch screen control.

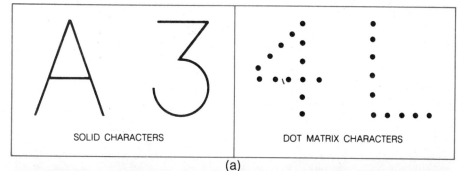

SOLID CHARACTERS   DOT MATRIX CHARACTERS

(a)

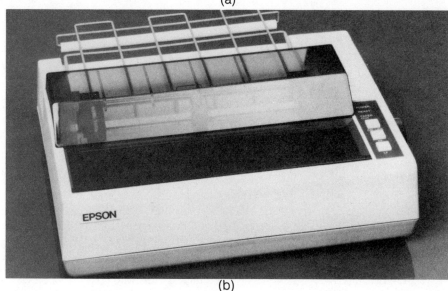

(b)

FIGURE 8.19
**Solid and dot matrix printing.
(a) Solid characters and dot
matrix characters. (b) Dot matrix
printer prints nine international
character sets.**

are concentrated in word processing, graphics, printing of bar codes and electronic mail (the electronic transmission of messages from one terminal to another without using a postal service).

The tour guide points out that serial dot matrix printers and ink-jet printers, the cost of which is about $500 to $800, are commonly used by those owning personal computers. **Ink-jet printers** use the dot matrix principle for printing. They are nonimpact printers which spray ink from a jet, enabling different colors to be printed. Laser printers are also available for use with microcomputers. The possible range of speeds and costs for various types of printers are shown in Table 8.1.

A summation of where the various types of printers are found is shown in Table 8.2.

CHECKPOINT **Can you:**

State how printers are classified?

Differentiate among the various types of printers?

TABLE 8.1.
Most Frequent Uses of Printers by Applications.

APPLICATIONS	PRINTERS		
	SERIAL	LINE	PAGE
Bar code printing		X	
Data processing	X	X	X
Electronic mail			X
Graphics	X	X	
Personal computer	X		
Portable terminals	X		
Word processing	X	X	

TABLE 8.2.
Minimum and Maximum Speed and Cost Comparisons for Printers.

TYPE	CHARACTERS PER SECOND				LINES PER MINUTE			
	MINIMUM		MAXIMUM		MINIMUM		MAXIMUM	
	SPEED	COST	SPEED	COST	SPEED	COST	SPEED	COST
Band					240	$8,000	500	$ 94,000
Belt					300	$4,000	500	$ 5,000
Chain					300	$5,000	2000	$ 69,000
Daisywheel	12	$ 800	400	$19,500	150	$4,500	600	$ 15,300
Dot matrix	1	$ 400	600	$13,500	40	$ 800	1000	$ 10,000
Drum	45	$1,000	4800	$23,000	20	$3,500	6000	$ 75,000
Electrosensitive	42	$ 400	960	$ 1,000	120	$ 600	18000	$ 53,000
Ink jet	20	$1,300	270	$ 2,700	50	$ 500	50	$ 500
Laser					1300	$9,000	21000	$315,000
Thermal matrix	2	$ 650	160	$ 1,500	63	$ 600	300	$ 20,000

Note: The speed and cost do not necessarily represent the same device.

GALLERY 4

Input

We've come a long way! That statement is certainly typical when analyzing the applications in which the computer is used. In the 1950s, the only form of input was that of numeric data. Let us investigate the many different forms of input that are transmitted to a computer for processing, whether it be numbers, words, or images. When faster central processing units and larger memory were available, a new type of input emerged where a computer received, stored, and processed visual images as well.

1. Phototypesetting uses a key-to-disk system. 2. An artist uses a light pen to make the drawings. 3. The use of voice synthesizers has made computers more usable to many.

4. A reader-sorter uses checks as its input. **5.** Optical recognition is used in grocery stores for ordering products. **6.** Point of Sale Terminal (POS) terminal.

(a)

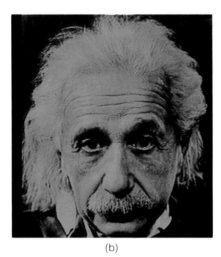

(b)

7. Although image processing is in its infancy, it is making headway into areas other than the taking of land photos by satellite, called LandSat, as shown in the gallery *Computers in Science and Technology*. A series of photographs of Albert Einstein is shown to emphasize the degree of flexibility that image processing has. By alterations, the image can be shown according to the needs of the user. The concepts are used in factory inspection systems yielding robotic vision and quality control on production lines. Or, it can be used in pattern matching and digital subtraction for inspecting integrated circuit boards. Another use is a nondestructive industrial X-ray inspection of a product. The medical field uses medical imaging by X-ray averaging and recording. Astronomy uses image processing for image averaging of telescopic images for tracking and identifying stars. This processing can also be used for general inspection where areas are measured, distances are measured, and uniformity is measured.
7(a). The noisy original which is generated by a scanning electron microscope is inputted. **7(b).** Averaged original. **7(c).** Phase contrast's enhanced. **7(d).** Thresholding the averaged original. **7(e).** Thresholding the low pass filtered image. **7(f).** Pseudo color applied to thresholded image. **7(g).** Pseudo color applied to low pass filtered image.

(c)

(d)

(e)

(f)

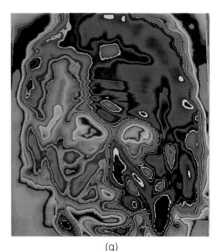

(g)

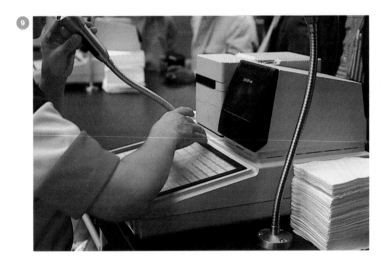

8. Keyboard input is used in a computer room. **9.** A touch screen is used in a fast food restaurant. **10.** A person using a mouse as an input device.

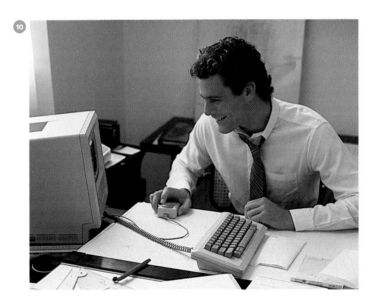

GALLERY 5

Computer Art and CAD/CAM

A new kind of art has emerged that is generated through computer graphics. The once used paint brush has been replaced by pictures represented in a digital form.

CAD/CAM has greatly enhanced an engineer's job by efficiently and very quickly laying out designs previously done by hand.

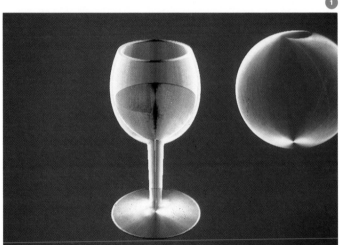

1. "Rendering of a glass" courtesy of Robert Bosh Corporation. 2. "Flower" by Kevin McMahon. 3. "Minneapolis Skyline" by Kevin McMahon.

4. and 5. Sample of color graphics work done on the Imaginator Design Console.

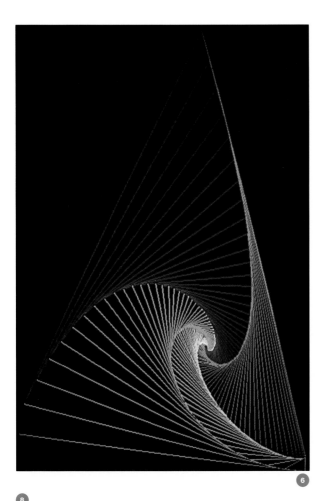

6. Color geometric art courtesy of Chromatics. **7. and 8.** The selection and intensity of the colors of the baboon and oriental rug were generated from instructions written by a programmer.

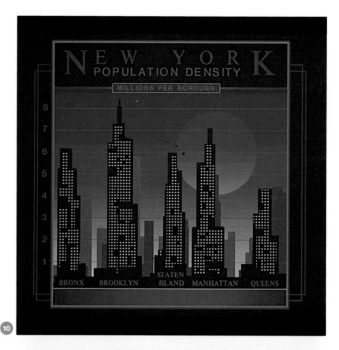

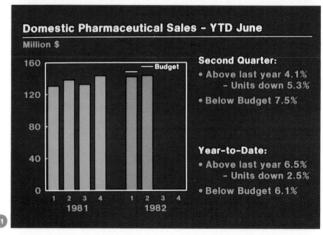

9. One example of an educational use of color graphics.
10. This New York population density graphic. **11. and**
12. Examples of business graphics.

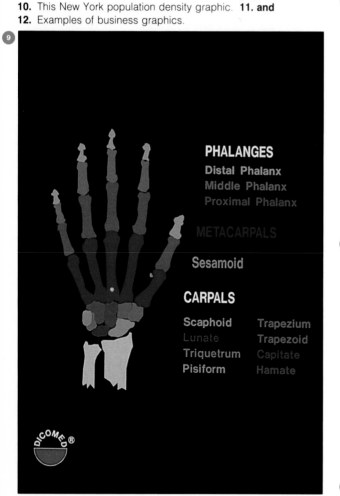

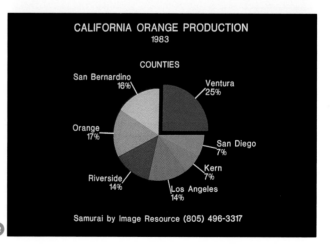

13. The IBM 5081 display screen. 14. The IBM 5080 Graphics System. 15. The Imaginator Design Console.

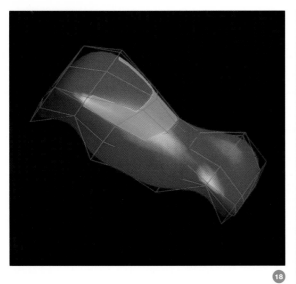

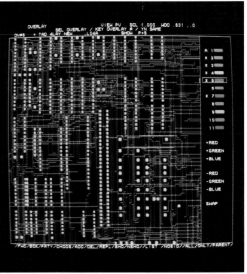

16. An application engineer uses a computer to design a numerical control tool. 17. A computer aids in the design of a process control plant. 18. A solid image design for a car. 19. An IBM-Compatible Adage 4250 Color Raster Workstation is used to design a printed circuit board. 20. An HP desktop computer with color CRT display tests a digital fuel-indicating system for a plane by simulating cockpit meters. 21. An automotive engineer conducts vibration tests on an automobile prototype using an HP structural dynamics analyzer.

22. The computerized control room of a nuclear power plant. **23.** Process control in a paper mill through the use of a computer.

COMPUTER OUTPUT MICROFILM (COM)

Our tour guide points out that we have talked about the use of teleprinters and printers, but there is a third type of hard copy device. **Computer output microfilm (COM)** is known as a micrographics technology; it provides the highest speed, brightest color, and the best reproduction quality because it uses 35 mm slides or 16 mm movies to copy data.

Computer output microfilm provides an alternative to the abundance of continuous forms that pose quite a storage problem for many firms. Business data requiring up to 207 pages of 11-by-14-inch paper for hard copy can be reduced and stored on one piece of film (called a **microfiche**) about the size of a postcard— 4 by 6 inches.

Computer output microfilm equipment converts data stored on magnetic tape into a form that is readable by a person sitting at a visual display terminal and can operate on-line from a central computer or off-line to a magnetic tape drive. This preparing of the microfilm can be done on-line or off-line. When COM equipment is off-line, the data that is to be printed is formatted by a program, with the microfilm tape resulting. This tape is next taken to the minicomputer, which oversees the preparation of the microfiche. Refer to Figure 8.20(a). If the procedure is to be done on-line, the data that is to be printed is formatted by a program and transferred over a channel to a micro-image minicomputer which prepares the film, as shown in Figure 8.20(b).

Computer output microfilm hardware is **plug compatible,** meaning that it can operate with several computer systems other than IBM. Originally computer output microfilm was designed for IBM mainframes, but other mainframes manufactured by Honeywell, Burroughs, Univac and others can now be used with the computer output microfilm minicomputer system. The city of Pittsburgh, Pennsylvania, found it beneficial to change all of its criminal records to this system. Before the switch, there were 90,000 file folders contained in eighty-nine four-drawer file cabinets. Now the storage is held in an area about the size of a small car.

CHECKPOINT **Can you:**

Explain why COM is used?

VISIT TO A RETAIL STORE

The next company visited is a large supermarket. At the front of the store, we find automated teller machines. Our attention is directed first to the point of sale terminals.

FIGURE 8.20   **Computer output microfilm. (a) Off-line operation. (b) On-line operation.**

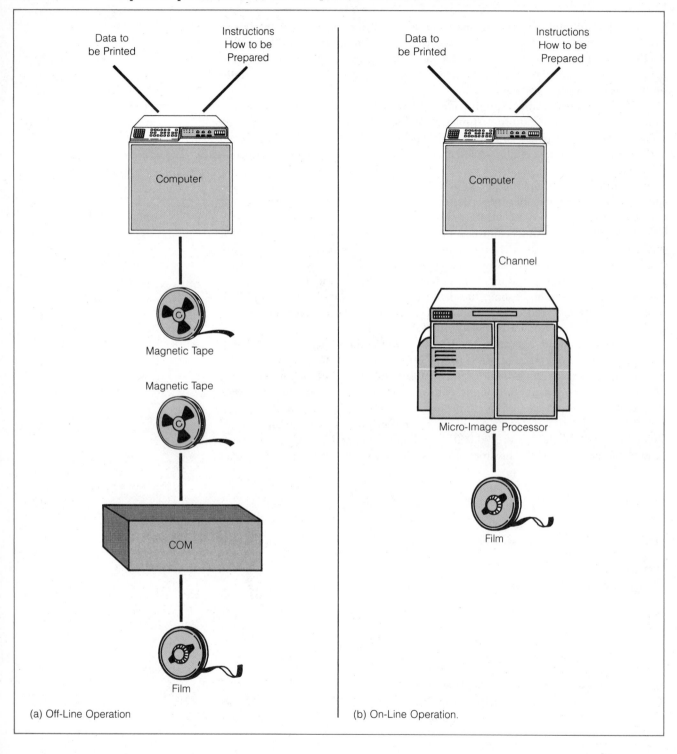

(a) Off-Line Operation

(b) On-Line Operation.

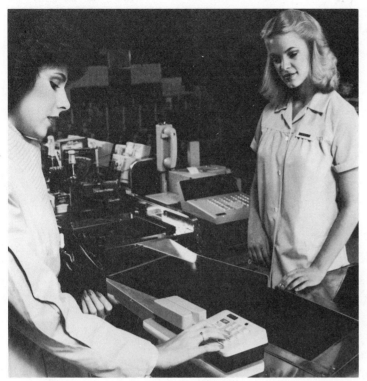

FIGURE 8.21(a)   **A Point of sale (POS) terminal at a supermarket check-out.**

POINT OF SALE (POS) TERMINALS

Point of sale (POS) terminals are those on-line terminals that are used in stores for capturing data on items purchased, the price of each, and the total customer bill. In other words, a point of sale terminal is an electronic cash register which also captures sales and inventory data for a computer; once relayed to the central processing unit, records are instantaneously updated. Our tour guide reminds us that we have probably seen point of sale terminals in other supermarkets, department and variety stores, and large self-service food stores.

Point of sale terminals as shown in Figure 8.21(a), read bar codes to identify the products, as was previously explained. When a checker serves you in a check-out line, he or she passes an item over a light source, making certain that the bar codes are visible to the optical bar code reader. When the bar code is recognized, a little beep is heard. When, however, a product is not correctly identified, a loud harsh beep is heard or no beep depending upon the equipment used. Either the checker tries again or keys in the product identifying number by hand on the electronic cash register. This number identifies that product, among all others in the store. We ask the tour guide how the terminal knows what to charge? Upstairs we go to a room that reveals the answer—a minicomputer which receives all the captured data from the point of sale terminals. The minicomputer has a magnetic disk that stores the needed records. A chart on the wall shows how the computer system is configured (see Figure 8.21(b)).

Our tour guide reminds us of a similar type of operation that is done in

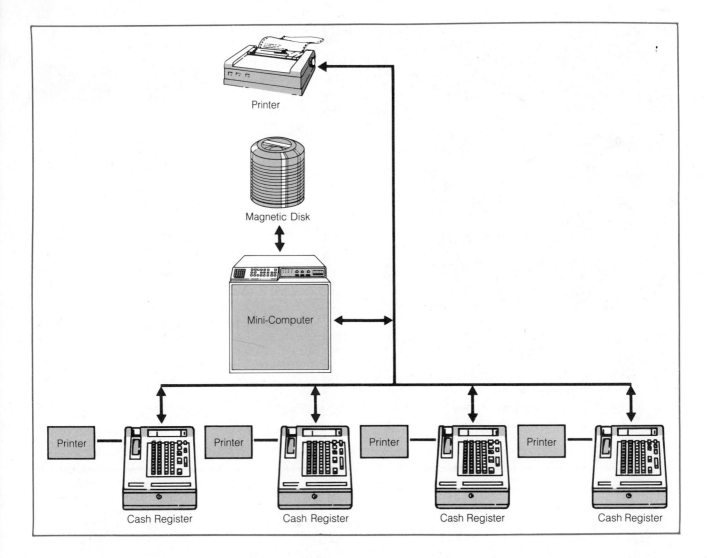

FIGURE 8.21(b)
Diagram of point of sale computer system.

department stores. Perhaps you have visited a department store where you have seen a sales clerk take an optical wand, (shown previously in Figure 2.9), and apply it to the ticket stub of the merchandise that is being purchased. The data contained on the ticket stub is then transferred to the point of sale terminal, where a paper receipt is prepared and given to the purchaser, listing the merchandise purchased and the amount of the transaction. Up to 100 characters can be read per second, a rate about twenty times faster than the manual method of data entry.

PORTABLE TERMINALS

As we leave the store, we see a salesman walking to the phone booth. He is carrying a **portable terminal** that can transmit data over telephone lines. He dials the computer's telephone number and hears a high-pitched whistle. He inserts the handset into two rubber-cups that allow the terminal's signals to be transmitted over the telephone line. Generally, on a portable terminal there is a small screen used for output. We notice, however, he has one that is equipped with a printer. You may have seen an executive using one of these on an airplane or in a hotel to prepare reports or write letters. Refer to Figure 8.22(a) for an illustration of a portable terminal.

You may also have seen employees in a supermarket using portable terminals to prepare orders. Most often their portable terminals consist of a keyboard and a light pen as shown in Figure 8.22(b); no printer is included.

CHECKPOINT **Can you:**

Describe how the POS terminal operates?

VISIT TO A COMMUNICATIONS COMPANY

A visit to a communications company is the next stop on our tour. Here we are told that we will see a different type of work and emphasis. A communications company designs the telephone equipment that we use as well as equipment used in microwave (radio) transmission. (The data communications topic is discussed

FIGURE 8.22
Portable terminals. (a) Terminal has built-in word processing and micro-cassette storage. (b) Light pen used for inventory control.

(a)

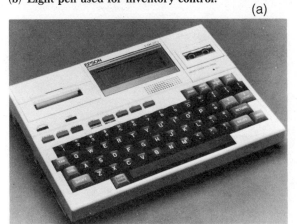

(b)

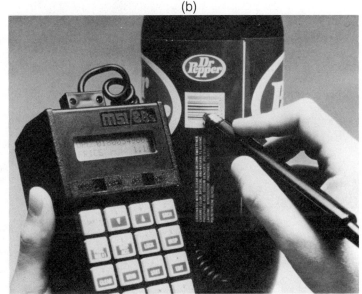

IBM Serviceman To Get Computer Aid

The field technicians of IBM will be given assistance when working on intermediate and large-scale information processing systems. When the serviceman needs parts, the order will be generated from that site immediately through the use of a portable terminal that weighs only 1½ pounds. The intention is to speed up processing orders and reduce drastically the paperwork involved in parts invoicing.

The network is to be in operation by mid-1985, servicing 250 cities. The terminal users will be able to communicate with each other through the computer that handles the parts orders and message traffic.

in Chapter 10.) Since this type of company stresses the way that data is transmitted from one location to another, engineers are continually designing new circuitry for improved service and reliability.

Our tour guide explains that the communications company we are observing designs new circuitry but also needs to use previously designed circuitry that perhaps is on a blueprint and is not stored in primary or secondary storage. To accomplish their task, the communications company will probably use, along with its visual display units and printers, a digitizer and a plotter.

DIGITIZER

We walk through the engineering department to view a digitizer. We are told that if we have seen people having their "picture taken" by a computer in a department store, we have seen a digitizer in operation. A **digitizer,** a flat and oval shaped device, as shown in Figure 8.23 is used with a graphics tablet, and a cathode ray tube for drawing simulation models, preparing architectural designs in simulation, designing statistical analyses, making maps, and designing integrated circuits.

The tour guide goes to the cabinet and removes a blueprint design for a building. This is to be stored in a computer's memory, however, so that this drawing can later be modified to fit another application. A digitizer would be used

FIGURE 8.23
Digitizer used with graphics tablet.

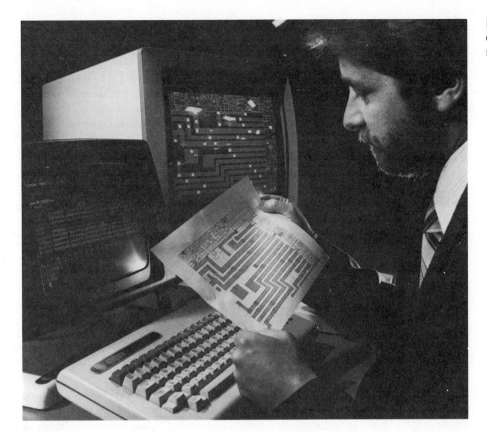

FIGURE 8.24
**Computer-aided design reduces
manual circuit design.**

to trace the drawing; that image, in turn, is converted to electrical impulses that
can be stored in a computer's memory. The engineer can later modify the drawing
as desired.

Computer-Aided Design

Another application for our communications firm might be that an engineer designs
a circuit board. Prior to the 1970s an engineer laid out a circuit using a mechanical
drawing board. Days and months were spent in doing such work. Rather than
work many days on laying out the circuit board manually, the engineer will use
a program called **Computer-Aided Design (CAD),** developed by Gerber Systems
Technology, Inc., of South Windsor, Connecticut. This program uses ½ megabyte
of memory and is a dedicated system for efficiently designing printed circuit
boards. A user specifies the components of the circuit and draws with the digitizer
any required placement of certain components, if any. Computer-aided design
automatically determines the best board design by considering the best positioning
of each component. It sets up a pattern with cross lines; it sets up a second pattern
of vertical lines or connections and then puts both of them together. The placement
of the components is constantly evaluated for efficiency when the circuit is used,
by placing the circuit in the smallest possible space on the board. The shortest
distance that electricity must flow, the faster and more efficient is the circuit,

resulting in faster operating speed of the computer hardware. Contrast the layout of the board under computer-aided design with the layout using engineer expertise alone; the former takes from one to five days from start to finish, whereas a manual design requires anywhere from five to thirty days or longer. Refer to Figure 8.24.

Our tour guide recalls the days at the communications company before computer graphics. Before the days of computers, a manual system was used; charts and graphs were pasted up on paper. In the late 1950s, an eleven-inch plotter was developed but it did not prove helpful to the engineers. To make the plotter operate required extensive programming; as each time the pen was to be moved a programmer's instruction was necessary. In addition, programmers were needed for making the plotter a useful tool. As a result, it was sometimes just as fast to have the artist prepare the drawing originally. In the late 1960s, the software was improved, but the ability to write a program was still needed. The drawings still left much to be desired. Today, however, the quality of the graphics is good, and the hardware is easy to use. A user can display the graphics on a graphic display terminal or have hard copy generated on a printer, plotter, or microfilm unit. Computer-aided design has created a need for computer graphics specialists.

PLOTTER

There are times, we are told, that some digital computer installations need graphical displays in the form of graphs, charts, or line drawings in order to get a picture of the meaning of data. A computer uses the data and presents a graphic display on paper. A computer, through a program, instructs the pen plotter as shown in Figure 8.25(a), when to raise and lower the pen on the paper, how far to draw the line, which colored pen to use, and whether to produce a solid line, dotted line, or crossed lines.

FIGURE 8.25(a)
Pen Plotter used with personal computer produces business graphics.

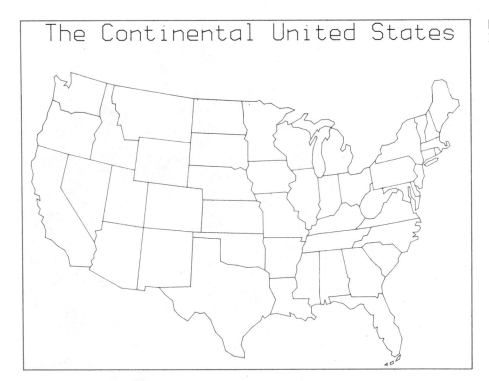

FIGURE 8.25(b)
Example of the output.

It is fascinating to watch the pen plotter perform. A user must input the size of the bar graph or pie-shaped plot that it is to prepare along with the data and the legends for the X and Y axes. A plotter works in three dimensions: the X axis, the Y axis, and the plane in which the pen moves. Some plotters can change pens for a different color almost as quickly as you blink your eyes. Refer to Figure 8.25(b).

Plotters are available in all sizes. Pen plotters use 8½-by-11-inch paper and produce drawings of excellent color and quality, but they operate at slow speed. The **electrostatic printer/plotters** use 200 dots per inch on paper as long as 24 feet. Their quality is very good; the use of color has just been introduced. How the printer plotter color is generated is shown in Figure 8.26(a). Electrostatic plotters, also known as nonimpact printer/plotters, are being used in increasing numbers, even though the purchase price is extremely high (roughly stated in terms of printed copy is about $1,000 per inch of printed copy). Refer to Figure 8.26(b). When a company has an electrostatic printer/plotter, they will many times have a digitizer as well.

CHECKPOINT **Can you:**

Explain why portable terminals are used?

Tell why a digitizer is used?

Explain why Computer-Aided Design is useful?

Identify the various types of printer plotters?

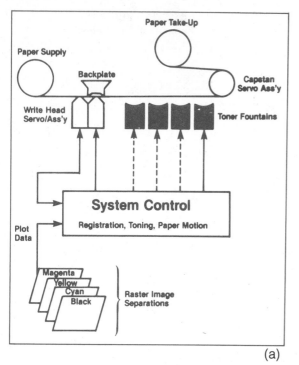

(a)

FIGURE 8.26
Electrostatic printer/plotter. (a) Color plotter diagram. (b) Electrostatic printer plotter being used.

(b)

SUMMARY

● Since the late 1960s input has been recorded on media other than punched cards.

● A terminal refers to an input or output device that can transmit data to or receive data from the computer.

● Peripheral devices refer to all hardware other than the central processing unit.

● When a peripheral device is on-line, it is connected to the central processing unit and controlled by it.

● When a peripheral device is off-line, it cannot transmit data to or receive data from the central processing unit. A peripheral device can be used off-line for data entry, for example, and then made on-line for transmitting the recorded data to the central processing unit.

● The user chooses the type of on-line terminal by considering the volume of data, the source of it, and the application involved.

● Several types of devices are used for keying data onto magnetic tape, thereby eliminating the need to use the computer to store the data originally on the magnetic tape. These devices are key-to-tape and key-to-cartridge.

● The operator keys the data using the key-to-tape system. The magnetic tape that is written is compatible with tapes used on computer systems and can therefore be mounted on a tape drive for processing.

● With the key-to-cartridge system, the keyed data is recorded on a small magnetic tape that is not usable on mainframes.

● The key-to-disk system is often controlled by a minicomputer.

● Teleprinters have keyboards for inputting data or programs. They also have a printer used for generating hard copy.

● A visual display terminal (VDT) contains a keyboard and a cathode ray tube. Sometimes a light pen is also used for altering graphic displays shown on the cathode ray tube. The visual display terminal is used frequently in many offices. Because of their flexibility for a variety of work purposes and the completeness with which they can debug programs, visual display terminals are referred to as workstations.

● Remote job entry refers to a card reader and printer located at a location previously where data is collected. Now RJE refers to data captured at a distant site from the central processing unit.

● Optical character recognition devices read magnetic ink characters, printed typed, or handwritten copy.

● Magnetic ink character recognition (MICR) equipment is used by banking installations for reading the account number and the amount of the check that have been encoded in magnetic ink characters.

● The proof inscriber and the reader-sorter are two magnetic ink character recognition devices.

● The proof inscriber is used for encoding the amount of the check onto the lower right hand corner of the check.

● The reader-sorter transmits the account number and the amount of the check to the central processing unit so the account can be updated. It also sorts the checks into a sequence.

● There are three types of optical readers: the optical mark sense reader, bar code reader, and optical character reader.

● An optical mark sense reader reads test score sheets.

● A bar code reader reads the bar code printed on grocery items and envelopes, which consists of a series of lines.

● The optical character reader can read handwritten, printed, or typed data.

● Automated teller machines (ATMs) are used outside of many large banks and in some supermarkets to provide a twenty-four-hour check cashing service.

● Electronic funds transfer (EFT) refers to the method of transferring funds electronically throughout the world without the actual passing of currency between parties.

● Printers are the busiest of all peripheral devices since most programs require the preparation of hard copy.

- Printers are classified as to how they prepare the printing on the paper (impact versus nonimpact), how they print the output (by character, line, or page), and how the character is formed (by solid type or dot matrix).

- As an alternative to printers, computer output microfilm (COM) is increasing in usage.

- COM uses a program to convert the data on magnetic tape to a form that is usable by the minicomputer—the microfiche. The storage of data on microfiche instead of as hard copy reduces the storage space required for reports by 95 percent.

- Point of sale (POS) terminals are commonly used in large supermarkets and department stores. In supermarkets they use the bar codes marked on products to identify the price to be charged for the product.

- Optical wands are used for reading the printed merchandise information that appears on clothing labels, for example. The sensed data is then transmitted to an electronic cash register.

- Optical wands and POS use optical readers to analyze the dark and light spots on a bar code or on printed characters respectively so characters can be differentiated.

- The digitizer is a device used for preparing simulation models, designing statistical analysis, and making maps.

- Computer-aided design (CAD) is a program to help the engineer to efficiently lay out a circuit board. This program uses a half million characters of code to instruct the computer on the various options for design of the board. A digitizer and visual display terminal that has a wide screen is usually used with CAD.

- The plotter is a tool used for preparing line drawings, charts, or graphs.

- A pen plotter uses regular sized paper and has the capability to use colored pens.

- The printer plotter can print a design up to twenty-four feet long that has been prepared by CAD. These printers' costs are based roughly on the inches of paper generated on output, costing $1,000 per inch.

STUDY GUIDE

REVIEW OF TERMINOLOGY

The following terminology was discussed in this chapter:

automated teller machine (ATM)
band printer
bar code reader
batch totals
chain printer
character printer
computer-aided design (CAD)
computer output microfilm (COM)
daisywheel printer
digitizer
dot matrix printer
drum printer
electronic funds transfer (EFT)
electrostatic printer/ plotter
impact printer
ink jet printer
key-entry devices
key-to-cartridge
key-to-disk
key-to-diskette
key-to-tape
laser printer
line printer

magnetic ink character recognition (MICR)
microfiche
nonimpact printer
off-line
on-line
optical character reader
optical mark sense reader
page printer
parallel printer
pen plotter
personal identification number (PIN)
pixel
plug compatible
point of sale (POS) terminal
portable terminal
proof inscriber
reader-sorter
remote job entry (RJE)
serial printer
solid-character printer
teleprinter
teletypewriter
visual display terminal (VDT)
wheel printer
workstation

MULTIPLE CHOICE

Circle the item that completes each statement correctly.

1. This type of device cannot send or receive data from a central processing unit:
   a. bar code reader
   b. optical character reader
   c. off-line
   d. on-line
   e. impact printer

2. This type of device is used for inputting data or programs, but it also has a printer:
   a. bar code reader
   b. teleprinter
   c. dot matrix
   d. point of sale terminal
   e. automated teller machine

3. Magnetic tape measuring ¼ inch wide is used for copying the recorded data in a:
   a. key-to-tape system
   b. key-to-cartridge system
   c. key-to-diskette system
   d. key-to-disk system
   e. key-entry device

4. Data transacted at an electronic cash register is often copied on a:
   a. key-to-tape system
   b. key-to-cartridge system
   c. key-to-diskette system
   d. key-to-disk system
   e. tape cassette

5. Encoding of the dollar amount on a check is done by:
   a. an impact printer
   b. a nonimpact printer
   c. a computer output microfilm
   d. a proof inscriber
   e. a key-to-tape system

6. Remote job entry hardware includes:
   a. computer output microfilm and minicomputer
   b. plotter and key-to-tape system
   c. card reader and printer
   d. printer and plotter
   e. proof inscriber and magnetic ink character recognition device

7. These terminals are found in stores, performing as electronic cash registers:
   a. point of sale terminals
   b. automated teller machines
   c. electronic funds transfer
   d. magnetic ink character recognition devices
   e. remote job entry equipment

8. These terminals use a minicomputer for looking up storage and a bar code as input for determining the price:
   a. point of sale terminals
   d. magnetic ink character

b. automated teller machines   recognition devices
c. electronic funds transfer   *e*. remote job entry equipment

9. These use 8½-by-11-inch paper and produce drawings that are of excellent color and quality:
   a. electrostatic printer/plotters
   b. pen plotters
   c. optical character readers
   d. bar code readers
   e. optical mark sense readers

10. Probably the most commonly used device that contains a screen with up to 512 by 512 dots:
    a. teletypewriter
    b. digitizer
    c. visual display terminal
    d. automated teller machine
    e. soft copy

11. This device electronically copies drawings:
    a. teleprinter
    b. reader sorter
    c. optical character reader
    d. digitizer
    e. electrostatic printer/plotter

12. Magnetic ink character recognition devices are commonly used in:
    a. grocery stores
    b. department stores
    c. banks
    d. schools
    e. government offices

13. When checks must be placed in a sequence, the device used is:
    a. an automated teller machine
    b. a point of sale terminal
    c. an electronic funds transfer
    d. a reader-sorter
    e. a proof inscriber

14. Test sheets that contain small dotted line areas that can be darkened by pencil are read by:
    a. an optical wand
    b. a bar code reader
    c. an optical mark sense reader
    d. an optical character reader
    e. a proof inscriber

15. Printed data is read by:
    a. workstations
    b. a bar code reader
    c. an optical mark sense reader
    d. an optical character reader
    e. a proof inscriber

16. Printers are classified one of three ways, as:
    a. impact, character, or dot matrix
    b. impact, line, dot matrix
    c. impact or nonimpact; character, line, or page; and solid-character or dot matrix
    d. plotter, impact, or electrostatic
    e. plotter, laser, electrostatic

17. Which of the following is magnetic ink character recognition equipment:
    a. proof inscriber only
    b. reader-sorter only
    c. proof inscriber and reader-sorter
    d. automated teller machine only
    e. ATM and reader-sorter

18. When its printing mechanism strikes against the paper, the printer is classified as:
    a. an impact printer
    b. a nonimpact printer
    c. a daisywheel printer
    d. a dot matrix printer
    e. a solid-character printer

19. Which of the following reduces the volume of hard copy:
    a. daisywheel printer
    b. computer output microfilm
    c. electronic funds transfer
    d. automated teller machine
    e. plotter

20. The fastest of all printers is:
    a. the daisywheel printer
    b. the line printer
    c. the character printer
    d. the page printer
    e. the serial printer

TRUE/FALSE QUESTIONS

1. **T/F** Key-entry devices include the key-to-tape, key-to-disk, and proof inscriber.

2. **T/F** The use of key-entry devices is often times found in the major department stores for entering customer purchases.

3. **T/F** With the increased use of on-line processing, key-to-tape systems are being used less frequently today than they were used in the 1970s.

4. **T/F** A proof inscriber is used for encoding the amount of the check and also for calculating meaningful totals.

5. **T/F** Optical readers permit the source document to be used as input.

6. **T/F** Test sheets which students complete by marking in the dotted lines are read by an optical character reader.

7. **T/F** Printers can print in only English characters.

8. **T/F** Some printers print by lasers or by drum.

9. **T/F** Computer output microfilm uses 35 mm slides or 16 mm movies to copy data.

10. **T/F** The pieces of film used with computer output microfilm are called microfiche.

11. **T/F** In computer output microfilm a minicomputer is used for transforming the magnetic tape's data to hard copy.

12. **T/F** Banking installations are the only companies that use computer output microfilm.

13. **T/F** Remote job entry devices are always located at the computer site.

14. **T/F** The only purpose of the point of sale terminal is to capture data.

15. **T/F** POS is the acronym for point of sale.

16. **T/F** When POS terminals are used in a grocery store, the captured data is transmitted to a large-scale computer.

17. **T/F** PIN is used with POS or visual display terminals.

18. **T/F** Cathode ray tubes can be used to display text or graphics.

19. **T/F** The screen of the cathode ray tube is made up of little dots called dot matrix.

20. **T/F** A light pen can be used with a visual display terminal for graphics.

21. **T/F** Computer-aided design is a program developed by Gerber Systems Technology, Inc., that uses ½ megabyte of storage.

22. **T/F** The use of the computer-aided design program has theoretically replaced the mechanical engineer's drawing board.

23. **T/F** The plotter is used for drawing graphs in only one color.

24. **T/F** Electrostatic printer/plotters are very inexpensive.

25. **T/F** Companies that prepare patterns for clothes would use a plotter for output.

26. **T/F** Automated teller machines are very simple to use and are foolproof against tampering.

27. **T/F** CashWire is the newest electronic funds transfer system available for bankers.

28. **T/F** Laser printers use bands for printing.

29. **T/F** All plug compatible hardware is always on-line.

30. **T/F** Batch totals are generated when digitizers and computer-aided design are used.

31. **T/F** An advantage of a daisywheel printer is that the wheel can be changed to a different style font.

32. **T/F** If you use a visual display terminal and want hard copy, you might have a teleprinter prepare the hard copy.

33. **T/F** The speed of printers is stated in 1pm or ppm.

34. **T/F** A terminal could be a teleprinter, a teletypewriter, an optical mark sense reader, or a workstation.

35. **T/F** The small dots that make up the printing on a dot matrix printer are called pixels.

ANSWERS

Multiple Choice: 1. **c** 2. **b** 3. **b** 4. **e** 5. **d** 6. **c** 7. **a** 8. **a** 9. **b** 10. **c** 11. **d** 12. **c** 13. **d** 14. **c** 15. **d** 16. **c** 17. **c** 18. **a** 19. **b** 20. **d** *True/False:* 1. **F** 2. **F** 3. **T** 4. **T** 5. **T** 6. **F** 7. **F** 8. **T** 9. **T** 10. **T** 11. **T** 12. **F** 13. **F** 14. **F** 15. **T** 16. **F** 17. **F** 18. **T** 19. **F** 20. **T** 21. **T** 22. **T** 23. **F** 24. **F** 25. **T** 26. **F** 27. **T** 28. **F** 29. **F** 30. **F** 31. **T** 32. **T** 33. **T** 34. **T** 35. **F**

REVIEW QUESTIONS

1. Why are punched cards and paper tape becoming obsolete?

2. When are peripheral devices on-line? Off-line?

3. What devices are used for the direct keying of data onto a secondary storage medium?

4. What are the major differences between key-to-tape and key-to-disk equipment?

5. When is magnetic ink character recognition equipment used? Where is it used? What type of equipment is it?

6. Name the three types of optical readers. What are the purposes of each?

7. What are the three characteristics used for classifying printers? Identify the types of printers within each classification.

8. What type of device is called a workstation? Why is it so named?

9. What is a point of sale terminal? Where is it used? Why is it used?

10. What does ATM stand for? Where is an ATM used?

11. What does EFT stand for? What are the basic goals for this system? How will it affect society?

12. What kinds of plotters are there? What is the capability of each plotter?

13. What types of applications make use of a digitizer?

DISCUSSION QUESTIONS

1. Which peripheral devices use the source document for input? Identify the type of input for each of these devices.

2. What type of hardware do banking installations use for processing checks? For Christmas club membership? For storage of check data?

3. If you decided to buy a printer for your computer, what would be some of the questions that you would ask before deciding on a product?

4. What are the differences between a nonimpact and an impact printer?

5. Describe how the computer output microfilm system operates both on-line and off-line.

6. How has computer-assisted design revolutionized engineering work? Which peripheral devices are used to perform this type of work?

7. Cite some applications for which an electronic funds transfer system could be used successfully. Which peripheral devices would be needed to make the system operate successfully?

8. Why has the trend been away from punched cards?

9. Explain the statement: "A company has a choice as to the types of input and output devices used."

People in Computing

Tom Mowery

COMPANY
Western Microfilm, Inc.

POSITION
Branch Manager, Sales and
Operations

EDUCATIONAL BACKGROUND
Bachelor of Arts, California State at
Los Angeles

Working in the information
management technology explosion
is indeed challenging and
interesting. For each dollar in the
gross national product, 46 cents is
spent on information-related
technology and services. I have
been involved with the
micrographics industry since 1967,
a brief time in the historical
development of the micrographics
industry. Although the first microfilm
camera was invented in 1926, a
French optician developed the first
microimage much earlier. The first
practical, known use of microfilm
was to communicate spy messages
via courier pigeons during the
Franco-Prussian war in 1870.

The integration of micrographics
and computer technology offers a
major opportunity for increased
productivity in information handling.

Computer-assisted retrieval (CAR)
combines the low-cost and space-
saving features of micrographics
with the fast and accurate indexed
capability of data processing. CAR
systems work hand-in-hand with
other information-handling
technologies such as word
processing, electronic mail, and
communications.

The integration of technologies in
today's offices is replacing the
single word processing system, and
electronic mail (the transmitting of
electronic messages) is more widely
used, thanks to the interconnection
of workstations. True electronic filing
occurs as electronically stored
information is transmitted through
the system together with
computerized indexes to information
which is more suitably stored on
micrographic media. With an
automated workstation, consisting of
an electronic terminal and a
microfilm reader, a person can use
the visual display terminal to enter
information into the computer files,
receive electronic mail, search for
needed microfilm documents, and
communicate to other computers
and data bases. Using the microfilm
reader, the person can view needed
source documents with COM
(computer output microfilm).

As large volumes of information
are created on the word processor,
disk storage of outgoing
correspondence becomes less and
less economical. The disk contents
can be outputted via COM to
microfiche. Large volumes of
incoming paper documents can be
converted to source document
microfiche in the same format as
COM. The microfiche images of
both outgoing and incoming
correspondence can be retrieved
using CAR.

How would you manage a large,
growing volume of correspondence
records—a backlog of 80,000
documents with an additional 4,000
each month—that must be copied
and distributed to four different
offices for storage and retrieval over
the next ten years? Due to
government regulations, some
documentation on a project might
require storing for up to ten years.
By converting the paper files to
microfiche, the correspondence
record is imprinted with a unique
address. An index (like a pointer) is
generated by the corporation's
mainframe computer to cross-
reference the microfiche addresses
of each document with key
information such as the name of the
person generating the document,
the date of the transaction, and the
specific project component
discussed in the correspondence.
The index is printed in catalog form
via computer-aided publishing. The
computer-generated indexing
provides fast and accurate retrieval
of any needed documents.

As for the future of micrographics,
there will always be a need. The
telephone companies have, for
example, over 26,000 microfilm
readers used for directory
assistance. Many of today's needs
using microfilm very likely will give
way in the future to optical disk,
which is similar to the laser optical
video disks sold for home use.

9 Secondary Storage

OUTLINE

PROLOGUE

Realizing that she failed to have her savings account activated by either a withdrawal or a deposit for the last two and half years, Helen goes to the savings and loan near her home.

When entering the savings and loan, she tells the teller that she wishes to have all her interest credited first and then withdraw $10. The teller smiles at her and takes the passbook, noticing that she has not been in for quite some time. No problem, the teller states, as she places the passbook into the terminal after depressing several keys.

The printing begins on the correct quarter, calculates the beginning balance correctly, and does not miss recording any interest. Helen looks at the passbook in amazement.

HOW DOES IT DO THAT?

READ ON.

OBJECTIVES

After studying this chapter, you should be able to:

1. Identify the physical properties of magnetic tape.

2. Explain the differences between logical and physical records.

3. Identify the various labels used with magnetic tape and the purposes of each.

4. Identify the physical properties of magnetic disk.

5. Explain why the cylinder concept is used for addressing.

6. Differentiate between the ferrite and thin-film read-write head technologies.

7. Explain why optical disk will make an important contribution in the storage of data.

8. Identify the possible users of mass storage.

9. Identify the various file organizations and the advantages and disadvantages of each.

INTRODUCTION

Regardless of how large the primary storage is, there is always a demand for more storage capacity. Some job might need a small amount of storage; another job might use the entire primary storage capacity. Secondary storage is used to handle requests for large amounts of data. Recall that all secondary storage can do is hold data; the data must be brought from secondary storage into primary storage for decision making and calculations. Secondary storage is dependent upon primary storage for any processing; hence, its name is appropriate. Secondary storage is also often called auxiliary storage.

There are many types of secondary storage devices available for use, such as those shown in Figure 9.1. Magnetic tape works according to concepts much like those involving tapes used on a home tape recorder. Magnetic disk works much like a stack of phonograph records that are used for writing (storing) data or reading (recalling) data as many times as desired by the user. Optical disk works rather like a phonograph record in concept too, but its primary concentration is on writing data once and reading it thereafter. Mass storage, which combines the magnetic tape and magnetic disk technology, operates like a juke box in concept, pulling one of many magnetic tapes from storage, reading it, and sending the data to magnetic disk for processing.

You probably are wondering why there are so many types of secondary storage. Looking from the viewpoint of the manufacturers, the various user needs must be considered: cost, capacity, and **access time** (the time required from a request for data to the delivery of it to primary storage). One company may be more concerned with reasonable cost and very large capacity than with access time. Another company may need extremely fast access time and be willing to pay for the speed with which data is provided to the user.

The manufacturers must also provide a variety of ways for users to get at the data. If the data is to be processed sequentially using one pass (run) through a

FIGURE 9.1(a)
Magnetic tape.

FIGURE 9.1(b)
Magnetic disk.

computer, magnetic tape or mass storage is used for that application. If, however, on-line processing (which requires processing data in random order) is used, magnetic disk and optical disk are appropriate to the application.

Let us begin the secondary storage discussion by looking into the physical properties of magnetic tape. Later, many of these same properties are noted as being used on the other media.

The discussion regarding diskettes in Chapter 6 explained how a programmer instructs a computer to write, or store, a character. To read a character means to retrieve data from a storage device. Data is written or read at various densities; density refers to the number of characters in an area on the secondary storage medium. The higher the density, the greater the capacity.

MAGNETIC TAPE

Magnetic tape has long been a popular medium for storing data since it is so reasonably priced, costing usually about $20 and up per reel. Even as late as the early 1970s, magnetic tape usage was extremely popular, but today its usage is declining because of the popularity of magnetic disk. Most computer centers usually have both magnetic tape and magnetic disk for secondary storage. We noted previously in Chapter 5 how tape cartridge and tape cassettes are used on microcomputers. Our concentration here is on the reels.

PHYSICAL PROPERTIES

Magnetic tape is generally ½-inch wide. The lengths vary from mini-tapes, which are about 200 feet long, to full-length tapes, which are about 2,400 feet long. It

A company makes backup records for a day's data input in case a computer system fails during the next work day. Even though much of today's secondary storage data is stored on magnetic disk, magnetic tape is used for backup of those magnetic disk records.

Companies often discover that software purchased from the computer manufacturer for use in copying data is inadequate. Some programs in the operating system are cumbersome, which means that the installation either rewrites the program, modifies it as needed (if this is allowed under the terms of the contract), or purchases a new software package. Many of the software packages sold today offer improvements over already-existing software packages.

The experience of a relatively small company serves as an illustration. This example is duplicated in concept across the country. For the company to backup its records, four and a half hours were spent each night, resulting with six reels of tape. With the new backup system purchased, the backup tape preparation takes less than a half an hour a night and uses only one reel of tape.

FIGURE 9.2(a) **Magnetic tape drive.**

is possible to store over 270 million bytes on one magnetic tape reel. A **tape drive,** as shown in Figure 9.2(a) is a device used for holding the magnetic tape as the data is read or written on a tape. Figure 9.2(b) shows a schematic of the tape being fed from a file reel to a take-up reel. The vacuum columns, the long narrow columns, are used on most tape drives to ease the tension placed on tape when the tape starts and stops.

Magnetic tape is coated with a dust-like substance on one side. These small particles can be shuffled to either a magnetized state (recorded as a 1) or a nonmagnetized state (recorded as a 0).

Recall from Chapter 6 that 0s and 1s are stored on a diskette similar to a string of beads; the bits are stored in concentric circles called **tracks.** Since magnetic tape is long and narrow, a character's coding is stored in columns which run the width of the tape. Chapter 7 discussed how a character is coded using 6, 7, or 8 bits. Each bit in a byte is coded on a track on magnetic tape. Tracks run the length of the tape. Tapes are either seven-track or nine-track. A seven-track tape, as shown in Figure 9.3(a), uses BCDIC, while a nine-track tape uses EBCDIC or ASCII.

The most popular densities are from 800 up to 6,250 bytes per inch (bpi). The faster each column passes under the read-write head, the higher the density. To give you some idea of how fast the tape moves, when a tape is written at 1,600 bpi, about 200 inches of magnetic tape is passing per second under the read-write head. Once tape is written in a certain density, it must be read in that

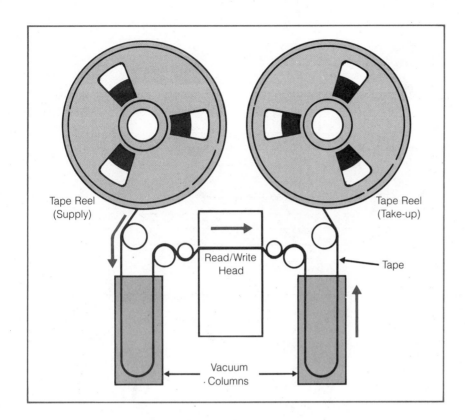

FIGURE 9.2(b)
Schematic of magnetic tape drive.

density; otherwise, invalid characters are detected, and processing stops.

Figure 9.3(b) shows a protective ring that is placed in the back of a tape reel when a file is to be written. Without a protective ring, no data can be written on a tape. This safeguard is used for protecting data from a programmer's incorrect usage of the word *write* (rather than *read*).

CHECKPOINT **Can you:**

Tell how long and how wide magnetic tape is?

Tell what the greatest density is?

Tell why tracks are used and how many there are?

Tell the purpose of using a file protective ring in the back of the reel?

TYPES OF RECORDS

Records can be grouped into two types: logical records and physical records. Recall the discussion about logical and physical in Chapter 2; logical was defined as how we perceive something to be; physical as how it truly is. A **logical record** is information that is defined in terms of its content rather than its physical

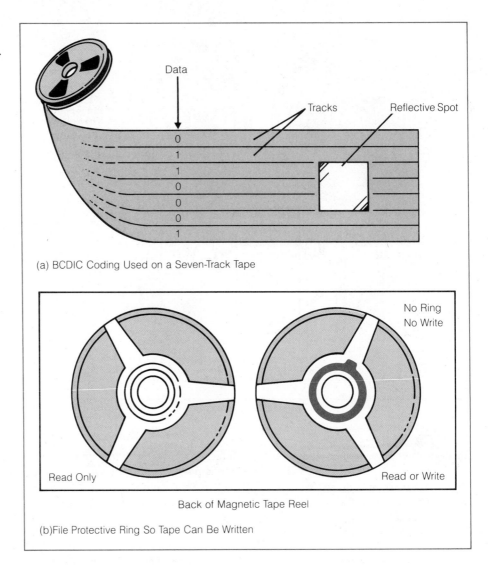

(a) BCDIC Coding Used on a Seven-Track Tape

(b)File Protective Ring So Tape Can Be Written

attributes. A logical record relates to data about one person, one inventory item, one charge account, and so on. For efficient reading and writing of records in secondary storage, five or six logical records are usually grouped together to form a **physical record.** The number of logical records grouped together depends upon the number of characters in each logical record. Generally, there is no set rule as to how many or how few characters are stored in a logical record. The length of the record varies according to the job being processed and sometimes varies in the same processing job, as shown in Figure 9.4. The logical record and physical record in this example are the same; the word length (the number of bytes in each logical record) is considered as **variable word length.** Figure 9.5 shows that logical records can be of equal length or **fixed word length** within a file. Variable word length records use primary storage more efficiently than fixed word

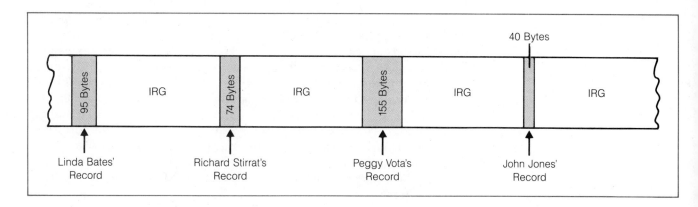

length records. The welfare records of San Francisco are set up as variable word length records since there is such diversity as to the number of dependents listed per welfare recipient.

FIGURE 9.4
Variable word-length records.

FORMAT OF RECORDS

The question becomes how can logical records be stored on a magnetic tape? If we think of each logical record as being like a box, assuming we had many boxes, we could lay each one out directly next to each other, end to end. If we had to transport these many boxes into another room we would find that we could not carry all of them at one time. A type of separator would be needed to divide them into groups (physical records). It would be far easier to move them in groups of five or six at a time, for example, than to move them one by one.

FIGURE 9.5
Fixed word-length records for blocked and unblocked records.

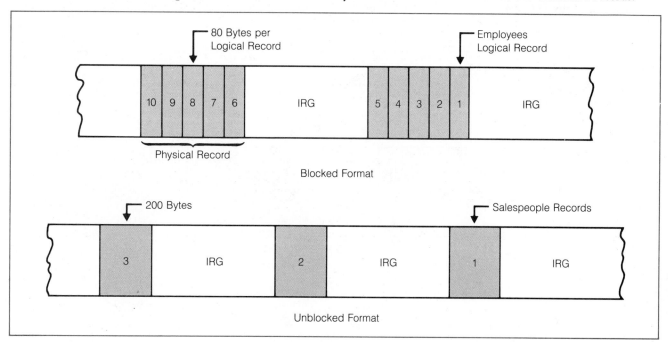

Logical records are arranged using blocked or unblocked records. Figure 9.5 also shows that logical records can be grouped together for faster processing. This grouping results in **blocked records.** The question becomes how can the computer tell where a physical record begins and ends? A type of data or a spacing is used by the computer for designating the area between physical records; this is called an **interrecord gap (IRG)** or **interblock gap (IBG).** Using Figures 9.4 and 9.5, the interrecord gap appears between physical records; the size of the interrecord gap is 0.6 inch long. Have you ever seen the way a magnetic tape reel turns then stops, turns then stops? The program is asking for data to be read, which makes the tape reel start moving. The stopping occurs because an interrecord gap is recognized by a computer, which then stops data transmission between primary storage and a magnetic tape drive.

The format appearing in Figure 9.6 illustrates **unblocked records** where logical records are separated from each other by the interrecord gap. Remember the starting and stopping just discussed regarding interrecord gaps? In Figure 9.6, since a logical record is read and is followed by an interrecord gap, the magnetic tape is continually starting and stopping. Notice how the read-write head is positioned halfway in the interrecord gap before John Jones's logical record is read; notice where the read-write head is positioned after the read of John Jones's data. If the interrecord gap is 0.6 of an inch long, 0.3 is used for getting the magnetic tape to its proper speed before transmission of data occurs. The other 0.3 of an inch after the logical record is read is used for stopping the magnetic tape. Each time a physical record is read, there is a type of internal checking for an interrecord gap. Once the record is read, data transmission from the secondary storage medium to primary storage is terminated. The transmitted data that is sent to primary storage is stored in a **workarea,** an area set aside by the programmer's instructions for holding the data in a logical record. Unblocked records require greater processing time on a computer since more time is required to transfer the data contained in the records from secondary storage to primary storage or from primary storage to secondary storage.

FIGURE 9.6
The tape stops halfway in the interrecord gap.

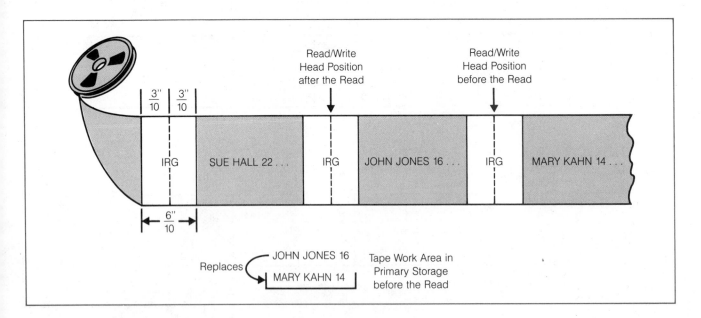

Consider the situation where a logical record is 800 bytes. Assume that the density of the tape—the number of bytes written per inch of tape—is 1600 bpi. Each interrecord gap would be 0.6 inch long. For each unblocked record, the actual data would be stored in one-half linear inch of magnetic tape.

When logical records are blocked, less storage space is used, faster transfer speed is achieved, and the amount of time needed to use a computer is reduced. Blocked records use fewer interrecord gaps; these gaps take up a large area of the magnetic tape if it is not efficiently formatted.

Using the same 800-byte logical record example and assuming that six logical records were grouped as a blocked record, the physical record would use 3 inches of magnetic tape to store the data. The interrecord gaps would use 0.3 inch before the physical record and 0.3 inch after it.

You might ask, how long does it take to transfer the data from magnetic tape to primary storage? The speed of the transfer of data, called the **data transfer rate** or **transfer rate,** depends upon the density of the tape and the speed with which the tape moves under the read-write head. If the tape moves at 200 inches per second (ips) and the density is 6,250 bpi, the data transfer rates of up to 1,250,000 bytes per second can be achieved.

CHECKPOINT **Can you:**

Explain the difference between logical and physical records?
Tell how logical records are formatted?

TYPES OF LABELS

The discussion of systems commands in Chapter 6 explained how a file was saved (created) through the use of the systems command SAVE and a file name created by the programmer. The file could be read at a later time by supplying the file name that was created.

When using magnetic tape, since each magnetic tape is a volume, each volume is given a type of identification (a number) to clearly identify it from other volumes. Assume that you have prepared a program that writes the original recording of data; this tape is considered the **grandfather tape.** The name of the tape file is STUDENT-ID. The data in the file is considered very important information; it must be kept for a year. Assume also that there are 1,752 students' data that are to be incorporated into this file; 1,752 logical records will exist. Also assume that the file is created on January 2, 1985. After the file is written on reel 66712 (the volume number), the tape might appear as shown in Figure 9.7.

The volume number that was assigned to this entire tape applies to all files using it. The **header label,** which precedes each file, includes the name of the file, the date the file was created, and the number of days the file is to be kept without being destroyed. All dates are recorded by the Julian calendar. The Julian date is composed of five digits—two for the year and three for the numbered day

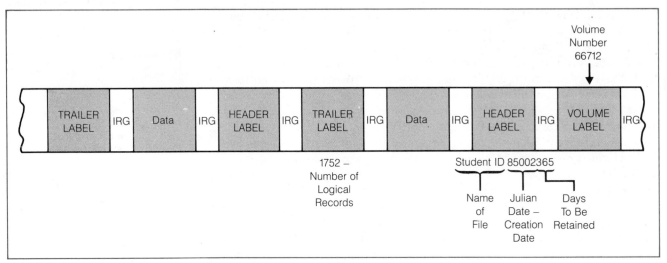

FIGURE 9.7 **Use of volume, header, and trailer labels.**

of the year. If the file was created on January 2, 1985, the Julian date is 85002. If the file was created on February 1, 1985, the Julian date is 85032 since February 1 is the 32nd day of the year.

A systems program that handles the file labelling and retrieval work in an operating system uses the current date (inputted each day), the creation date, and the retention period (days the file is to be retained without destroying data). The program determines if the contents of the tape can be just read. The retention period must be exceeded or met before any changes can be made to the contents of the tape. In our example in Figure 9.7, no data can be changed until one year after the creation date. This is a type of file protection to avoid losing data that must be kept intact.

The **trailer label** is often used by programmers for storing some batch totals accumulated throughout the processing. Examples could be the number of logical records written in the file or the total dollars accumulated for all salesmen's records stored in the file.

The volume label identifies a tape from all others. This label is used by a computer operator or tape librarian in locating a tape in the tape library. Figure 9.8 shows an automated tape library where the system stores and accesses data on about 8,000 magnetic tapes. The data is accessible in less than 20 seconds.

CHECKPOINT **Can you:**

Identify the various labels used for magnetic tape?

Tell the purpose of each?

FIGURE 9.8 Automated tape library. 8,000 tapes can be accessed and data can be accessed in less than 20 seconds.

MAGNETIC DISK

There are applications that require immediate updating and handling of records at a company. In light of such needs, magnetic disk has become the most popular of all secondary storage devices, for it allows direct access. That is, magnetic disk is a **direct-access storage device (DASD)**; a user can access data for a specific record on magnetic disk directly, without reading the previous records in the file.

Given the current business climate, such a feature is essential. Information must be processed as it is needed by management so that split-second decisions can be accurately made. Some information has a higher priority than other data and, therefore, requires immediate processing. Some data requires current, up-to-date figures that must be available at a moment's notice. Some jobs have such a large volume of data that it is sometimes easier to process the data as it is received rather than to batch it.

PHYSICAL PROPERTIES

Magnetic disks are large flat platters that are usually made of aluminum. Many platters are generally mounted as one unit; these are referred to as a **disk pack.** A disk pack has read-write heads that function much like a needle on a record player with a major difference—read-write heads do not physically touch a magnetic disk platter.

Many disk packs are removable. A removable disk pack, as shown in Figure 9.9, can be taken from a disk drive and replaced with another disk pack. A

FIGURE 9.9
Removable disk packs.

computer operator is instructed by programmer's instructions as to the disk pack that is to be mounted for a specific application. When a disk pack is mounted in the drive, its platters rotate at a rate of approximately 3,600 revolutions per second.

The number of platters included in a disk pack varies with equipment. In the mid-1960s six platters with ten recording sides were commonly used; two surfaces in the disk pack were not usable for recording data. In the 1970s eleven platters and twenty recording sides were commonly used. Today, with the latest developed technology (to be discussed shortly), as few as two platters may be used, with four recording sides yielding increased storage capacity.

Data on disk is stored in **tracks,** which are concentric in shape as they are for a diskette. Refer to Figure 9.10. Each track is numbered, beginning with 0. Disks manufactured in the late 1960s had 200 usable tracks per platter. Disks manufactured in 1980 had 800 tracks per inch; in 1984 there are 1,200 tracks per inch. Technology currently under development plans for 2,000 tracks per inch; this disk equipment is scheduled for release in 1985 or 1986.

The same concepts of blocked and unblocked records are used on magnetic disk as on magnetic tape. Interrecord gaps separate the physical records on a disk but, unlike magnetic tape, which stopped when an interrecord gap was encountered, magnetic disk revolutions continue at a constant rate.

Volume, header, and trailer labels are also used; their function is the same as was discussed in the magnetic tape discussion.

CHECKPOINT **Can you:**

Identify some of the physical properties of magnetic disk?

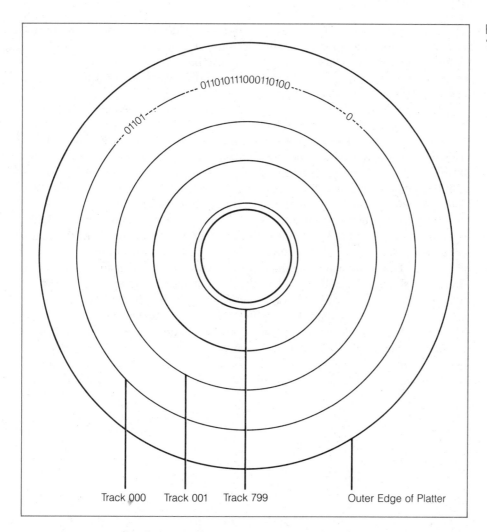

FIGURE 9.10
Tracks on a platter.

Addressing Scheme

To read or write just the desired logical record, a direct-access storage device requires an addressing scheme which references the cylinder, recording surface, and record number. Other equipment uses a sector number and a block number. Let us briefly look into how addressing is achieved.

Cylinder Method of Addressing

If there are twenty recording surfaces in a disk pack, there are then twenty tracks numbered 000, twenty tracks numbered 001, twenty tracks numbered 002, and so on. All the read-write heads are positioned on an access arm assembly. The access arm assembly positions all read-write heads on the same track on all platters. All tracks having the same track number are referred to as a **cylinder.** All tracks

010 are referred to as cylinder 010, for example. The correct positioning of the read-write heads is accomplished through the use of the **servo tracks** which are written magnetically on the bottom side of the bottom platter of the disk pack. These servo tracks are prerecorded by the manufacturer and point to any track on the platter.

Refer to figure 9.11. Notice how the disk access arm assembly, which is stationary, moves all the read-write heads into the same track position on all recording surfaces. The positioning of the read-write heads on the same track takes the longest period of time; this movement of the read-write heads to the desired cylinder is called **seek time.** Once the read-write heads are correctly positioned on the desired cylinder, one read-write head merely is turned on (called **head selection**), allowing any of the different tracks to be read or written without repositioning the read-write heads. The disks are rotating at approximately 3,600 revolutions per minute. There is **rotational delay** or **latency** involved; the read-write heads wait for the disk to turn and pass the desired data under the read-write head. The read-write head that is turned on senses the data for transmission to primary storage. If another track in the same cylinder is to be read or written, head selection is accomplished in the speed with which light travels.

Using the cylinder method, a cylinder number, a recording surface, and a record number provide an address for directly locating a logical record. Other equipment uses a cylinder number, a recording surface, and a sector number. A sector number refers to that portion of the platter that is divided electronically into wedges, much like slices of pie as previously discussed in Chapter 5.

FIGURE 9.11
Cylinder method of addressing.

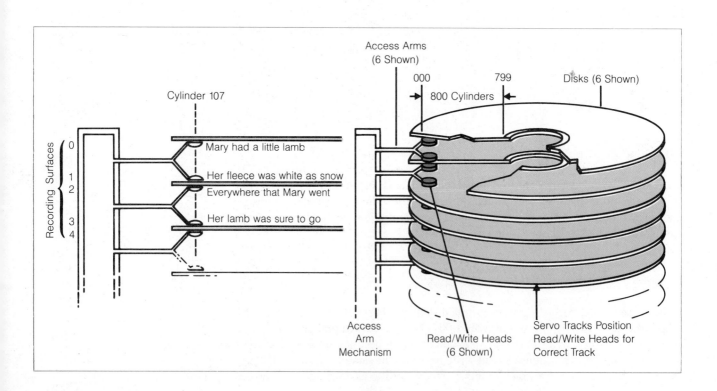

GALLERY 6

Secondary Storage

When secondary storage devices were first introduced with digital computers the emphasis was on greater storage capacity. However, today, constant improvements are needed to accommodate greater capacity, faster operating speeds, faster locating of the data, and less cost per bit to store the data.

The optical disk, recognized as the disk of the future, is shown on the following four pages. (Compliments of Optical Storage International—A joint venture of N. V. Philips and Control Data). The automated tape library is shown on the next four pages. (Courtesy of The Braegen Corporation). The automated tape library is increasing in use in installations which require massive volumes of data.

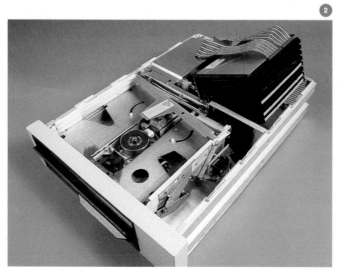

1. Laser Drive 1200 Digital Optical Disk Drive (19″ × 25″ × 6″) with 1 gigabyte per side of interchangeable 12″ diameter Laser Drive Media Cartridge. **2.** Laser Drive 1200 (top view with cover off and cartridge removed). Main modules of the modular design include the printed circuit card cage (rear), power supply (rear), base plate assembly (front), and laser carriage assembly inside of base plate. **3.** Laser Drive 1200 with 1 gigabyte per side. Digital Optical Disk is out of the cartridge which is inserted 70% into the base plate.

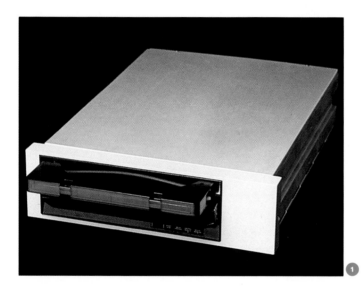

4. Close up of Laser Drive 1200 (top view) with cartridge in place over laser carriage assembly with optical disk removed from cartridge. **5.** Close up of Laser Carriage assembly with fine servo motor next to a quarter for size comparison. **6.** Assembled and unassembled Laser Drive 1200 laser pen with standard lead pencil for size comparison.
7. Semiconductor Laser Diode developed by N. V. Philips with pencil eraser for size comparison.

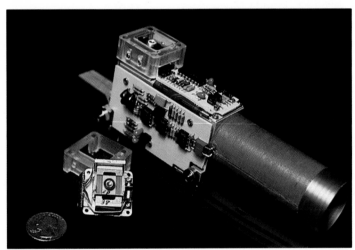

8

8. Laser Drive 1200 Digital Optical Disk (media only, no cartridge with reflected image in disk). Disk is semi translucent with mirror image characteristics.

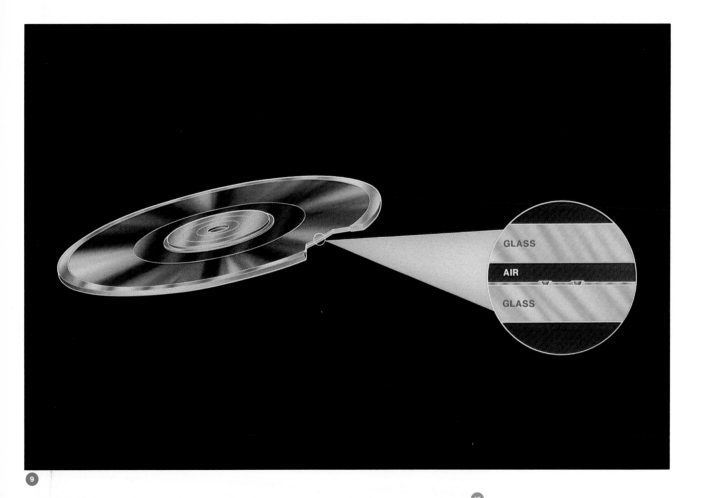

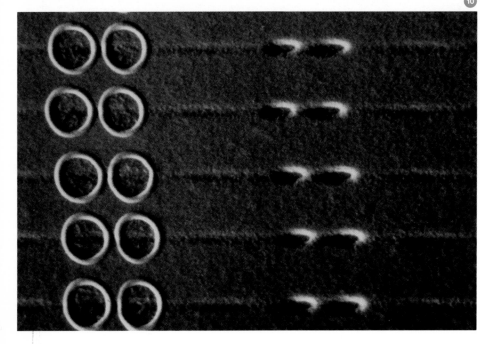

9. Laser Drive media consists of two glass substrates with a layer of tellurim alloy in which 1 micron holes are recorded (DRAW) and read with semiconductor laser. **10.** Actual cylindrical burn holes with timing modulations photographed on an electron microscope at 10,000× (holes are approximately 1 micron in diameter).

11. The automated tape library housing is about five feet wide and less than seven feet high. Each section is 67½ inches deep; many sections can be joined together. **12.** The automated tape library can store from 746 to more than 8,000 magnetic tape reels.

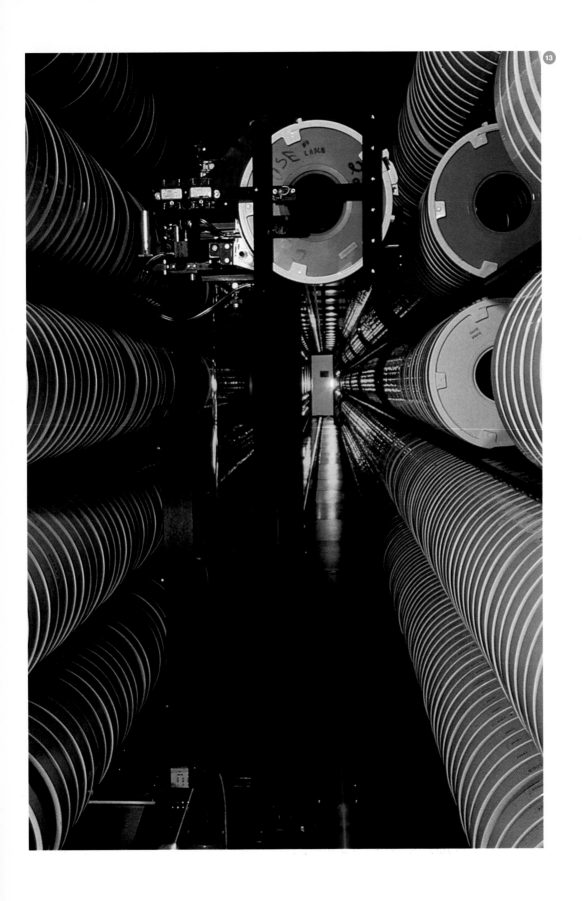

14

13. The reel selector mechanism moves at 100 inches per second. It selects a magnetic tape and mounts it on the station. About 150 tape mounts and dismounts can be performed in one hour. **14.** The reel station reads or writes the data onto magnetic tape. **15.** The manual operation of magnetic tape takes about 75 to 90 seconds to hang a tape in a tape drive. The automated tape library requires about 15 to 20 seconds.

15

16. The mass storage device resembles a honeycomb. Each data cartridge that appears in the honeycomb-like structure can be hand held. **17.** A disk pack. **18.** Here we see removable disk packs in their disk storage units.

CHECKPOINT **Can you:**

Explain how addressing is possible using the cylinder concept?
Identify seek time? Head selection? Rotational delay?

Ferrite and Thin-Film Read-Write Head Technologies

The read-write head technology of magnetic disk is divided into two groupings: the ferrite technology and the thin-film technology. All magnetic disk read-write heads manufactured before 1979 use the ferrite technology; both thin-film read-write heads and ferrite read-write heads are being manufactured today.

The ferrite technology uses magnetic disks that are fourteen inches in diameter and have a head disk assembly (HDA) where the read-write heads are located. The surface of the disk is metallic oxide particles. The thickness of the disk has been over the years reduced to 35 millionths of an inch. Oxide particles on the disk must be polished to a smoothness smaller than the diameter of human hair for efficient storing and recalling of data. The read-write head is used for either magnetizing (writing) or sensing (reading) data stored on tracks on the platter.

The oldest type of disk hardware, used in about 1965, had the aluminum substrate with the read-write head disk assembly positioned over the disk pack. The storage capacity was 7.25 megabytes; the access time was about 50 milliseconds (MS). Because the disks were rotating very fast, the air generated from the disk movement theoretically kept the read-write head from touching the disk. Users placed more demands on disks when on-line processing increased in popularity. Manufacturers, to meet these increased hardware requirements, had to produce read-write heads having higher density; more bits had to be stored in a smaller circumference area of the disk. Also, the number of tracks had to be positioned closer together. These efforts advanced the technology, and the Winchester drives were introduced, which had the disk and read-write head fixed in a dustproof, contamination-free enclosure. The Winchester drive, often known as **Winchester technology,** is shown in Figure 9.12(a). Some of the larger disk storage units are called **data modules.** The shape of the ferrite read-write head disk assembly was designed differently with these Winchester drives; the end was cut at an angle rather in the previously used 90-degree shape. A schematic of the Winchester technology is shown in Figure 9.12(b). The read-write head was then positioned within 20 millionths of an inch from the disk. Because the read-write heads could fly closer than previously (the sawed-off portion allowed a different pattern of air to circulate in helping to hold up the read-write heads from the disk), the number of bits on the tracks and the number of tracks were increased. Notice the coil shown in Figure 9.12(b); this coil is used for magnetizing (writing) or sensing (reading) the data on the desired tracks. Technological demands increased for greater **aerial density** (that area measured in a square inch of a disk surface). The maximum number of bits allowed with the ferrite technology was 9,000 bits per inch on a track because of the limitations of the magnetic field and other factors beyond the scope of this material.

FIGURE 9.12
The Winchester technology.
(a) Winchester drive. (b) Schematic
of the Winchester technology.

(a)

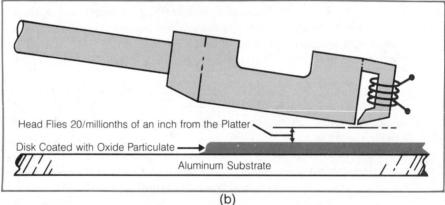

Head Flies 20/millionths of an inch from the Platter

Disk Coated with Oxide Particulate

Aluminum Substrate

(b)

Cache memory, an extremely fast semiconductor storage, was included in the disk drives for holding information recently updated or requested by the user. It was found that a high percentage of requests for data occurring in a period of time were often for the same file (data set). By using cache memory, the contents of which reflected the most current information, perhaps recently updated, the response could be sent to the requester using the contents stored in the cache memory wherever appropriate, rather than looking up the data on the disk. This disk storage also further reduced the access time; it, however, was not good enough.

The scene was set for a new technology, that is, the **thin-film technology,** in which various alloys of iron and nickel replace the ferrite material used. The changes bring about a lower flying head assembly. The thin-film heads have been developed and are currently being used. Figure 9.13 shows a woman looking through the microscope at the wafer that holds 500 sets (two are used in case one becomes inoperative) of the thin-film read-write heads. Figure 9.14 shows a close-up of the thin-film head. This thin-film head is mounted on a head assembly.

In 1984 at the time of this writing, 15,000 bits were stored per inch on a track; the aerial density was 12 million bits. Approximately in 1985, the new

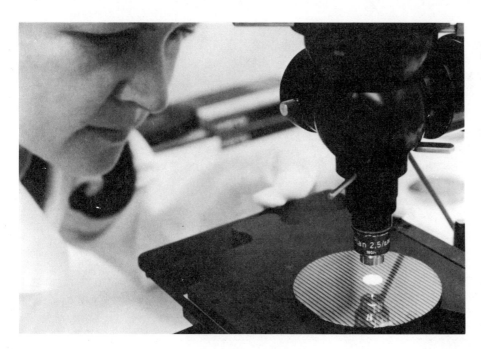

FIGURE 9.13
A woman inspects the integrated circuit wafer.

technology is gearing for 25,000 bits to the inch on a track with a track density of 2,000 tracks per inch. A contrast of the ferrite read-write head technology and the thin-film read-write head technology is revealing. A maximum of 9,000 bits can be stored to the inch on a track using ferrite technology; the upper limit is not known as yet on thin-film. Compare the storage capacity: 635 megabytes written in ferrite read-write heads to 1,260 megabytes for thin-film. As for access

FIGURE 9.14
Thin-film head close-up positioned on a dime.

TABLE 9.1.   **Approximate Capacities of Disk Storage Devices.**

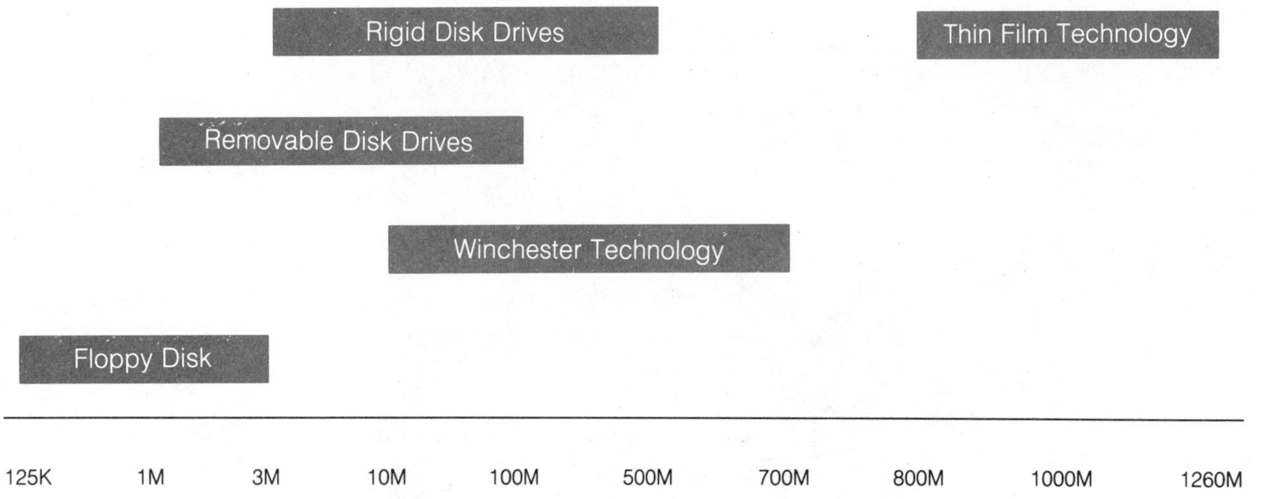

Rigid Disk Drives

Thin Film Technology

Removable Disk Drives

Winchester Technology

Floppy Disk

125K	1M	3M	10M	100M	500M	700M	800M	1000M	1260M

time, ferrite technology needs 22 to 27 milliseconds; thin-film technology's latest developed read-write heads need 16 milliseconds. The data transfer rate for ferrite technology is about 1.2 megabytes per second; thin-film technology transfers 3.0 megabytes per second. Today, even though this new technology is in its infancy, disks using the thin-film read-write heads technology can store 10 gigabytes using a floor space that allows storage of only 2.5 gigabytes with ferrite technology.

The thin-film technology will show rapid improvements when the new disk surface is developed. The disk is to be smoother and more rigid; its surface is being sputtered or sprayed on, making it more uniform and smoother than that available today. Also under development is Memorex's vertical or perpendicular recording method, for which vertical magnets are used for storing 200 million bits per square inch.

Refer to Table 9.1 for a summarization of the disk capacities.

CHECKPOINT **Can you:**

Differentiate between the ferrite and the thin-film read-write head technology?
Explain why Winchester drives became so widely used?

OPTICAL DISKS

Laser technology has also made its entrance into laserdisc or optical disk. **Optical disk,** as shown in Figure 9.15, is the disk of the future, opening up applications that were never thought possible. Its storage capacity is enormous. A fourteen-inch disk can store 100,000 pages of documents and an eight-inch disk can store about 10,000 letter-size documents. Near the end of 1984, the capability of storing data on both sides of the disk was announced, yielding approximately 2.0 gigabyte memory capacity.

Optical disk operates with a laser that does not burn micron-sized holes into a coating on its surface as often stated, but rather makes an indentation in the disk about a few millionths of an inch. The optical disk stores the data; any changes to the existing data require that a new area be used for the recording. It was not until April 1983, that the first erasable optical disk was announced. This announcement has not caused great change at this time since the concentration of

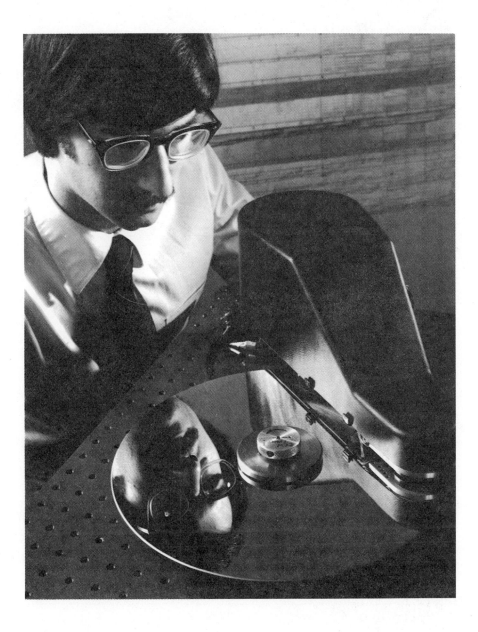

FIGURE 9.15
Optical disk.

Would you ever have use for 100,000 planetary images? The National Aeronautic and Space Administration (NASA) and the Jet Propulsion Laboratory seem to find uses. These two organizations have stored their planetary images on optical disk. Certainly an erasable storage is not critical for this type of data storage.

The Bureau of Census with its hundreds of thousands of magnetic tapes could certainly reduce the number by using optical disk as an archival storage. The Internal Revenue Service could store the many tax returns on optical disk.

What types of applications could be suggested for optical disks in public libraries? In schools? Evaluate if possible, whether these applications are new ones for computer usage or would be replacing the current disk storage.

the optical disk is on historical, or archival, storage. The optical disk is currently under development and probably will require several more years' work before it is perfected.

The primary use of an optical disk is archival. Primary commercial users are banks, libraries, and insurance companies. It is envisioned that this type of medium will be used by all of us in one form or another in the near future. We will carry megamemory cards on our person that record our medical history and may even include x-ray images. There can be about four pages of information recorded on a strip, the size of which is equivalent to the magnetic strip currently used on credit cards.

The future will probably find many optical disks being used in networks of

TABLE 9.2. **Comparison of Secondary Storage Devices**

DEVICE	PURPOSE	PHYSICAL SIZE (in Inches)	STORAGE CAPACITY
Optical Disk	Archival; mostly not reversible	14	2.0 gigabytes per platter
Magnetic Disk	On-line processing; two or more users use same disk simultaneously	1200 tracks per inch 14	Up to 1026M bytes
Floppy Disk	Used in small business	8	800K single sided
Floppy Disk	Used in micros, small business systems, word processing	5¼	Up to 1M double sided
Floppy Disk	Used in micros, for back up for Winchester drives and large capacity jobs	5¼	Up to 2M double sided
Micro Floppy	Used in intelligent instruments portable computers	3½	Up to 1M
Winchester Drives	Word processing, graphics, spreadsheets	8	Up to 140M
Hard Disks (Winchesters)	Word processing, graphics, spreadsheets; used on personal computers	5¼	About 10M
Magnetic Tape	Backup, utility I/O, initialization	½	6250 bytes per inch

computers to store all kinds of forms and records which can be examined and reproduced on many different peripherals in the network.

Table 9.2 shows the capacities and sizes of various disks and diskettes.

CHECKPOINT Can you:

Tell why optical disks will make an important contribution when perfected?

MASS STORAGE

Mass storage, as shown in Figure 9.16, combines features of magnetic tape and magnetic disk. It provides a company with an alternative to magnetic tape medium, but yields extremely fast access time.

PHYSICAL PROPERTIES

When using magnetic tape, the computer operator mounts (hangs) the tape, which might take a minute or much longer, depending upon how successful he or she is in finding the tape in the tape library. In the mass storage facility, however, no mounting of tapes is required by the operator; this is done automatically.

FIGURE 9.16
Mass storage.

The honeycomb-type structure houses the data cartridges; a close-up is shown in Figure 9.16. A magnetic tape is contained in a data cartridge. In this data cartridge up to 50 million bytes of data can be stored, with the magnetic tape being 770 inches long and 3 inches wide.

Mass storage operation can be compared to juke box operation. The desired data cartridge is pulled from its honeycomb-type structure, called **staging,** and the magnetic tape is then read or written. Depending upon the mass storage device used, there can be one or two read-write stations used for reading and loading the tape. Using the IBM mass storage system, the magnetic tape is read and the data is transferred to either a magnetic disk drive 3330 or 3350, which then transmits the data to primary storage.

The access time for this mass storage is about 20 milliseconds if the tape is already staged, or 1 to 2 minutes if the data cartridge is to be pulled from its staging. Although the mass storage can cost up to $500,000, it provides an extremely cheap storage medium per bit, since up to 472 billion bytes can be stored. Which companies use this type of storage medium? An insurance company's volume of data is enormous; it must record a great deal of data on every policyholder. This type of company can adequately use mass storage, as can banking institutions, which need a tremendous amount of storage for processing their clients' savings, checking, and credit cards accounts.

CHECKPOINT **Can you:**

Tell how magnetic disk and magnetic tape are used in mass storage?

Tell who would use this type of storage?

FILE ORGANIZATIONS

Suppose a friend has been taking many courses of various subject matters. The stacks of lecture notes are enormous. Last time you visited your friend, he was trying to find some way to place those lecture notes in an orderly fashion in a four-drawer file. Your friend is concerned that once he places the papers away in the four-drawer file, he will never be able to find notes on any given subject quickly.

One possible way is to organize all the lecture notes by subject taken, filing the individual papers by date within each course. The only trouble with this method is later locating the desired material; much searching would be required before the desired topic was located. Probably a search for data would begin at the beginning of the file and proceed in order until the desired material was found.

Another possible way to organize the notes is by course taken and then by subtitles under the course. These subtitles would form an index for ease in referencing the notes.

The third possible way would be to prepare a numbering system to identify the course taken, the material covered in that particular lecture, and the respective manilla folder number in which the lecture notes are placed (in essence, a key to the material).

Many variations to these plans could be prepared. Each of these plans, however, centers around filing the material by an application, which is, in this case, a course taken. The three file organizations (sequential, direct, and indexed sequential) used on secondary storage devices focus on the application as the means for file organization. The operating system includes a data management program that manages the various addressing schemes and file organizations.

To meet the different processing needs, files of data can be arranged using different methods. In the following discussion let us concentrate on the advantages and disadvantages and some particular uses of each file organization.

SEQUENTIAL FILE ORGANIZATION

A **sequential file** is a file organization in which the information is stored in a sequence, usually by key. The processing is done one record after the other. This is a popular file organization since much of industry's reports are generated in a sequential order.

A sequential file organization is used when capacity is limited since records can be blocked effectively without jeopardizing the processing. Some applications, such as payroll or student grades, work best with batching.

When the sequential file is created, its logical records must be in a sequence, which usually requires sorting. Two types of sequential files are illustrated for processing magnetic tape and magnetic disk.

Magnetic Tape Processing

Suppose that the Step-Ease Company has many sales people selling their shoes door to door in a wide geographical area. During the day the sales person records his or her sales on a terminal that is carried in an attaché case, often called a portable terminal. At the end of a work day, each sales person calls in orders to the computer located at the home office. According to company policy, each sales person must call in his or her orders during the time slot from 6 to 6:30 P.M. The company has a magnetic tape hung on a tape drive to accept these orders in random order. Refer to Figure 9.17. Scheduling is set up so that at 7 P.M. the magnetic tape that collected all the incoming orders is to be used as input to a sort program. Each record is read from the magnetic tape; the input file is read sequentially, one record right after the other. Sorting is performed. Refer to Figure 9.18. Figure 9.18 shows three workareas used in primary storage. The sorted transaction workarea is not used until the tape is to be written.

The sorted data are written on a new tape that is now in sequential order. Refer to Figure 9.19. This tape represents a sorted transaction tape since each order is considered a transaction (an event or a happening).

The sorted transaction tape for the day is to be used as input along with the last current master file, which records all the current sales (in dollars) by each sales person. The original recording of the master file (referred to as the **grand-**

FIGURE 9.17
Writing a magnetic tape in random order.

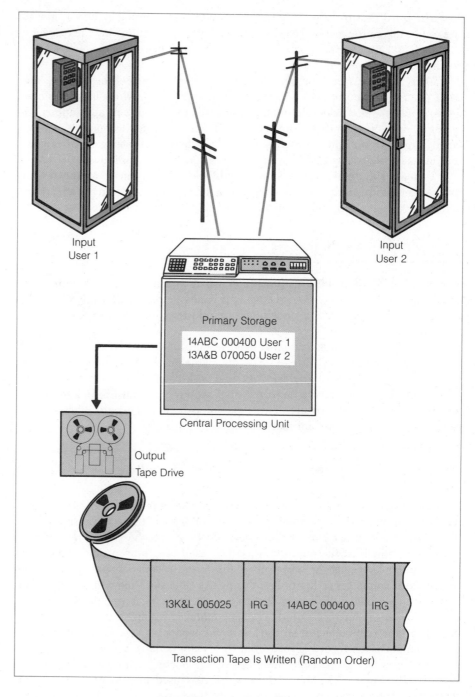

Input
User 1

Input
User 2

Primary Storage

14ABC 000400 User 1
13A&B 070050 User 2

Central Processing Unit

Output
Tape Drive

| 13K&L 005025 | IRG | 14ABC 000400 | IRG |

Transaction Tape Is Written (Random Order)

father tape) was created two days ago. Yesterday, the grandfather tape was used as input; the results from processing would be stored on the **father tape** as output. Each day a new master file is created (after the father comes the **son tape**). All previous tapes are kept for backup just in case a back-trail is needed. This back-trail is referred to as the **grandfather-father-son tape** concept.

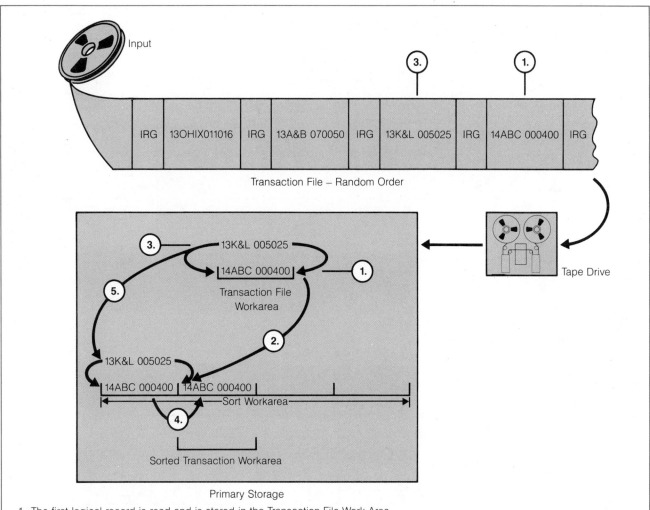

1. The first logical record is read and is stored in the Transaction File Work Area.
2. The first logical record is also stored in the Sort Work Area.
3. The second logical record is read, replacing the first logical record in the Transaction File Work Area.
4. A comparison is made between salesperson's numbers. Since 13 in the Transaction File Workarea is less than 14 in the Sort Workarea, the logical records must be rearranged in order.
5. The lowest salesperson's logical record is stored as the first logical record.

FIGURE 9.18   **Sorting the contents of magnetic tape.**

Refer to Figure 9.20, which uses the father tape and the sorted transaction tape as input. Notice how both input tapes are in the same sequence (sales person's numbers are in ascending order). Figure 9.20 shows three workareas used in primary storage: the master file father tape workarea, the sorted transaction tape workarea, and the master file son tape workarea. Only one logical record is ever stored in any of these three workareas at any one time.

This example illustrates batch processing; note that most records are updated in the newly created master file. Also notice that records in the master file not updated are written to the newly created master.

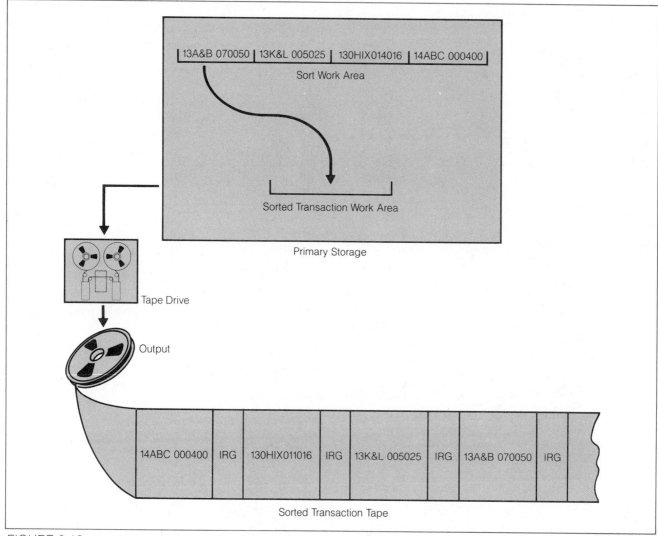

FIGURE 9.19 **Writing a sorted transaction tape.**

Key: For Figure 9.20

1. The first record of both files is read.
   A sales person's number of 13 in the sorted transaction tape is compared to a 12 in the father tape.
2. An unequal comparison results, requiring that the first record in the master file written to the new master file tape (son tape in this example).
3. The next record in the father tape is read. A comparison of salesperson numbers (13 versus 13) is performed. Since the comparison is equal adding of dollars sold is done.
4. The next record in the sorted transaction file is read. Since an equal comparison of salesperson numbers exists, adding is performed.
5. Same as step 4.
6. After the next record in the sorted transaction file is read, an unequal comparison of salesperson numbers exists. The previously calculated record's data must be prepared for output.
7. The data written to the son tape comes from two sources (Arithmetic-Logic Unit and the Master File Father Tape Workarea).
8. A new father tape record is read and compared with the salesperson's number in the sorted transaction tape. Since an equal comparison results, adding is performed.
9. The last logical record is processed. Since the end of file occurs on both input files, the last logical record is written to the output tape.

FIGURE 9.20   **Writing an updated master file.**

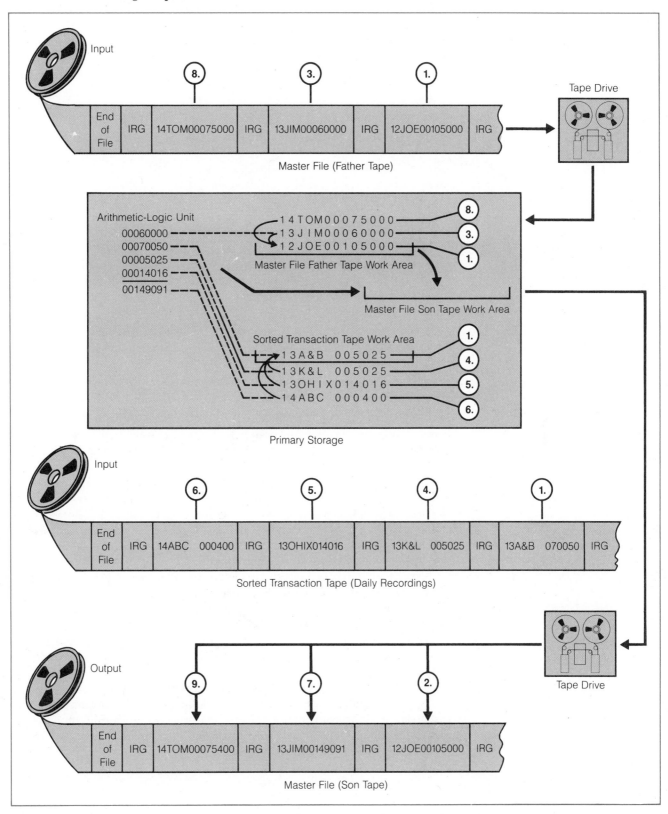

The reason this file organization works efficiently when most records are read is due to the fact that each record must be read to determine which data is stored there. The key is contained within the record.

To retrieve data from a sequential file requires reading sequentially through the file, one record after another, to find the desired record. If any additional records are to be included in the file, or any records updated or removed from the file, the entire file must be rewritten.

We can equate the processing of this file to the reading of a book. In a sequential file organization you must start at the first "page" (record) and read each before you get to the end of the "book" (file).

Magnetic Disk Processing

When a sequential file is written on magnetic disk, it is stored beginning with the first cylinder and the first recording surface that is assigned to the file and continues for as many cylinders as needed. When additions or deletions are to be made to the file, the entire file is rewritten. The same concepts are followed as discussed for magnetic tape.

DIRECT FILE ORGANIZATION

Many times industry needs immediate answers to questions, with these requests being in random order. Reading each logical record as is done in a sequential file organization is time consuming and becomes too costly for locating desired information that is in random order. For that reason a **direct file** organization is set up, which allows a user to locate just the required logical record. If a merchant, for example, asked the bank that handles credit card information about the status of a charge account, just that record is read by using the account number as the key for retrieving data in secondary storage. **Hashing,** or **randomizing,** uses a mathematical equation for arriving at an address in secondary storage, providing the cylinder and recording surface locations.

Records are unblocked in a direct file organization, resulting in an inefficient use of secondary storage since some areas of secondary storage are unused or other areas become crowded. When the file organization becomes cumbersome, it must be reorganized which is difficult to do. Refer to Figure 9.21.

Direct file organization is used where there are many additions and deletions that result from processing. The number of additions and deletions determine the **volatility** of the file. When volatility is high, direct file organization works best since the file does not require rewriting as in sequential organization.

To adapt our Step-Ease Company example to a direct file organization, the transmission of the record from a sales person would automatically be used for updating the direct file. Whenever a record were to be retrieved, the key would be randomized to find the desired record.

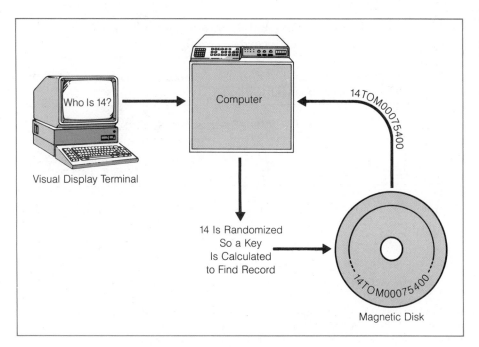

FIGURE 9.21
A key is calculated by software to locate desired record.

INDEXED SEQUENTIAL FILE ORGANIZATION

An indexed sequential file organization offers a user the capability of processing or inquiring about data in random order like the direct file organization, but it provides a more efficient use of secondary storage than the direct file. The indexed sequential file organization, however, needs pointers to be stored along with the data to be able to find the data randomly, and so is less efficient than sequential file organization. An indexed sequential file organization also offers the advantage of preparing reports that are generated in sequential order without requiring any sorting before printing.

Indexed sequential file organization uses indexes which act as pointers so a cylinder and a recording surface in the file can be referenced. The indices require storage space, so this is a disadvantage. When the program for creating an indexed sequential file is prepared, the programmer must identify which field or fields in the record are to be used as a key. The key then allows the systems software to later access the correct record in the file. These indexes (pointers), prepared when the file is created by the systems program, are created in a table where the highest key is noted, as shown in Table 9.3.

Think of the table that holds the indexes of the highest key on each cylinder and track in the disk pack as resembling a table of contents. By comparing the desired key versus the highest key in each track, the track holding the desired record can be located. Each record on that track is read sequentially until the record is located. Each time a user requests a record from the file, the table is referenced by the systems software.

An indexed sequential file can be used for retrieving or updating data in either a sequential or random order, depending upon the needs of a user. This file organization does not demand the rewriting of the entire file when additions

TABLE 9.3. **Data Management Program Uses a Table for Referencing Records.**

Data Management Software Stores Indexes on Magnetic Disk for Each Application in Indexed Sequential File

Example, Customer Transaction Records	
CYLINDER NUMBER	HIGHEST KEY FOR CUSTOMERS
100	6724
101	7358
102	8410
103	10000

Indexed sequential file:
1. Must be created in an order so indexes for the customer data can be prepared.
2. Can be updated in either a sequential order or in random order.
3. No rewriting is required for additions to the file or deletions from the file.
4. No randomizing is done as in direct file.
5. Key number of 9000 is located on cylinder #103.

TABLE 9.4. **Comparison of File Organizations.**

	ADVANTAGES	DISADVANTAGES	ACCESSING DESIRED RECORD	READ JUST DESIRED RECORD	READ FILE SEQUENTIALLY
Sequential	Easy to use; fast access when using batching	No record additions to already existing file; requires rewrite	Compare of key in storage versus desired record	No; direct access not available	Yes
Indexed sequential	Allows direct or sequential access to data; additions or deletions can be made without rewrite; can be used to process sequentially	Must be created sequentially; processing slow	Key is given; indexes point to storage area	yes	yes
Direct file	Processing is fast	File space inefficiently set up	Uses hashing; key is calculated or taken from certain positions of record number	yes	no

or deletions are made; the systems software handles this for the user by setting up indices to point to records that are added or deleted after the file is created.

An indexed sequential file organization is useful when sequentially outputted reports must be prepared daily or frequently. Consider a factory that produces detergent products. Many raw materials are used in these products. It is of utmost concern that sufficient quantities of all raw materials are available for use; otherwise, production will be halted. Each time a quantity of raw materials is removed from the warehouse, the raw materials amount on hand must be updated instantly, so that materials inventory always reflects the true amount. It is important that only the required raw material record be read and updated without the system having to examine the thousands of records of raw materials. At the end of the day, a current list is made available. The hard copy is far more usable if it is in a sequential raw material order. If a direct file organization were used, the manner of addressing would be similar except for the indexes. However, sorting would be required first so that the daily report could be outputted in sequential order.

In our Step-Ease Company example, if the firm used an indexed-sequential file organization, records would be updated as the sales person submitted the data. Only that record requiring any updating would be retrieved from secondary storage.

Table 9.4 shows a comparison of the three file organizations.

CHECKPOINT Can you:

Identify the three types of file organization used?

Differentiate among them as to how they are accessed?

Differentiate among them as to how additions to the file are handled?

SUMMARY

● Secondary storage, often called auxiliary storage, provides the needed storage capacity so that different jobs can be processed in primary storage.

● There are several different types of secondary storage devices, such as magnetic tape, magnetic disk, optical disk, and mass storage.

● Magnetic tape is a popular medium although it is not as popular as it was in the early 1970s.

● Magnetic tape is one-half inch wide and can be up to 2,400 feet long.

● Data is coded the width of the tape in columns. The number of columns depends upon the density of tape, which can be from 800 bytes per inch (bpi) to 6,250 bpi.

- Seven- or nine-track tapes are used where a track runs the length of the tape. EBCDIC and ASCII use a nine-track tape; BCDIC uses a seven-track tape.

- Appropriate data about one person or thing is recorded in a logical record.

- Many logical records can be grouped together, forming a physical record.

- When logical records are grouped together, they are referred to as blocked records. Other times one logical record is separate; this is an unblocked record.

- Interrecord gaps (IRGs) are used to separate physical records.

- When logical records in the file have the same number of bytes, the word length is fixed word length.

- The interrecord gap, or interblock gap (IBG), separates logical records from each other when the format is unblocked; and separates physical records from each other when the format is blocked.

- Logical records are usually blocked since less time is required for transferring the data to primary storage.

- The data transfer rate is that time required to send the data from primary storage to be written on the track or to transfer the sensed data from the track to primary storage. The data transfer rate depends upon the speed of the device and the density used for storing the bits.

- Each magnetic tape is a volume; hence it has a volume number to identify it.

- A header label is primarily used for recording the name of the file and the creation date.

- A trailer label is used for storing batch totals.

- A magnetic disk consists of a set of platters that are housed as one unit (disk pack). Some disk packs have only four recording sides, while others have twenty.

- Many disk packs are removable; that is, they can be taken from the disk drive and replaced with another disk pack.

- Data is stored in tracks which are concentric in shape. The number of tracks used on a disk varies, but 200 tracks were commonly used for equipment introduced in the mid-1960s; up to 1,200 tracks per inch are used with the latest developed thin-film technology.

- Because on-line processing demands fast access time, addressing of direct access storage devices (DASD) such as magnetic disks must be achieved quickly. Addressing is achieved by using a cylinder, recording surface, and record number. Other equipment uses a sector number and a block number or sector number and the key to locate the desired record.

- The cylinder addressing scheme requires that all tracks be numbered. All tracks numbered 0 on their recording sides make up cylinder 0.

- The optical disk is viewed by most experts as the disk of the future. It stores about 100 times more data than the currently developed ferrite disk technology.

Some experts view the applications as being those not currently on computer storage.

● Magnetic disk provides direct access, and hence, fast access time, and large capacity. Its disadvantage is it currently is not the fastest and the largest storage medium.

● Mass storage uses cartridges that contain magnetic tape. Each cartridge can hold about 770 inches of magnetic tape. The maximum storage capacity is 472 billion characters for the entire device.

● There are three types of file organizations: sequential, direct, and indexed sequential.

● The sequential file organization stores records in a set order. When the file is to be read, the first logical record is read, then the next logical record, then the following logical record.

● When new records are to be added to the already existing sequential file, another file is created.

● When records are to be deleted from the already existing sequential file, another file is created.

● A direct file organization uses a key for locating the desired record.

● The direct file organization stores data so that it can be retrieved in any order. It does not require sequential processing or creation of a new file when there are any additions or deletions.

● The direct file works best with requests that require an immediate answer and are in no particular order.

● The number of additions and deletions made to a file determine its volatility.

● The indexed sequential file organization is a combination of both the sequential and direct file organizations. Its use avoids the disadvantages of the sequential file organization.

STUDY GUIDE

REVIEW OF TERMINOLOGY

The following terminology was discussed in this chapter:

access time	magnetic disk
aerial density	magnetic tape
blocked records	mass storage
cache memory	optical disk
cylinder	physical record
data modules	randomizing
data transfer rate	rotational delay
direct-access storage device (DASD)	seek time
	sequential file
direct file	servo tracks
disk pack	son tape
father tape	staging
fixed word length	tape drive
grandfather-father-son tape	thin-film technology
	tracks
grandfather tape	trailer label
hashing	transfer rate
head selection	unblocked records
header label	variable word length
indexed sequential file	volatility
interblock gap (IBG)	Winchester technology
interrecord gap (IRG)	workarea
logical record	

MULTIPLE CHOICE

Circle the letter of the item that correctly completes a statement.

1. Which storage device is a combination of two of the more popular types of secondary storage:
   - *a*. magnetic tape
   - *b*. magnetic disk
   - *c*. optical disk
   - *d*. mass storage
   - *e*. Winchester technology

2. The time used from the sending of a request for information until it is received is referred to as:
   - *a*. access time
   - *b*. transfer time
   - *c*. direct access
   - *d*. volatility
   - *e*. fixed block architecture

3. The data fields making up facts about an event or a person are referred to as:
   - *a*. a physical record
   - *b*. blocked records
   - *c*. an unblocked record
   - *d*. a logical record
   - *e*. staging

4. Spacing used between logical records is called:
   - *a*. an inter block
   - *b*. an interrecord gap
   - *c*. a physical record
   - *d*. an unblocked record
   - *e*. a channel

5. When logical records contain different numbers of characters, the word length is:
   - *a*. blocked
   - *b*. unblocked
   - *c*. variable
   - *d*. fixed
   - *e*. fixed blocked architecture

6. A number of logical records are grouped together to form:
   - *a*. unblocked records
   - *b*. variable word length
   - *c*. fixed word length
   - *d*. a physical record
   - *e*. a track

7. Which type of format is most inefficient:
   - *a*. unblocked records
   - *b*. blocked records
   - *c*. actuator
   - *d*. high volatility
   - *e*. staging

8. The density of the tape and the speed with which the tape moves is called the:
   - *a*. access time
   - *b*. transfer rate
   - *c*. length of the header and trailer labels
   - *d*. servo tracks
   - *e*. cylinder, track, and sector number

9. Hard disk is often referred to as:
   - *a*. magnetic disk
   - *b*. Winchester technology
   - *c*. mass storage
   - *d*. actuator
   - *e*. disk pack

10. The many tracks on a disk pack that have the same track number are referred to as:
    - *a*. a servo track
    - *b*. a transfer rate
    - *c*. ferrite technology
    - *d*. a cylinder
    - *e*. a physical record

11. The newest type of disk read-write heads use the:
    - *a*. ferrite technology
    - *b*. thin-film technology
    - *c*. track
    - *d*. randomizing method only
    - *e*. hashing method only

12. When records are processed sequentially one directly after the other, the file organization can never be:
    a. a direct file
    b. a sequential file
    c. an indexed sequential file
    d. a direct-access storage device
    e. a fixed block architecture

13. When records can be processed either in order or randomly, their file organization is:
    a. direct
    b. sequential
    c. indexed sequential
    d. randomizing
    e. none of these

14. New records are to be added to a file, requiring that the entire file be rewritten; the file organization used is:
    a. direct
    b. sequential
    c. indexed sequential
    d. fixed block architecture
    e. data management

15. Which file organization uses pointers in a table so a record can be referenced directly:
    a. direct
    b. sequential
    c. indexed sequential
    d. fixed block architecture
    e. none of these

16. Which file organization uses calculations to arrive at the address:
    a. direct
    b. sequential
    c. indexed sequential
    d. randomizing
    e. hashing

17. The positioning of the read-write heads on the correct cylinder is accomplished by the use of:
    a. a channel
    b. a track
    c. a servo track
    d. staging
    e. a hard disk

18. These run the entire length of magnetic tape:
    a. a track
    b. a file protective ring
    c. a servo track
    d. a label
    e. an interrecord gap

19. This is used in the back of magnetic tape to prevent any destroying of the contents:
    a. a channel
    b. a file protective ring
    c. a servo track
    d. a label
    e. an interrecord gap

20. Its storage capacity is in hundreds of billions of characters:
    a. magnetic disk
    b. magnetic tape
    c. mass storage
    d. hard disk
    e. Winchester technology

TRUE/FALSE QUESTIONS

1. **T/F** The optical disk is the latest developed technology in secondary storage.
2. **T/F** Access time refers to the time it takes for the data to be located once the request is given.
3. **T/F** A company selects secondary storage devices by considering cost per bit, access time, and capacity.
4. **T/F** The programmer determines how many characters are to be in a logical record.
5. **T/F** The number of logical records grouped together is never greater than 10.
6. **T/F** The programmer instructs the computer as to where the interrecord gap is to be written and the length of it.
7. **T/F** An interrecord gap is always less than one inch long.
8. **T/F** It is the interrecord gap on the magnetic disk that makes the disk start and stop, start and stop.
9. **T/F** Winchester technology disks are less reliable than conventional disk drives.
10. **T/F** Data is stored in tracks on magnetic disk, which are equivalent to concentric circles.
11. **T/F** All the tracks numbered 147, belong to cylinder 147.
12. **T/F** The programmer cannot use the servo tracks for storing data.
13. **T/F** The mass storage facility is really made up of a magnetic disk system and four magnetic tapes.
14. **T/F** Sequential file organizations are best for applications that require batching.
15. **T/F** Indexed sequential file organization can be updated sequentially or randomly.
16. **T/F** The direct file organization easily handles requests for retrieving and storing data in random order.

REVIEW QUESTIONS

1. Why is secondary storage so named? What is another name for it?
2. What three factors are used in selecting a secondary storage device?
3. What are tracks on magnetic tape? How many are there?
4. What is the highest density of characters that can be stored on one inch of magnetic tape?
5. Why do the magnetic tape reels start and stop, start and stop?
6. What is meant by blocked records? What is meant by unblocked records?
7. What is a track? A sector? A cylinder?
8. What is the difference between a logical record and a physical record? When can these be the same?
9. Identify a header label and a trailer label. When is each used?
10. Explain how the grandfather-father-son tape concept works.
11. Although cache memory is an internal memory, why was it mentioned with magnetic disks?
12. What is the difference between variable word length and fixed word length?
13. What is a workarea? Can there be more workareas than one when secondary storage is being used? Explain your answer.
14. What is transfer rate? Is it the same as access time? Explain your answer.

DISCUSSION QUESTIONS

1. What is the most important advantage and disadvantage of each secondary storage device?
2. Why is the cylinder concept important for use on direct access storage devices?
3. Explain why the ferrite technology has given way to thin-film technology used on magnetic disks.
4. Explain why the mass storage device acts similar to a juke box in retrieving data.
5. Explain how and why the magnetic tape uses the file protective ring.
6. Differentiate among the file organizations. Explain when each might be used.

People in Computing

Gary Kildall

COMPANY
Digital Research Inc.

POSITION
Chairman of the Board

EDUCATIONAL BACKGROUND
B.S., M.S., and Ph.D. in Computer Science, University of Washington

Some of my recent work at Digital Research Inc. has centered around the laserdisc technology.

Videodiscs are an entertainment device in many cases although there are other applications such as educational and archival uses. The sales of those discs has got to be based on the material that is recorded on them, not the way that it is recorded or the fact that you are able to record gigabytes of information. Much of the information must be good material for people to be interested in buying and that will lead to success in the videodisc industry.

Videodiscs can be interactive through a remote control unit. That is how we are going to promote our first product called *Vidlink* that will give a very low cost solution to a computer-controlled interactive videodisc situation. *Vidlink* is a very

Courtesy of Sybex Pioneer Days

simple solution; all we have is a very inexpensive computer system, a Commodore, controlling a videodisc player that lets you switch between the computer-generated videodisc and output. This will lead to the first level of applications. The intention is to have this system grow to the point where we have digital information recorded on a videodisc that is downloaded (transferred from the main central processing unit to the terminal). This information will contain such things as data structures for a big data base system, and programs to process the data bases. What we are seeing right now is an emergence of various standards promoted by companies like Pioneer and Phillips for Laserdiscs and JVC. In the case of the VHD standard they use AHD (Audio High Density) for digital storage. These standards are still evolving. We don't really have them yet, but it will be sometime in 1985 when we will see large amounts of digital information recorded on videodisc that is accessible to the computer market.

Where is this going to go? What real benefit are consumers going to see from videodisc controlled by computers? First of all, we have to have a notion that a videodisc is an archival or read-only kind of device. It stores lots and lots of information. Take, for example, still frames on videodisc where you can store 100,000 frames on a videodisc; this amounts to a stack of books about five or six feet high.

Let's take some examples of what you can do with that. You have random access to over 100,000 pages of visual information if you are storing just visual information. We are not even talking about storing digital information. One of the standard examples used is, if you have that much storage, you can put the entire *Encyclopedia Britannica* on a videodisc and have storage left over. If you do that, you can produce a very interesting data

base system that could be very useful in the home. You could simply have a query on your computer keyboard that states that you would like to find out all about the solar system of everything that was known, say between the years 1600 to 1900. From the result of that, you might show the planets and their names as a still frame. To add to that, you might have a little video segment where an actor, dressed up like Galileo, explains the Copernican theory. This adds a very dynamic dimension to a dictionary. You do not have to look up all the different pages for some topic since the data base program gets all those sections for you automatically. This shows you the information very succinctly and in a colorful way; it even gets some live action video which even explains it better. It makes a learning experience a lot of fun. There are many examples like that but, the important example is that the videodisc is being used as a read only device. You are reading from it much like reading from an encyclopedia; you do not write into it. Although we are going to see writable disks in the very near future (in fact there are writable disks right now called DRAW Disks), these probably will not be a very important consideration in the near future. The kinds of applications that we are going to see for videodiscs will be for read-only access. We don't need to write onto these disks anymore than you would write into your encyclopedia.

Videodiscs are not going to displace hard disks. A hard disk can coexist very nicely in the same computer system as a videodisc. The hard disk is more expensive on a bit by bit basis than the videodisc and it realistically cannot store any live video. We want to think of these things as being different types of storage devices. The applications that use videodiscs are going to be new and different.

10 Data Communications With Distributed Data Processing

OUTLINE

PROLOGUE

Tymshare Corporation of Palo Alto, California, has very sophisticated computer systems and software. The systems operate much faster than many computer systems. To prove how fast and efficient their systems are, they give this example.

A bank in London, England, transmits its daily data to Tymshare in Palo Alto at the end of its banking day. All record keeping for that bank is done in Palo Alto. Certainly you realize what volume of data a bank handles. When the bank closes in London, the data for the day is transmitted to Palo Alto. Tymshare updates all the necessary records and transmits all information to the bank before it opens the next morning. The amazing thing is that no one in London would ever dream that their bank balances were calculated in California.

HOW DOES IT DO THAT?

READ ON.

OBJECTIVES

After studying this chapter, you should be able to:

1. Identify the types of communication facilities.

2. Identify the types of bandwidth and the communication facilities that each uses.

3. Explain why modems or acoustic couplers are needed.

4. Differentiate between dial-up lines and leased lines.

5. List various ways of reducing telephone costs for a firm.

6. Differentiate among the various types of circuits.

7. Differentiate among the types of networks.

INTRODUCTION

The world of data communications is growing very fast and is in many instances an experimental technological field because the demand for communication facilities has almost surpassed the supply. Extensive studies are currently being conducted to find satisfactory substitutes for the readily available telephone. The impact of satellite communication is being felt in the data processing world, but for most consumers, heavy usage is near the late 1980s.

This chapter deals with the data communications industry's basic concepts. It explains how the available communication facilities operate and how they are used.

Consider a company's processing needs. An accounting clerk is using a terminal in the home office to inquire about the number of boxcars in a yard that contain cottonseed oil. A buyer in a buying department is using real-time processing to help make a purchase of some cottonseed oil; she makes queries about past quality of oil received from a supplier. A shipping clerk at a distant warehouse prepares the input for those shipping orders received today that are to be batch processed. Later in the evening each warehouse in this company will get a turn to transmit its processed data about shipments to its home office. A sales person receives a payment from a customer for a product just purchased, requiring that inventory be reduced by the quantity purchased. A programmer is busy making changes to an existing program due to a change in state taxation laws recently passed. A user is running programs that were purchased from a software company for handling sales forecasts based upon the state of the economy, the prevailing interest rates, and the market share figures that each product in the company presently has.

What links these points together? The worlds of data communications and data processing, once separate from each other, are now blending into one industry.

DATA COMMUNICATIONS AND TELEPROCESSING

Data communications is a transmission of data, pictures, or voice from one processing point to another over telephone, telegraph, or some other medium. When the transmission is over a long distance, it is called **telecommunications.** No processing is necessarily involved when data communications occur. For example, a file can be transferred from one point to another; this involves data communications. Or your transcripts might be transmitted from one college to another, assuming that the college computer systems are interconnected.

Not all processing is done at the main computer site (location); much computing is done remotely (from a location other than where the main central processing unit is located). Here is where the distinction is made between data communications and teleprocessing. **Teleprocessing** involves data processing and data communications. A teller in the bank that uses your passbook to make a withdrawal from your account and then transmits this withdrawal over miles to the main office is involved in teleprocessing. When BART (Bay Area Rapid Transit) in San Francisco transmits messages on its electronic message boards to the various stations telling of a train being late, or the arrival time of the next train and its destination, this only involves data communications although the messages are transmitted by computer equipment throughout the entire subway system. Some texts treat data communications and teleprocessing as the same. They are quite close in concept, but they do differ slightly.

In all data communications, regardless of the communication medium used, there is always a sender, a message, a receiver, and a communications facility. In Figure 10.1, these aspects of data communications are illustrated for the portable terminal used in grocery stores. In Figure 10.1(a) the portable terminal is used for entering the product number and the quantity to be ordered. The portable terminal sends sounds over the telephone line. The telephone receiver is placed in something that looks like a rubber cup. This is an **acoustic coupler,** which sends data by sounds and puts the sounds on speakers; in effect, it links a computer at one end of a telephone line with a peripheral device at the other. The transmission does not exceed 300 bits per second. Placing a telephone in an acoustic coupler permits the use of a regular telephone for data transmission. In Figure 10.1(b) the communication facility used is microwave which sends by radio signals to a computer located at the maximum 8 miles away.

Figure 10.1(c) shows a **facsimile (fax)** machine which uses an already prepared document at a sender site and generates paper copy at a receiver site. The fax machine scans the paper lengthwise, determining where markings are placed. If the original that you are using for transmission contains smudges or dirty spots, these are transmitted along with the message that was intended for transmission. How embarrassing when you explain the coffee stain! No acoustic coupler is needed for the data transmission as the facsimile machine has the necessary hardware already wired inside it for transmitting the data to a computer. The terminal is considered as being hardwired.

COMMUNICATION FACILITIES

On-line processing has increased the demand for telecommunications. A user has several choices as to the kind of **communication facility** (the means by which data communications can be made easier) that can be used for the transmission of data, pictures, or voice. These are the telegraph, microwave, satellites, or telephone.

TYPES OF FACILITIES

Telegraph is that service provided by Western Union for the sending of messages over wire; no voice transmission occurs. The number of bits per second that can be transmitted—up to 300 bits per second—is very slow when compared to other communication facility speeds, but the telegraph offers the advantage of low cost.

Western Union has a nationwide network for data communications called **Telex.** To use this service, all you need is a terminal, an acoustic coupler, and a telephone line. When you wish to transmit data to some location, you dial the number of the desired location and the Telex exchange equipment automatically makes the direct connection for you.

Microwave is radio transmission. The advantage of using microwave is that no wires or cables have to be strung between points. Microwave has been used for many years by American Telephone & Telegraph (AT&T) for its long distance calls. Any calls requiring transmission over 500 miles or any calls over mountainous

(a)

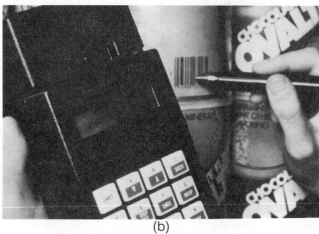

(b)

(c)

FIGURE 10.1

Terminals transmit messages. (a) Portable terminals used in grocery stores with acoustic coupler. (b) Portable terminals used with microwave. (c) Facsimile machine.

FIGURE 10.2   **Microwave station.**

WHAT'S NEW

**Some Light
On The Subject**

The cities of Boston, New York, Philadelphia, Washington, and Richmond have one thing in common: a fiber optics network, the first of its kind. On two thin strands of glass, 1,300 simultaneous telephone conversations can be carried on. A regular telephone wire carries only 24 conversations.

AT&T plans to include other cities in the United States in its network. AT&T is not the only company using fiber optics; MCI Communications Corporation has planned a network to extend from Washington to New York.

areas travel by microwave. Although microwave was introduced in the 1940s, terrestrial (earth) microwave began only in the 1950s. AT&T, Microwave Communications Inc. (MCI), and Western Union are the large users of microwave; they have replaced coaxial cable with the more economical microwave. Electrical signals may travel up to 100,000 miles per second over microwave radio paths. Approximately 45 megabits per second can be transmitted.

There is a problem, however, in using microwave transmission if some large structure is constructed in the path along which the radio signals are being beamed. As with a flashlight beam aimed at an object, the microwave beams are blocked when something large gets in the way, and the signals do not get to their desired target. Refer to Figure 10.2.

Satellites are used for large volume data transmission and for broadcasting. The satellites may be from 100 miles to 65,000 miles above the earth's surface. The ones closer to earth detect storms, survey land, and take photos. The satellites 65,000 miles high are used for detecting nuclear explosions in space and for infrared detection of missile launches. A **geosynchronous satellite** has an altitude of about 22,300 miles and is the specific type designated for data transmission. It orbits the earth in about twenty-four hours and therefore appears to be standing still; since they are synchronized with the earth, tracking of these satellites is unnecessary. The geosynchronous satellite aims narrow beams of concentrated microwave energy at certain earth stations, as shown in Figure 10.3. An antenna is aimed electronically at the satellite and electronic transmission occurs in a few microseconds.

A satellite has a wing span of about twenty feet but the size of a satellite itself is about the size of one or two kitchen tables. Refer to Figure 10.4. Computers are used to control the environment of a satellite for any one of three purposes: (1) to orient a satellite in respect to the sun for heating and cooling; (2) to orient

The telephone company uses re-peaters, those little black boxes that hang on telephone poles usu-ally positioned near railroad tracks, for the sending of voice or data over the telephone line. Posi-tioned about a mile apart, the re-peaters increase the signal so that the transmission can occur.

Amateur radio enthusiasts are using the repeaters in order to in-crease their range so that others may receive the digital signals from their computers. A ham connects his or her computer to the radio equipment which then transmits digital signals. The repeater re-ceives the radio signals and for-wards them on to the next repeat-er.

In 1984, the hams launched a satellite that is in an orbit lower than that of the geosynchronous satellites. Since the satellite moves quickly around the earth, a ground transmitter receives a signal for only fifteen minutes as it passes overhead. The advantage here is that the satellite provides elec-tronic mail ability around the world, transmitting mail messages as it passes over each transmitter lo-cation.

FIGURE 10.3   **Satellites use earth stations.**

solar cells to get power to change the direction; (3) and to fire the engines when a satellite is to be moved.

When data is transmitted, a satellite acts as a relay station, reading signals and forwarding them to the microwave (earth) station. Electronic pulses are usually exchanged at a rate of 63 megabits per second.

Many ventures are being undertaken to provide other communication facil-ities than the telephone. **Satellite Business Systems (SBS)** is a joint Comsat, IBM, and Aetna Casualty venture. The satellite, launched by the space shuttle in 1983, transmits voice, data, facsimile, and video at a speed up to 63 megabits per second. A customer has an earth station on the roof that is used for transmitting to another earth station or satellite.

When satellites were first launched, many believed that the satellites would "bump" into each other in space. This is no longer a realistic concern. The satellites are separated into radians enabling them to orbit very close to one another. An antenna is used for tracking the desired satellite.

A **telephone** can be used for voice and data transmission; a telephone used in homes uses **voice-grade lines.** There is another type of telephone line that is used, however; this is a digital line which is used for strictly transmitting data. There is no telephone used but merely a telephone wire and a black box that digitizes any data and transmits it to a telephone company's office. AT&T's Da-taphone Digital Service (DDS) offers this direct digital service, but it is not available in all parts of the country. Data is transmitted at a rate of 56 Kilobits per second using DDS. A variation of the digital lines are discussed later.

To accompany these communication facilities, two kinds of communication links are used: coaxial cable or fiber optics. **Coaxial cable,** made of strands of copper, is used in cable TV (called CATV) as well as in data transmission. Coaxial cable has been in use for many years; transcontinental networks were constructed

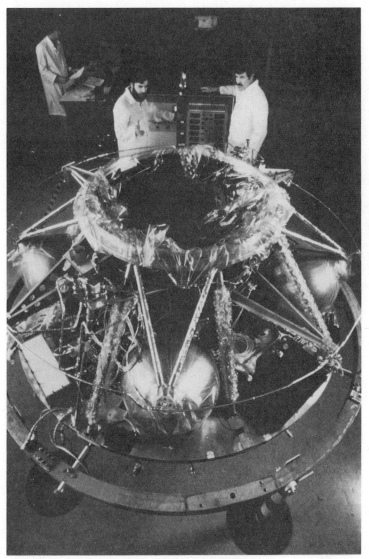

FIGURE 10.4 **A Satellite being constructed.**

WHAT'S NEW

Satellites Come Out On The Short End Of The Comparison

A comparison of satellites versus cable transmission is rather eye-opening. The cost of the satellite's half-duplex circuit is $13,500; the cost of a coaxial cable's half-duplex circuit is $8,300. Some fiber optics are in operation; the cost is $2,500 per half-duplex circuit. These figures are based on 1984 data.

Coaxial cable and fiber optics life span is almost infinite. Since a satellite's power pack wears out in 10 years, the satellite tends to get off orbit. There are plans on the drawing board to set on a tether—plans to repair satellites by being able to "capture" them. The Looks West Satellite, used for forecasting the weather in the western part of the United States, is an example of problems that can plague a satellite's communication facilities. As you will recall, there is one satellite covering the entire United States' weather forecasting. If there is a problem with a cable, located even in the middle of the ocean, a boat could be used to get to the cable.

Conversations transmitted on satellites are also found annoying by users. A one-half second delay exists in the conversation. If you say "Hello", you must wait. The person to whom you are talking must also wait and then answer you; this results in a one-half second delay. The reason the delay is so long is the signal must go up 22,300 miles and then come down another 22,300 miles. All that to just say "Hello!" Since light travels at 186,000 miles per second, the resulting delay would be one-fourth of a second if the communication was being sent only one way.

in the 1940s. Data transmitted via coaxial cable travels in electric waves over a metallic wire, with approximately 64 megabits (million bits) being transmitted per second.

Fiber optics is used today to either replace coaxial cable or to supplement it. A fiber optics cable contains strands of glass thinner than hair, and the cable itself is generally thinner than a lead pencil, depending upon the application. A fiber optics cable could have eighteen fibers which would carry over 6,148 calls at one time and be one inch in diameter. The number of voice transmissions depends upon the number of fibers in a cable. Cables containing the fibers can be strung pole to pole above-ground or laid within a duct underground which the telephone and utility companies are already using. Refer to Figure 10.5.

Fiber optic systems use light waves travelling in glass fibers to transmit messages. Pulses from a light source, flashing 90 million times per second, travel

An Educational System That Is Up In The Air

Hughes Communication, Inc., and IBM have joined forces in funding a venture to provide a customer and employee education program by satellite. The communications network will be composed of terrestrial microwave and earth stations that beam to the Galaxy II satellite launched in September 1983. The IBM educational centers receive video, voice, and data transmission from this communications medium.

IBM also uses its Satellite Business Systems (SBS) for its voice and data applications throughout the corporation. SBS is a joint venture of Aetna Casualty, Comsat, and IBM.

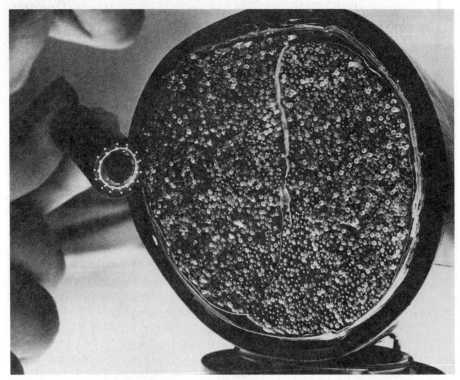

FIGURE 10.5 **Fiber optics.**

through a cable and are bounced and bent as they pass through it. Signals travel in a cable at the speed of light—186,000 miles per second.

Since fiber optics industry is in its infancy, much experimental work is being conducted to transmit the beams of light over long distances. The shorter the distance the bits travel, the more bits can be transmitted per second. For a two to three mile distance, 1000 megabits have been transmitted per second. For longer distances of, say, 30 miles, 1.544 megabits, 6 megabits, or 45 megabits have been transmitted per second. The reason for the wide variation is because different messages are grouped together; this is discussed shortly. Current research is being conducted to avoid the use of repeaters. **Repeaters** are those devices that you are perhaps familiar with that are used in telephone transmission. You see black boxes hanging on many telephone poles; they magnify the voice signals as they pass from one repeater to the next until the signals get to the destination. In September, 1984 it was reported that Bell Laboratories was transmitting two billion bits per second over 80 miles of glass strands without repeaters. Another study reported that Bell Laboratories transmitted 420 million bits per second over 126 miles without repeaters.

Fiber optics usage is increasing day by day and is expected to be heavy in the mid 1980s. Fiber optic systems can be supplied to certain users as they build new power cable housings, but any rewiring of already existing cable systems would be an astronomical expense, except for replacement.

Refer to Table 10.1 for the summation of the communication facilities used and the appropriate transmission rates.

GALLERY 7

Telecommunications

The world of telecommunications represents great technological advances. Let us view some of these advancements in this section.

1. Lightwave communications systems now carry high-speed information across neighborhoods and continents. The world's longest lightwave route, stretching 776 miles from Massachusetts to Virginia, uses cable similar to that shown. The cable, seen in across-section, contains flat ribbons (vertical in photo), each with a dozen glass fibers. One fiber pair can transmit 1,344 voice conversations.

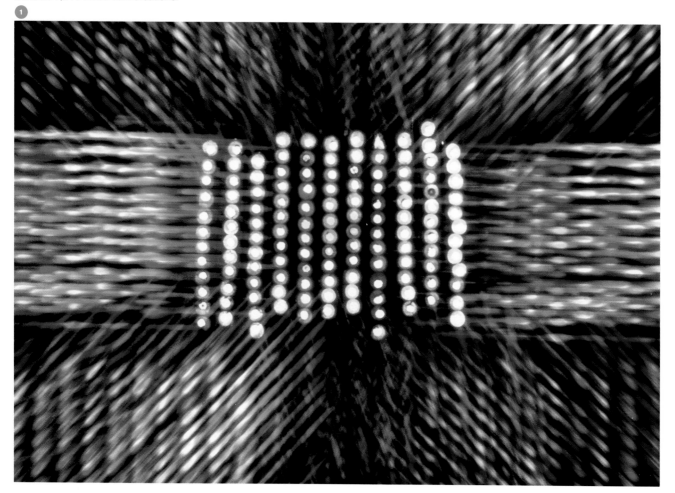

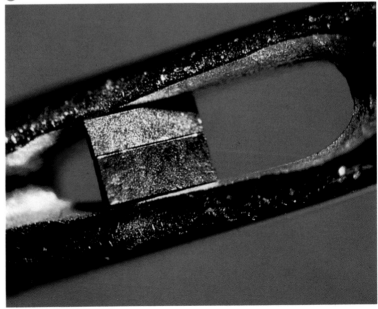

2. Fibers are drawn from glass preforms such as the one held here. Red laser light projected through the side if a preform (wavy lines) is used to determine its optical quality. **3.** An AT&T team assembled leading-edge components into an experimental system that sent 420 million bits of information per second through 100 miles of AT&T glass fiber. Shown are the cleared coupled-cavity laser light source (bright spot near center), optical fiber (at left), and some of the electronics (at right) used to drive the system. **4.** A C3 laser is a semiconductor device that can be turned to emit a range of ultrapure frequencies; it has important implications for future generations of lightwave communications system.

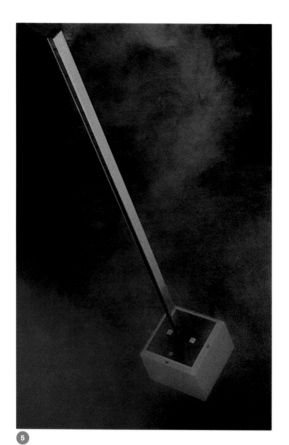

5. Invented and developed at Bell Labs, this microphone can pick up normal speaking voices from across a room. **6.** The Bell microphone at work in an actual teleconference. **7.** An engineer writes on a GEMINI electronic blackboard. His handwriting appears on a remote monitor as it does on the monitor at left.

8. A videotelephone. **9.** An automobile phone. **10.** In 160 Florida homes, participating families obtain news and other information from a centralized database. They also can use the system to pay bills, shop or buy tickets. **11.** A salesperson transmits data over the telephone lines with a small keyboard and modem. **12.** A brokerage firm is virtually held together by a computerized telecommunications network. Brokers are made instantaneously aware of price fluctuations. **13.** The new Telstar satellite will be able to transmit digital signals. **14.** A rear view of a transmitter—a 60 foot "dish antenna."

15. The RCA-6 communications satellite undergoes checkout and alignment of some of its instrumentation before installment in its canister and subsequent transfer to the launch pad. **16.** This view shows technicians at the complex 17-B launch site on the Cape Canaveral Air Force Station as they prepare the RCA SATCOM 1-R for a scheduled launch aboard a Delta rocket. The 24-channel spacecraft is an advanced second generation domestic communications satellites. **17.** The RCA Satcom IIR communications spacecraft was launched on a Delta 3924 launch vehicle from Launch Complex 17-B, Cape Canaveral Air Force Station. **18.** An overall view of activity in the mission operations control room (MOCR) of the Johnson Space Center's mission control center at work. **19. and 20.** These false color photos were taken by a SMS NASA weather satellite. The series of pictures on the Satellite's tapes could trace the movement of a hurricane across the Atlantic Ocean during a 72-hour period and show where it is on the day the tapes are distributed. From its vantage point, the spacecraft can see most of the Western Hemisphere, North and South Atlantic oceans, and the west coast of Africa.

18

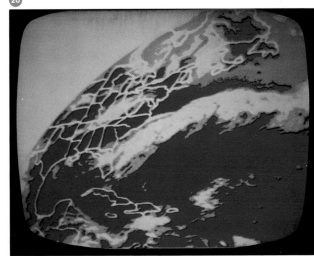

20

19

21.

21. Only advanced computer telecommunications technology made this Viking 1 photograph of the Martian surface possible. 22. Voyager 1 took this photo of Jupiter and two of its satellites (Io, left and Europa). 23. Voyager 2 returned this view of Saturn and its ring system when the spacecraft was 13.9 million kilometers away.

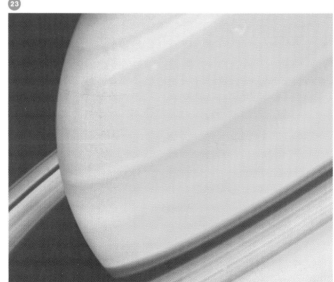

23.

22.

TABLE 10.1. **Comparison of Communication Facilities.**

COMMUNICATION FACILITY	TYPE OF TRANSMISSION	ADVANTAGES	DISADVANTAGES	TRANSMISSION RATE PER SECOND
Telegraph	Wire	Cheap; readily available	Slow	300 cps
Coaxial Cable	Copper strands of wire	Transcontinental cable system; easily available; fast transmission	Costly	up to 64 megabits
Fiber Optics	Glass strands	Light-weight; less costly than coaxial; very compact; extremely fast transmission	Limited availability	up to 1000 megabits for 2–3 miles
Microwave	Radio signals	Usable in mountainous areas and for telephone calls over 500 miles	Interference; large objects can obstruct transmission	45 megabits
Satellite	Relay stations in upper atmosphere and earth stations	Handles large volume of data; easily makes possible a world communications system	Limited atmosphere use; extremely costly	63 megabits
Telephone: Voice-Grade Lines	Wire	Regular telephone lines readily available to almost anywhere; reasonable costs	Bottleneck in getting data from user's site to telephone company office	4,800 bps dial-up lines; 9,600 bps leased lines
Telephone: Digital Lines	Wire	Fast transmission; requires no modem	Not readily available	up to 56K bps

CHECKPOINT **Can you:**

Differentiate among the various communication facilities?

Tell why coaxial cable and fiber optics are important?

VOICE-GRADE LINES TELEPHONE TRANSMISSION

There are many ways that data, voices, or images can be transmitted by telephone. A telephone message can be transmitted over lines strung from pole to pole, over cables laid under the ocean and underground, over microwave beamed from one place to another, or over satellite (signals beamed to it and then back to earth).

Your voice is put on a telephone line, amplified (magnified), and sent to a central office which might be only a few miles away. That distance between you and your central office is called a **local loop** or **subscriber's loop.** It is this local loop that creates the bottlenecks for data transmission since most transmission relies on a telephone before other communication facilities are used. After your voice goes to your central office, it sends the signal on to another office of the telephone company until finally your friend's telephone receives your voice. Your call is sent with other calls over the same wire to an appropriate central office, a process called **multiplexing.**

When Alexander Graham Bell invented the telephone in 1876, he never envisioned that bits (0s and 1s) would be transmitted. Bits are digital signals that are sent in the form of pulse trains, as shown in Figure 10.6. The telephone was designed, however, for voice transmission which is sent in analog signals that appear as sine waves (also shown in Figure 10.6).

Since a telephone was designed for voice, hardware adjustments are needed before a computer can use a telephone for data transmission. The hardware to be adjusted includes a modem, an acoustic coupler, and a touch-tone data phone. Some hardware is shown in Figure 10.7.

Since computer equipment uses digital signals and voice-grade telephone lines use analog signals, a sender needs a digital-to-analog conversion, while a receiver requires an analog-to-digital conversion. The role of a receiver and sender can be reversed, so messages can flow the other direction as well. Refer to Figure 10.8.

A **modem,** (short for **mod**ulator-**dem**odulator), changes a computer's digital signals to analog signals so they can be transmitted over a telephone line (a process called **modulating**). Or analog signals can be changed to digital signals, when located at a receiver location (this process is called **demodulating**). Refer to Figure 10.8, noting how modems work in a pair. Modems can transmit at varying speeds but do not exceed 9600 bits per second (bps) for voice-grade lines. Believe it or not, but modems might also be used at an earth station for transmitting the analog signals to a satellite. The modem at the earth station could transmit at 9,600 bps to the satellite. Another example could be that a sender uses digital

FIGURE 10.6
Digital and analog signals.

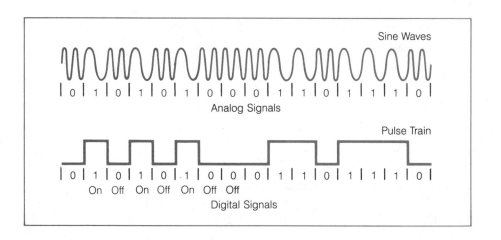

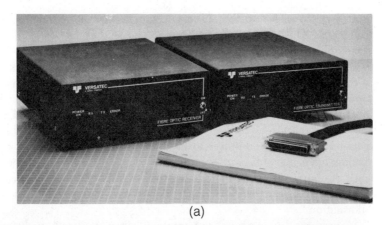

(a)

FIGURE 10.7
Some hardware needed for data transmission over telephone lines.
(a) Fiber optics modems.
(b) Digital feature telephones with automatic dialing.

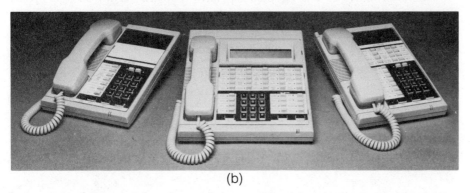

(b)

lines; no modem is used at the sender site. When the message is transmitted at 56 kilobits per second to the earth station, the earth station combines the message with other messages and remodulates the signals to a satellite at transmission speeds of 112 kilobits per second. Before the receiver site gets the message, the earth station nearest the receiver site demodulates the message for further transmission to the site.

A **touch-tone data phone** (as was shown in Figure 10.7) gives different frequencies for characters used for data transmission. Think of changing frequencies

FIGURE 10.8   **A sending device uses modulating; a receiving device uses demodulating.**

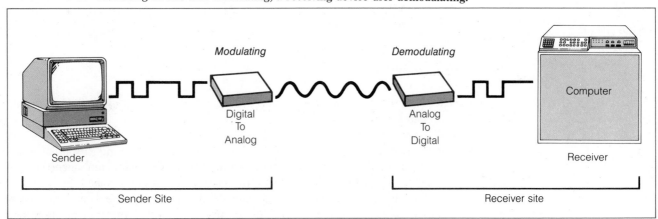

as being like selecting the station of your choice on a radio dial by dialing its frequency. The touch-tone data phone allows a sales person, for example, the option of keying in information which is then sent to a computer. The advantage of this direct keying on the telephone eliminates the paperwork normally done at the originating site. The touch-tone data phone can also be equipped with a tape cassette for recording the transmitted data sent to a computer. Another option available for use is the automatic dialing of telephone numbers. Depending upon the equipment selected, many telephone numbers can be stored in the memory; a user identifies the number to be automatically dialed. Some touch-tone data phones have the option of continuously dialing a number at specified intervals until the line is available. The touch-tone data phone is ideally used for checking credit on credit cards, requesting balances of savings accounts, or requesting loan information.

Some terminals do not use modems since they are **hardwired;** this means that their logic design is set up on integrated circuit chips so their functions are specific and cannot be changed.

CHECKPOINT **Can you:**

State why modems are needed?

TRANSMISSION OF BITS

The speed with which bits are transmitted is measured in **bits per second (bps).** The number of bits that can be carried by a communications link (a cable or signal) is referred to as **bandwidth.** Pulse trains cannot be used because of the limitation of the frequency. Data is transmitted over a band (range) of frequencies. Think of bandwidth as being a multi-lane highway where a narrow lane is used for small vehicles and a wide lane used for truck traffic. A VW can travel in the wide lane but that certainly is not an efficient way to manage highway traffic. The narrow lane is much like narrowband and the wide lane is much like the wideband that is discussed next.

Bandwidth

There are three classes of service according to bandwidth. These are narrowband, voiceband, and wideband.

Narrowband is usually used by companies that have a low volume of input data. Data transmission rates are from 45 to 300 bits per second (bps). This class of service, used by Western Union, is only for data transmission since the frequency range will not accommodate the various pitches of a voice.

Voiceband, the most popular bandwidth, is used when the data transmission needs all or most of the channel. The facilities used for this transmission are either

Direct Distance Dialing (DDD) or Widearea Telephone Service (WATS). Many companies use WATS for telephone calling during office hours and then use the lines at night for data transmission. WATS is the 800 exchange number service that is used for credit authorizations, reservation systems, catalog merchandise ordering, and the like. From 1,800 to 9,600 bps can be transmitted, although 2,400 bps is very common on voiceband.

Wideband, or **broadband** features more than one voice channel and transmits 9,600 to 500,000 or more bits per second. Twelve voice-grade lines are frequently combined by the telephone company when voice or data is being transmitted. Assume you are calling from a city outside of Los Angeles to a city outside of New York City. Your call is combined with other calls going to New York City. In New York City, the message gets decoded and reconstructed at the other end, and is transmitted to a receiver on voiceband. See Figure 10.9 for an illustration of this process. These machines used by the telephone for combining calls and then splitting each out again to its original setup are called **multiplexors.** You may have heard another person's conversation when you are talking. This problem, called cross-talk, occurs when the multiplexor has not allocated enough pitch (frequency) for the voice transmission.

The three classes of bandwidth are summarized in Table 10.2.

CHECKPOINT **Can you:**

Name the three classes of bandwidth service?

Tell when each is used?

Carriers

The Bell Telephone System, divested itself in 1984 into many small telephone companies which provide services to the public as a common carrier for voice and data. The word **carrier** refers to the company that provides the means of transmitting the data from one location to another. Western Union and the many private telephone companies also supply such a common carrier service. You are probably aware of the common carriers of WATS and DDD that provide services to users for a fee.

Another class of carriers, called **specialized common carriers,** supply services along with the leased (private) channel—among these being Microwave Communications, Inc. (MCI), Telenet from GTE, Tymnet (a division of Tymshare), and International Telephone & Telegraph's (ITT's) Compak. Telenet and Tymnet, two companies that are called **value added networks (VANs),** provide a communication line to a user, the interface for any terminals, and a method for transmitting data in the network. Value added networks are so named because they take a communication line that is otherwise passive (inactive) and make it work for the user by adding software and needed hardware to accomplish data transmission. **Interface** can mean many different things, but in this example, think of it as being that common electrical connection that allows two pieces of hardware

FIGURE 10.9
Use of wideband and voiceband bandwidths.

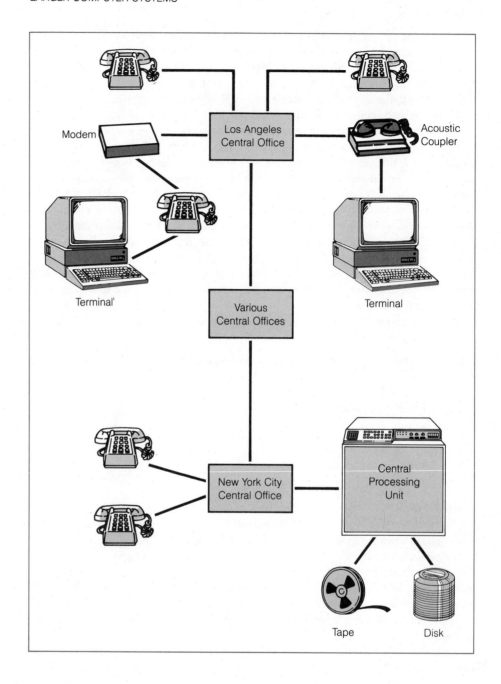

to be joined. These two companies operate in theory like dropping a packet into a hypothetical boxcar as it passes by. The **packet,** which is the temporarily stored message or data that is collected for transmission, is forwarded on a wire to its destination by both hardware and software provided by a carrier. The connection of the various communication points served by Telenet and Tymnet is called a **packet switching network.**

TABLE 10.2. **Comparison of Bandwidths.**

	NARROWBAND	VOICEBAND	WIDEBAND
Transmission of bits	45–300 cps	1800–9600 bps	Over 9,600 bps
Users	Western Union	DDD WATS VAN's	Telephone companies, coaxial cable, fiber optics, microwave, satellite, DDS

Types of Connections

Two choices for line connections are available to a user of voice-grade lines. These are dial-up and leased lines.

A **dial-up line,** often called a **switched line,** involves the use of a switching network that is provided by the telephone company so that different telephone lines can be called from one telephone. Charges for dial-up lines are based on either a flat monthly rate or a measured rate, depending upon the time that is used. WATS and DDD are the most popular facilities. Acoustic couplers must use dial-up lines.

A dial-up line certainly gives flexibility to a company since a telephone can be used for voice as well as data transmission. Its maximum data rate is 4,800 bps. Its strong disadvantage is that switching picks up noise, resulting in poorer transmission than leased lines offer. The repeaters (discussed earlier), located at intervals on telephone poles, contribute to the noise factor. Each time a repeater is used, there is a possibility of some noise being picked up; the noise is amplified as the voice or data is sent on to its destination.

Dial-up lines offer users this advantage, however; they can just hang up and try again if there is a poor connection. Routing of calls for dial-up lines changes constantly, so the chances of getting the same path are very slim. However, it might take several attempts to reach the computer since you are competing with other users for that computer's time.

Dial-up lines use a handshaking routine; **handshaking** is the connection of a line and later disconnection through the use of some pre-arranged signals. To successfully accomplish data transmission, users follow rules or standards for procedures that have been established to govern the transmission and exchange of information between two systems (or devices). These rules on how bits are transmitted and the needed signals to accomplish handshaking are called **protocol.** Whenever data is not transmitted correctly, determination must be made as to how data is to be retransmitted; this is spelled out clearly in the protocol.

Leased lines, often called **dedicated** or **private lines,** are available as a permanent circuit twenty-four hours a day, connecting a user with a computer center. Since these lines are permanently connected, they are always on-line and therefore require no switching equipment, resulting in better reception. They are like a pipe; a user controls both ends of the pipe because it is dedicated to that user.

Leased lines transmit up to 9,600 bps. Errors in transmission occur on the average of one bit per million bits transmitted, but they usually occur in bursts rather than in isolation. Handshaking is usually not present since there is a permanent connection.

CHECKPOINT **Can you:**

Differentiate between dial-up lines and leased lines?

List some of the other names that each is known by?

Mode of Transmission

In addition to considering the rate at which bits are transmitted and who provides the carrier for the transmission to occur, we must also consider the mode of transmission. From a data processor's viewpoint, concern is only with three types of circuits: the simplex, half-duplex, and full duplex circuit. A **circuit** refers to an electrical signal that is used in the telephone line for transmission. Refer to Figure 10.10.

A **simplex circuit** allows for a terminal to just send or just receive data, but never both. Simplex circuits are seldom used since two-way communication is usually preferred for transferring signals back and forth between a computer and a user to make certain correct data was transmitted. What you see is not necessarily what you get!

A **half-duplex circuit** gives the possibility for a two-way transmission, but

FIGURE 10.10
The various types of carrier circuits between central processing unit and terminals.

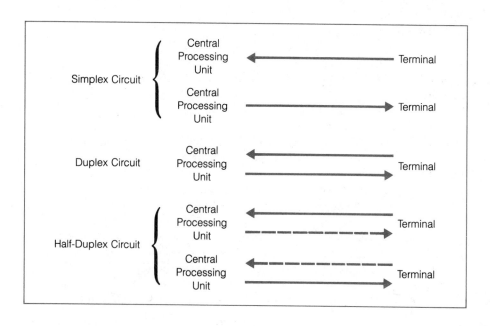

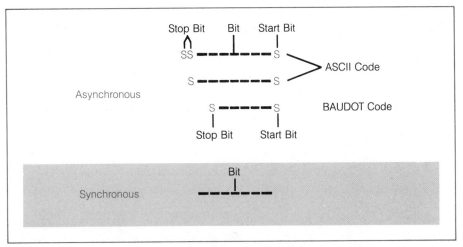

FIGURE 10.11   **Asynchronous and synchronous data representations.**

only one way can transmit at a time. It operates in a manner similar to a CB radio; one person has to listen while the other talks.

A **full duplex circuit,** or **duplex circuit,** can transmit data in both ways at the same time. If a full duplex circuit is used, a sending signal uses one portion of the frequency and a receiving signal uses the other portion.

CHECKPOINT **Can you:**

Differentiate among the various types of circuits?

Tell which type is rarely used? Why?

Synchronous or Asynchronous (Start/Stop) Transmission

Now let us look into another important point concerning how terminals transmit bits—by synchronous or asynchronous data transmission. Whether synchronous or asynchronous transmission is used depends upon the terminal and the speed of transmission. **Synchronous transmission** is the fastest transmission that exists between terminals and the computer. The transmission of the data between the terminal and the computer are synchronized by timing impulses (signals); both the terminal and the computer have a clock that runs continuously when the data is being transmitted to make certain that both the sender and the receiver are working in harmony (the timing and data rate are the same for both).

Asynchronous transmission offers a less expensive way of transmission between a terminal and a computer since the clocking mechanism used in the synchronous transmission is absent here. Because an asynchronous transmission does not use timing signals, a way of identifying where a byte begins in transmission becomes important. To accomplish this, additional bits are included within a byte to act as a divider; this means 10 or 11 bits in all are required to transmit one byte. Refer to Figure 10.11.

By 1986 in Florida, all 2,345 schools from kindergarten through college are to be linked by a communications network of computers. Think of a network as being all those terminals, computers, and input/output devices that are interconnected. The information available in the network will include data on the 1.5 million students in the state's sixty-seven school districts and the personal records for the staff and faculty.

To have information available for decision making, record-keeping, and analysis is quite an advantage. Personal data about each student need only be entered once in the system of computers since data can be shared by all school districts. The disadvantage, however, is that certain information must be kept confidential, or off-limits to users who are not privileged to see or change such records.

Student processing will include much information. Remember a computer is useful when the same type of processing occurs over and over again. What might be some examples of data commonly used in such a network?

Both synchronous and asynchronous transmission speed is stated in **baud** units (a baud is one signal per second). A rough estimation for the number of characters transmitted per second (cps) is to divide the baud by 10. The one exception to this rule of thumb that 10 bits represent a character applies when teletypewriters are used; they use a 5-bit code developed by Jean Maurice Baudot. Each character uses 5 bits rather than 10 or 11 bits.

There is no way of telling which type of transmission is used by the terminal by just looking at the equipment, with the exception of the teleprinters and teletypewriters. You must know how a terminal transmits its data.

Since asynchronous transmission is slower, it is less expensive, but a cost factor is more important to many companies than a speed factor. Acoustic couplers can be used for only asynchronous transmission. Data entry and editing of data are typical applications for an asynchronous transmission.

Synchronous transmissions are often used when forms are completed by filling in certain data; it would be easier for the entire screen to be filled in and then transmitted at one time.

CHECKPOINT Can you:

Differentiate between asynchronous and synchronous data transmission?

List some advantages synchronous transmission has over asynchronous transmission?

Physical Connections

Terminals can transmit data to a computer locally or remotely. **Local terminals** are positioned near a computer, anywhere from 50 feet up to 10,000 feet from it, depending upon the type of electrical connection that is used. Terminals positioned further from a computer are called **remote terminals;** they use either dial-up lines, such as we use every day, or leased lines that provide a twenty-four-hour connection to a computer center.

Telephone costs for some companies are overwhelming; monthly telephone charges can be from $200,000 and up. For this reason, the way that the telephone lines are hooked up is of utmost importance. Hardware that is specifically designed for efficiently managing the communication traffic includes the multiplexor, terminal controller, and concentrator. We have already mentioned the multiplexor as it is used in voice transmission, but let us look into each of these in some detail.

Let us suppose a company has offices located in three cities, as shown in Figure 10.12. There is one connecting telephone line used from a terminal to a **port,** which is an entry point of a computer. Ports for personal computers are usually found on the back and resemble an outlet. The physical hook-up of a terminal to a port is referred to as **point to point** data transmission. Using such a line configuration, this company's telephone bills will be extremely high, but management might feel it is important to have the fast response time that exists

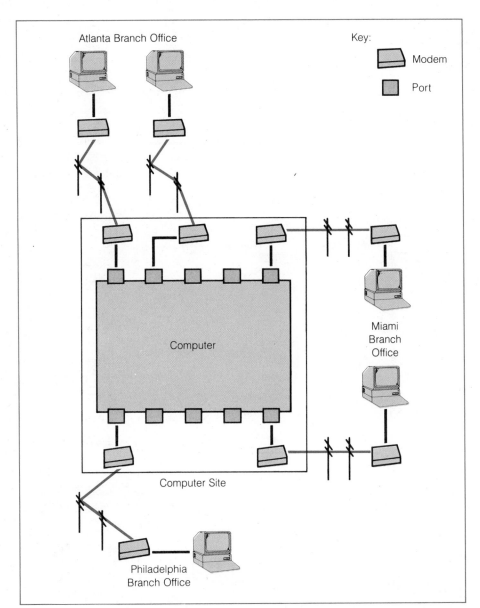

FIGURE 10.12
Point to point data transmission.

with this point to point line configuration. Maybe the amount of data traffic justifies the point to point configuration.

Multiplexors are used by many companies to reduce their transmission costs by sharing one telephone line with many terminals. Many terminals transmit 300 bits per second and more, and telephone line capacities allow up to 9,600 bits per second. Multiplexors manage the transmission of data over telephone lines much more efficiently by combining the data transmission from several terminals and then use one telephone line. To accomplish this transmission, multiplexors work in pairs—one at the computer site and the other at the terminal site. Refer to Figure 10.13. Not all multiplexors are programmable (able to change to fit a need); hence, they are not as efficient as they would be otherwise.

FIGURE 10.13
Use of multiplexor for reducing telephone line costs.

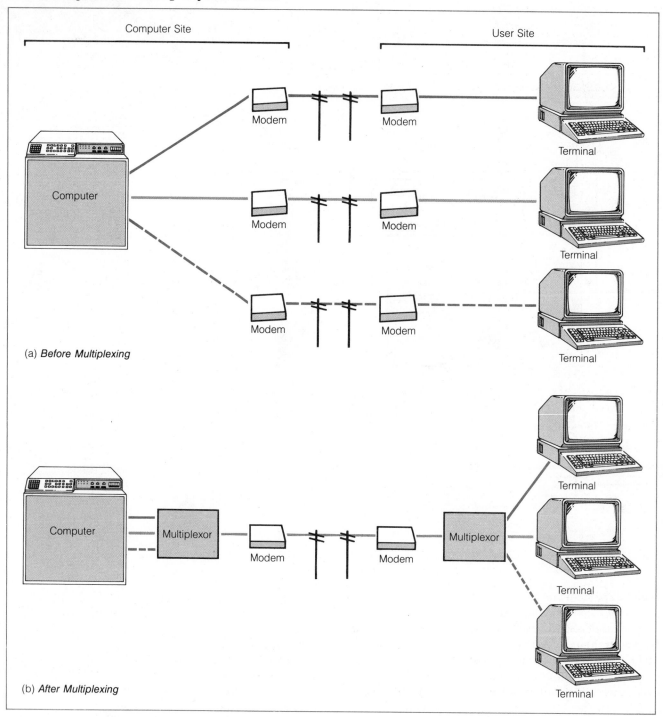

(a) *Before Multiplexing*

(b) *After Multiplexing*

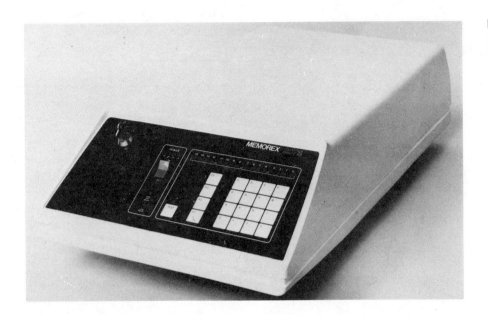

FIGURE 10.14
**Remote cluster controller—
Memorex 2076.**

Another way that a terminal can be connected to a central processing unit is through the use of a terminal controller. A **terminal controller** is a specialized minicomputer that accepts messages from terminals and then sends the messages to the central processing unit. In this way, the central processing unit only works with the terminal controller rather than each terminal directly. One terminal controller handles the input and output of these terminals, which are considered to be **clustered.** Refer to Figure 10.14. Notice in Figure 10.15(a) that six telephone lines are required for servicing the six terminals to the central processing unit. In Figure 10.15(b), illustrating point-to-point configuration with clustered terminals, there is just one telephone line that goes directly to the central processing unit. Each terminal has its own telephone line, however, to the terminal controller. Both of these examples represent a point-to-point configuration.

To further reduce telephone line costs, the number of telephone lines could be further reduced by the sharing of one telephone line among the clustered terminals, as shown in Figure 10.15(c). The terminals are still clustered in this configuration, because of the use of the terminal controller. The difference is that the terminals share the same telephone line to the terminal controller. The telephone line is then referred to as a **multi-point** or a **multi-drop line.**

As you sit at a terminal keying in data, you are waiting in line, but this is one line you are not really aware of. To maintain an efficient flow of data to the central processing unit, the terminal controller checks with each terminal it services to see if the terminal has any data to send. When there is data, the data is transmitted. The terminal controller goes to its list for the address of the next terminal it serves and asks if that terminal has data to send. The terminal controller is actually **polling** its terminals in a round-robin fashion, as illustrated in Figure 10.16. This polling activity works best when each terminal has data to send. If, however, the terminals are not equally busy, polling wastes a lot of time. To overcome this problem, **contention** is used; this means that when a terminal has

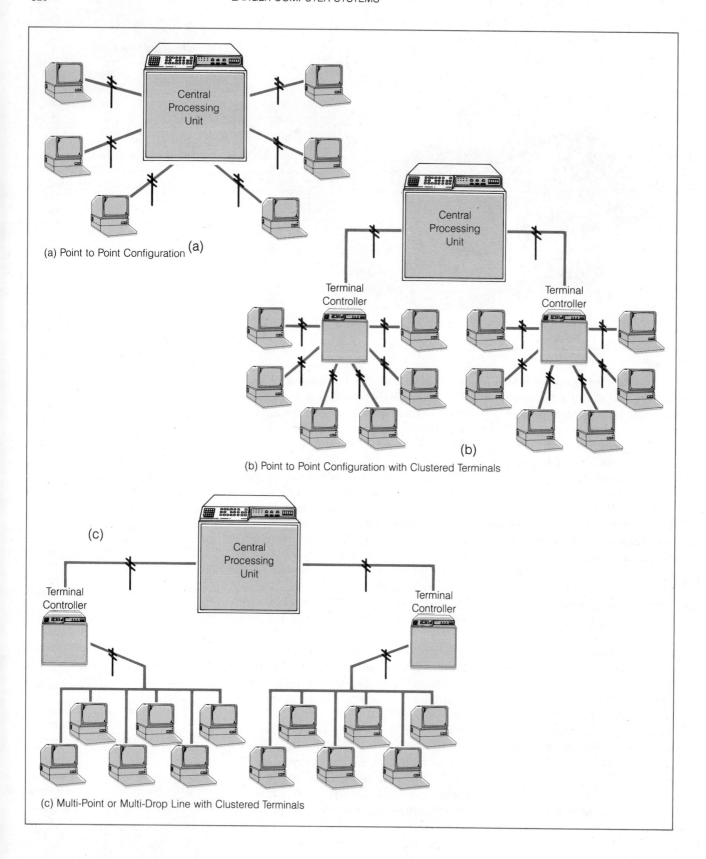

(a) Point to Point Configuration (a)

(b) Point to Point Configuration with Clustered Terminals

(c) Multi-Point or Multi-Drop Line with Clustered Terminals

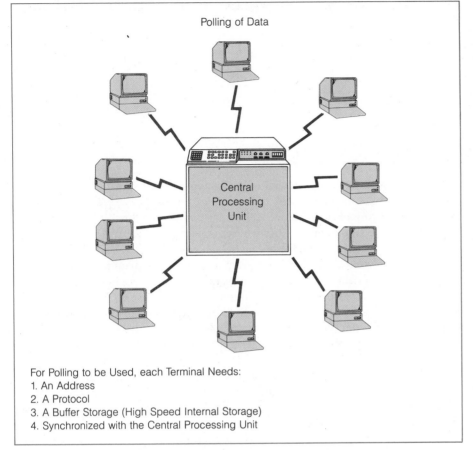

Polling of Data

Central
Processing
Unit

For Polling to be Used, each Terminal Needs:
1. An Address
2. A Protocol
3. A Buffer Storage (High Speed Internal Storage)
4. Synchronized with the Central Processing Unit

FIGURE 10.16 **Polling of synchronous terminals.**

data to send, several terminals contend (compete) for the same telephone line to
send data to the terminal controller.

Multiplexing is also performed by a concentrator, which has more flexibility
than a multiplexor. A **concentrator** is usually a microcomputer or minicomputer
that divides a data channel into channels of slower speed. Think of channels in
this respect as being like a data transmission highway that carries data from one
location to another. The main purposes are to maximize throughput (measured
work) and to reduce telephone line costs. A microcomputer or minicomputer's
program dynamically allocates channel space as the need arises. No terminal will
ever be transmitting every second of every day. When data traffic is heavy, a
temporary high-speed internal storage holds data to be transmitted later. When
the line is available, a concentrator sends the data, illustrating the concentrator's
store and forward capability. A concentrator allows more terminals to be connected
to one telephone line than multiplexing does. A concentrator has more flexibility
than a multiplexor in that it can also perform polling and contention.

◀ FIGURE 10.15   **Different telephone line configurations. (a) Point to point configuration. (b) Point to point configuration
with clustered terminals. (c) Multi-point or multi-drop line with clustered terminals.**

CHECKPOINT **Can you:**

Identify some of the ways that companies reduce their costs of telephone usage?

CLASSIFICATION OF TERMINALS

Terminals can be classified according to the types of work that they perform as dumb terminals, smart terminals, or intelligent terminals.

A **dumb terminal** contains no intelligence and is used for any entering of data and any inquiry. **Intelligence** exists where a microprocessor and primary storage capability are present. A **smart terminal,** as shown in Figure 10.17, has an internal processor (intelligence) that has been programmed by the manufacturer to accomplish some type of data entry, inquiry, or business graphics. An **intelligent terminal** has an internal processor that can be programmed by a user. One example of an intelligent terminal is a microcomputer. Smart and intelligent terminals do not require point to point line configuration to a host computer, but a dumb terminal requires its own telephone line to a host computer (the main central processing unit).

Intelligence is placed at many locations in a network, enabling files to be transferred from one site to another and communication to exist among these points. Intelligence can take the form of micros, minis, controllers, concentrators, or intelligent terminals. Each of these "intelligent sites" is then referred to as a **node.** The positioning of nodes and a host computer must be given careful consideration.

FIGURE 10.17
Smart terminal using a digital telephone.

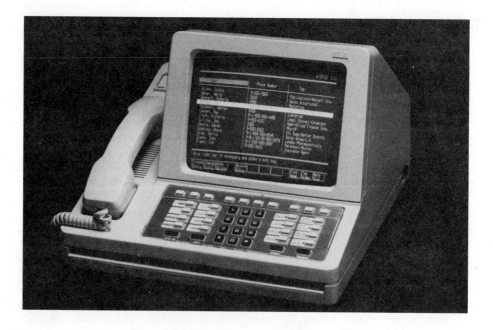

Types and applications of networking receive much attention in periodicals. Let us look at both of these aspects.

CHECKPOINT Can you:

Identify the three types of terminals by what work they can do?

Tell which type contains intelligence?

NETWORKS

As we discussed in Chapter 3, a distributed data processing system places its hardware where the data is needed. To accomplish a sharing of data, data must be formatted the same way. The same protocol as to how information is to be exchanged among sites must be followed.

A **network** ties together many **remote sites** (these sites are located a distance from the main computer). Essentially, the network represents a series of interconnected terminals (input/output devices), communication lines, and computer systems. A computer system at a central site is the main computer used for data manipulation; this is called the **host computer.** Another computer system that works with the host computer handles all communication among sites. This processor, which is usually a minicomputer, is called a **front-end processor (FEP)** and is located at a central computer site. Refer to Figure 10.18. A **back-end processor (BEP)** (shown in Figure 10.19) is often used for looking up and storing data in the data base. It is easier and more efficient to have the dedicated BEP and FEP than not. The host computer could do all the work alone, but not as efficiently.

Micros, minis, or terminals are placed throughout a network so that remote sites can communicate with the central site. This distribution allows local processing to occur and also permits transmittal of information around the network.

TYPES OF NETWORKS

Before we briefly discuss the types of networks available, a look into the history of data processing reveals that need dictates the degree of sophistication for the facilities and services rendered. The greater the demand for higher performing products and services the more sophisticated the hardware becomes. The more hardware sophistication, the more processing capability exists. The resulting networks of today become more encompassing as to how data is transmitted and how sites are connected to the network. Because of the cost factor and the unavailability of desired services, companies are setting up their own networks or having a software company develop their programs. There are, therefore, many variations to the three networks discussed here.

WHAT'S RIGHT

Campus Network Supporting 33,000 Students

San Diego State University has become part of history in the information world by becoming the first university campus using a local area network to tie the entire campus's facilities together. There are over 16,000 feet of coaxial cable used. A Cyber 170/750 acts as the host computer; a combination of Digital Equipment Corporation (DEC) 10 VAX and PDP computers are used for communications, time sharing, and processing capability; and an Apple computer is used as the network manager.

The 170 word processors and 90 visual display terminals are being used successfully to operate the library, registrar's office, and accounting services as well as to monitor computer classes on campus.

Future plans involve the use of electronic mail and a campus security system. It is anticipated that up to 32,500 terminals and computers will become part of the campus network.

FIGURE 10.18   **Two people stand in front of front-end processor.**

There are three major types of networks: a star, local-area, and ring. The star is the oldest and is, therefore, the least efficient. The local-area network is continually receiving more attention as it increases in popularity. The ring network is used by packet switching facilities that allow data to be entered at any point in the network.

Star Network

A **star network,** the oldest type of communication network, originated to fit the needs of a centralized company system approach; it is set up so that each **node** (a peripheral or computer system that connects to a network) communicates directly to a host computer through the use of a dial-up or leased line. A star network centers around a controller which supplies intelligence to the node which is the connecting point to the network. A controller connects any equipment together as shown in Figure 10.20(a). If a controller becomes inoperative, an entire node and all terminals connected to it are shut down. Usually the same manufacturer's devices are used in this network so the hardware is compatible.

A variation to the star network is the hierarchical star network as shown in Figure 10.20(b). Different levels of importance are attributed to the various computers.

Local-Area Network (LAN)

Companies have had networks of telephones for years. Such networks make use of a telephone operator, who answers telephone calls and plugs them to extensions in the company. All the telephones tie into the network. Any one telephone

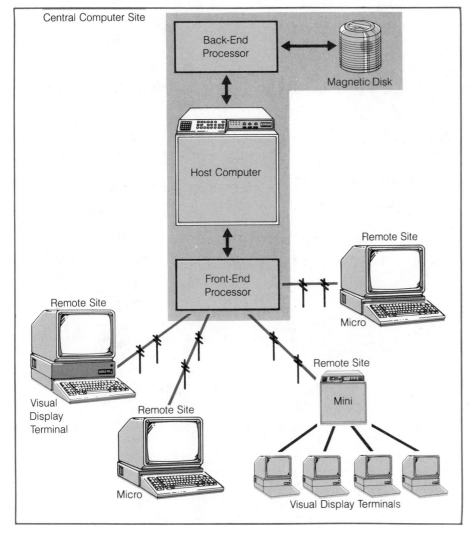

Central Computer Site

Back-End
Processor

Magnetic Disk

Host Computer

Remote Site

Front-End
Processor

Micro

Remote Site

Remote Site

Visual
Display
Terminal

Remote Site

Mini

Micro

Visual Display Terminals

FIGURE 10.19   **A network of computers.**

becoming inoperative has no affect on the other telephones' operation. The concept
of a local-area network is much the same, as terminals are added easily to the
network, and data and messages must be transmitted from one terminal to another,
even though one or more nodes are not operating correctly.

A **local-area network (LAN)** is developed to avoid the problem of the network
shutdown as mentioned. This network also permits a mix of many manufacturer's
products since hardware is easily attached to the network. Since a cable is passive
(inactive), programs are written to make it operate. Each node operates independently, which increases the system reliability. Refer to Figure 10.21.

A local-area network usually services a geographical area encompassing one
building or site. A popular local-area network is called **Ethernet** by Xerox; it uses
packets for transmission over coaxial cable. Refer to Figure 10.22. Another form
of local-area network is the **Private Automatic Branch Exchange (PABX);** this uses
telephone lines to link the hardware in the network. PABX, also called **Computerized Business Telephone System (CBX)** by some other manufacturers, is a digital

FIGURE 10.20
Star network variations.
(a) Controller used as intelligence.
(b) Hierarchical star network.

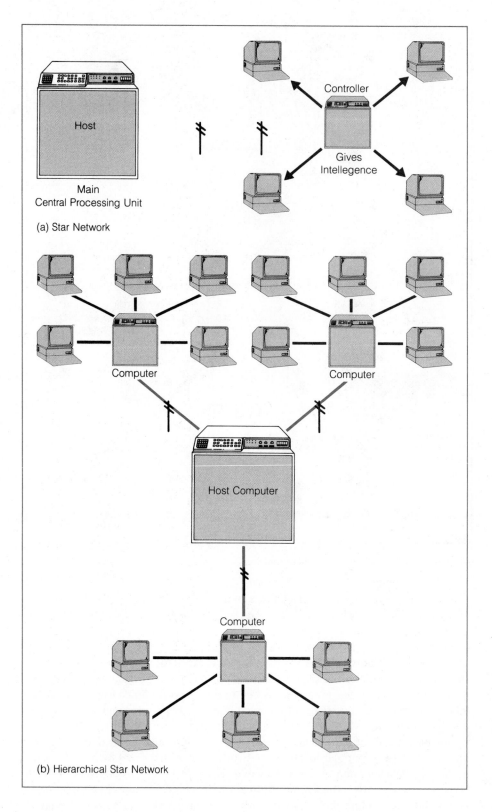

(a) Star Network

(b) Hierarchical Star Network

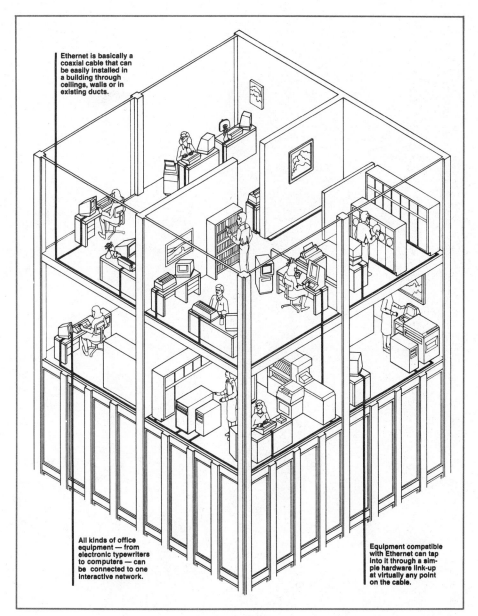

Ethernet is basically a coaxial cable that can be easily installed in a building through ceilings, walls or in existing ducts.

All kinds of office equipment — from electronic typewriters to computers — can be connected to one interactive network.

Equipment compatible with Ethernet can tap into it through a simple hardware link-up at virtually any point on the cable.

FIGURE 10.21
Local-Area Network (LAN).

transmission of voice and data that can be transmitted simultaneously over the same **twisted-pair** wiring (regular telephone line). CBX is a local-area network in and of itself; it can also be hooked up with another network of computers that is not CBX-oriented.

If we were using CBX, for eample, we could talk on the telephone and, at the same time, transmit data from our personal computers. In the conversation we could make reference to the screen shown on the visual display terminal,

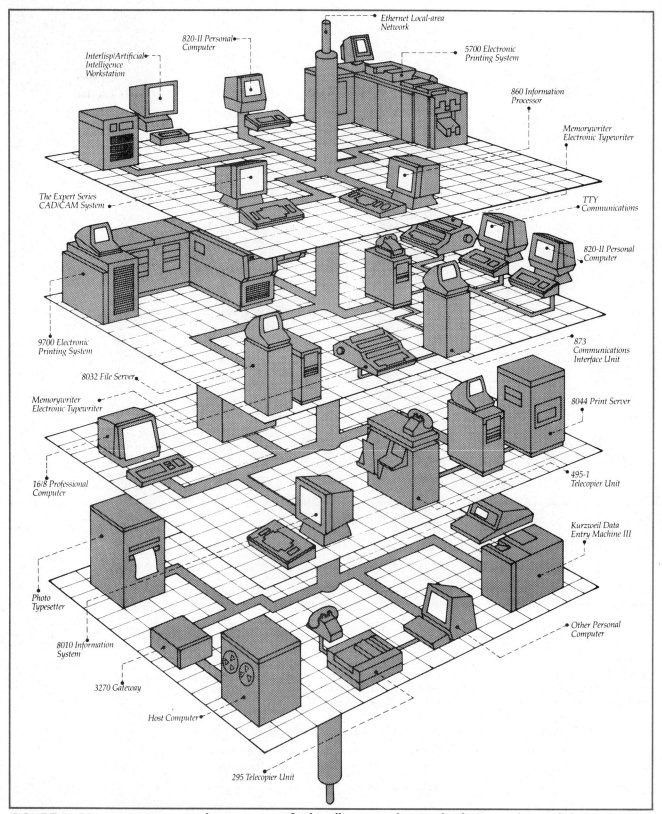

FIGURE 10.22   **LAN using personal computers, artificial intelligence workstation for decision making and electronic mail transmission, 3270s for synchronous terminals, and others.**

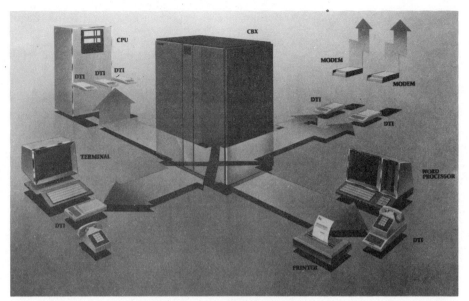

(a)

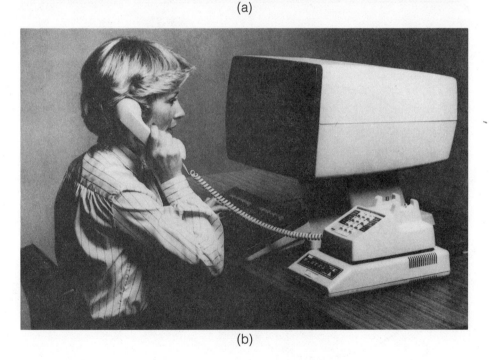

(b)

FIGURE 10.23
Computerized business telephone system. (a) Schematic for voice and data with data transmission up to 19.2 Kbps between computer points. DTI stands for data terminal interface. (b) A user communicates where voice is digitized within a local-area network.

perhaps making some comments about a particular set of figures that are shown on the screen. Refer to Figure 10.23(b).

Do not confuse PABX or CBX with Private Branch Exchange (PBX). PBX uses only analog signals. The operator hand-plugged a cord for interface (common type of connection). In a CBX the interface is controlled by data terminal interface (DTI). Refer to Figure 10.23(a); various modems can be pooled by several terminals. The CBX can handle 22,000 users at basically the same time. Software accompanying this system can spotlight abuse, report an analysis of trunk usage, and show cost allocations.

Ring Network

A **ring network** has no host computer; communication exists only between nodes. The communication is passed from one node to the next until it gets to its desired location. If a node becomes inoperative, it can be bypassed. It allows data to enter at any point of the network. Refer to Figure 10.24.

CHECKPOINT **Can you:**

Identify three types of networks used?

State how each one differs in operation and organization?

FIGURE 10.24
Ring network.

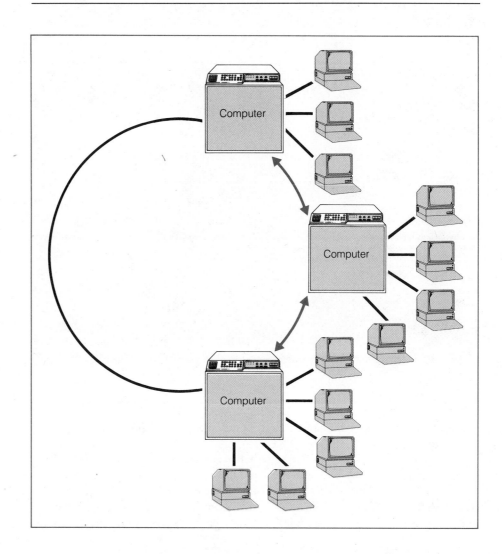

APPLICATIONS

Transmission problems can occur in any system. For an efficient networking system to be maintained, considerable effort must be expended. For example, newspaper data today is transmitted by satellite over a network for printing at different sites in the United States. As long as everything works correctly, the newspapers are available for sale at the newspaper stands. What happens if some communication problem occurs? What is an easy way to transfer files between sites? Let us look into two techniques developed to handle such transfer: down-line loading and up-line dumping.

DOWN-LINE LOADING

Because a new labor contract was negotiated last month, the central data processing staff at Belmont News needs to make changes in the program that calculates the payroll. The program changes are written and tested at the host computer site. These changes are now ready to be incorporated in each of the remote site's minicomputers. The transmission flow goes from the host computer to the nodes. The front-end processor at the host computer signals that it wants to transmit to the minis. They "come up," and the contents of the host computer's primary storage that is holding the new payroll data is transferred. The contents of the memory could be written onto magnetic tape and later read and transferred to the node, if desired. This technique is called **down-line loading.** Microcomputer networks refer to this as downloading. Refer to Figure 10.25(a).

Another application for using down-line loading would involve a direct transfer of information from the host computer's primary storage to the node. If something should happen in the data transmission or some kind of static occur, the whole system would crash (shut down). Bay Area Rapid Transit (BART) in San Francisco operates subway trains by the use of computers. BART insists that the schedule changes in the transmission do not use magnetic disk since disk does become inoperative occasionally. There are eighty nodes in the BART system that must be down-line loaded in one minute with information such as changes in train schedules, switching of tracks, emergency procedures, and train failures.

UP-LINE DUMPING

Management must provide protections within the distributed data processing system for data in case of a failure of hardware in the system. The host computer can down-line load programs or data from its storage to a remote processor. Or a remote processor can down-line load programs or data to the node. Ability to recover data or programs must be provided in the opposite direction in case a remote processor crashes, for example. This type of recovery is called **up-line dumping** where the node will transfer data or programs to the remote processor to get the remote processor's computer system up and running. Microcomputer networks are calling this uploading. Refer to Figure 10.25(b).

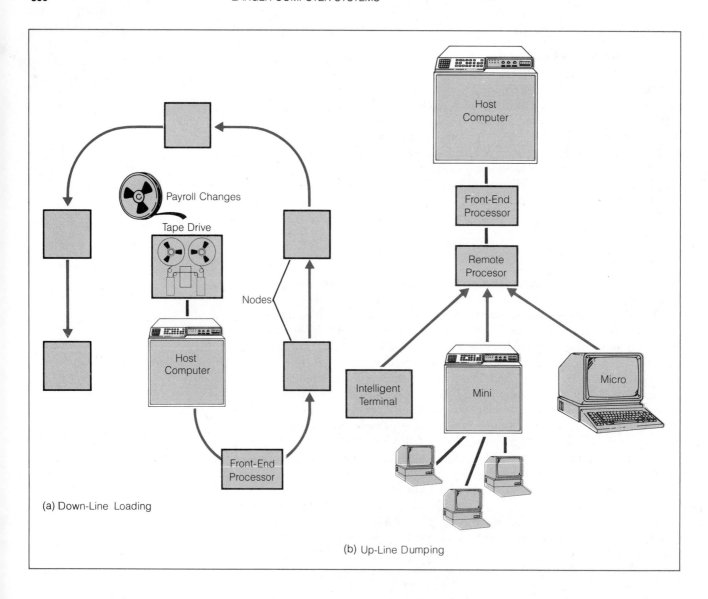

(a) Down-Line Loading

(b) Up-Line Dumping

FIGURE 10.25
**Transferring data in a network.
(a) Down-line loading. (b) Up-line
dumping.**

DISTRIBUTED DATA PROCESSING APPLICATION

Assume a company sells to wholesale outlets and there are two regional offices
located in the eastern and western part of the United States. All processing for
the eastern division is done at the host and remote processors. Remote processors
are located at warehouse sites in major cities of the territory. Some of the terminals
are located in smaller cities or rural areas where orders are placed. When a request
is received at the branch office, an inquiry is made to make certain the desired
shipment can be met. Upon making inquiry to the remote processor, it is evident
that the nearest warehouse cannot fill the shipment. An inquiry to the host computer is then made to determine where the item can be located. The host can
communicate with the other remote processor for the answer. Refer to Figure 10.26.

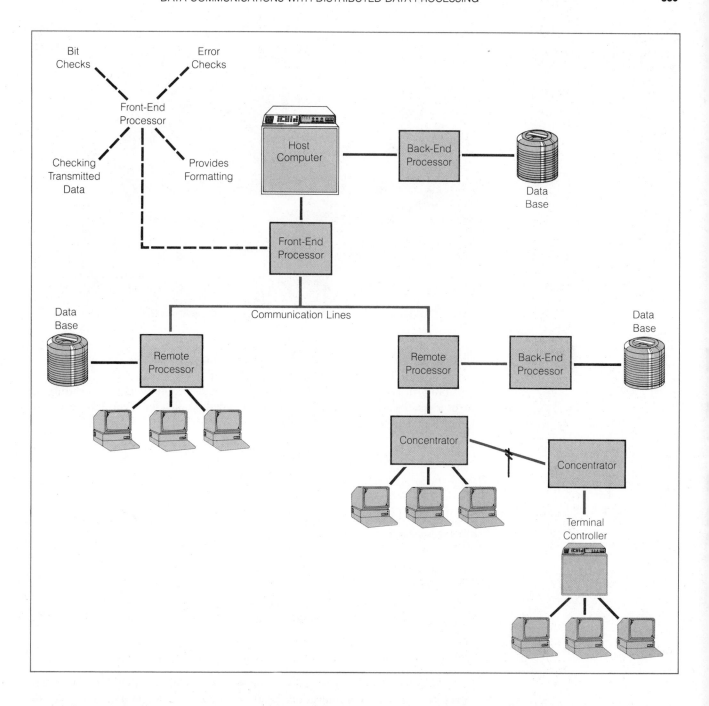

This last application not only shows the interaction of parts of a distributed data processing system but also shows how important it is to be able to access data easily.

Consider another example using distributed data processing. An engineering company positions several remote processors throughout a geographical area. Multiple sites are serviced from a remote processor. When calculations are made, the results are temporarily stored on secondary storage and then later printed

FIGURE 10.26
Some hardware used in a distributed system.

FIGURE 10.27
Remote processor used for spooling.

when either the results are needed or the printer is available for outputting a particular job. This is an example of **spooling.** Refer to Figure 10.27. Until the availability of laser printers that can be positioned in a network, the printing of the processed data was usually delayed, or spooled. Today, however, laser printers do not require the extensive spooling.

SUMMARY

• Data communications is a transmission of data, pictures, or voice from one processing point to another.

• Telecommunications is the transmission of data or pictures over a long distance. No processing is necessarily involved; only a transmission of data can be accomplished.

• Teleprocessing involves data processing and data communications.

• Regardless of communication medium used, there is always a sender, a message, a receiver, and a communication facility (telephone, telegraph, microwave, or satellite).

• An acoustic coupler is often used for sending data by sounds and puts the sounds on speakers so the data can be transmitted to the computer located perhaps miles away.

• Some terminals are hardwired which means the terminal has the necessary hardware already wired inside it for transmitting the data to the computer.

- A user has several choices as to the kind of data communication facility that can be used; telegraph, microwave, satellite, and telephone are some choices.

- The telegraph is the service provided by Western Union for the sending of messages over wire; no voice transmission occurs.

- Microwave is used for sending voice or data over mountainous areas or for transmission to a satellite.

- Microwave, a very heavily used medium, transmits via a digital or analog radio. Microwave is used by AT&T to transmit telephone calls that extend over 500 miles.

- Geosynchronous satellites are used for data transmission. Much developmental work is being conducted on the usage of satellites, but the telephone and broadcast companies are already using them for relay stations.

- Coaxial cable, used for years to communicate data, is being replaced by fiber optics systems which are faster and, at the same time, cheaper to install. Fiber optics is in its infancy, but it holds much promise for extensive use in the 1980s.

- Voice-grade lines are those regular telephone lines that are used for voice and data transmission.

- Digital lines are not usually intended for voice transmission.

- The local loop or subscriber's loop is that distance between you and your central office; transmission bottlenecks occur in this area.

- The telephone company efficiently combines many voice-grade lines (regular telephone lines) for transmission over one telephone cable; this is multiplexing.

- Voice-grade lines require the use of a modem (modulator-demodulator) that changes digital pulses transmitted by computer equipment to analog signals for telephone transmission. Analog signals at the other end of a transmission are changed back to digital signals.

- An acoustic coupler can be used instead of a modem, but it is only used on dial-up lines. Transmission rates are 300 bps or less. A touch-tone data phone gives different tones for characters used in the data transmission. The touch-tone data phone can be equipped with a tape cassette for recording transmitted data. Automatic dialing of numbers can also be accomplished.

- Bandwidth refers to the speed with which bits can be transmitted over a communication facility. The classes of service according to bandwidth are narrowband, voiceband, and wideband.

- Narrowband is used by Western Union for its telegraph transmission. Its frequency range will not allow voice transmission.

- Voiceband is used for telephone transmission; it allows both voice and data to be transmitted.

- Wideband, combining numerous voice-grade lines, is used for cable, microwave, and satellite transmission.

- For data transmission using voice-grade lines, a user has a choice of a dial-up or leased line.

- Dial-up (switched) lines are cheaper, but their transmission is of poor quality because they involve switching, which can pick up noise.

- Widearea Telephone Service (WATS) and Direct Distance Dialing (DDD) are the most popular dial-up line carriers.

- Leased lines (dedicated or private lines) are private lines that supply twenty-four-hour service to one computer center. There is a lack of switching in these leased lines which makes for better quality transmission.

- Three types of circuits are used for transmission of data: simplex, which provides only for one-way transmission and is rarely used; half-duplex, which allows data to flow in either direction but only one direction at a time; and, full duplex, which allows data to flow in both directions at the same time.

- Synchronous data transmission is the fastest transmission that exists between terminals and the computer. The sender and receiver sites are synchronized by impulses so that timing and the data rate are the same for both. Polling is possible with this data transmission.

- Asynchronous transmission offers a less expensive transmission. Handshaking is used in this data transmission. The sender and receiver sites work together through the use of additional start and stop bits included in a byte.

- Local terminals are those that are positioned near a computer, anywhere from 50 feet up to 10,000 feet from it, depending upon the type of electrical connection that is used.

- Remote terminals are those terminals positioned further from a computer. They use either dial-up lines or leased lines for data transmission.

- Western Union has introduced a data communications network that furthers the Telex network currently available to 1.5 million subscribers. This network called EasyLink allows personal computer owners to joining the network for a minimum monthly service charge of $25 per month.

- For a user to use EasyLink, the user must use asynchronous data transmission, even parity, half-duplex or full duplex, ASCII code, 300 or 1200 baud, 80 or 132 column character field, and Direct Distance Dialing line with either a rotary or touchtone dialing capability.

- Reducing telephone costs can be reduced by using terminal controllers, multiplexors, or concentrators.

- Multiplexors are used to reduce transmission costs by sharing one telephone line with many terminals.

- A terminal controller is a specialized minicomputer that accepts messages from terminals and then sends the messages to the central processing unit. A terminal controller handles input and output for certain terminals; these terminals are clustered.

- A telephone line can be shared among the clustered terminals; the telephone line is referred to as a multi-point or multi-drop line.

- A multi-drop or multi-point line is one communication line that can serve several terminals at the same time. Each terminal has an address so polling can be done.

- A concentrator is usually a microcomputer or minicomputer that divides a channel into channels of slower speed. The purpose is to maximize throughput and reduce telephone costs.

- The concentrator has a store and forward capability which allows its internal storage to hold data for later transmission when the line is busy and send the data when the line is available.

- Terminals are classified as dumb, smart, or intelligent, categories that relate to the work they perform.

- A dumb terminal is used for only data entry (keying of data) and for inquiry.

- A smart terminal is programmed by the manufacturer. It can be used for data entry, inquiry, or business graphics.

- An intelligent terminal is programmable by a user.

- Networks are formed so communication can exist among different users at the same site or different sites. There are several types of networks available for use: the star network, ring network, and local-area network (LAN).

- The star network is set up so that each node communicates directly to a host computer. A controller, supplying intelligence to each node, is subject to losing communication when a malfunction exists, leaving the remote site helpless.

- A ring network contains no host computer but allows messages to pass around the network, thus avoiding the problem a controller can pose in the star network setup.

- The local-area network allows a mix of many manufacturers' products on a network. This network is usually limited to the same building or the same site.

- A host computer is that large-scale computer, usually a mainframe, located at a central site.

- Before a distributed data processing system is set up, a tremendous amount of planning must be done to ensure that data flow will not be disrupted and major software adjustments are not required.

STUDY GUIDE

REVIEW OF TERMINOLOGY

The following terminology was discussed in this chapter:

acoustic coupler
asynchronous
    transmission
back-end processor (BEP)
bandwidth
baud
bits per second (bps)
broadband
circuit
clustered terminals
coaxial cable
concentrator
contention
Dataphone Digital
    Service (DDS)
data communications
dedicated line
demodulate
dial-up line
digital line
Direct Distance Dialing
    (DDD)
down-line loading
dumb terminal
duplex circuit
EasyLink
Ethernet
facsimile (fax)
fiber optics
front-end processor (FEP)
full duplex circuit
geosynchronous satellite
half-duplex circuit
handshaking
hardwired
host computer
intelligence
intelligent terminal
interface
leased line
local loop
local terminal
local-area network

microwave
modem
modulate
multi-drop line
multiplexing
multiplexor
multi-point line
narrowband
network
node
packet
packet switching
point to point
polling
port
Private Automatic Branch
    Exchange (PABX)
private line
protocol
remote terminal
ring network
satellite
Satellite Business
    Systems (SBS)
simplex circuit
smart terminal
specialized common
    carrier
spooling
star network
subscriber's loop
switched line
synchronous transmission
telecommunications
telegraph
telephone
teleprocessing
Telex
teletex
terminal controller
touch-tone data phone
twisted pair
up-line dumping

value added network
    (VAN)
videotex
voice-grade line

voiceband
Widearea Telephone
    Service (WATS)
wideband

MULTIPLE CHOICE

Circle the letter of the item that correctly completes each statement.

1. When data, pictures, or voices are transmitted for processing from one location to another, this is called:
   a. bandwidth
   b. data
       communications
   c. analog
       transmission
   d. digital
       transmission
   e. broadband

2. Strands of glass are used for transmitting data in:
   a. coaxial cable
   b. satellite
   c. microwave
   d. telephone
   e. fiber optics

3. Which of the following are classified as to the bit rate capacity that can be used:
   a. narrowband
   b. wideband
   c. voiceband
   d. broadband
   e. all of these

4. Regular telephone lines that are used for transmission of data and voice are called:
   a. voice-grade lines
   b. voice lines
   c. digital lines
   d. switch-up lines
   e. leased lines

5. A way of connecting a terminal to a port can be through the use of:
   a. twisted-pair
       wiring
   b. dial-up lines
   c. switched lines
   d. leased lines
   e. all of these

6. Voice-grade lines transmit voice by analog signals but bits are transmitted in the form of a:
   a. pulse train
   b. switched line
   c. concentrator
   d. multiplexor
   e. multidrop line

7. Which of the following is used for efficient management of data traffic:

a. terminal
      controller
b. multiplexor
c. concentrator

d. all of these
e. none of these

8. Which of the following uses voiceband bandwidth:
   a. telegraph
   b. telephone
   c. satellite
   d. microwave
   e. coaxial cable

9. Which of the following uses radio transmission:
   a. telegraph
   b. satellite
   c. microwave
   d. coaxial cable
   e. fiber optics

10. A modem is not needed on:
    a. dial-up lines
    b. leased lines
    c. subscriber's loop
    d. digital lines
    e. voice-grade lines

11. An acoustic coupler can only be used on:
    a. dial-up lines
    b. leased lines
    c. subscriber's loop
    d. digital lines
    e. voice-grade lines

12. Which of the following uses light sources for its transmission of data:
    a. voice-grade lines
    b. digital lines
    c. coaxial cable
    d. satellites
    e. fiber optics

13. One telephone line can be shared with other users through the use of a:
    a. simplex circuit
    b. multiplexor
    c. point to point line configuration
    d. modem
    e. half-duplex circuit

14. When one communication line serves several users at the same time, this telephone line is referred to as a:
    a. concentrator line
    b. leased line
    c. point to point
    d. multi-drop line
    e. dedicated line

15. No switching ever occurs on this type of telephone line:
    a. dial-up line
    b. multi-drop line
    c. multi-point line
    d. leased line
    e. multiplexing

16. When analog signals are changed to digital signals, this is referred to as:
    a. modulating
    d. concentrating

b. demodulating
c. multiplexing

e. multidropping

17. When data can be transmitted in two directions but not at the same time, this is called:
    a. simplex circuit
    b. full duplex circuit
    c. modulating
    d. multiplexing
    e. half-duplex circuit

18. Which telephone lines are cheapest but yield poor transmission quality:
    a. private lines
    b. switched lines
    c. dedicated lines
    d. full duplex circuit
    e. multi-drop lines

19. Reducing telephone costs is accomplished by using:
    a. multi-drop lines
    b. multi-point lines
    c. multiplexing
    d. concentrating
    e. all of these

20. Which of the following is the 800 exchange dial-up line carrier:
    a. WATS
    b. Telex
    c. EasyLink
    d. Ethernet
    e. LAN

21. Satellites and cable use this type of bandwidth:
    a. narrowband
    b. voiceband
    c. wideband
    d. Ethernet
    e. VAN

22. The rules elaborating how bits are to be transmitted in data communications are called:
    a. WATS
    b. packet switching
    c. VAN
    d. node
    e. protocol

23. The capability to store and forward is found in:
    a. remote terminals
    b. local terminals
    c. a concentrator
    d. a multiplexor
    e. clustered terminals

24. The connection of a line and the later disconnection of it is referred to as:
    a. DDD
    b. protocol
    c. handshaking
    d. VAN
    e. LAN

25. A type of network that has its intelligence concentrated only in the center of it is called a:
    a. local network
    b. star network
    c. ring network
    d. LAN
    e. packet switching

26. Which network allows a mix of several manufacturers products:
   - *a.* local-area network
   - *b.* star network
   - *c.* ring network
   - *d.* WATS
   - *e.* DDS

27. Which network contains no host computer:
   - *a.* local-area network
   - *b.* star network
   - *c.* ring network
   - *d.* WATS
   - *e.* DDS

28. Tymnet and Telenet offer this type of transmission:
   - *a.* local-area network
   - *b.* star network
   - *c.* packet switching
   - *d.* digital lines
   - *e.* acoustic couplers

29. The site where intelligence is placed in a network is called a:
   - *a.* local terminal
   - *b.* remote terminal
   - *c.* star network
   - *d.* node
   - *e.* value-added network

30. Each terminal must have an address and a protocol for a computer to do:
   - *a.* multiplexing
   - *b.* concentrating
   - *c.* polling
   - *d.* networking
   - *e.* handshaking

TRUE/FALSE QUESTIONS

Circle the T next to a true statement; the F if it is false.

1. **T/F** There are three types of bandwidth that are used: narrowband, voiceband, and wideband.
2. **T/F** The most popular bandwidth is voiceband since it is used with telephone transmission.
3. **T/F** Local terminals are those that are located at a host computer site.
4. **T/F** Remote terminals must use dial-up lines.
5. **T/F** A port is an entry point for a telephone line to connect to wideband.
6. **T/F** When terminals located at different sites share the same telephone line, the physical connection is called multi-point.
7. **T/F** When terminals share the same telephone line and are at the same site, these terminals are clustered.
8. **T/F** If you decide to use Telenet or Tymnet, you are using company services called value added network.
9. **T/F** When using value added networks, all you need to provide is a personal computer and telephone line; they provide the programs for running your application.
10. **T/F** Slow-speed terminals usually use handshaking.
11. **T/F** Terminal controllers and concentrators are the same hardware.
12. **T/F** DDS is a digital service used for all types of data transmission.
13. **T/F** A user is most concerned with which type of cable is used and its required protocol.
14. **T/F** A local-area network is usually located at one site.
15. **T/F** Acoustic couplers can be used by any terminal.
16. **T/F** Point to point is the cheapest type of telephone hook-up.
17. **T/F** The word *modem* refers to the modulating and demodulating that are used in data transmission.
18. **T/F** The conversion of digital to analog signals is called demodulating.
19. **T/F** WATS uses digital lines.
20. **T/F** The latest developed cable used for data transmission by light impulses is called fiber optics.
21. **T/F** Full duplex carriers allow only a one-way transmission at one time.
22. **T/F** Only one manufacturer's products are usable in a local network.
23. **T/F** Microwave is used by the telephone company for transmitting calls over 500 miles.
24. **T/F** Another name for leased lines is private lines.
25. **T/F** For a computer to call up a terminal for data, that terminal must have an address.
26. **T/F** Down-line loading is the transferring of data or programs to a terminal controller.
27. **T/F** Spooling handles the printing of the results from some program at a later time; the results are temporarily stored on secondary storage.

REVIEW QUESTIONS

1. What are voice-grade lines? What can be transmitted over these lines?
2. What are digital lines? What can be transmitted over these lines? When can voice be transmitted over these lines?
3. What is a dial-up line? What other name is it known by? What is a leased line?
4. What are the advantages and disadvantages of using dial-up lines? Of using leased lines?
5. What is handshaking? When is it used?
6. What does the word *modem* stand for? What are the functions of a modem?
7. What is protocol? Why is it important? What types of terminals use it?
8. Name the three types of circuits used for data transmission. How does the transmission flow in each circuit?
9. When are terminals considered clustered?
10. What is multiplexing?
11. What two types of cables are used for data transmission? Which one is the most popularly used at the present time? Which one is in its infancy?
12. What is a geosynchronous satellite? What is it used for?
13. What is a dumb terminal? A smart terminal? An intelligent terminal? State how each is used.
14. What is a network? What are the three types of networks? Identify each.
15. What is down-line dumping? Up-line loading?

DISCUSSION QUESTIONS

1. Explain the differences between teleprocessing and data communications. Give four examples of each to support your answer.
2. The telephone is an instrument for analog transmission. What adjustments are made so it can be used for data communications? What kind of telephone lines are there?
3. How does the use of voice-grade lines differ from the use of digital lines?
4. What techniques are used by companies to reduce their telephone costs for data transmission? Explain how each technique accomplishes this.
5. When you visit an airport, you see telephones that might have the hotel's name printed over them. What kind of lines are these? Why? What are the major differences between these and your home telephone?
6. Assume that your college wishes to establish data communication facilities with a college located several hundred miles away. What type of communication facilities could be used? Why? What additional hardware would be needed? Where would these be located?
7. Using the same problem, let us change the number of miles for transmission to 1,500 miles. What type of communication facilities could be used? Why?
8. Discuss the differences among the various networks, explaining how each is used.

People in Computing

Mitchell R. Schrudder

COMPANY
The Middleburry Group

POSITION
President

EDUCATIONAL BACKGROUND
Degree in Business Administration,
University of Cincinnati

I have been in the data processing field since 1969. My experience includes computer operations, programming, systems, data processing management, teaching, and numerous speaking engagements. For four of the past six years, I have been in the consulting field, and currently I serve as president of the Middleburry Group, Inc. Prior to my current consulting position, I managed Corporate Systems and Programming for Cincom Systems, which is the world's largest independent software firm.

As president of a small management consulting firm, it is important to stay involved at all operating levels. In addition to staffing and administrative duties, client contacts and actual consultiing work are in competition for my time and energies. It is obvious that, in order to maintain a successful practice, self-discipline, scheduling, and planning are required personal attributes.
I recently took on a very large air cargo company as a client. Problems began for this client when their product line underwent extensive modification. Consumer oriented, overnight delivery with its high-volume individual clients and

shipments was added as a new service to an existing industrial client base generating fewer shipments but higher dollar value. Aside from the obvious strains on terminal operations to gather, sort, and deliver the higher volumes, an additional strain was placed on the existing computer system. Most airlines have huge data processing facilities and resources, with massive networks installed to accomplish high-speed real-time data transmission. This client was certainly no different. The problem here was how to increase airbill, manifesting, billing, sales analysis, and reporting tenfold without adding additional data entry personnel and resources.

By the time I arrived on the scene, the symptoms of excessive volumes for current system capabilities were already surfacing. Late reporting, slow airbill entry, and concern over a growing accounts receivable were evident. The new product line required more sales information and analysis, which were also lagging. The biggest problem of all was the growing error rate in data entry. This rate was as high as 42 percent. The errors resulted in increased accounts receivable, as customers refused to pay incorrect billing. Distorted sales analysis and trends were also a by-product. Since this network included 1,200 visual display units, 650 printers, and 500 employees nationwide, the problems had to be addressed and solved quickly.

My personal view of distributed data processing includes what I refer to as a "vested interest." What that means basically is: don't require any user to input data, even if it

resides on their own source, if that data is not pertinent to that users' functional responsibilities. In this client's case, terminal agents were inputting all data on the airbill. After all, the airbill is their source document, and this surely makes distributed data processing sense. But does it? Look more closely at the data on the airbill, and you'll find that only 25 of the 260 fields entered into the system are related to actual freight loading. These were the only pieces of data that held interest to the agent. The balance of the entries were related to finance, sales, marketing, billing, and so on. There was no "vested interest" in making sure these entries were 100 percent correct upon entry. Sure, many edits existed in this system; however, when the volumes grew so quickly, shortcuts were developed and errors increased.

Without getting into great detail, the answer here was to keep the freight entries in the terminals and move the sales and financial entries to a central data entry point where they could be edited, validated, and monitored for accuracy—a disbursement in accordance with the vested interest viewpoint. The tasks involved in such a data reorganization were broad in scope and certainly not without complications; however, this client now processes ten times the inputted data with no increase in the number of traffic agents and a maintained and manageable 8 percent error rate. The financial/sales entries are accomplished by fifteen data entry people at a single facility.

Application

AVON PRODUCTS

AVON uses minicomputers to support its business. The Representative Order Control System (ROCS) is used to provide process control automation to distribution facilities in the shipping systems division. From these facilities, orders are shipped to AVON representatives at the rate of approximately 10,000 orders a day from each of six facilities.

Avon Products has developed a system for handling its orders called ROCS (Representative Order Control System). ROCS provides efficient, accurate, and economic processing of representatives' orders in the Avon Branch. The main objectives for this system include:

1. decreasing branch controllable lost orders

2. decreasing delivery company lost orders

3. catching gross order errors and correcting them before shipment

4. providing a data base for future automated subsystems

5. keeping the status of representatives' orders updated in the IBM mainframe.

The data base includes a master representative file which includes information such as the representative's name and address, truck codes, and package data. Other information includes item data such as the item number, location, weight, and description, and order data including the group number, representative number, billing sequence number and the quantity.

The complete ROCS system is planned to be installed in phases. Below is the flow of how the complete ROCS System will operate.

Mechanical Assembly System (MAS) releases and prepares the order. The order then passes through the MAS order start function where a label is applied to the first tray of the order and is then scanned. The billing sequence number, ROCS number, and number of trays are then transmitted to the ROCS minicomputer. Orders are then diverted to the Set Table Area or directly to the Manual/Station Lighting Lines. The purpose of this subsystem is to reduce assembly errors and increase productivity by simplifying and improving the manual assembly of products in a station through the use of computer aided display indicators and control of the conveyor belt. In the event of error (missing items, broken trays, etc.,) the order can be flagged by pressing the error correct button on the panel. On leaving the line, the order can be corrected in an error correction area.

Completely assembled orders leaving the Manual/Station Lighting Lines move to the automatic checkweighing subsystem. High speed scales weigh each order to detect errors based on the calculated weight stored in the ROCS computer. The orders failing this check will divert to an Error Correction Area. Here they are manually examined using the enclosed list.

Orders leaving Error Correction

are then merged back with the non-error orders to the Packing and Closing Area where packing is done by shrink wrapping a plastic film over the order through heat tunnels.

After packing is complete, the order then goes through the closing area where Auto Addressing spray prints the shipping labels and the dock sortation bar code on each tray of the order. Completed orders are strapped and conveyed to Dock Sortation, where each package is tracked and diverted to its preassigned door. An operator assigns all on-schedule trucks to their appropriate dock doors using the daily run screen. The Dock Sortation subsystem uses this daily run information in conjunction with information contained in the off-schedule matrix to generate a convert table of all possible bar codes and signed door numbers. This table is then down-loaded to the sortation microcomputer which, in turn, uses the table to divert packages. As packages are correctly diverted, the sortation microcomputer sends divert messages back to the dock sortation subsystem. The dock subsystem then evaluates these messages and merges this information with manually sorted package information received from the manual input screen. This information is then sent to the ROCS system to close the control loop by updating its files with the shipping status.

At 'truck out' time, shipping documents, Bills of Lading, and shipping manifests are generated for each truck by entering appropriate operator commands through the operator's terminal. Copies of these documents are sent with the trailer for delivery companies' use while the originals are kept in the branch as record of shipment. At the end of the day, a shipping receipts tape is created during the file purge operation. The tape is then used to update the representative information file stored on the IBM mainframe.

You might ask what are some of the reports and information needed by employees during the day? The system must accommodate many different types of reports such as the manifests for the current day, all truck codes for a given day, manifests from previous days, bills of lading statistics, all data relating to an order inquiry, types of errors and messages for corrections.

Routines must also be set up to accommodate all purging (eliminating of old records) from the file, the contents of which are transferred to a scratch tape that is kept for history. Last but not least, there has to be methods established to restore the data base.

PART FOUR

Software

11 Beginning Programming

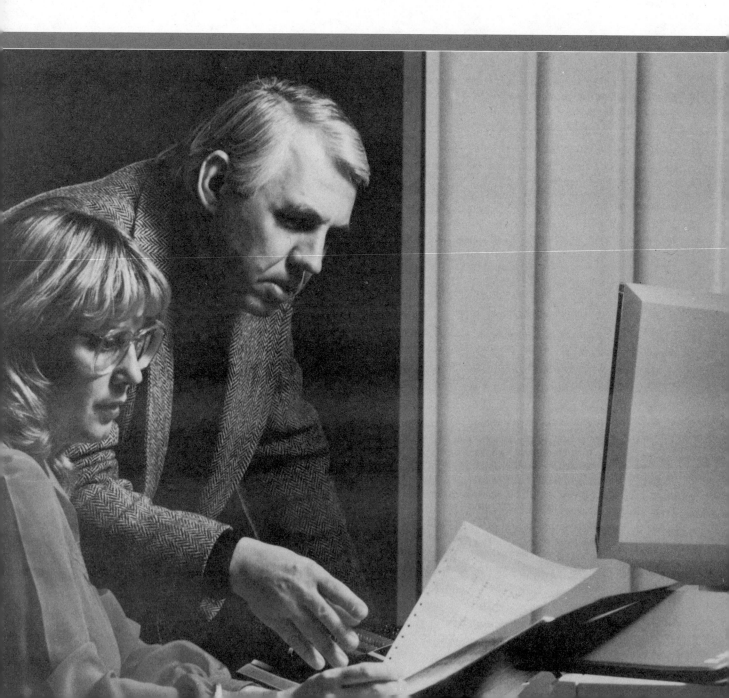

OUTLINE

PROLOGUE

John needs to wake up at 5:30 each morning. It seems as though his wife has trouble reading the clock that early in the morning. Sometimes she has gotten him up at 4:30 instead, and once it was at 3:30 A.M. After several rude awakenings in the early morning hours, John decided to take the situation in hand.

Down to the computer store he went. For $40, John got a small device that measures about 4 inches by 4 inches. It certainly keeps the peace in the household now. The talking clock automatically announces the time every hour. If you want to find out what time it is, you merely push a button.

There is an alarm that can be set. Five minutes before the alarm is to ring, a voice tells John, "It is 5:25." At 5:30 it plays a melody for about ten seconds.

If you have four hours to clean the house before company comes, you can set the dials to give you an hourly countdown as to the hours you have remaining.

HOW DOES IT DO THAT?

READ ON.

OBJECTIVES

After studying this chapter, you should be able to:

1. Differentiate between bottom-up design and top-down design.

2. Explain how structure charts are constructed and be able to construct some.

3. Identify each of the symbols used in a flowchart and be able to prepare some flowcharts.

4. Differentiate among sequence, selection, and repetition constructs.

5. Write pseudocode to represent some straightforward algorithms.

6. Explain the parts of a decision table and why it is used.

INTRODUCTION

A program is rarely executed correctly by a computer unless considerable problem solving time has been involved in the program's writing. After problem solving is completed, the computer language is then coded from that plan. As discussed in Chapter 6, planning to solve the problem at hand involves developing a series of instructions referred to as an algorithm.

An algorithm is prepared so the problem at hand can be solved in a systematic way. It is necessary to sit at the drawing board and think. If a step is placed at the wrong spot in the logic, the problem may not be solved correctly. Many times after thinking the problem through, we find an easier way to do it. The adjustment is then made so that the problem is solved in the quickest and most efficient way.

The first step in setting up an algorithm involves determining the objectives. The second step is to specify the input and output data formats. The third step involves developing the overview of the logic. A detailed plan, however, must also be established to guide the programmer when the computer language instructions are written.

Let us look into each type of problem-solving methodology, noting how each is used. The discussion centers on the use of structured walk-throughs, a structure chart, flowchart, pseudocode, and documentation.

TOP-DOWN DESIGN AND STRUCTURED PROGRAMMING

The beginning programming techniques developed in the early 1950s centered around the solving of a problem using **bottom-up design,** in which the extreme details of the programming solution are investigated first, as opposed to beginning with a breakdown by broad objectives. Each program was written in isolation to solve a particular problem. The problems became obvious when the various programs for the complete system had to work together to produce the desired processing. In those days computer memory was often a limiting factor in processing programs. Program logic was designed for a program to fit in primary storage. Programmers were also concerned with executing programs in as fast an execution time as possible, thus producing programs that were often done in a far less than straightforward way.

For an example of bottom-up design, assume that a programmer is assigned to create a system for an analytical laboratory. The laboratory handles all types of chemical analyses for products that the company produces. Various chemical engineers submit for analysis samples of improved company products or of competitor's products. The programmer must prepare a program for charging the engineers for the analyses requested, so the appropriate accounting charges can be made to the respective departments. The programmer completes this task.

To make the system more efficient in the laboratory, the programmer wishes to signal the various technicians in the laboratory that certain preparatory work must be done so that the submitted samples can be thoroughly and quickly analyzed. The programmer writes a program to accomplish this. At this point, two individual, complicated programs have been written and tested separately. Both of these programs must now be successfully tied together so that the accounting and the signalling of future analyses applications can be implemented simultaneously. If the programmer did not thoroughly think the problem through at the beginning, the joining of the programs will be a problem. This is one of the major problems involved with bottom-up design.

As the example suggests when programming began in the early 1950s, programmers worked individually on problems, solving them the best way that the programmers knew. Most of the programs, although very large in size, were individually created. Today applications become so large that several programmers are involved in solving one. Project teams are often set up, consisting of several programmers and a project leader. Programmers often move to other jobs and, hence, leave the company before a project is completed, requiring another programmer to begin work in midstream. So that a programmer can begin work in the middle of a project, there is a definite need for preparing an English summary of how a problem was solved. Also, there is a need for using straightforward programming techniques so the project can be carried through successfully.

Today, computer memory is not such a limiting factor; the emphasis is placed on the programming technique rather than on how long the program requires for execution, as was done in the 1950s and 1960s. Programs can thus be written in a far more structured (highly organized) manner, producing code that is easier to read and to change later, if the need arises. With the increasing demands for programming efficiency and standardization, the problem-solving technique has changed in approach: programmers examine the problem as a whole, outlining the major steps that must be completed (in other words, getting the complete picture first), then breaking these main functions into greater detail. This is referred to as **top-down design** and is used in structured programming.

Today **structured programming** is used; it is a set of techniques designed to improve the organization of the program, to facilitate solving a problem, and to make the code easier to write and read in both an individual and group project environment. There is a definite need for efficient and standardized approaches so other programmers can later modify a program to incorporate some desired changes. This technique of changing or updating programs that are already written is called **program maintenance.** It is estimated that 80 percent of programmers' activities involve program maintenance rather than original program creation. The attempt to keep things simple and straightforward, coupled with high programmer turn-over and a trend toward large programs, have led to the structured program approach.

Using structured programming, the problem solving is divided into segments called **modules.** Each module entails processing of data that are logically related. Modules are the functional parts that make the processing work. Ideally, each module works independently of the other modules, although this sometimes is impossible. Relate the concept of using modules to the baking of a cake. The various modules or steps that could be listed would be the purchasing of the necessary ingredients, the preparation of the ingredients, and the baking of the cake. Under each of these three modules, the details would be listed.

Modules are ranked by hierarchy as to importance. The lower the module on the structural organization plan, the more detail is given as to the programming steps involved. The top module level is the control module, which gives the overall view of structure for the program. The program is designed so that at each level of modules, more detail is given.

A module is coded and tested and is then added to the other tested modules. This procedure makes program integration easier since there is one entry and one exit point per module. Think of a module as being like a room. Inside the room we do all work pertinent to calculation of the grade point average (GPA), for example. We enter the room through one door, do the calculation, and then leave the room through only one other door. This makes any future modification of a program easy since we know there is only one way to enter the module and one way to exit.

The effect of the top-down design and structured programming has been to lower the cost of programming overall. Although salaries are constantly increasing because of inflation, the top-down design and structured programming have had their marked effects on increasing programmer efficiency and reducing costs. Formerly, when programmers coded traditional programs using the bottom-up design, it was estimated that about ten to fifteen lines of code were written and tested per day. With structured programming design, about twenty to forty lines of code are written and tested per day. The latest developed languages (to be discussed in Chapter 18) allow programmers to write and debug about 100 lines of code.

CHECKPOINT **Can you:**

State the differences between bottom-up design and top-down design?

Tell why structured programming is used today?

PROBLEM-SOLVING METHODOLOGIES

Five methodologies as to how logic is designed for problem solving are presented in this chapter: structure charts, structured walk-throughs, flowcharts, pseudocode, and decision tables. Structure charts (like organization charts) and structured walk-throughs (like evaluation sessions) are prepared to set forth the overall ideas of how a problem is to be solved. As soon as a problem is presented to a data processing professional, that person must think the problem through, breaking the problem into modules.

After the overview is completed, the details are worked out, with flowcharts (like blueprints), pseudocodes (like English written instructions), or decision tables (a way of processing set in columns).

Structure Chart

A **structure chart,** or **hierarchy chart,** is developed by the programmer as one of the first methods of deriving the algorithm. Since structured programming uses

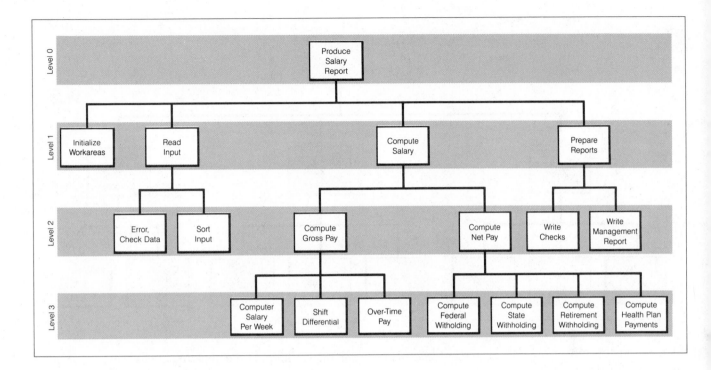

FIGURE 11.1

Structure chart for producing a salary report.

the top-down design, each program is designed by first developing the overall picture of the program, with its major topics set up in modules.

Figure 11.1 shows a structure chart. The control module is the top level, called Level 0. Notice how Level 1 deals with **initialization,** (the setting up of various values for data), inputting, and updating according to the conditions needed for their use. Level 2 deals with more detail, such as sorting and error protection (making certain that data is accurate).

Development of a Structure Chart. Accepting the premise that getting to school some days poses a problem not only for the teacher but also for the student, let us develop a structure chart to show the process by which this procedure is accomplished.

The control module is called GETTING TO SCHOOL and is of a Level 0 importance. Thinking of major concepts, the problem could be broken into three modules: (1) getting up, (2) preparing for school, and (3) arranging transportation to school. Refer to the structure chart shown in Figure 11.2. Level 2 shows procedures that are routinely performed; notice that these read left to right in the order in which they are performed. It must be pointed out that this left to right ordering is not followed on all structure charts. Pay particular attention to the fact that the preparation for school involves dressing and eating, and these functions are associated only with this module. Eating while driving or on the bus to school disrupts the existing concept of modules, which separates eating from the other modules exclusively.

The structure chart closely resembles the organization chart of a business or a school. Control is passed from the control module (the college president) to the next level of modules (the vice-presidents), and so on (just as it is passed in turn

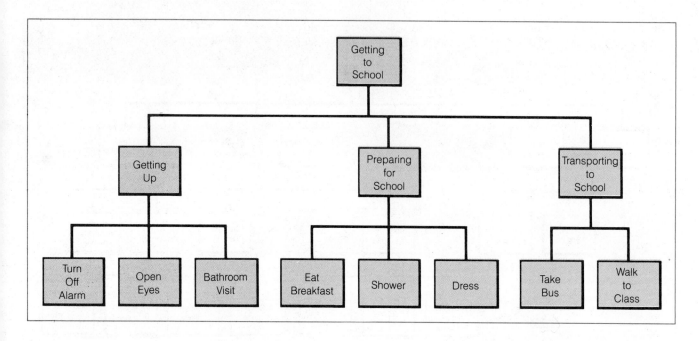

FIGURE 11.2
Structure chart for getting to school.

to the deans, who oversee the workings of the department chairpersons). Notice that the structure chart does not show any flow of data or the order of its execution. Also notice that there is no indication as to when each module is to be performed and how often it is to be done. The chart's sole purpose is to indicate planning and implementation.

The overall importance of the structure chart as a programmer's tool is not evident when straightforward problems are solved. However, when the logic for a problem deals with a large processing concept—one that has several program-mers working on the same programming team to solve the problem—then its significance is clear. The structure chart breaks the major ideas into smaller parts in a meaningful way. When programming teams are assigned to a project, one module might be assigned to an individual or several programmers, depending upon its complexity. The length of a module in many companies seems to be about fifty lines of code; it is felt that longer modules tend to become burdensome.

CHECKPOINT **Can you:**

Explain how a structure chart is constructed?

Structured Walk-Throughs

A method for testing the proposed solution to a problem is called a **structured walk-through.** This programming methodology uses peer review of a programmer's proposed solution. Sometimes a programmer's logic in determining how to get from one point in a program to another point is flawed. The proposed algorithm is discussed, evaluated, and adjusted if needed. Discussion is held to determine if any errors in program design are apparent. This method produces a more efficient program design and, it is hoped, reduces design time.

Another advantage of using a structured walk-through is to provide a program that can be easily modified at a later time to meet new user needs or requirements of law. Recall that any changes made to an existing program are referred to as program maintenance. Most of a programmer's time involves program maintenance rather than the creation of new programs. Any modification is made easier if the program is originally set up without "tricky" code. Most times the KISS principle is the easiest: keep it simple, stupid!

Chevron Corporation uses a very interesting idea in its structured walk-throughs. The programmer plans how a problem is to be solved and then places color-coded cards with appropriate words noted on the cards on a conference room wall, showing the over-all solution to a problem. Each colored card represents a different type of processing. At points in the logic where a programmer is uncertain as to the correct development of logic, a card with a question mark is placed. The systems analyst then views the algorithm. It is easy to change the logic pattern by merely shuffling the cards, producing the best overall solution to the problem. A real problem exists, however, when a systems analyst sees a sea of question marks upon entering the conference room.

After the plan is finished, the programmer then codes these steps into a language that the computer can understand. The programmer is the designer of logic that must be followed by the computer. Any designer of a product, whether it be a bridge, a dress, or a computer program, must lay out the design carefully and accurately.

Flowcharts

There has to be some easy and quick way to put the program logic down on paper; it would be very tedious indeed to write all a program's steps down in longhand. Nor would such a process pinpoint the steps in a concise method. For this reason, the flowchart was devised. Flowcharting explains the processing done in the module.

A **flowchart** is a graphic display of logic to solve a problem. It describes, by the use of symbols and words, how data is to flow (be used) when processing is done. The programmer traces the outer edges of a symbol from a **template** onto paper as it is needed in the problem logic. Phrases are written inside the symbol designating the activity that is to be performed. The combination of the symbols and short phrases, placed in a certain order, tell the logic. The various symbols that are used on most flowcharts are shown in Figure 11.3.

Construction of a Flowchart for Listing Data. Assume that a diskette or magnetic disk contains a file of student data, such as the name, address, and age, but the number of records is unknown. A printout of all records stored in the file is needed. Refer to Figure 11.4(a) for an example of input and output data. What type of processing is needed? The record must be read. The line must be printed.

The first symbol used in the flowchart is the oval with the word *START*

FIGURE 11.3
Symbols used to denote specific functions in flowcharts.

Symbol	What It Represents
	Shows input and output that is not oriented to any device.
	Shows when magnetic tape is to be read or written.
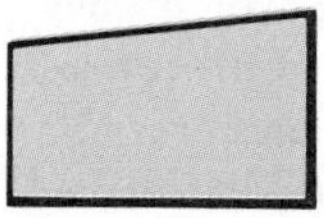	Identifies any on-line keyboard activity.
	Identifies any calculations that are to be done or any initializing of workareas to a specified value, also used (depending upon the language) for opening and closing files.
	Identifies any decisions that are to be done in logic.
	Shows an off-page connector when the flowchart exceeds one page.
	Shows the entry or exit point of logic in the flowchart.
	Identifies the beginning and the end of the flowchart. Shows the start and end of a module identified by a pre-defined process symbol.
	Identifies the beginning and the end of the flowchart. The start of a module identified by a pre-defined process symbol.
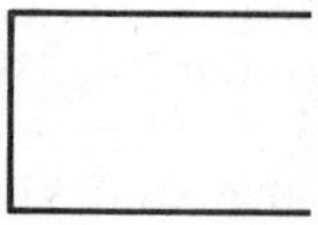	Shows any comments included in the logic.

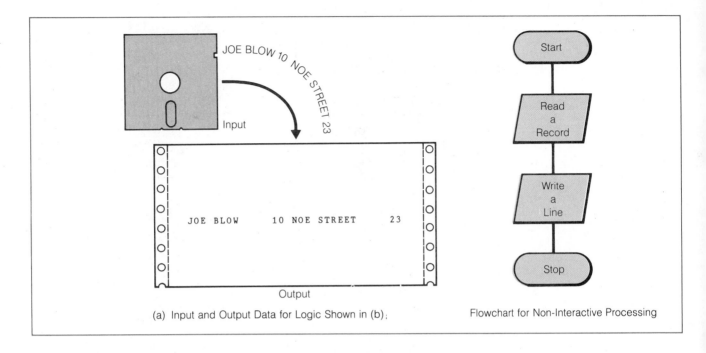

(a) Input and Output Data for Logic Shown in (b).

Flowchart for Non-Interactive Processing

written inside as shown in Figure 11.4(b). The next thing that must be done is to read a record. Inside the record symbol the words *READ A RECORD* are written. Unless the record is read, the computer could not work on the data. The next symbol is the *WRITE* symbol. Inside that symbol the fields to be printed are noted. Notice how the line connects the symbols together. The oval with the word *STOP* is also included.

Figure 11.4(b) illustrates **non-iterative processing,** in which just one record is read and processed with no repeating of successive steps. Reading and processing one record could never be cost justified on a computer. The repetition of steps that makes it feasible to use a computer is called **iterative processing.** In Figure 11.5(a), notice how the directional line is drawn so that the processing of reading and writing continues. When certain processing is to be done over and over again, this is called **looping.** As the logic is stated in parts a and b of Figure 11.5, the computer is never instructed to stop processing on this problem. When there are no more records to process, the computer should stop processing this job. Figure 11.5(b) shows the same processing but uses connectors instead of the directional line used in Figure 11.5(a).

To check whether there are any more records to process, a question is asked of the computer. **A decision** asks a question and provides an answer; it uses the diamond-shaped symbol with the phrase *END OF FILE? (EOF)* written inside the symbol as shown in Figure 11.6(a). The two possible answers are true or false. (Some companies use yes or no answers rather than true or false, but the meaning is the same.) Each answer can be represented by drawing a line from the symbol and then labelling the line as to the condition it represents.

Notice in Figure 11.6(a) how a read of a record appears twice in the flowchart. The first read is used to initially input data into the computer system. It is called a **priming read,** and merely "gets the ball rolling" before the loop is encountered.

FIGURE 11.4
Example flowchart and input and output it generates.

FIGURE 11.5
Endless loops.

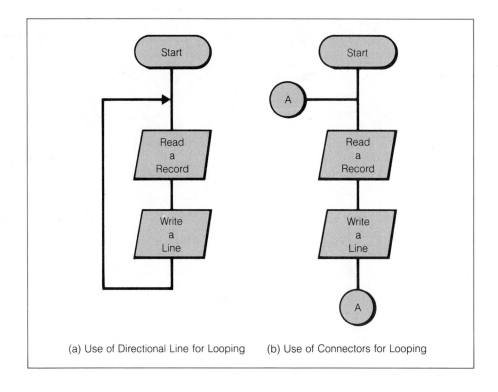

(a) Use of Directional Line for Looping   (b) Use of Connectors for Looping

The second read is used within the loop or iterative processing. The second read is dictated by the rules for looping. The loop always begins with a decision or ends with one; the choice is explained later. You cannot stay in revolving doors forever. At some time you must leave them, but you must leave them always at the same point. Loops are left, then, at the point of decision, placed either at the beginning or at the end of the loop. In this case, it is at the end of the loop.

The flowcharts that we have used so far have no modules included in them. Let us use that processing included in the loop in Figure 11.6(a) to change the flowchart to one that is slightly more structured. The **predefined process symbol** used for showing modules is a rectangle that has a set of vertical lines on its left- and right-hand sides. Inside the predefined process symbol is a name representing that module. The symbol communicates that the processing of that module is illustrated in a separate section elsewhere in the flowchart. This section begins with an oval bearing the same module name stated in the predefined process symbol, followed by the desired processing symbols and instructions. After the processing in the module is completed, flow returns to the main flowchart for the next processing. The return always points back to the symbol following the predefined process symbol. Refer to Figure 11.6(b). The same concept is used in this figure as was done in Figure 11.6(a). More complex flowcharts have many modules included, each one of which uses a predefined process symbol with a unique name, a separate processing section beginning with an oval bearing the same name and ending with a return to the main flowchart.

Use of Decisions on Data. Decisions (questions) about data use the diamond-shaped symbol. From that symbol, lines are drawn which direct the logic to

FIGURE 11.6 **Same processing is shown in two different ways of flowcharting.**

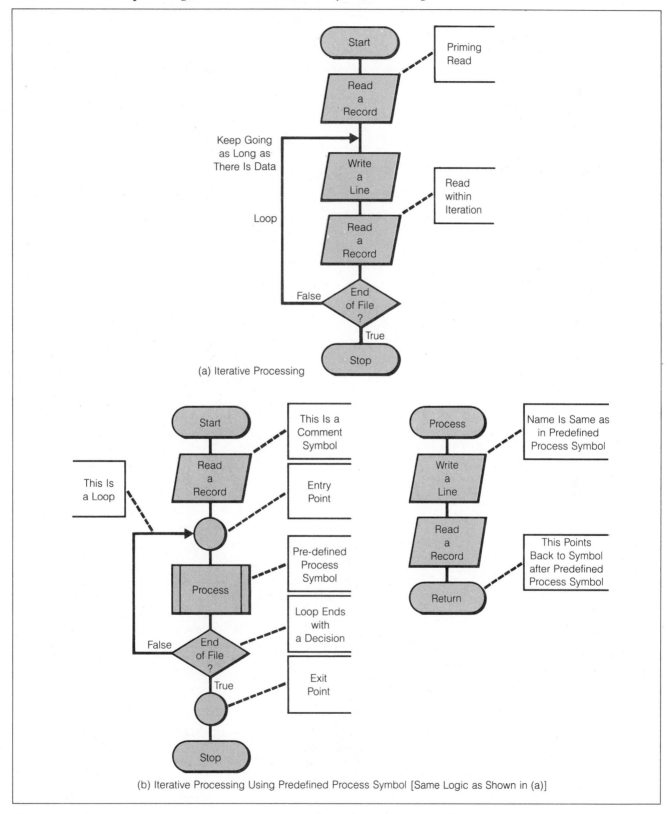

(a) Iterative Processing

(b) Iterative Processing Using Predefined Process Symbol [Same Logic as Shown in (a)]

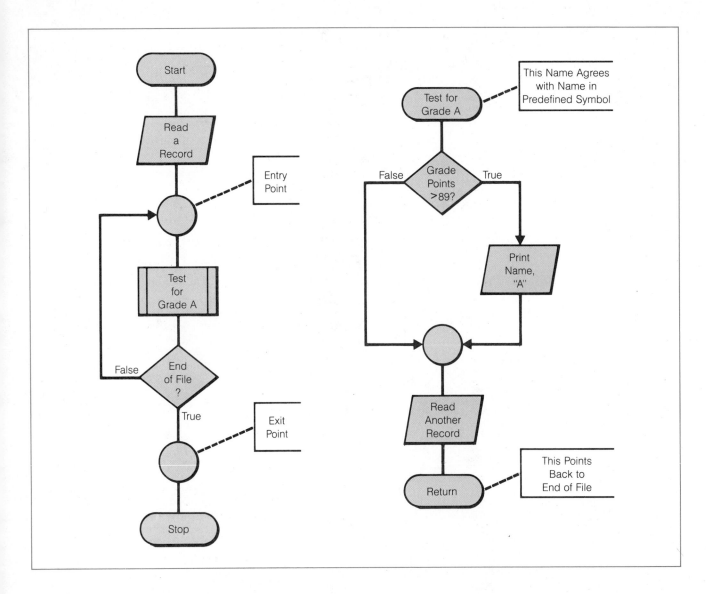

FIGURE 11.7
Printing only names of A students.

different paths. In structured programming questions can be formed in several ways, but answers to these questions are always either true or false. The practice today in flowcharting is to make the true leg run to the right from the decision symbol.

Some possible ways of asking questions about data or a condition involve comparing for relative value, using these symbols:

equal to ($=$)
unequal to ($\neq$)
greater than ($>$)
less than ($<$)
less than or equal to ($<=$)
greater than or equal to ($>=$)

Assume, for the sake of example, that Mrs. Pritchard wishes to assign letter grades based upon the scores earned by her students. If the score is greater than 89, the letter grade of an A is to be printed. No other grades are to be printed. Figure 11.7 illustrates one way of asking the question about the data: GRADE > 89? The question could have been asked in this way: GRADE <= 89? In this case, the print of name and the letter A would appear on the false leg rather than on the true leg.

CHECKPOINT Can you:

Identify each of the symbols used in flowcharting?

Explain how decisions are constructed?

Constructs of Structured Programming. The most common techniques, used in structured programming to solve all problems are called **constructs.** Sequence, selection, and repetition constructs are illustrated graphically in Figure 11.8. Note that sequence processes one instruction after another, selection asks questions, and repetition provides looping. These three constructs are examined and appropriate flowchart examples given in the sections that follow.

● Sequence. **Sequence** refers to an instruction or a series of instructions that does a required calculation or allows input or output of data. These steps are executed by the computer one after the other since there is no change to the flow of logic. On a flowchart, the rectangle symbol is used to show sequence.

The idea of sequence can be related to everyday life in the process of getting a glass of milk. Using the example in Figure 11.9, note the sequence of steps: the refrigerator door is opened, the carton of milk selected, and so on, before the milk is drunk. Many steps are taken before the milk is drunk, none of which can be omitted. In the sequence construct, notice there is one entry and one exit.

Figure 11.10 presents two examples of sequence processing, one of which deals with employee records and the second, with three numbers. For the employee record, the data pertains to the hours worked, the rate of pay, and the tax deduction in dollars. The input and output data prepared when developing the algorithm is shown in Figure 11.10.

Figure 11.11 gives another example of sequence. The input is shown in Figure 11.11(a); the output is shown in Figure 11.11(b). In this example, the output is more meaningful since a heading is included along with the output data. Part d of Figure 11.11 shows a printer spacing chart for the positioning of the data as well as the heading. The complete flowchart is shown in Figure 11.11(c).

● Selection. **Selection** refers to testing for a certain condition or asking a question about data. In structured programming, there are only two possible answers to questions—true or false (or yes or no). One selection technique variation is known as the **IF-THEN-ELSE.** The instructions that are to be executed when the condition is true follow the IF-THEN alternative. The instructions following the ELSE alternative represent what is to be executed when the condition is false. On a flowchart, the selection uses the diamond-shaped symbol. The true alternative is

FIGURE 11.8 **Three constructs.**

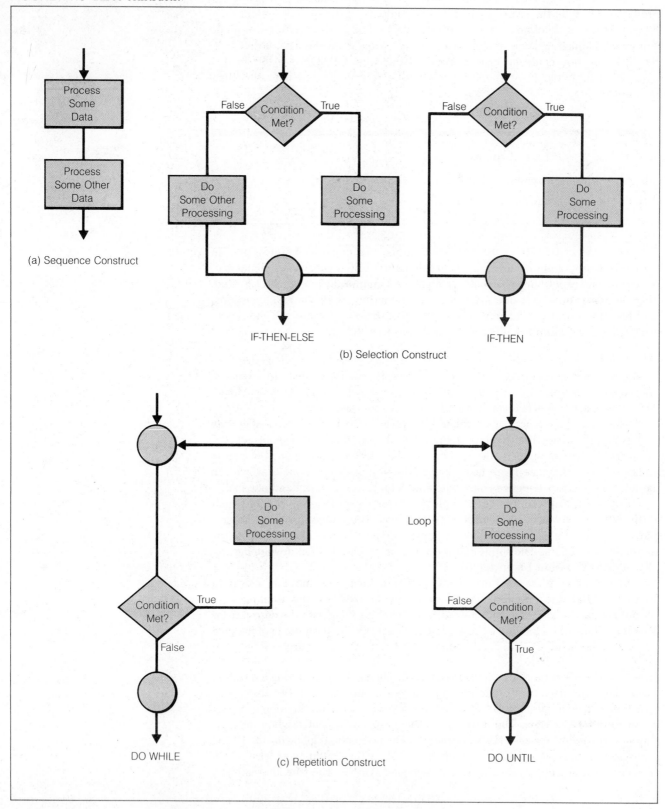

(a) Sequence Construct

IF-THEN-ELSE

IF-THEN

(b) Selection Construct

DO WHILE

(c) Repetition Construct

DO UNTIL

noted as a line that usually runs to the right from the diamond-shaped symbol. The false alternative is usually shown by a line running to the left from the diamond-shaped symbol. The other selection variation is made whether a condition is true or false which requires some processing when the condition is only true; this is referred to as the **IF-THEN.** Refer again to Figure 11.8, and notice how the connector symbol (the small circle) is used to end the selection. Putting it another way, there are as many connectors to end the selection as there are decisions to begin it.

Let us begin the discussion on selection with an example using just one record. We will then change to iterative processing later in the discussion.

Assume that the Ludkey Furniture Store wishes to reward employees who have performed satisfactory work during their tenure with the company, giving a one-time bonus to those employees. The company decides to code a 3 in the record of the employee who has performed satisfactory work during tenure with the company. The input data is shown in Figure 11.12(a); the output is shown in Figure 11.12(b). The employee whose performance is coded as a 3 is to receive a $500.00 increment. If the employee's record does not contain a code of a 3, that employee is to receive only a $50 increment. Refer to part c of Figure 11.12 for the complete flowchart showing the IF-THEN-ELSE variation of the selection construct.

Referring to part d of Figure 11.12, let us suppose that the Ludkey Furniture Company wishes to give a bonus to only employees whose job performance is rated a 3; other codes receive no bonus. This flowchart uses the IF-THEN variation of selection construct.

The Quick Dating Bureau has a prospect named Freddie who only wishes to join the dating bureau if there is a lady member who has red hair. The dating bureau desperately needs new members so they agree to bet Freddie that the first record in the file of lady members has red hair. When there is a **hit,** which means that the data that you were looking for compares equal to the data being examined, the computer will print a message stating that the color of hair is red. In this example, a message will be printed in either case, the contents of the message depending upon what color hair is entered in the first record of the file. Figure 11.13 reads just one record.

Freddie is still not happy as he claims it was just dumb luck that there was a hit. Now he wants to know the name of the lady and whether she has red hair and green or blue eyes. Refer to Figure 11.14. Two IFs used together are called **nested IFs:** the second IF statement is only tested when the first IF statement is true. Notice how the connector symbol is used for each decision.

In the examples for the Ludkey Furniture Company and Quick Dating Bureau, only one record was shown and inputted. Efficient computer usage is based, however, upon the computer being used to process the same kind of data over and over again. Variations as to the way that a problem is solved can be achieved by selection, but the repetitive processes of a computer are needed.

● Repetition. **Repetition** involves the use of a series of instructions that are repeated over and over again (looping) until a certain condition is met, until there is no more data, a desired amount is calculated, or a hit is made. Sometimes the user wishes a series of instructions to be repeated a certain number of times. Most frequently, however, the user wishes to do repetitive work for as long as there is data to process.

FIGURE 11.9
Example flowchart use.

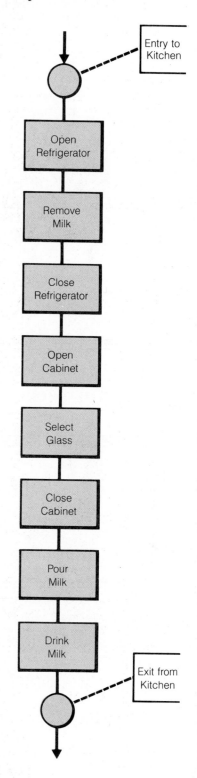

FIGURE 11.10 **Examples of input, flowchart, and printed data.**

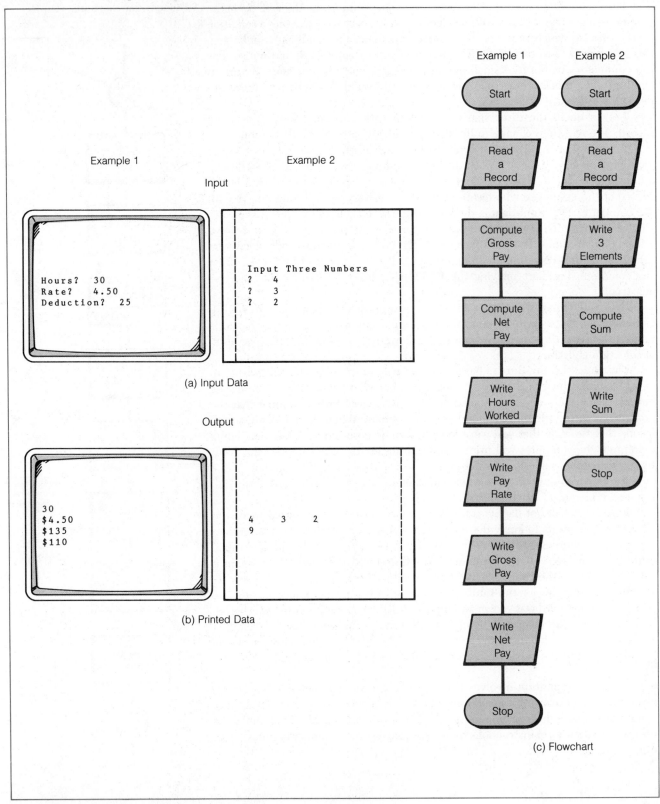

Example 1

Example 2

Input

```
Hours?    30
Rate?     4.50
Deduction?    25
```

```
Input Three Numbers
?    4
?    3
?    2
```

(a) Input Data

Output

```
30
$4.50
$135
$110
```

```
4       3       2
9
```

(b) Printed Data

Example 1

Start → Read a Record → Compute Gross Pay → Compute Net Pay → Write Hours Worked → Write Pay Rate → Write Gross Pay → Write Net Pay → Stop

Example 2

Start → Read a Record → Write 3 Elements → Compute Sum → Write Sum → Stop

(c) Flowchart

FIGURE 11.11 **Example of input, flowchart, and printed data for a record.**

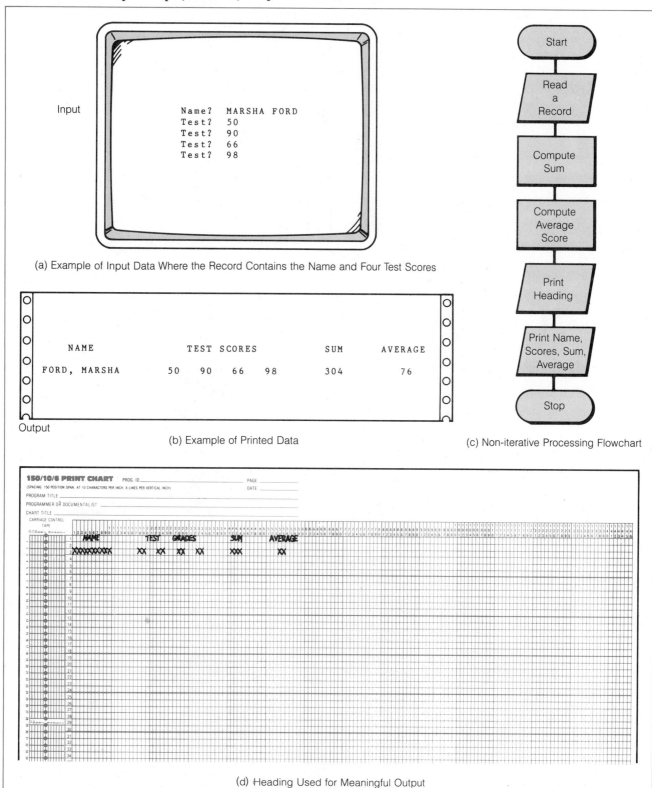

(a) Example of Input Data Where the Record Contains the Name and Four Test Scores

(b) Example of Printed Data

(c) Non-iterative Processing Flowchart

(d) Heading Used for Meaningful Output

FIGURE 11.12 **Example of selection used on input to accomplish output for a record.**

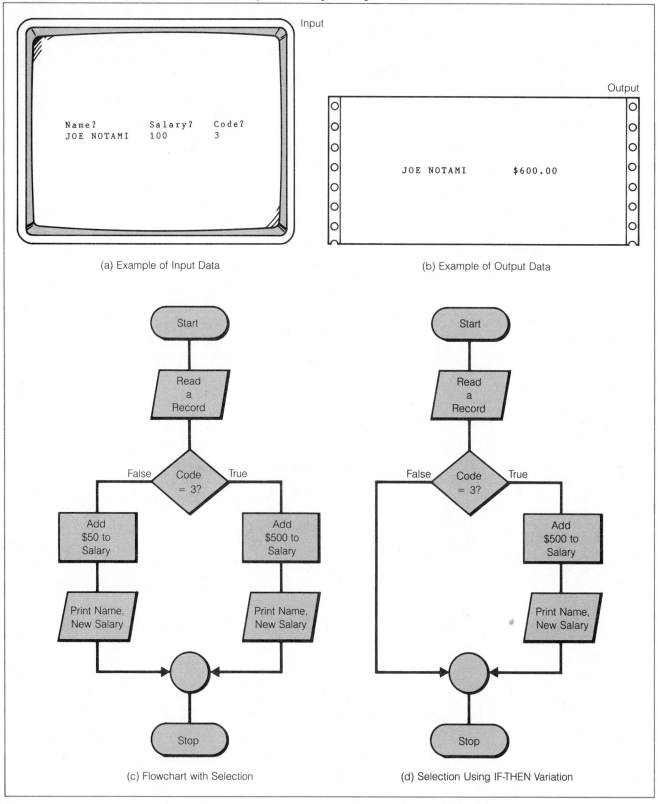

Input

```
Name?        Salary?    Code?
JOE NOTAMI   100        3
```

(a) Example of Input Data

Output

```
JOE NOTAMI        $600.00
```

(b) Example of Output Data

(c) Flowchart with Selection

(d) Selection Using IF-THEN Variation

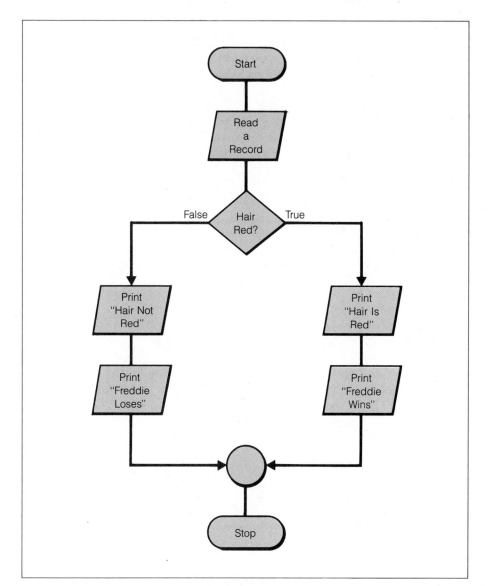

FIGURE 11.13
**Non-iterative processing with
selection.**

Repetition involves two methods: the DO WHILE and the DO UNTIL. The DO WHILE can be likened to the testing of the swimming pool water with your big toe to determine if the temperature of the water is suitable for swimming. If so, you jump in and keep swimming until the water is no longer suitable. The DO UNTIL is more bold in that you jump in the water and then determine if you want to stay in there!

Repetitive work is shown on a flowchart easily by using a directional line or a connector, as noted previously.

Usually the entire file is to be inputted, but the user is not certain as to the number of records in the file. The DO WHILE construct provides an open-ended way of looping without the need to know the number of records in the file.

The **DO WHILE** states that a function be done as long as the condition is true. As long as there is data (and the condition is true), the instructions in the loop are to be repeated. When there is no more data (and the condition becomes

FIGURE 11.14
Flowchart using nested IFs.

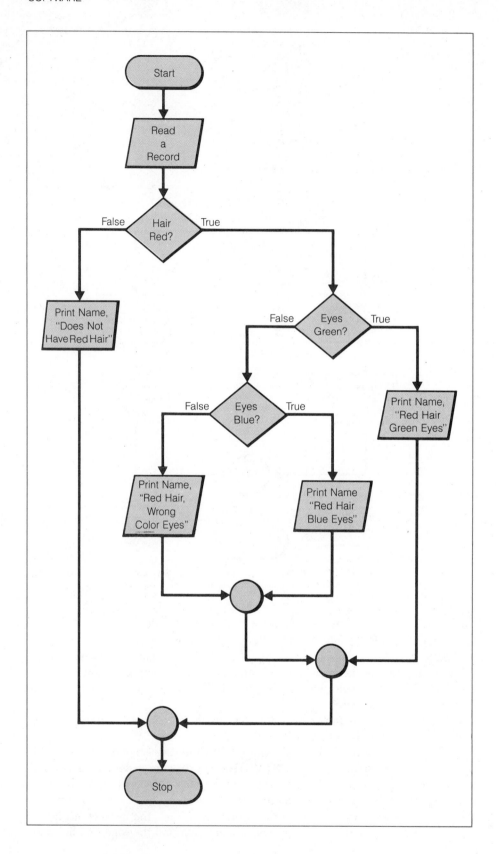

false), the loop is exited and the next sequence is done. A memory aid to keep these DO WHILEs and DO UNTILs straight might be DWT for DO WHILE TRUE.

Repetitive work is involved in daily chores such as dish washing. We can wash the dishes until there are no more dirty dishes to wash. (Although in fact there are times we might stop washing the dishes if we run out of soap, or when we run out of time, or maybe run out of patience.) If we ask: Is there a dish to wash? and then we wash it, we have done repetitive work using the DO WHILE because we have asked the question first and then processed as long as the answer was true. If, however, we wash a dish and then ask if we are finished to which we answer false, we have done the repetitive work by using the DO UNTIL. Remember the big toe example. Refer to Figure 11.15. Testing first and then processing as long as the condition is true is the DO WHILE. Processing first and then testing and continuing as long as the condition is false is the DO UNTIL. Do not forget that looping must either begin or end with a decision.

When data is processed on the computer, the same option of processing all of the data, none of it, or just some of it is possible. When all of the data is to be processed, meaning all records in the file are to be inputted and processed, the DO WHILE construct is done for as long as data remains. The repetitive processing continues as long as there is data—the true alternative. The end of file is only reached after all data records are inputted.

Let us return to the Ludkey Furniture Company example, using the input data as shown in Figure 11.16(a). The output is shown in part b, while part c

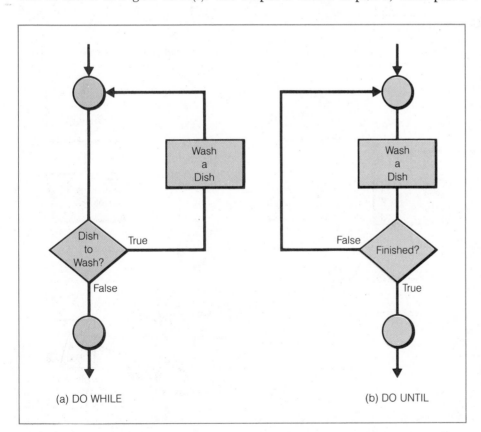

(a) DO WHILE   (b) DO UNTIL

FIGURE 11.15
Repetition using the two forms.

FIGURE 11.16 **DO WHILE used for repetition that tests if data remains.**

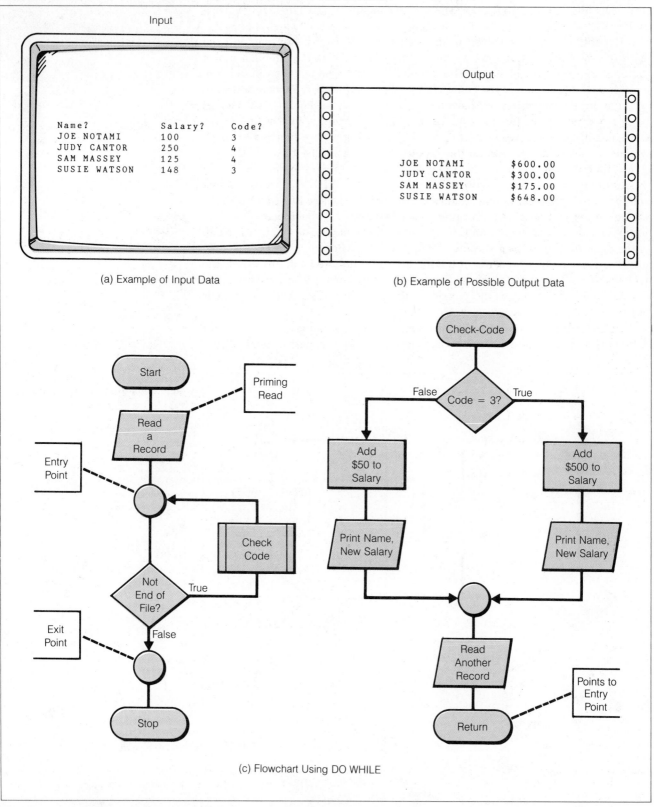

Input

Name?	Salary?	Code?
JOE NOTAMI	100	3
JUDY CANTOR	250	4
SAM MASSEY	125	4
SUSIE WATSON	148	3

(a) Example of Input Data

Output

JOE NOTAMI	$600.00
JUDY CANTOR	$300.00
SAM MASSEY	$175.00
SUSIE WATSON	$648.00

(b) Example of Possible Output Data

(c) Flowchart Using DO WHILE

shows an example of the DO WHILE. Notice in Figure 11.16(c) that the *READ A RECORD* symbol is used. This is a priming read. Let us use the input data as shown in Figure 11.16(a) with the first record being Joe's data. Now the loop is entered. The code in Joe's record is tested and the $500 bonus added to his salary. Now, the next record is ready to be processed. Notice that the *READ ANOTHER RECORD* symbol is used after the end of the selection. Let us assume this is Judy's record, which is next to be processed. The looping continues, and Judy's record is now tested for a bonus.

Another technique often used with the DO WHILE construct is to set up, as the last record of the file, some imaginary data that does not exist normally, which is referred to as a **trailer value** or **end of data tag.** If, for example, using the employee records illustration, the last employee's name could be recorded as XXX. The way that the programmer is certain that no more data remains to be processed is to use a selection, testing for the employee's name of XXX. Remember with the DO WHILE the condition must be asked first with the answer for looping being true. As long as the employee's name is not equal to the trailer value, the processing continues, for the condition is true. Refer to Figure 11.17(a), noting that the input data is changed, with the last record containing a name of XXX as the trailer value, with all other numeric fields entered as zeros. Figure 11.17(c) shows the completed flowchart. The same output is prepared in Figure 11.17(b), however.

Another way to use looping with the DO WHILE is to count the number of times that the program should pass through the loop. Equate it to running around the block a certain number of times. Let us assume we wish to pass through a loop three times. Referring to Figure 11.18, the counter is set to a 0 initially before the DO WHILE construct is begun. Because the question is asked first, the data is processed and then the counter is increased by 1. Processing has occurred once, and the counter registers a 1. The loop is again processed and the question asked if the counter is less than 3. Yes, the counter is at 1, so the processing continues. A 1 is added, making the counter register 2. The processing in the loop is now done two times. The question is again asked: Is the counter less than 3? Yes, so processing continues. We have now passed through the loop three times. Now when the question is asked, the counter is equal to 3. The answer to the question is false, so the exit is taken.

Because of the structure of such a construct, it is possible to bypass the entire processing setup in the loop. This can be done by setting the counter to a 3 initially. The test condition is then false, so the exit is taken and no processing of data occurs, as shown in Figure 11.19.

Looping can be stopped by setting up the last data record with some imaginary data. Figure 11.20 shows the structure chart. Figure 11.20(b) shows the input data for employee records. Figure 11.20(c) shows a complete flowchart using the three constructs of sequence, selection, and repetition using the DO WHILE. Notice that there is more than one module, and a module is contained within another module. Notice the employee identification number of 99999 is randomly chosen since the programmer knows that no such employee number exists. This testing by employee identification number is then used for determining when the loop is to end, with the program exiting the loop.

The **DO UNTIL** provides the negative voice of the DO WHILE. The DO UNTIL has the same looping capability as the DO WHILE, but it processes first and then tests. Looping continues until the condition is met, or becomes true. The exit from the loop is then taken on the true leg. It is advisable to get some

FIGURE 11.17 **DO WHILE used for repetition that tests for trailer value.**

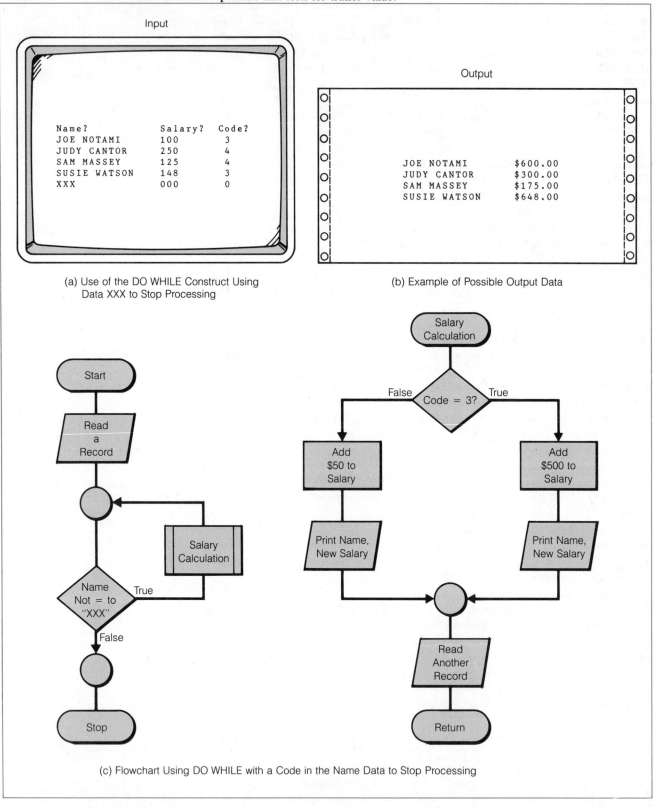

(a) Use of the DO WHILE Construct Using Data XXX to Stop Processing

(b) Example of Possible Output Data

(c) Flowchart Using DO WHILE with a Code in the Name Data to Stop Processing

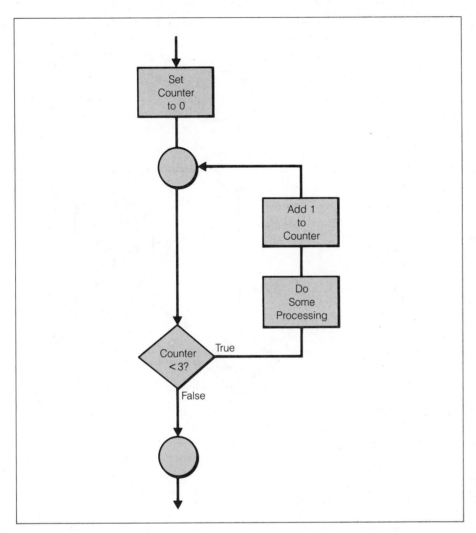

FIGURE 11.18
DO WHILE with the question asked first.

memory aid for the difference between the DO WHILE and the DO UNTIL; otherwise, you can easily be a candidate for the padded walls! Refer to Figure 11.21.

Figure 11.22 shows the same problem as shown for Figure 11.20(c) but uses the DO UNTIL instead of the DO WHILE. Only the main flowchart section is shown since the other modules remain the same.

The counselor's office at your college wishes a printout of the names and addresses of the students who are ages 18 through 25 inclusively. The data for ages other than 18 through 25 is of no concern to the counselors at this time, and should be ignored. The age data is of prime concern. Each record must be read; the age data must be analyzed to determine if printing is to be done or not.

Figure 11.23 shows the completed flowchart. The comparison for the age 25 could be asked first instead of last. It makes no difference in flowcharting as long as the desired processing is accomplished.

Refer to Table 11.1 for a comparison of the looping operations in the DO WHILE and DO UNTIL constructs.

FIGURE 11.19
DO WHILE with no processing
done in loop.

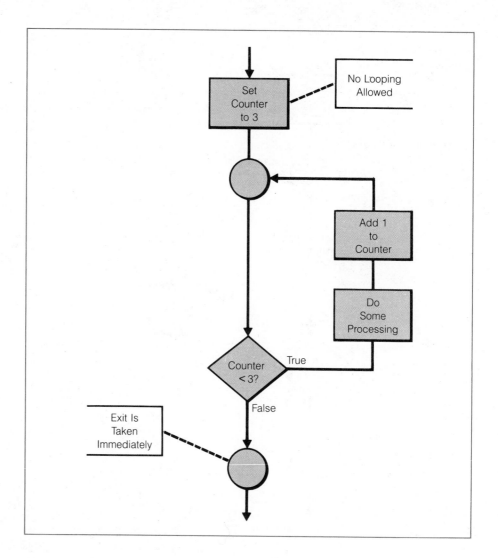

CHECKPOINT **Can you:**

Identify the constructs used in structured programming?

Differentiate among them?

Explain the differences between DO UNTIL and DO WHILE?

Pseudocode

Pseudocode provides, through English statements, a description of the steps in a problem's solution. Pseudocode is used by some companies in place of the flowchart for producing the algorithm. The statements are written in a general format, not following the rules of the language that will be used for actual code. The pseudocode is not tested on the computer since its only function is to spell out the direction that the program is to follow.

Pseudocode is a narrative language that merely tells what the programmer wishes to accomplish in the required processing. The choice of the words used in pseudocode varies, but there is a definite format; indentation shows which pseudocode instructions are subordinate to instructions that are higher in the hierarchy or have greater importance.

Certain words in pseudocode are significant. *Input* or *read a record* means that data is made available to the computer for processing. The input data is generally in the form of a record, for which several fields of data pertaining to a person or a thing are inputted as one line or one item. If various bowlers' performances on a given night at a bowling alley were to be analyzed, the various fields of data for each bowler might be the name, the score of each game rolled, the handicap that the bowler carries in the league, and the name of the team to which the bowler belongs. If, however, the data pertained to employee records, a record might contain the social security number, the department to which that employee is assigned, the number of hours worked, the date, the rate per hour, and the tax deduction.

The word *set* or *assign* is often used in pseudocode to initialize values to a desired amount. Calculations frequently involve independent and running totals. Each time a hand-held calculator is used, it is necessary to ask if this total is for an entire series of numbers that requires subtotalling (running total) or one calculated for a person's account or one subject matter (independent total). When using the hand-held calculator, the accumulator is set to a certain value (usually zero). This process of setting starting values is referred to as initialization.

The word *if* is used in pseudocode for selecting certain data, or determining if a condition is true, or checking the accuracy of input data as to whether it is within a certain range of data.

Another word used in pseudocode is *compute* which means to calculate. Sometimes the words *add, subtract, divide,* or *multiply* appear in the pseudocode but this often is the choice of the programmer or company that sets the standards for the pseudocode generated by the programmers.

Another word used in pseudocode is *print,* which means that data is to be prepared as output on the printer.

Other words, such as *DO, ENDDO, DO WHILE,* and *ENDWHILE,* are used. These will be explained as we progress through the discussion of the three constructs of structured programming.

TABLE 11.1.   **Comparisons of DO WHILE and DO UNTIL.**

LOOP BEGINS WITH		LOOP ENDS WITH		ITERATION CONTINUES FOR AS LONG AS CONDITION IS	
DO WHILE	DO UNTIL	DO WHILE	DO UNTIL	DO WHILE	DO UNTIL
decision	processing	processing	decision	true	false

FIGURE 11.20   Structure chart, flowchart, and input data for a payroll problem.

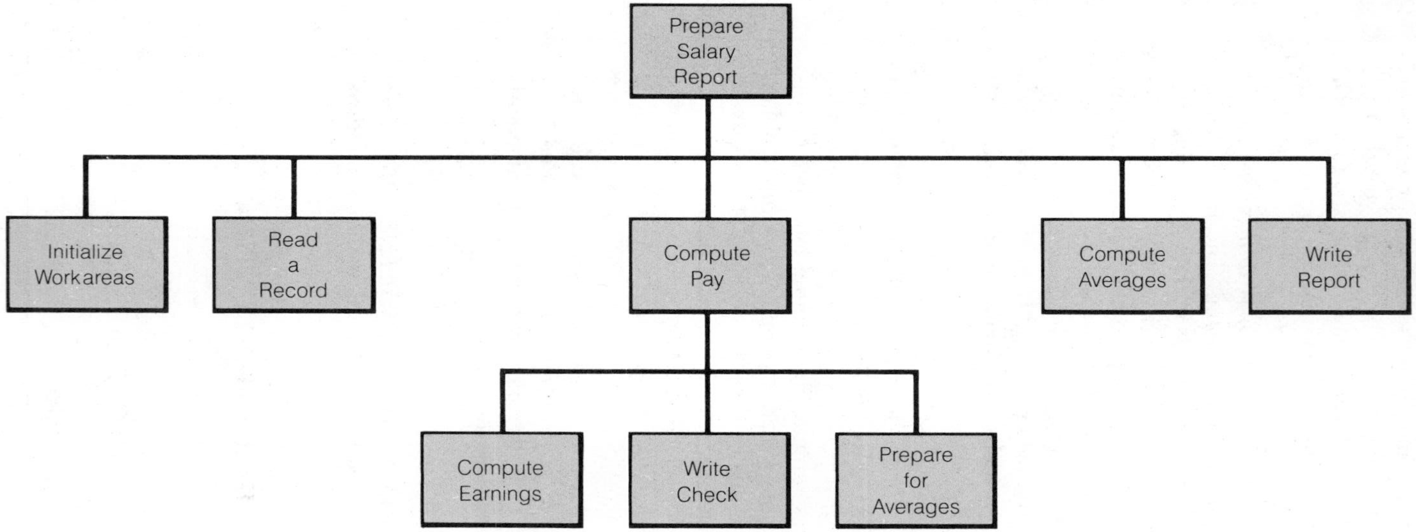

(a) Structure Chart

EMPLOYEE NUMBER	NAME	HOURLY PAY	WEEKLY HOURS WORKED	% FEDERAL TAX	% STATE TAX
11324	SMITH GERTRUDE	0516	38	15	.03
17456	FOWLER JAMES	0700	45	22	.03
18632	MORGAN HENRY	0800	30	24	.03
13133	HAINES JUNE	1200	25	24	.04
99999	XXXXX	0000	00	00	.00

(b) Input Data

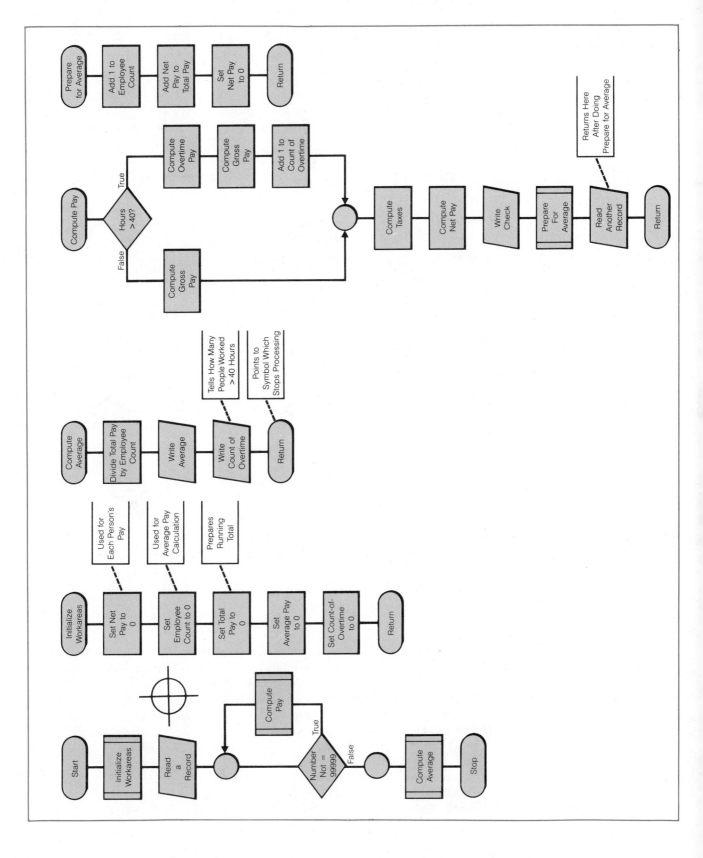

FIGURE 11.21
DO UNTIL construct.

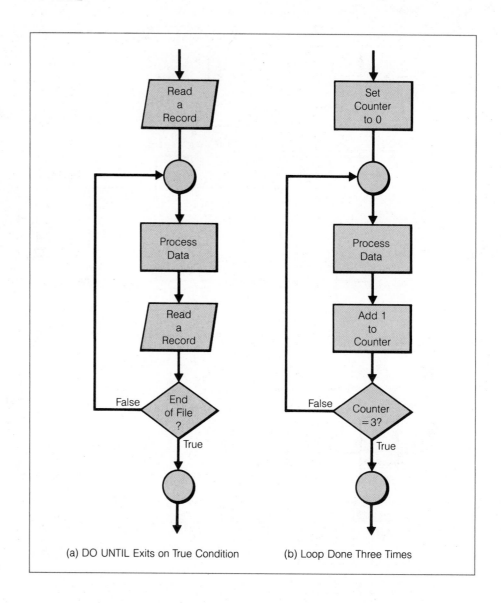

(a) DO UNTIL Exits on True Condition   (b) Loop Done Three Times

Let us follow the same sequence of presentation as we did for the flowcharts. The skeleton for the *DO* is shown in Figure 11.24(a). The sequence for getting a glass of milk is shown in Figure 11.24(b). Notice how the **DO** and **ENDDO** (pronounced as two words) show the boundaries for the sequence construct. They are aligned, while the instructions for the sequence are indented. Many students find sequence easier to follow in pseudocode than in flowcharts. Figures 11.25 and 11.26 show pseudocode for the same processing as shown in Figures 11.10 and 11.11, respectively.

The selection construct uses the IF-THEN-ELSE and IF-THEN. Notice the format for each in Figure 11.27(a). The ENDIF (say the words separately) is always shown. There are as many ENDIFs as there are IFs. The ENDIF is equivalent

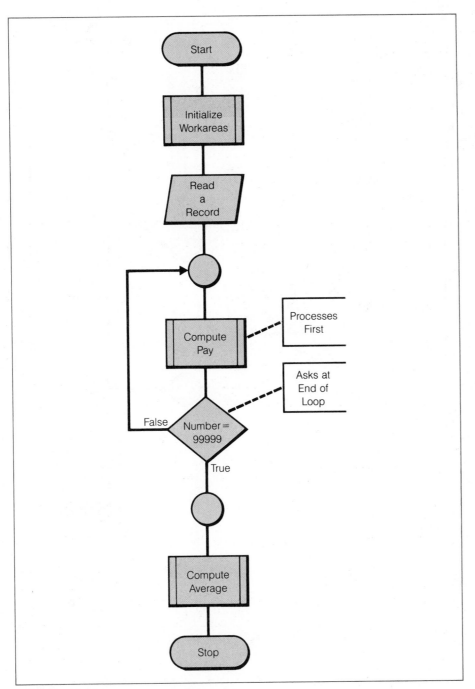

FIGURE 11.22
**Example of DO UNTIL using the same
processing as shown in Figure 11.20(c).**

FIGURE 11.23
**Printing only those records
with the age being 18 through 25.**

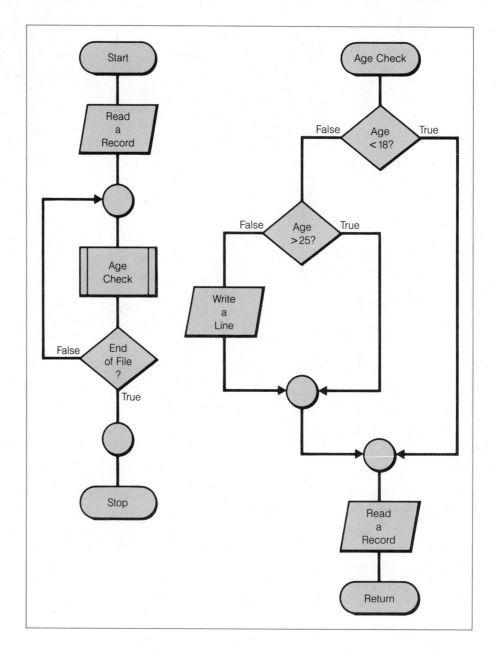

to the connector used in the flowchart. Figure 11.27(b) shows the pseudocode for the Ludkey Furniture Store example that was previously discussed and illustrated in the flowchart in Figure 11.27(c). Figure 11.28 shows the pseudocode for the Quick Dating Bureau example; a flowchart was shown in Figure 11.14.

The **DO WHILE** is fairly straightforward in pseudocode. This construct begins with "**WHILE** there is data DO" and ends with the **ENDWHILE** statement. Notice that statements that are to be performed as long as the condition is true

Entry Point

DO
.
.
. Instructions
.
.
ENDDO
Exit Point
(a) Structure

Enter Kitchen

DO
. Open Refrigerator
. Remove Milk
. Close Refrigerator
. Open Cabinet
. Select Glass
. Close Cabinet
. Pour Milk
. Drink Milk
ENDDO
Exit Kitchen
(b) Example of DO

FIGURE 11.24
Structure and example of DO construct.

DO
. Read a record—hours worked, rate, tax
. Compute gross pay
. Compute net pay
. Print hours worked
. Print pay rate
. Print gross pay
. Print net pay
ENDDO
END   (a) Example 1

FIGURE 11.25
Example pseudocode using processing shown in Figure 11.10(c), Example 1 and Example 2.

DO
. Read a record of three numbers
. Print elements in record
. Computer sum of elements
. Print sum
ENDDO
END
(b) Example 2

DO
. Read a record of name and hour scores
. Compute sum of hour scores
. Compute average score
. Print heading line
. Print name, scores, sum of scores, average
ENDDO
END

FIGURE 11.26
Example pseudocode using processing shown in Figure 11.11(c).

FIGURE 11.27
Structure and example pseudocode for selection construct.

Selection Starts with

   IF   What Is Being Tested Goes Here

   .   **THEN**
   .   .
   .   .   This Is What Is Done When the Condition Is True
   .   .
   .   .
   .   **ELSE**
   .   .
   .   .   This Is What Is Done When the Condition Is False

   ENDIF

            (a) The IF–THEN–ELSE Structure

- -

   DO
   .   Read a record
   .   **IF** code = 3
   .   .   **THEN**
   .   .   .   Add 500.00, salary giving new salary
   .   .   .   Print name, new salary
   .   .   **ELSE**
   .   .   Add 50.00, salary giving new salary
   .   .   Print name, new salary
   .   **ENDIF**
   ENDDO

   END
        (b) Pseudocode Using One Record Showing IF–THEN–ELSE
            and Sequence for Processing Shown in Figure 11.12(c).

FIGURE 11.28
Nested IF pseudocode, showing same processing as done in Flowchart in Figure 11.14.

   DO
   .   Read a record
   .   **IF** color of hair is red
   .   .   **THEN**
   .   .   .   **IF** color of eyes is green
   .   .   .   **THEN**
   .   .   .   .   Print name, "has red hair and green eyes"
   .   .   .   **ELSE**
   .   .   .   **IF** color of eyes is blue
   .   .   .   .   **THEN**
   .   .   .   .   .   print name, "has red hair and blue eyes"
   .   .   .   .   **ELSE**
   .   .   .   .   print name, "red hair, wrong color eyes"
   .   .   .   **ENDIF**
   .   .   **ENDIF**
   .   **ELSE**
   .   .   Print name, "Does not have red hair"
   .   **ENDIF**
   ENDDO
   END

are indented. Notice also how the WHILE and ENDWHILE are aligned. Referring to Figure 11.29, note that the priming read is used before the DO WHILE. The read of another record is contained within the iteration (loop). Do not lose sight of the fact that if Joe's record is the first record, Joe's data is read by the priming read. The loop is encountered and Joe's record is processed. Judy's record is now read. The loop is repeated.

The same problems used for the flowcharts shown in Figure 11.17 is shown in pseudocode in Figure 11.30.

CHECKPOINT Can you:

Identify some of the words used in pseudocode?

Structured Flowcharts

Some feel that pseudocode is difficult to write or takes too much time. Others feel that flowcharting requires too much time to prepare and is difficult to modify. It appears, however, that others prefer a type of graphical analysis, especially for the selection construct.

Isaac Nassi and Ben Schneiderman devised the structured flowchart presentation which is commonly known as the **Nassi-Schneiderman diagram,** or **structured flowchart.** There are other methods, such as Chapin Charts and Warnier diagrams, both of which are beyond the scope of this text.

Many feel that the Nassi-Schneiderman flowcharts are easier to draw than the traditional flowcharts. They are not difficult to modify if prepared using a word processing program. If they are done by typewriter or by hand, they too present a problem when modification is needed.

Structured flowcharts are a combination of flowcharting and pseudocode; two are shown in Figures 11.31 and 11.32. They use the English phrases shown in pseudocode with some graphical analysis as shown in flowcharting. There are no flow lines used, however, for showing looping.

In Figure 11.31, the same problem appears as shown previously in Figures 11.17 and 11.30. If you refer to the flowchart in Figure 11.17 you will notice that the structure flowchart follows the flow as in the order which it will execute on the computer. Notice how the module SALARY-CALCULATION is boxed on the structure flowchart. Notice that only two symbols appear. The rectangle used for the sequence takes a shape of that which will accommodate the material or words it must include. The second symbol, used for decisions, is an inverted triangle, with the "no" alternative shown on the right and the "yes" on the left. The size of the triangle and the slant of the line under the decision depends upon the required space to write the desired processing. Also notice how the pseudocode follows an implied left margin in both structured flowchart examples.

WHAT'S RIGHT

A Consultant's Viewpoint

The consulting field is one that has experienced exceptional growth over the past ten years. The current trend is toward specialized consulting, where a potential client will seek out a firm with specific strengths such as data processing, financial, legal, and so on.

The type of individual being sought out for careers in consulting is very similar to the data processing professional. It's important in either profession to be organized, disciplined, logical in thinking, and problem-solving oriented. To develop good written communicative skills is a definite plus. Hyperactive personalities rarely do well in data processing, as the ability to calmly think things through is imperative. You should be the type of person who enjoys starting a problem-solving approach and sticking with implementation through completion, which includes long-term follow-up.

Don't forget that computers are driven by systems and systems are made up of procedures and programs which are developed and written by people.

```
DO        shows beginning                              DO
    .                                                      .   Read a record
        WHILE There Is Data DO                             .   WHILE there is data DO
    .       .                                              .       IF code = 3
    .       .   These Are the Instructions in the Loop     .       .   THEN
    .       .                                              .       .   .   Add 500.00, salary giving new salary
    .       .                                              .       .   .   Print name, new salary
    .       ENDWHILE   shows end                           .       .   ELSE
                                                           .       .       Add 50.00, salary giving new salary
ENDDO                                                      .       .       Print name, new salary
                                                           .       ENDIF
DO                                                         .       Read another record
    .                                                      .   ENDWHILE
    .       These Are Other Instructions for Another Sequence  ENDDO
    .                                                      END
ENDDO
END                                                        (b)  Use of DO WHILE Construct For As Long As There
                                                                Is Data. Example Data Shown in Figure 11.16.
(a)  Skeleton of Structure for DO WHILE
```

FIGURE 11.29   **Structure and example use of DO WHILE construct.**

FIGURE 11.30
**Use of the DO WHILE construct
for looping using certain data to
stop processing. Refer to Figure
11.17.**

```
DO
    .   Read a record
    .   WHILE name is not equal to "XXX" DO
    .   .   IF code = 3
    .   .   .   THEN
    .   .   .       Add 500.00, salary giving new salary
    .   .   .       Print name, new salary
    .   .   ELSE
    .   .           Add 50.00, salary giving new salary
    .   .           Print name, new salary
    .   .   ENDIF
    .   .   Read another record
    .   ENDWHILE
ENDDO
END
```

In flowcharting, the oval with the phrase *START* and all of the other symbols
through the oval with the phrase *STOP* constitute the control module. Other
modules use the predefined process symbol. In structured flowcharts, the name
of the module is labelled at the left of the instructions that make up that module.
Notice how the module name is boxed in, with the top and bottom horizontal
lines showing the boundaries of that module. This area is shaded in the figure for
your ease in reference. The control module appears at the top of the structured
flowchart. Any additional modules that are included in the structured flowchart
are presented in the order in which they are executed in the control module.

    Let us use the data from the flowchart shown in Figure 11.17(c), the Ludkey
Furniture Company example, to illustrate a structured flowchart. Refer to Fig-

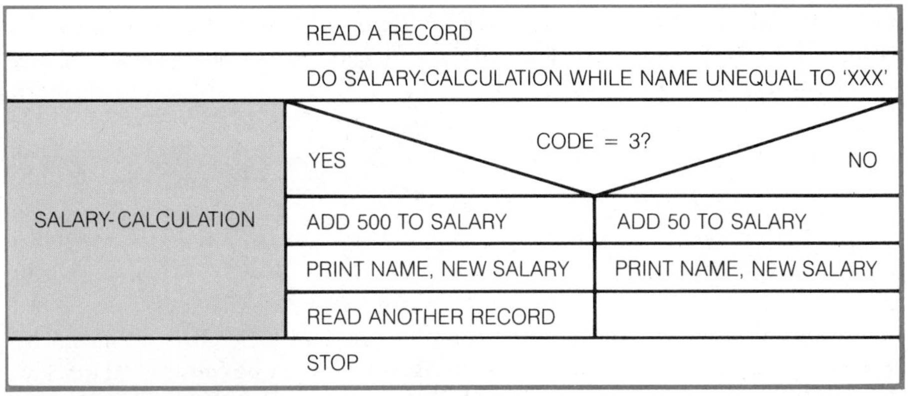

READ A RECORD		
DO SALARY-CALCULATION WHILE NAME UNEQUAL TO 'XXX'		
SALARY-CALCULATION	CODE = 3? YES / NO	
	ADD 500 TO SALARY	ADD 50 TO SALARY
	PRINT NAME, NEW SALARY	PRINT NAME, NEW SALARY
	READ ANOTHER RECORD	
STOP		

FIGURE 11.31
Nassi-Schneiderman diagram showing same processing as shown in the Flowchart in Figure 11.17(c).

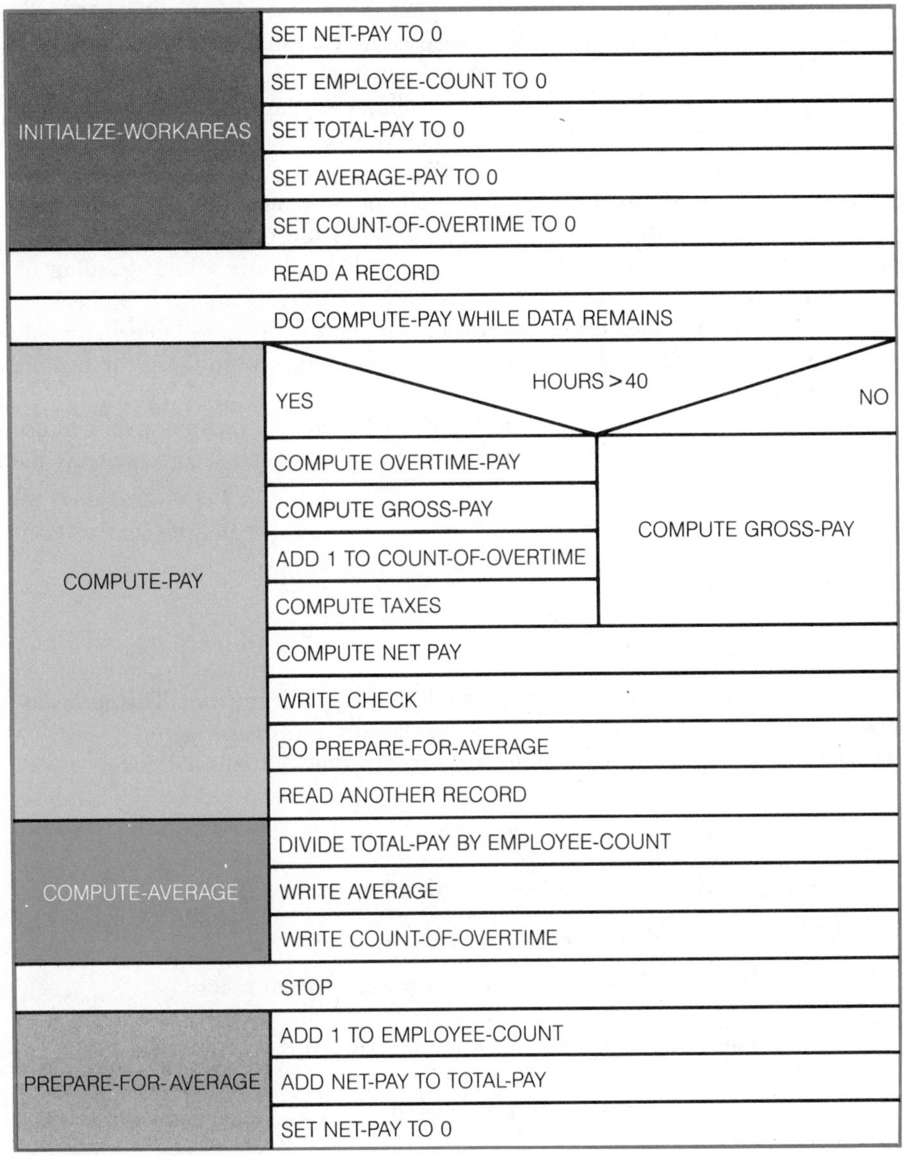

INITIALIZE-WORKAREAS	SET NET-PAY TO 0	
	SET EMPLOYEE-COUNT TO 0	
	SET TOTAL-PAY TO 0	
	SET AVERAGE-PAY TO 0	
	SET COUNT-OF-OVERTIME TO 0	
READ A RECORD		
DO COMPUTE-PAY WHILE DATA REMAINS		
COMPUTE-PAY	HOURS > 40? YES / NO	
	COMPUTE OVERTIME-PAY	COMPUTE GROSS-PAY
	COMPUTE GROSS-PAY	
	ADD 1 TO COUNT-OF-OVERTIME	
	COMPUTE TAXES	
	COMPUTE NET PAY	
	WRITE CHECK	
	DO PREPARE-FOR-AVERAGE	
	READ ANOTHER RECORD	
COMPUTE-AVERAGE	DIVIDE TOTAL-PAY BY EMPLOYEE-COUNT	
	WRITE AVERAGE	
	WRITE COUNT-OF-OVERTIME	
STOP		
PREPARE-FOR-AVERAGE	ADD 1 TO EMPLOYEE-COUNT	
	ADD NET-PAY TO TOTAL-PAY	
	SET NET-PAY TO 0	

FIGURE 11.32
Nassi-Schneiderman diagram showing processing as in flowchart in Figure 11.20(c).

ure 11.31 and contrast it to Figure 11.17(c). Refer to Figure 11.20(c), our payroll example flowchart, and contrast it with the structured flowchart shown in Figure 11.32, which uses the same data.

Decision Tables

A **decision table** is used for defining complex program logic. It is preferred by some companies to flowcharting because decision tables can be constructed quickly. One advantage of using a decision table is that it is easier to construct than a flowchart since no symbols are involved. Phrases are not as difficult to use on a decision table, which is not as limited in space as a flowchart.

A decision table provides a way of looking at all of the alternatives that can exist for some application. Its chart format allows for easy checking as to applicability of the elements. The decision table has a selection feature built into it.

The decision table is divided into two parts. The upper part deals with **conditions**—the questions that would normally be used on a flowchart. The lower part deals with **actions**—what is to be done when the condition is true. Since there can be many alternative paths from which to choose when deciding on appropriate actions, many columns are provided for a programmer to check off the alternatives. (A Y means yes, an N means no on the decision table.) The **rule** is a column on the table which represents a path of logic used upon the making of a decision.

Let's take an example. A company named P-Marshall Center wishes to use the computer to calculate each account's new balance. Each record contains the following fields:

- account number
- amount owed

- purchase/credit
- code

The coding system has been pre-established by the company. The company uses only two codes: a 4 or a 5. No other codes are permissible.

The following processing is done for a record that contains a 4 code:

1. Consider the record as a purchase record.

2. The purchase/credit field data is considered as a purchase.

3. The purchase should be added to the amount owed.

4. Print the account number and total owed for each record.

The following processing is done for a record that contains a 5 code:

1. Consider the record as a return record.

2. The purchase/credit field then represents a credit.

3. The credit should be subtracted from the amount owed.

4. Print the account number and the total owed for each record.

An independent total is to be calculated for each record, requiring initialization for each record. **Error protection,** a way of providing checks on input data to make certain it is as accurate as possible, is to be included in case a code other than 4 or 5 is found. This erroneous data could result from someone incorrectly coding the source document or making a data entry error. Since it is extremely important that the user is signalled of any incorrect data that might exist when the program is run, an error message will be generated on the printer when an error condition occurs.

The input and output data are shown in Figures 11.33(a) and 11.33(b) respectively. Notice how the EOF (End of File) is used in the pseudocode shown in Figure 11.33(c). This line of pseudocode says to process the loop as long as data remains. The decision table is shown in Figure 11.33(d).

CHECKPOINT Can you:

Tell what comprises a decision table?
State when it is used?
State how it is used?

Refer to Table 11.2 for a comparative summary of the features of the various problem-solving methodologies presented in this chapter.

DOCUMENTATION

Documentation refers to an organized presentation of materials that substantiate the accuracy of a debugged program. All sources of data and references that can be helpful to someone later using the program is included in documentation. Often times documentation is a forgotten item in a data processing shop because programmers do not enjoy performing this task as they did preparing the code and logic to solve the problem. When, however, a program must be modified— either because of improper code included in the program or because of new requirements demanded of the program—the job of patching is far easier if documentation is included.

FIGURE 11.33 **Calculation of amount owed.**

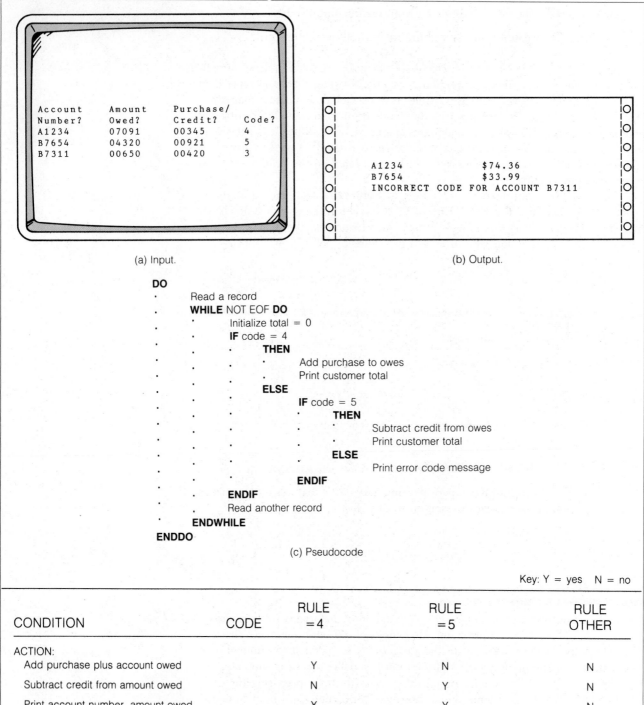

(a) Input.

```
Account     Amount    Purchase/
Number?     Owed?     Credit?     Code?
A1234       07091     00345       4
B7654       04320     00921       5
B7311       00650     00420       3
```

(b) Output.

```
A1234              $74.36
B7654              $33.99
INCORRECT CODE FOR ACCOUNT B7311
```

DO
  ·   Read a record
  ·   **WHILE** NOT EOF **DO**
  ·   ·   Initialize total = 0
  ·   ·   **IF** code = 4
  ·   ·   ·   **THEN**
  ·   ·   ·   ·   Add purchase to owes
  ·   ·   ·   ·   Print customer total
  ·   ·   **ELSE**
  ·   ·   ·   **IF** code = 5
  ·   ·   ·   **THEN**
  ·   ·   ·   ·   Subtract credit from owes
  ·   ·   ·   ·   Print customer total
  ·   ·   ·   **ELSE**
  ·   ·   ·   ·   Print error code message
  ·   ·   ·   **ENDIF**
  ·   ·   **ENDIF**
  ·   ·   Read another record
  ·   **ENDWHILE**
ENDDO

(c) Pseudocode

Key: Y = yes   N = no

CONDITION	CODE	RULE =4	RULE =5	RULE OTHER
ACTION:				
Add purchase plus account owed		Y	N	N
Subtract credit from amount owed		N	Y	N
Print account number, amount owed		Y	Y	N
Print error message, account number		N	N	Y

(d) Decision Table

TABLE 11.2. **Comparisons of Problem-Solving Methodologies.**

	STRUCTURE CHART	FLOWCHART (TRADITIONAL)	PSEUDOCODE	DECISION TABLE	NASSI-SCHNEIDERMAN DIAGRAM
Purpose	Overview	Detail	Detail	Detail	Detail
Uses (for format)	Rectangles and lines	Various symbols and phrases	English and indentations	English set in columns	English, lines, and inverted triangle
Show	Modules only	Sequence, selection, repetition, and modules	Sequence, selection, repetition	Selection	Sequence, selection, repetition, no directional flow
Primary concentration	Level of importance	Order of steps in problem solution	Order of steps in problem solution	What is to be done when selection is performed	Straightforward presentation to be done on word processing system

Documentation, although not standardized in approach, usually includes the following:

1. An English presentation of the description of the problem along with the desired objectives.

2. The source program listing.

3. The formats for input and output data.

4. The test data that was used for substantiating the program as being debugged.

5. Any flowcharts, decision tables, structure charts, and pseudocode that were prepared for determining the logic used in the program.

6. Any error conditions that can occur when processing the program.

7. A list of instructions for the computer operator to follow when the program is being executed.

If you were a programmer who had to do program maintenance, you would be most gratified to have the above information.

SUMMARY

● Program writing that was done up to the 1970s was mostly performed by one person, although some project teams did exist. The programmer was solely responsible for developing the code for the computer language.

● The methodology commonly used before the 1970s for problem solving was called bottom-up design, in which the details were worked out first.

● Programs using the bottom-up design were written separately and not linked together until the complete problem was near solution. Flaws in logic were then detected at a very late stage of testing.

- The problem solving methodology being used more commonly now involves top-down design and structured programming.

- Top-down design divides the problem to be solved into segments, or phases, called modules, with the top-level modules representing more general concepts. The control module is the top level. The program is designed so that each successive level of modules takes on more detail.

- A module is coded and tested and is then added to the other tested modules.

- Much of today's programming involves program maintenance rather than the actual creation of programs.

- Structured programming uses a set of techniques to improve the organization of a program, to improve readability, to generate better programming techniques, and to make program maintenance easier.

- Structure charts are used by many programmers. Such a chart consists of a series of rectangles that are arranged by levels. The lower the level, the more detailed is the level of processing.

- Structured walk-throughs are a programming methodology used for checking program design with peers in order to avoid faulty program design that might otherwise not be detected until the program was tested on the computer.

- Three techniques, or constructs, used in structured programming are called sequence, selection, and repetition.

- Sequence refers to statements that do such data manipulations as calculations, initializing workareas, and inputting or outputting data; the series of instructions is executed in order, with no break or change in logic flow.

- Selection refers to a choosing between alternatives. A question is asked and the answer to the question—true or false—is used to initiate one of two processing steps.

- The selection technique is known as the IF-THEN or IF-THEN-ELSE.

- Repetition involves use of a series of instructions that are repeated (looped) until a condition is met.

- The repetition technique is often referred to as the DO WHILE or DO UNTIL technique.

- The DO WHILE technique always tests a condition first and while the condition is true, the loop is continued. When the condition becomes false, the logic exits the loop.

- The DO UNTIL technique always does some processing first and then tests the condition. If it is false, the loop continues. If it is true, the logic exits the loop.

- Decisions are used for problem solving by testing fields of data to determine the appropriate path of logic that is to be followed.

- Pseudocode is English-type statements that are written to describe the steps in a problem's solution (an algorithm). The pseudocode does not follow the specifications of the language that is to be used for coding; it merely spells out the program in a form easily read.

● Flowcharts are used in place of or along with pseudocode for writing the detailed logic into a code.

● A flowchart is a graphic display of logic, using symbols and words to identify how the data is to flow and when processing is done.

● A template is used for drawing the symbols. Some of the more commonly used symbols are the oval, rectangle, parallelogram, triangle, and connector (a small circle).

● The oval is used for identifying the starting and stopping places in the main flowchart. The oval is also used for showing the start of the module that uses a pre-defined process symbol. The pre-defined process symbol, shown with a rectangle and two parallel lines contained within it on either side, identifies a series of processing steps that are to be executed as a group or routine.

● The rectangle is used for calculating and initializing data.

● The parallelogram is used for input and output.

● The triangle is used for decisions. The question is asked within the triangle. From the points of the triangle, lines (called legs) are drawn and labelled; true and false (yes or no) are used in structured programming.

● The false leg and true leg, after necessary steps are identified on the respective legs, are joined at the connector (the small circle). The connector is positioned in line with the triangle.

● Decisions are used for problem-solving by testing fields of data. The contents of the fields determines the appropriate path of logic that is to be followed.

● Structured flowcharts, also called Nassi-Schneiderman diagrams, use English phraseology along with two symbols (rectangle and inverted triangle) for showing their logic pattern.

● Decision tables are used by some companies in place of flowcharts to define complex program logic. The decision table is divided into two parts; the upper part deals with conditions (questions on a flowchart) while the bottom part deals with the actions that are to be taken when the condition is true.

● No symbols are used on the decision table. It uses columns (called rules) that are used to represent a path of logic when a decision is made. The programmer answers in the columns by noting a Y for yes if the action is to be done; a N is used for denoting that the action is not to be done.

● Documentation is an organized presentation of materials that includes the objectives for the problem that requires solution, the source program listing, the formats of input and output data, the test data used to debug the program, and any flowcharts, decision tables, structured flowcharts, or the like, to show the logic used to solve the problem.

STUDY GUIDE

REVIEW OF TERMINOLOGY

The following terminology was discussed in this chapter:

actions
bottom-up design
conditions
constructs
decision table
decisions
DO
documentation
DO UNTIL
DO WHILE
end of data tag
error protection
flowchart
hierarchy chart
hit
IF-THEN
IF-THEN-ELSE
initialization
iterative processing
looping
modules

Nassi-Schneiderman
   diagram
nested IFs
non-iterative processing
predefined process
   symbol
priming read
program maintenance
pseudocode
repetition
rule
selection
sequence
structure chart
structured flowchart
structured programming
structured walk-through
template
top-down design
trailer value

MULTIPLE CHOICE

Circle the letter for the item that correctly completes each statement.

1. A programming technique developed and used in the 1950s and 1960s was:
   a. structured programming
   b. top-down design
   c. bottom-up design
   d. decision tables
   e. structure charts

2. A graphic display using various symbols and phrases is the:
   a. decision table
   b. flowchart
   c. structure chart
   d. predefined process
   e. template

3. The processing of just one record without any repetition of statements is called:
   a. looping
   b. non-iterative processing
   c. iterative processing
   d. structured programming
   e. bottom-up design

4. The first read that is used before the loop is encountered to initially input data is called:
   a. iterative processing
   b. non-iterative processing
   c. looping
   d. iterative read
   e. priming read

5. When calculation workareas are set to a certain value or to zero, this is called:
   a. priming
   b. priming read
   c. initialization
   d. program maintenance
   e. a modular value

6. Structured programming solves its problems by breaking the problems into different functional parts called:
   a. modules
   b. templates
   c. top-down designs
   d. pseudocodes
   e. actions

7. Peers evaluate how a programmer plans to solve a problem in the:
   a. top-down design
   b. condition
   c. rule
   d. structured walk-through
   e. action

8. Problems are solved by looking at the most important and the broadest view of the problem first. This approach is called:
   a. structured flowcharting
   b. program maintenance
   c. structured walk-throughs
   d. top-down design
   e. actions

9. The rectangle on the flowchart is used for:
   a. calculating
   b. decision-making
   c. showing the entry point
   d. showing the beginning
   e. reading data

10. Questions are asked on a flowchart by using a:
    a. connector
    b. oval
    c. diamond-shaped symbol
    d. predefined process symbol
    e. parallelogram

11. All problems are solved in structured programming using:

a. selection, sequence, and IF-THEN-ELSE

b. IF-THEN-ELSE, DO UNTIL, and DO WHILE

c. sequence, IF-THEN-ELSE, and selection

d. repetition, DO WHILE, and DO UNTIL

e. selection, sequence, and repetition

12. When a decision is asked first and then processing is done, this repetitive processing uses:
    a. looping conditions
    b. DO UNTIL
    c. DO WHILE
    d. actions
    e. rules

13. When a decision is made after the processing is done, this repetitive processing uses:
    a. looping conditions
    b. DO UNTIL
    c. DO WHILE
    d. actions
    e. rules

14. When this type of processing is used, looping is stated in the negative voice:
    a. iterative processing
    b. DO UNTIL
    c. DO WHILE
    d. non-iterative processing
    e. none of these

15. This is used in place of a flowchart's diamond shaped symbol and legs for showing various alternatives:
    a. structure chart
    b. documentation
    c. program maintenance
    d. decision table
    e. pseudocode

16. When one instruction follows directly after the one preceding without any change in flow of logic, this is called:
    a. nested IFs
    b. conditions
    c. actions
    d. rules
    e. sequence construct

17. Questions normally asked on a flowchart are shown on decision tables as:
    a. decisions
    b. diamond-shaped symbols
    c. conditions
    d. selection
    e. IF-THEN-ELSE

18. A sequence in pseudocode begins with the word:
    a. DO
    b. ENDDO
    c. IF
    d. WHILE
    e. ENDWHILE

19. When instructions are written within a loop and an exit is taken when the condition becomes true, this is an example of:
    a. DO UNTIL
    b. DO WHILE
    c. DO
    d. selection
    e. IF-THEN-ELSE

20. On a structure chart, the control module is considered as:
    a. level 0
    b. level 1
    c. level 2
    d. the most detailed
    e. level 3

TRUE/FALSE QUESTIONS

Circle the T next to a true statement; the F if it is false.

1. **T/F** Structured programming was developed to make coding easier to read and programs easier to code.

2. **T/F** Structured programming concepts were needed in industry because there was a shift from individually constructed programs to those designed by project teams.

3. **T/F** Another advantage of structured programming is that it eliminates program maintenance.

4. **T/F** Most of a programmer's activities involve changing an already existing program to meet some new processing requirements.

5. **T/F** When programming began in the early 1950s, problems were solved by working with the details first and then completing the overall concepts.

6. **T/F** In the 1950s, the problem solving was done using the bottom-down design.

7. **T/F** When programming first began, programs had to be written very concisely since the capacity of memory was a problem.

8. **T/F** Today, programs are written in a more straightforward manner, with emphasis on clarity.

9. **T/F** The technique used today for problem solving is called top-down design.

10. **T/F** A structure chart is usually prepared after the logic is developed.

11. **T/F** There are several levels used in a structure chart, the top of which is called the control module.

12. **T/F** The higher the level number in the structure chart, the more detailed work is involved in programming.

13. **T/F** A level 1 module on a structure chart may have a level 2 module subordinate to it.

14. **T/F** A level 0 always has three or four level 1 modules.

15. **T/F** Pseudocode is a popular type of program description using English statements to represent an algorithm.

16. **T/F** When a series of instructions is executed one right after another, this construct is called sequence. It is represented as beginning with a DO in pseudocode.

17. **T/F** When questions are asked in structured programming, only two alternative answers exist: true and false.

18. **T/F** When a programmer uses selection, the true portion represents the THEN, while the false portion represents the ELSE.

19. **T/F** If a programmer uses selection in pseudocode, the word IF is used along with the word ENDIF to show where the logic pattern begins and ends.

20. **T/F** When a hit is made, there is always initialization and error protection used.

21. **T/F** Two or more IF statements cannot be used together.

22. **T/F** When the same pattern of work is done many times, the usage of the computer can be justified.

23. **T/F** The way a programmer keeps a computer inputting and processing new data is through looping or repetition.

24. **T/F** Repetition uses a DO WHILE construct, which means that a series of instructions is continually executed while there is data to process.

25. **T/F** A priming read refers to the reading of only one record in the program.

26. **T/F** A way that the programmer can determine when no more data remains to be processed is by using a record that contains data that does not normally exist in the file.

27. **T/F** A rectangle is used on a flowchart for instructions in a sequence construct.

28. **T/F** The diamond-shaped symbol is used for asking questions and determining if there are any more data to process.

29. **T/F** Very little discussion is held in a structured walk-through.

30. **T/F** The purpose of a structured walk-through is a peer evaluation to determine a programmer's worth.

31. **T/F** The avoidance of tricky code is desirable.

32. **T/F** If a programmer wishes to do looping, a count of the number of times the loop is to be executed can not be initialized to any value other than 0.

33. **T/F** If a loop is to be done 5 times, the decision testing if the loop is complete can be written IF THE COUNT IS < 5. In this case, the adding of 1 is done after the data is processed. The decision begins the loop. The count is set to zero before the loop is begun.

34. **T/F** If a loop is to be done 5 times, the decision testing if the loop is complete can be written IF THE COUNT IS $= 5$. This assumes that the count is initialized to 0 and the incrementing of the count is done before the decision, which appears at the end of the loop.

35. **T/F** Using the wording of item 33 above, the question could be asked IF COUNT IS LESS THAN 6, with the count being initialized to a 1.

36. **T/F** Item 33 assumes that the DO WHILE construct is used.

37. **T/F** The DO UNTIL construct processes first and then asks the question.

38. **T/F** If the loop was to be executed 10 times, using the DO UNTIL construct, assuming the count is set to 0, the question to exit the loop would then test if the COUNT IS EQUAL TO 10.

39. **T/F** The DO UNTIL exits the loop when the condition is false.

40. **T/F** Decision tables are used in place of flowcharts for the selection of data.

41. **T/F** A rule is a column on the decision table which shows the logic as to how work is to be processed.

42. **T/F** Nassi-Schneiderman diagrams are the same as traditional flowcharts.

43. **T/F** Structured flowcharts never contain predefined process symbols.

44. **T/F** Structured flowcharts never show a module name.

Multiple Choice: 1. **c** 2. **b** 3. **b** 4. **e** 5. **c** 6. **a** 7. **d**
8. **d** 9. **a** 10. **c** 11. **e** 12. **c** 13. **b** 14. **b** 15. **d** 16. **e**
17. **c** 18. **a** 19. **a** 20. **a** *True/False:* 1. **T** 2. **T** 3. **F**
4. **T** 5. **T** 6. **F** 7. **T** 8. **T** 9. **T** 10. **F** 11. **T** 12. **T**
13. **T** 14. **F** 15. **T** 16. **T** 17. **T** 18. **T** 19. **T** 20. **F**
21. **F** 22. **T** 23. **T** 24. **T** 25. **F** 26. **T** 27. **T** 28. **T**
29. **F** 30. **F** 31. **T** 32. **F** 33. **T** 34. **T** 35. **T** 36. **T**
37. **T** 38. **T** 39. **F** 40. **T** 41. **T** 42. **F** 43. **T** 44. **F**

REVIEW QUESTIONS

1. What is meant by bottom-up design? How does it differ from top-down design?
2. What is program maintenance?
3. What is looping? When is it used?
4. What three techniques are used in structured programming? Explain what each technique involves.
5. How is a structure chart designed?
6. What is the top level in a structure chart called?
7. In which level of a structure chart will the greatest amount of processing work be done?
8. Identify the use of the following symbols used on a traditional flowchart: oval, rectangle, diamond-shaped symbol, rectangle with parallel lines on either side, connector.
9. Which symbols are used on a structured flowchart?
10. On structured flowcharts, how are modules shown?
11. What is pseudocode? Why is it used?
12. What are some of the words used in pseudocode? What does each mean?
13. Why do programmers use both structure charts and pseudocode?
14. What is looping? When is it used?
15. Why are structured walk-throughs helpful as a problem-solving methodology?
16. What is the difference between DO WHILE and DO UNTIL?
17. What is a decision table? What are its parts?

DISCUSSION QUESTIONS

1. What are the advantages of using structured programming?
2. What are the major differences between top-down design and bottom-up design?
3. Your instructor asks you to prepare a report about the smoking habits of your peers. It is your responsibility to determine who is to be interviewed for the survey, which age group is to be surveyed, how the report is to be prepared, and what statistical analyses are to be done. Set up a structure chart illustrating how you plan to solve the problem. Next, discuss what processing is involved in preparing the pseudocode.
4. A sequence has one entry and one exit point. Explain what this means.
5. Explain the meaning of the words DO WHILE.
6. What are the major differences between a traditional flowchart and a decision table?
7. Explain how DO WHILE and DO UNTIL are used for looping.

PROJECTS

1. Life is not always as straightforward as discussed in sequence. The purchase of ice cream involves a DO function, but many times it might also involve an IF-THEN-ELSE. A frequent problem is if you have the money to pay for the ice cream or if your diet will allow such a purchase. Write the pseudocode to determine if your available cash allows you to purchase a pint or a cone. If you are on a diet, include this option also.
2. Assume that you hire a taxi. When you enter the taxi, the meter is set to zero for counting the miles travelled. The pricing policy of this taxi company has been set at a minimum fare of $2.50 for any distance travelled, even if you merely travel one block. The charge is based upon the metered fare plus any tip you wish to give. Set up the input data. Prepare the flowchart, and the pseudocode so the total amount paid is based upon what percentage of a tip you wish to give, if any, plus the metered fare; make certain that the metered fare exceeds $2.50.

3. Write the pseudocode for the module EAT BREAKFAST. Limit yourself to eating cereal with milk or toast and coffee (the pseudocode will become too complex if all possible options are presented). Prepare a flowchart for the same module.

4. The Acme Manufacturing Company pays its workers according to the hours worked and the rate per hour. If the hours worked are 40 hours per week, the salary is based upon the rate multiplied by the 40 hours. If the hours worked are between 41 and 48 hours, the rate is calculated as time and a half. If a worker exceeds 48 hours in a week, the rate is doubled per hour. Set up your work record for one week, including your name, the hours worked, and the rate for the Monday of that work week. Prepare the structure chart, flowchart, and the pseudocode so your name, the date, and the salary before deductions is printed on one line.

5. Using project 4, include other worker's data. Adjust the pseudocode and flowchart to reflect other records. Determine how you are going to signal the end of the file. Prepare the solution to this processing, including the printing of the average number of hours worked by all workers represented in your data.

6. An instructor's introductory data processing class has forty students in it. Each student's record has the format (presented using some possible data) shown in Table P-1.

Prepare a flowchart and pseudocode to accomplish the following processing:

a. Read a record.
b. Calculate the total score for each student.
c. Print out the student's data originally contained in the record (student number, name, test 1, test 2, test 3) along with the calculated total score.
d. Process all records in the file.

e. Set up the printer spacing chart according to your desired output. Include headings over the columns of data.

7. The manager of the stamp redemption store wishes an up-to-date listing of the items that are to be included in the next catalog edition. Because of a fire loss, the manager arbitrarily decides to raise the price of the coupon books by 20 percent on all items to be included in the new catalog. The input fields of data along with some examples of data are shown in Table P-2.

The printout should contain the fields shown in Table P-3. Space out the fields of data on output for ease in reading. Use the printer spacing chart if desired.
Prepare a flowchart and pseudocode for the problem.

8. The Ace Sporting Goods Store sells five lines of sporting goods equipment. There are two branches—one located in New York City and the other in Chicago. The company has coded every item in its inventory by using a five-digit stock number. The first position of the stock number designates the line of the equipment while the remaining four digits identify the particular manufacturer and item in the line. The coding for the five lines of equipment is as follows: 1XXXX for golf, 2XXXX for baseball, 3XXXX for tennis, 4XXXX for archery, and 5XXXX for fishing.

If a stock number was a 43267, it would be archery equipment. All archery stock numbers range from 40000 through 49999. A stock number of 39882 designates some item of tennis equipment; the 9 could refer to MacGregor line, the 88 to balls used for playing on clay courts, and the 2 to green color.

An example of some input records is shown in Table P-4.

Do the following processing (first prepare a structure chart, flowchart, and pseudocode):

Table P-1.

STUDENT NUMBER	NAME	TEST 1	TEST 2	TEST 3
A12345	Denise Hall	30	25	28
X77776	Dennis Scott	24	31	29

Table P-2.

STOCK NUMBER	DESCRIPTION	UNIT COST	DATE SHIPPED	COUPON BOOKS
1X234	rubber ducks	0525	0817	2
2A355	towels	0300	0923	1

Table P-3.

STOCK NUMBER	DESCRIPTION	NEW NUMBER OF COUPON BOOKS

a. Calculate the ending inventory for the month as follows for all stock other than archery:

Beginning Inventory + Purchases − Sales = Ending Inventory

b. Print out the following data for all stock except archery equipment:

stock number   ending inventory

c. For the archery stock data, count the number of records that are read, and print out this total after all data is processed.

9. Adjust your solution setup in item 8 above to calculate only the stock records at New York City, ignoring all non-archery stock records at Chicago. The invoice numbers beginning with a B denote New York City. For the archery stock data calculated in point *c* above, prepare a separate total for Chicago and New York, presenting both totals when all data is processed. The invoice numbers that begin with an A denote Chicago. Also assume that any invoice number not beginning with an A or B is incorrect data and no processing is to be done other than directing that

an error message be printed out stating the coding error. Set up the structure chart, flowchart, pseudocode, and printer spacing chart.

10. Assume that a file of data is to be used to prepare a printout of all those students who have a grade point average (GPA) between 2.5 and 3.6, inclusively, printing the name, address, and age on a line. For those students whose GPA is not between 2.5 and 3.6 inclusively, calculate the average GPA and print this average after all records are read. Set up the structure chart, flowchart, and pseudocode.

11. You are elected as secretary of the computer club at your college. The club decides to charge a $2.00 fee for all those students who are more than twenty-five years old. An additional $1.00 fee is to be charged for those students not currently enrolled in a computer class at the college. Prepare some input data and possible output that informs the students of the charges accessed. Set up the structure chart, flowchart, and pseudocode along with the input and output data. Step the logic through for each set of data, making certain the logic follows exactly the pattern it should.

Table P-4.

INVOICE NUMBER	STOCK NUMBER	BEGINNING INVENTORY	PURCHASES	SALES	MONTH AND YEAR
A-2345	13457	025	013	007	0982
B-3333	46789	100	007	045	0982
B-8888	54321	004	098	032	0982
A-7777	23389	058	010	023	0982

12. You are hired as a ticket taker at an amusement park's automobile parking lot. The management informs you that there are 500 parking stalls available for compacts, 10 for recreational campers, and 400 for full-sized automobiles. The charges for parking are $1.00 for compacts, $4.00 for recreation vans, and $1.25 for full-sized automobiles. Compute the money collected in a day. Make sure you have room in the lot before you collect the fee, as management does not allow you to return any parking fee. Print out the results at the end of your shift. Prepare the structure chart, flowchart, and pseudocode.

13. The Star Car Sales Company has five salespersons who sell used cars. The salesperson earns a 16 percent commission on the sales price of the car if the sales price is under $5,000 and the car is more than two years old. If the sales price is over $5,000 and the car is two years old or younger, the salesperson earns 20 percent commission. All other car sales earn a 12 percent commission rate. Calculate the amount of profit made on each car, printing out this amount. The transaction record includes such data as the following: license number, make of car, year, sales price, cost price, salesperson number. The cost price indicates the price paid by the company to the owner and does not include the commission. Prepare the flowchart.

14. The Shelbyton National Bank has forty checking account customers. Two types of checking accounts are offered, one carrying no service charge as long as the balance does not go below $500 and a savings account balance of $1,000 is maintained. The other type of checking account charges a flat fee of 25 cents per check. Any returned check for insufficient funds is charged a $5.00 service fee. Prepare the structure chart, flowchart, and pseudocode.

a. Set up some input data for several accounts. Consider how a deposit and a written check can be processed.
b. Read a record.
c. Calculate the balance of the account, deducting the fee for each check, if appropriate.
d. Print out the pertinent data about this customer's account along with the new balance.
e. Process all records in the file.

15. Using information from 14 above, adjust your flowchart to include an average bank balance for each customer's data that is read. Print out this data at the end of the customer's monthly statement. Also calculate the number of accounts that have more than a $750 daily balance. Print out this average after all records are read and processed.

16. Using project 15 information, prepare another flowchart, using the DO UNTIL method for looping. Use the predefined process symbol.

People in Computing

Jo Ellen Dufresne

COMPANY
TRW, Inc.

POSITION
Software Test Engineer

Computer programming is only one part of putting together a computer system. Software engineering takes care of getting the parts together, and software test engineering is responsible for making sure that they function as a whole and as the customer specifies.

I work as a software test engineer for a company which designs and develops large computer systems. I enjoy my work very much because it offers me responsibility, a wide variety of technical challenges, and contact with our customers.

Software test engineering is the discipline whereby a software system's functional requirements are verified in the working product. For this to be done thoroughly and effectively, testing must be considered at the onset of a software development project.

A good test program starts with a test group which is independent of the development organization, and which provides a different perspective in the test process. The developers, in their unit and development testing, have an interest in proving that their products work correctly. The independent testers, on the other hand, are interested in finding any and all areas in which the product does not meet its functional requirements.

The tester begins by analyzing the software requirements for testability, revising those requirements which are ambiguous or qualitative rather than quantitative. He or she then defines acceptance criteria—those conditions which must be true for a requirement to be considered satisfied. He or she includes these requirements and acceptance criteria in a test plan, which defines and drives the entire test program.

The tester then generates test cases which verify groups of functional requirements. The test case defines the exact hardware and software environment in which the test will be run. It also includes the step-by-step procedures which must be followed, including inputs and expected responses, to verify that the requirements have been satisfied.

When all of the test cases have been satisfactorily executed, it has been demonstrated that the software satisfies its requirements, and the customer formally accepts the product.

Software test engineering is a satisfying profession because it is applied to a wide variety of software applications, and it is necessary on every software development program. The software test engineer needs to have a good understanding of how the whole system is meant to operate, as well as a broad knowledge of how individual software and hardware entities function. This opportunity and need to understand the total software/hardware picture is much more interesting and exciting to me than concentrating on the design and coding of one small software component. I recommend this line of work to anyone who is detail conscious and who is interested in a computer science career which provides variety, responsibility and challenge.

12

Applications and Systems Programs

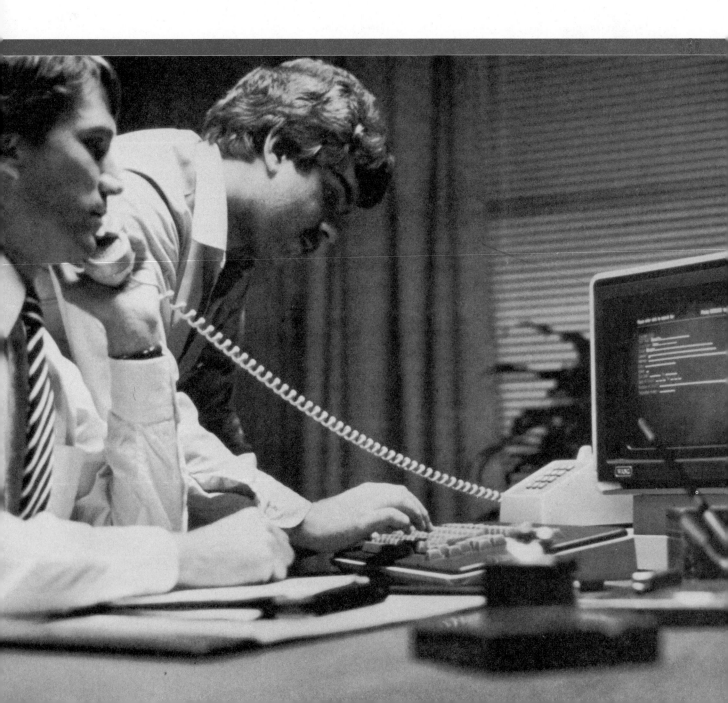

OUTLINE

PROLOGUE

A book salesman named Don Partenfelder visits a student computer club at the club's request. The club wishes to see some of the computer language books that he has to sell. A club member asks the salesman to identify one word in a computer language that makes him think of that particular language. "Well", Don answers, "there is *picture* in COBOL; *format* in FORTRAN, *perform* in COBOL, *begin* in Pascal and Ada, *loop* in Ada, *let* in BASIC—"

"Oh, no" says Mildred. "I thought that computer languages would have advanced at the same pace as hardware. Why, I thought all instructions would be written in almost the same way."

"Keep going, Mr. Partenfelder," said Jack. After five minutes, the club stopped their guest from answering the question.

HOW DOES IT DO THAT?

READ ON.

OBJECTIVES

After studying this chapter, you should be able to:

1. Differentiate between assembly language and high-level language.

2. List the major advantages and disadvantages of various high-level languages.

3. Differentiate among the systems programs as to the function each performs.

4. Explain the various steps a program passes through before an applications program can be used for executing data.

INTRODUCTION

This chapter deals with the two worlds of programming: those programs used to solve everyday problems, and those programs that make up the operating system, called systems programs.

In this chapter we will look into the advantages and disadvantages of various selected applications programs. Some of the programs are illustrated with a complete, straightforward program. In other cases, however, only the same data is set up and used for multiplication. This is done so you can see how each language has its own specifications for identifying data, creating names to identify the data, and accomplishing the writing of the instruction to multiply the data. The purposes for using systems programs are also investigated.

STORED PROGRAM BACKGROUND

We communicate with computers by the use of words or symbols which form instructions. From these instructions, electrical paths are formed; then and only then can the computer operate. Such instructions, in program form and located in primary storage, are called a stored program. Without a stored program, there would be no electrical signals and so no computer operation.

Let us assume that you are visiting Paris and speak only English. You wish to ask a Frenchman for directions, but he speaks only French. The only way both of you can communicate is through an interpreter who must know both English and French. In a similar manner, the computer's translator program interprets, or bridges the gap between the language a programmer writes, and the computer's own language, which is called machine language. If a programmer wishes to write a program other than the machine language of that particular computer, a translator program is needed.

This is true because the only language the computer can really understand is the machine language. The translated program, in machine language, is often called the **object program.** It is from the object program that the electrical signals are generated. The machine language, unique to a computer type since it is set up for the electrical circuitry for that computer, is made up of 0s and 1s. An IBM 370 object program is different from a Honeywell object program. The mainframes, the large computer systems, have unique object programs. A microcomputer, however, does not; rather, the object program used depends upon the microprocessor chip that is used. Refer to Figure 12.1.

A user has a choice of writing in assembly language, which is closest to machine language, or a high-level language that is more English-like. The high-level language is easier to write and is designed to solve some specific type of problem. Examples of these high-level languages are those that are used to solve scientific problems algebraically, or, simply, algebraic mathematics problems. Business-oriented problems use a different type of high-level language since the decimal points and signs are fixed in position in the solution. These English-like languages demand more of the translator program than they demand of the pro-

GALLERY 8

Computers In Science and Technology

This color gallery is dedicated to the men and women who have worked tirelessly and mostly have gone unrecognized for their scientific contributions. So much of our world around us we take for granted. There are many times, however, that we realize the important contributions made by these scientific-oriented individuals when we seek help or wish to further our knowledge of the world around us. Computers and computer technology are an integral part of their research.

1. The field of space exploration relies on computer technology. Numerous computer devices are shown in this "fish-eye" lens view of the flight deck of the space Orbiter 102 Columbia. Between the two seats are the flight computer and navigation aid console. Immediately in front of the console are the three cathode ray tubes (CRTs) used to display computer data and information for the crew. **2.** *T-Minus Three Hours and Holding*—An acrylic painting by Ron Cobb of the Space Shuttle Columbia preparing for her fourth flight into space. **3.** A computer tracks the Voyager I's trip to Saturn.

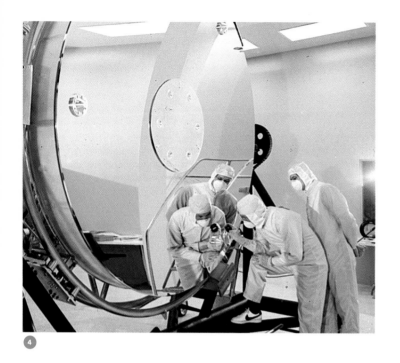

4

6

5

4. A space telescope developed by NASA will enable scientists to see seven times further into the universe. A computer was used to polish the 94-inch diameter optical surface. **5.** Technicians are moving the mirror after it was polished. **6.** Forecasters in NOAA's National Weather Service rely heavily on computers in order to provide almost two million predictions a year. **7.** Artificial intelligence experts are trying to design robots that are able to simulate the human thought processes. The experimental robot ARGON attracts the curiosity of a group of children. **8.** High-speed computers advance quantum research. Using theories based on the Schroedinger wave equation, quantum chemists can describe molecules with great accuracy. This color image is a graphical representation of the electrostatic potential produced by a molecule. **9.** At GE, scientists use computer graphics to study a polymer's molecular structure in order to judge its properties.

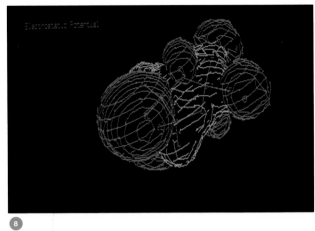

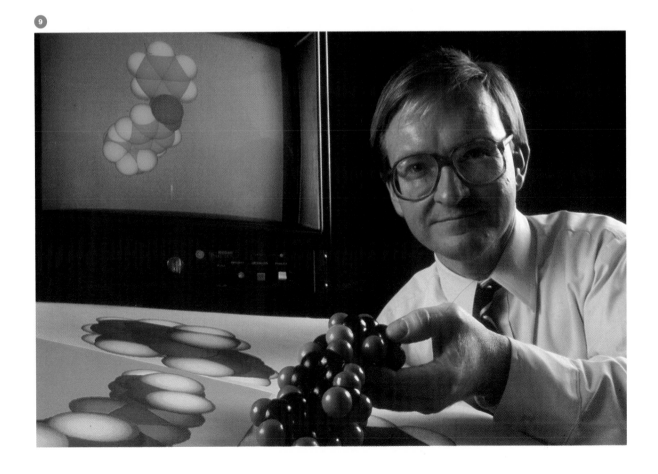

10. A computer generated landstat picture taken from a satellite and the corresponding map produced. **11.** A computerized cartographic work station aids cartographers in the making of maps. **12.** HP's critical-care monitoring system checks a patient's vital signs from a bedside terminal for more immediate care. **13.** Computers are used by surgeons to monitor a patient's progress during surgery. **14.** Computers are used in laboratories for analysis of specialized tests. **15.** A lab technician uses "Hemotrak" to analyze a patient's blood sample.

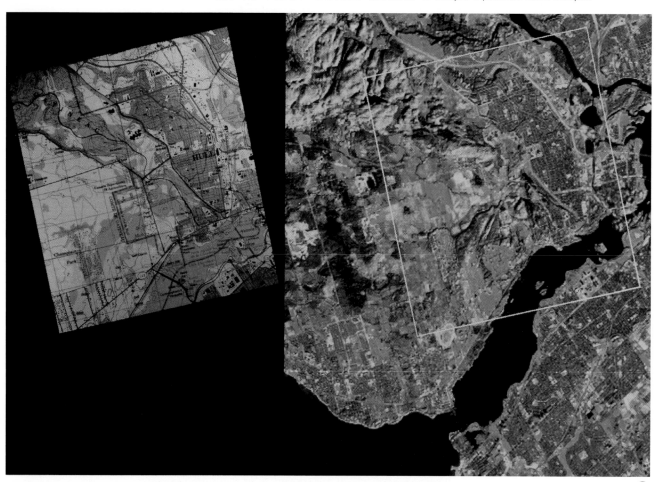

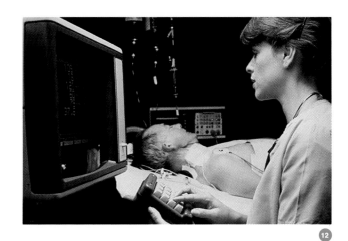

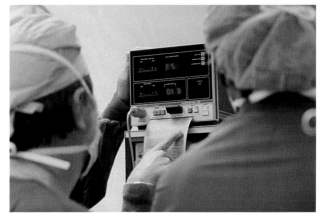

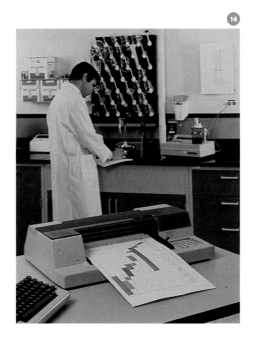

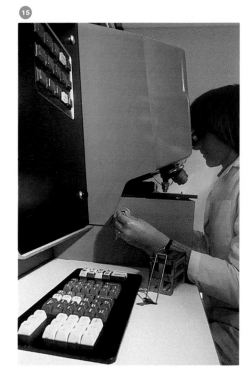

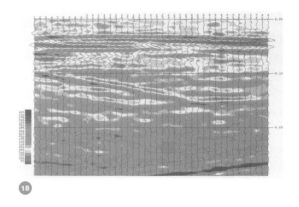

18

17

16. and 17. Computers are used to develop laser technology. **18.** Computers are used to record vibrations within the earth. A computer generated seismograph is shown here. **19.** A patient undergoes a CT scan computer operated CT device. **20.** The results of a CT scan are shown here.

16

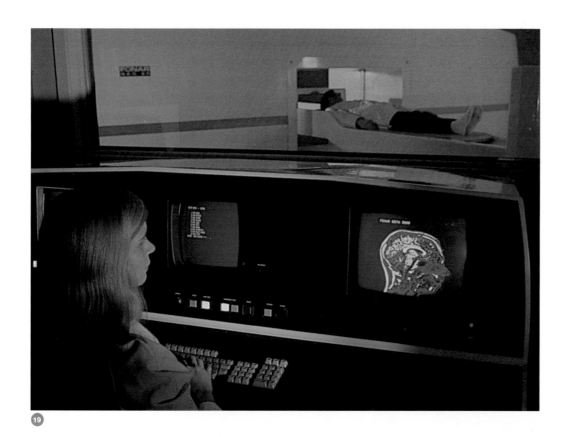

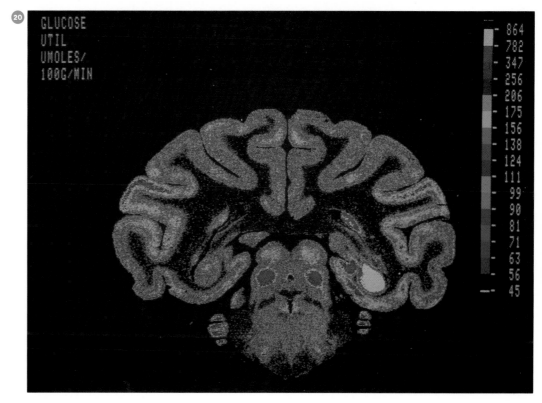

GLUCOSE
UTIL
UMOLES/
100G/MIN

864
782
347
256
206
175
156
138
124
111
99
90
81
71
63
56
45

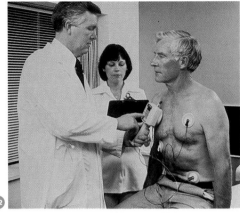

21.

22.

21. The computerized Kurtzwell Reading Machine reads aloud to the blind. **22.** A physician uses a computer to adjust the rate of this patient's pacemaker. **23.** With the "computerized stimulation and feedback system" developed by Dr. Jerrold Peltrosky at Wright State University, Nan Davis, A WSU student paralyzed from the waist down, has taken several steps.

23.

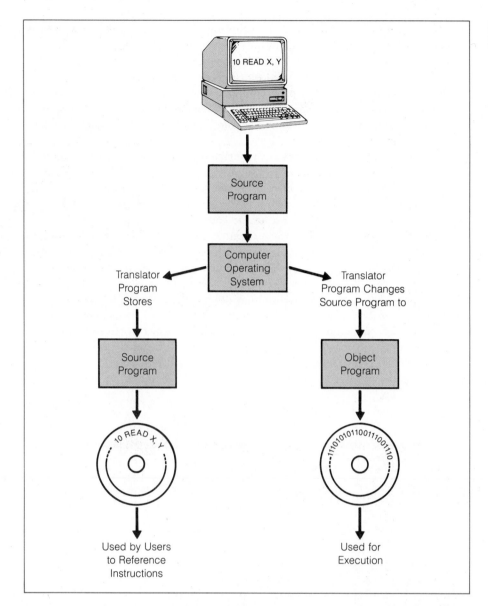

FIGURE 12.1
Role of a translator program.

grammer; hence, they do not demand a close, technical knowledge of the computer's workings.

After the programmer completes a program, the instructions are keyed and checked to make certain they are entered as intended. Test data is prepared to substantiate the authenticity of the program. The program is then used as input to the computer, with the source program being translated to machine language by the compiler or interpreter.

The word *compile* means to bring together parts into a new, organized format. **A compiler** is a program designed to translate a high-level (source) program to a machine language (object) program.

There is no resemblance between the high-level language and its machine language. Any details about the computer being used are handled by the compiler when the translation is done to machine language. Specifics such as registers (those high-speed storage areas used by the control section) and their manner of usage are of no concern to the programmer.

Another translator program, called an **interpreter,** does the translation work of changing the source program into machine language just like a compiler does, but on a statement-by-statement, not a whole-program, basis. The interpreter translates each instruction to machine language when the user depresses the RUN command on the keyboard (that is, as the instruction is executed). Once executed, each statement's object code is discarded, not saved. The compiler, by contrast, does the translation after the entire program is entered and saves its object program, making for more efficient use of the computer.

After the program is run on the computer, the programmer is given a **source program listing,** which contains the source program as written by the programmer as well as any diagnostics, which point out syntax errors made by the programmer. A syntax error results from incorrect keying of an instruction or use of the wrong design of an instruction. The programmer debugs the program by removing and correcting any instructions that produced diagnostics or any instructions that produced incorrect execution of data. Should any logic be incorrectly written, these logic errors must be corrected at this time, too. The corrected program is again submitted to the computer for translation to machine language and for execution of the test data, with the hope that this time it will execute correctly.

CHECKPOINT Can you:

Differentiate among object program, source program, compiler, and interpreter?

HISTORICAL DEVELOPMENT OF LANGUAGES

In the late 1950s the IBM 305 RAMAC, the first disk-oriented computer system developed, was introduced. The programmer learned the instructions oriented to the IBM 305. It took weeks for the programmer to efficiently write the language of this computer. Instructions of R99Y9900 (to write a record to disk storage), W04J9905 (to seek a record in disk storage), and W04X0405C1 (to compare certain data) eventually meant something to the programmer.

When the company changed computers in the early 1960s and it became possible to lease the IBM 1401 instead of the IBM 305, the programmer again returned to school to learn the language acceptable on the IBM 1401, a popular second-generation computer. This time the programmer could write instructions of 4, C068004, /299. Again the machine language was full of symbols meaningless to all but the highly trained. Rather than having the programmer learn such cumbersome instructions, a **symbolic language** was written which was closely related to machine language. SPS, a symbolic programming language for the IBM 1401, was a low-level language that closely resembled the machine language but was easier to write since English-type symbols were used. The programmer also had the option of writing in assembly language rather than SPS or machine language. The assembly language, called Autocoder, was easier to write than SPS because it gave more flexibility and capability in programming. For example, the programmer would write an R for the symbol to read a card, a CS for the symbol to clear storage, a W to write a line on the printer, and so on. Autocoder, like SPS, was still **machine-oriented.** In other words, this language was acceptable and understood only by IBM 1401s.

Programmers grew weary of going to school to learn a new language each time the company leased a new computer system. The company grew weary of sending programmers to school and waiting for them to become proficient in writing the new language. The stage was set for movement toward some uniformity in computer languages.

In 1957 IBM introduced the FORTRAN language. IBM supplied a translation program for the language to each installation using their computers. FORTRAN was then acceptable on all IBM equipment; today it is acceptable on all larger computer systems and even many microcomputer systems. **FORTRAN** (an acronym derived from **FOR**mula **TRAN**slation) is a language geared to scientific applications, although it has been used in some business applications as well.

In 1959 a group of business people met to create a language that was geared to strictly business applications. **COBOL** (short for **C**ommon **B**usiness **O**riented **L**anguage) was developed. Each manufacturer has some of its own rules that apply to the language. These variations are slight, however.

Today most business-oriented programmers write programs in COBOL, while scientific-oriented programmers write programs in FORTRAN. BASIC was developed at Dartmouth College in 1965 to teach students how to write programs using a straightforward language. BASIC soon became the most popular language used on microcomputers.

The trend is well established for the programmer to write the high-level languages to solve most applications. High-level languages such as FORTRAN, COBOL, BASIC, and Pascal take much of the detail work to accommodate hardware away from the programmer and give it to the translater program. Refer to Figure 12.2.

Some applications require that programs be written in assembly language because of the efficiency in executing the program on the computer. To be able to write assembly language requires that the programmer have very detailed knowledge of that computer. The highly specialized programmer, such as the systems analyst, is machine-oriented and can write assembly language. The systems analyst is concerned with the actual working and capability of the computer system. The typical programmer concentrates his or her efforts on solving applications.

In the remaining part of the chapter, let us investigate the two levels of programming that are available, namely the low-level (the assembly language) and the high-level.

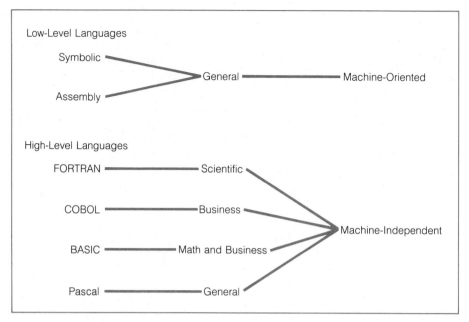

FIGURE 12.2 **Types of languages.**

ASSEMBLY LANGUAGE

Assembly language closely resembles machine language since one instruction exists in assembly language for each instruction written in machine language. In other words, there is a 1 to 1 ratio when the assembly language is translated to machine language, the translation of which is done by a program called the **assembler.**

When a programmer writes assembly language, he or she is working directly with the registers (the high-speed storage used by the control section) of that computer, these varying according to the computer. Because the programmer is dealing with low-level language, a more efficient program is generated in terms of both processing time and allocation of primary storage. Some of the very large programs that are scheduled for daily execution in some companies are written in assembly language for efficiency and economy. The programmer might require a longer time to write the program because of the detail that is involved, but in the long run, this program uses considerably less time for processing the data. On the other hand, many times when a short program is to be written, assembly language is far quicker and easier than writing some of the high-level languages.

A marked disadvantage of writing in assembly language results because of the extreme detail that is involved. It can be more difficult to debug an extensive program written in assembly language. Other times, when a programmer writes a high-level language and cannot debug the program successfully, the programmer, if knowledgeable in both, might use the assembly language for debugging the high-level language. Certain systems commands can be given to the operating system to translate the high-level language written by the programmer into assembly language. The programmer examines the printout of the assembly language.

For purposes of example, we will use the assembly language of the IBM 370 family of computers, called Basic Assembly Language. You need not concern yourself with asking why the assembly language handles calculations in the way that it does, since the example is made only for comparative reference with other languages to be discussed in this chapter.

In the overall discussion regarding the various languages, let us assume we wish to set up two fields that are whole numbers. RATE has a value of 3 and TIME has a value of 2. We wish to multiply RATE by TIME to calculate DISTANCE.

When writing assembly language to multiply data, the programmer must load, or put in, the multiplicand in an odd-numbered register and the multiplier in an even-numbered register. The instructions to accomplish the multiplication might look like the following:

```
        L      7,RATE          Puts a value of 3 into register 7
        M      6,TIME          Multiplies a value of 2 in register 6
        ST     7,DISTANCE      Stores from register 7 into PRODUCT


TIME      DC   F'2'            Sets up a value of 3 in 32 bits
RATE      DC   F'3'            Sets up a value of 2 in a full word
DISTANCE  DS   F               Sets up one storage word 32-bits long
```

HIGH-LEVEL LANGUAGES

There are hundreds of high-level languages developed for use on the computer. Let us just list briefly some of the popularly used languages, so that if you see the name, you can readily identify it as to purpose.

Let us group the languages according to the degree of structure they possess. A structured computer language calls for structured programming techniques. In other words, can the language be tested in small modules? Can it be written with top-down design? Does it use the control structures of sequence, selection, and repetition? Does it avoid the use of GO TO instructions which are used for changing the flow of the logic as discussed in Chapter 11?

Many of the languages designed before structured programming existed in the early 1970s have been redesigned so that they are partly structured. To be classified as a **structured language** in this discussion, the language has procedures that allow processing to be done in a module; it also has selection and an iterative provision for looping. If one of these characteristics is missing, the language is considered as semistructured. If the IF-THEN-ELSE and DO WHILE are not included, we will consider the language to be unstructured. Report Program Generator (RPG) is the only language discussed in this chapter that is unstructured.

The following discussion will illustrate how data can be set up (initialized) and how two fields of data can be multiplied. Contrast these instructions for various languages as we pass through the discussion. In a program we make up names to identify data. Some languages have limitations as to the number of characters used in naming the data; some allow thirty characters in naming the data, others just two characters.

UNSTRUCTURED OR SEMISTRUCTURED LANGUAGES

The following unstructured and semistructured languages are discussed briefly in the sections below: COBOL, FORTRAN, Report Program Generator, BASIC, SNOBOL, LISP, and Logo.

COBOL

COBOL is an internationally accepted programming language that is designed for solving business problems. In 1959 the Department of Defense organized a Conference on Data Systems Languages called **CODASYL,** attended by many representatives from government, computer manufacturers, and interested individuals. This committee set the standards for the language. Thousands of COBOL programs have been written over the past twenty years. This language will be popularly used for many more years.

Two versions of COBOL have been standardized—the 1968 and the 1974 versions, with the latter being the more commonly used. A later version of the 1974 standards was set up, but at this time of writing it has not been released because of a pending lawsuit.

Textbook and manual mentions of **ANSI COBOL** refer to the standardized COBOL language, the specifications of which were approved by the American National Standards Institute (ANSI). The purpose of the specifications was to establish a standardized COBOL language that was consistent for all manufacturers, so that the same COBOL program could be executed on many computers, hence making COBOL machine-independent. This has not been totally accomplished; the 1974 standards did not incorporate all of the desired capabilities of the language, so each computer manufacturer has included some additional capabilities.

COBOL was designed for business applications, with the hope that many business people who are not programmers by profession would be able to read it and understand its use. To accomplish this, COBOL uses English-like statements, which make the language easy to read and self-documenting.

The machine-independent characteristic of the language contributes to its popularity since it can be executed on most computers as long as a translator program is available. COBOL, like most other high-level languages, does not make efficient use of computer storage.

Let us set up a data name for RATE, TIME, and DISTANCE. The statements that set up the data could be written as follows:

```
05   RATE        PICTURE 9      VALUE 3.
05   TI-ME       PICTURE 9      VALUE 2.
05   DISTANCE    PICTURE 999    VALUE ZEROS.
```

To make the multiplication occur, the following statement could be written:

```
MULTIPLY RATE BY TI-ME GIVING DISTANCE.
```

COBOL is divided into four divisons: identification, environment, data, and procedure, with each division serving a specific purpose in the program. No COBOL program can exist without all four divisions. The identification division gives a program name. The environment division identifies the file with the logical unit used (for example, magnetic disk, terminal, printer, and so on). The data division specifies the file designed as an FD in the program. The record is set up as a 01 level number in the program. The fields in the record are identified as 05 level numbers. The procedure division specifies the data manipulation that is to be done.

The program in Figure 12.3 prints all input data when the age data is between the ages of 18 through 25. An average age is calculated for all records read.

FORTRAN

FORTRAN, as has been mentioned, is a standardized programming language designed for solving scientific and mathematical problems. Its usage is widespread in the scientific sector.

Its popularity is based upon its ease of use for writing instructions to do calculations. FORTRAN, as introduced, was cumbersome, however, for handling input and output but was made far more flexible and easier to use when the 1977 standards were released for the language.

There have been many versions of the FORTRAN language, each of which is geared to fit more modern methods of programming sophistication.

FORTRAN is a fairly easy language to write since it does not deal with words as much as COBOL. Geared to scientific data, the language is very flexible in the use of decimal points on input and output, allowing different decimal positions in the same field from record to record. Positive and negative signs are also handled easily in the language. Numbers can also be expressed in exponential form.

Although some people prefer writing in other languages, FORTRAN is used for a tremendous number of programs. There are still positions available for maintaining FORTRAN programs although some companies are electing to write in other languages.

To initialize the value of RATE, TIME, and DISTAN, we could write these instructions:

```
INTEGER TIME, RATE, DISTAN
RATE = 3
TIME = 2
```

To accomplish multiplication, we could write the instruction as follows:

```
DISTAN = RATE * TIME
```

WHAT'S RIGHT

TI-ME Rather Than Time; Distan Rather Than Distance

Computer languages have their individuality. COBOL, for example, has a long list of reserved words that are part of the COBOL language. From a beginning programming standpoint, it is just easier to place a hyphen in a word created to identify data rather than to reference the long list of reserved words. It is only a few of these reserved words that contain a hyphen. Your chances of selecting a data name is then slim. If, by accident, you named data that was the same as the reserved word, your program would not execute data correctly. An example of this is the reserved word of TIME. In the discussion, the data name was changed to TI-ME.

In FORTRAN, only six alphabetic characters can be used to identify the name for data. In FORTRAN, these names for data are called variables. The variable called DISTANCE is illegally formed since DISTANCE uses eight characters. To meet the specifications of the language, the variable was shortened to six characters—DISTAN.

FIGURE 12.3
Sample COBOL program with output.

```
IDENTIFICATION DIVISION.
PROGRAM-ID. PROB1.
AUTHOR.   CHU CHU SMITH.
ENVIRONMENT DIVISION.
INPUT-OUTPUT SECTION.
FILE-CONTROL.
      SELECT INPUT-FILE ASSIGN TO CD.
      SELECT PRINT-FILE ASSIGN TO PR.
DATA DIVISION.
FILE SECTION.
FD    INPUT-FILE
      LABEL RECORDS ARE STANDARD
      DATA RECORD IS INPUT-RECORD.
01    INPUT-RECORD.
      05    I-STUDENT-NAME                PICTURE X(20).
      05    I-STUDENT-ADDRESS             PICTURE X(30).
      05    I-STUDENT-AGE                 PICTURE 9(02).
      05    FILLER                        PICTURE X(28).
FD    PRINT-FILE
      LABEL RECORDS ARE STANDARD
      DATA RECORD IS PRINT-RECORD.
01    PRINT-RECORD.
      05    P-STUDENT-NAME                PICTURE X(20).
      05    FILLER                        PICTURE X(10).
      05    P-STUDENT-ADDRESS             PICTURE X(30).
      05    FILLER                        PICTURE X(10).
      05    P-STUDENT-AGE                 PICTURE 9(02).
      05    FILLER                        PICTURE X(60).
WORKING-STORAGE SECTION.
01    END-OF-JOB-SWITCH    PICTURE X(01) VALUE 'N'.
01    CALCULATION-WORKAREAS.
      02    RECORD-COUNT    PICTURE 9(05) VALUE ZEROS COMP.
      02    TOTAL-AGES      PICTURE 9(05) VALUE ZEROS COMP.
      02    AVERAGE-AGE     PICTURE 9(02) VALUE ZEROS COMP.
PROCEDURE DIVISION.
00/-PRODUCE-NAME-LIST.
      OPEN INPUT INPUT-FILE OUTPUT PRINT-FILE.
      READ INPUT-FILE
           AT END MOVE 'Y' TO END-OF-JOB-SWITCH.
      PERFORM 100-PRODUCE-NAME-LINE
           UNTIL END-OF-JOB-SWITCH IS EQUAL TO 'Y'.
      PERFORM 200-CALCULATE-AVERAGE-AGE.
      CLOSE INPUT-FILE PRINT-FILE.
      STOP RUN.
100-PRODUCE-NAME-LINE.
      IF END-OF-JOB-SWITCH IS NOT EQUAL TO 'Y'
           PERFORM 110-PRINT-NAME-LINE
           PERFORM 120-CALCULATE-AGES.
      READ INPUT-FILE
           AT END MOVE 'Y' TO END-OF-JOB-SWITCH.
110-PRINT-NAME-LINE.
      IF I-STUDENT-AGE IS GREATER THAN 17
         IF I-STUDENT-AGE IS LESS THAN 26
           MOVE SPACES              TO PRINT-RECORD
           MOVE I-STUDENT-NAME      TO P-STUDENT-NAME
           MOVE I-STUDENT-ADDRESS TO P-STUDENT-ADDRESS
           MOVE I-STUDENT-AGE       TO P-STUDENT-AGE
           WRITE PRINT-RECORD AFTER ADVANCING 1 LINE.
120-CALCULATE-AGES.
      ADD +1 TO RECORD-COUNT.
      ADD I-STUDENT-AGE TO TOTAL-AGES.
200-CALCULATE-AVERAGE-AGE.
      DIVIDE TOTAL-AGES BY RECORD-COUNT GIVING
           AVERAGE-AGE ROUNDED.
      MOVE SPACES         TO PRINT-RECORD.
      MOVE AVERAGE-AGE TO P-STUDENT-AGE.
      WRITE PRINT-RECORD AFTER ADVANCING 2 LINES.


KIRK GIBSON        50 PHELAN AVENUE           24
MARY CANN          17 HAPPY LANE              20
JOYCE SON          10 CLAY STREET             25

                                             23
```

Report Program Generator

Report Program Generator (RPG) is an unstructured language designed primarily for solving business applications that are fairly straightforward. The language is not standardized, but it is similar on IBM and Univac computers or other small systems. While the language is not as readily meaningful to the untrained user as FORTRAN and COBOL, it is quickly learned.

As its name implies, Report Program Generator prepares reports. The programmer prepares the input, calculation, and output specifications. The programmer writes these types of instructions as well as those specifying how the data is to be manipulated. Report Program Generator, however, generates its own processing procedures. The programmer communicates with the translator program by using various coding formats which in turn dictate how the processing is accomplished. Report Program Generator offers a very straightforward and quick way of writing a program. The program that is generated is quite efficiently prepared by the translator program.

Figure 12.4 shows some of the completed coding forms that are used by a programmer to specify the desired processing. The same program is presented that was used for COBOL.

BASIC

Although the BASIC language has been mentioned in several parts of the text, it is important enough to mention here again. The BASIC language works in a time-sharing environment. BASIC was the first **interactive language,** which means that a user is given an immediate response from the computer as to the accuracy with which each instruction is written. A type of conversation exists between computer and user. This does not mean, however, that you positively wrote the instruction correctly for processing a program. What it does mean is that you wrote the syntax correctly. As soon as you depress the return key, the syntax (the rules for forming an instruction) is checked. If there is an error, the computer outputs a diagnostic immediately on the next line on the monitor.

It is easy to learn to write this, the most popular of all the computer languages used. There are many versions to the language.

To set up our same problem for multiplication, the data would be initialized as:

```
10   LET R = 3
20   LET T = 2
```

To accomplish the multiplication, we could write:

```
30   LET D = R * T
```

BASIC is discussed and illustrated in depth in Appendices A and B.

FIGURE 12.4 **RPG II file description, input calculation, and output specifications.**

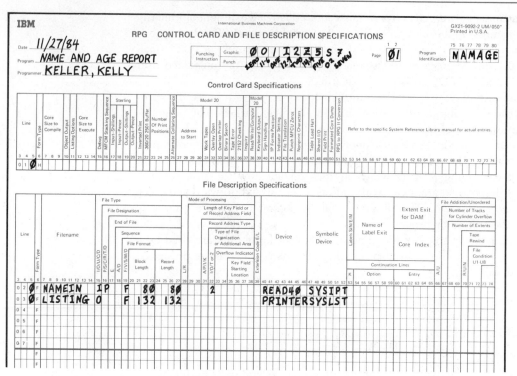

(a) File Description Specifications

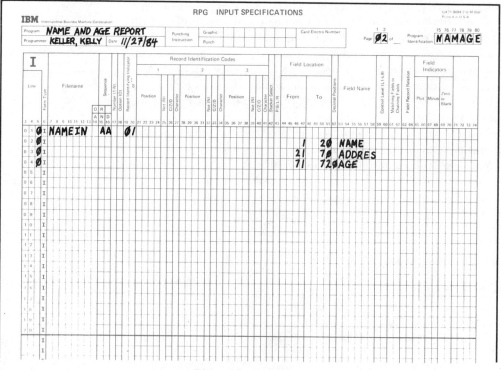

(b) Input Specifications

FIGURE 12.4 (*Continued*)

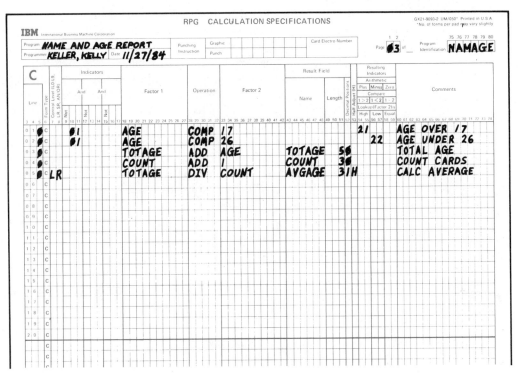

(c) Calculation Specifications

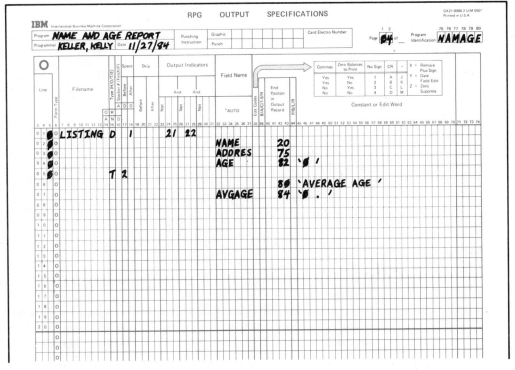

(d) Output Specifications

SNOBOL

SNOBOL was developed at Bell Telephone Laboratories in 1962 for handling strings; a string can be defined as any data that is to be set up with some type of value. SNOBOL is both a string processing and an algebraic language which also does pattern-matching. When patterns are matched, a character or characters can be replaced with new data. If, for example, the data contained some 7s that you wanted to remove and replace with Zs, this would be pattern matching. SNOBOL has the capability to **concatenate** data, that is, to join or add together data as specified by the programmer.

A person's name, for example, can be set up as a string, by simply using an equation such as NAME = "JOE BLOW". If you wished to change text and insert your name instead of Joe's name, an equation would be prepared. Just for fun, let us assume that RATE has a value of 3 and TIME has a value of 2. To set up these values we would write:

```
RATE = 3
TIME = 2
```

To perform the multiplication, we could write:

```
DISTANCE = RATE * TIME
```

To add two numbers together the instructions could be written:

```
A = 5
B = 6
C = A + B
```

The answer would be 11. If, however, to illustrate its string processing ability to concatenate, we wrote:

```
C = A B
```

The answer would be 56.
If, we set

```
A = "SNO"
B = "BOL"
```

and we set

```
C = A B
```

C would then be equal to SNOBOL. How about C = A A B B? What would you get? How about C = A"B"? In this example, you would get SNOB.

This language can be used for writing assemblers, compilers, and interpreters because of its easy associations using strings. SNOBOL can also analyze for similar patterns in text and make changes as directed by the use of equations.

LISP

The **LISP** (derived from the words **LIS**t **P**rocessing) language was developed in the 1960s by John McCarthy for nonnumeric computation. Massachusetts Institute of Technology (M.I.T.) first used LISP to process data that consisted of lists of symbols. LISP is used for symbolic calculations in such applications as electrical circuit theory, mathematical logic, and game playing—often as a research tool.

It has proven valuable in artificial intelligence development; artificial intelligence, sometimes defined as creating "thinking machines," is being developed to help humans by providing expert decision making. Artificial intelligence is discussed in Chapter 18.

LISP is a functional as well as a list processing language. If you wished to add the values of 3 and 2 together you would merely write:

```
(SETQ RATE 3)
(SETQ TIME 2)
 PLUS (RATE TIME)
```

If you wished to multiply these values instead you would write:

```
TIMES (RATE TIME)
```

When you see a LISP program, you will find a long list of words that are enclosed within pairs of parentheses, as many as nine in a single statement. This language certainly has individuality.

Logo

In 1967, Seymour Papert began developmental work at the Massachusetts Institute of Technology on a language that was suitable for children. The language was **Logo;** its name was derived from the Greek word *loglike*, meaning logic. Handicapped and gifted children were taught abstract concepts through the use of the Logo language which uses graphics and animation. The child, using a terminal or microcomputer, moves a "turtle" on the graphics display screen, thus giving instructions to the computer. The turtle, resembling an arrowhead, can be moved upward or downward on the screen or to the right or left.

This language can be taught in several minutes. It gives marvelous reinforcement to youngsters who have deficiencies in spatial relations. It offers a fantastic experience to a youngster when investigating the world of graphics.

Logo has been refined many times. This language has the advantage of teaching programming concepts that can be applied to any programming language. It is not scientifically line-oriented as BASIC; hence, the popularity of this language will increase at the expense of the BASIC language as the first language taught. Logo provides the opportunity for children to learn difficult mathematical concepts and explains these concepts to children in a way which they can relate to. There are Logo learning kits that can be purchased for the teaching of math and spelling. Programs are also being sold for Scholastic Aptitude Tests (SAT) preparation. It is envisioned by some software experts that Logo will be used for expert systems (discussed in Chapter 1) and artificial intelligence systems. Logo is based upon LISP.

STRUCTURED LANGUAGES

The following structured languages are discussed next: ALGOL, PL/I, Pascal, FORTH, C, Ada, and Modula-2. Illustrations showing programs in C and Ada are included in the material because of those languages' popularity and interest level.

ALGOL

ALGOL, the name of which was derived from **ALGO**rithm **L**anguage, is a language designed for handling numerical calculations on larger computer systems. Its original version was introduced in 1960. In 1968 another version was presented which became an international standard for programming numerical processes. It has a very strict logical structure that must be defined exactly. The intent in using this language is so everyone writing this language can communicate with each other. ALGOL's popularity has been concentrated in educational environments—especially in European universities. It did form the backbone for the FORTRAN and Pascal languages, however.

For our RATE and TIME example, the integer (int), or whole number, would be specified as well as the name of the data and the data itself. The instructions could be written as follows:

```
int RATE := 3; int TIME := 2; int DIST := 0;
```

To accomplish multiplication, it would be written as:

```
DIST := RATE * TIME;
```

PL/I

PL/I (short for Programming Language One) was originally developed by a group of scientific users and business users in 1963 to be a general-purpose language. They hoped to create a structured language that would be meaningful to both groups and thus make communication between both groups easier. The advantages of COBOL, FORTRAN, and ALGOL were considered when this language was designed. Some users feel there is no better language available; others feel it is difficult to learn.

To initialize the values for our common problem, the maximum number of positions are written inside the parentheses. Also it is important to specify whole numbers by the use of the word *FIXED*. The instructions are:

```
DECLARE RATE      DECIMAL FIXED (2);
DECLARE TIME      DECIMAL FIXED (2);
DECLARE DISTANCE  DECIMAL FIXED (4);
RATE = 3;
TIME = 2;
```

To perform the multiplication, the following could be written:

```
DISTANCE = RATE * TIME;
```

Pascal

Pascal, named after the famous French mathematician, Blaise Pascal (1623–1662), was created by Niklaus Wirth in Zurich, Switzerland. Wirth developed the language for several years; it was released in 1971. Its roots grew out of ALGOL, (1960 version) although it is a much easier language to write than ALGOL.

Pascal was designed for use in scientific, business, and educational environments with an interactive capability. It provides an easy but yet powerful language that utilizes the structured programming approach. Its acceptance at the time of writing is mostly in the educational environment, but Pascal compilers are available on some of the large computer systems. Currently Pascal is used primarily on microcomputers.

It is a very easy language to learn once you have mastered its structure. Learning pseudocode helps in the writing of this language since Pascal follows the same concepts.

Pascal was developed after considerable research. The aim was to produce a language that would solve problems on the computer in a desirable way. The language has achieved that. Some computers accept Pascal at this time of writing: Apple, IBM, SuperPet, and even the Honeywell mainframe. Pascal is a language that must be compiled to be understood by the computer. That takes time and requires a large size compiler. This poses no problem for minis and mainframes but it can be a problem for some microcomputers.

A disadvantage of the language is data that is defined as real (numbers with decimal points or those stated with a negative or positive sign) must remain exponential throughout the program. The language does not accommodate a change of type from real to integer (whole numbers) or integer to real.

To set up RATE, TIME, and DISTANCE, the following instructions could be written:

```
CONST
    RATE = 3;
    TIME = 2;
VAR
    DISTANCE : INTEGER;
```

To perform the multiplication, we could write:

```
DISTANCE := RATE * TIME;
```

Pascal is a structured language; the structure was built into its design. Pascal programs are divided into two parts: the heading and the body. The heading gives the name of the program. The body contains the statements that are used to identify the processing that is to be done. The body forms the procedure division, identifying the instructions precisely. For example, the CONST represents constants which are those values that do not change in the program. The VAR (variables) are those names created by the programmer. The CONST and VAR are shown in the Pascal program in Figure 12.5. Notice how procedures are set up which are modules, each having one entry and one exit point. A similar program, used for COBOL and Report Program Generator, is also shown for Pascal.

FORTH

FORTH was developed by Charles Moore, who worked on its design for many years. In 1978 the language became part of the public domain, meaning it could be copied without copyright problems. In 1978 a committee called FORTH Interest Group (FIG) set up a standard for the language. Another group, however, called FORTH-83, set up a standardized approach that has become the standard of the industry.

This language can be used for writing systems programs as well as applications programs for graphics, games, communications, and robotics. It can be used on different systems, making it very flexible and efficient from the software standpoint. It is an interactive language. When you write the instruction according to the language specifications, the interpreter replies "ok" on the next line.

Most high-level languages have the advantage of **portability** which means that the same program can be easily adaptable to other computers. This means that an application is written once and can then be understood by other computers. FORTH has a distinct feature of allowing a programmer to be able to build up a dictionary of programs that are called by a name. After each program is stored in the dictionary, the programmer can always call up that program by simply giving its name.

To initialize our values, the following statements could be written:

```
3    VARIABLE RATE
2    VARIABLE TIME
0    VARIABLE DISTANCE
```

To perform the multiplication, we could write:

```
RATE @ TIME @ * DISTANCE.
```

C

The **C** language was developed by Bell Telephone Laboratories for the purpose of writing systems programs for the UNIX operating system. The C language is, however, very flexible and can also be used for solving business, scientific, word processing, data base and financial applications. Some less complex C compilers

FIGURE 12.5

A sample Pascal program.

```
(*****************************************************************)
(**        A PASCAL PROGRAM USING A PROCEDURE STATEMENT        **)
(*****************************************************************)
PROGRAM LISTING;
    TYPE
      LENNAME = PACKED ARRAY[1..20] OF CHAR;
         (* SET UP A FIELD FOR NAME HAS MAX. OF 20 CHARACTERS   *)
         LENADDR = PACKED ARRAY[1..40] OF CHAR;
         (* SET UP A FIELD FOR ADDRESS HAS MAX. OF 40 CHARS.    *)
   VAR (* SET UP THE VARIABLES                                  *)
      NAME : ARRAY[1..100] OF LANNAME;
      ADDR : ARRAY[1..100] OF LENADDR;
         (* SET UP MAX. NUMBER OF RECORDS (UP TO 100)           *)
      TEMPNAME : LENNAME (* TEMPORARY INPUT BUFFER FOR NAME      *);
      TEMPADDR : LENADDR (* TEMPORARY INPUT BUFFER FOR ADDRESS   *);
      COUNT : INTEGER;
(*****************************************************************)
(* THIS PROCEDURE READS A PERSON'S NAME AND ADDRESS.  SIGNALS *)
(* END OF FILE WHEN YOU ENTER * FOR NAME AND PRESS RETURN KEY *)
(*****************************************************************)
PROCEDURE DATAIN;(* NOTE DATAIN IS THE PROCEDURE NAME         *)
BEGIN
   WRITELN (* ADVANCE A LINE *);
   WRITELN ('PLEASE ENTER THE PERSON''S NAME:');
   READLN(TEMPNAME);
      WHILE TEMPNAME[1] <> '*' DO
        BEGIN
          WRITELN('ADDRESS:');
          READLN(TEMPADDR);
          COUNT := COUNT + 1;
          NAME[COUNT] := TEMPNAME;
          ADDR[COUNT] := TEMPADDR;
          WRITELN;
          WRITELN('PLEASE ENTER THE PERSON''S NAME:');
          READLN(TEMPNAME);
      END (* OR WHILE DO LOOP *);
 END (* OF PROCEDURE DATAIN *);
(*****************************************************************)
(*     THIS PROCEDURE PRINTS THE NAME, ADDRESS.  AT          *)
(*      END, IT PRINTS THE TOTAL NUMBER OF RECORDS           *)
(*****************************************************************)
PROCEDURE DATAOUT;
   VAR
      LOOP : INTEGER (* USE FOR FOR...DO LOOP                   *);
   BEGIN
      WRITELN;
      WRITELN;
      WRITELN('NAME':8,'ADDRESS':35);
      WRITELN;
      FOR LOOP := 1 TO COUNT DO
         WRITELN(NAME[LOOP],ADDR[LOOP]:49);
      WRITELN;
      WRITELN;
      WRITELN('TOTAL NUMBER OF RECORDS: ',COUNT:4);
   END (* OF PROCEDURE DATAOUT                                  *);
(*****************************************************************)
(*                  MAIN    PROGRAM                           *)
(*****************************************************************)
(* NOTE: DATAIN--CALLS SUBROUTINE NAMED DATAIN AT END RETURNS *)
(*            TO THE NEXT INSTRUCTION FOLLOWING DATAIN.        *)
(*      DATAOUT--CALLS SUBROUTINE AT END RETURNS.             *)
(*****************************************************************)
BEGIN
   COUNT :=0; (*SET COUNTER TO ZERO                            *)
   DATAIN;
   IF COUNT <> 0 THEN DATAOUT
   ELSE WRITE('NO DATA HAS BEEN INPUTTED.');
END (*             OF MAIN PROGRAM                              *).
*

PLEASE ENTER THE PERSON'S NAME:
MOON WONG
ADDRESS:
858 WASHINGTON STREET

PLEASE ENTER THE PERSON'S NAME:
CHARLES MEZLER
ADDRESS:
1212 NOE STREET

PLEASE ENTER THE PERSON'S NAME:
CARL WONG
ADDRESS:
1723 OCEAN AVENUE

PLEASE ENTER THE PERSON'S NAME:
*

     NAME                        ADDRESS

MOON WONG              858 WASHINGTON STREET
CHARLES MEZLER         1212 NOE STREET
CARL WONG              1723 OCEAN AVENUE

TOTAL NUMBER OF RECORDS:    3
*
```

```
main()
{
    int sum, a,b;              In this program,
    a = 15;                    1) the integer values for a, b,
    b = 32;                       and sum are declared
    sum = a + b;               2) If the sum is less than 45,
    if (sum < 45){                the word "low" is printed.
        printf("low");         3) If the sum is equal to 45 or
    }else{                        greater than, the word "high"
        printf("high");           is printed.
    }                          4) Notice how the { and } form the
}                                 boundaries for the statements and
                                  how these are paired.
```

FIGURE 12.6 **C program.**

can be purchased for less than $50. Ron Cain deserves much of the credit in placing the C compiler in the public domain (for public use).

A highly structured, portable language, C often executes with remarkable speed. Compared with BASIC, C might take only 2 percent of the time required for running a BASIC program.

C differs from most languages since it uses lower-case symbols for its writing. Most other languages use upper-case symbols exclusively. C reserves the upper-case for the words that make up its instructions.

Because of the popularity of this language, a short program is provided in Figure 12.6.

Ada

The language **Ada** is named to honor Augusta Ada Byron, Countess of Lovelace, who worked with Charles Babbage in the 1840s when he was developing the Analytical Engine (mentioned in Appendix D). She is recognized as the first programmer.

Ada is sponsored by the Department of Defense, (DOD), which has been setting standards for many computer languages. Since 1978, the DOD has concentrated on the Ada language that it hopes will be the dominant language used in the military for the next twenty to twenty-five years. The language must have one-hundred percent standardization, being designed identically, so that Ada can run on different microprocessors without any translation problems. Often times, software companies will provide "bonus" options for users. These options, when run on a different computer, cause severe errors and prevent execution. Another feature of Ada is it provides **transportability,** the capability of running a program designed for a 8-bit microprocessor to be run and successfully executed on a 16-bit microprocessor.

Although its original intention was for applications dealing with military systems, Ada is being used for business applications such as payroll. Translator programs are being designed by several companies with the hope that the language will be in common use in the mid to late 1980s.

Ada is a highly structured computer programming language; it incorporates into its structure those ideas set up for software engineering. **Software engineering** refers to the scientific principles used to develop programs; it encourages programs to be set up in an efficient, understandable, modular, and reliable structure that can be easily modified when the need arises. Software engineering uses the visible tools of structured walkthroughs, structure charts, and pseudocode, referred to by software engineers as **Program Design Language (PDL)**, but it goes further to make programming a science. Since programs become very large in the number of instructions needed to meet the application's requirements for processing, programming becomes unmanageably complex. The software techniques advanced in Ada are hopefully viewed as providing a basis through which software can be designed in a scientific approach. There must be a way to manage the complexity of the program. Since humans work efficiently with a limited number of parts (variables) at one time, these parts must be handled to accomplish the desired effect but at the same time make it manageable. Ada accomplishes part of this by using modularity where each module is a subprogram (a small program) or task. Ada stresses that the extreme details be worked with only at that lower level. As was discussed in structure charts in Chapter 11, the lower the module, the more detail exists. The higher the module, the more machine-independent it is. Each module in Ada is considered independent from other modules, being logically and functionally independent. Each module should be understandable by a reader. The higher-level modules are developed without regard for the lower-level modules' detail; this has not always been the case in the past using other languages as details sometimes dictated a solution.

Because of the interest in this language, a subprogram is shown in Figure 12.7.

Modula-2

One of the newer languages on the structured programming scene is **Modula-2**, designed by Nicklaus Wirth, the father of Pascal language. There is a great similarity between Modula-2 and Pascal, yet there are distinct differences. It is said that anyone familiar with Pascal can learn Modula-2 in about four hours and can begin programming efficiently in a few days.

The concept of the language began with the idea that operating systems and translator programs could be written in the same high-level language as used for solving applications. Mr. Wirth developed this concept, beginning with the language called Modula-1 and after modifications, developing the newer version, Modula-2.

Key words are shown in all upper-case letters, while identifiers (how data is named) can be shown by a combination of upper- and lower-case or just by lower-case. The statements of Rate, Time, and Distance, which we have been developing through the chapter, are like those of Pascal. A main difference is that a program written in Pascal is replaced with a module in Modula-2; the Modula-2 language is modular in design.

Refer to Table 12.1 for comparison of some of the languages discussed.

```
declare
  package INTEGER_IO is new DIRECT_IO(ELEMENT_TYPE => INTEGER;
  use INTEGER_IO;
  INPUT_DATA      : INTEGER_IO.FILE_TYPE;
  OUTPUT_DATA     : INTEGER_IO.FILE_TYPE;
  AGE             : INTEGER;
  TOTAL           : INTEGER := 0;
  AVG             : INTEGER := 0;
  COUNT           : INTEGER := 0;
begin
  OPEN   (INPUT_DATA,IN_FILE,"INPUT_DISK_FILE");
  CREATE(OUTPUT_DATA,OUT_FILE,"OUTPUT_DISK_FILE");
  while not END_OF_FILE(INPUT_DATA)
    loop
      READ(INPUT_DATA,AGE);
        if AGE >= 18 then
            TOTAL := TOTAL + AGE;
            COUNT := COUNT + 1;
        end if;
    end loop;
  WRITE(OUTPUT_DATA,TOTAL);
  AVG := TOTAL / COUNT;
  WRITE(OUTPUT_DATA,AVG);
  CLOSE(INPUT_DATA);
  CLOSE(OUTPUT_DATA);
end;
```

An Ada program.
In this program,
1) A disk file is used.
2) The input data is read which is a list
    of ages
3) If the age is greater than or equal to
    18, the total age and the count of items
    are calculated
4) When there is no more data,
    a) the total age is written on the
        new disk file
    b) the average age is calculated
    c) the average is written on the new
        disk file

FIGURE 12.7   **An Ada program.**

CHECKPOINT Can you:

List the advantages and disadvantages of COBOL? FORTRAN? RPG? BASIC?
SNOBOL? LISP? Logo? ALGOL? PL/I? Pascal? FORTH? C? Ada? Modula-2?
State the major usage of each one?

SYSTEMS PROGRAMS

An operating system includes all those programs that are needed for executing
applications programs and does work such as scheduling jobs, controlling the input
and output needed for jobs, and performing the data management of secondary
storage, to name a few. The purpose of the operating system is to manage the
flow of jobs that are to be executed on the computer.

AGNES SCOTT COLLEGE

Bi-Weekly Employment Time Report

THIS REPORT MUST BE COMPLETE AND CORRECT OR IT WILL BE RETURNED

NAME OF EMPLOYEE Amanda D Smith

FIRST MIDDLE LAST

DEPARTMENT Chemistry ACCOUNT NUMBER 11 - 01104

WEEK ENDING April 28 19 89

	TIME IN	TIME OUT	HOURS WORKED
MONDAY	2:00	5:00	3
TUESDAY	9:00	1:45	4 hr 45 min
WEDNESDAY	2:00	5:00	3
THURSDAY	10:00	12:30	2 ½
FRIDAY			
SATURDAY			
SUNDAY			
		WEEKLY TOTAL	13 hrs 15 min

WEEK ENDING May 5 19 89

	TIME IN	TIME OUT	HOURS WORKED
MONDAY	2:00	5:00	3
TUESDAY	10:30	1:00	3 ½
WEDNESDAY	2:00	5:00	3
THURSDAY	9:30	12:00	2 ½
FRIDAY			
SATURDAY			
SUNDAY			
		WEEKLY TOTAL	12

PAY PERIOD TOTAL 25 hr 15 min

I certify that the student indicated has worked the number of hours listed and that the work has been performed in a satisfactory manner. Work has **not** been performed in a satisfactory manner. ☐

May 5, 1989

DATE

SUPERVISOR'S SIGNATURE

Amanda Smith

EMPLOYEE'S SIGNATURE

5 hrs and 15 minutes

TABLE 12.1 **Comparison of Some Languages.**

LANGUAGE	PURPOSE	INITIALIZE VALUES	MULTIPLICATION INSTRUCTION
Ada	Portable, structured, transportable language for military, business, and possible general use	RATE : INTEGER := 3; TIME : INTEGER := 2; DISTANCE : INTEGER;	DISTANCE := RATE * TIME;

ALGOL	Standardized international programming language for numerical processes	int RATE :=3;
		 int TIME :=2;
		 int DIST;
			DIST = RATE * TIME;

BASIC	Interactive language for first programming language	10 LET R = 3 20 LET T = 2	30 LET D = R * T
Basic Assembly Language	Solving high-priority problems and writing of operating systems	RATE DC F'3' TIME DC F'2' DISTANCE DS F	L 7,RATE M 6,TIME ST 7,DISTANCE

C	Highly structured, portable language designed for writing applications and systems software	int rate, time, distance;
		 rate = 3;
		 time = 2;
			distance = rate * time;

COBOL	Self-documenting business-oriented language	05 RATE PICTURE 9 VALUE 3. 05 TI-ME PICTURE 9 VALUE 2. 05 DISTANCE PICTURE 9(2) USAGE IS COMPUTATIONAL.	MULTIPLY RATE BY TI-ME GIVING DISTANCE.
FORTH	Interactive, portable, structured language for writing applications and, systems software	3 CONSTANT RATE 2 CONSTANT TIME VARIABLE DISTANCE	RATE @ * TIME @ DISTANCE !
FORTRAN	Standardized scientific-oriented language	INTEGER RATE, TIME, DISTAN RATE = 3 TIME = 2	DISTAN = RATE * TIME
LISP	Nonnumeric computational language used with artificial intelligence problem solving	(SETQ RATE 3) (SETQ TIME 2)	TIMES (RATE TIME)
Pascal	Interactive language used for teaching structured programming and for executing programs on micros	CONST RATE = 3; TIME = 2; VAR DISTANCE : INTERGER;	DISTANCE := RATE * TIME
PL/I	General-purpose structured language used for solving applications and writing systems programs	DECLARE RATE DECIMAL FIXED (2); DECLARE TIME DECIMAL FIXED (2); DECLARE DISTANCE DECIMAL FIXED (4); RATE = 3; TIME = 2;	DISTANCE = RATE * TIME;
SNOBOL	String processing, pattern matching, and algebraic language	RATE = 3 TIME = 2 DISTANCE = 0	DISTANCE = RATE * TIME

Let us briefly investigate the steps needed for executing the program. Let us begin by briefly discussing which programs make up an operating system and the purposes of each.

PROGRAMS IN THE OPERATING SYSTEM

The operating system's set of programs is usually supplied by the computer manufacturer, but software companies could also supply them. On occasion, the operating system is written by the programmers at the installation. This latter practice is, however, rarely carried out; there is really no need for an installation to write the same programs as those available for a fee. Years ago this procedure was followed. To avoid duplication of effort at every installation, operating systems were then supplied along with the hardware.

The programs that make up the operating system can be divided into two parts, namely the control programs and the processing programs, as shown in Table 12.2.

Control Programs

The **control programs** supervise and schedule the programs that are to be executed on the computer; they process no data. Examples of the control programs are the initial program loader and the supervisor program.

TABLE 12.2 **Programs in the Operating System.**

CONTROL PROGRAMS	PROCESSING PROGRAMS
• Initial Program Loader	• Language Processors or Translators
• Supervisor	• Interpreters
• Priority scheduler	• Compiler for each procedure-oriented language assembler
• Sequential scheduler	• Linkage Editor or Loader
• Assigns base	• Creates load module
• Checks legitimate users	• Loads
• Times job	• Brings in subroutines
	• Utility Programs
	• Tape to disk
	• Disk to tape
	• Sort/merge
	• Librarian and Editors

Initial Program Loader (IPL). The **initial program loader,** usually referred to as **IPL,** is the program used by the computer operator at the beginning of each work day. This program brings the supervisor program into primary storage so the computer can begin its work. It also initializes accounting records at this time. The Initial Program Loader, also referred to as **bootstrapping,** may reside in read-only memory (ROM) or programmable read-only memory (PROM). On micro-computers, you will hear that a user must "**boot up**" the system, meaning that the bootstrap program is called into primary storage which, in turn, calls in the supervisor program.

Supervisor Program. The **supervisor program** is all-important in the operating system, for its jobs are many. This program protects the users by timing jobs so no one can monopolize the computer's time. The supervisor also checks the legitimacy of each user according to account number and password. It also allocates primary storage by assigning a base (starting address) for each program and handles multiprogramming as well. It schedules work by one of two methods: a **priority scheduler,** which means the user pays an additional cost for faster service; or a **sequential scheduler,** which services jobs in the order in which they are received, according to the **first-in, first-out (FIFO) principle.**

Processing Programs

All programs other than the initial program loader and the supervisor program are processing programs. These **processing programs** are written by the user or by the manufacturer of the computer or a software company with the purpose of processing data. Examples are the language processors, linkage editor or loader, utility programs, sort/merge programs, librarian, and user-written programs.

Language Processors or Translators. The source program must be translated into machine language. Depending upon the language written, the processor program to accomplish the translation will either be a compiler—such as a FOR-TRAN, COBOL, ALGOL, or PL/I—an assembler, or an interpreter. Examples of languages possibly using an interpreter are BASIC and Pascal, but these languages, for production runs, will use a compiler.

The compiler or assembler creates an **object program,** or **object module,** which is the machine language for those instructions written in the source program. The object module contains, however, requests for subroutines. **Subroutines** are small programs that are usable by all users for accomplishing some required processing. Examples are a calculation of a square root or some predefined set of instructions needed for reading data records. A programmer writes a series of instructions that make up some desired processing; the subroutine is called SUB, for example, by the programmer. When the object module is created, it contains the call instruction for the subroutine, (for example, CALL SUB), not the instructions that make up the subroutine. Think of the subroutine as being stored as a footnote. When reading a paragraph, a footnote is noted. You find the footnote, read it, and then return to the next place where the call of the subroutine was initiated. The computer operates the same way as it needs a program to go out and get the

WHAT'S RIGHT

A Computer Operator Tells about the Job.

From the operational standpoint, a computer operator really does not care what the program is doing as long as it does not tie up any other job on the computer system. Each job is not running continuously; they swap in and out of memory since the mainframe is running under a multiprogramming environment.

The statistics kept by the operating system show that a program began running Tuesday night at 10 P.M. and it is now noon on Friday. The job has used about sixteen hours of processing time but the programmer has instructed the computer operator to abort the job at 5 P.M. today if it has not reached a successful completion on its own.

Many large computers run twenty-four hours a day, but on Saturday they may shut down about two hours to boot the system. When the system is booted it is reset. Everything on the magnetic disk is saved and the contents are stored on magnetic tape. A boot will also reset the number of new jobs that have been run in the system since the last boot. The total time where the processors are idle and the total number of lost interrupts are also accumulated. A lost interrupt can be information lost when faulty data transmission occurred or an integrated circuit chip malfunctions. Whenever something goes wrong that is not supposed to go wrong, the system will list that in its history. The total number of jobs that are run at the terminals, the number of lines printed, cards punched, and jobs swapped, are all part of the counters that are reset during the boot. All the instructions that have been executed, all the lines that have been printed, all the users that have been served, all the interrupts, and all the jobs that have been swapped out of memory are maintained as part of the history.

subroutine's instructions. The object module cannot process data because it only sees the call instruction, not the instructions that make up the subroutine.

Linkage Editors or Loaders. The **linkage editor** or **loader** program creates the executable program called a **load module.** It brings the source program into primary storage from secondary storage, looks up all the CALL instructions and gets these necessary subroutines from secondary storage, and incorporates all these into a load module. The load module contains the machine language generated from the compiler's, interpreter's, or assembler's translation. It also contains the machine language for the subroutines (the missing instructions in the object module).

Utility Programs. **Utility programs** are those programs, usually supplied by the manufacturer of the computer, that perform such work as copying data from one medium to another, sorting data, sorting and merging data, and tracing errors throughout the source program.

Most operating systems include a **sort program** which arranges data into a prescribed sequence by the programmer. A **sort/merge program** is also included; it allows two or more files of data to be brought together in a prescribed order.

Librarian and Editors. The **librarian** is a set of routines that handle any deleting, adding, or renaming of programs that already exist as users' programs. The **editor** is a program that allows users to input data or instructions from keyboards and alter or delete as necessary. When users key in data, a line editor or a text editor is used. The text editor works much like that used in word processing. In fact, the text editor was the forerunner of word processing as we know it today. When a user uses a line editor, each instruction or line of data is given a line number to identify it from all others. The editor uses the line numbers for deleting, inserting, and rearranging data or instructions in a program as directed by the user.

User-Written Programs. **All** of the user-written programs that are tested and executable at the installation are stored in the system's library for later reference. These programs include all applications software as previously noted.

CHECKPOINT Can you:

Identify the various systems programs in an operating system?

Explain why each is needed?

EXECUTION OF A PROGRAM

Computer operators and all users communicate with the operating system through the use of control statements that are keyed on the console typewriter, terminal, or punched cards. These commands, called **job control language (JCL)** or job control, identify the steps that the computer is to follow for each task. The job control language is written differently than a source program's instructions. The job control language command usually has a /, $, or other special character in the first position, thus differentiating it from the source program instructions and the data. Each mainframe has a different type of job control language. Refer to Figure 12.8 to see how the many systems programs interact.

USING PREPARED SOFTWARE PACKAGES

The preceding discussion has assumed that a programmer writes the source program and then has the source program executed. Before we leave this discussion, however, let us briefly focus our attention to the already-prepared software packages that are purchased for use on microcomputers. Most packaged software (prepared software packages) has a stipulation that the software developer is not liable for any changes made to the prepared software. What this means is that a user cannot alter the machine language and hold the software developer responsible for any malfunctions in the program. Obviously, the already prepared programs are in load module format rather than requiring compilation each time; assembly language or machine language is frequently used as the source program.

To the user of a packaged software, the compilation and the bringing in necessary subroutines to the object module is then unnecessary; this has been previously completed by the software developer.

CHECKPOINT **Can you:**

Identify the different steps a program passes through so data can be processed?
Tell why these steps are not present at the time the user uses packaged software?

TYPES OF OPERATING SYSTEMS

There are as many operating systems basically as there are mainframe manufacturers. **Disk operating system (DOS)** and **operating system (OS),** the two most popular operating systems, exist in many versions. Operating System is the most complex of the operating systems in that it provides greater processing power for scheduling, multitasking, and multiprogramming than the others. The programs of Operating System might require six megabytes of storage. Disk Operating System does not have the full capability to perform all of these functions.

Recall from the Chapter 3 discussion that an operating system usually handles multiprogramming and multiprocessing environments. Many users want answers

WHAT'S RIGHT

Engineering Analysis At An Automobile Manufacturer

Ford uses structural analysis in its evaluation of its automobiles. Customers demand more; competition demands state-of-the-art technology.

A car loses a front wheel because of faulty engineering or the bumper falls off because some part cannot take the continual rough ride, or the engine has a faulty part—it is hoped that such problems can be averted through structural analysis. New cars are subjected to extensive tests to prevent such disasters. You are probably aware of manufacturers' crash tests, but structural analysis goes further than that. Weak spots are detected through simulation and extensive analysis only made possible through extensive computer usage. These weak spots or points of stress are pointed out to engineers by a color coding system built into the computer program.

Extensive analysis requires that 12,000 individual elements on a car body be tested. Over 11,400 individual parts that make up an engine block are also tested. The analysis is a continual twenty-four-hour process involving plants in the United States as well as those located in the United Kingdom and Germany. Because of the different time zones, time sharing works very efficiently, permitting the plants in Germany and the United Kingdom to transmit data beginning at 1 A.M. Michigan time. By the time that the final data is transmitted by satellite to the main headquarters, the engineers are just coming to work there. Computers are then available for use in the U.S. plants for the batching, on-line processing, and time-sharing environments essential to a large corporation's efficient operation.

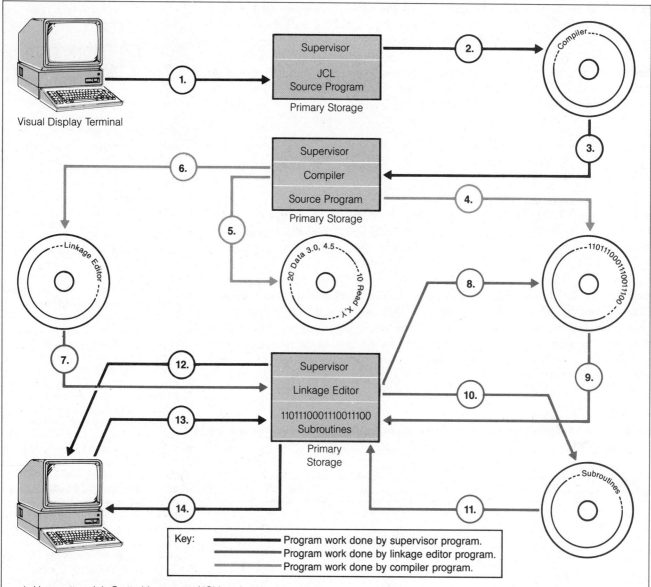

1. User enters Job Control Language (JCL) and source program.
2. JCL calls in compiler for translation.
3. The compiler program is loaded into primary storage.
4. The compiler program translates source program to an object module; the object module is stored on magnetic disk.
5. Compiler stores source program on magnetic disk.
6. Compiler passes control to the linkage editor program.
7. The linkage editor program is brought into primary storage.
8. The linkage editor gets the object module.
9. The object module is then loaded into primary storage.
10. The linkage editor goes through the object module and finds any requests for subroutines. These are then called in from secondary storage.
11. The subroutines are stored in primary storage. The subroutines and object module make up the load module.
12. The linkage editor passes control to the supervisor program which, in turn, gives central processing unit time to the user.
13. The user inputs data.
14. Results are returned.

FIGURE 12.8   **Interworkings of programs in an operating system.**

to their questions, need calculations performed, and must have records updated. To accommodate this type of direct access processing (giving answers immediately), the operating system needs to service as many users as possible.

Because a computer is serving many users at the same time, a signal is sent to the central processing unit when a user requests more data, needs to process a high-priority program, or requests more instructions in a program. An **interrupt** occurs (the stopping of some current processing in such a way that it can be resumed at a later time). The central processing unit's time is divided into small portions called **time slices.** To assure the many users of good service and to acknowledge and handle the interrupts, the clock in the central processing unit allocates so many time slices to each job which approximates 15 or 20 milliseconds in a round-robin fashion.

The operating system handles the systems interrupts. There must be a way available to keep all users happy in a multiprogramming environment. To accomplish this, a user's program is divided into small equal parts, called **pages.** The capacity of a page can be 2K or 4K, for example. We know that a computer can only execute an instruction when it resides in primary storage. To serve many users in a fast round-robin fashion, only one page of a user's program is in primary storage at any one time. When the computer finishes the required processing on a page of a program stored in primary storage (called **real storage**), the next page of the program is brought very quickly from secondary storage (called **virtual storage**) to real storage. The new page from virtual storage is swapped (traded) with the page in real storage. The operating system handles the swapping of pages very quickly. To a user it appears that the storage of a computer seems virtually unlimited; hence, its name of virtual storage (virtual memory).

SUMMARY

- A stored program is a series of instructions that tells the computer precisely what to do. It is from these instructions that electrical signals are generated.

- A source program is a program written by a programmer to solve a problem, but not yet translated into machine language.

- Another name for the machine language version of a source program is the object program. Each type of mainframe, except those in a computer family, have unique object programs. This is not true, however, for microcomputers; most use the microprocessors by Zilog, Intel, or Motorola.

- Different levels of programming language can be used. The low-level, which is one step up from machine language, is an assembly language.
- Assembly language deals with the various registers of the computer to accomplish the desired manipulation. The programmer must have a thorough knowledge of that computer.

- Assembly language is machine-oriented.

- The assembler is the translator program that is used for changing assembly language into machine language.

- High-level languages are those English-type languages that are easier to write, sometimes are self-documenting, and are machine-independent.

- Examples of high-level languages are COBOL, FORTRAN, Report Program Generator, BASIC, Pascal, ALGOL, C, and Ada, to name a few.

- COBOL is a language geared for solving business problems. Currently there are two versions standardized, the 1968 and 1974 versions. The 1980 COBOL version is currently being evaluated as to adoption. COBOL is designed so that it is a self-documenting language; it contains mostly English statements for ease in reading.

- FORTRAN is a standardized programming language for solving scientific and mathematical problems. The new 1977 standards version provides for a more flexible language. This is the most popular language used in solving scientific applications.

- Report Program Generator (RPG) is designed primarily for solving business problems. The language is readily learned although it uses up to six different forms for specifying input, output, and calculations specifications.

- BASIC is an interactive language, originally designed for use on mainframes; it currently is the most popular language used for microcomputers.

- SNOBOL is a language used for checking certain patterns that might exist in data, for concatenating (joining certain data together), and for calculating data.

- Text can be edited by the use of languages that deal with strings, such as SNOBOL, which can change words in a text, and LISP, which works with symbols.

- Logo is a language used for teaching children basic programming concepts. Learning kits for teaching spelling and mathematical concepts are available for sale.

- ALGOL is an internationally standardized, high-level language that was designed in 1960. The language concentrates on complex calculations.

- PL/I was developed in 1963 by a group of scientific and business users. The advantages of COBOL's input and output file structures, FORTRAN's ease in handling calculations, ALGOL's modular form were combined in designing this language.

- Pascal is a general-purpose structured language released in 1971 by Niklaus Worth. Much of its use centers in the educational field.

- FORTH is a portable, structured, interactive language that can be used for writing applications software involving graphics and robotics.

- C language is a high-level structured language developed by Bell Telephone Laboratories for the purpose of writing operating systems and application programs.

- Ada is a language developed for the U. S. Department of Defense. Its purpose is to provide the military with a language that is usable by all departments. The specification set up by the Department of Defense is that all microprocessors must be able to understand the language.

- Software engineering solves a program using a scientific approach. Its purpose is to produce programs that are set up in an efficient, understandable, modular, and reliable form.

- Software engineering uses the tools discussed in Chapter 11 but also stresses modularity. Lower-level module details are not considered when higher-level modules are set up.

- Software engineering also stresses that modules be independent of each other so each are logically and functionally independent. Each module should stand on its own merits, being understandable to the reader.

- An operating system consists of many programs which work together to control and run the computer system.

- The purpose of the operating system is to manage the flow of jobs as they pass through the computer.

- Programs in the operating system can be divided into two major classifications: control programs and processing programs.

- Control programs include the initial program loader (IPL) and the supervisor program.

- The initial program loader is used by the computer operator each day to initialize the system for accounting purposes and to bring the supervisor program into primary storage.

- The supervisor program times jobs, checks legitimacy of users, allocates primary storage, assigns the base to each program, handles multiprogramming, and schedules jobs.

- Processing programs include language processors (the translators), the linkage editor or loader, utility programs, the librarian, and user-written programs.

- The language processors refer to those translator programs that convert the source program into machine language; the resulting program is called an object module or object program.

- The linkage editor or loader program creates the load module. This represents the object program that was translated and all machine language instructions used in subroutines; the load module executes data.

- Utility programs, which can work on any data, are supplied by the computer manufacturer or software company. They include system programs that do such work as copying data from one medium to another, sorting data, sort/merging of data, and tracing of errors in a program.

- The librarian program handles for the user any adding, deleting, and renaming of programs.

- The editor program helps the user in working with lines of code in a source program, allowing insertions, deletions, or rearrangements of instructions.

● Job control language, or job control, communicates to the operating system the steps that are to be performed by the computer for a job. These commands are totally different in form from instructions of application programs.

● Mainframe manufacturers have different versions of operating systems, depending upon the computer's processing power and capability. The most popularly used versions are disk operating system (DOS) and operating system (OS).

● Many larger computer systems use virtual memory, which causes these programs to be divided into equal small amounts of storage called pages. One page is in primary storage (called real storage) for a user at one time. When the page is completely processed, the next page is brought in from secondary storage (called virtual storage) and the instructions on this new page are then executed.

STUDY GUIDE

REVIEW OF TERMINOLOGY

The following terminology was discussed in this chapter:

Ada
ALGOL
ANSI COBOL
assembler
BASIC
bootstrap
boot up
C
COBOL
compiler
concatenate
control program
disk operating system (DOS)
editor
first-in, first-out (FIFO) principle
FORTH
FORTRAN
initial program loader (IPL)
interactive language
interpreter
interrupt
job control language (JCL)
librarian

linkage editor
LISP
load module
loader
Logo
machine-oriented
Modula-2
object module
object program
operating system (OS)
pages
Pascal
PL/I
portability
priority scheduler
processing programs
program design language (PDL)
Report Program Generator
sequential scheduler
SNOBOL
software engineering
sort program
sort/merge program
source program listing
structured language

subroutines
supervisor program
symbolic language
transportability

unstructured language
utility programs
virtual storage

MULTIPLE CHOICE

Circle the letter of the item that correctly completes a statement.

1. The only language the computer can understand is:
   a. Ada
   b. Pascal
   c. machine language
   d. high-level language
   e. assembly language

2. A translator program is called:
   a. an assembler
   b. a compiler
   c. an interpreter
   d. all of the above
   e. none of the above

3. Which language is very close to machine language:
   a. Ada
   b. program design language
   c. unstructured language
   d. structured language
   e. assembly language

4. A translator that gives you an immediate response as to the accuracy of each instruction as it is keyed is called:
   a. a transportable language
   b. a compiler
   c. a portable language
   d. an interactive language
   e. an interpreter

5. Which of the following languages cannot be used for applications and systems software:
   a. Ada
   b. FORTH
   c. C
   d. COBOL
   e. Modula-2

6. A programming language that is used in the European universities and formed the foundation for FORTRAN is:
   a. Pascal
   b. C
   c. COBOL
   d. ALGOL
   e. SNOBOL

7. This programming language was the first general-purpose language designed that used structured programming concepts:
   a. Pascal
   b. ALGOL
   c. PL/I
   d. SNOBOL
   e. C

8. This programming language has proven valuable in developing machines as a research tool:
   a. LISP
   b. FORTH
   c. Ada
   d. C
   e. PDL

9. This language originally began for writing systems programs for UNIX:
   a. Ada
   b. C
   c. Pascal
   d. FORTH
   e. ALGOL

10. This language is known for solving business-oriented applications:
    a. ALGOL
    b. SNOBOL
    c. COBOL
    d. Basic Assembly Language
    e. Ada

11. A scientific language that is decreasing in use:
    a. Pascal
    b. Ada
    c. FORTRAN
    d. LISP
    e. C

12. This programming language is known for its capability to concatenate (join data):
    a. COBOL
    b. SNOBOL
    c. FORTRAN
    d. software engineering
    e. Logo

13. The first interactive language used on microcomputers is:
    a. BASIC
    b. Ada
    c. C
    d. LISP
    e. Logo

14. This language's original intention was for use in military installations:
    a. BASIC
    b. Ada
    c. C
    d. LISP
    e. ALGOL

15. A turtle is moved on the screen:
    a. BASIC
    b. SNOBOL
    c. FORTH
    d. Logo
    e. Ada

16. All systems programs other than the initial program loader and supervisor programs are called:
    a. priority schedulers
    b. sequential schedulers
    c. FIFO
    d. control programs
    e. processing programs

17. This program prepares the load module so data can be executed:
    a. supervisor program
    b. initial program loader
    c. sort/merge program
    d. linkage editor or loader
    e. editor

18. A user wants to change a name of a program. This is handled by the:
    a. editor
    b. loader
    c. supervisor
    d. initial program loader
    e. librarian

19. These programs are often supplied by the manufacturer of the computer for copying data and tracing errors:
    a. utility programs
    b. supervisor programs
    c. subroutines
    d. load modules
    e. object modules

20. This program type schedules the work on the computer:
    a. processing programs
    b. service programs
    c. utility programs
    d. control programs
    e. initial program loader

21. Commands given to identify the steps that are to be followed for compilation or execution of a program are called:
    a. high-level language
    d. an assembler
    e. a supervisor program

b. an interactive
    language
c. job control
    language

22. Software engineering considers a program as:

a. a programmer's
    right to structure
    as desired

b. a well-thought out
    process that uses
    scientific
    methods

c. using just
    structure charts,
    pseudocode,
    program design
    language, and
    structured walk-
    throughs

d. being used for
    solving scientific
    problems

e. being set up in
    modules such as
    done in COBOL,
    FORTRAN, and
    Ada

TRUE/FALSE QUESTIONS

Circle T if a statement is true; F if it is false.

1. **T/F** The object module cannot execute data
   because it is not a complete program.

2. **T/F** It is more efficient as far as computer time
   goes to write in assembly language than in
   such languages as COBOL or BASIC.

3. **T/F** FORTRAN and COBOL have been modified
   by different versions to make the languages
   more structured in concept.

4. **T/F** C is becoming a popular language used for
   writing applications software and systems
   software.

5. **T/F** Languages designed after the mid 1970s are
   usually considered as structured languages.

6. **T/F** Many of the languages used today have been
   improved because their designs draw from
   the advantages of other languages.

7. **T/F** Software engineering stresses that modules
   can overlap in processing as long as the
   reader is able to clearly understand the
   solution attempted.

8. **T/F** Software engineering hides the details when
   the high-level modules are set up.

9. **T/F** Systems programs can be divided into two
   groups: control programs and high-level
   programs.

10. **T/F** The initial program loader or a bootstrap may
    reside in read-only memory.

11. **T/F** A load module is a complete executable
    program that can be used to process data.

12. **T/F** A linkage editor or loader program uses the
    program that has been translated and stores it
    in primary storage for execution.

13. **T/F** If a programmer wished to copy data from
    disk to tape, the programmer must first write
    the program to direct the computer to do so
    or use a control program.

14. **T/F** Files can be deleted, renamed, and changed
    by using language processors.

15. **T/F** Virtual memory allows more users to have
    their programs stored in primary storage at
    one time.

16. **T/F** Large blocks of primary storage are set aside
    in virtual memory called pages.

ANSWERS

Multiple Choice: 1. **c** 2. **d** 3. **e** 4. **e** 5. **d** 6. **d** 7. **c**
8. **a** 9. **b** 10. **c** 11. **c** 12. **b** 13. **a** 14. **b** 15. **d** 16. **e**
17. **d** 18. **e** 19. **a** 20. **d** 21. **c** 22. **b** *True/False:*
1. **T** 2. **T** 3. **F** 4. **F** 5. **T** 6. **T** 7. **F** 8. **T** 9. **F**
10. **T** 11. **T** 12. **T** 13. **F** 14. **F** 15. **T** 16. **F**

REVIEW QUESTIONS

1. What is a stored program? Why is it needed?

2. What is machine language?

3. What types of source programs can be written?
   Give examples of eight possible languages that can
   be used to write a source program.

4. Which is easier to write, assembly language or
   high-level languages? Why?

5. Which high-level language is designed for math
   and scientific processing? When was this language
   introduced? What did IBM do to make this
   language acceptable on its computers?

6. Which language is designed strictly for business
   and gives great flexibility and capability? When
   was it introduced? When was it standardized?

7. Identify the principal use to which each of these
   languages is put: assembly language; COBOL;

FORTRAN; Report Program Generator; BASIC; SNOBOL; ALGOL; PL/I; Pascal; FORTH; LISP; C; Ada; Logo.

8. What is software engineering's purpose?

9. What is the purpose of an operating system? Are there many kinds? Explain your answer.

10. What are the two major classifications of programs in the operating system? Which programs are included in each type?

11. Identify the purposes of each of the processing programs.

12. What is the program that is generated by the language processors called? Is it a complete program that can execute data? If not, why not?

13. What is a subroutine? Is it usable by others at the installation?

14. Why is the linkage editor program an important program?

15. How is communication with the operating system accomplished?

16. What are some of the tasks done by job control language?

17. What is virtual memory?

7. What are some of the utility programs that are supplied in the operating system? Why are these included?

DISCUSSION QUESTIONS

1. What are the advantages and disadvantages of each of the following languages: FORTRAN, COBOL, Report Program Generator, Pascal, assembly language, Ada, and C.

2. Why would assembly language be used?

3. Why do most programmers write programs in high-level languages rather than assembly language?

4. Did programmers always write high-level languages? Explain your answer.

5. Discuss how the various processing programs interact with each other.

6. What jobs are performed by the supervisor program? Why is each job important to the user?

BIBLIOGRAPHY

Bates, Frank, and Douglas, Mary L. *Programming Language/One*, 3d ed. Englewood Cliffs, New Jersey: Prentice-Hall, 1975.

Booch, Gary. *Software Engineering with Ada*. Menlo Park, California: Benjamin Cummings, 1983.

Griswold, Ralph E., and Griswold, Madge T. *A SNOBOL4 Primer*. Englewood Cliffs, New Jersey: Prentice-Hall, 1973.

Krasner, Glenn. *Smalltalk-80, Bits of History, Words of Advice*. Palo Alto, California: Addison-Wesley, 1983.

Lewis, T. G. *Pascal Programming for the Apple*. Reston, Virginia: Reston Publishing Company, 1981.

Maurer, Ward Douglas. *The Programmer's Introduction to LISP*. London: MacDonald/American Elsevier Computer Monographs, 1972.

Maurer, Ward Douglas. *The Programmer's Introduction to SNOBOL*. New York: Elsevier Publishing Company, 1976.

McGettrick, Andrew D. *ALGOL 68: A First and Second Course*. London: Cambridge University Press, 1978.

Purdum, Jack. *C Programming Guide*. Indianapolis: Que Corporation, 1983.

Siklossy, Laurent. *Let's Talk LISP*. Englewood Cliffs, New Jersey: Prentice-Hall, 1976.

Watt, Daniel. *Learning with Logo*. New York: McGraw-Hill, 1983.

Welburn, Tyler. *Structured COBOL, Fundamentals and Style*. Palo Alto, California: Mayfield Publishing, 1981.

Winfield, Alan. *The Complete FORTH*. Wilmslow, Cheshire, U. K.: Sigma Technical Press, 1983.

Zaks, Rodnay. *Introduction to Pascal (Including UCSD Pascal)*, 2d ed. Berkeley, California, Sybex, 1981.

Zaks, Rodnay, *Your First BASIC Program*, Berkeley, California, Sybex, 1983.

People in Computing

Barbara Y. Mathiasen

COMPANY
G. E. Calma Company

POSITION
Product Manager, Full Custom IC

EDUCATIONAL BACKGROUND
B.S. in Information Systems
Management (Computer Science)

As a marketing product manager for G. E. Calma Company, I am involved in the definition, design, and development of new Computer Aided Design/Computer Aided Manufacturing (CAD/CAM) systems. My product specialty and the tools that I help to define and market are used primarily in the development of full custom integrated circuits for the semiconductor industry. Essential to my job is an understanding of the needs for CAD/CAM tools within the marketplace.

Prior to my current position in marketing, I was the CAD Manager in the semiconductor divisions of Atari and Data General. In that role, my job was to identify the requirements of the design engineers, layout designers, and CAD software engineers and provide the best products available in support of their tasks. This involved an industry survey for specific applications, recommending, justifying, procuring, installing, and supporting software and hardware for each requirement. For example, layout designers require a graphics system that can be used for topology layout of semiconductor chips. Since there are several manufacturers of equipment in this field, benchmark tests are run on each system, identifying ease of operation, capabilities, reliability, cost, delivery dates, service, and functionality of the system.

In general, a CAD manager should have extensive hardware and software knowledge. I spent several years programming using a variety of software languages and computer systems. I also acquired a basic background in electrical engineering, which enabled me to conduct meaningful discussions with design engineers and layout designers and contributed to my understanding of their job requirements for hardware and software.

A survey of new hardware must answer such questions as: What are the screen capabilities? Will a mouse, puck and tablet, or touch tablet be required? Will the user require function keys and programmable keys on the keyboard? What type of printers and plotters will be necessary? How much memory and disk capacity are needed? Software considerations must include: What types of programs are needed? What languages should be available for general programming? (High-level, structured?) Will it be necessary to use machine or assembler code to perform tasks? What type of software simulation tools and CAD verification tools are needed? How "user-friendly" are these software packages? What are their reliability factors? Will the code have to be modified to meet specific needs of the users? How much of a job will it be to modify existing code or write new code to perform tasks? What is the expected delivery date of hardware or software? Will the date meet the timeline required to complete work?

As a marketing product manager, I have been given the opportunity to help define the ultimate system today that will be the most useful to the engineers designing integrated circuits. This gives me the chance to design the system that I would have purchased as a CAD manager if it had been available.

My previous position as CAD manager has given me insight into a variety of hardware and software products available in today's marketplace. It has also given me an excellent overview of that market, which has been extremely helpful in my new position, evaluating what the competition may have.

There will be many advances in the integrated circuits marketplace for CAD/CAM and associated applications in the future; we are just now beginning to tap those applications. How will silicon compilers be incorporated into the future development of integrated circuits? What is the ultimate end-to-end design solution? Will it be an engineering workstation, a personnel computer, an intelligent terminal interfaced to a large mainframe computer, or some combination of these? There are also many applications which have not yet been pursued by any of the existing CAD/CAM companies. I am looking forward to a very exciting future in this field.

There will be numerous employment opportunities in the CAD/CAM field for hardware design engineers, software programming engineers, customer support engineers, and marketing and sales personnel.

Application

DESIGNING SOFTWARE FOR THE INTERNATIONAL MARKET*

HEWLETT PACKARD

Users of office software products are generally not technically trained. They want a user interface that is as easy as possible to understand. On the most fundamental level, an office product such as a word processor must interact with the user in the user's native language. To make this possible, office products must be designed so that they can be localized. Localization is the adaption of a software application for use in different countries or environments.

What problems do we face when trying to design localizable products? It is important that the user of the localized product does not suffer reduced functionality. Nor should any restrictions be imposed as a result of localization of the product.

The person who localizes the product should not have to touch the source code. Localization should be possible without taking the chance of introducing new bugs. This means that a localizable application will not have any functions within the source code that are dependent on the local language or the customer.

Although many of HP's products are menu-driven, there are some that are command-driven. Let us consider how we might detect when the user wants to delete something if we have a command-based interface. In our program we could have a statement something like this:

if userinput = 'DELETE' then. . .

Then, when the French localize the product they could change that line of code to read:

if userinput = 'DETRUIRE' then. . .

If we use this method, we're again faced with having to change the program code.

Localization of command recognition presents us with other problems. HPDesk is an electronic mail system that runs on the HP 3000 Computer.* It allows users to create, send, file, and work on electronic messages. Within HPDesk there exists the concept of the current message. If I'm sent a message, I might read it, decide it is not worth keeping, and so decide to delete it. I could do this by typing delete it. Were I French, I would like to say le détruire because détruire le does not make sense. It is like asking me to type it delete in English! I therefore want to be able to tell my command recognizer which order to expect the verb (delete) and the object (it) in. And I do not want to have to change the program when the French want the order to be object, then verb.

If a product is going to be used in an English speaking country, then only ASCII characters need be displayed. However, problems arise if that product is then localized into French. If the ASCII character set is used, there is no way that you can display or store é. This is a serious problem, since é is the most common character in the French language.

Thus, a localizable program must be able to recognize and process all local character sets. It must display, take as input, and print each local character set. When localizing an electronic mail system, for example, the system should be able to send a message in one local character set and still be able to display that message at a destination where another local character set is being used.

Localization would be a lot simpler if all terminals were able to display and transmit HP extended ASCII characters. Then, we would not need to know which terminal we were talking to. Unfortunately, because our current ideas about localization did not arrive overnight, all terminals are not the same.

Having so many terminals presents many problems for a product that has to try to store and display all European characters as best it can given the capabilities of the terminal.

Office products face many localization problems when information they produce crosses either time or language boundaries. HPTelex is an HP 3000 office product that allows the user to create the text of a Telex message using a word processor, and then to ask the computer to send this message whenever it thinks best. The Telex network transmits only a very limited character set—capitalized ASCII characters and a few other characters. What these "few other characters" are varies from country to country. For example, @ is valid in most but not all countries. Because Telex messages often travel across country boundaries, all characters that are not standard across the world must be filtered out by the HPTelex software.

An HPDesk user must specify to whom electronic mail is to be sent. Suppose an HPDesk user in the U.S.A. wants to send mail to a Mr. Förster in Germany. We really cannot expect the American sender to know that the o has an umlaut over it. However, were we to just upshift all names as they were input this would lead to problems, Å is a totally different letter from plain A in Finnish, for example. So people with an Å in their names would have their names changed when upshifted.

As one might imagine, a diary product hits problems at time boundaries. With HPDesk there is a time management facility which, among other things, allows users to send messages requesting appointments. To record the appointment so that HPDesk will produce a reminder of it later, the recipient simply types file it in diary. If I, in Britain, request a conference with some people in California for 5:00 p.m. on 13.12.84 British time, those people in California must see an appointment for 9:00 a.m. on 12/13/84. Making this appointment highlights two problems. The first problem is that the date format in Europe is day/month/year but it is month/day/year in the U.S.A. The second problem is that there are time differences between countries that we must compensate for.

Let us see how we can overcome the problems that we have outlined. The solutions we shall offer are those we have used for office products. They may, however, be readily applied to other fields.

ASCII character representation uses only seven bits if no parity checking is required. The Roman8 European character representation standard developed by HP uses all eight bits of a byte. All ASCII characters remain as they were, except that the eighth bit is always off. When the eighth bit is on we are able to represent another 128 characters. So the ç character is the ASCII 5, but with the eight bit set. Documents and messages should, wherever possible, be stored in Roman8 form.

The Application Centers translate the message file into their languages. All characters in the message file are stored in Roman8 form. Some terminals, can only display ASCII characters. So, if one of our messages contains an é (decimal 197) we must translate the character to an e (decimal 101) before we output it to the terminal.

If we do not have a menu-based user interface, we must be able to recognize commands. To allow localization of commands, HPDesk uses yet another file, which it calls a dictionary. This file contains a list of verbs (like create), objects (like text), and connectors (like of) that HPDesk will accept in the local language.

Let us now try to solve the date and time problems that diary products face. The date format problem can be easily overcome by allowing the Application Centers to specify the format. A stickier problem is that of time differences. HPDesk solves this by making each computer keep a record of its offset from Greenwich Mean Time (GMT). The date and time on a message requesting an appointment are stored in normalized GMT form. When a date or time is displayed on a specific computer it is corrected by deducting that computer's GMT offset from the normalized GMT date and time. So, when an appointment request message for 5:00 p.m. on 13th December is sent from Britain to California, that date and time is stored in the message because Britain is on GMT in December. However, when the message is displayed in California, eight hours are subtracted because California is eight hours behind GMT.

It is obvious that it is not easy to make software applications easy to localize. Message lengths, character sets, time and data formats, and the syntax of commands must all be taken into account. All of these and more must be easy to change without having to touch the source code of the product. Once you change the source code, the result is a new product.

PART FIVE

Systems

13

Management Information System

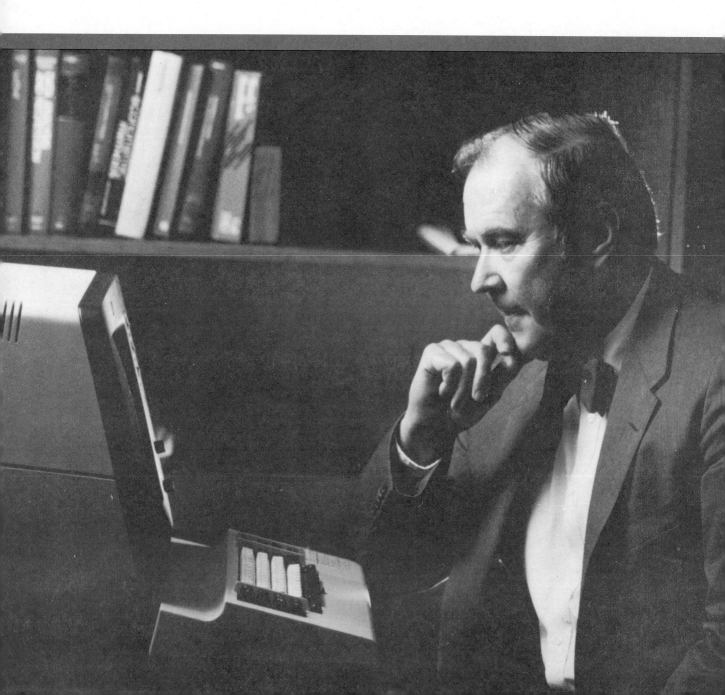

OUTLINE

PROLOGUE

In the executive dining room of the Snazzy Manufacturing Company, three executives are bent over cups of coffee. Joshua is telling the other two how his buying department must change to meet the times. The batch processing requires that too much stock be kept on hand because up-to-the-minute stock figures are not available.

Michael says that his needs in the accounting department have changed, also. The president wants him to prepare other reports that are just not available in already-prepared software. He tells how the company's programming staff is always busy; he needs information but what can he do.

Jack tells the other two that their problems are the minor ones. His department spent $8,000 for microcomputers, and now he can't get the reports he needs after all that. He doesn't know where to find the data.

Henry, at the next table, overhears the conversation. "Many companies have the information arranged and provide service to users in such a way that information is available instantaneously. Why, Timothy down at Sunshine Motors has a tremendous number of reports available for his recall. And Sally at Times Square gets advice on her microcomputers to buy. And. . . ." Jack, Michael, and Joshua leave without finishing their coffee.

HOW DOES IT DO THAT?

READ ON.

OBJECTIVES

After studying this chapter you should be able to:

1. Explain how the need for information has changed for both small businesses and large corporations.

2. Define a system.

3. Differentiate among the three levels of management as to their purposes and positions.

4. Discuss some of the decisions made every day when business is conducted.

5. Discuss how information flows within a corporation.

6. Explain what a management information system is and why it is needed.

INTRODUCTION

Look back in history to when the business community in the United States was composed of mostly small businesses. The business person held all of the facts in his or her head. When a question was asked to recall facts, many times the data was inaccurately stated. In this day and age, competitive forces are more keen than they were in the past. The small business person of the past survived in spite of inaccurate facts.

As competition grew in intensity, the small business person became less common, the corporation, more common. Facts were demanded of many individuals rather than just of one person. Some type of information system had to be set up so that the facts could be located without any great loss of time. The facts had to be accurate! Businesses were pressured into keeping detailed records as the government reports required of them became more complex. Numbers of manufacturing and research firms increased drastically, and such firms required very detailed information. The upsurging demand for distributive services reached an all-time high—more services, more data, and more confusion. Join these demands for facts to rising clerical costs and the decreasing cost of data processing machines, and you understand the logical move to machines for record-keeping tasks.

Today, computer use affects virtually all individuals, small businesses, and corporations. Complex organizational structures have emerged in the last couple of decades as a result of diversification within the companies. The day has gone when a company just sells one product, such as soap. Today we find a one-time soap company successfully competing with other companies in, say, food and paper products.

This complex type of organization requires clear lines of management. It is an important responsibility of management to use its data about its products, manufacturing processes, customers, suppliers, and competitors in a highly structured way so that the company maintains an edge over other competitors. To achieve this competitive edge requires the use of computers, not merely for record-keeping as was done two decades and more ago, but as the center of its information system. An **information system,** or a **management information system (MIS),** can be described as the apparatus established to provide finished data to aid management in making decisions on a day-to-day basis as well as to plan, to forecast future trends, and to avoid any future pitfalls. A management information system is discussed in detail later in this chapter.

As was discussed previously, data refers to unprocessed facts about some person, item, or event. Information refers to data after it has been organized into a meaningful form. Having all the data about the grades assigned by an instructor to a class is not meaningful until the particular grade is distributed to the appropriate student.

Input data is analyzed, edited, and corrected; it then becomes information. Before computers were used extensively, punched card data processing equipment (those individual machines that sorted data, merged data, or printed reports) prepared the necessary data manipulation to generate reports. Someone had to analyze the reports, however, to determine their meaning and the accuracy of their data. Decision making was done by the reader of the report. At its earliest, computer usage served only this processing and a record-keeping function. When, however, management found that the computer could aid in forecasting and determining consumer trends, computer usage evolved to an information system designed for helping management.

There are other reasons why information systems have come of age. Computer users have become aware of the tremendous advantages of using a computer to analyze and to keep information current. General user awareness of this value and of the availability of information through increasingly sophisticated computer equipment are the other necessary factors in the acceptance of computer-based management information systems.

CHECKPOINT **Can you:**

Explain how the need for information has changed the structure of small businesses and the large corporations?

SYSTEMS APPROACH

The systems approach, when used successfully, involves constantly modifying procedures and changing plans as the company's operations continue. It is used in business, in data processing—in fact, in much of our world today. A **system** encompasses the entire method and plans that are formulated to accomplish a logical way of doing something. In a business system, the combination of the procedures, goals, personnel, machines, and materials blend together for the purpose of conducting the operations of the company. The desired end of the business system is the preparation of reports and information in a form that is meaningful and helpful in the successful operation of the company.

Let us use an example to illustrate a systems approach. If, for example, some sales forecasts are to be changed, the change is affected in the sales department. The change, however, is also reflected in departments that handle transportation costs, estimates of salespeoples' commissions, and scheduling of shipping. For a systems approach to be effective, there must be feedback so that control and any needed action taken by management can be implemented quickly and accurately. **Feedback** refers to the process of modifying, correcting, and improving a result by exchanging ideas. **Constraints** are controls or limitations placed upon the operation of a system. Management exercises constraints such as those shown in Figure 13.1 to optimize the business environment.

Since the systems approach affects all levels of personnel in a company, it is wise to begin by investigating an organizational structure of a company with the purpose of identifying the different levels of management along with the possible decision-making processes of each level.

WHAT'S RIGHT

A Recycling Center Is A System?

A system maintains equilibrium and processes input into output. There are many types of systems, some of which you may never even have thought of before as being systems. For example a recycling center for bottles and cans is a system. The advertising, collecting, packing, storing, and money collection all comprise a system.

In order for the recycling system to operate successfully, each group must perform the assigned duties. If the advertising is not done effectively, there will be fewer cans and bottles to collect, pack, store, and account for monetarily. If, after the cans are collected, the group that stores them does not perform adequately, the system's success becomes threatened. Without a committment from all people involved, a system cannot reach its anticipated goals.

In the data processing world, the systems analyst (that person who helps users in solving and trouble-shooting applications) must work with human resources and data resources to make the system operate successfully and efficiently.

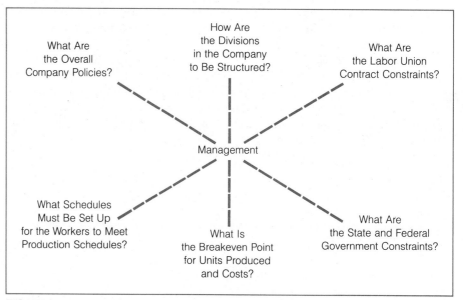

FIGURE 13.1 **Management constraints.**

ORGANIZATION OF A COMPANY

The organization chart of a company is the blueprint for its management structure. No one organizational structure is perfect for all companies. The type of organizational structure depends upon many variables, such as the type of business activity of the company, the size of the company as measured by number of employees hired and capital investments made, to name a few. The organization chart of a company is hierarchical in structure. The closer the position is to the top rectangle (usually the president or chairman of the board), the higher the level of the position.

For our discussion, let us suppose that the Going Bankrupt Fast Company manufactures and sells typewriters. Its organization chart is shown in Figure 13.2 highlighting the three vice-presidential categories of marketing, manufacturing, and finance.

The vice-president in charge of the marketing division is responsible for the market research, sales, and advertising departments. Coordination must exist, however, with the manufacturing and the finance divisions.

The vice-president of the manufacturing division is responsible for the production, buying, shipping, and engineering departments. The production department creates the finished product using materials and labor. All materials used in production must be accounted for, as must all on-hand raw materials; this function is performed by the buying department. The transporting of the finished product to the customer is performed in the shipping department. Any new product development and design is performed by the engineering department.

The vice-president in charge of the finance division is responsible for the accounting department, controller, and auditor. The finance division affects all transactions dealing with payroll, personnel, accounts receivable, accounts payable, fixed assets, and general ledger.

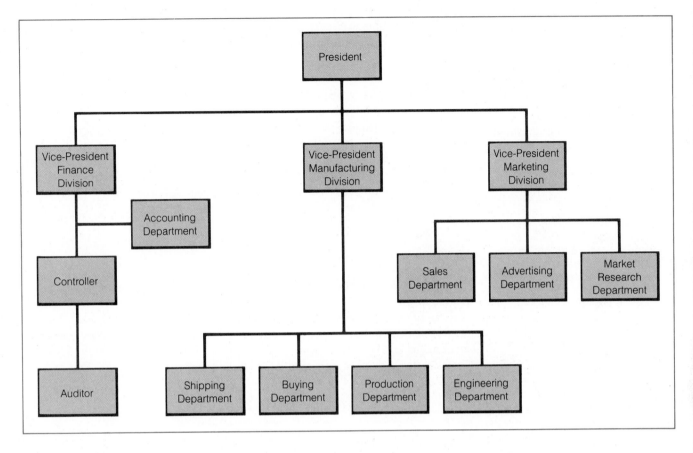

The three vice-presidential positions that we have mentioned so far are classified in the top-level management category. Let us look into the different levels of management along with the responsibilities of each.

FIGURE 13.2
Organization chart.

CHECKPOINT **Can you:**

Define a system?

MANAGEMENT LEVELS

The three management levels are top-level, middle-level, and lower-level management.

Top-Level Management

The **top-level management** is involved in organizing, planning, and forecasting for the overall business organization; the president and the vice-presidents comprise this level of management. These executives usually work in a timeframe that projects five years in the future.

Middle-Level Management

The **middle-level management** is responsible for organizational structure at the departmental level. This level of management concentrates on planning usually within a one-year timeframe. Many companies require weekly or bimonthly progress reports from each staff member, which are forwarded for evaluation to middle-level management. The middle-level management positions can be a regional director, plant manager, or district director.

Lower-Level Management

The **lower-level management** concentrates on the everyday decision-making processes, dealing with personnel problems, inventory control, training, scheduling, and the functional organization of the personnel that report to this level. Lower-level management positions are usually supervisors who, in turn, report to middle-level managers.

The three levels of management are usually shown as depicted in Figure 13.3;

FIGURE 13.3 **Levels of management, purposes, and positions.**

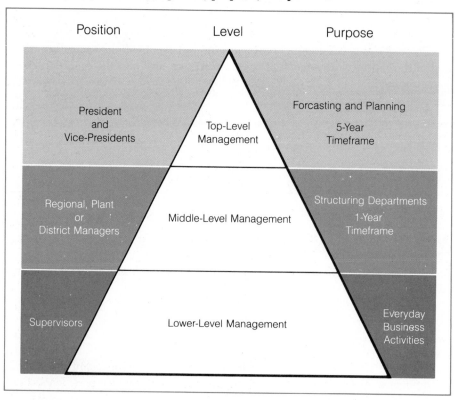

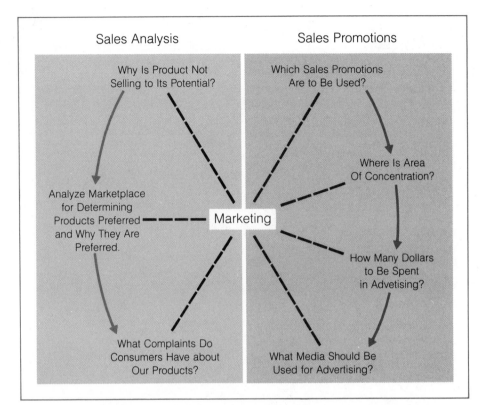

FIGURE 13.4
Marketing division's decision making.

note that the widest range of decision making occurs at the lower management level. The higher the level of management, the more essential it is for those executives to have knowledge of the interworkings of the business.

To get a better picture of the activities of each managerial division and how their departments interact with each other, let us first look at the activities of each and then concentrate on the flow of information among them.

DECISION-MAKING PROCESSES

The **marketing division** concentrates on ideas for promoting and selling products. The **advertising department** creates the advertising, chooses the media for the coverage, and prepares sales promotions that have been agreed upon by the marketing division vice-president. The **market research department** investigates customer response to the finished product and checks public sentiment about existing or proposed products. Refer to Figure 13.4.

One of the purposes of the **sales department** is to monitor all sales of typewriters to the customers. Another is to maintain an accounting of all customers wishing additional service warranties when the original warranty of ninety days expires. And still another is to control any planned promotions for increasing the sales of all company products. Refer to Figure 13.5. The sales department is continually in contact with the advertising department and frequently in contact with the market research group.

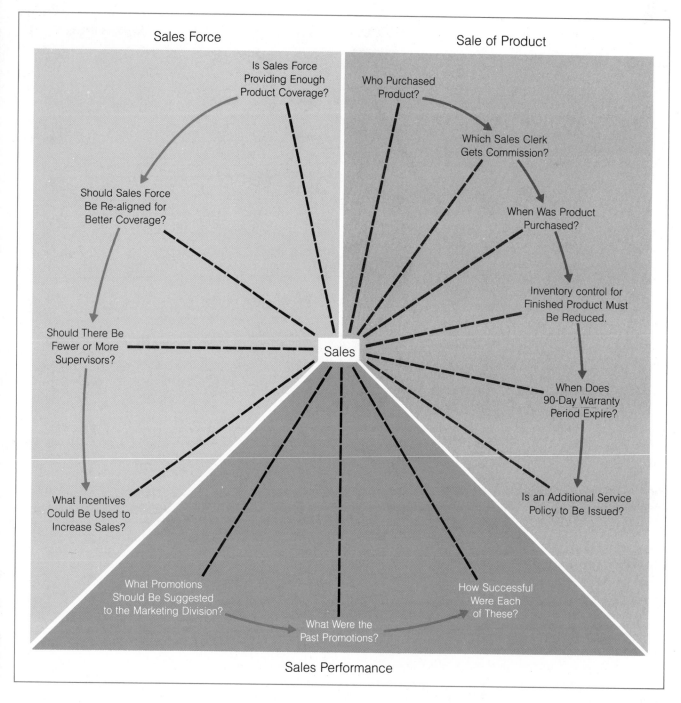

FIGURE 13.5
Sales department's decision
making.

The **manufacturing division** concentrates on designing, testing, manufacturing, and shipping the product. The **engineering department** tests the current
products on the market as well as designs any future products. New product
development is also an integral part of this department's activities. Refer to
Figure 13.6. The engineering department communicates frequently with the sales,
advertising, production, and market research departments.

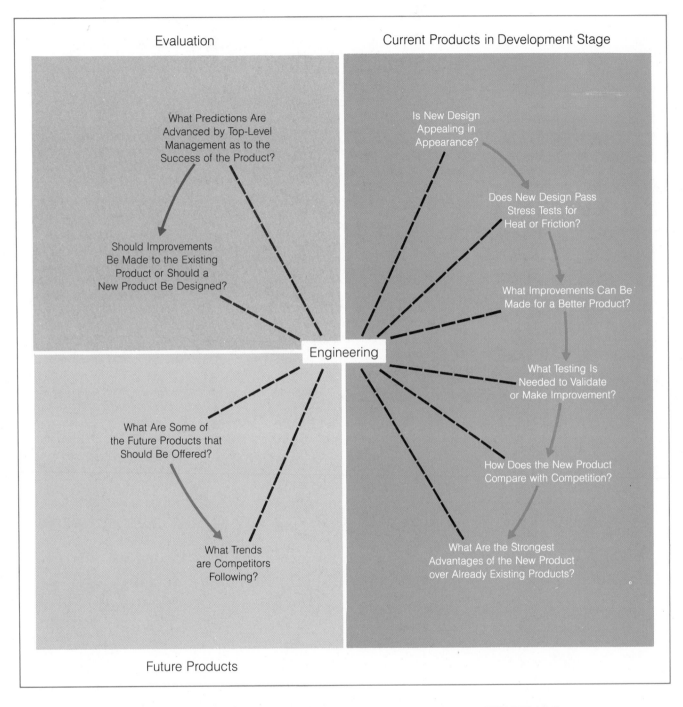

Evaluation

Current Products in Development Stage

What Predictions Are Advanced by Top-Level Management as to the Success of the Product?

Should Improvements Be Made to the Existing Product or Should a New Product Be Designed?

Is New Design Appealing in Appearance?

Does New Design Pass Stress Tests for Heat or Friction?

What Improvements Can Be Made for a Better Product?

Engineering

What Testing Is Needed to Validate or Make Improvement?

What Are Some of the Future Products that Should Be Offered?

How Does the New Product Compare with Competition?

What Trends are Competitors Following?

What Are the Strongest Advantages of the New Product over Already Existing Products?

Future Products

The **production department** produces the finished product. The production department works hand in hand with the **buying department,** which maintains inventory control for adequate raw materials. Refer to Figure 13.7 for some examples of decision making by a manager of the buying department. The production department must have close coordination with the marketing division and the finance division to check feasibility in cost and production decisions.

FIGURE 13.6
Engineering department's decision making.

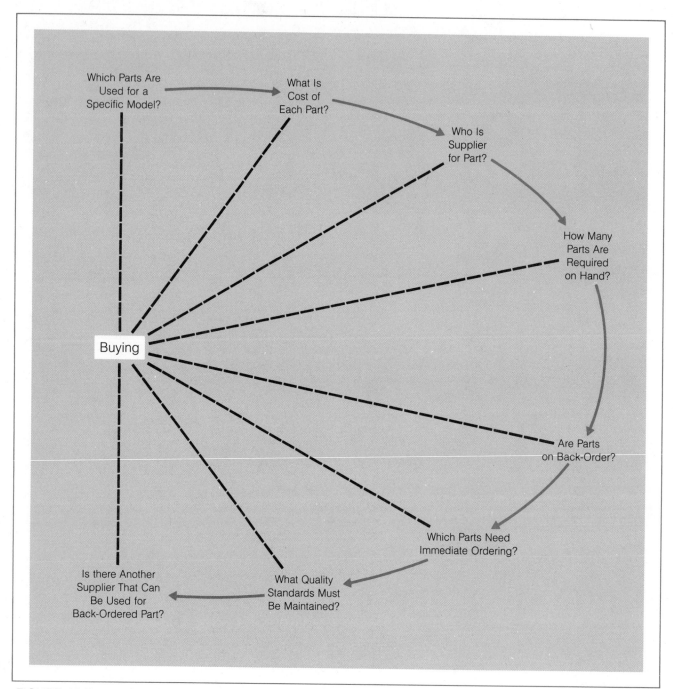

FIGURE 13.7 **Buying department's decision making.**

The **shipping department** prepares the finished product for delivery to the customer. Refer to Figure 13.8.

The **finance division** handles all monetary aspects of the company as well as all auditing. The **accounting department,** a vital part of an organization, must

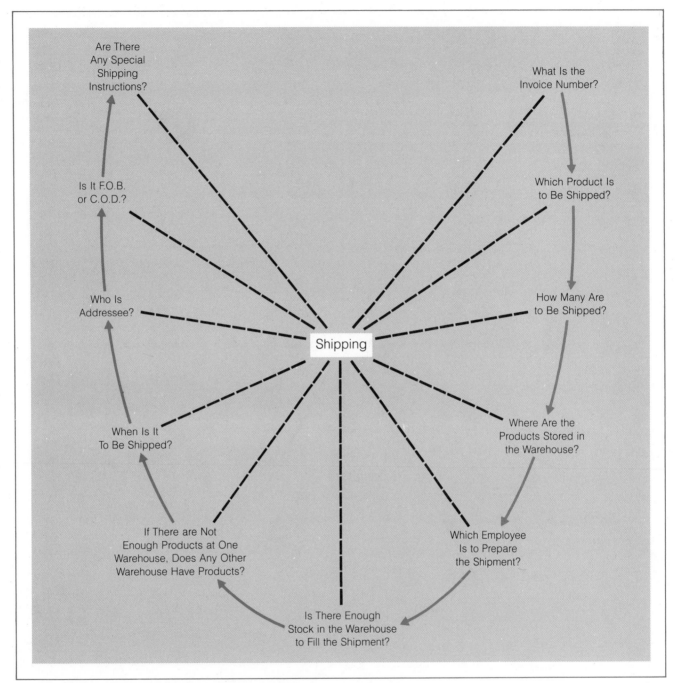

FIGURE 13.8 **Shipping department's decision making.**

accurately determine the costs to establish the profit and loss of the company. All departments must accurately communicate with the accounting department, for this is the key to the business's success or failure. Accounting department figures influence many management decisions. Refer to Figure 13.9.

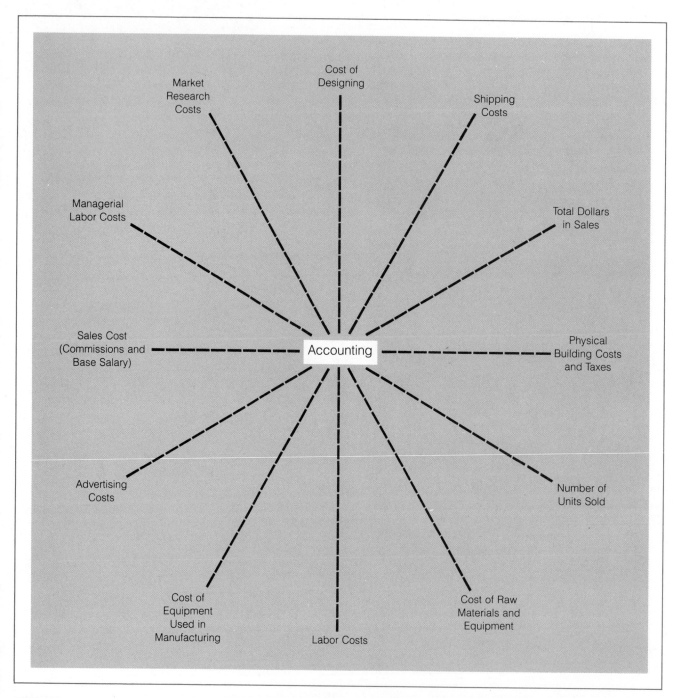

FIGURE 13.9
Accounting department's decision making.

CHECKPOINT **Can you:**

Differentiate among the levels of management?

Explain what timeframe each level works in?

Explain what type of work each level concentrates on?

FLOW OF INFORMATION IN A COMPANY

This discussion stresses interdepartmental information flow and the interaction of the departments in an information system rather than levels of management. We will note that much of the information flows in all departments and that many of the departments use the same information for decision making. In addition, we will note that some of the data is independent to each department. Unless the top-level management coordinates the activities of all departments, the company will not achieve success.

Examples of Flow of Data

Several examples are given to illustrate data flow. These are the sale of the typewriter to the consumer, the sales promotion of the product, and the improvement of an existing product.

Sale of Product. Let us begin our discussion with the customer purchasing a typewriter. Figure 13.10 explains the steps involved before the customer is shipped the typewriter. When the customer signs the invoice to authorize the billing process, notice the checking done by the sales clerk to authorize the sale. This data retrieval is done on-line to the computer. Refer to Figure 13.10(a). On-line processing, as was discussed in Chapter 1, allows users to query information from the computer's storage.

If there is an insufficient quantity of the desired typewriter model on hand, a report is generated, which alerts the buying and production department of the problem. When authorization is given for shipment, notice how the clerk's input data is stored on magnetic disk at the computer center as shown in Figure 13.10(b).

All sales follow the same pattern, with checking performed on-line, but the actual processing of the order is not executed until that evening, allowing all orders for the day to be forwarded to the computer center. This type of processing, you recall, is called batch processing. After all orders are processed in a batch, the various departments are notified of the transactions, as shown in Figures 13.10(c) and 13.10(d).

The sales clerk in this discussion does not need to know any other pertinent information about the flow of data in the organization other than what affects the processing of the order. The supervisor in the lower-level management, however, checks the performance of the clerk. And the input data generated by the sales clerk is evaluated by middle- and top-level management with regards to forecasting and planning.

Sales Promotion. Let us explore the interaction of the departments when a sales promotion is to be run. The company has a sales convention including all its sales personnel, asking at the time for feedback on products. Which products need improvement? What were the reasons for lost sales? Is there any other pertinent information that the salespeople can pass on to management?

Much discussion is held regarding which typewriter should be used for a sales promotion. The middle-level management authorizes the sales promotion of a certain product, which necessitates communication among all divisions of the

FIGURE 13.10 **Authorization through shipping a product.**

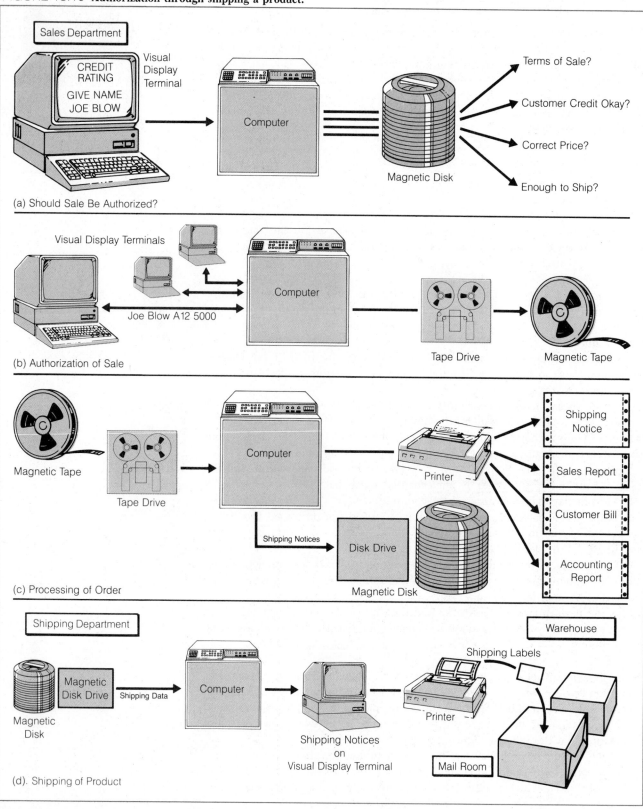

(a) Should Sale Be Authorized?

(b) Authorization of Sale

(c) Processing of Order

(d). Shipping of Product

company. Refer to Figure 13.11. Perhaps it might be more feasible from the company's standpoint to have the sales promotion focus at one plant rather than another one. Communication with the accounting department is vital; cost figures must be evaluated so that the correct judgment is made. The sales department works closely with the rest of the marketing division in planning the promotion. Frequent evaluation is made by middle-level management, which weighs alternatives to set up the best possible advertising campaign with the greatest consumer acceptance, while at the same time striving to achieve the greatest cost effectiveness.

With plans firmly set, the marketing department must communicate with the buying department that is part of the manufacturing division to be certain that ample materials are available for the manufacture of the designated typewriter. The buying department must check with the engineering department to make certain that its list of components for the designated typewriter is accurate, since occasional changes are made in the specifications for the manufacture of the product. The buying department must communicate with the production department to establish schedules for production.

FIGURE 13.11
Sales promotion emphasizing feedback.

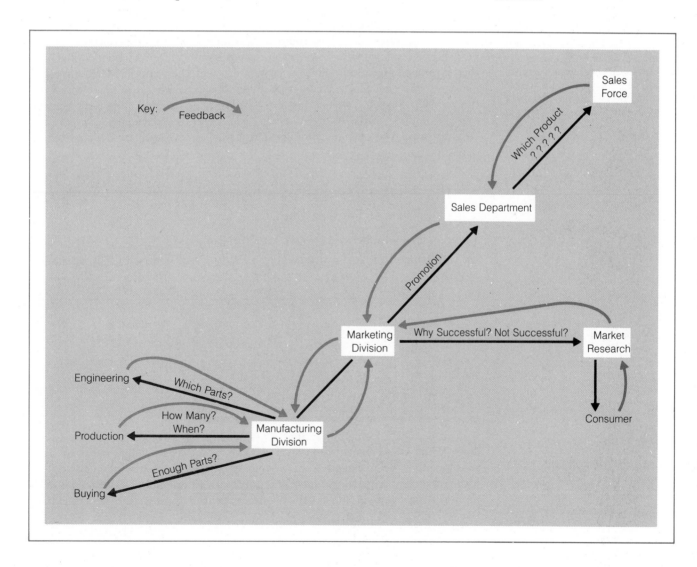

WHAT'S RIGHT

What To Do With Micros?

Believe it or not, the presence of the microcomputer has posed problems for information center managers. The information center is that group within the department that helps end-users to solve some of their own programming needs. The information center provides education to the end-user on how to buy some packaged programs.

The problem that many information center managers are having is what to do with the microcomputers. Should the information center have end-users purchase their own microcomputers and then try to help them solve the problems on how the micros are to be used? Or should the center restrict the growth in numbers of microcomputers by placing the needed processing on the mainframes? Some information center managers feel that the use of the mainframe is easier than the use of microcomputers. Some feel that the microcomputers do not meet all of the processing needs of the user.

The way the microcomputer problem is solved is not clear, but information center managers feel that there is an urgent need for providing the means for solving the communication problem that exists between microcomputers and mainframes. It is then that the successful management information system will "touch" all users.

The production department must communicate with the sales department as to the extent of the promotion and with the shipping department to make certain that the proper packaging of the sales-promoted product is correctly implemented.

Sales Analysis. Using one more example, the sales department analyzes its sales figures for the company's various models of typewriters. Of the six models of typewriters manufactured and marketed by the company, two models sell exceedingly well, but one other model's sales figures are sharply declining. The sales department manager communicates his or her concern to the marketing vice-president, pointing out that no reasons for this poor performance can be detected. It is then decided that the market research department should test consumer responses to the performance of the three models, evaluate the problems that the consumers have had with the models, investigate how the product could be improved, and identify the advantages of using the product. The market research department carefully prepares its questionnaire, determines which consumers are to be interviewed, and initiates the interviewing process.

Results from the interviews are finalized and forwarded to the engineering department for comments. The engineering department carefully analyzes the comments, re-evaluates the design of the products, and makes changes based on the consumer responses. New company specifications for the manufacture of the product are established by lower-level management. These may be modified and then approved by middle-level management, and then approved by top-level management. The design changes are then incorporated in the manufacture of the product. Buying, engineering, accounting, sales, and shipping departments must be notified of the changes, as they affect each department—although in a different way. The changed product information sheets must be updated by all departments.

CHECKPOINT **Can you:**

Describe how information flows within a company?

Identify some of the major departments of a company along with the major role of each?

MAKING A MANAGEMENT INFORMATION SYSTEM WORK

A management information system must include top-level planning that filters down to the lower management level. Human resources as well as hardware and software must be managed if the system is to operate successfully. Top-down planning is very critical for a successful corporation's operations. This means that top-level management must use the data captured through the generation of reports as a corporate resource for modeling and forecasting.

A management information system must be very carefully planned and organized so that it is accurate, available when needed, concise, and correct. It does not spring up in six or seven months, but takes many years to successfully complete. Management must know how to structure information so it can be called upon and used by anyone in the company who needs it. Information processing must be optimized; this requires careful planning by management as to the hardware and software required, and the best way for organizing the data. The information system does not remain static; changes are constantly being made in the interests of clarity, accuracy, better distribution of information, and efficiency.

The key ingredient in an information system is feedback, which provides management with the opportunities for controlling and altering courses of action. Data must be used in different ways to provide answers to questions that are unanswered at this time. Data must be made available so that this type of evaluation can take place.

An information system to benefit the company in the next decade should provide capabilities for word processing, data entry, inquiry, use of graphics, the preparation of reports, and the inclusion of an expert system for decision making and factual analysis. These reports show the normal business activities of the company in its everyday operations. Also shown are the exceptions that result from the analyzing, correcting, and processing of the data, any desired information requested by users, and the information necessary for predictions and determining trends. Figure 13.12 summarizes some of the activities that surround the use of the computer as discussed in our typewriter example. All of these activities surrounding the use of data and the computer must be carefully structured and planned for a successful information system to exist.

For a company to attain a successful management information system requires many years of preparation and dedication to its development. To achieve a highly integrated and successful management information system, management must carefully set standards by which the company will operate. Without a sound commitment of the users to make the information system work, to participate in its use, and to give feedback, a management information system will not operate successfully. An organization chart for a management information system is shown in Figure 13.13.

As has been shown in the typewriter company example, data flows in many directions and to many sources. Some of the data that is used in all departments is the same; other data differs—is uniquely useful to a specific division or department. Common data can be shared by the various departments in an information system; this is accomplished by the use of a data base (discussed in the next chapter).

CHECKPOINT **Can you:**

Explain what a management information system is?

Tell why it is needed?

FIGURE 13.12   **A management information system.**

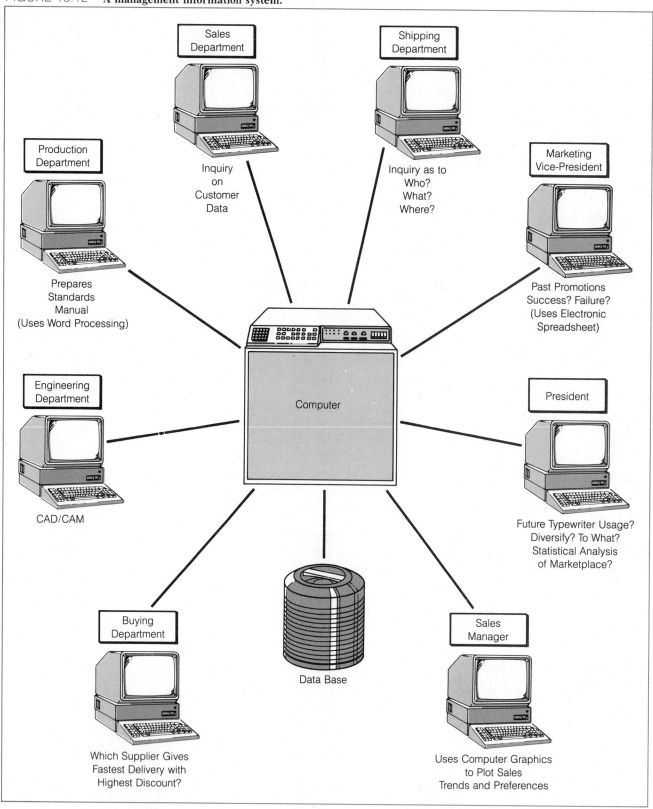

Sales Department

Inquiry on Customer Data

Shipping Department

Inquiry as to Who? What? Where?

Production Department

Prepares Standards Manual (Uses Word Processing)

Marketing Vice-President

Past Promotions Success? Failure? (Uses Electronic Spreadsheet)

Engineering Department

CAD/CAM

Computer

President

Future Typewriter Usage? Diversify? To What? Statistical Analysis of Marketplace?

Buying Department

Which Supplier Gives Fastest Delivery with Highest Discount?

Data Base

Sales Manager

Uses Computer Graphics to Plot Sales Trends and Preferences

FIGURE 13.13   **Organization chart with a management Information system included.**

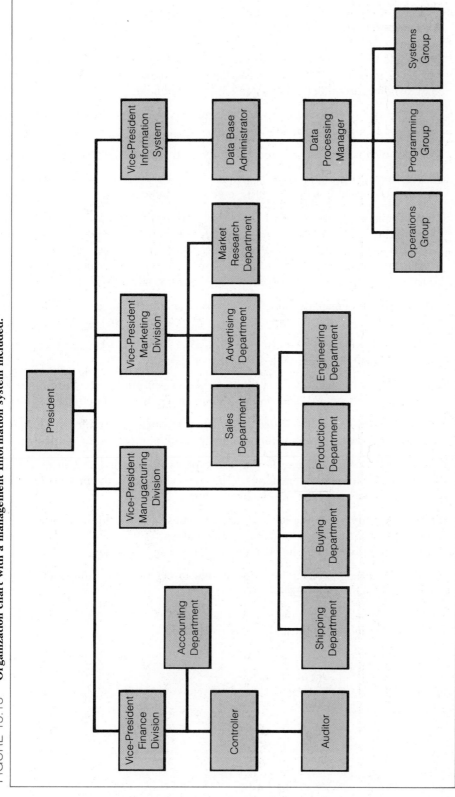

SUMMARY

- An information system provides processed data to aid management in making decisions on a day-to-day basis as well as in planning, forecasting future trends, and avoiding any pitfalls the business future may hold.

- Data refers to raw, unprocessed facts. Information refers to data that has been organized in a meaningful way.

- Input data is analyzed, edited, and corrected. It then becomes information.

- A system is a group of basic principles and related goals that are performed in an organized fashion to accomplish some desired end.

- A company has many departments that work together to accomplish its goals. Some of these departments handle the marketing aspects of the business, such as advertising, sales, and market research. Others handle the finances: the accounting department, controller, and auditor. The manufacturing division handles the production, shipping, and buying of raw materials for producing the finished product.

- Three levels of management exist: top-level, middle-level, and lower-level management.

- Top-level management concentrates on forecasting and planning for the organization, usually working with a five-year timeframe.

- Middle-level managers concentrate on the organizational structure of the departments that they head. Planning is done on a one-year timeframe.

- Lower-level management deals with everyday business problems. This group consists of the supervisors who monitor the work of much of the workforce.

- Data flows among departments. The type of information that flows and the direction that it follows depend upon the type of company, the product or service of that company, and the information system's structure.

- A management information system (MIS) must provide information that is accurate, concise, available for all users, and current. To accomplish this efficiently and successfully, it must be thoroughly planned and organized.

- For the management information system to be successful, top-level planning and involvement are essential.

- A management information system will only offer the benefits and reach the goals it is supposed to through user participation.

STUDY GUIDE

REVIEW OF TERMINOLOGY

The following terminology was discussed in this chapter:

accounting department
advertising department
buying department
constraints
engineering department
feedback
finance division
information system
lower-level management
management information
   system (MIS)

manufacturing division
market research
   department
marketing division
middle-level management
production department
sales department
shipping department
system
top-level management

MULTIPLE CHOICE

Circle the letter of the item that correctly completes each statement.

1. The process of exchanging ideas or responding to information with the purpose of modifying, correcting, or improving a result is known as:
   a. constraints
   b. information
   c. feedback
   d. system
   e. none of these

2. Government rules and limitations placed on companies are referred to as:
   a. laws
   b. constraints
   c. feedback
   d. system management
   e. management information systems

3. The buying, shipping, and engineering departments make up a division called:
   a. production
   b. manufacturing
   c. financial
   d. accounting
   e. management information system

4. All payroll and matters dealing with money are handled by the:
   a. production department
   b. manufacturing division
   c. accounting department
   d. management information system
   e. marketing division

5. Which of the following is required for a successful management information system?
   a. the data must be accurate
   b. the data must be available for use
   c. the data must be current
   d. the system must be well planned
   e. all of these

6. Assuming the company is operating successfully, a president's major emphasis is on:
   a. overseeing how departments operate
   b. how data is inputted, analyzed, and corrected
   c. forecasting and planning for next year
   d. making plans for five years from now
   e. overseeing how data can be made useful

7. A supervisor deals with:
   a. training
   b. personnel problems
   c. inventory control
   d. scheduling
   e. all of these

8. A supervisor belongs to which level of management:
   a. lower-level
   b. middle-level
   c. higher-level
   d. corporate-level
   e. top-level

9. A management information system will only reap benefits when:
   a. management and users both participate
   b. a lot of money is spent in creating it
   c. expensive hardware is purchased
   d. management participates exclusively
   e. communication exists only within groups

10. Which department checks consumer demands?
    a. marketing division d. market research
    b. buying   e. advertising
    c. sales

11. Which department maintains adequate raw materials?
    a. accounting   d. advertising
    b. buying   e. production
    c. market research

12. Which department receives information regarding activities dealing with production and sales?
    a. accounting   d. advertising
    b. buying   e. production
    c. marketing

13. Very careful planning and organization must be accomplished for this to operate successfully:
    a. management information system
    b. lower-level management
    c. middle-level management
    d. top-level management
    e. none of these

REVIEW QUESTIONS

1. What is data? How does it differ from information?
2. What is a system? What must be present in a system for it to be successful?
3. Give five examples of departments in a business system. State the primary purposes of each department.
4. What are the three levels of management? What is the major responsibility of each level? Give an example of a type of position held in each level.
5. What is a management information system?

DISCUSSION QUESTIONS

1. What type of activities in a business are included in a management information system?
2. Consider your college and its use of information. What possible ways could information be used by administrators at your college?
3. Assuming the information from question 2, identify the various levels of management, citing examples for personnel at each management level.
4. Explain the hierarchy of an organization chart.
5. Describe how a management information system supports management in decision making.
6. Before setting up a management information system, company standards and constraints must be examined and evaluated for all departments of a company. Explain why this is important.
7. The three management levels of a company each have different responsibilities, yet they all aim at the successful operation of the system. Describe some of these responsibilities and rules that are followed so the system operates to benefit the company.
8. A system has its constraints and feedback mechanisms built into it. Explain how this is true in your school environment.

TRUE/FALSE QUESTIONS

1. **T/F** The accounting department determines the number of parts to be ordered for a product.
2. **T/F** The supervisor group is the middle-level management.
3. **T/F** Top-level management forecasts and plans in a five year timeframe.
4. **T/F** The top-level management represents the regional or district managers.
5. **T/F** Lower-level management works in a one year timeframe in planning.
6. **T/F** The engineering department tests current products.
7. **T/F** The market research department measures the pulse of the marketplace to determine what consumers want.
8. **T/F** The goals and procedures that are set up by management to achieve a desired end is called a system.

People in Computing

H. Clair Althouse

COMPANY:
VLSI Technology, Inc.

POSITION:
Director of Information Systems and Services

EDUCATIONAL BACKGROUND:
B. S. in Mathematics, Lehigh University, Graduate Studies in Computer Sciences/Operations Research, American University

In my current position as the Director of Information Systems and Services for a new start-up electronics company, I am responsible for the design and implementation of the company's information structure with respect to information data bases and for the development and operation of MIS, Computer and Network Operations, Office Services and related information system organizations. My job requires that I be involved with, and sometimes, responsible for, the structure, the type, and the quality of the information that is used within my company. The accuracy and timeliness of information is one of the major resources of a new, high-growth company.

The execution of these responsibilities is rewarding, if you enjoy creating systems and environments for people to communicate, to grow, and to do exciting jobs or functions, while working in a fast-growing company and industry. In this type of environment, the challenge is to choose and to create the correct system and to live through the implementation and application in order to measure your success. It is your own objective measurement that will give you the experience to make the next decision in a new and changing technology, like information systems.

A sound technical training helps immensely. This permits confidence in technical areas in order to learn and gain experience as a manager in the skills of human communication and interpersonal relations. These skills can be read and lectured about, but they can only be understood in actual experience to achieve satisfactory goals in a management career.

The change in data processing in the next few years will be a move from data processing to information processing systems. This is not just a play on words; it implies that the scope will broaden in the areas of human communications and the structure and use of information; that is, the total solution to the problem. The reason that we will concentrate on the solution is because the technology will progress to such a level that it will relieve the need for developing the tools, but it will create the need for applying the tools.

This path means that we will need people who are more "implementers" than "architects." Architects will and are necessary, but they will be employed in the development of the new technology which is used by the implementer. It is in the world of the implementers where the career and future employment growth will take place. These people must be trained and be prepared to apply the technology to problems, environments, and people to make reasonable and economic solutions.

For what skills and for how long do you train people for these new horizons? The prerequisites are education, training, experience and objective self-evaluation. Education should provide the formal foundation in computer sciences, business management, and engineering. Training provides the concepts for interpersonal skills, human communications, and other behavioral disciplines. Experience is the application of education and training and the measurement of the success (or failure) of these skills by objective self-evaluation. Positive experience is a continual learning process.

One of the most interesting possibilities is the development of a new executive position within the structure of private business called the chief information officer (CIO). This person will be responsible for the information systems in a manner similar to the chief financial officer and financial systems. The areas that would be involved are corporate information and organization structures, management information and office automation systems, and overall integrity of the relationships and consistency of corporate coding structures. The CIO needs to understand the business for which he works and to know how to apply the tools of information systems for solving the information problems of the company. His position will be important for fast growing, new companies as well as for large, established companies and will become recognized as a major management position.

14 Data Base Processing

OUTLINE

PROLOGUE

A lawyer representing a client remembers a point of law that would help in the courtroom hearing. What she needs to do is to find out about the finding in a particular case related to the current one. She is granted a recess, rushes to the telephone, dials a telephone number, gives some words, and later hears the recitation of the case.

The lawyer returns to the courtroom with the pertinent rulings. Her client's case is dismissed.

HOW DOES IT DO THAT?

READ ON.

OBJECTIVES

After studying this chapter, you should be able to:

1. Explain the limitations of a file management system for establishing new data relationships.

2. Discuss the advantages and disadvantages of using a data base.

3. Identify what makes up a data base system.

4. Explain how data is viewed physically and logically in a data base.

INTRODUCTION

In a distributed data processing system, the placement of the data as well as the accessing of it are extremely important. Since the distributed systems share data among the many users through the use of a data base, it is important that we understand the fundamental concepts involved. As was discussed earlier in the text, a data base is a community type of file organization, often used by a company, that structures all the data for that company—usually on one storage medium—in a way that makes access easy and efficient. Computers are also accessing data in public data bases.

In this chapter, the emphasis is centered on why a data base is needed, how it is created and used, and how a user finds data by establishing relationships (associations) to desired data.

FILE MANAGEMENT VERSUS DATA BASE PROCESSING

Traditionally, an application was programmed where the data was associated to a particular program. It was the programmer's responsibility to create, update, and maintain the file, as was discussed in Chapter 9. The file was owned (updated) by one department, so it was application-oriented.

Let us illustrate differences in file management and data base processing through an example, say, a company that sells typewriters as well as typewriter service. Just for the servicing of the typewriters, there would be a file maintained by the service department to keep track of the repair personnel's master records as shown in Figure 14.1(a). The service department also would need to identify the customers' master records, which are kept in a separate file, as shown in Figure 14.1(a).

For the repair personnel file, the normal relationship is the repair person's number and name. For the customer file, the normal relationships are the customer number with the customer name and the customer number with the repair person's number. These pairings show who the customer is and which repair person (by number, not name) calls on that customer. Refer to Figure 14.1(b).

If the service department wants to find out the name of the repair person who services a particular customer, both files must be called up by the programmer. If this type of relationship is to be made continually, both files could be combined, as shown in Figure 14.1(c). This results, however, in an abundance of data, not all of which is needed by the service department. We have looked at just the service department. The sales department would have records regarding each sale with much of the same data that appears in the service department's records. The awkwardness and inefficiency of the separate files are clear.

Consider the telephone company with the various information it supplies to users of the telephone system. The telephone company provides a white pages listing, a yellow pages listing, and a city directory. Much of the same data appears in these three types of listings. For each file, the data is sorted in the order in

FIGURE 14.1 **An application-oriented set of files using file management.**

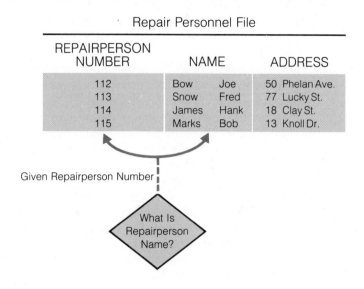

Repair Personnel File

REPAIRPERSON NUMBER	NAME		ADDRESS
112	Bow	Joe	50 Phelan Ave.
113	Snow	Fred	77 Lucky St.
114	James	Hank	18 Clay St.
115	Marks	Bob	13 Knoll Dr.

Given Repairperson Number

What Is Repairperson Name?

Customer File

CUSTOMER NUMBER	NAME		ADDRESS	TYPEWRITER SERIAL #	SERVICING REPAIRPERSON #
C6666	Henry	Joe	1 Noe St.	S 7272888	114
C7777	Able	Sue	6 A St.	K 1111111	112
C8888	Tom	Fay	8 1st Ave.	S 6666666	114
C9999	Poe	Tim	7 C St.	M2222222	115
D1111	Jacks	Tom	2 S St.	Y 7777777	115

What Is Customer Name?

Given Customer Number

What Is Repairperson Number?

(a) Master Files and Relationships

Combined File

CUSTOMER NUMBER	NAME		ADDRESS	TYPEWRITER SERIAL #	SERVICING REPAIRPERSON #	SERVICING REPAIR PERSONNEL NAME	
C6666	Henry	Joe	1 Noe St.	S 7272888	114	James	Jim
C7777	Able	Sue	6 A St.	K 1111111	112	Bow	Jim
C8888	Tom	Fay	8 1st Ave.	S 6666666	114	James	Hank
C9999	Poe	Tim	7 C St.	M2222222	115	Marks	Bob
D1111	Jacks	Tom	2 S St.	Y 7777777	115	Marks	Bob

(b) Combined File

which the key or keys are used. In the case of the white pages listing, the data fields are related by name of the customer. In the yellow pages listing, the data fields are related by the category or service they provide to customers. In the city directory listing, the data fields are related by street name and house number on the street.

If a composite of all the telephone numbers in the entire telephone system were to be listed, each of the three listings previously mentioned would require sorting into telephone number sequence. The telephone numbers would be compared if unique and those would be included in the newly created file. Under file management, a file is used for each listing. Much repeated data appears not only wasting secondary storage space but also requiring the maintenance of all files for any additions or deletions.

With a data base, however, separate files do not exist as they do with file management. All data for the applications at the company are contained in the data base and are usable by different departments or individuals.

Under file management, the programmer manipulates the physical records in a file. In a data base, this responsibility is shifted to the software that manages the data base—called the **data base management system (DBMS).** This frees the programmer for more productive work. Since the data base management system handles the creation, maintenance, and retrieval of physical records from disk storage, it provides an interface (a type of connection) between the programmer's application programs and the data base (the data). Refer to Figure 14.2.

The users of the data base are concerned with the logical records (how they perceive the records as meaningful units) rather than the physical records (how the records are actually laid out). Refer to Figure 14.3.

The use of data bases is growing considerably; not only are there small data bases that contain thousands or tens of thousands of records, but there are also large data bases that might contain hundreds of thousands of records.

Let us look into the elementary concepts that surround the use of the data base with the intention of gaining a general idea of what it is and how it is used.

FIGURE 14.2
Data base management system's responsibilities.

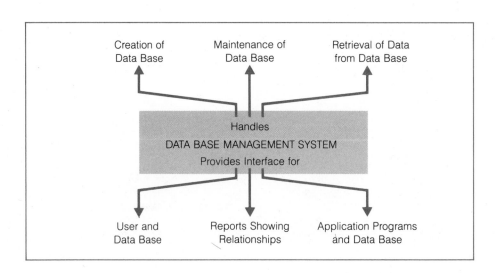

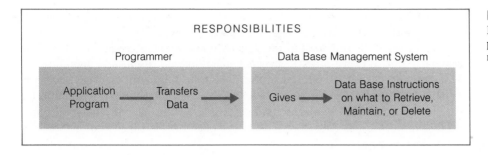

CHECKPOINT **Can you:**

Explain why file management inhibits the setting up of new data relationships?

REASONS FOR USING A DATA BASE

In a data base management system, many features are built into the software package. These features provide protections and efficiencies that are not available under file management. Let us first list these features and then look into each one individually. These features include the:

1. Insuring of data integrity and security.

2. Elimination of most redundant data.

3. Sharing data.

4. Reduction of secondary storage space.

5. Achieving data independence.

6. Providing data relatability.

7. Including dumping, backup, and recovery routines.

DATA INTEGRITY AND DATA SECURITY

Data integrity assures that data is complete, accurate, and secure from tampering. Since data is an important corporate resource, the data chosen to be in the data base must be accurate. A problem of data integrity exists in the following example. If your college used file management and your name was to be changed, what files might require updating? As a matter of course, your instructors' records need changing. Records in the registrar's office, testing office and counselor's office also need updating. If all of these records are not changed or if they are not changed at the same time, there is a problem of data accuracy.

Data security is provided in the data base management system by the use of passwords and software locks to prevent unauthorized disclosure, modification, or destruction of the data stored in the data base. Certainly you have heard in the news and read in the newspapers how frequently illegal entry and tampering with data in a data base is attempted. People like to "browse" through a data base and look at the various data stored. This type of activity is a threat to the accuracy and privacy of data.

ELIMINATION OF MOST REDUNDANT DATA

Redundant data refers to excessive or repeated data. The elimination of redundant data is another reason for using a data base. Data such as your name, telephone number, address, student number, or social security number are needed by the registrar's office or counselor's office. Why have the same data appear in each office file? The data can be stored once in secondary storage but can be referenced by any of the offices that require it. Certain data that make up the keys, such as a social security number and student number, for example, will be repeated. There is no need, however, to repeat the name, address, and other fields of a person's record.

SHARING OF DATA

Sharing data is a primary concern in using a data base. It can pose a problem in companies that formerly used file management, where each department had its own data and felt it totally owned the data. When data is to be shared, decisions are made as to how data is to be accessed. For example, one department might want to access data by social security number while another department might want to access the same records by employee number.

REDUCTION OF SECONDARY STORAGE SPACE

The number of secondary storage positions needed to store the data is reduced by the use of a data base. This reduction cannot be expected overnight since the data base is created in stages. A particular application's file or files are converted from the existing file format to the data base format. Programs for such conversion are included in the data base management system package. Certainly a company needs a smooth transition period so its operations are not disrupted.

DATA INDEPENDENCE

As was stated previously, a user deals with logical records and not physical records. The user is not concerned with the physical devices, the number of bytes in a physical record, or the number of blocks in a physical record. **Data independence** refers to the user's ability to use only the logical records and to think in those terms rather than the physical records. Data independence is the separation of the data from the hardware specifications. This goal is not fully reached in the data base management systems available since most of them are geared to specific hardware. Constraints are placed on the users, perhaps on the language that is usable for the applications program to reference the data base or on the format of the record that requires fixed word length. When a data base management system is selected, it must be carefully scrutinized for advantages and disadvantages.

DATA RELATABILITY

Data relatability refers to the way that data are integrated and interrelated. Data in a data base can be related (associated) to each other in different ways. In file management the high cost involved in programming these relationships prevents much of the data from being associated; files have to be sorted, compared, and merged to accomplish the desired relationships. For the sake of example, suppose it is critical for management of an insurance company to be able to find out how many people with red hair and brown eyes, who were born in 1952 and own a Mercedes, have purchased automobile insurance from the company. In this example, color of hair, color of eyes, year of birth, and make of car are the relationships established. Once these relationships are set up for processing using a data base management system, the color of hair, eyes, birthdate and car model can change for each request of data by simple instruction changes on the part of the end-user. No programming help is needed.

Determining relationships is one of the first objectives of a total information system. The purpose of the information system is to provide for management planning as well as record-keeping and document preparation. Management planning involves decisions made on the basis of data relationships. Relationships should be set up in a way that helps management solve existing problems.

DUMP, BACKUP, AND RECOVERY

Dump, backup, and recovery are supplied by the data base management system, in case the system has a failure. The word *dump* here means to make a copy of the data. The data base management system provides for periodic dumps of the data base, just in case there is a need for rebuilding the data base. All changes made to the data base are recorded on a log tape. This, too, can be used if the need arises. If there is a problem, the tape is backed up to see the last data that was updated. The log tape and the last dump are used to rebuild the data base if it has been entirely lost. This activity then provides the needed recovery to start up again.

REASONS FOR NOT USING A DATA BASE

One of the main reasons for not using a data base is that familiar story about cost. A company must weigh the benefits of using a data base against the drawbacks. The high cost for the extensive study made before selecting a data base management system, coupled with the cost of the system itself and the salary of the data base administrator (the person who manages the data base), discourages many companies from using data bases. A data base alone could cost from $20,000 (for a small system) to $150,000 (for a large system). Once a data base commitment is made, it must be viewed in a long-term perspective. That is the only timeframe in which significant advantages will be forthcoming.

CHECKPOINT Can you:

State the advantages of using a data base?

Tell some of its disadvantages?

DATA BASE SYSTEM

The total data base system includes a data base, a data base management system (DBMS), a data base administrator (DBA), and a data base model.

DATA BASE

A **data base** contains the data that is used by all members of a company and is not limited to just one application. Recall the distinction between *physical* and *logical* entities in Chapter 2: *physical* refers to how a thing really is set up and *logical* to the way we perceive the thing's setup.

A data base provides a way to store data in a set of logical files that follow relationships to the real world. The data base evolved as a sophisticated community-type of file in which the relationships were set up on a one-to-one basis, much like those shown in Figure 14.1. Currently, the data base has evolved into an extensive cross-reference file that handles complex relationships that are not limited to a one-to-one relationship between physical and logical records. The user does not deal with physical records, only with logical records. By handling the records logically, the user can do a variety of analyses on data. Data integration is the key ingredient in the technology.

DATA BASE MANAGEMENT SYSTEM

The data base management system is the software system that organizes data in logical files so that they can be entered or retrieved quickly, formatted, and reported. Popularly used data base management systems for mainframes are TO-TAL by Cincom, Information Management System (IMS) by IBM, Integrated Data Base Management System (IDMS) by Cullinane Corporation, ADABAS by Software AG of North America, and SYSTEM 2000 by MRI Systems, Inc. The popularly used data base for personal computers is dBASE II and dBASE III by Ashton–Tate. These software packages differ in the way they structure data and the access method they use for getting at the data.

DATA BASE ADMINISTRATOR

The **data base administrator** (**DBA**) is the person responsible for managing and controlling the data base, defining and organizing it, and preparing documentation for users so they can access the data base successfully. The data base administrator supplies necessary instructions to the data base management system to make the data base usable.

The data base administrator determines how data is to be accessed, establishes the data formats, and sets standards for company-wide use. He or she interviews users to determine their views as to the type of data relationships that are needed for processing. The interactions of people and source documents must be scrutinized as well as all manual and automated processes. These act as inputs. The output is the picture of relationships which act as a blueprint for determining how data is used.

Uses of Data Dictionary

A **data dictionary,** used by the data base administrator at the time the data base is created, is a type of rule book that is used for documenting the field formats as they exist in the physical records.

Formerly, the data dictionary was maintained by hand or by software but was separate from the data base management system. Today, however, the data dictionary is frequently integrated with the entire system as one package. Each time an application program wishes access to the data base, its queries or references go through the data dictionary.

DATA BASE MODEL

A **data base model** is the vocabulary of the data base. It takes two forms: the data definition language and the data manipulation language.

The **data definition language** (**DDL**), written by the data base administrator, inputs the data structure of the data base into the data base management system including such information as the field names, the type of data, the length of the field, some values and relationships. In other words, the data base administrator is defining the physical records as to how the data is set up; this is the **schema.**

FIGURE 14.4
**Reasons for using data
manipulation language.**

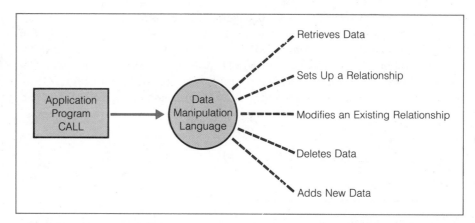

The data base administrator is the only person concerned with writing the data definition language.

The **data manipulation language (DML)** provides a way for users to access the data in the data base. Let us think of the data manipulation languages as being used from two viewpoints: the applications programmer's and the end-user's. Application programmers, usually at the host site (main computer site), use COBOL, FORTRAN, PL/I, or assembly language to access the necessary data in a data base. Refer to Figure 14.4. End-users get access to the data in a data base by using **query languages,** the instructions of which are written as English sentences. Since the query languages are easy to use, the end-user does not need a programmer's help in accessing the data base. To even further help the end-users, **report generators** are included with the data base management system. These are programs that format the responses back to the end-user in a form dictated by the end-user. Refer to Figure 14.5 for an example of a query language written by a user.

Recalling that the physical records are of secondary importance in a data base, the end-user and programmer deal with the logical records, called **subschemas.** These are specified in the data manipulation language. The logical records are set

FIGURE 14.5
**Query languages used by non-
programmers.**

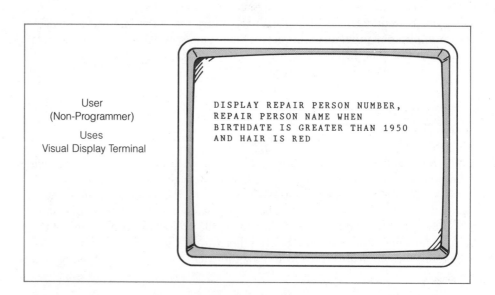

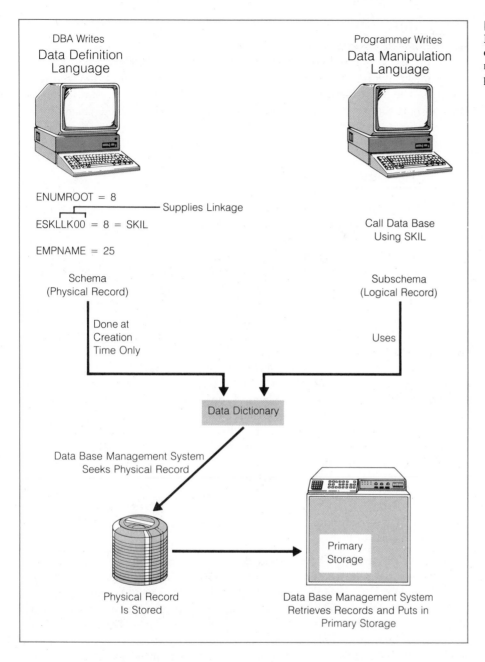

FIGURE 14.6
Data definition language used by data base administrator; data manipulation language used by programmer.

up differently than the physical records. That is of no concern to the user as all he or she wants is the requested data. Refer to Figure 14.6 for a summation.

CHECKPOINT **Can you:**

Define data base model? Data base management system? Data dictionary? Explain the role of the data base administrator?

VIEWING OF DATA

Let us discuss very briefly the physical and logical ways of viewing data. The data base subject involves great detail, and an entire course could be devoted to its learning. The following discussion is not comprehensive but is meant to remove the mystique that seems to surround the use of a data base in the layman's mind.

PHYSICAL VIEW

The data base management system locates the physical records for the user through programs. To illustrate, consider one possible method of passing through a data base, via linked lists. **Linked lists** create a single path of data that is used to get from one physical record to the next. Think of a linked list as being a chain that ties the physical records together. Each record contains a link value which points to the next record; these pointers are called linked lists. Other access methods use indexes or calculations but these methods are beyond the scope of this material.

Let us assume that the payroll department has data associated with the employees organized by departments for which they work, by salaries they earn, and by skill levels they have achieved. We wish to request records of all employees who have a skill of steno. The employee's name and social security number are to be printed. In Figure 14.7, notice that a table exists showing the skills with the starting disk address for each chain of records. The first record of the steno skill chain is located, and the data is formatted for output. The first physical record in the steno chain contains the pointer (a disk address) for the next record in the steno chain. The next record is searched, and the procedure continues until the end of the chain is encountered.

LOGICAL VIEW

To begin the discussion of how a data base is viewed logically, let us use an order entry system as an illustration. If we asked some of the people in the marketing department how they view the data in the data base, they would tell us they relate the data by customers. The customer data is set up in a hierarchical structure where the customer number is the entry point to the data. The different fields of data, called **data elements,** are chained (grouped) together. One possible chain is the orders that each customer has ordered; this chain provides an easy method of accessing data of common characteristics at some later time. Another chain could be set up by a product that is ordered by all the customers.

If we visited the people who maintain the inventory production control and asks them the same question about the same data, they would tell us they relate the data from the standpoint of the product. The product number provides the access to the logically related files. The product number is the entry point to the data which then points to the orders that must be shipped, the dates of these shipments, and any special instructions. The hierarchy is tiered in this viewpoint as it was in the marketing people's viewpoint; the tiering is different since multiple

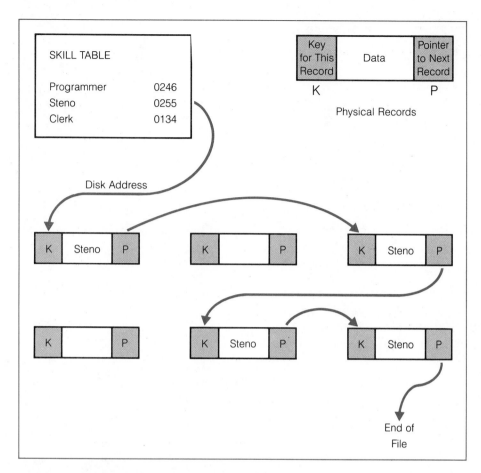

FIGURE 14.7
**Physical records are linked
together.**

questions are being asked about the same data. There is an integrating and interrelating of data.

A user associates data elements together which are linked logically by data relationships to form a **data structure.** A data structure can primarily be of one of three types; network data structures, hierarchical data structure (trees), and relational data structures. Sometimes the data structure is referred to as a data base, such as, a relational data base.

Network Data Structure

In a network data structure there is a hierarchical structure used for showing levels of importance. The **root** contains the basic information. A **network data structure** allows a user to have a different entry point other than the root. The network data structure allows a user to pass through the data base in different directions.

Let us suppose a customer file and an item file are set up with the basic data. The customer number in the customer file is the root. This customer number is used to link to the order file. The item file has its item number used to link to

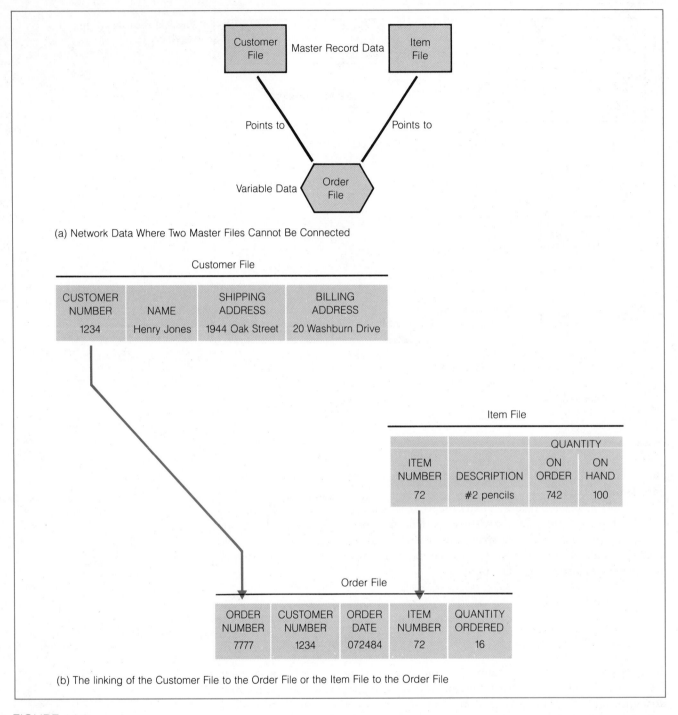

(a) Network Data Where Two Master Files Cannot Be Connected

(b) The linking of the Customer File to the Order File or the Item File to the Order File

FIGURE 14.8

Network data structure. (a) Two master files cannot be connected. (b) The linking of the customer file to the order file or the item file to the order file.

the order file as well. Notice in Figure 14.8(a) that the linkage is provided between the customer file and item file only through the use of the order file. The order file is considered the variable data (transaction data); the customer file and item file are considered the sets of master records.

As previously stated, pointers allow a user to access data from different entry points. Refer to Figure 14.8(b). If we wanted to find out what outstanding orders for a certain customer were yet to be filled, we could get that information by looking at the customer file for a particular customer record. This record links to the orders that are outstanding for that customer.

Hierarchical Data Structure

A **hierarchical data structure** sets up the data in different tiers. As you might expect, you start at the root, or the main part, and branch out from there. That is why this data structure is often referred to as a **tree structure.** The further you go away from the root, the more detailed is the data. The marketing people in the previous discussion viewed their data in a hierarchical data structure.

There would be three files set up, as shown in Figure 14.8, but different levels of importance are assigned to the data. The first level, called the root, contains basic information for that file. There are pointers stored within the records that then point to the next level. The second level of importance gives a different dimension to the basic information and contains data that is variable. Note in Figure 14.9 that the customer file's root data contains the customer number and name. The second level of the hierarchy contains the customer's addresses; for each customer, two addresses are filed—one for shipping and one for billing purposes. Since the secondary storage addresses are contained within the physical records, a chain of new data relationships can be supported by the data structure. The user needs to understand the use of pointers and the relationships that are used to get out on the tree limb!

Relational Data Structure

Since, from a user's standpoint, most of the processing is done at the terminal, there is a need for a data base that can easily display its data in a form of a table

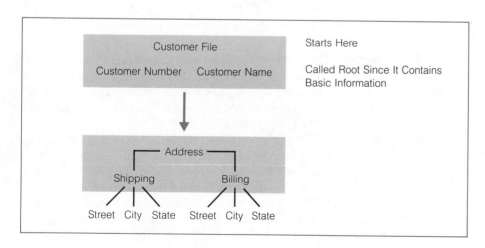

FIGURE 14.9
A hierarchical data structure.

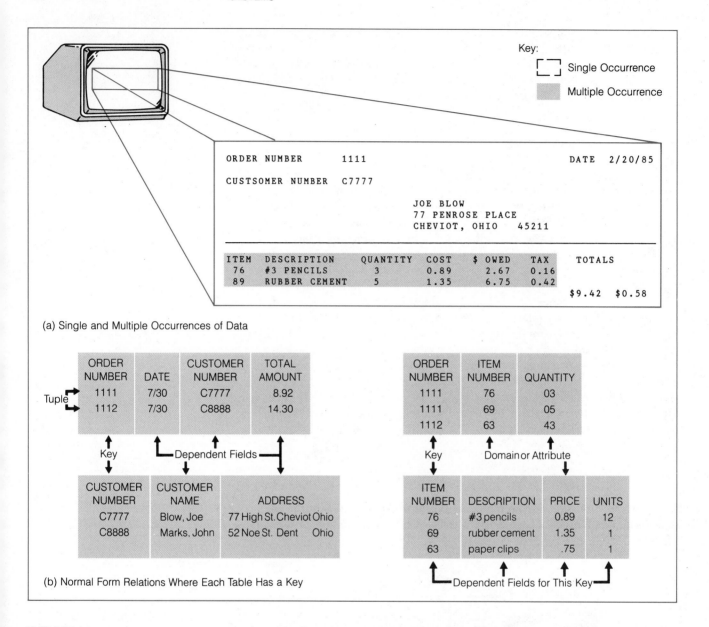

(a) Single and Multiple Occurrences of Data

(b) Normal Form Relations Where Each Table Has a Key

FIGURE 14.10
**Relational data structure.
(a) Single and multiple
occurrences of data. (b) Normal
form relations where each table
has a key.**

on the cathode ray tube. This is where the **relational data structure** comes into use. One of its purposes is to meet the demands for data relatability at any time—even after the data base is created. It is designed for flexibility. The tables that are used in this data structure can be linked physically together. As is the case in the other data structures, linked lists are used.

The relational data model uses a **flat file** structure, which means it has no repeating fields of data and has fixed word length (the same number of bytes for each record). The data appears as a table as shown in Figure 14.10(a).

Figure 14.10(a) shows an order with its particular details. Certain data occurs only once, but data referring to the individual items occurs more than once. The item data is split into two tables so that the flat file structure is maintained. Each table has a key for ease in entering. Refer to Figure 14.10(b).

Calculations done in calculus are used for navigating (passing) through the data base. These are performed by the data base management system and need not concern the programmer or user. A tremendous amount of storage is needed, however, for this data structure since its overhead (the needed code to make it work) is high. Many experts predict that this type of data structure will set the trend for future data base usage. Two of the most popular relational data bases are dBASE II for microcomputers and Structured Query Language (SQL) for mainframes.

CHECKPOINT **Can you:**

Identify the ways that data is viewed physically in a data base?

Identify the structures through which data is viewed logically in a data base?

dBASE II. The very popular data base program used for microcomputers is **dBASE II;** a later version, called dBASE III, was released in mid-1984. Let us look briefly into a program that uses an existing data base. There is a data base that contains questions used for testing. Two types of questions can be used: multiple-choice and other. The multiple-choice question alternative is coded as an M-type, while the other is coded as an O-type for short review and discussion questions.

Referring to Figure 14.11(a), note that a control program is given a name, (HGOTQ) followed by a .PRG notation. We will look at the program that makes the operation execute. Howard Granger names the program HGOTQ.PRG; the HG standing for his initials, the O for other questions only, the TQ for test questions, followed by the .PRG. The data base file of questions is named as HGQUES.DBF. The .DBF stands for data base file and identifies the name of the file that will be used to hold the list of questions that will make up the data base. Notice in Figure 14.11(a) that the questions are in the order in which they have been entered into the data base file. Also notice that the complete question appears in the data base file.

A user must also specify the form that is to be used for displaying each question on a printer or monitor. The user has a choice if multiple choice or review questions and discussion questions are to be inputted. Since this program works with the other type of questions (review and discussion questions), the user must make up a name followed by a .FRM. The control program and the format (form) use the same name but are differentiated by the characters following the period.

The user must specify the index which becomes the pointer for locating the desired question from the data base. Notice how the index appears in sequence by question number since this is the way that Howard wishes to access the questions. Use of an INDEX file automatically keeps your file in order. For example, when using a dBASE II file, adding a new record (such as a new question) always causes that record to be put at the bottom of the data base file (the complete set of questions), regardless of its question number. However, in the index, entries are always in order. Note particularly that the index only lists the question number and the type of question used.

WHAT'S RIGHT

Whose Data Base Is Best?

Data processors are willing to take sides in a hurry as to which data base is the best. Some will proclaim TOTAL as their salvation; others will sing the praises of SQL (pronounced C-QUL); others will praise their IMS data base, and so on.

An argument for the relational data base is that the data base handles requests for data relationships regardless of whether they have been previously used in the data base structure. Pro—relational data base people claim that the network and hierarchical data structures are designed for handling planned activities. The relational data base, because of the structure using tables, is able to accommodate any needs.

Network and hierarchical data base users say that simplicity is more their goal. The logically-related files, such as are used in both of these data structures, allow high performance. But the relational data base users point out that the tables used in their data structure can be separate or can be physically connected or stored near one another in storage to accommodate better run time.

The relational data base uses a high amount of overhead, that coding needed to make it work for users. It allows users to access the data easily, however. The network data structure allows a user to enter any logically-related file and refer to any other related file, which yields simplicity in accessing data. The hierarchical data structure requires that the searching through it begin at its root.

Tune in again. Many users out there still want the relational data bases. There must be some reason.

A Subscription Company's Need For a Data Base

You are president of a company that wishes to keep its employees current on the on-going world of engineering advancements, business, data processing, research experiments—in fact, the world of work. A subscription to many periodicals is considered an important contribution to furthering employees' education. What can you expect as a subscriber to a very large subscription service?

You expect the capability to request any one of 160,000 unique titles from over 55,000 publishers located anywhere in the world. Information about the articles of interest should be available within four seconds if your company is an already established user, providing such information as complete pricing and bibliographic data. To place an order should take no longer than thirty seconds, even though the subscription company handles over 130,000 daily transactions.

From the subscription company's viewpoint, the company must continually add 17,000 titles per year to its already existing data base. There are about 10,000 record changes involving pricing that must be made in the year, but the company must maintain up-to-date records. The company must be prepared to bill over 50,000 organizations but also be able to ship desired periodicals to over 420,000 different shipping addresses. Shipping addresses and billing address data are certain to change, so this, too, must be kept current. It is critical that staffing be adequate; therefore, over fifty-eight people are employed to process the subscription work.

Two 8-megabyte minicomputers are used with 25 gigabytes of magnetic disk storage. There are over 250 visual display terminals used in 14 countries throughout the world.

Referring to Figure 14.11(b), let us look briefly at each line of a program that allows Howard to output, either on the printer or on the monitor, the questions in the data base. Line numbers have been written on the source program listing shown in Figure 14.11(b) for our discussion purposes. Also notice how the various loops are marked on Figure 14.11(b) for ease in presentation. Figure 14.11(c) shows the pseudocode for the program.

Let us refer to the discussion by line numbers, using Figure 14.11(b) as the reference. Line 1 asks that the program be listed by entering the word TYPE followed by the control program name. Line 2 of the program turns the screen display off so that it will be less confusing to the viewer. If you do not turn the screen display off, everything the computer does is shown on the screen. Line 3 uses ERASE, which clears the screen. On line 4, the USE instruction identifies the data base file as well as the index, specifying that they are accessible from disk drive B.

The three STORE statements of lines 5, 6, and 7 store blanks (spaces); thus, they are initializing variables in primary storage to a one-position field. As you will recall, variables are names made up by the programmer to identify data so that data can be referenced in primary storage by the computer. The variables chosen were WATE for waiting for the user to press any key; RESP and RESP1 are used for waiting for a particular response from the user, such as Y or N (yes or no).

The DO WHILE statement on line 8 signals the beginning of a loop, whose finish is indicated by the ENDDO on line 12. This causes the computer to repetitively do the contents of this loop as long as the condition following the DO WHILE is true. The .NOT. RESP$ 'PS' is the condition. The dollar sign character is used to specify a string. Recalling a discussion of BASIC, a $ is used in a variable to name any kind of characters not used in calculation. In this program, as long as the user does not type a P or an S as a response, the loop continues.

On line 9, the @ 22,0 is a way of writing, either to the screen or to the printer. In this case, the printer is not on, so this message, which is included within single quotes, goes to the monitor, starting at vertical line 22 of the screen and position 0 for the horizontal spacing. The GET RESP on line 9 does two things. First, it saves whatever is already in the variable named RESP and, secondly, it allows you to change the value of the variable or to fill it in. Instead, if the coding was, say, RESP instead of GET RESP, it would not allow you to change the contents of RESP. READ on line 10 accepts whatever the user keys in and stores it in the variable named RESP.

On line 11, STORE ! (RESP) TO RESP makes certain that the user responds in capital letters. Recalling that ASCII code recognizes 128 different possible characters, some being upper- and others being lower-case, a programmer must check to make certain that just upper-case are acceptable.

ENDDO on line 12 signals the end of the loop.

Let us briefly discuss another part of the program. If the RESP is a P, as stated on line 13, line 14 tells how the output should be positioned. On line 14, the @ 23,0 means that the response goes to vertical line 23, beginning at position 0 of the horizontal line. We are assuming that the output for the program will be generated on the screen only if the answer is false. The GET WATE, READ, and ERASE statements on lines 14, 15, and 16 receive the response, input it, and then erase the screen. On line 17, the REPORT FORM statement identifies the name used for the form (HGOTQ, in this case). When the report form was created,

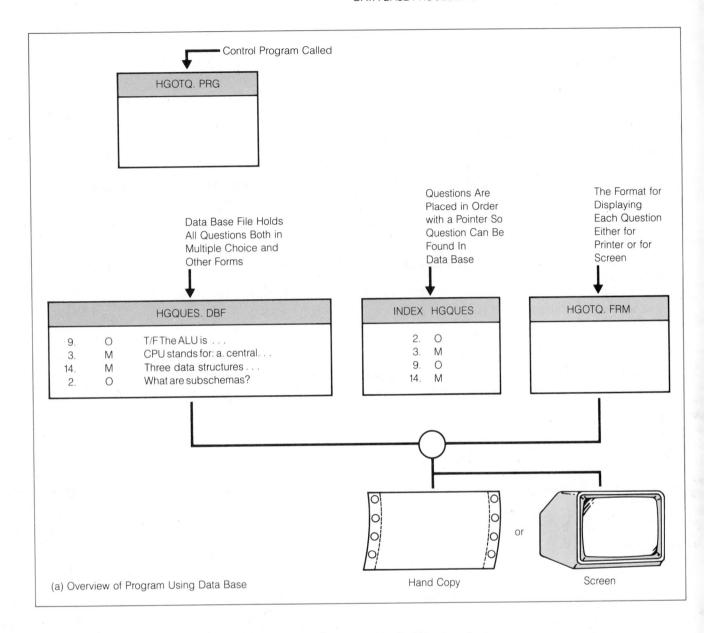

(a) Overview of Program Using Data Base

Control Program Called

HGOTQ. PRG

Data Base File Holds
All Questions Both in
Multiple Choice and
Other Forms

Questions Are
Placed in Order
with a Pointer So
Question Can Be
Found In
Data Base

The Format for
Displaying
Each Question
Either for
Printer or for
Screen

HGQUES. DBF

9.	O	T/F The ALU is . . .
3.	M	CPU stands for: a. central. . .
14.	M	Three data structures . . .
2.	O	What are subschemas?

INDEX HGQUES

2.	O
3.	M
9.	O
14.	M

HGOTQ. FRM

or

Hand Copy

Screen

FLD3 was set up to O for other questions. Since this program deals with only the other question type and since we assume that the printer is not on, the **ELSE** option is followed which represents the processing needed for output on the screen, namely lines 18 through 31. The **ERASE** on line 19 clears the screen.

DO WHILE .NOT. EOF on line 20 sets up the beginning of a loop that is finished by **ENDDO** on line 30. This loop will continue as long as the end of the file has not yet been reached. This loop is necessary because of the limited length of the screen. It causes the computer to stop from time to time. Whereas the length of the printer area is essentially unlimited, the length of the screen is limited. Therefore, ever so often the computer will stop and tell the user to press the carriage return key to continue or to press the X key to exit this part of the program.

FIGURE 14.11
dBase II. (a) Overview of program using a data base.

```
1   TYPE HGOTQ.PRG
2   SET TALK OFF
3   ERASE
4   USE B:HGQUES INDEX B:HGQUES
5   STORE ' ' TO WATE
6   STORE ' ' TO RESP
7   STORE ' ' TO RESP1
8   DO WHILE .NOT. RESP$ 'PS'
9   @ 22,0 SAY 'OUTPUT TO PRINTER OR TO SCREEN (P/S)  ' GET RESP
10  READ
11  STORE !(RESP) TO RESP
12  ENDDO
13  IF RESP = 'P'
14  @ 23,0 SAY 'PREPARE PRINTER, PRESS RETURN KEY WHEN READY' GET WATE
15  READ
16  ERASE
17  REPORT FORM B:HGOTQ FOR FLD3 = 'O' TO PRINT
18  ELSE
19  ERASE
20  DO WHILE .NOT. EOF
21  REPORT FORM B:HGOTQ FOR FLD3 = 'O' NEXT 10 PLAIN
22  @ 23,0 SAY 'PRESS RETURN KEY TO CONTINUE OR  X  TO EXIT' GET RESP1
23  READ
24  IF RESP1 = 'X'
25  ERASE
26  RETURN
27  ENDIF
28  ERASE
29  SKIP
30  ENDDO WHILE NOT EOF
31  ENDIF RESP = 'P'
32  RETURN
```

FIGURE 14.11. (*Continued*) **dBase II. (b) Sample program.**

The REPORT FORM statement on line 21 tells the computer to go to disk drive B and find the report form which is named HGOTQ. Also notice the statement NEXT 10; it limits the number of lines that appear on the screen. Without NEXT 10 the program would just scroll on by and keep on rolling. With NEXT 10, it stops after ten records and waits for a pressing of the return key or an X key. The word PLAIN on line 21 deletes such information as the date and headings which are normally sent to the printer.

Line 22 of the program positions the message enclosed within single quotes on the twenty-third line of the monitor and accepts the response from the user, as shown on line 23 of the program.

Line 24 tests the response. If the user depresses an X key, the screen is cleared and a return is made to the control module, which in turn stops processing (lines 24, 25, 26, and 27). The RETURN on lines 26 and 32 is a command in dBASE II, which is a user's way of communicating with the data base management system. The computer exits this program and goes to whatever program called this program for execution. In effect, this entire program is a subroutine which is a small program usable by others for processing some particular task.

Referring to line 28, if the response is not an X, the screen is cleared. On line 29, SKIP causes the computer to input the next record since the program is still inside the DO WHILE .NOT. EOF loop.

ENDDO, on line 30, causes the computer to go back to the beginning of the loop since we are not yet at the end of the file. Ten records are outputted. The computer waits for the response, and if it does not get an X, it skips one record, goes to the top of the screen, and prints the next ten questions.

Notice how the ENDDO WHILE NOT EOF, on line 30, is used. This programmer likes to label each ENDDO the same as its starting DO. This simplifies program review and debugging, by making it easier to identify which DO is matched with which ENDDO.

ENDIF RESP = 'P', on line 31, ends (closes) the IF statement shown on line 13. Here again, the RESP = 'P' is used to help the programmer match the end of the range of the IF that was started by IF RESP = 'P'.

RETURN on line 32 puts the computer back again to the menu after all records are processed.

SUMMARY

• Using file management, a programmer sorts, compares, and merges files to establish relationships—associations of meaningful data as used in everyday activities.

• Relationships are limited under file management to those written in a program. Other desired relationships are frequently not processed because of the cost of hardware and programming.

• The advantages of using a data base are many, such as data integrity and security; non-redundant data; sharing data; reducing requirements for secondary storage; data independence; data relatability; and dumping, backup, and recovery routines.

- Data integrity refers to the accuracy of data and to the protecting of data from accidental destruction.

- Data security is provided to protect the data base from unauthorized users by the use of passwords and software locks.

- Using a data base keeps redundant data to a minimum since users share common data.

- Sharing data is a primary concern in using a data base.

- Data independence is the separation of data from the computer hardware. The user is not concerned with the physical devices or physical specifications, but is only concerned with logical aspects. Limitations built into the data base management system, however, prevent this from being totally achieved.

- Data relatability is an important aspect of using a data base, as it provides a means of tying various logical files together. It provides an effective management information system environment.

- Dumping, backup, and recovery are provided in a data base management system for rebuilding the data base in case of a system failure.

- Data integration is a key ingredient in data base technology. This is accomplished when data is viewed logically rather than physically.

- The only person at the computer installation who actually deals with physical records is the data base administrator (DBA), whose role is to set up, maintain, and administer the data base. He or she sets up the physical records by preparing the data definition language (DDL).

- The programmer deals with logical records and prepares the data manipulation language (DML) so the applications program can transfer the data to the data base management system.

- The data base management system handles the creation, maintenance, and retrieval of physical records on magnetic disk.

- The data base management system provides the interface so the operating system, the applications program, and the data base can work in harmony.

- The data dictionary, used by the data base administrator, contains the documentation of the system. In some data base management systems, the data dictionary is an integral part, while others do not use it at all. The usage depends upon the availability of money to spend on a data base system.

- The data dictionary holds the data relationships that are established for a particular job's processing requirements.

- Physical records are often linked together by pointers that can be included in the record. These pointers are called linked lists.

- Data can be viewed logically by three data structures: network, hierarchical, and relational. All three structures place importance on basic data (the root) and separate the variable data (the transactions) from the basic data.

- The network data structure allows a user to enter the data base in any of the several logical files used.

- The hierarchical data structure allows a user to enter the data base through the main part, called the root. The user must proceed further along the tree-like (branching) structure to find more detailed data.

- The relational data structure uses a table to display data to a user. A relational data structure uses a flat file structure.

STUDY GUIDE

REVIEW OF TERMINOLOGY

The following terminology was discussed in this chapter:

data base
data base administrator
  (DBA)
data base management
  system (DBMS)
data base model
data definition language
  (DDL)
data dictionary
data elements
data independence
data integrity
data manipulation
  language (DML)
data relatability

data structures
dBASE II
flat file structure
hierarchical data structure
linked lists
network data structure
query language
redundant data
relational data structure
report generator
root
schema
subschema
tree structure

MULTIPLE CHOICE

Circle the letter of the item that correctly completes each statement.

1. The data that is shared by the users at a company is called:
   a. a data base
   b. a data model
   c. schema
   d. subschema
   e. tree structure

2. When data is repeated many times, the data is considered to be:
   a. logical
   b. physical
   c. redundant
   d. modelled
   e. linked

3. When data is accurately remembered, the data has:
   a. redundancy
   b. relatability
   c. integrity
   d. recovery
   e. linking

4. Associations are made as to how we wish to look at the data. The data has:
   a. integrity
   b. independence
   c. recovery elements
   d. redundancy
   e. relatability

5. A data base is often copied in case of machine failure. The process of protecting the data in the data base is done by:
   a. dump and
     recovery
   b. data manipulation
     language and
     data definition
     language
   c. query and
     generators
   d. schema and
     subschema
   e. flat file structures

6. The person who creates the data base is the:
   a. data base
     management
     system
   b. data base
     administrator
   c. programmer
   d. user
   e. end-user

7. The physical records (used for defining how the data is set up) are called the:

a. root
b. table
c. schema

d. subschema
e. data model

8. A user or a programmer uses only these for accessing data in a data base:
a. root
b. table
c. schema

d. subschema
e. report generator

9. When data elements are grouped together to form data relationships, the logical linking is called:
a. relatability
b. a data structure
c. integrity

d. a data model
e. recovery

10. The data base administrator uses this to set up the physical records:
a. DML
b. data manipulation language
c. data dictionary

d. report generator
e. flat file structure

11. A programmer uses this to see what data relationships are already set up in the data base:
a. data model
b. data dictionary
c. schema

d. query language
e. DBA

12. The entry point is at the root; the more detailed data branch out from the root. This structure describes a:
a. network data structure
b. linked lists
c. relational data structure

d. hierarchical data structure
e. data base management system

13. An end-user can set up his or her own data relationships by using:
a. a data dictionary
b. dump recovery
c. a query language

d. a linked list
e. data manipulation language

14. Pointers included in records, that then provide means of linking the physical records along a single data path, are called:
a. DDL
b. DML
c. DBMS

d. DBA
e. linked lists

TRUE/FALSE QUESTIONS

Circle T if the statement is true; F if it is false.

1. **T/F** For new data relationships to be set up under file management, the data requires sorting, comparing, merging, and making new files.
2. **T/F** Data relationships can be set up under file management, but the problem is the programming time involved and the extreme high cost.
3. **T/F** An effective management information system can be accomplished by having data shared and related among many files.
4. **T/F** Data security is a problem when using a data base.
5. **T/F** Data independence means that no department updates its own data.
6. **T/F** Data in a data base is viewed logically by users rather than physically.
7. **T/F** When data is viewed logically, this means that the user is only interested in setting up the desired data relationships so data can be accessed.
8. **T/F** The data base administrator is the only person who generally works with the data's physical setup.
9. **T/F** The data base management system handles the creation, updating, and maintaining of data in a data base.
10. **T/F** The data base management system gets its instructions on what to do from the data base administrator writing the data definition language.
11. **T/F** Programmers write data manipulation language to access the data and set up data relationships.
12. **T/F** End-users are only concerned with writing query languages for accessing the data base.
13. **T/F** Writing in query languages requires programming experience.
14. **T/F** A network data structure allows a user flexibility in accessng data by allowing the user to work with several logically related files.
15. **T/F** A hierarchical data structure requires that a

user understand the way that data are related.

16. **T/F** A relational data base is less costly and more efficient to use on a computer system than other data structures.

17. **T/F** Regardless of the way that data is viewed logically, linked lists are still used as a means of navigating (passing) through the data base.

ANSWERS

Multiple Choice: 1. **a** 2. **c** 3. **c** 4. **e** 5. **a** 6. **b** 7. **c** 8. **d** 9. **b** 10. **c** 11. **b** 12. **d** 13. **c** 14. **e** *True/ False:* 1. **T** 2. **T** 3. **T** 4. **T** 5. **F** 6. **T** 7. **T** 8. **T** 9. **T** 10. **T** 11. **T** 12. **T** 13. **F** 14. **T** 15. **T** 16. **F** 17. **T**

REVIEW QUESTIONS

1. Define each of the following terms: data independence, data integrity, data relatability, data security, and data recovery.

2. What are the advantages of using a data base? Why is each advantageous characteristic important?

3. Who is a DBA? What does a DBA do?

4. What is a network data structure? How does a user get at the data using such a structure?

5. What is a hierarchical data structure? How does the user get at the data in this instance?

6. What is a relational data structure? Why does this data structure have such high overhead?

DISCUSSION QUESTIONS

1. A data base system consists of several parts. Describe these.

2. Contrast the three types of data structures.

3. Discuss the advantages and disadvantages of using a data base.

4. Can you envision ever using a data base with your personal computer? Explain your answer.

PROJECTS

1. The *Congressional Record* is published for the general public giving information on the activities of Congress with regards to bills and voting records of the various congressmen. Play the role of the data base administrator and determine various relationships that could be meaningful for the voting public at election time.

2. You are a school administrator who has just been appointed to determine what new courses should be offered at your college. These are to be set up as short-term courses. The only restriction placed on you by the governing board is that you must hire instructors who already are part of the faculty to teach these courses. How can you make use of the data base to solve this problem?

3. Investigate some of the large corporations which are using data bases and are located in your area. Discuss ways in which their various departments share data.

People in Computing

Mark A. Masson

COMPANY:
Cincom Systems, Inc.

POSITION:
Manager, Level-I Support Center

EDUCATIONAL BACKGROUND:
Bachelor of Arts, St. Joseph College

I joined Cincom Systems in 1980 as a programmer/analyst in the internal data processing group called Corporate Systems & Programming. My work involved gathering requirements from users, developing and designing the system, and then programming it. For example, we developed an on-line customer information system that enabled Cincom's field offices to access and update information about their customers. Such information included the type of hardware each customer used, the other Cincom products used, other competitive products used, and the customer name and address information. These categories of information provided the means of searching a data base.

I have also performed in the role of teacher and consultant for such Cincom clients as Xerox, ACLI International, and the Department of Defense. I also have developed a media management system which lets libraries put books in the system. It replaces the use of the card catalog and prepares reports on circulation and budgeting. I used dBase II for the data base management system. Currently, I am rewriting the application programs used in the library application into a language called Pascal so the program executes faster.

I am also developing the first level of a multi-tiered customer support structure at Cincom. Level-I will screen all incoming customer calls and resolve them if possible. Those that can't be resolved in a timely manner will be dispatched to four other technical service centers (in Cincinnati, Fairfax, St. Louis, and San Francisco). This project is being put in place to improve the level of service we provide our customers.

Our goal is to provide quick response to customer problems. For example, a high-priority problem such as a down-production system will require a fast response from Cincom in order to get the customer back up and running. A down-production system would result from a data base software bug or a hardware problem. Maybe the magnetic disk drives had a crash or invalid data was transmitted by a surge in the line.

Working in a data base environment is very challenging because it requires that we coordinate all of the users' information needs. We must continually try to get all the requirements together by developing a system that meets these needs.

Verbal and written communication are the two most important skills for individuals entering the data processing field. Good conceptual skills and a desire to never stop learning come in second.

My philosophy about data processing and life is "knowledge transferrence." Simply stated, this is the concept that "knowledge greatly increases in value when shared with others." Success in data processing demands that we develop our ability to share ideas with others.

15 Systems Analysis and Design

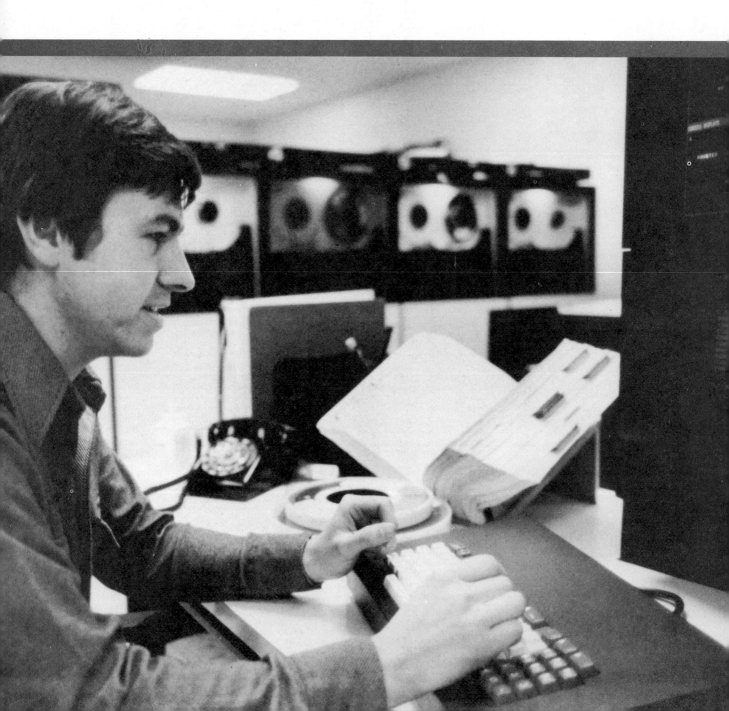

OUTLINE

PROLOGUE

"Hello, Ron. This is Jack Spencer in Buying. Got a minute? I've got a problem."

"You know how short Z Paper Company is on supplies lately. I overheard from the competition, of all things, that Z is allowing any of its privileged customers to first query the data base to see if enough paper is on hand to ship before the customer orders. That way it saves us the trouble of placing an order if it can't be filled. If they don't have the paper, we can seek another supplier. As I understand it, all that we must do is to identify our account number, the computer sees that we are a privileged account, and then we find out if there is enough stock for our needs. But, I understand, we must set up the necessary hardware and software to make this thing work. You know me about computers! Can you help me?"

"Jack, we need to talk and find out the details. We'll get on it tomorrow."

HOW DOES IT DO THAT?

READ ON.

OBJECTIVES

After studying this chapter, you should be able to:

1. Describe the traits that a successful systems analyst should possess.

2. Explain what a life cycle is.

3. Differentiate between the preliminary analysis and the feasibility study.

4. Describe the activities involved in the systems design stage.

5. Explain how a system progresses through the development phase.

6. Explain the activities involved in the implementation and execution phase.

7. Explain why the systems analyst's job is never finished.

INTRODUCTION

The ever-changing world of computers continually makes demands for change. Some uses of computers must be updated; others require the initial use. The evolution of change is discussed in this chapter from the standpoint of how it is evaluated, undertaken, and accomplished.

ROLE OF SYSTEMS ANALYST

A system is a group of interrelated elements or activities that operate in an environment to some common purpose. For a successful system to operate, goals must be clearly established. The system maintains itself as it becomes self-regulating; that is, it adjusts and corrects itself according to the feedback that is provided. Nothing in this world is static; any viable system keeps adjusting and changing to meet new needs and demands. Change in a business organization is, therefore, inevitable. To meet the new needs change causes, **analysis** is done; that is, a problem is studied before any action is taken. The person, who does the analysis and who develops and designs the system, is called the **systems analyst.**

For a successful system to exist, the activities in the business organization must be interrelated in such a way as to run smoothly. Different departments or individuals should not pull against the managerial decisions that are made to influence change in the company. There has to be one individual who serves as the agent of change and bridges the gap between management and the staff when new policies are implemented or developed. The systems analyst is the person who provides such an interface. At the same time, however, the systems analyst is the very person who brings about change. The change is not for change's sake but for efficiency and better operation of the organization. The systems analyst is in the unique position of trying to satisfy both management, which decides if the system is to be implemented, and staff, who must follow the directives.

Unless an atmosphere of teamwork exists in a business organization, any new system is doomed to difficult times or failure. Often a system will fail because its users do not like it or management does not feel a total commitment to it. As we will discuss in this chapter, the systems analyst's position is to keep the communication lines open among all personnel in the company. At the same time, the analyst must provide a system that is usable, acceptable, and workable.

Before any new system is implemented, a thorough analysis must be done. The analyst's position is one of liaison between the application and the available technology. The systems analyst is the architect of the system—its hardware, software, programming languages, and standards. The user knows best how the business operates, while the systems analyst knows best how to accomplish the operation. The systems analyst must provide services to the many users at the company, shaping the system to satisfy all users.

PERSONAL CHARACTERISTICS NEEDED BY A SYSTEMS ANALYST

The systems analyst must have very good communication skills, both orally and in writing. He or she must collect facts through questionnaires or interviews, or both. The interviews are usually conducted in an informal way, so as not to strain relationships between the user and the analyst. After the interview, the analyst makes recordings of facts and observations. Often, the analyst will spend time observing operations within departments to detect any noticeable bottlenecks that can be alleviated. These observations and results from interviews and questionnaires are combined, studied, and used to compile written reports for management use. Many times these facts are given to management in the form of a presentation, where charts, visual aids, and graphs are displayed and discussed to help management in reaching a decision as to whether the system should be implemented.

The systems analyst must be tactful and pleasant to work with, since most of the job responsibilities require working with people. People resist change, fear losing jobs, and fear the unknown; these human reactions make the job of the analyst more difficult. A good analyst never loses sight of these points.

CHECKPOINT **Can you:**

Identify the desirable traits of a good systems analyst?

LIFE CYCLE OF A SYSTEM

A **life cycle,** those many changes in form that exist from the beginning to the end of a series, is evident in all aspects of our world. Data processing is no exception, and the systems analyst uses a highly structured life cycle in his or her work. There are four phases in the system life cycle: the problem definition phase, the design phase, the development phase, and the implementation and execution phase. Often the phases tend to overlap each other as the system is conceptualized, designed, and developed. Let us investigate each of these phases, noting the work involved in each. Figure 15.1 gives an overview of the four phases.

CHECKPOINT **Can you:**

Tell what a life cycle is?
Name the phases of a system's life cycle?

FIGURE 15.1
The four phases of the life cycle.

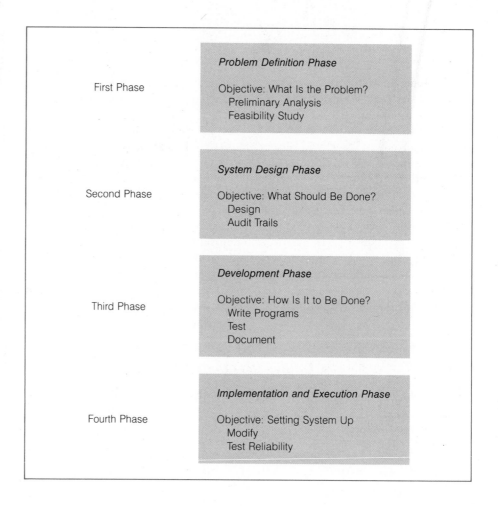

First Phase

Problem Definition Phase

Objective: What Is the Problem?
  Preliminary Analysis
  Feasibility Study

Second Phase

System Design Phase

Objective: What Should Be Done?
  Design
  Audit Trails

Third Phase

Development Phase

Objective: How Is It to Be Done?
  Write Programs
  Test
  Document

Fourth Phase

Implementation and Execution Phase

Objective: Setting System Up
  Modify
  Test Reliability

PROBLEM DEFINITION PHASE

The **problem definition phase** can involve two levels of analysis, depending upon the outcome of the initial one. First, interviews are conducted for a preliminary analysis. Second, if necessary, a feasibility study is conducted.

Many times a department alerts the systems analyst to some operational problem. Perhaps the department wishes to have on-line processing capability or needs other information for adequate management decision making. It may be that the current systems approach is outdated, stressing record-keeping more than the availability of information to the users of a department. Possibly the department wishes more information than it has available in the current system. With additional information, the department head feels he or she could evaluate more efficiently consumer trends and preferences for a product. This additional information could prove profitable to the company since aligning products with the trends could lead to recapture of lost business. Perhaps all the department needs is a faster way of receiving information.

GALLERY 9

Office of the Future

Places of work have changed drastically in appearance. The filing cabinets and typewriters are being replaced with terminals and workstations. As offices change in outward appearance, the workers must change to meet the new technology head-on to take advantage of the technology and not be swept away by it.

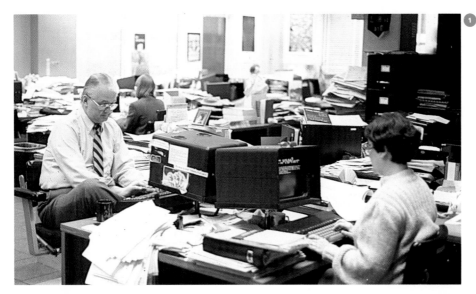

1. Reporters use computers for aiding them in the preparation of their articles. The reporters article preparation is made easier through the use of a word processing program and a data base for historical facts. **2.** The facsimile machine has been used in offices for years for generating hard copy. The electronic transmission of documents, however, has greatly increased in the past several years. **3.** As homes become the workplace of many individuals, the home becomes known as an electronic cottage.

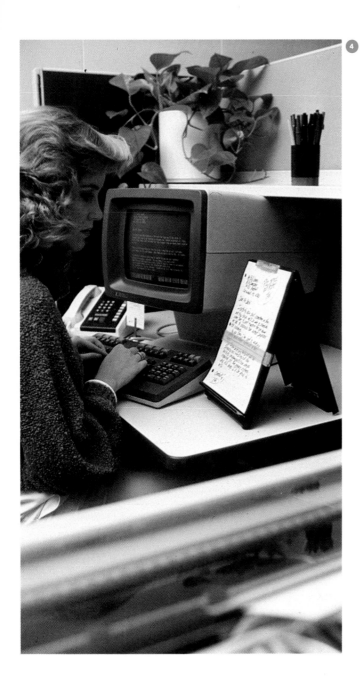

4. Typewriters have been replaced by terminals or personal computers. 5. Although a secretary's duties of preparing letters is still prominent, the tide is shifting to executives doing their letter writing. 6. Personal computers are used in offices for the preparation of customer bills and correspondence.

7. People of all ages have the opportunity to produce programs at home for self-satisfaction as well as for profit. 8. Personal computers offer those people, whose responsibilities require them to be at home, to be part of the world of work. 9. A couple uses a computer at home for the preparation of the financial status of their company and for aiding them in decision making of future transactions.

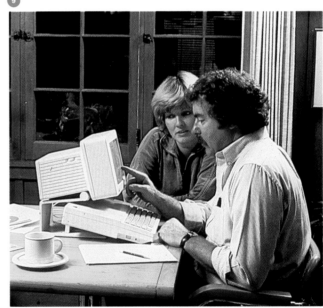

10. Users of personal computers find that generating histograms and pie-shaped graphs of important data makes communication easier. **11.** Computers are used for generating graphs by executives for that all-important business meeting. **12.** Computer generated graphics makes a very effective and impressive presentation.

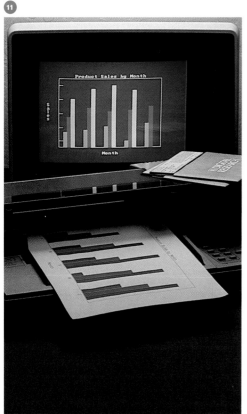

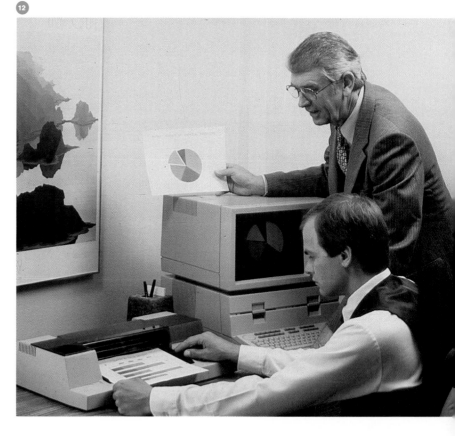

13. Law offices use computers for preparation of wills and legal forms. The data base aids tremendously in the searching of records for previous rulings. **14.** Workstations are used by executives for preparation of documents, signalling of meetings, inquiring the computer, and for receiving and forwarding electronic messages.

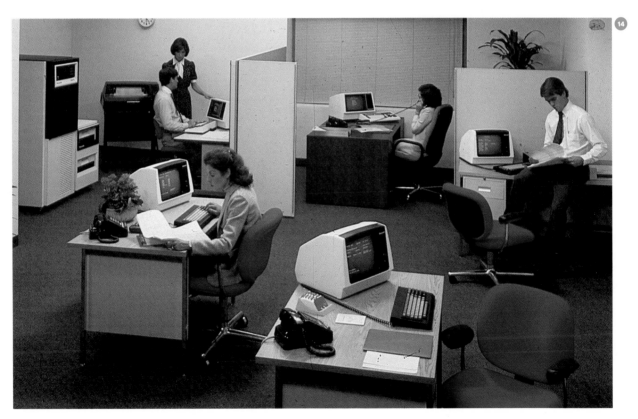

15. As middle-level management and top-level management become more accustomed to using a computer, the management information system becomes more important and useful to all in the company. **16.** Executives use computers for generating those much needed reports when the need for information arises. **17.** The computer becomes an executive's electronic briefcase.

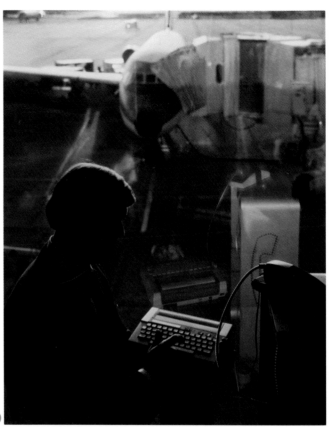

18. The need for information and for filing of reports often takes place at unusual locations. Portable computers offer these opportunities. **19.** A freelance artist uses a computer to keep track of expenses and hours. **20.** A cattle farm in Missouri puts the Apple II to use.

21. Through the use of the computer's tremendous speed and storage capabilities, decision support tools for management are readily available. The executive can organize, manipulate, and extract the information needed for effective planning and controlling the business.
22. Business executives use their computers at business meetings and conventions.

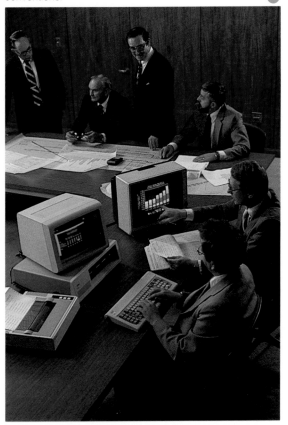

Preliminary Analysis

The typical day in the life of the systems analyst involves communication with nontechnical people—both management and staff—who have a technical problem. It is the systems analyst's job to think the problem through. When a need is communicated to the systems analyst, an initial investigation is started, which is referred to as a **preliminary analysis.**

Let us assume the users have expressed a need to the systems analyst. The expressed need must be closely analyzed to determine what the problem really is and how it can best be solved. Sometimes the preliminary analysis can present an easy solution, and the analyst need only suggest some modification of current procedures. Sometimes, however, the constraints (limitations) placed upon the users and the analyst by management make the needs of the users impractical or impossible to meet. If the needs of the user do bear investigation, the analyst looks into the problem from a cost standpoint. Projected costs must be considered, as hardware, software, and overhead costs will weigh heavily upon the decision to solve, modify, or forget this problem. Some of the factors that influence the systems analyst's decision at this preliminary analysis stage are shown in Figure 15.2(a), with the recommendations shown in Figure 15.2(b).

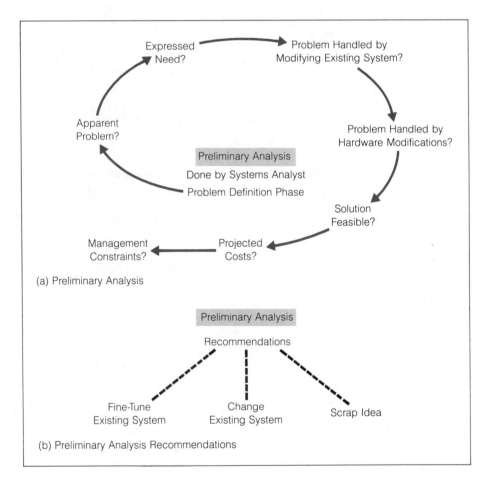

FIGURE 15.2
Stages of Preliminary analysis.

Feasibility Study

The recommendations that result from the preliminary analysis may produce a decision to conduct a **feasibility study**—a very detailed analysis of the problem. The study is usually conducted with a panel of company executives, users, systems specialists, and the systems analyst. It is important that the panel consist of highly trained and knowledgeable individuals since any system change in the organization can be very costly.

In the past, the systems analyst was the only interface between the users and the system. Today, however, the systems analyst cannot be knowledgeable in all technical fields. With the tremendous technological expansion and the ever-increasing demand for computer usage, the systems analyst must consult with specialists in various aspects of the technology. These specialists analyze the aspect of the problem fitting their expertise, decide whether the desired solution can be accomplished, and determine if it fits within the constraints set up by management.

The feasibility team, because of its important work, needs individuals who can cooperate and communicate. The team must determine the needs of the user and the way the proposed system meets those needs. The recommendations of this team can have an impact company-wide, for there might be a need for new equipment, requiring retraining of existing personnel, or possibly the hiring of new personnel. The recommendations could also lead to the replacing of some personnel. It is the feasibility team's responsibility to make the final recommendation as to whether the proposed plan is to be implemented. The team might suggest modifications to the current system so that it can operate efficiently and still meet the needs of the users without having a major impact upon the business organization.

A summary of the problem definition phase is shown in Figure 15.3.

CHECKPOINT **Can you:**

Differentiate between the preliminary analysis and the feasibility study?

SYSTEMS DESIGN PHASE

How much does the new system cost? This is a vital question. The proposed system must be judged to be cost justifiable by weighing the current system's costs against the proposed system's cost. The proposed system will probably demand a large amount of money, which necessitates a careful study of the break-even point for comparable cost of the current and the proposed systems.

What are the advantages of the proposed system? Will the users accept it? Both of these questions need answering. Acceptance by the users of the new system can make or break it. The new system certainly must possess simplicity and flexibility. Feedback (give and take) also must be an integral part of the new system so that changes and modifications can be ongoing.

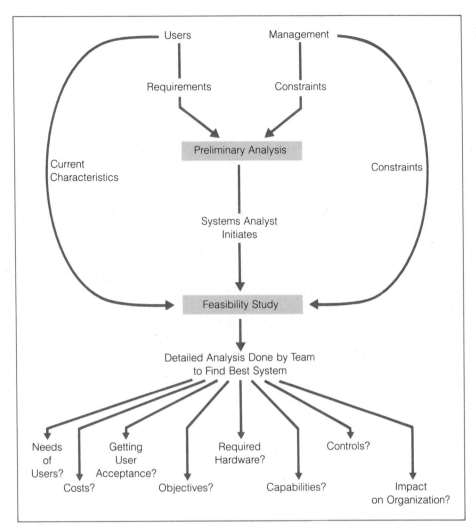

FIGURE 15.3
Problem definition phase.

Planning and development of the actual mechanics of the system operation and how the work is processed is referred to as the **systems design.** The design of the proposed system requires extensive planning, taking into consideration the objectives of the system, what constraints are imposed, what output is needed, what input is to be used, which computer language is used for programming, and how the logic is to be structured. These require close scrutiny for an accurate and thorough treatment of the problem. Changing the system to meet one department's needs might disrupt another department's needs; the entire organization's integrated functioning must be considered. An overview of the results that should be achieved in the systems design is shown in Figure 15.4.

The **systems design phase** includes important decisions regarding input, output, data structure, system controls and backups, scheduling of jobs, and costs. Just planning the input and output data is not enough. The data structure must also be planned. The systems analyst must determine if data is to be set up in a data base format or as files. Data will have to be interrogated, so the users must

FIGURE 15.4
Designing the system.

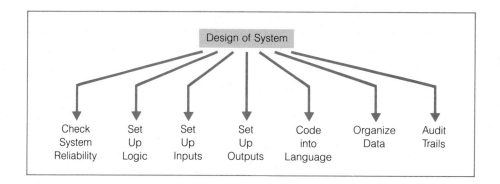

be able to reference the data without problems. The systems analyst decides how records can be deleted from the data structure, changed, or added to it. Very careful planning is needed since the analyst must know how the users wish to use the data and what data they normally seek. The analyst establishes ways that data are associated or related by the users, then determines how the data is referenced. For example, in a school environment, data is referenced by student identification number, that being the key that ties the data together. In a personnel office, the employee number or social security number becomes the key for relating such data as the name, address, salary, department, skill, years of service and so on.

The new system must also have controls to determine the accuracy of the data. The controls must be built into the system. Audit trails are used to check the efficiency and the accurateness of the system. Usually a magnetic tape is written of all the data as it flows into the system. The magnetic tape is read by an audit program, which checks the accuracy of the system.

The outputs are evaluated as to what is needed to be accomplished, what information is needed by the various users, and what the information means to them. The systems analyst sets up printer spacing charts and cathode ray tube screen displays which give prompts and menus. The design of the inputs depends largely upon what processing is desired and what output is to be generated. The source document that is used for recording the original data is set up by the systems analyst so that it is easily read when the data is keyed from it.

The more specifications that are clearly laid out in this phase, the easier the job of developing the system and testing the system later to determine its effectiveness.

CHECKPOINT **Can you:**

Identify the activities involved in the design phase?

DEVELOPMENT PHASE

The **development phase** involves such important aspects as scheduling the work, programming the project, testing, and documenting the system.

The development phase involves hardware and software considerations that have required time schedules. Any hardware that must be purchased or leased is ordered, and, often, a new office layout must be set up.

As far as software is concerned, the detailed logic as to how the system is to operate must be planned. Several tools are available for this planning: systems flowcharts, application flowcharts, structure charts, pseudocode, and decision tables (discussed in Chapter 11).

Refer to Figure 15.5, noting that the **systems flowchart** deals with the overall

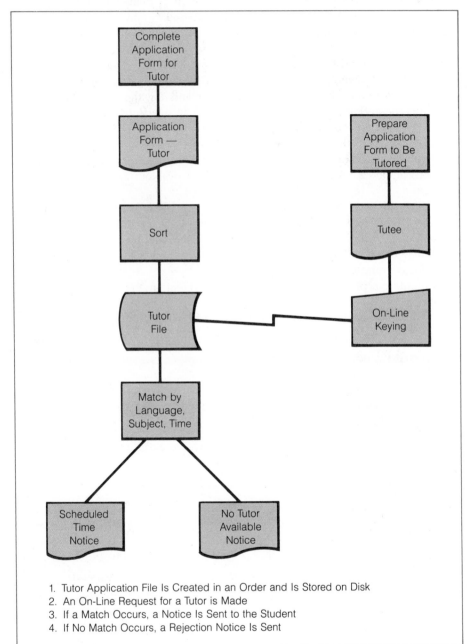

FIGURE 15.5
Systems flowchart.

1. Tutor Application File Is Created in an Order and Is Stored on Disk
2. An On-Line Request for a Tutor is Made
3. If a Match Occurs, a Notice Is Sent to the Student
4. If No Match Occurs, a Rejection Notice Is Sent

ideas of the operation of the system and how the system parts fit together for the flow of data.

The systems analyst determines the detailed specifications that must be followed by the programmers to meet the systems requirements. Since the systems analyst is the interface between the corporate management, the programmers, and the users, he or she must respond to the needs for information or clarification. The progress of the programs in development must be evaluated for meeting target dates. At the same time, the analyst must establish a basis for determining the reliability of the new system by building in checks which show whether the new system is dependable and operates as intended.

Documentation encompasses all the written words and graphical representation that show what is being done in the system. It includes a graphical analysis of the proposed logic to design the system, the printer spacing charts, the pseudocode, the debugged programs, examples of the input and output data, and the written words to tell what is being accomplished and how the system should work.

Documentation reaches into different areas of the business organization. What are the clerical procedures? Where is the data prepared? What are the corporate procedures? All of these questions must be answered. Documentation also tells the computer operator what should be done at certain points in the processing of the application. Alternative steps are given if a problem exists in running the program.

All of this work involved in the development phase is set up with carefully laid out time schedules. A time schedule for hardware delivery and software completion is evaluated and set. The system is tested first by testing the programs individually and then grouping them. Next, the system is set up on a small scale as a pilot system, where all aspects are checked to make certain it works. By first implementing a pilot or small-scale model, the company may avert many future headaches.

A summary of the development phase is shown in Table 15.1.

CHECKPOINT **Can you:**

Identify the activities involved in the development phase?
State why each is important?

TABLE 15.1. **Development Phase Summary.**

TIME SCHEDULES	LOGIC DEVELOPMENT	TESTING	DOCUMENTATION
• Hardware	• Systems flowchart	• Individual programs	• Clerical
• Software	• Structure charts	• Pilot or small-scale testing of system	• Data preparation
	• Application flowcharts or pseudocode	• The complete system	• Corporate procedures
	• Decision tables		• Computer operations

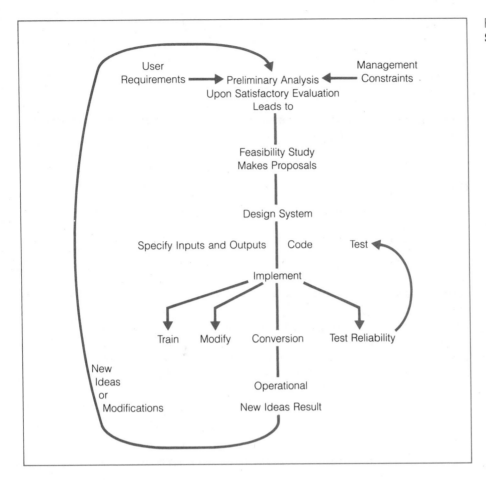

FIGURE 15.6
Systems implementation.

IMPLEMENTATION AND EXECUTION PHASE

The proposed system is now ready to be processed on the computer. Figure 15.6 shows the progression to the **implementation and execution phase** as well as its purpose. This stage is one of modifying and testing the reliability of the new system. **Conversion** refers to the changeover from the existing system to the new system. The files, procedures, standards, and programs must be converted to handle the new system. The changeover from the old to the new system can be done in stages. One option, in which the old system runs at the same time as the new system, is called **parallel conversion.** After an application is successfully converted to the new system, another application is then changed over. **Direct conversion** works more abruptly; the old computer system is immediately replaced with the new system's hardware and programs.

Training personnel about the new system is a very important aspect of implementing the system because the users will determine the system's success or failure. The new procedures that have been documented are discussed in detail. During the changeover to the new system, personnel must be instructed as to how data is collected and edited, the codes that are to be used, the required format of data for programs, and the various required program runs needed to accomplish the reports.

How do you know the new system works? The systems analyst must use the tools of auditing, evaluation, and maintenance to make certain everything is working as planned. Any problem areas must be cleared up to the satisfaction of both management and staff.

CHECKPOINT Can you:

Tell what is involved in the implementation and execution phase?

Differentiate between parallel conversion and direct conversion?

OPERATION OF THE SYSTEM

When the system becomes operative, there is a constant ongoing evaluation as to the success of the system. Reliability of the system is continually being tested. When modifications are found to be needed, the entire process of going through the life cycle stages is then followed to make certain that the proposals are needed, are within the constraints of the system, and meet the desired current characteristics needed by users in the system.

It is clear from this description that the work of the systems analyst is ever challenging and ongoing.

CHECKPOINT Can you:

Explain why a systems analyst's job is never finished?

TABLE 15.2. **Comparison of Disadvantages in Options Changing an Existing System.**

DEVELOP FROM SCRATCH	BUY A PACKAGE	MODIFY PACKAGE
1. Long development time	1. Must alter company policies to fit designed system	1. Need for additional reports or changing of reports
2. Extremely costly	2. Cost savings from purchase of package offset by costs to alter company policies and procedures	2. Need to change screen formats for data entry
3. Error prone to improper definition of system	3. Package may prove unsatisfactory	3. Need for additional file or files than what is proposed
4. Users might not accept system		4. Vendor help in making desired modifications may be offset by cost of changes made by vendor
5. Needs program maintenance later to keep current		

Table 15.2 lists disadvantages or possible drawbacks to consider when deciding which option to take in changing an existing system: (1) develop a new system, (2) buy a package from a manufacturer, or (3) modify the existing system.

SUMMARY

- For an information system to be an effective tool of management, data must be used in different ways to solve existing problems. Data must be analyzed for possible answers where data otherwise might not be investigated.

- The process of systems analysis must be done in a systematic and highly structured manner.

- Four phases make up the life cycle for systems analysis: the problem definition phase, design phase, development phase, and implementation and execution phase.

- The problem definition phase involves two types of analysis: the preliminary analysis and the feasibility study.

- The preliminary analysis involves initial interviews with users who probably desire additional computing power or wish to change some existing procedure.

- The systems analyst must determine the requirements of all users as well as the constraints set up by management. The judgment must be made as to whether a user request is justified as far as costs and efficiency of the company's operation are concerned.

- When the preliminary analysis produces satisfactory options, a feasibility study is undertaken to provide a very detailed analysis of the proposed system.

- Proposals for the new system must consider the desired objectives, the necessary controls, the mandated constraints, the costs for the new system versus the old system, and the capabilities that are to be included.

- The design phase of the system includes setting up the inputs and outputs, coding the program, testing the logic, and checking the reliability of the system. The hardware, although specified in general terms in the feasibility study, must be selected.

- The development phase involves the purchasing or leasing of the hardware. Documentation is an ongoing process but has its finishing touches placed on it at this time. For example, such documentation is needed for the computer operator's successful operation.

- The implementation and execution phase involves the conversion to the new system.

- Direct conversion can be used, in which case the changeover is done at once with the old system being replaced entirely. Other times parallel conversion is used; this means the application is converted by stages, with the old and new system operating simultaneously.

STUDY GUIDE

REVIEW OF TERMINOLOGY

The following terminology was discussed in this chapter:

analysis
conversion
development phase
direct conversion
feasibility study
implementation and
  execution phase
life cycle

parallel conversion
preliminary analysis
problem definition phase
systems analysis
systems analyst
systems design
systems design phase
systems flowchart

MULTIPLE CHOICE

Circle the letter of the item that correctly completes each statement.

1. Changes in form that evolve from the conception of an entity to its completion or end are known as the:
   a. design phase
   b. analysis
   c. life cycle
   d. audit trail
   e. preliminary analysis

2. Constraints upon users and the systems analyst are usually not relevant at this stage:
   a. life cycle
   b. feasibility study
   c. design phase
   d. implementation and execution phase
   e. preliminary analysis

3. A team is set up in this activity to suggest possible modifications, propose a new system, or to forget the whole idea:
   a. feasibility study
   b. design phase
   c. implementation phase
   d. operation phase
   e. preliminary analysis

4. Extensive documentation is prepared in the:
   a. feasibility study
   b. design phase
   d. development phase

   c. implementation phase
   e. future whenever the analyst and programmers have time

5. The system is checked for accuracy and efficiency in the:
   a. problem definition phase
   b. systems design phase
   c. development phase
   d. operation phase
   e. implementation and execution phase

6. A way of checking the system for accuracy is through the:
   a. systems analyst talking with management
   b. documentation
   c. feasibility team
   d. audit trails
   e. parallel conversion

7. Time schedules for hardware and software are set up in the:
   a. problem definition phase
   b. systems design phase
   c. life cycle
   d. development phase
   e. implementation phase

8. The overall ideas of how the system is to operate are shown on:
   a. a life cycle chart
   b. a systems flowchart
   c. an audit trail
   d. a systems design graph
   e. a feasibility study document

9. Training of personnel is involved in the:
   a. problem definition phase
   b. systems design phase
   c. implementation and execution phase
   d. operation phase
   e. feasibility study

10. The input and output, the data structure, and the system controls are some of the activities involved in the:
    a. implementation and execution phase
    b. execution phase
    c. systems design phase
    d. operation phase
    e. problem definition phase

11. The life cycle begins with the:

a. implementation phase
b. execution phase
c. systems design phase
d. operation phase
e. problem definition phase

12. The programming language to be used for coding the proposed system and the way the logic is to be solved are selected in the:
a. feasibility study
b. systems design phase
c. preliminary analysis
d. development phase
e. implementation phase

TRUE/FALSE QUESTIONS

Circle T if the statement is true; F if it is false.

1. **T/F** A system must always have a purpose.
2. **T/F** The systems analyst must know all things relating to data processing.
3. **T/F** The systems analyst must have a good background in business and data processing.
4. **T/F** A systems analyst makes changes, whether the changes are justifiable or not, since change keeps people on their toes.
5. **T/F** The personal characteristics of a systems analyst should be patience, friendliness, ability to listen, ability to communicate, and ability to provide services.
6. **T/F** Only systems analysis has a life cycle.
7. **T/F** The problem definition phase can stop the new system before it ever gets started.
8. **T/F** The problem definition phase includes a preliminary analysis and, possibly, a feasibility study.
9. **T/F** The feasibility study is conducted by a team of experts who evaluate whether the system can work in the company.
10. **T/F** The feasibility study is only concerned with the first-expressed needs of the department or departments that need some new proposals for change.
11. **T/F** The feasibility study might suggest scrapping the entire project because of management constraints.

12. **T/F** The way the system is to operate is set up in the feasibility study.
13. **T/F** When the system is designed, the input and output data formats are designed exclusively by the users.
14. **T/F** The design of the input is solely determined by how the data is to be entered.
15. **T/F** Job scheduling and system controls and design are important considerations when the system is designed.
16. **T/F** When the system is designed, considerations are given as to how the system is to be controlled and how backups are prepared in case of system failure.
17. **T/F** The systems analyst will report to management to answer questions on the system design.
18. **T/F** The systems analyst has full responsibility for reporting to management and following the management's directives as to whether the plan is to be developed or not.
19. **T/F** When the system is developed, schedules must be met for software and hardware.
20. **T/F** If the programmers fall behind in the schedule, the documentation is cancelled.
21. **T/F** Programmers should only test in their programs what they feel will work so that they can prove their effectiveness and productivity.
22. **T/F** Documentation is used for later reference if the existing system needs modification.
23. **T/F** When the system is implemented, the files are converted one at a time. This is known as direct conversion.
24. **T/F** The training of personnel is the last thing done before the system is implemented since the users probably will not be too happy about using it anyway.
25. **T/F** If the company is certain that the new system will work, parallel conversion must be done.
26. **T/F** Often a pilot run is made, which means that the new system is tested on a small scale.
27. **T/F** Once the new system is operative, it never needs changing.
28. **T/F** Without the systems analyst being able to gather data, prepare questionnaires, conduct interviews, and make intensive observations, much of the systems analyst's evaluation would be thwarted.

REVIEW QUESTIONS

1. What is meant by analysis?
2. What is meant by a life cycle?
3. Name the various phases of the life cycle as it applies to a development of a business system.
4. What is a preliminary analysis? Why is it used?
5. What are the possible conclusions reached from the preliminary analysis?
6. When is a feasibility study used? Who conducts this study?
7. What might be the conclusions reached from a feasibility study?
8. Why is the use of data so important in the systems design?
9. How can a system be checked to make certain it is operating as planned?
10. What is a systems flowchart? How does it differ from an applications flowchart?
11. In which phase are time schedules prepared? What do these time schedules pertain to?
12. What is documentation? Why is it needed?
13. What is meant by conversion? By parallel conversion? By direct conversion?

DISCUSSION QUESTIONS

1. Why is the job of systems analyst such an important one? What are some of the analyst's duties?
2. A systems analyst must be a well-adjusted person. Explain this statement, discussing the various roles of the analyst.
3. Explain how the life cycle concept applies to systems analysis. Identify the cycle stages and explain the purpose of each.
4. Contrast the preliminary analysis versus the feasibility study as far as types of information gathered and decisions made.
5. When detailed analysis is done, user acceptance, the necessary hardware, and the design of the system are of utmost importance. Explain why this is true.
6. Once the system is operational, is the systems analyst finished working with the project? Explain your answer.
7. Would you like to be a systems analyst someday? If so, what types of business and data processing experience would be most helpful to you in performing your duties?
8. The systems analyst is the catalyst of change. Explain this statement.
9. At which stage does the life cycle become technically oriented? Explain your answer.
10. Communication is a required skill for a successful analyst. When is this skill used by the systems analyst?

People in Computing

Ronald Armijo

COMPANY
Chevron Corporation

POSITION
Senior Systems Analyst

EDUCATIONAL BACKGROUND
Bachelor degrees in accounting and data processing, University of New Mexico

I enjoy being a systems analyst because it affords me a variety of assignments, as I adapt from one job environment to another. Great satisfaction is derived when I see clients use a system that solves their business problems and wonders how they ever did their work before having the system.

In analysis work, you really get a good look at how a company operates. You must find out exactly what the client is trying to do and how the problem can be solved by computer usage—if it can be, that is. In some cases, the solution may be a change in the way they operate rather than bringing in a new computer system.

My greatest challenges have centered on employee earnings, the corporation's accounting system, and marketing. The marketing project dealt with installing minicomputers at warehouses for an inventory control system for all of our packaged petroleum products plus our tires, batteries, and auto accessories. (TBA) I "lived" at the oil refinery for six months, looking at the current system and how a system could be developed for handling all facets of inventory control from production scheduling to product sales. This system dealt with capturing the data for the proposed sale, generating all documents, ordering of the item, and instructions for picking up the item and placing it on the conveyor belt for delivery to a certain customer. Customers call a number to place an order. The system checks the inventory on hand in case there is insufficient quantity to honor the order. If the item is not available, it is back-ordered.

The warehouse project was staffed with twelve people—Chevron employees and contractors. The contractors helped in the design but were used primarily for the programming. When implementation actually occurred, there was a coordinator and analyst at the warehouse site and also a client user who acted as trainer. All users of the new system were trained as to how orders are taken, how the warehouser uses the reports, and how management willl use the system. Every six months the inventory is physically counted and compared with the computer records. If there is any difference, the system is made current.

The warehouse project is part of the overall Chevron Product System that ultimately includes all bulk terminals that supply service stations with gasoline and jet fuel for airports—in fact, everything to do with marketing, pricing, and taxing for domestic petroleum and tires, batteries, and accessories products. It supports the Chevron, U.S.A., marketing policies.

The future for systems analysis is influenced by two factors. First is the basic formula for analysis work, which won't change. You identify the business need, the alternatives for satisfying the need (whether it is computer solvable or not), study the economies (whether it is justified), and then develop and implement the selected alternative.

On the other side of the coin, however, are the tools that are used. The tools get more sophisticated. The goals are improved productivity and better systems. Analysts are becoming more specialized. Even now, we have these specialists: the data base designer, a person who deals strictly with job control language; programmers at module level; and analysts to integrate the design. The position of analyst will continue to evolve at a higher level. We get more removed from the computer every day. I know the computer (a box) is out there somewhere; it is something that makes my terminal beep and places characters on my screen.

The pressures in the job will not noticeably change. The pressures placed upon the analyst come from two sources. From top management the pressure is to complete the job on time and to do it right. Many of the projects require quick solution. For example, government requirements must be handled promptly. The other pressure comes from business itself, which dictates the priority. One example deals with a personnel department needing an on-line system to maintain employee data. The software must be developed to support it. Changes in the market place present new opportunities for the company but may require quick access to large volumes of data. Computers can solve these problems which help improve the company's profits.

Our activities are committed for business, to support its needs in an efficient yet negotiable manner.

The Automated Office

OUTLINE

PROLOGUE

What a day Sally had at work today. First, she had to prepare a message to send electronically to London. Next, she typed a manuscript for her boss's article, which is to appear in the newspaper. After that, she set up the communication channels for the conference to be held at one o'clock.

After lunch, she had an electronic conference with the marketing department head who had many answers for her business problems. At three o'clock she began setting up the input for an application that the marketing manager told her how to do. Right now she begins preparing a speech on how to avoid stress in her job. She stops and sighs "Thank heavens, I didn't have to leave home today."

HOW DOES IT DO THAT?

READ ON.

OBJECTIVES

After studying this chapter, you should be able to:

1. Describe the office of the future.

2. Explain what is involved in the automated office.

3. Describe how the business environment must change to meet the challenges of the automated office.

4. Describe the roles of the data processing department, end-users, and decision support system.

5. Explain why the integration of the data processing department and the decision support systems is needed to provide a strong corporate strategy.

INTRODUCTION

Automation has had influences upon the way we work, live, and have fun. The home, too, is gradually being influenced. Some homes are becoming what is known as **electronic cottages;** that is, they are being used for office space. The electronic cottage term can also refer to a remote site that is used for housing office workers, usually in the suburbs, rather than in the downtown office building as was the rule for over fifty years. But the impact of automation has gone beyond that as offices are becoming highly integrated with computer hardware, software, and systems.

Let us think of the **automated office** as being that group of individuals who use computer hardware and software extensively to carry out everyday business activities. The automated office concept has been with us since the introduction of the terminal in the office. The automated office's major purpose is to increase productivity. When distributed data processing began, terminals appeared at many sites, thus changing office equipment somewhat. But this was just one step toward the fully automated office. More technology breakthroughs were needed; the microcomputer began the movement. In the 1970s, the automated office's theme centered on the use of word processing and microfilm.

The use of data bases, improved communication facilities, and the integration of voice and video all have had a profound influence upon the automated office. Evidence of that influence continues to increase, little by little. The filing cabinets are replaced by disk storage. The paper and pencils, calculators, and typewriters are replaced by workstations. The real growth probably will be in the next few years, however.

Much of the activity in the automated office centers around such work as typing, filing, communications, retrieving information, calculating, and preparing reports. The office areas that are then involved are those of the file clerks, book-keepers, secretaries, typists, bank tellers, and insurance workers, which account for about 35 percent of the jobs in the workforce. Many critics of the automated office feel that it destroys the variety of work that is available to the office worker by controlling the type of work that is to be done in the office. Workers in an automated office often express boredom and stress.

Certainly a retraining program must be undertaken to allow the workers displaced by automation to find their niche in industry. A program named **Programmed Inquiry Learning or Teaching (PILOT)** is designed to help people seeking training and education.

Management likes the automated office from the standpoint that the automated office supports decision making and relieves people of the rote and repetitive aspects of their jobs. Far more important, however, from the management's standpoint are the other opportunities that automation makes available. Let us look at each of these.

CHECKPOINT **Can you:**

Explain the major purpose of the automated office?
State how the revolutionary change in offices began?

WHAT THE AUTOMATED OFFICE ENCOMPASSES

The fully automated office will use data processing, image processing, graphics, forecasting and modeling, electronic messaging, text processing, electronic conferencing, and data bases. This can be thought of as being the **office of the future.** When will the office of the future appear? Some experts predict not until the 1990s.

The office of the future is geared to increase productivity and improve working conditions, just as the automated office is. Involved in this movement is the office technology that originally began with the use of word processing and microfilm. The office technology expanded into the use of electronic mail and electronic filing.

Let us look into how the automated office is evolving through various applications used in offices today. Then let us look at the problems that are confronting the office of the future.

The automated office concept has captured the attention of industry. The total sales in the United States of office automation equipment in 1982 was over $7 billion. If the monies spent on the automated office are to be fruitful, the whole automated office concept must work as an integrated comprehensive system including teleconferencing, electronic filing, electronic messaging, word processing, administrative support, and local area networking, along with the regular data processing functions.

TELECONFERENCING

Teleconferencing involves three or more people from two or more locations who communicate electronically. Some systems transmit only voice; others, voice plus

FIGURE 16.1
A teleconference in session.

visuals, text, or images. From management's viewpoint teleconferencing can be cost effective. It has been estimated that over $290 billion per year was spent by corporations on meetings in the last several years. This figure represents about 40 percent of the total expenditures of corporations. Those office worker's joys of having the boss go away might soon be negated. Studies indicate that about 65 percent of the executive's time is spent in meetings, so teleconferencing in the automated office understandably takes on significance both in monetary savings and in increased productivity.

ELECTRONIC MESSAGING

The office of the future will operate (and many present-day offices already do) with decreasing amounts of paper since much of the communication is handled by telecommunications. The communications facility used depends upon the availability of the facility to the desired site, the charges for its services, the types of hardware needed to use each type of communications facility, and how critical it is for the electronic message to be transmitted within seconds, minutes, or hours.

All types of messages in this type of environment are distributed electronically throughout the communications facility or facilities, a process referred to as **electronic messaging** or **electronic mail.** The message is stored and later forwarded to the receiver of the message. Years ago, the message would have been sent through the postal service or transmitted verbally over a telephone line. An **electronic bulletin board** is also used as a means of communication. It can take two forms. One form is the sending of messages throughout the system so all terminal users can just read the text, similar in concept to broadcasting a message. Another form is an actual blackboard that is used for transmission in teleconferencing as shown in Figure 16.2. Amazing, is it not, but an electronic bulletin board was planned and developed in the early 1970's. It is only now that there is use for it.

The **executive workstation** has an electronic mailbox in a message system allowing messages to be sent or received electronically and stored until the user wishes to reference them. The executive workstation's special type of terminal offers additional features; for example, it can receive and send voice as well as keyed messages and can also store telephone numbers and appointments for easy reference.

Two companies offering services for in-house message systems are Telemail by GTE and On-Tyme-II by Tymnet.

WORD PROCESSING

Word processing involves the use of computer equipment for processing letters or text materials. The use of the word processing program makes typing easy, for the user is not concerned with depressing the return key as on a typewriter or with keeping track of the last line on a page. However, the user must learn how to communicate with the word processing program. This is usually done by the

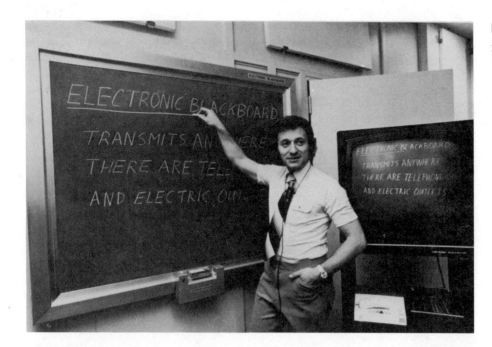

FIGURE 16.2
A teacher uses the AT&T blackboard.

use of the control key and an additional key or keys that indicate to the word processing program what is to be done.

Prompts are given throughout the keying, if a user desires help. Menus are supplied that are equivalent to pointers for various types of instructions that can help the user in performing the keying task. Many menus that are available list the various options for, say, moving the cursor, changing the length of the line to be keyed, getting the printing performed, moving paragraphs around in the text, deleting paragraphs, and so on.

Let us briefly discuss how a user instructs the WordStar program on what is to be done with the text. Let us first see how to create a file. You look at the first menu called the no-file menu, and find that the D communicates that editing is to be done. A prompt appears that says NAME OF FILE TO EDIT? and the user responds by looking at the **directory,** a listing of all file names of previously edited files. The user selects a previously edited file or creates a new file. The main menu then appears on the monitor. It is from the **main menu,** which all future commands originate. A list is presented on the main menu of the various activities that can be used. The cursor movement pertains to how the cursor is moved from one line to another or how it is moved forward or backward on a line. Scrolling is the movement of the cursor from one line to the next or the movement either forwards or backwards of 12 lines at a time. When any deletion is to be done, the user glances at the main menu for directions. Notice how the ^ character appears on the menu. This character refers to CTRL key (or its appropriate marking on a terminal or microcomputer). The user depresses the CTRL key along with the appropriate key to accomplish the desired processing. For example, if the user wishes to move the cursor one line down from where it currently is positioned, the CTRL and the X key are depressed once.

FIGURE 16.3
An example of word processing.

After WordStar opens the file for your use, the margins can be set. The CTRL key is again the means of communicating with the WordStar program; the main menu shows the ^ and the O as the Onscreen. This menu is used for changing margins. For example, if a 60-position line rather than the standard 65-position line is desired, the user depresses the CTRL key and the O key and then depresses 60 and the RETURN key.

There are many word processing programs available for purchase. WordStar is used for many brands of personal computers developed by MicroPro; AppleWriter is used for Apple computers; EasyWriter is used for the IBM Personal Computer; and Scriptsit is used for TRS-80 computers from Tandy Corporation. WordStar can be purchased for about $400; it is registered to each user. Some users have explained that after one and a half years of use, they still are not completely versed in all the possible commands of the program. A user can learn the basics, however, in about an hour. It certainly beats the typewriter!

Word processing systems can be categorized as stand-alone systems, shared-logic systems, or shared-resource systems. A **stand-alone word processing system** is usually a microcomputer or a minicomputer comprising a single system that uses the diskettes for storage of data, the microprocessor, and the printer for output.

The minicomputer offers the **shared-logic word processing system.** In this system there are many workstations for keying the text, but the logic (central processing unit) is shared. A problem with this system occurs when the central processing unit of the minicomputer fails, making the workstations inoperable.

The **shared-resource word processing system** combines the best of both worlds in that each workstation has its own logic and storage, but the printers and large disk storage are shared. Each workstation is independent of the others.

ELECTRONIC SPREADSHEET PROGRAMS

Financial analysis is an important aspect of the business office, as it includes the budget and financial statement analysis, system modeling, portfolio charting, cash flow, and production forecasting. In the automated office, this type of work centers around the use of spreadsheet packages, as was discussed in Chapter 6. Some of the programs now available are VisiCalc by Visi Corp, Multiplan by Microsoft, and Calcstar by MicroPro.

EXTENSIVE USE OF DATA BASES

The use of data bases by both offices and individuals has been increasing. A wealth of information is available for executive's forecasting and modeling. For example, every meaningful word of 110 electronic newsletters from 50 independent publishers has been indexed for use by Newsnet data base which began in 1982. Stock market quotations, business and economic news, United Press International news briefs, and financial and investment service news items are available for purposes of forecasting and keeping current. Refer to Figure 16.4.

WHAT'S RIGHT

Phase Two Of Ethernet

Xerox Corporation has improved upon its Ethernet network by introducing a second phase. The user has the option of creating documents and transmitting them by electronic mail in any one of nine different languages: English, Russian, Japanese, German, French, Spanish, Chinese, Italian, and Portuguese. To use Japanese and Chinese requires a special keyboard for the workstation and font for the printer.

The user can use the electronic spreadsheet in the network.

FIGURE 16.4
In Minnesota, all legislation before the House and Senate is easily accessible through database.

In Chapter 14, report generators were noted as being those programs used in data base management systems for formatting the responses back to the end-user in a form dictated by the end-user. Several other variations of generators exist; the purpose of these programs is to write programs for a user.

An increased demand for generator programs is being felt because end-users wish to develop programs that are geared to their specific data. They do not wish to become programmers, however. The software generator prepares the programs you need after you give the layout of your input and output data on the screen. The software generator does the programming work for you. It is user-friendly. The generator makes the computer work for you rather than requiring you to work for the computer.

Not only can generators prepare reports and screen and record layouts for your use, they also can be used to create summary tables for use with the electronic spreadsheet.

Newspapers are selling the use of their data bases to those who want to locate certain photographs and stories. Other companies are providing film and video projects for different subject matters. The film and video subjects are available for use by referencing the desired titles through the use of a data base.

Economic forecasts for particular industries are available from Data Resources, Inc., and Visi Corp. Through the use of Visi Corp's spreadsheet program, the data in the data base can be down-loaded (transferred) to the microcomputer. There it can be used for forecasts or statistical work, as needed.

NETWORKS

In an automated office environment, data is shared. The network must be able to support the microcomputers to supply needed information when it is requested. Some of the minicomputer networks—such as Ethernet by Xerox Corporation, Wangnet from Wang Laboratories, Inc., and Arcnet from Datapoint Corporation—are being used with microcomputers. Some of the microcomputer firms offer network facilities; Z-net is offered by Zilog Corporation, and CP/Net is available from Digital Research, Inc.

Some microcomputers use the Telenet and Tymnet communication networks that are available for public use. These two companies supply the communication facility, the interface, and the needed programs so that the user at the microcomputer can transmit over the network. EasyLink was previously mentioned as a network available from Western Union. There are disadvantages to using these networks, with the current state of the art. The microcomputers send or receive data at 300 bps or 1,200 bps, which is very slow for the use of such facilities. Also, the microcomputers do not have the standard protocol used in these networks. This protocol must be built into the next generation of microcomputer products. The use of satellite transmission will continue to increase for teleconferencing and the transmission of data among different sites.

NEED FOR INTEGRATED SOFTWARE PACKAGES

So far in this chapter we have mentioned each of the major office functions handled with individualized programs. Some offices that are becoming automated have introduced these piecemeal. The users later find that none of the programs work together. When the data is transmitted over the network, how can it be used with a spreadsheet program? Many times the information has to be keyed again. Can some of the data that was keyed with the word processing program be used for spreadsheet data?

Certainly the use of graphics will also increase in the automated office. All of these programs involving graphics, word processing, electronic spreadsheet analysis, data base, and data communications need to work together harmoniously. There is a definite need to make the computer "transparent" to the user. Although all will know the computer is there, software that makes the integration of office activities simpler will remove the hesitancy that many office workers feel regarding the use of a computer. Many companies are developing integrated software that accomplishes these goals. One of the more popular software packages of this kind is called Lotus 1-2-3.

CHECKPOINT **Can you:**

Explain how teleconferencing, electronic messaging, word processing, electronic mail, data bases, and networks are used in an automated office?

MICROCOMPUTERS AND THE CHANGING DEMANDS IN THE BUSINESS WORLD

In Chapters 5 and 6, the discussion about microcomputers was slanted to personal computers. Although much of this information holds true for the microcomputers used in the business world, let us just briefly point out some additional hardware considerations and needed improvements for microcomputers used in the business world.

Microcomputers use 8-bit, 16-bit, or 32-bit microprocessors. One time main-frames used 32-bit processing power exclusively; now it has come to the micro-computer. This is a measure of the rapid technological growth in the microcom-puter and minicomputer industries. The 8-bit microprocessor, which serves excellently in the personal computer, is not as fast as the 16-bit microprocessor. To a user in the business world, this is important. To the user at home, this speed and capability are not as important as price.

Because the emphasis is shifting from single users to multi-users, new op-erating systems are created to handle the multiprocessing environment. Storage is also affected. Primary storage capacity has increased from the previous standard 64K to 256K bytes and more. Hard disk systems can hold up to 20M bytes, while new floppy disks have progressed to 400K bytes. Flexible floppy disks will be giving way to rigid ones measuring 3¼ inches or 3½ inches rather than the stan-dard 5¼ inches.

Input devices other than the keyboard and trackball are needed. Digitizing tablets, mouse, light pens, and voice synthesizers are all being used in the office. The voice synthesizer's technological advancements that are currently being an-nounced and implemented will certainly open up the office of the future to middle-level management and top-level management, primarily. The keying of infor-mation seems, to some of these executives, beneath their position.

When a microcomputer is used as a stand-alone, the data for that user is available on the diskette (floppy disk). No problem exists as the user has easy access to the data. With multi-users, however, the data needs to be shared and at the same time protected from unauthorized users.

The problem then becomes: how can these microcomputers be operationally combined so that communication can exist among different users? To accomplish

A multi-user system must possess a way to prevent errors aris-
ing when one user interferes with
another user. This means then that
a fail-safe mechanism must be
built into the hardware. Such a
mechanism keeps one user's
mistakes from interfering with
someone else's use of the computer and keeps data secure from
unauthorized users as well.

To keep unauthorized users
from accessing the system, each
user is assigned an account number, which is then checked when
the user wishes time on the computer. Certain users have permission to write and read data; other
users can only read data. A protection must be built into the system in case two users who have
the capability of writing data wish
to access the same record at one
time for making the contents of
the record current.

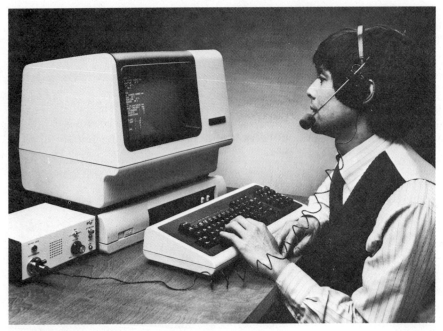

FIGURE 16.5 **A voice input device.**

this, the management information system personnel must use their expertise to
provide the needed interface.

To meet the needs of the multiprocessing system, high-speed bus lines are
used to connect the various microcomputers. The front-end processor is used with
the host computer (main computer) in order to allow a mix of different operating
systems. This enables communications to exist and keeps the host computer busy
processing jobs. Each microcomputer gets a time slice, a portion of the host central
processing unit's time. Say, for example, that a task requires 3 microseconds to
complete. The operating system might decide to give the microcomputer four
1-microsecond time slices since time must be allotted to the program that schedules the jobs. For more efficiency, however, the operating system might allot a
single 4-microsecond segment to this task.

FOURTH-GENERATION SOFTWARE

In today's office atmosphere, too many applications that require solving are being
delayed because of programming restrictions. End-users need to specify their
programming needs, but, unfortunately, they are neither programmers nor systems analysts. They are, however, the people who need to use the computer.

As was discussed previously, the language needed to communicate with the
operating system, the applications program, the use of the files and their organization—all need attention in the currently developed system. If we look at the
history of software development, the first-generation software accompanied the
very early computers, for which many instructions were hand-wired. Second-

generation software began when assembly language was used. Third-generation software includes those high-level languages discussed in Chapter 12.

The **fourth-generation software,** although mostly in its infancy, is centered around the use of English statements that require no translation and no control language. A user is helped with the correct writing of the language by an interactive program that is included as part of the software. Also, **data encryption** is included to protect the program from unauthorized users by scrambling the message when it is transmitted. The message, once received, is then unscrambled, kept intact without any unauthorized alteration. The programmer must still follow syntax and set up relationships, however, using the available fourth-generation software. Examples of this software now on the market include Nomad 2 (a relational data base) from National CSS, Inc., Ramis II from Mathematica, Inc., Focus from Information Builders, Inc., and Inquire from Infodata Systems, Inc.

The productivity of the workers using fourth-generation languages is increased where a programmer writes about one hundred lines of code per day. Contrast this figure with the approximate 40 lines of code written with third-generation languages. Computer usage increases to accommodate the needed processing of these programs. But, because of technological advancements, the greater use of primary storage and processing time increases is negated because of increased processing power of the computer.

The fourth-generation software also has its effect upon the system life cycle, for users now control the processes more than formerly was possible. The user has a very significant say in the desired specifications and preparation of the documentation. The documentation standards in the organization and the developing system's life cycle must be modified.

CHECKPOINT Can you:

Identify the changing demands for hardware and software?

INFORMATION RESOURCE MANAGEMENT

The previous discussion dealt with the automation of the office. The topics discussed centered on applications.

The discussion is incomplete, however, without an examination of information resource management as a vital role in the office of the future. The office of the future—that projected as a reality in the 1990s—must be committed to information handling and dissemination in the most efficient and timely manner possible. The concentration will be on **information resource management,** which views information as a company resource equivalent in stature to financial resources, and which achieves this level of importance through pointed management efforts. For example, top-level management must direct its efforts to setting goals and pro-

WHAT'S NEW

The Programming Problem

The need for programming assistance has been prevalent for as long as there have been computers to program. A centralized programming staff was set up to handle all types of programming requests. Then programmers were assigned to a specific department, some being a part of that department and never being a part of the programming pool. The backlog of applications needed is tremendous.

To solve or to help relieve some of the backlog problem for demanded applications, the end-user should be turned loose to use fourth-generation languages for developing desired applications. The information center can aid the end-users by helping them fine-tune their programs for better machine efficiency. The role of the information center is indeed important, as it can help in reducing the troublesome backlog.

FIGURE 16.6
An executive using a database.

cedures for the company. A long-term commitment must be made to provide data resources to many users.

The move toward the described office of the future is not taking place without a struggle, however. To investigate the climate in which the struggle exists, let us focus on the points of view of three different groups within the office environment, whose emphases differ: the data processing department, the end-users, and the decision support system.

DATA PROCESSING DEPARTMENT

End-users in the 1960s and early 1970s were few in number, compared to the present-day. Typically, the end-users were those involved in accounting, sales, purchasing, buying, and other departments involved with financial transactions. All requests for any new system or any change in the computer system went through the data processing department.

When the data processing department began back in the 1950s, it probably occupied an office in the basement of a building or was found in some area away from the mainstream of people. The data processing department did not achieve its proper recognition with top-level management for the work it was doing. Certainly recognition for the data processing department's importance grew, but it still is not granted its full due for the important role it plays in the corporate structure.

Over the years, the data processing department became the center for applications development. The department, rightfully so, has always concentrated on the following aspects:

- The selection, training, and assigning of programmers and systems analysts to projects requiring solution were the sole responsibility of the data processing department.

- The hardware and software were selected based upon the company's overall data processing plans. The hardware and software were managed and protected according to the stipulations set up according to the overall company plan.

- Data bases were created and managed. Emphasis was geared to satisfying department needs.

- Programs were written in COBOL, assembly language, or some other high-level language such as PL/I for the problem solution.

- The overall plan concentrated on compatibility for all users.

- The selection of protocols and communication facilities were carefully considered by the data processing department for the company's overall good.

- The Management Information System was developed from the company's standpoint.

As the use of computers increased in popularity, users wanted their applications to be processed on the computer. The backlog of these applications grew; the trend continued for many years with unrest brewing. Each month, there were more and more applications that were felt useful. Although the intentions of the data processing departments were good, there were not enough programmers and analysts to handle the demand for information and services. An extensive backlog resulted.

END-USERS

Each day seemed to compound the problem; unrest of the end-users increased. They were aware of terminals being used. They realized that microcomputers could be used easily. They also knew of the benefits of on-line processing since many had seen applications being successfully implemented and executed.

The end-users wanted to use the microcomputers. Various departments ignored the suggestions of the management information system and purchased their own microcomputers, not concerning themselves with the questions of compatability, portability, and the security of data. The end-users had been thwarted for years by not having their application demands satisfied. They wanted to use word processing, electronic spreadsheets, and data bases that are external to the company's data. In no way do they wish to be regulated by the management information system department. The end-users set out on their own to purchase the needed software and hardware for their own application solutions. These were **ad hoc applications** since they were for a single purpose or user.

Some companies tried setting up a company computer store to allow end-users to purchase the desired microcomputer equipment through the company. Gillette Corporation provided this service, eliminating some of the problems with protocols and compatability that exist in some other corporations at the present time. Other companies are setting up information centers, conceptually much like libraries, which supply all types of learning aids for end-users to become knowledgeable in computer usage.

DECISION SUPPORT SYSTEM

Enter the decision support system (DSS) personnel. Beginning in 1975, the decision support system personnel listened to the end-user's needs and tried to help; they were marketing and finance-trained individuals. The **decision support system** group worked independently of the data processing department. Since the end-users were interested in the terminal, the decision support system concentrated on it. As is true for so many things, you have to be at the right time and the right place, but know you are there. This is certainly true of the decision support system personnel.

The decision support system worked with easy applications. They set up the ad hoc model in about two days, solving the specific request of the end-user. The language used for coding was probably APL since it is easy and fast to write, taking perhaps only one-tenth of the time required for COBOL. The prototype, the original model, was usually working in about another day. Basically, it took a week or less to provide the end-user the desired solution.

The decision-support system has satisfied many of the needs of the end-users. However, it cannot satisfy the needs of the end-users who want to use the corporate data or to gain access to the mainframe. Certainly the end-user's goal is to become an on-line mainframe terminal user. Although the decision support system group met the short-term needs of end-users, end-users want access to the corporate data by using the company's mainframe. Decision support system personnel cannot supply this access. The data processing department must provide personnel to handle these applications needs of end-users. How can the problem be solved?

CHECKPOINT **Can you:**

Describe the roles of the data processing department?
Describe the informational concerns of the end-users?
Describe the roles of the decision support system group?

INTEGRATION OF DATA PROCESSING AND DECISION SUPPORT SYSTEM

The time has come when the decision support system and the data processing department must integrate to provide the best overall strategy for the company. The time has come when the argument that exists in many instances between these two groups must stop for the good of all. The applications must be blended so that there is purposeful direction.

The corporate data base must be made available for end-users as well as those individuals who have been carefully screened by the data processing department. The entire purpose of the office of the future is to increase productivity and improve the quality of work. Direction must come from the top-level management to enforce these principles.

The top-level management must make a commitment to extend information resource access to all employees, not strictly concentrating on the secretarial and office worker. Middle-level management as well as top-level management must also become involved in the process.

The best of both worlds of the data processing department and the decision support system group must be brought together. Since the latter specializes in knowing the business details and the former knows about the hardware and software complexities, the mix of talents they could offer might bring the office of the future from concept to reality.

CHECKPOINT **Can you:**

Explain why the data processing department and decision support system group must integrate?

SUMMARY

● Until recently, the office had changed only slightly for over fifty years.

● The truly automated office uses data processing, image processing, graphics, forecasting and modeling, electronic messaging, text processing, and electronic conferencing.

● Employees such as file clerks, bookkeepers, secretaries, typists, bank tellers, and insurance workers will feel the effect of the automated office.

● Retraining of workers must be accomplished when this automation takes hold. A program called Programmed Inquiry Learning Or Teaching (PILOT) is used for retraining or educating employees displaced by automation.

● Teleconferencing involves three or more people who communicate electronically from two or more locations.

● Teleconferencing will drastically reduce travel expenses of companies.

● Electronic messaging and electronic mail involve the store and forward concept where a message is sent electronically throughout a communications facility.

● An electronic bulletin board is used in transmission of messages. It takes two forms. One form sends messages to terminals similar to broadcasting a message. The second form is an actual blackboard used for transmission in teleconferencing.

● An executive workstation has an electronic mailbox in a message system allowing messages to be sent or received electronically and stored until the user wishes to reference them.

● Word processing involves the use of a minicomputer or a microcomputer for preparation of text. A mainframe can be used for this type of activity, but it is in limited use.

● Electronic spreadsheet programs are another example of the changing style of work in an automated office. These are used for budgets and financial statement analysis.

● A real need is present for networks that are equipped to accommodate data transmission from microcomputers.

● A wealth of information is available for forecasting and modeling through the use of a data base. Newspapers are selling their data bases to those who want certain photographs or stories. Film and video are also being sold for referencing desired titles in a data base.

● Word processing systems are categorized as stand-alone systems, shared-logic systems, or shared-resource systems.

● Stand-alone word processing systems comprise a single system that uses a microcomputer for processing.

● Shared-logic word processing systems contain many terminals for keying the text; the central processing unit is shared.

● With a shared-resource word processing system each workstation has its own logic and storage, but the printers and large disk storage are shared.

● Because of the increased use of microcomputers in the industry, there is a need for integrated software packages which combines word processing, data base, graphics, and spreadsheet capability into one software package. This allows an interchange of data between these programs without a compatibility problem.

● The microcomputers must be able to communicate with each other. To accomplish this, a front-end processor can be used to accept a mix of different operating systems in the network.

● The multiprocessing system needs high-speed bus lines to allow communication among different microcomputers.

● A time slice is that portion of the host central processing unit's time that can be shared by the many users.

● Fourth-generation software is available which uses English for communicating with the computer as to what is to be done. Nomad 2 is an example of this software. It is a relational data base.

● Information resource management stresses that data is an important corporate asset.

● The emphasis of the data processing department, end-users, and decision support system are different.

- The data processing department has traditionally been geared to solve department problems, usually using COBOL as the language.

- The data processing department cannot meet all of the demands for processing because of its extensive backlog.

- The end-users want to use the mainframe's data as well as the microcomputer. They turn to the decision support system (DSS) personnel—marketing, finance, and strategic-planning oriented individuals, who take simple applications and turn them into completed systems within a period of a week.

- The data processing department and the decision support system have been at odds as to who has the power and who has the responsibilities.

- Time has come for the office of the future technology to emerge. Both data processing and decision support system people must work harmoniously to achieve top-level dictated policies.

STUDY GUIDE

REVIEW OF TERMINOLOGY

The following terminology was discussed in this chapter:

ad hoc applications
automated office
data encryption
decision support system (DSS)
electronic bulletin board
electronic cottage
electronic mail
electronic messaging
executive workstation
fourth-generation software

information resource management
office of the future
Programmed Inquiry Learning Or Teaching (PILOT)
shared-logic word processing system
shared-resource word processing system
stand-alone word processing system
teleconferencing

MULTIPLE CHOICE

Circle the letter of the item that correctly completes each statement.

1. The home used for office space is called:
   a. PILOT
   d. electronic
   b. teleconferencing
   c. an electronic cottage
   messaging
   e. a shared resource

2. When a message is to be transmitted throughout a system so all terminal users can read it, this is called:
   a. electronic messaging
   b. shared resource
   c. electronic cottage
   d. electronic bulletin board
   e. executive workstation

3. This was designed for scrambling the transmission of messages:
   a. electronic messaging
   b. executive workstations
   c. electronic bulletin board
   d. data encryption
   e. fourth-generation software

4. Today the offices that use computer hardware and software extensively are:
   a. offices of the future
   b. shared resource word processing systems
   c. shared-logic word processing systems
   d. teleconferencing
   e. automated offices

5. When data is considered a resource equal in importance to dollars, a managerial concept exists called:

a. the office of the
future
b. the automated
office

c. information
resource
management
d. teleconferencing
e. ad hoc
applications

6. Fourth-generation software uses:
   a. job control
   language
   b. translator
   programs
   c. English
   statements for
   job control
   language
   d. only English
   e. no relational data
   bases

7. The data processing department has concentrated on:
   a. training
   programmers
   b. development of
   data bases
   c. selection of
   protocols
   d. batch processing
   and department
   problems
   e. all of these

8. End-users' requests are usually for a single user. These are called:
   a. information
   resource
   management
   b. information
   centers
   c. ad hoc
   applications
   d. data encryption
   e. decision support
   systems

9. Decision support systems emphasize:
   a. problem solving
   for end-users
   b. department
   problem solving
   c. hardware and
   software
   development for
   the company
   d. the training of
   programmers
   e. development of
   management
   information
   systems

10. Decision support systems began to operate in:
    a. 1950s
    b. 1960s
    c. 1970
    d. 1975
    e. 1980

TRUE/FALSE QUESTIONS

Circle T if a statement is true; F if it is false.

1. **T/F** The intent of the automated office is to reduce the amount of rote and repetitive work.
2. **T/F** Many critics of the automated office feel that it greatly reduces the variety of work done in an office.
3. **T/F** The automated office involves teleconferencing, electronic filing, and data processing.
4. **T/F** Although teleconferencing is expensive, it is felt that this medium of communication will save companies considerable money.
5. **T/F** The amount of paper used in an automated office should continue at its present level.
6. **T/F** Word processing programs differ significantly in the kinds of work they do.
7. **T/F** When dealing with a word processing program, the user uses only words and never images.
8. **T/F** A control key is a resource for giving instructions to the word processing program.
9. **T/F** The spreadsheet package is used in the automated office for budgets or other financial statements since any changes made in a column of numbers can be easily calculated and modified.
10. **T/F** Networking is an area that needs technological improvements so that microcomputers can communicate readily and efficiently with mainframes.
11. **T/F** Microcomputers do not have a standard protocol.
12. **T/F** Store and forward capability, an advantage of sending information electronically, is used in electronic messaging.
13. **T/F** Fourth-generation software uses English symbols that need no translation.
14. **T/F** Printers are shared by many users, but each user works independently at his or her own workstation to key text in a shared-logic word processing system.
15. **T/F** An integrated software package that includes graphics, word processing, spreadsheet, data base, and data communications is most desirable in an automated office.

ANSWERS

Multiple Choice: 1. **c** 2. **d** 3. **d** 4. **e** 5. **c** 6. **d** 7. **e** 8. **c** 9. **a** 10. **d** *True/False:* 1. **T** 2. **T** 3. **T** 4. **T** 5. **F** 6. **F** 7. **T** 8. **T** 9. **T** 10. **T** 11. **T** 12. **T** 13. **T** 14. **T** 15. **T**

REVIEW QUESTIONS

1. What is considered as the automated office? How does it differ from the office of the future?
2. What is the electronic cottage?
3. What is teleconferencing? Why is it used?
4. What is involved in electronic messaging? Which companies provide such services?
5. Why is there a need for integrated software?
6. What is fourth-generation software? Why is it used?
7. What is information resource management?
8. What is a decision support system? Why is it useful?

DISCUSSION QUESTIONS

1. The automated office will change much that is standard in today's offices. Explain your answer.
2. What types of activities are involved in an automated office? Differentiate these.
3. Explain why retraining of office workers will be needed.
4. How is the concept of the automated office changing the way that microcomputers are used?
5. Using your field of interest, investigate how some large company in that field has set up its organizational structure for computing power. Find out if the company plans any changes in the near future or has made such changes recently.
6. Explain why direction must come from top-level management for the integration of the decision support system and data processing department. Explain the differences in emphasis and outlook of each group.

People in Computing

Arthur K. Przybyl

COMPANY
Beatrice Foods Company

POSITION
Assistant Vice-President, Corporate
MIS Operating Services

EDUCATIONAL BACKGROUND
Bachelor of Business Administration,
Western Illinois University, Masters
of Business Administration, Western
Illinois University

My responsibilities include strategic
planning and operational direction of
the corporate MIS department
consisting of systems development,
data administration, training and
education, data center operations,
technical support, office automation,
and telecommunications.

My favorite experiences resulted
from serving as an internal
consultant for nine years, which
enabled me to see business and
data processing from both a
domestic and international
perspective; from developing one of
the first large-scale integrated
decision support systems of its type
in use today, and being on the
leading edge of new developments
in the use of information processing
technology; from proposing,
implementing, and managing an
evaluation project to perform a
structured test of a new generation
of computers, resulting in the
preparation of an extensive report
which has been called
"outstanding" by peer professionals.

Success for me has resulted from
a combination of factors: a
willingness to go beyond the limits
of any position or assignment to
help co-workers resolve business
problems; a desire to know more
about something than may be
apparent; thoroughness in the
performance of an assignment; and
a willingness to work hard at any
activity in spite of personal
shortcomings or deficiencies, and
compete with others on a
professional basis without giving up
or giving in. Support from a superior
and encouragement to continue my
educational training resulted in the
attainment of my bachelors and
masters degrees. These credentials,
in combination with my experience,
helped to open doors and make
opportunities available to me. I have
been willing to take some risks to
attain goals.

Advances in technology will
permeate the business enterprise,
removing more of the mystique
which has previously surrounded
data processing technology. This
greater understanding of technology
coupled with increased levels of
understanding from new generations
of workers will increase the
importance of business skills. The
systems builder of the future will be
distinguished by his or her business
skills instead of technical skills. It
will be the effective management
and application of technology which
will be important, not the
understanding of it. Business
leaders of the future will have to be
as comfortable and knowledgeable
with information processing
technology as with any other
business skill, or they will find it
exceedingly difficult to succeed.

The best future positions will go to
those who enter the areas of fourth-
generation languages, artificial
intelligence (involving use of a
computer for expertise in decision
making), and higher-level tools and
techniques. These positions will not
be the largest in terms of numbers,
but the best in terms of their
challenges, opportunities, interest,
and professional development.
Exceptionally good people in these
areas will achieve the highest
rewards in terms of compensation,
job satisfaction, and career
advancement opportunities.

Students must cultivate many
skills, always remembering that
success in business requires
diversity. Effective business
leadership is as dependent on oral
and written communications,
interpersonal skills, and related
items as it is on the understanding
of technology. Students who
concentrate solely on the technical
aspects of their education will
further the stereotype of the
"technician," and find that many
opportunities may not be made
available to them. Business people
are evaluated on many attributes,
and so they must make every
attempt to develop all their skills.
Major weaknesses are apparent in
many recent graduates in the areas
of grammar and language skills,
verbal communications, business
knowledge, and other nontechnical
areas. A well-balanced educational
program is an essential element for
success, but often this is not
realized by students until long after
they have left the academic
environment which is capable of
providing that which they need for
success.

As a final note, students entering
the business field must understand
that it is a competitive environment
requiring hard work, dedication,
creativity, and commitment to
succeed.

Application

ACCOUNTING MANAGEMENT INFORMATION SYSTEM (AMIS) CHEVRON CORPORATION

CHEVRON

Chevron Corporation's Computer Services Department (CSD) began in 1981 the step-by-step implementation of its Accounting and Management Information System (AMIS). This system is designed to collect, allocate, and distribute charges for various Computer Services Department (CSD) services to the Chevron family of companies. Another purpose of AMIS is to facilitate and control data received from various feeder systems that gather resource usage data. Sources that make up the feeder systems include batch, data base and data communications; the time-sharing network; disk storage, which uses a mass storage system; tape storage; manpower time allocations; publications; and training.

AMIS is supported by an on-line system which provides users with access to billing and resource usage information. The system was justified because it improved the capture of resource usage data, increased accuracy for client billing and reporting, improved audit control from the feeder systems to the billing system, and provided management with better information for making management decisions.

Figure A.1 shows an overview of the daily processing. Several data bases are used, some of which are more important in our understanding of AMIS than others. The archive data base holds information about projects, phases, and tasks that have been removed from the charge number data base and placed in an

inactive status. Access to this data base is through the use of a charge number. The charge number data base is the heart of the system. The data base contains all project information such as authorized subjects, actual costs, budget supplements, scheduling information plus much more project control information. The data base also carries names of the project management team; the project manager, project leader, and client manager. The manpower data base holds all data about employees in the Computer Services Department. The plan data base holds information about project activities—the development plan, the personnel assigned to the project, and the expected and maximum development costs. The sessions data base deals with tracking daily and monthly adjustments made to client accounts in the charge number data base.

Input comes from various sources as shown in Figure A.2. Several acronyms need explanation.

CSS is Chevron's time-share environment. This systems is a licensed product from National CSS, Inc. The time-share system is used by all CSD employees to develop programs and integrate these programs into a system for a client. Clients also have access to CSS. They use this system for many types of business applications. In some cases, clients write their own programs in languages such as BASIC and Nomad.

MICS stands for MVS Integrated Control System. It is a licensed product from Morino Associates, Inc. This product is used to store detailed resource usage data generated by the various computer operating systems. The data is subsequently used for: Capacity Planning; Performance Improvement; Problem Tracking; Management Reporting; Client Billing and Reporting; and Special Studies.

Two systems are input to MICS, namely RMF and SMF. **RMF** is the acronym for Resource Management Facility. It is an IBM term. RMF monitors the system for performance. Every 15 seconds a snapshot (a memory dump) is taken to determine how busy the control units are, how many jobs are being executed by the computer at this given period of time, and how many programs are stored in primary storage.

SMF is an acronym for Systems Management Facility. Its emphasis is on the time that the central processing unit is busy, idle, and productive. It also analyzes the time that the printer, tape drives, and disk drives are busy. Data provided by SMF is the basis for billing clients for computer usage.

IMS, Information Management System, is a widely used on-line processing system used for entering data as well as making inquiries. This type of environment must support the processing of data in random order and the processing and execution of programs dynamically. To accomplish this type of processing and to eliminate the programmer's need for familiarity with the teleprocessing network, many manufacturers offer a type of programming capability to handle the control of files, terminals, and programs that act as a data communications operating system. Any prompts appearing on cathode ray tubes for aiding the user in data entry as well as in inquiry of data are generated through IMS. The user has the menu shown which gives a choice as to which activity is to be performed. The programming for such an activity is done with IMS through programs written in COBOL, assembly language, or PL/I.

Figure A.2 shows an overview for the monthly processing. There are several input acronyms used.

● **MSS** MSS stands for mass storage system. This mass storage system is used for storing billing information that can be retrieved quickly and easily.

● **TLMS** TLMS stands for the tape library management system. This keeps track of the thousands of magnetic tape reels.

● **Converse** Converse refers to the permanent secondary storage that is allotted and charged to a user. If you have 50 cylinders, you are charged for the 50 cylinders whether you use them or not.

● **Score** Score stands for the System for Computer Resource which keeps track of all hardware managed by the Computer Services Department. It tracks such items as IBM 3270's (intelligent terminals), the control units, the microcomputers, and other hardware, along with the various software.

The **CRC** acronym is used on output. CRC stands for Chevron Resource Company which is a Chevron Corporation operating company. Each month CSD must provide CRC with a file containing all CRC computer charges. CRC

processes this file to generate general ledger entries for their accounting system.

The system was implemented in six phases; each phase replacing a portion of the current system. The first implementation phase replaced the data capture system used to capture computer resource usage. The second implementation phase dealt with client billing; invoice formats and month-end processing were improved. The third implementation phase dealt with the changeover to an account number that allows clients access to the computer. The fourth implementation phase completed replacement of all the remaining data captures systems, which provided a single source for billing resource usage, and supported joint venture accounting. The fifth implementation phase provided an improved project control and management information reporting system, which is shown in Figure A.3.

FIGURE A-1. **Daily Processing handled by AMIS.**

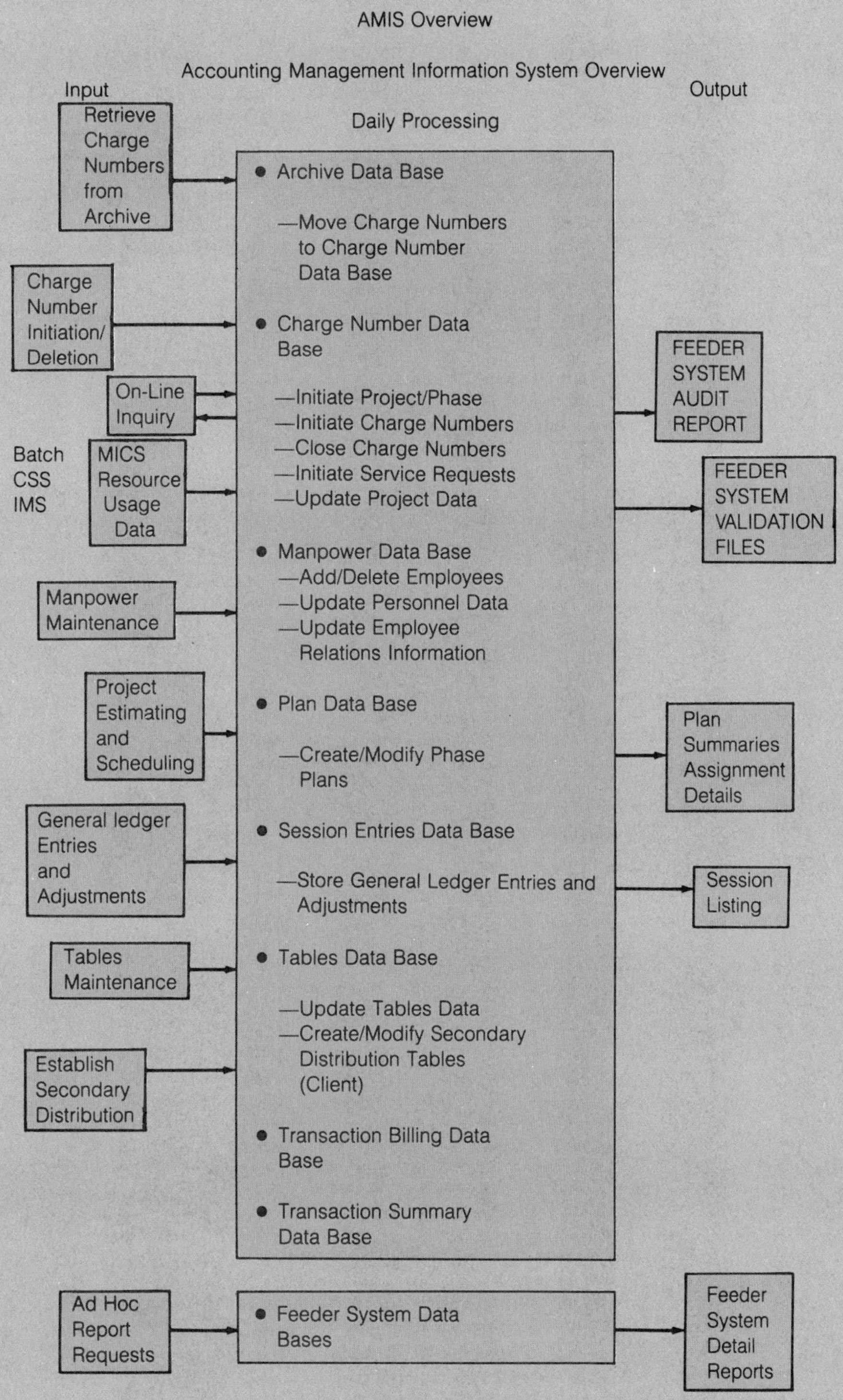

AMIS Overview

Accounting Management Information System Overview

Input — Daily Processing — Output

Retrieve Charge Numbers from Archive

- Archive Data Base
  —Move Charge Numbers to Charge Number Data Base

Charge Number Initiation/Deletion

On-Line Inquiry

Batch CSS IMS

MICS Resource Usage Data

- Charge Number Data Base
  —Initiate Project/Phase
  —Initiate Charge Numbers
  —Close Charge Numbers
  —Initiate Service Requests
  —Update Project Data

Manpower Maintenance

- Manpower Data Base
  —Add/Delete Employees
  —Update Personnel Data
  —Update Employee Relations Information

Project Estimating and Scheduling

- Plan Data Base
  —Create/Modify Phase Plans

General ledger Entries and Adjustments

- Session Entries Data Base
  —Store General Ledger Entries and Adjustments

Tables Maintenance

- Tables Data Base
  —Update Tables Data
  —Create/Modify Secondary Distribution Tables (Client)

Establish Secondary Distribution

- Transaction Billing Data Base

- Transaction Summary Data Base

Ad Hoc Report Requests

- Feeder System Data Bases

FEEDER SYSTEM AUDIT REPORT

FEEDER SYSTEM VALIDATION FILES

Plan Summaries Assignment Details

Session Listing

Feeder System Detail Reports

FIGURE A-2.   **Monthly Processing handled by AMIS.**

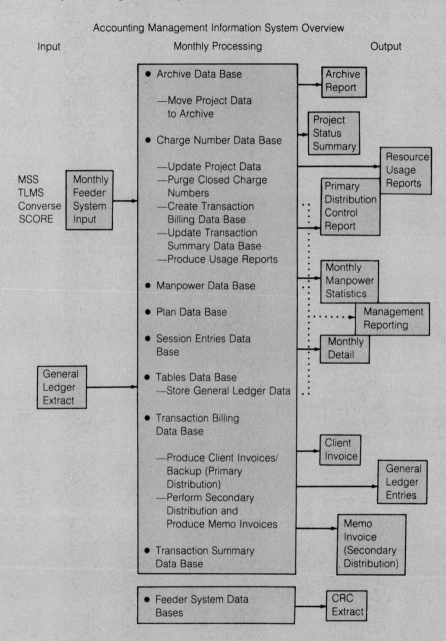

Accounting Management Information System Overview

| Input | Monthly Processing | Output |

FIGURE A-3. **Fifth Stage of Implementation.**

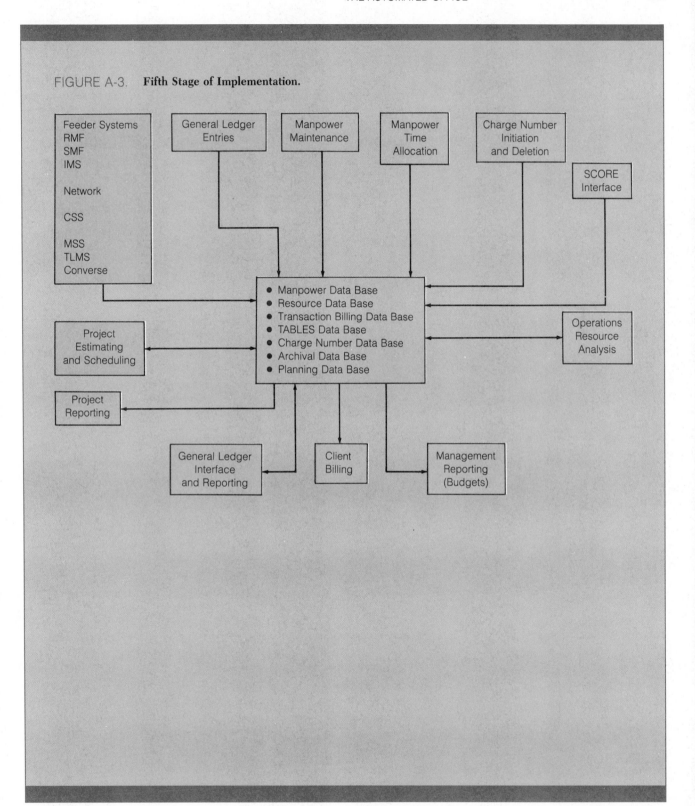

PART SIX

Today and Tomorrow

17 Computers and Society

OUTLINE

PROLOGUE

Sally's dream vacation has materialized—a trip on an ocean liner bound for faraway places. The captain calls in to the U. S. Coast Guard Automated Merchant Volunteers Emergency Rescue Systems (AMVERS) to tell of the ship's destination, departure time, proposed speed, and intended route. Every four hours the ship relays by radio its speed and location to AMVERS. What a vacation, free from cares.

Next morning, she slips and breaks a leg. The ship's doctor cannot fix fractures, so help is summoned on the radio. An orthopedic doctor in the vicinity leaves his ocean liner and joins Sally's ship to assist her. As she lies in her bed, she wonders.

HOW DOES IT DO THAT?

READ ON.

OBJECTIVES

After studying this chapter, you should be able to:

1. Discuss the ways that computers have affected medicine, government, entertainment, retailing, transportation, finance, education, and research.

2. Explain the goals of artificial intelligence.

3. Discuss the problem of computer crime.

4. Discuss the problems of privacy and security raised by computer technology.

INTRODUCTION

The affects that computers have had on society are far-reaching. Rare is the case where computers have not changed the way that work is done. They have had an impact on social applications as well as on issues affecting an individual. These issues are discussed in this chapter.

The personal computer is used for solving problems such as balancing the bank account, performing equations used in some math class at school, or completing programming exercises for class, fun, or business. At the other end of the spectrum, government, banks, stock exchanges, research institutions, department stores, and hospitals use computers for solving their everyday problems as well as problems occurring weekly, monthly, or only occasionally.

Some of the institutions that have been affected by the computer are discussed below.

SOCIAL APPLICATIONS

The far-reaching usage of the computer has touched all facets of our world today. Society is, to some extent, at the mercy of machines. When the computer "goes down" (stops operating), business sometimes comes to a screeching stop. For example, a credit union using computer equipment is unable to prepare a check. The launching of the space shuttle, Columbia I, was halted for two days when the computers could not communicate with each other. A company cannot tell the customer if enough parts are on hand to ship a product because the computer is down.

Any machine, whether it be in the multi-million dollar class or in a few hundred dollar class, is subject to breakdowns. Sometimes a part that costs $2 will halt a million-dollar machine. At Cape Canaveral, which houses the most sophisticated computer system available in the world, personnel must cope with this failure problem. Every part is checked three times, but failures still occur. There are backups, and even backups for those backups.

MEDICINE

The computer has made great inroads into the medical field, not only in diagnosis and treatment, but also in support for handicapped and disabled people. In a hospital, one thinks of a computer being used for the calculation of bills, tracing or updating of the history of patients, and monitoring of the administrative, clerical, and equipment costs to operate the office—all record-keeping functions.

Consider also the reports that hospitals must send to Blue Cross, the U. S. Government, and the state government. The same data is sent to all three, but it is on different forms. Changes are dictated by any of these three; they must be handled smoothly by the computer.

In addition to these reports, the hospitals must maintain patient admissions records, including logistics which list such things as care given, dismissal or transfer data, patient accounting and billing, patient accounts receivable, accounts payable, and general ledger. Each of these must be kept in detail for later auditing.

The computer has moved, however, from a totally record-keeping function to one of helping diagnose diseases. No doctor can know all things needed for every possible diagnosis but a computer can specialize in holding certain types of information that can be retrieved, analyzed, and used to make diagnosis more efficient and accurate. Over 4,000 symptoms of about 500 diseases can be analyzed, merely by the doctor referencing information from the memory of a computer that is available for all those users who are part of the network maintained by Stanford or Rutgers Universities.

In hospitals, anesthetists, doctors, and nurses can use computers to monitor a patient's vital signs such as pulse, blood pressure, heart beat, and amount of carbon dioxide exhaled. Refer to Figure 17.1.

The computer has opened doors that were firmly shut for handicapped people. Through the use of the computer, active minds can be put to productive work. The use of a specialized keyboard or specially designed device—such as a voice synthesizer, which is used for speaking to the computer, or a braille terminal, which is used for sending messages to or receiving them from the computer— allow the handicapped to enter programs, test them, and even sell them for fees.

The computer also helps those with pacemakers by monitoring the pacemakers. People with diabetic problems can use computers to test the insulin levels in their blood. Deaf people can detect sound vibrations through the use of the computer, which opens an entirely new world to them.

Administrators of a hospital need information about its business for complying with laws regarding the new Medicare rate system that became effective on January 1, 1984. The hospital must now supply information on history of patients as well as charges for a specific treatment made by the hospital. For example, the administrators need to know about those patients who have had appendectomies.

FIGURE 17.1
A computerized analysis of blood.

If all relevant information on these patients were to be referenced manually, the patient's name would be looked up in a file, and then the various information would be extracted—operating surgeon, length of patient stay in the hospital, charges made, patient's address, insurance company involved in payment, and so on. This manual method would take a week-long study or more. The computer, through its programs, can produce the information in about a minute.

Laboratory work also needs to be analyzed for the amount of work done by a technician in a day. Assuming that a hospital laboratory processes about 1,000 services a day, there would be, in an eight-week period, 56,000 slips requesting a service of the laboratory. A computer can sort about 300 to 600 slips per second, accomplishing the workload study in one and a half to three minutes.

CHECKPOINT _Can you:

State how computers are used in medicine?

GOVERNMENT

A very big user of computer equipment in the federal government is the U. S. Weather Bureau. Its extensive satellite communication system monitors the entire United States. In late 1982, Looks West, a satellite used for weather forecasting for the western portion of the United States, became inoperable. The satellite that monitored the eastern portion of the United States had to be repositioned in its orbit so it could serve both portions of the country. The movement of the satellite was accomplished through complex calculations performed by a computer that followed the program written for such a manuever.

One user of the U. S. Weather Bureau's information is the U. S. Coast Guard. They give free service for routing of ships that cross the ocean, helping them avoid storm areas or areas of high winds. In an international agreement among nations whose coasts touch on the North Atlantic Ocean, each nation will keep track of iceberg location and movement in a specified area. The weather bureau predicts where and when storms will happen; the U. S. Coast Guard alerts the ships.

Closer to home, we are all familiar with the income tax collection done by the Internal Revenue Service (IRS). The IRS processes 90 million tax returns each year. How embarrassing it is to receive a tax return corrected by a computer, with a very neat report stating which lines were calculated incorrectly. The IRS has a wealth of information at its disposal and can check amounts of interest shown for a mortgage and savings account interest, income of those receiving veteran payments, income of those claimed as dependents—more facts than we could ever imagine.

City and state governments use computers, many of which are used to aid in the collection of income tax, property tax, and license fees. These applications have been used for quite some time.

Computers are used for traffic control by many city governments. At many street corners there are induction coils placed in the pavement. When a car passes over a coil, it picks up an impulse and registers it as one car passing over. It can count the number of cars that use a street. It might be programmed (instructed) that the red light can stay on no longer than thirty seconds on a particular street. Or, at the intersection of a busy throughway and a quiet street, the light might stay green for the busy street and only turn red when a car approaches on the other street. New York City has implemented a computer-controlled traffic system whose 8,000 traffic signals are regulated completely by computer. Use of the computer system lead to greater understanding of traffic flow problems. It was noted that in Manhattan over 2,700 intersections are extremely busy and require monitoring for efficient traffic control. If one or two of the main intersections become blocked, the traffic bottleneck affects other intersections, and they become blocked, too.

To overcome this problem, the system's Vehicular Traffic Control System software monitors the intersections for speed, volume, and density of traffic. The loop sensors, which are placed in the street below the surface of the pavement, accumulate the data and pass it over the coaxial cable to a computer located in Long Island. The computer makes timing adjustments at the necessary intersections.

The city of Anaheim, California, uses a computerized crime system that has resulted in an increase in arrests. All reports of crimes are prepared so a computer can analyze the data for patterns. Humans live by patterns, so the police have used statistics to show the patterns for such crimes as homicide, rape, robbery, and motor vehicle theft. In analyzing the details regarding the reported crimes, a computer pinpoints the areas where these crimes occur, also noting the time of day. Maps are generated for easy viewing to show where certain crimes occur in the city. Thus trouble areas in the city, types of crimes, and the usual times that these crimes occur can be adequately predicted by the police department, enabling the administration to position police personnel strategically. The public is better served because the computerized method provides information that would not normally be available.

A computer also prepares reports on stolen property and recovered property in Anaheim. Information regarding the stolen property can be sent electronically to alert pawn shops. As technology advances and costs decrease, it may become possible for these pawn shops to be directly hooked up to a police network that allows for exchange of such information.

The computer is used for collection and analysis of criminal records. In a city or state, various areas are designated for holding criminal records, the data of which is shared among various police departments. In San Francisco, for example, all criminal records recorded for crimes committed in the Bay Area are grouped by severity of crime and area in which the crime was committed.

A record of a wanted criminal can be checked in the police computer system in the state of California. When a motorist is stopped for a traffic violation while driving on a freeway, the California Highway Patrol (CHP) officer either calls in the motorist's driver's license on a radio or keys in the motorist's license on computer equipment. The information is sent to a police computer system, and the driver is checked for outstanding parking tickets, suspension of driver's license, or criminal activity that would have placed him or her on a current wanted list.

The automobile's license might be checked for illegal registration or to see if it is stolen property.

CHECKPOINT **Can you:**

State how computers are used by government agencies?

ENTERTAINMENT

The entertainment field also has felt the impact of computer use. When you are watching a football game on television and the kicker tries for the field goal, you may note statistics shown on the screen—how many successful tries he has made from 35 to 39 yards away, from 50 yards, from over 50 yards. These statistics are flashed on the screen from a computer's storage.

The multi-billion-dollar market that encompasses the use of computer video games has its impact on society. Not only have people used their television sets for game playing, but they have enjoyed those video games that appear in grocery stores, drug stores, and arcades across the country. Even the speak/spell games have brought hours of entertainment to children.

For photography buffs, the computer-operated lens has increased the quality of picture taking. Development of film is now carefully controlled by computer equipment. Eastman Kodak, for example, will not even speak about the process control used for picture development because the field is so highly competitive and technically oriented.

Computer camps are becoming the fashionable way for enjoying vacations. Some camps offer parents and children the opportunity to learn about computers together. Some camps offer about four hours of formal instruction per weekend plus two hours of computer time to reinforce the learning. Other camps provide a weekend entertainment schedule including swimming, tennis, golf, and computer instruction.

The famed performing center of Carnegie Hall in New York City has also changed its mode of operations. Before 1979 all accounting procedures, recording of donations, and assigning of seats were handled manually. In 1983, Carnegie Hall became computerized; now all donations, pledges, subscriptions, and seat assignments are handled through a computer.

The sports field has changed, too. Professional football teams analyze the success of various plays by statistically analyzing each play's performance. The Dallas Cowboys professional football team pioneered the use of computers in professional sports. The computer is used for helping in the drafting of players by cataloging their performance on tests such as the 40-yard dash, the number of pounds lifted, and the shuttle run test. Professional scouts are not dependent solely on their own perception. The computer has made itself felt in the professional baseball arena by analyzing a player's performance through fielding, batting, and pitching statistics and also analyzes weather (via simulation), field conditions, and positioning of players.

CHECKPOINT **Can you:**

State how computers are used in entertainment?

RETAILING

We have already discussed the point of sale terminals used in grocery stores and department stores. Those terminals have changed the physical appearance of retailing outlets as well as the way they process data.

The retailing world is changing its emphasis as to how it does its advertising; direct mail is being emphasized more. The personal information about customers are stored in a computer's memory and can therefore be recalled for mailing purposes. Some companies have devoted their complete activity to providing direct mail service. Because the United States Postal Service feels this is economically beneficial to the department's financial status the direct mail houses receive lower postage costs. Those users who like the services or products presented through direct mail benefit.

There is another side of the coin regarding the use of direct mail. Companies sell a customer name list to a direct mail house. Once a name is sold or given to a direct mail house, it is a difficult task to get the name removed from the list. The department that handles driver's licensing in many states sells information from its driver's license data. Grocery stores frequently sell the names and addresses of those who have completed forms for check cashing privileges. One gentleman made an interesting experiment. Each time he completed a form for either a new charge account or a check cashing service, he filled in his middle initial differently. When the direct mail ads arrive, he is then able to identify the source. This junk mail, as it is called, has a presort identification number on the label, enabling these direct mail houses to enjoy lower postal expenses.

CHECKPOINT **Can you:**

State how computers are used in retailing?

TRANSPORTATION

Car rental agencies often advertise that a car will be waiting at an airport upon arrival without the renter having to wait in line. Once an application form is completed and approved, the person uses his or her credit card for identification purposes. Before computers were available for processing of car rental requests, the time required for approval of the application was time consuming.

FIGURE 17.2
BART at work.

Computers run a complete subway system in San Francisco (see Figure 17.2). A visit to the Bay Area Rapid Transit (BART) control room reveals quite a sight. The electronic board is several hundred feet long; its lights blink on and off as each train passes through the system. People constantly monitor the operations of all trains in the subway system, just in case a malfunction occurs. Changes in time schedules because of train breakdowns, poor scheduling, rush-hour traffic, or an abundance of riders because of some special event are signalled throughout the system by the many computers that work together for the operation of the subway system. This information is passed in a matter of seconds from the main computer to other computers used in the subway system.

The trucking industry, long associated with the movement of household goods, has felt the impact of computers also. A new technique had to be systemized for the moving of electronic equipment, for example. In addition, the 1983 deregulation of the trucking industry by the federal government as to the charges for its services has had an impact on trucking companies' computer usage. An increased demand for computer time for the calculation of the rates has placed such an increased load on its computers that United Van Lines of Fenton, Missouri, changed its entire computer system to meet the ever-increasing demand for on-line dispatching of its specialized fleets as well as the calculation of all of its rates.

CHECKPOINT **Can you:**

State how computers are used in transportation?

FINANCE

Banks certainly have changed to meet the demands of computer processing. In October 1982, the Shawmut Bank of Boston made history by being the first bank to provide at-home computerized services to its banking customers who have microcomputers. The microcomputer is connected by telephone lines so that transactions can flow between bank and customer. Interest on a savings account can be displayed on the microcomputer screen, and the customer need not leave the house. Account balances are also available upon demand.

The computer has been used in stock market dealings for many years. In March 1982, the Kansas City Board of Trade introduced a new way of playing the stock market. Instead of dealing with individual stocks, the investor deals in the whole market of approximately 1,700 stocks, betting on the entire market going up or down. The volume of data dictates that a computer be used. Other firms have enlarged upon the idea, generating a very lucrative and active business.

Two risk-taking options are available: futures or index options. When dealing with futures, the investor can lose an unlimited amount of money, depending upon the performance of the market. When dealing with the index option, the investor can lose only that amount of money actually put in. The index option can be handled by some 100,000 brokers across the country. Futures contracts are traded at the Kansas City Board of Trade, the Chicago Mercantile Exchange, and the New York Futures Exchange. Index options markets are the American Stock Exchange and the Chicago Board Options Exchange.

CHECKPOINT **Can you:**

State how computers are used in finance?

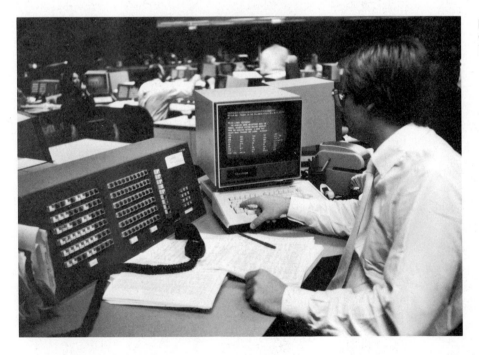

FIGURE 17.3
Computers are used extensively by stockbrokers.

EDUCATION

Colleges and universities across the country are receiving free computer equipment from hardware firms which have been given the incentive by the government. The hardware is not given to just those colleges or universities which concentrate on teaching the art of computing. Brown University at Providence, Rhode Island, received fifty microcomputers for use by its 6,600 liberal arts students in July 1983. Their purpose is to provide a campus-wide communications network serving the 126 buildings on campus. This gives scholars and educators of all disciplines accessibility to computers.

Computers are used in classrooms to aid in instruction, a method called **computer-assisted instruction (CAI).** At the present time, most computer-assisted instruction deals with drill and practice work. Computers are also being used for "mental exercises" for those suffering from brain damage; this topic was discussed in Dr. Acord's the *People In Computing* article following Chapter 2. Computer illiteracy, poorly written programs, and inadequate funding are noted as principal reasons that the computer-aided instruction movement has not yet gained momentum.

CHECKPOINT **Can you:**

State how computers are used in education?

RESEARCH

Researching articles, journals, newspapers, and the papers presented at professional meetings in order to set up new techniques in experiments and treatments has been made easier, more efficient, and extremely fast through the use of the computer. Reference material that previously took weeks to locate is now available in minutes. Other research applications include the search for ways of using computer equipment for plowing fields, for translating one language to another, for aiding in surgical operations, for solving problems, and more.

The libraries have felt the impact of the computer, too. Many records, formerly held on 3-by-5-inch cards and retrieved manually, are now available by searching the computer's storage. The records kept on these index cards were changed to a machine-readable version for computer use. Because the computer is used, records can be easily cross-referenced into various categories that would never have been possible through manual methods because of the tremendous volume of data. The cross-referencing of journal articles and research reports, called citations, are grouped by topic so anyone using a computer who has access to these citations can retrieve the printed indexes and abstracts. The files searched by a computer are called bibliographical data bases.

There are hundreds of data bases available for use, with Lockheed's DIALOG System being a prime source. For example, if a research person wishes to know the references in the periodicals, the written summaries that proceed from meetings, reports, monographs, and theses pertaining to cancer, the researcher would use the name of the data base called CANCERLIT. The librarian uses a computer to sort the large number of citations and to produce a printout of all citations dealing with a specific area of interest. The user is charged 33 cents per minute plus 15 cents per printed page. The library can prepare a printed report or produce the output on a user's screen, depending upon the capability of the computer system. The research person has references that can now be used to pinpoint selected areas of concentration.

Another example is a business management and administration data base called ABI/INFORM which has been available for use since 1971. The user is charged $75 per hour plus 7½ cents per citation. Most citations include the title and the abstract.

Criminal records that are maintained by a city or state government, as was mentioned previously, are stored in a data base. If the police wish to know, for example, the names of those suspected of stealing Porsches within the last six months, of those pushing drugs in a certain area of town, or of those accused of child abuse within the last four years, the names can be outputted. The person searching the data base must know how to ask for the desired information from the program that manages the data stored there.

Another aspect of research deals with the way computers can help society in intelligent problem solving and doing repetitive work. **Artificial intelligence,** is a science associated with automated decision making and robotics.

Automated Decision Making

A great emphasis in the science of automated decision making deals with how people reason and make decisions. Humans make decisions based upon thinking, reasoning, and relating present problems with what they have been exposed to in the past. The aim of researchers then is to include this type of activity in a computer program.

Stanford Research Institute (SRI), Fairchild Industries, and Yale University, among others, have been working to develop a computer with the intelligence and expertise to answer questions in some particular field. Artificial intelligence incorporates all possibilities that can happen and then includes them in its logic. Often referred to as a "thinking machine," its reasoning process includes handling of a large degree of uncertainty and incomplete data.

To illustrate with a very simple example, assume that you stop at a fast-food diner. After standing in line, you select and are served a hamburger and a small order of french fries. The amount of the purchase is keyed on the cash register, the amount is paid, and the change, if any, is returned to you.

This process could be programmed fairly easily, but the assumption would be that every time you walk into the diner, you would automatically purchase a hamburger and an order of french fries. Artificial intelligence goes further. All types of uncertainty must be accounted for in the process. What might some of these be? A hold-up could occur while you were in line, thwarting your purchase. A fire could occur in the kitchen, so no one could serve you. There may be no hamburgers ready at that time, or all french fries might have been sold, leaving no more for the entire day. Another factor could be that you do not have enough money to purchase both items or that you do not even want a hamburger, only a cup of coffee.

A September 3, 1982, article in *Science* reported that an artificial intelligence program successfully located concentrations of an ore called molybdenum. The program demonstrated a degree of expertise, intuition, and judgment that would normally be attributed to an expert in the field for locating the ore deposits. An expert gave a tremendous amount of knowledge to the program so the computer could complete the reasoning process.

In no way will artificial intelligence eliminate the need for experts, but it will help to improve decision-making processes. Development in this area has just begun.

Robotics

Artificial intelligence dealing with robotics has already had its impact upon the world of work. Robots are being used in factories across the country. Cameras have been developed, so the robot can "see" where it is going.

As the price of labor in the United States increases, the enhancement of robots increases. The robots' costs are continually decreasing; the payback period is estimated to be about two and a half years. Each time there is a one-dollar-per-hour increase in wages, the use of robots becomes more economical. It was estimated by the chairman of General Motors that a one-dollar per hour increase in wages in a large company makes the use of 1,000 robots economically feasible.

The use of robots has just begun. Refer to Figure 17.4. Those blue-collar workers who have been displaced by robots must seek retraining. Strange as it might seem, the wide-open field for which they might train involves repair of robots; there will be great demand for robotic technicians.

FIGURE 17.4
The robotic industry is just beginning.

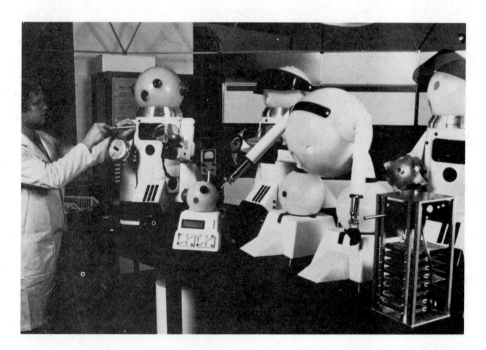

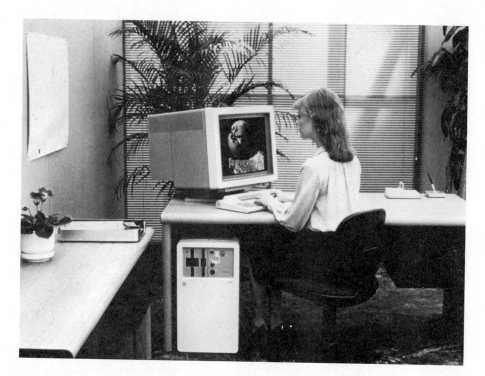

FIGURE 17.5
Artists are beginning to explore the computer as a new medium.

CHECKPOINT **Can you:**

State how computers are used in research?

Explain artificial intelligence?

State what its goals are?

ART

In 1982 the artist's stylus and video screen were made available as options or alternatives to the paintbrush and canvas. The painting by electrons was designed so that the stylus is pressure-sensitive, yielding a range of lines from the very fine to thick strokes. The digital paint box allows the user to make full use of a complete range of colors, even allowing the artist to mix new colors, which are then stored in the memory of the computer. This advance in technology can be used for retouching or for filling in missing parts of images.

Consider also the world of computer graphics. Each pixel, or small dot on the monitor, can be turned on or off. When the pixel is on, it can be combined with any of the other pixels to form an image, a line, or a character. Any pixel can be assigned a color and an intensity of that color. Software allows this pixel identification and choice and intensity of the color, opening possibilities for truly computer-generated art.

Walt Disney amazed the world with his image reproductions—of Donald Duck and Bugs Bunny, for example. Commercial artists were employed by the hundreds to produce the many needed drawings so Bugs Bunny could jump across the walk. The many animated drawings were synchronized in such a way that when they were fanned, or run in rapid succession, we saw Bugs Bunny moving. Enter computer technology. How has it changed the cartooning art? The computer is programmed to produce the drawings for animation. Amazing!

CHECKPOINT Can you:

State how computers are used in art?

COMPUTER CRIME

As has been discussed, the computer has aided society greatly. Unfortunately, there is another side of the coin. The use of computers to commit crimes is also evident. The illegal use of computers to invade the privacy of individuals and to manipulate records in a computer's storage are two serious examples of such crime. Other computer crimes involve the theft of hardware and software, the illegal use of software that is copyrighted, and the illegal use of software that is designed only for one person's use.

The criminal who zeroed out a savings account without the real account owner even knowing it happened until much too late is but one common example of computer crime. A less common incident involved a man who received a $12,000 deposit to his account that was generated in error by a computer. He told the issuing bank that the balance of his account had to be in error. The bank checked the account and stated that the amount was correct. The man later cashed a check for the $12,000, only to later wind up behind bars.

The programmer, who writes a program and sells it for profit under copyright laws, expects the program to be used by the purchaser, only to find out much later that the program has been illegally copied. Sometimes individuals who buy these programs copy them; other times software houses may have sold the illegally copied program to an unsuspecting person.

Even schools are being sued by software houses; one major university is being sued for several million dollars because it violated a licensing stipulation for a program. The program, when purchased by the university, was to be used by just one user. Instead the university used the program for hundreds of users at the school.

A publishers' association is suing a school for violating the copyright laws. The school reproduced the first chapters of a textbook on its computer equipment, ran off the shortened version of the text, and sold it in its book store.

The banks, because of federal restrictions, have lagged behind on the protection of their software and data. They have often been the targets of crime. The time has come when the banks must change the policies set forth to protect their software and data. Thefts are becoming more prevalent every day as unauthorized people find out clients' passwords (codes made up by the users which supposedly are known by only the user and the computer). Another weakness is that banks are continually looking for programmers with bank programming experience. Sometimes the bank will hurriedly hire a person with the desired experience without thoroughly checking that person's ethics.

CHECKPOINT **Can you:**

Explain how computer crime affects society?

PRIVACY

Because of the technological advancements which brought about enormous computer storage and increased usage of computers, the privacy problem becomes important to all of us. **Privacy** is the right to control who uses personal information and the way in which it is used. The federal government has passed several laws to protect individuals' privacy rights. These are the Fair Credit Reporting Act of 1970, the Freedom of Information Act of 1970, the Education Privacy Act of 1974, and the Privacy Act of 1974.

If you are ever denied credit, check the Fair Credit Reporting Act for your rights to inspect your credit records. If you wish to check the information stored about you in the federal government, you have this right under the Freedom of Information Act. If anyone ever wishes to keep school records private, that person is protected under the Education Privacy Act.

The Privacy Act touches all of us in one way or another. If any organization is in the practice of collecting data about individuals, those individuals must be told as to the nature of the data collection and the uses of such data. If an organization incorrectly represents your data, they can be held responsible for problems resulting from that false information.

How can you as an individual protect your right to privacy? Hope that people input the correct data, that programmers write good programs for updating records, and that no one maliciously "plays" with computer storage. How often have you heard of a "computer freak" gaining access to a large data base and "browsing" through the data base, sometimes trying to change data at will? Hope that security provisions at the computer site are good and well thought out to protect your data as well as others'.

In our fast-moving world, the ever-present computer is used to chronicle many facts about you, some of which you would just as well forget, and some of which may be inaccurate. Now, however, the problem of so many things being remembered in a computer's memory can come back to haunt you, long after you have either forgotten about the incident or it has become unimportant in your life. Many times it is not even the incident that is important but the faulty facts that were reported or the intentional misrepresentation of them that is bothersome. A person has to be concerned about who possesses these faulty facts and what they plan to do with them.

Say, for example, that an unfair charge is made against a person's account because of a computer misrepresentation or factual error. Feeling threatened with a possible tarnished credit record, the person pays the unjust charge and keeps his or her name off a creditor's list. The least fact held in a computer's memory can be brought back to haunt someone. For example, if you write a check and your account has insufficient funds, the store accepting the check will tag your account in its computer as being a "bad account" since a check was returned to them. You may have written hundreds of good checks, but because of one error in arithmetic or the like, your credit is tarnished. The frightening thing is that, even though you pay the charge for a returned check to the store, unless you are extremely careful, the bad account stigma can remain on your records indefinitely. How can you be sure that records about you are accurate? Many others want to find out the same answer.

SECURITY

Looking at a problem from the other perspective, the computer center manager is deeply concerned over the security of the computer hardware. Years ago, magnets were considered the ultimate threat in a computer room. Today, the concern for any damage to hardware, whether intentional or accidental, is pronounced. Most people do not even see the mainframe; it is located at some well-protected site. Formerly, data processing departments were located in the basements of many companies due to their unimportant role. Now, they have been returned to a location off the beaten path, but this time, for a different reason.

Security poses a problem even in Silicon Valley, where the integrated circuits are abundantly produced. The People in Computing feature for this chapter supports this contention.

SUMMARY

• The impact of computers has been felt in many facets of our world today.

• In the medical field, computers are used to process patients' accounting and billing records, dismissal or transfer data, and forms needed for processing Blue Cross, federal, and state forms.

• The medical field uses computers for diagnosis and treatment, too, as a patient's symptoms and history background can be studied.

- Handicapped persons are benefitted through the use of special devices that allow them to input programs or data to a computer for analysis.

- The federal government uses computers extensively. Some of the most commonly known uses involve weather prediction and processing of tax returns.

- City and state governments use computers for processing tax forms. Their uses involve, however, additional services to the community, such as traffic control, scheduling of police manpower, record-keeping of stolen goods, and maintenance of criminal records.

- The entertainment field has felt the impact through the wide use of computer games. In addition, most professional athletes' performances are analyzed as to the degree of success or failure.

- The desire to learn about computers is made fashionable through the computer camp vacation.

- Retailers use computer equipment to price merchandise, as is evident in many grocery stores.

- Direct mailing is used in retailing for the circulation of advertisements.

- The transportation industry uses computers for operation of subways, for car rental arrangements, for dispatching truck fleets, and for calculation of rates for the deregulated trucking industry.

- Banks use computers for calculation of savings and checking account balances and for computerized services to those customers who have their own microcomputers.

- The stock market has long been a user of computers. It, however, has included another way of playing the stock market by allowing individuals to buy options that deal with all stocks in the exchange rather than with an individual stock.

- Education has benefitted from gifts of hardware given by manufacturing firms, with incentives from government.

- Drill and practice work performed on computers fall into the category of computer-assisted instruction (CAI).

- Research has definitely benefitted from the use of the computer; articles, periodicals, monographs, records from meetings, and reports are more readily available for inspection. Through the use of a data base, the user only needs to know what topics are desired so the desired data can be accessed.

- Artificial intelligence, a method of endowing computers with certain human abilities—such as decision making—is under development. It bases its theory on the use of a computer for making decisions given incomplete data and a large degree of uncertainty.

- Computer crime takes many forms from theft of individual data or money to theft of copyrighted programs, hardware thefts, and illegal use of programs.

- Privacy involves the right of individuals to control the facts that are being stored about them.

● Privacy is protected by laws such as the Fair Credit Reporting Act of 1970, the Freedom of Information Act of 1970, the Education Privacy Act of 1974, and the Privacy Act of 1974. These laws have been passed to protect individuals from the misuse of information, and use of faulty information, and to control the extent to which the information is to be disseminated.

● Security of computer hardware from unintentional or deliberate misuse is very important, yet it has become a problem that is difficult to resolve.

STUDY GUIDE

REVIEW OF TERMINOLOGY

The following terminology was discussed in this chapter:

artificial intelligence (AI)
computer-assisted
   instruction (CAI)
privacy

MULTIPLE CHOICE

Circle the letter of the item that correctly completes each statement.

1. If you ever want to inspect your credit records after being denied credit you should check the following:
   a. artificial intelligence
   b. CAI
   c. Education Privacy Act
   d. Fair Credit Reporting Act
   e. AI

2. A person has a right to control the accuracy of his or her personal information. This is called:
   a. security
   b. privacy
   c. artificial intelligence
   d. CAI
   e. none of these

3. The Freedom of Information Act is associated with the problem of:
   a. security
   d. CAI

   b. privacy
   c. artificial intelligence
   e. none of these

4. If anyone ever wishes to keep records of school behavior private, this is protected under:
   a. CAI
   b. AI
   c. Freedom of Information Act
   d. Education Privacy Act
   e. Fair Credit Reporting Act

5. The science of automated decision making is associated with:
   a. AI
   b. CAI
   c. privacy
   d. security
   e. none of these

6. Having a computer with the intelligence and expertise to answer questions in some particular field is associated with:
   a. CAI
   b. computer-assisted instruction
   c. Artificial Intelligence
   d. privacy
   e. security

7. This programmed instruction helps in drill work of mathematics:
   a. AI
   b. CAI
   c. computer-assisted instruction
   d. all of these
   e. none of these

TRUE/FALSE QUESTIONS

Circle the T if a statement is true; F if it is false.

1. **T/F** A computer is used for diagnosing diseases.

2. **T/F** Stanford and Rutgers Universities' computer facilities can provide a reference for symptoms of about 500 diseases.

3. **T/F** Hospitals use computers only for record-keeping.

4. **T/F** A computer is used for changing the positioning of a satellite.

5. **T/F** One of the biggest users of computers is the IRS since it processes 90 million tax returns a year.

6. **T/F** The IRS has limited computer power for checking data.

7. **T/F** A computer can be used for traffic control but only for a few intersections.

8. **T/F** When a computer system is used for detecting patterns in criminal behavior, it is effective for analyzing crime types and times the crime is committed.

9. **T/F** Some highway patrol officers are able to find out to whom an automobile is registered by looking up data stored in a computer's storage.

10. **T/F** Some highway patrol officers are able to find out from a computer if an automobile is reported as stolen property.

11. **T/F** Professional sports are using computers for calculating batting averages or field goal percentages, but that is the extent of current use.

12. **T/F** Mass mailings have decreased in recent years.

13. **T/F** Computers have been used in the stock market since the Kansas City Board of Trade introduced a new method of playing the stock market.

14. **T/F** The use of robots affects the positions of the white-collar workers.

15. **T/F** Each time a dollar per hour increase in wages occurs in a large company, 1,000 robots become an economically attractive alternative to management.

16. **T/F** Computer-assisted instruction deals with research projects.

17. **T/F** Artificial intelligence requires a complete set of data and circumstances in order to be operative.

18. **T/F** Artificial intelligence will replace the need for people to be experts in their fields.

19. **T/F** Laws have been passed to protect computer hardware from misuse but little has been done to protect individuals.

ANSWERS

Multiple Choice: 1. d 2. b 3. b 4. d 5. a 6. c 7. b *True/False:* 1. T 2. T 3. F 4. T 5. T 6. F 7. F 8. T 9. T 10. T 11. F 12. F 13. F 14. F 15. T 16. F 17. F 18. F 19. F

REVIEW QUESTIONS

1. How are computers used in the medical field?
2. How are handicapped and disabled people helped through the use of computers?
3. How does the federal government use computers?
4. How does the usage of computers at the city and state government level differ from that by the federal government?
5. How do professional baseball and football use computers?
6. How are computers being used for retailing?
7. What sources does the direct mail industry use for obtaining lists of names and addresses?
8. The transportation industry uses computers for reservations. Identify some possible uses.
9. What are some of the ways that a computer can be used in the operation of a subway system?
10. Some people playing the stock market have enjoyed a new method of capital investment. Explain this method and tell why a computer is needed for this type of activity.
11. Banks have become computerized by offering personal, in-home services to some of its customers. How do these services work?
12. Do you foresee that the worker will be staying at home rather than commuting to work? If so, why?
13. Do persons involved with research use a computer? If so, how can computer-provided information be helpful?
14. Identify seven possible types of computer crime occurring today.
15. Is artificial intelligence closely related to computer-assisted instruction? Why or why not?
16. Why is privacy important to an individual in a society making extensive use of computers?

DISCUSSION QUESTIONS

1. Educators use computers in many ways. Discuss some of these uses.

2. Direct mail houses affect us all. Explain this statement.

3. The use of computers is highly concentrated in government. List and explain some of the many uses.

4. The use of computers in the library has changed the way that articles are accessed. Explain this statement.

5. Enumerate some of the questions that a highway patrol officer might ask a motorist stopped for a violation. Explain how the answers could be checked for accuracy.

6. Can you think of any large institution that is not affected by computers?

7. What far-reaching effects could artificial intelligence have on society?

8. Discuss the needs to safeguard individual privacy and maintain computer security and the issues that have arisen regarding these two problematic areas in the computer age.

People in Computing

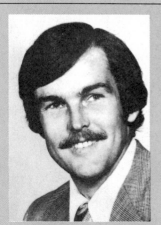

Douglas K. Southard

COMPANY
County of Santa Clara, California

POSITION
Deputy District Attorney

EDUCATIONAL BACKGROUND
Degree of Philosophy, Stanford University, Hastings College of the Law, J. D. University of California

In recent years, high technology thefts have made headlines across the country, and particularly in Silicon Valley, Santa Clara County, California, where high technology electronics is centered. So what's the fuss about? In the period of 1979 through 1982, I would estimate that in excess of $100 million of technology and products have been stolen, illegally copied, or counterfeited from Silicon Valley firms. Most of that theft is by employees. The cases we handle involve technicians, inventory clerks, draftsmen, and engineers. Quite commonly, security personnel are also involved. They steal circuit designs, process information, precious metals, and the chips themselves. There is also an increasing propensity to steal finished goods, such as computer disk drives, and personal computers, which have become increasingly smaller in size and therefore easier to steal.

When the integrated circuit chips are produced, there is about a 30 to 40 percent rejection rate, especially for the more complicated devices, and a good number of bad parts have to be disposed of in some fashion. This is normally done by a reclamation process which involves grinding up the parts in a shredding machine and flushing out the precious metals in an acid bath. Although some companies maintain their own reclamation facilities, most subcontract this task to metal reclaimers. Varying degrees of security are used to insure that the parts are in fact ground up.

These measures are taken because the manufacturers want to maintain a reputation for quality. One obviously doesn't sell defective products with one's logo on them. Nor would a company normally want to put its unmarked rejects on the market. They could easily have counterfeit markings printed on them, and be sold as good parts. The resulting warranty claims and injury to reputation would be costly. As a result the manufacturers almost uniformly maintain a policy of not selling unmarked or rejected parts. Thus an unmarked part should be presumed stolen.

If this were in fact the case, the job of enforcement would be easier. Unfortunately, the truth is more complicated. Many parts which do not meet specifications—and are therefore technically rejects—are usable for lesser tasks and thus still have value, often above their scrap value. For example, a 16K EPROM may not meet factory specs, yet still have 4,000 or 8,000 bits of usable memory capacity. As such it may not be usable in, say, computer or guidance system applications, but it would be usable in less critical applications—for instance, a video game. If it were cost effective, the company might sell it with special customer markings or no markings at all. In such a case the part could be remarked and fraudulently sold as a first-grade product. Or, if a company were particularly cash poor at a given time, it (or an unauthorized department head) might be tempted to sell the unmarked parts for the short-term benefit involved. This has happened on numerous occasions.

All in all, however, the primary problem with the unmarked parts market involves consumer safety, not national security. When defective chips installed in medical equipment, airplanes, microwave devices, and the like start failing, people are going to be hurt. Hopefully the problem can be cured before that happens.

Trade secrets thefts pose a potentially more serious security problem than theft of product, since such thefts provide the very means of obtaining the technology upon which to establish an industry and develop competitive expertise. I've heard it authoritatively said that the United States at one time possessed a ten-year lead over the Soviet Union in microelectronics technology, but that that lead has already shrunk to maybe five years, based primarily on the easy access the Soviets have had to our technology. I'm not in a position to attest to the veracity of that proposition, but what I have seen would certainly not negate it.

By its very nature, trade secret theft is the most difficult to detect and solve. What is taken is generally not a physical thing, but an idea. Original documents, computer tapes, and technical drawings can be easily copied by any of a number of photographic or electronic means without anything corporeal ever being taken. Hence, it is never missed.

As a result of this, it appears unreasonable to expect local law enforcement agencies to be up to the job of such specialized investigations. Some sort of national or regional approach is necessary. The Santa Clara County experience with various cases suggests that creation of a central intelligence clearinghouse is a mandatory first step toward combatting high tech crime. The "gray market" in particular consists of large numbers of interconnected companies and individuals, whose activities and relationships can only be established by a continual monitoring effort, much like a narcotics bureau. Since these people operate on at least a regional scale, it is impossible for a local agency to keep track of them. By a pooling of information into a central intelligence unit, a broader, more complete picture can be constructed. From this vantage point, the major problem can be isolated and addressed.

Although the problems as outlined are often centered in California, they are becoming increasingly material in scope as the industry spreads out across the country. Most western and eastern seaboard states have an electronics manufacturing industry of some sort. This trend will continue as the industry seeks new locations with relatively cheap labor pools and inexpensive employee housing opportunities—both commodities that are becoming extremely scarce in California.

GALLERY 10

Computers In Sports

The performance of athletes in competition is statistically documented when an athletic event is watched on television. Another side of computer usage in sports involves the evaluation of performance, endurance, form, and stress.

1. Photographer Dan McCoy gives an artist overview of how computers have been used in a wide variety of sports to analyze and help an athlete improve his or her performance.

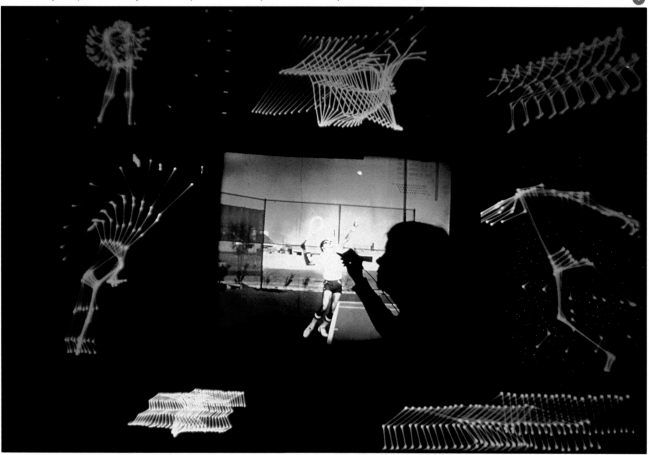

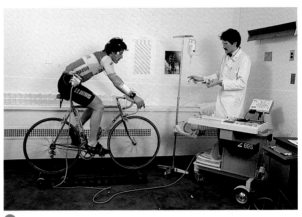

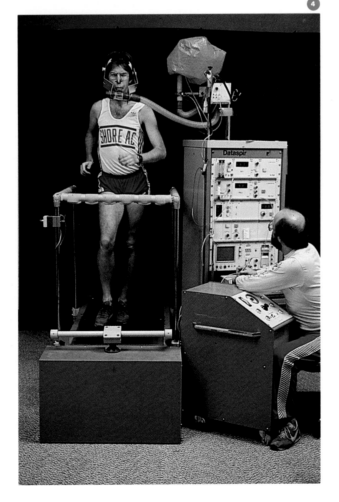

2. and 3. First a bicyclist's leg strength and then his cardiovascular condition are monitored by computer. **4.** A jogger's lung capacity is measured through the use of a computer.

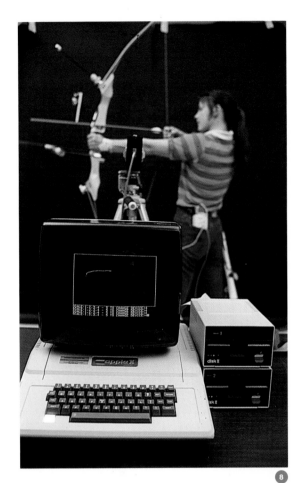

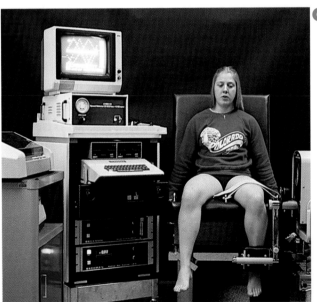

5. A portable data recorder records the heart rate of the runner in the background. **6.** A weightlifter's leg strength is measured and compared to previous tests to assess progress. **7. and 8.** The form of both these athletes is analyzed by feeding the computer with video input.

9. In Minnesota, Defenseman Dan
Mandich of the Minnesota North Stars who
suffered a severe knee injury undergoes
stress analysis of his knee. Coplin Physical
Therapy of Minneapolis operates this state
of the art equipment. They work closely
with the North Stars and other professional
and amateur athletes to help assess and
improve athletic performance. 10. A
close-up of the monitor which has
generated a graph of the knee's progress.

18 The Future?

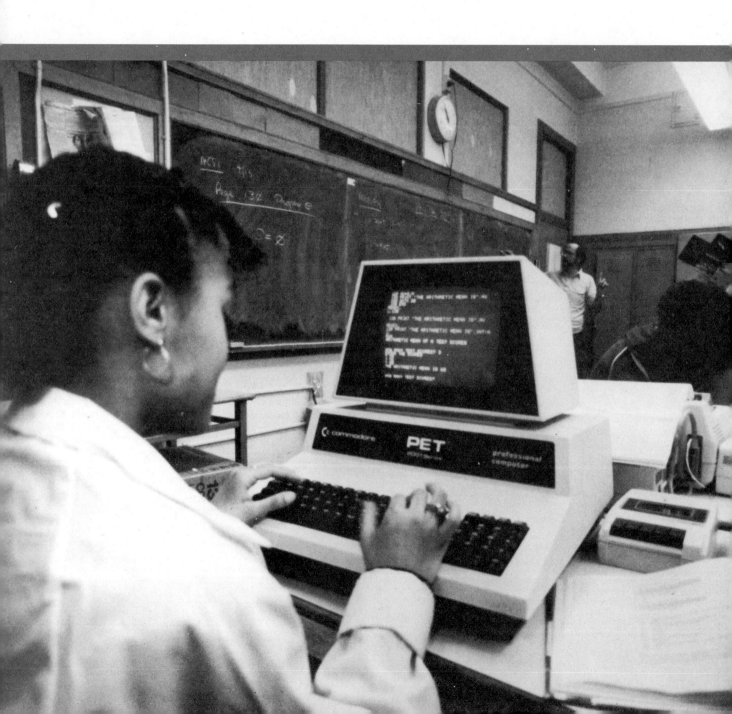

OUTLINE

PROLOGUE

"Ladies and gentlemen. May I have your attention please. As we usually do on Monday mornings at our company gathering, we introduce any new employee. Today, there is an unusual—umhh, well, it is different. You know how you have all been unhappy about the mail delivery, having to wait until a certain mail person gets through having coffee. And you remember the other mail person who was so slow at delivery of the mail.

"What I am trying to say is we have a new approach. Our office is to become automated. That is right; everything will be electronic— except you, of course. We plan to cast paper aside and become more productive. We might as well start with the mail delivery.

"After three months of trial, I think you will fondly call our mail delivery robot, PG, meaning pretty good."

HOW DOES IT DO THAT?

READ ON.

OBJECTIVES

After studying this chapter, you should be able to:

1. Realize that the future for computerization holds capacities for revolutionary change.

2. Open your imagination to express possibilities for the future.

INTRODUCTION

The concepts that form the basis of computing began centuries ago. What took so long to even envision an information age like ours? What took so long to develop hardware and software that can carry out some of the tasks that amaze us today? If we analyze the "why," we notice that it is frequently the smallest detail that often is the stumbling block to success and, therefore, to change. Charles Babbage certainly had his ideas and dreams (see Appendix D for details); he was thwarted not by his own ideas but because of the metallurgy problem he encountered. Similarly, the people who will shape the computers of the future—and, therefore, the future itself—are formulating ideas from dreams, and seeking to overcome stumbling blocks to realize those dreams.

To hazard a guess at what the future will bring is risky but certainly fun. In ten years, we can look back and see how right or wrong we were. The one certain thing is that the computing concept is only beginning to find its range of applications. The current advancement of technology, which seems to be moving so rapidly, will in a few years seem to have been moving very slowly.

WHAT WILL IT BE LIKE IN 1990?

Let us look with unbounded imagination into the home, education, computer services, and libraries of 1990 and guess what they will be like.

IN THE HOME

The use of the microcomputer will certainly have its effect on the design of new homes and the remodeling of older ones. Security systems will use the speech synthesizer for entering and locking the home rather than the old fashioned key and lock. Temperature will be controlled by a microcomputer which regulates both heat and cooling. Fences that will be constructed around the property line will probably be unlocked by fingerprint scanners.

Will the day come when a loan application is completed on the screen of the microcomputer? The desired questions could be answered and transmitted to the bank. The bank would signal later that the amount of the loan had been deposited in the account. The major problem with this type of transaction is security—the bank must be certain that the person applying for credit is truly who he or she claims to be. Identities can be checked by verifying signatures transmitted over the telephone line. Other methods might include the transmission of a fingerprint or use of a speech synthesizer, which would analyze a person's voice for pitch and speech patterns.

Can you see a microcomputer on most kitchen tables? Stacks of floppy disks will take the place in the cupboard that was formerly reserved for newspapers. Newspapers will not be much in evidence. The way we will get the news is by

turning on our microcomputer for reading the news releases. In the kitchen we
will probably find talking teapots and microwave ovens. How about the dishwasher? The oven? The refrigerator? It is difficult to think how these might change
because of computer technology, but it is reasonable to imagine that in the kitchen
you might see a robot taking the dishes from the dishwasher and stacking them
in the cupboard or scrubbing the floor and polishing the vinyl.

The television will look different from what we know today. The screen will
be much larger to accommodate conference calls and teleconferencing. This will
virtually eliminate Christmas cards as the holiday good cheer will be transmitted
via computer rather than sent in the mail. The much-used telephone of today will
have additional buttons that will be labelled "transmit" and "receive."

Housetop microwave earth stations will be the new status symbol. Those in
this elite group will have twenty-four-hour access to new material from the library
without leaving their homes, and will also subscribe to an electronic mail distribution service for a monthly fee. The servicing corporation will launch a satellite
about 100 miles in the air which will travel over certain large cities at the same
time each day. The satellite will broadcast the mail to the prescribed customers
as it passes over the city. Each customer will have a receiving device that will
copy the transmitted data for later viewing. The following day, the customer will
transmit the answer as the satellite again passes over at the same time.

An additional room will probably have to be constructed in the home or one
room converted to become the computer room. The microcomputer and floppy
disk storage were beginning to be a problem in the kitchen. There will be several
workstations, each of which has its own cubicle. Filing cabinets will be in the
shape of trays to accommodate the thousands of floppy disks (diskettes) that we
own. Oh, the size has changed. It is down to one inch rather than the 5¼-inch
diameter common now. The capacity is many megabytes. Each family will have
an old 5¼-inch diskette mounted in gold as a relic.

The call to dinner will be initiated via the electronic bulletin board signal, which also electronically transmits the menu. The electronic bulletin board will have replaced the intercom system that was formerly in place.

Those who have heart problems will have various computer equipment in their bedrooms. They may do treadmill exercises nightly, being monitored by the computer at the doctor's office.

IN EDUCATION

Some colleges will demand that students own a microcomputer before they are admitted. The entrance examination will also test the student's capabilities at using word processing.

Many of the universities will be "totally wired" for computer communications. A university may have its own satellite for broadcasting to its students. A student might sign up for an electronically transmitted course at any time during the semester. To earn credit for the course, the student must finish the course by completing the prescribed exercises and taking a final exam at the instructor's office.

Counseling will be of primary concern in this atmosphere, as a student's performance on various tests taken for measuring satisfactory skill level will be evaluated often. Any skill that is lacking will be improved by any of the dial-up courses in English composition, mathematics, and English literature—all available from the student's home microcomputer. Classes given throughout the day will be monitored by students.

IN COMPUTER SERVICES

A visit to a computer service department at a company will be utterly amazing. The central processing unit will be as big as a couple of shoe boxes. All the magnetic disks will be gone, as they will have been replaced by optical disks. Printers, all of the laser type, will be printing at the minimum 21,000 lines per minute. Because of security reasons, no one will ever be allowed into the computer room unless he or she is a computer operator or the data processing manager.

You will never find a programmer at the company, as each programmer will work strictly at home in a truly electronic cottage. The programmers will be utterly relieved of having to learn new computer languages; all of them will be written in English.

The information center will have become the hub of learning and help for end-users. The decision support system and data processing group will have been blended into one information group that helps end-users as well as departments. The top-level management will have recognized the need for a chief information officer (as was discussed in the People in Computing feature for Chapter 13). The top-level management will have a firm policy in place that has given needed direction to the company, resulting in drastic reduction of application backlogs.

FIGURE 18.2
Like the handheld calculator did ten years ago, the student's work environment will be revolutionized by the personal computer.

IN LIBRARIES

Incidentally, don't count on getting a job in the library for the twenty-four-hour shift that we previously mentioned. Robots will be pulling the desired books from the shelves and turning to the requested page. The contents of the page will then be transmitted and shown on the monitor of your microcomputer. These libraries, of course, will be more backward than some of the larger libraries. There, everything will be stored on optical disk, allowing material to be referenced in less than a minute, after the library recognizes you as a taxpayer or a resident.

FIGURE 18.3
**The new Josephson technology
was once thought it would replace
the silicon chip.**

Libraries will have many artificial intelligence systems available for a fee. These will be extremely busy as people of all ages clamor to learn the art of using computers. The demand for information will be increasing, not decreasing.

IN RESEARCH DEALING WITH HARDWARE AND SOFTWARE DEVELOPMENT

Foreign governments subsidize their research and development, but the United States does not. For that lack of extensive monetary support, much activity exists to keep in competition with foreign governments, particularly the Japanese. The Japanese are spending billions on the development of the new processor. It is indeed a race between the Japanese and the United States, with Germany running a distant third.

The **fifth-generation software** might make its debut by the turn of the century. This new software would be used on a new processor which has been under development and will probably take anywhere from ten to twenty years to perfect. There already has been a tremendous amount of energy and dollars spent on research and development for the hardware. It is estimated that IBM spent $3 billion in 1983 alone for commercial applications. The new software certainly would include the use of artificial intelligence and a very easy type of language format.

As for hardware development for defense applications, the United States Department of Defense set up a research group called Defense Advanced Research Projects Agency (DARPA) to fund $50 million in the fiscal year of 1983 and $95 million for the fiscal year 1984. This money was spent for the research and development of a new processor. Control Data Corporation (CDC) is also looking toward the 1990s. It has had much success in developing its super-computers. Two of its leading architects, Neil Lincoln and Lloyd Thorndyke, were released with the company's best wishes to form their own company and develop a new processor. This new company is called ETA Systems, Inc.

Hardware and software development are underway at corporations, universities, and research laboratories as well. A consortium has been set up in Austin, Texas, called the Microelectronics Computer Corporation (MCC). Corporations included in the consortium are Honeywell, Micro Devices, Mostek, National Cash Register (NCR), National Semiconductor, Sperry, Allied, and Rockwell International. Research and development money is being donated to universities and research laboratories for their involvement.

Molecular Computing

In October 1983, thirty scientists met in Santa Monica, California, to establish guidelines for research using molecular computing. **Molecular computing** uses the proteins and enzymes that make the chemistry of living cells in the creation of **biochips.** The signals that pass through a biochip would be sent much like those in our brains are. The absence of heat with these biochips could alleviate a problem that is prevalent with silicon chips. Artificial organic compounds must be developed to carry the electrical signals. The researchers feel that the signals would travel at the speed of light, which is the speed of computers operating today.

The operating speed is to be in trillionths of a second, which is the speed of super-computers at the present time. Could all of today's computer data be stored on one biochip? Some of the researchers feel it is possible. One biochip, about the size of a sugar cube, is projected to store a million billion molecular gates for accommodating the on and off states. For comparison, integrated circuits use a million transistors that act as switches that are either "on" or "off." The projection for accomplishing the biochip design with its artificial proteins might be completed sometime before 1987. This would be a beginning.

Researchers dealing with this technique feel that this type of computing would come closest to simulating the thinking and emotional processes of humans. Ultimate plans involve this molecular computing in performing types of "miracles," for example, where the output is actually muscle movement for paralyzed patients, restoring full natural motion. Another projected goal is restoring sight to the blind.

As for computing as such, the molecular memories would provide tremendous storage capacities, enabling a vast amount of data to be stored for analyses of patterns and trends. This large amount of data would provide the means to make the necessary associations between what is currently happening and what has happened in the past. These associations would allow the expert systems to operate successfully; users could avail themselves of judgments based on some carefully evaluated decision making process.

SERIOUS NOW

It is fun to imagine; it is fun to guess. Only by keeping abreast of the latest happenings will you be able to evaluate the truly amazing, fascinating, and ever challenging world of computers.

WHAT'S WRONG

−273 Degrees Centigrade

That is cold. Colder is the fact that after hundreds of millions of dollars of research, the Josephson Junction will not work. The **Josephson Junction** is an integrated circuit that provides spectacular speeds, outdoing the mainframes on the market today.

The problems center on how the circuits can be integrated in the computer system and how the circuits could be kept at the cold temperature required for proper functioning. The problem of maintaining this temperature caused the scientists at Bell Laboratories, Sperry, and IBM to give up on these integrated circuits. The Japanese, however, are still trying to use helium and the circuits in a computer system.

People in Computing

Martin Kral

COMPANY
Cincom Systems

POSITION
Product Manager

EDUCATIONAL BACKGROUND

As computers have evolved in hardware configurations and operating systems, so too have the languages used to program a task. The era of *fourth generation software* is now upon us and it is geared to utilizing the technology of today's computers in a simpler way.

Fourth-Generation Languages (4GL's) is a generic term which basically represents several different categories of high-level languages used for application development. The primary purpose of each of these categories is to provide more computing power to their users, thus making them more productive.

Presentation Languages are those that allow for the display of data in some meaningful form. These languages are normally very simple in syntax or very English like. They are most commonly found in formal and natural query systems, report writing systems, graphics, etc.

The community of users for this language should have some computer awareness and their needs can be addressed by simple inquiry tasks.

Specification Languages come in basically two types. *Actual Code Generation,* that is language code (COBOL, PL/1, etc.), which is generated from a high-level language where you specify what you want, the task to do, and how the information is to look. The second type is similar to code generation in specifying the criteria, only the language code is not generated. A composite of the application is generated from a library of precoded functions based on the selected specifications. The library of precoded functions is extendable and the functions can be written in a compiler language or better yet, a high-level procedural language.

The traditional Management Information System (MIS) community would most likely take advantage of these languages to improve their productivity in generating applications that are structurally static in design and usage. However, the fairly sophisticated end user could take advantage of these languages, especially precoded functions, to develop simple to somewhat complex tasks.

High-level procedural languages should have the capabilities and flexibility of compiler languages but without the levels of translation for executable codes. High-level procedural languages are fully interactive and interpretive with powerful commands to simplify the instruction set. These languages normally insulate themselves from any dependencies on hardware or operation environment. *That is:* the procedure code is executable on IBM, DEC, Wang, PC's, etc. equipment and fully portable without change to the procedural code.

A user of these high-level procedural languages does need to understand the basic concepts of computer languages; this is the ability to think out the logical process flow of the task. Although a higher level command set than traditional compiler language, these languages, still require the author (programmer) to control the logic. Sophisticated end-users could utilize these languages, but they would need training similar to that which an MIS programmer would receive for the language.

Specialty Languages are those that are unique to a specific application area. Examples of this type would be spreadsheet systems, modeling system, simulation sytems, etc. These are more like utility languages and are very beneficial in addressing their application types. These languages are specifically designed for a specialized end-user base.

Fourth-generation languages have greatly improved application development productivity; there is no question about that. No one category is a complete cure by itself, so it is important to look at fourth-generation languages as a system which offers appropriate languages in each category. This fourth-generation system approach should be inter-related or better yet, integrated, so that movement through it is simple and straightforward.

Application

SAN FRANCISCO POLICE DEPARTMENT —CRIME LABORATORY

The San Francisco Police Crime Laboratory views its two million dollar fingerprint computer as a filing system that digitally places all fingerprints of arrested people in San Francisco into its data base. The hard copy of the fingerprint cards has the ten fingers printed on a card. These are fed into a fingerprint reader that digitizes and electronically stores the fingerprint on a disc. Technically, the 0s and 1s could be viewed but the crime lab is only interested in the individual characteristics called *minutia* which consist of ending ridges and "y" formations (*bifurcations*—the ending edges and splitting of these ridges as shown on a fingerprint). The print is measured for angle, measuring many times over the fingerprint; the print is produced on a X-Y axis.

If, for example, the department wanted to do a 10 fingerprint search on some offender, the input fingerprints are encoded and the data base is searched. A score is outputted anywhere from 1 through 9999. If a score of 3000 or more is achieved, it is felt that the correct fingerprint has been matched.

In the past when the police got to the crime where they find a "beautiful print on a smoking gun" there was no possible way for the police to go through the files and search for this one fingerprint. There are over 250,000 fingerprint cards which means a total of 2,500,000 prints. Crimes were solved usually by some lead as to the criminal. Now, however, they can take one fingerprint on that smoking gun, use a black powder and scotch tape and place it on a white card. The fingerprint can be directly entered into the computer but preferably a photograph is taken to enlarge the fingerprint by five times. The photograph is then covered with a piece of acetate and traced by hand. This produces a clearer drawing, eliminating dirt and smudges. This acetate tracing is then reduced to its original size, and it is cut out and put on a fingerprint card. The computer records that fingerprint into a temporary storage which can hold approximately 350 prints. When time allows, the crime lab uses the monitor and brings out the fingerprint from temporary storage.

If the police department does not know the sex, race, and year of birth and which finger the print is of, a search against the data base takes fifty minutes. If, however, the fingerprint pattern type of the finger is known, the search takes only about six minutes. If the sex and finger number are known, a search throughout the data base takes only three and a half minutes.

Cases that have been dormant for many years have been solved suddenly and with great speed. As an example, a burglary case was committed on June 2, 1981. Because of the statute of limitations in California on June 2, 1984 the offender would be free of any charges. However, on May 30, 1984, a search was made through the data base and in six minutes the suspect was identified.

The fingerprint computer was installed in the early part of 1984. In the first six months of operation, the computer helped to identify over six hundred suspects.

BASIC Programming

OUTLINE

PROLOGUE

"Today, class, we will learn to add, multiply, divide, and subtract," says Mary Mitchell.

"But I know how to do that. I learned that in second grade," says Rachel.

"On a computer?" asks Mrs. Mitchell.

"Will I be able to make up a computer guessing game after this chapter?" asks Rodney.

HOW DOES IT DO THAT?

READ ON.

OBJECTIVES

This chapter discusses the elemental instructions used in the BASIC language as well as pseudocode and flowcharting, which show how the problem is to be solved.
After studying this chapter, you should be able to:

1. Identify the various types of variables.

2. Explain how calculations are performed.

3. Explain how data can be printed and the various options available for printing.

4. Identify different ways of inputting data.

5. Explain how selection is accomplished.

6. Explain how programs use looping.

7. Identify some of the functions available.

INTRODUCTION

Many people are mystified about what actually makes up a computer program. To dispel this mystery, an examination of a simple BASIC program is in order. BASIC, a computer language developed for solving math problems and business problems, is an acronym for Beginner's All-Purpose Symbolic Instruction Code. This language is suitable for a user without prior programming training. Although BASIC originally was executed on mainframes, it has become the most popular of all the computer languages written on microcomputers.

Like all computer languages, BASIC has its own rules as to how an instruction is to be formatted. When we fail to follow the rules of how an instruction is formatted, a computer prepares diagnostics which are English messages generated for the purpose of helping the user debug the program. A user communicates to the operating system through the use of systems commands such as LIST, RUN, and SAVE. (These topics were discussed in Chapter 6.) You might ask, how do we as users or programmers communicate with the computer through the use of a program? We must communicate what data manipulation is to be done in the program, what the data is named, and what the actual data is. (Parents name a child to differentiate him or her from the other brothers and sisters. The same concept is used with naming data used by a computer.)

Let us begin by first investigating the format of an instruction.

FORMAT OF AN INSTRUCTION

Each instruction is composed of three parts: the line number, the statement, and the variable or variables. Refer to Figure A.1.

LINE NUMBER

A **line number** or **statement number** identifies the instruction and makes it easy to reference, from both the programmer's and the computer's points of view. A

FIGURE A.1.
Three parts of a BASIC instruction.

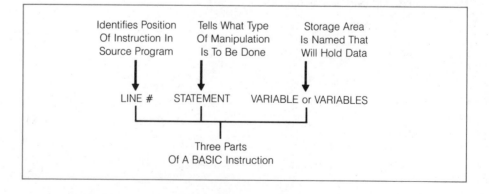

line number is generally stated in multiples of 10 so that additional instructions can be inserted easily, if needed. This is the more common practice, although line numbers can be numbered consecutively from 1 through 99999 on most computers.

There are many versions of the BASIC language; each mainframe has its form of BASIC, and C-BASIC, Microsoft BASIC, (also called M-BASIC), and BASIC Plus name just a few of the variations that are available on microcomputers. Although the BASIC language has been standardized, different computer manufacturers offer special features. The instructions introduced in this chapter are fairly consistent throughout the language variations. The intent of this material is to familiarize you with some instructions so that programs can be written and tested, if desired. Please understand that your version of BASIC might be different on some details; consult your reference manual for details.

STATEMENT

The statement identifies the data manipulation that is to be performed. To communicate with the computer, we use reserved words that it "understands." **Reserved words** are those words used in the language which specify a certain operation that the computer is to perform. The programmer chooses the correct reserved word, already defined in the computer language, for a specific data manipulation that is needed. Some of the reserved words that are discussed in this chapter are listed here, along with their purposes:

REM   Used for inserting remarks within the program for clarity and documentation purposes.

READ   Used to name the data that is inputted in the program. READ works with the DATA statement.

DATA   Provides the actual data used for manipulation. This statement is used along with the READ statement to identify what data is to be worked with in the program.

INPUT   Used in place of the READ and DATA statements when the programmer wishes to ask questions of the user or when you wish to make an inquiry of the computer.

PRINT   Used for preparing output on the monitor from the data that has been manipulated. Used when you wish to have the computer print some message or some value that was inputted or calculated.

LET   Used to make some calculation or assign some value in a program. The arithmetic operators used are the * for multiplying, the / for dividing, the + for adding, and the − for subtracting.

GO TO   Used for changing the flow of logic in the program by directing the computer to some particular line number.

IF THEN   Used for asking a question and giving a line number that is to be transferred to when the condition is true.

IF THEN   Used for asking a question and giving a statement or statement num-
ELSE   ber for the next step when the condition is true or false.

END   Used to tell the computer to stop processing the program.

USE OF VARIABLES

The user must identify the data that is to be used in the program. To do this, the user creates a name for the data, which is called a **variable.** The variable is not the data itself, but it does represent the data and becomes the name of the storage area that is reserved by the computer to hold that data. Think of a storage area as a post office box; the variable is the number on the outside of the post office box. Certainly this number is important, for it enables us to distinguish "post office boxes." More important, however, is the data that is inside the box. After all, it is the data that we wish to process. As an example, consider the variable named A. The data for A might be a 2, a 3.8, or a 1.777, for example. A pro-grammer's responsibility is to tell the computer the name of the variable as well as the data.

Let us analyze what type of data we work with in a program. There will be numeric data that is used for calculation and other data used for display purposes (as hard copy or soft copy shown on a cathode ray tube). The display data can take the form of messages or text, which is then considered a **string.** For example, if you wish to calculate the balance of your checkbook, the numeric data would be the dollar amount of the check used in the calculation. The name of the person to whom the check is paid would be considered a string. Variables can be of two types: (1) numeric or (2) string. Numeric variables identify numeric data which can be composed of numbers only, a sign and numbers, or a sign, numbers, and decimal point, as shown in Figure A.2. String variables identify the messages or text (in the case of the checkbook example, the payee's name).

FIGURE A.2.
Types of variables.

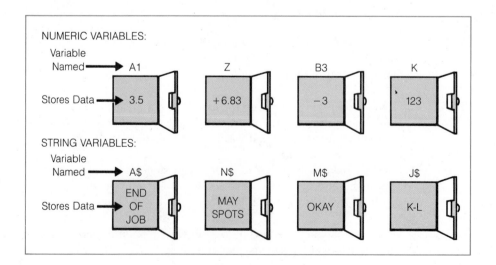

For naming variables, numeric data may use an alphabetic, an alphabetic and a number, or an alphabetic and the % symbol. The last combination is used to change a real number (one that has a decimal point in the data) to an integer (whole number). For example, suppose you have made a calculation that is expressed as whole numbers and decimals. All you are interested in, however, is the whole number. For the truncation (the cutting off) and the possible rounding of the decimals from the answer, all you would have to do is end the variable name with a %, for example, A% or Z%. (This is illustrated later in Figure A.3).

Any time we wish to set up messages and later have them printed, we must name these messages under the rules set forth for naming string variables. A variable used to identify alphanumeric data begins with an alphabetic character but has the second character as a dollar sign ($). All variables that contain a $ are considered a string.

It must be pointed out that BASIC run on the DEC System 20 and the IBM personal computer using the BASIC version called Microsoft BASIC allow thirty-five and forty characters, respectively, in the variable. For our purposes here, we will use just the single variable and a $ for representing strings. Numeric data will be designated using a single variable and possibly a number.

CHECKPOINT Can you:

Identify the types of variables that can be used?

Tell when the $ is used? The %?

SOME ELEMENTAL INSTRUCTIONS

Let us begin our discussion of BASIC statements by covering a few of the more elementary ones. Having just discussed naming variables, let us look into how the values can be assigned to a variable through the use of the LET statement. After that let us look into how the READ and DATA statements can be used. Certainly we wish to see the results from any processing so we will next briefly cover the PRINT statement. A complete BASIC program is then discussed.

LET Statement

You might ask, how does a person writing a BASIC program associate the variable with the data? One way to do so is to use a LET statement.

A LET statement takes as its format a line number, followed by LET, the variable name, an = symbol, and the data in question. A sample format follows:

Line # LET Variable = Data

Note particularly that the numeric variable or string variable appears on the left-hand side of the equal sign.

Data which does not change in value in the program is referred to as a **constant. A numeric constant** can represent numeric data that is used for setting a value to a predetermined amount for looping (repeating a series of instructions many times) or for calculations used in the program. The LET statement is called an assignment statement because it assigns or gives a value to a particular variable shown on the left-hand side of the equal sign. Refer to Figure A.3 for some examples of LET instructions.

The LET statement is also used for calculation. Most of the time a user does not have to enter the word LET when doing calculations but we will use LET each time.

Calculations are performed using the arithmetic operators of + to add, − to subtract, * to multiply, ^ to raise to a power, and / to divide. The rules of hierarchy of arithmetic are followed for BASIC as in algebra. The order in which calculations are performed is listed below.

1. Parentheses are used in BASIC as in algebra. The calculations set within parentheses are cleared first before any other calculations are performed in the equation.

FIGURE A.3.
LET instructions.

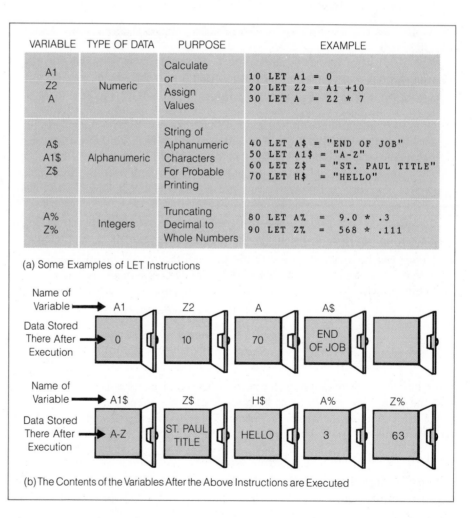

VARIABLE	TYPE OF DATA	PURPOSE	EXAMPLE
A1 Z2 A	Numeric	Calculate or Assign Values	10 LET A1 = 0 20 LET Z2 = A1 +10 30 LET A = Z2 * 7
A$ A1$ Z$	Alphanumeric	String of Alphanumeric Characters For Probable Printing	40 LET A$ = "END OF JOB" 50 LET A1$ = "A-Z" 60 LET Z$ = "ST. PAUL TITLE" 70 LET H$ = "HELLO"
A% Z%	Integers	Truncating Decimal to Whole Numbers	80 LET A% = 9.0 * .3 90 LET Z% = 568 * .111

(a) Some Examples of LET Instructions

Name of Variable → A1   Z2   A   A$

Data Stored There After Execution → 0   10   70   END OF JOB

Name of Variable → A1$ Z$ H$ A%   Z%

Data Stored There After Execution → A-Z   ST. PAUL TITLE   HELLO   3   63

(b) The Contents of the Variables After the Above Instructions are Executed

```
RUNNING TOTAL

010   LET T = 0           Initializes value to 0

020   LET S = 0           Initializes value to 0

030   LET S = S + 1       Notice how the same variable appears on both sides of the
                          equal sign. Each time the instruction is executed, a 1 is added
                          to variable S.

040   LET T = S + T       This adds whatever data is stored in S plus whatever data is
                          stored in the variable T. The result is stored in T.
```

2. Any exponential work is done next.

3. Multiplication and division are done in the order that they are stated in the equation. The important point in using division is that the first variable becomes the dividend and the second variable becomes the divisor. As an example, if A = 20 and B = 4 and the calculation statement is written as 010 LET C = A / B, after execution, the value held in C would be 5. The line number of 010 is equivalent to line number 10.

4. Adding and subtracting are performed in the order that they are stated in the equation.

Using Figure A.3(a) examine the example instructions. Refer to Figure A.3(b) for the variable and its contents after the instructions are executed.

When we think of calculation, a running total is frequently used. Refer to Figure A.4. Whenever a running total is to be used, always initialize the variable used for storing the running total to a predetermined value. In our example in Figure A.4, the variable named S is initialized on line 020 to a zero. When running totals are used, notice how the same variable appears on both sides of the equal sign as shown in lines 030 and 040. For example, the first time line 030 is executed by the computer, the variable named S is set to a 1. After line 040 is executed, the variable named T will hold a 1 also. If just lines 030 and 040 are executed again without executing lines 010 and 020 again, S will be storing a 2 while T will be storing a 3. If, for example, the variable named T was not initialized to a 0 as shown on line 010, there would be no guarantee that the running total calculated and stored in the variable named T would be correct.

Figure A.5 shows other examples of calculations using the LET instructions.

CHECKPOINT **Can you:**

Identify the arithmetic operators used for calculations?
List the rules of hierarchy of arithmetic?

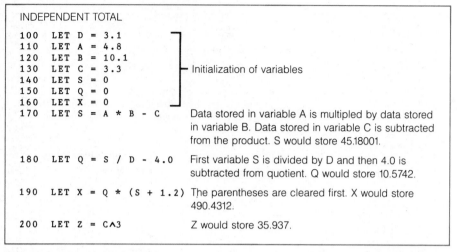

```
INDEPENDENT TOTAL

100   LET D = 3.1
110   LET A = 4.8
120   LET B = 10.1       ⎤
130   LET C = 3.3        ⎥── Initialization of variables
140   LET S = 0          ⎥
150   LET Q = 0          ⎥
160   LET X = 0          ⎦
170   LET S = A * B - C      Data stored in variable A is multipled by data stored
                             in variable B. Data stored in variable C is subtracted
                             from the product. S would store 45.18001.

180   LET Q = S / D - 4.0    First variable S is divided by D and then 4.0 is
                             subtracted from quotient. Q would store 10.5742.

190   LET X = Q * (S + 1.2)  The parentheses are cleared first. X would store
                             490.4312.

200   LET Z = C∧3            Z would store 35.937.
```

READ and DATA Statements

Data can also be inputted through the use of the READ and DATA statements, which work together. Referring to Figures A.6 and A.7, we note two formats are usable. Beginning with the READ instruction shown in Figure A.6, the format is a line number followed by the READ statement followed by a variable. In this example, there is only one variable to be read as input. In Figure A.6 the variable named H is used; we know from previous discussion that H is a numeric variable. Examining the format of the DATA instruction in Figure A.6, note that the data stored at the variable named H is 3.86.

As is shown in Figure A.7, several fields of data can be inputted on one READ instruction. Pay particular attention, however, that commas separate the variables on the READ instruction when multiple variables are inputted. No comma appears after the last variable name in Figure A.6 or A.7, however.

The DATA instruction works with the READ instruction. Figure A.7 shows that the variable named A stores the data 4. If the list of variables appeared on the READ instruction as:

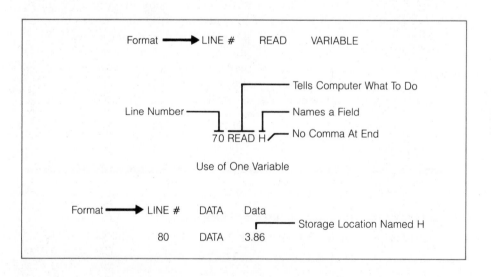

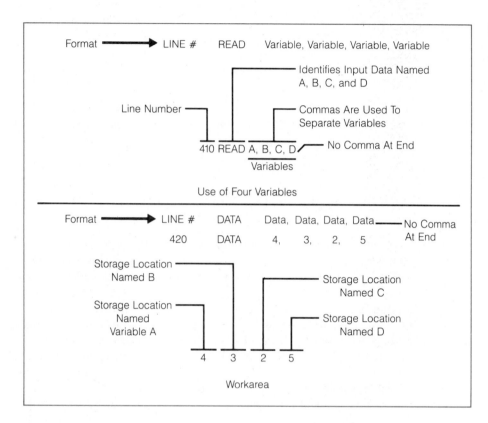

FIGURE A.7.
**More than one variable used with
a READ statement.**

```
10   READ D, C, B, A
20   DATA 4, 3, 2, 5
```

the variable D would then store the value of 4, the variable C would store the value of 3, and so on. In other words, the variable is listed in the same order as the data it represents.

PRINT Statement

We can input and calculate data all day long. Unless we output the results, we never know the answers. The PRINT instruction has two formats. When we wish to output just one variable, we would use the format of line number, the reserved word PRINT, followed by a variable. Let us try expressing the format of this instruction in a slightly shortened form where L# stands for line number and V stands for variable.

L# PRINT V or LINE # PRINT VARIABLE

Using this format for the PRINT statement, an instruction could be written as 30 PRINT H. For example,

```
10    READ H
20    DATA 8
30    PRINT H
40    END
```

the data displayed would be an 8. As you will recall from discussion in Chapter 6, the END statement tells the computer to stop processing the program. If, however, the instructions were:

```
100    READ A, B, C, D
110    DATA 4, 3, 2, 5
120    PRINT A, B, C, D
130    END
```

the PRINT instruction would use the format of L# PRINT V,V,V,V. The program and the output are shown in Figure A.8. Spacing is automatically generated between fields of data for easy reading. The shaded area represents the output from the computer.

On a printed line, just the data can be printed, or just an English message can be printed; or a combination of both can be printed. The last alternative identifies the data most clearly. Notice that in Figure A.9 the string variable is used as well as the PRINT statement; it uses the double quotation marks to enclose the message.

Refer to Table A.2 for the format for various instructions. Once again, L# stands for line number, V stands for variable, and D stands for data. Where V,V,V appears, this means that more than one variable can be used. In no way does it imply that just three variables can be used. To make certain we understand the convention used, look briefly at the PRINT instructions in Table A.1. There are three versions to the print instruction:

```
L# PRINT
L# PRINT V
L# PRINT V,V,V
```

The first example shows a line number but no variable. This statement is used in case you wish to generate a blank line. The second example shows a line number, the statement PRINT, and one variable. The third example shows the line number, the statement PRINT, and many variables, each of which is separated by a comma.

FIGURE A.8.
A complete BASIC program with system command and output.

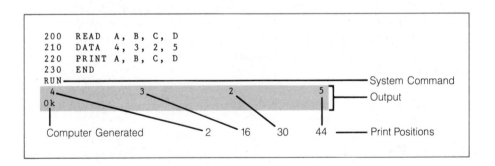

```
010   READ   A, B, C, D
020   DATA   4, 3, 2, 5
030   LET S = A + B + C + D
040   PRINT S
050   LET P$ = "VALUE OF PRODUCT IS "
060   LET P = A * B
070   LET Q = P / D
080   PRINT P$, P
090   PRINT "VALUE OF QUOTIENT IS ", Q
100   END
RUN ─────────────────────────────────────── System Command
```

```
        14
        VALUE OF PRODUCT IS          12
Output  VALUE OF QUOTIENT IS         2.4
        Ok ─────────────────────────────── Computer Generated
```

Discussion of a Program

Assume that three checks have been written on a checking account in the month. The service charge is 25 cents per check written. Also assume that the balance before these checks were written is known. Given this problem, let us calculate the new balance. The structure chart, the pseudocode, the flowchart, and this introductory program are shown in Figure A.10. Notice how the pseudocode statements closely parallel the instructions written in the BASIC program. The BASIC program is shown in Figure A.10(d).

When a program is to be written, it is far easier in the long run to name the variables so they are easy to remember. That is why the variables beginning with a C and a number are used for identifying the check amounts. Each variable must be different so that the computer knows what it is to work with. The balance is called B in the program, and the service charge is called S.

Can you imagine that at some later date, you wish to use the program again and are immediately confused as to what each variable represents? That is why documentation is included in programs. Refer to Figure A.11 for the same program with documentation included. The use of the REM statement in Figure A.11(a) tells the computer to never use this statement in processing. We use it, however, to make sense of a program. The programs shown in Figures A.10 and A.11 are equivalent in processing; it is only the documentation that differentiates them. If you are interested in keying the programs included in the appendix, omission of the REM instructions does not affect the processing. It is strongly suggested, however, that the same line numbers be used for successful execution of many of the programs presented later in the appendix. Figure A.11(b) shows how two instructions on lines 220 and 230 could be replaced with one instruction instead (line 225).

Discussion of Another Program

Let us use a payroll problem that calculates gross and net pay. The BASIC program is shown in Figure A.12(a). The pseudocode and flowchart are shown in Figure A.12 parts b and c, respectively. Comments are inserted in the program

TABLE A.1.   **BASIC Instructions Format**

The format for the instructions are set up with the following convention:

L#	stands for line number
V	stands for variable
V,V,V	stands for many variables; three variables are not the limit
D	stands for data
D,D,D	stands for many sets of data that can be used

The statements are not related to each other in the following table.

STATEMENT	PURPOSE	FORMAT	EXAMPLES
DATA	Used with READ statement to identify data assigned to single variable	L# DATA D	390 DATA 6.777 400 DATA 144
	Used with READ statement to identify data assigned to each variable	L# DATA D,D,D	410 DATA 4, 5.9, 6.8
GO TO	Used for changing the flow of logic	L# GO TO L#	420 GO TO 520
IF THEN	Used for selection by testing a relation; it points to a line number to be executed when condition is true	L# IF relation THEN L#	430 IF A = B THEN 50
	Used for selection by testing a relation; it provides a statement to be executed when condition is true	L# IF relation THEN statement	510 IF A = B THEN PRINT "EQUAL" 530 IF A > = B THEN LET C = C + 1
LET	Assign values to a variable	L# LET V = D	610 LET A = 5 620 LET A$ = "OK" 630 LET A$ = "5"
	Used for adding values	L# LET V = D + D L# LET V = V + D	640 LET A = 3 + 8 650 LET X = A + 8.7 660 LET C = C + 1
	Used for subtracting values	L# LET V = V − D L# LET V = V − V	670 LET Y = X − 4 680 LET Z = X − Y
	Used for multiplying	L# LET V = V * D L# LET V = V * V	690 LET D = Y * 9 700 LET E = D * X
	Used for dividing	L# LET V = V / D L# LET V = V / V	800 LET F = X / 5 810 LET M = Y / X
	Used for functions	L# LET V = function	820 LET C = SQR(A) 830 LET D = COS(X)
PRINT	Prints one blank line	L# PRINT	910 PRINT
	Prints one line with one field of data	L# PRINT V	920 PRINT A
	Prints one line with several fields of data using zone spacing	L# PRINT V,V,V	930 PRINT A,B,C,D
	Prints one line with one field of data; the positioning controlled by the number used with TAB	L# PRINT TAB( );V	940 PRINT TAB(3); A
	Prints one line with spacing determined by the number used with TAB	L# PRINT TAB( );V;V;	950 PRINT TAB(4);A; TAB(35);B; 960 PRINT TAB(59);C
READ	Input large volume of data with one data field per record	L# READ V	200 READ A
	Input large volume of data with many data fields per record	L# READ V,V,V	210 READ A, B, C

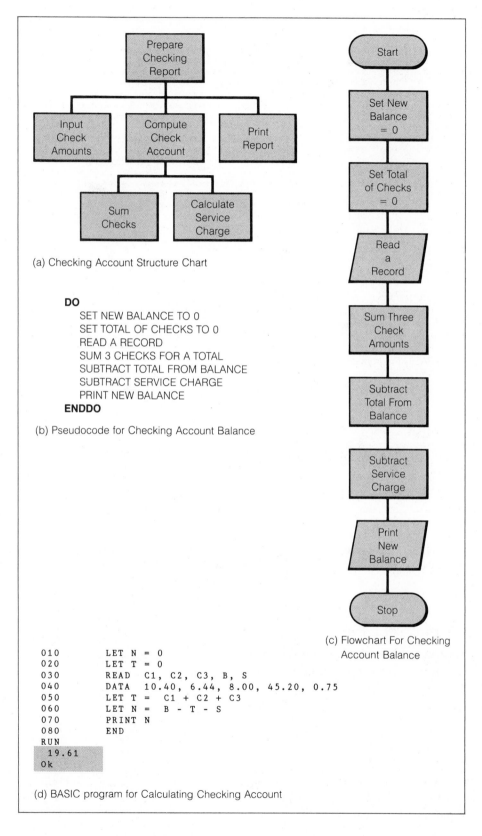

FIGURE A.10.
BASIC program for calculating a checking account.

(a) Checking Account Structure Chart

```
DO
    SET NEW BALANCE TO 0
    SET TOTAL OF CHECKS TO 0
    READ A RECORD
    SUM 3 CHECKS FOR A TOTAL
    SUBTRACT TOTAL FROM BALANCE
    SUBTRACT SERVICE CHARGE
    PRINT NEW BALANCE
ENDDO
```

(b) Pseudocode for Checking Account Balance

(c) Flowchart For Checking
Account Balance

```
010        LET N = 0
020        LET T = 0
030        READ   C1, C2, C3, B, S
040        DATA   10.40, 6.44, 8.00, 45.20, 0.75
050        LET T =   C1 + C2 + C3
060        LET N =   B - T - S
070        PRINT N
080        END
RUN
 19.61
Ok
```

(d) BASIC program for Calculating Checking Account

FIGURE A.11.
BASIC program for calculating checking account balance.

```
010   REM
020   REM                    ****************************
030   REM                         SYMBOL SECTION
040   REM                    ****************************
050   REM
060   REM                    C1  =  FIRST CHECK AMOUNT
070   REM                    C2  =  SECOND CHECK AMOUNT
080   REM                    C3  =  THIRD CHECK AMOUNT
090   REM                    B   =  BALANCE
100   REM                    S   =  SERVICE CHARGE
110   REM                    N   =  NEW BALANCE
120   REM                    T   =  TOTAL CHECK AMOUNT
130   REM
140   REM                    ****************************
150   REM                        PROCESSING SECTION
160   REM                    ****************************
170   REM
180         LET N = 0
190         LET T = 0
200         READ  C1, C2, C3, B, S
210         DATA  10.40, 6.44, 8.00, 45.20, 0.75
220         LET T =  C1 + C2 + C3
230         LET N =  B - T - S
240         PRINT N
250         END
RUN
 19.61
Ok
```

(a) BASIC Program With Documentation

```
    Line            Variable              Data That
   Number        Holds Result          Is Calculated

    225          LET   N = B - (C1 + C2 + C3) - S


    220          LET   T =  C1  +  C2  +  C3  ]  These Two Instructions
                                                ├ Are Equivalent To The
    230          LET   N =  B  -  T  -  S    ]  One Above
```

(b) The Combining Of Two Instructions Into One LET Instruction

through the use of the REM statement; these simply supply documentation and do not ever enter into processing. REMs make for easier program reading.

IN-DEPTH DISCUSSION OF INSTRUCTIONS

Let us now work in detail on the instructions, showing variations of each with many programs to explain the programming function.

PRINT STATEMENT

Printing can be accomplished in different ways, namely using variables and literals, strings and variables, zones for formatting data, the TAB statement, and # signs for editing data on some versions of BASIC.

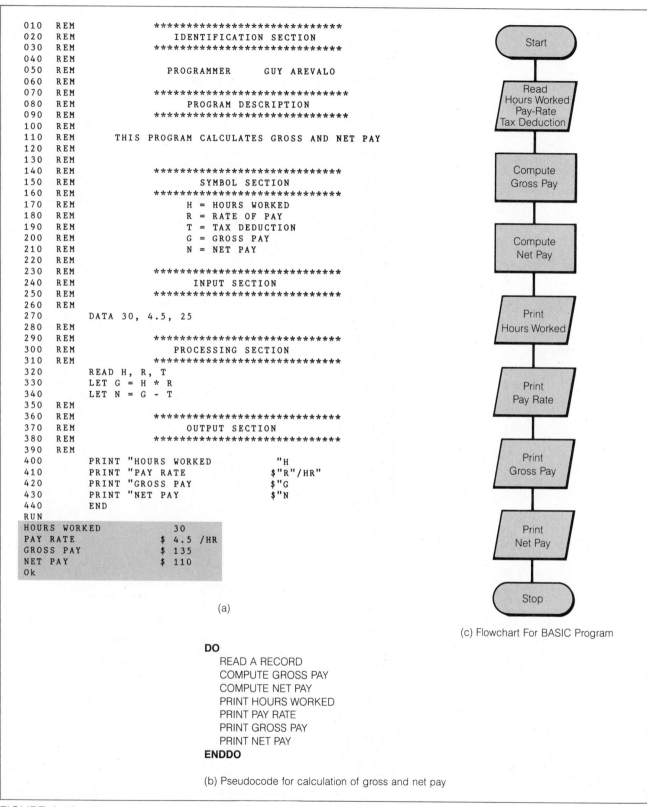

```
010   REM             ****************************
020   REM                   IDENTIFICATION SECTION
030   REM             ****************************
040   REM
050   REM                   PROGRAMMER     GUY AREVALO
060   REM
070   REM             ****************************
080   REM                   PROGRAM DESCRIPTION
090   REM             ****************************
100   REM
110   REM       THIS PROGRAM CALCULATES GROSS AND NET PAY
120   REM
130   REM
140   REM             ****************************
150   REM                   SYMBOL SECTION
160   REM             ****************************
170   REM                   H = HOURS WORKED
180   REM                   R = RATE OF PAY
190   REM                   T = TAX DEDUCTION
200   REM                   G = GROSS PAY
210   REM                   N = NET PAY
220   REM
230   REM             ****************************
240   REM                   INPUT SECTION
250   REM             ****************************
260   REM
270         DATA 30, 4.5, 25
280   REM
290   REM             ****************************
300   REM                   PROCESSING SECTION
310   REM             ****************************
320         READ H, R, T
330         LET G = H * R
340         LET N = G - T
350   REM
360   REM             ****************************
370   REM                   OUTPUT SECTION
380   REM             ****************************
390   REM
400         PRINT "HOURS WORKED        "H
410         PRINT "PAY RATE            $"R"/HR"
420         PRINT "GROSS PAY           $"G
430         PRINT "NET PAY             $"N
440         END
RUN
HOURS WORKED             30
PAY RATE          $  4.5 /HR
GROSS PAY         $  135
NET PAY           $  110
Ok
```

(a)

```
DO
    READ A RECORD
    COMPUTE GROSS PAY
    COMPUTE NET PAY
    PRINT HOURS WORKED
    PRINT PAY RATE
    PRINT GROSS PAY
    PRINT NET PAY
ENDDO
```

(b) Pseudocode for calculation of gross and net pay

(c) Flowchart For BASIC Program

FIGURE A.12.   **BASIC program for calculating gross and net pay.**

In the program in Figure A.12(a), a mix of variables and literals are used with a PRINT statement. Think of **literals** as being those messages that we set up within quotation marks.

FIGURE A.13.
Program and output for printing zones.

```
010    REM              **********************************
020    REM                  PROGRAM DESCRIPTION
030    REM              **********************************
040    REM
050    REM              DATA PRINTED IN ZONES WITH USE OF COMMA.
060    REM
070    REM                  ***************************
080    REM                      PROCESSING SECTION
090    REM                  ***************************
100            READ   A,  B,  C,  D
110            DATA   4,  3,  2,  5
120            PRINT  A,  B,  C,  D
130            END
RUN
    4              3              2              5
Ok
```
(a) Printing Using Zones

```
122            LET  S  =  A  +  B  +  C  +  D
123            PRINT  S,  A,  B,  C,  D
RUN
    4              3              2              5
   14              4              3              2              5
Ok
124            PRINT
125            PRINT  S,  " ",  A,  B,  C,  D
RUN
    4              3              2              5
   14              4              3              2              5

   14                             4              3              2
    5
Ok
```
(b) Skipping a Zone

```
LIST
010    REM              **********************************
020    REM                  PROGRAM DESCRIPTION
030    REM              **********************************
040    REM
050    REM              DATA PRINTED IN ZONES WITH USE OF COMMA.
060    REM
070    REM                  ***************************
080    REM                      PROCESSING SECTION
090    REM                  ***************************
100            READ   A,  B,  C,  D
110            DATA   4,  3,  2,  5
120            PRINT  A,  B,  C,  D
122            LET  S  =  A  +  B  +  C  +  D
123            PRINT  S,  A,  B,  C,  D
124            PRINT
125            PRINT  S,  " ",  A,  B,  C,  D
130            END
```
(c)

Use of Zones

All BASIC language output is automatically spaced according to built-in zones, so the user does not have to be concerned with spacing data. This automatic spacing is triggered by use of commas on the PRINT instruction to separate variables. As shown in Figure A.13(a), such use of commas between variables results in data printed in columns. Generally, five zones are set for one printed line, with the length of each zone being either fourteen or fifteen positions. Graphic representation of these zones appears in Figure A.14.

In Figure A.13(a), lines 010 through 130 were originally entered to illustrate zones used in printing data. The output appears in the first shaded area. Lines 122 and 123 were entered to calculate a total and then to print the total. Notice how the line numbers are chosen so they are correctly positioned for processing. The RUN systems command is given; the output for the complete program appears in the second shaded area. Line 124 was entered to illustrate that a blank line can be generated on output. Line 125 shows that a zone can be skipped through the use of quotation marks; in this example, use of the skipping function results in the carryover of some data to the zones of the next printed line. The output appears in the third shaded area.

Since we inserted additional instructions, let us now look at the complete source program. We can add instructions then perhaps become concerned about what the source program really contains. Notice in Figure A.13(b) how the systems command LIST is entered by the user. After the RETURN key is depressed, the computer generates a complete listing of the source program that is in primary storage, with the line numbers in sequential order.

Examine the program in Figure A.15. Notice that as long as numeric and alphanumeric data are enclosed within quotation marks, the computer left justifies the data (that is, uses a left margin).

Use of Semicolons

When the programmer wishes to format his or her own line of data on output, semicolons are used in the PRINT instruction between variables, as shown in Figure A.16. The number of spaces set aside within quotation marks determines the number of blank positions assigned by the computer. Many BASIC versions

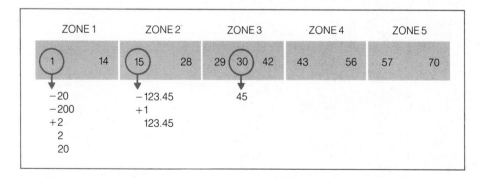

FIGURE A.14.
Zero used in signed data.

FIGURE A.15.
Alphanumeric and unsigned data.

```
010   REM                ******************************
020   REM                      PROGRAM DESCRIPTION
030   REM                ******************************
040   REM
050   REM      ZONES ARE BYPASSED WHEN SEMICOLONS ARE USED.
060   REM
070   REM                ******************************
080   REM                         INPUT SECTION
090   REM                ******************************
100   REM
110         DATA 4, 3, 2, 5
120   REM
130   REM                ******************************
140   REM                      PROCESSING SECTION
150   REM                ******************************
160         READ  A, B, C, D
170         PRINT A; " "; B; " "; C; " "; D
180         LET   S = A + B + C + D
190         PRINT "SUM IS "; S
200         END
RUN
 4      3     2      5
SUM IS     14
Ok
```

allow a blank position before a number for the possible printing of a sign. A user should check this detail as it varies according to the BASIC version used. For example, if the instructions were written as:

```
10    READ A, B
20    DATA -7.687, 578.9
30    PRINT A; B
40    END
RUN
```

FIGURE A.16.
**Use of semicolons on PRINT—
statement.**

```
010   REM
020   REM                ******************************
030   REM                      PROGRAM DESCRIPTION
040   REM                ******************************
050   REM
060   REM                 LEFT JUSTIFICATION OF DATA
070   REM                  IS USED WHEN THE DATA IS
080   REM                INCLUDED WITHIN QUOTATION MARKS.
090   REM
100   REM                ******************************
110   REM                      PROCESSING SECTION
120   REM                ******************************
130   REM
140         PRINT "FRED JONES"
150         PRINT "6000 GREAT HIGHWAY"
160         PRINT "ST. LOUIS, MO."
170         PRINT "63166"
180         END
RUN
FRED JONES
6000 GREAT HIGHWAY
ST. LOUIS, MO.
63166
Ok
```

the output data would be printed with the − sign beginning in position 1, the 7 in position 2, the decimal in position 3, and so on; the 5 of 578.9 would be printed beginning in position 8. The output would appear as:

```
-7.687 578.9
```

However, if the print instruction was changed above to read:

```
30   PRINT A; "  "; B
```

the − sign would print in position 1; the 5 of 578.9 would print in position 9. The output would appear as:

```
-7.687    578.9
```

Use of TAB

To better position data, a PRINT instruction can use the word **TAB,** which positions the data on a line. Figure A.17 uses the TAB statement, which requires semicolons with the PRINT instruction. When the TAB statement is used on the PRINT instruction, a number is placed in parentheses following the word TAB. If the PRINT instruction shows a TAB(5); A the data for the variable A will be printed beginning in print position 5; some BASIC versions would begin in position 6.

Use of Headings

In Figure A.18(b) which illustrates the pseudocode, notice that a blank line is to be printed between the heading line and the data line which gives the name,

```
010   REM              ****************************
020   REM                 PROGRAM DESCRIPTION
030   REM              ****************************
040   REM
050   REM              THIS PROGRAM ILLUSTRATES PRINTING
060   REM                 DATA WITH THE USE OF THE TAB.
070   REM
080   REM              ****************************
090   REM                 PROCESSING SECTION
100   REM              ****************************
110   REM
120        PRINT TAB(19);"FRED JONES"
130        PRINT TAB(19);"6000 GREAT HIGHWAY"
140        PRINT TAB(19);"ST. LOUIS, MO."
150        PRINT TAB(19);"63166"
160        END
RUN
                       FRED JONES
                       6000 GREAT HIGHWAY
                       ST. LOUIS, MO.
                       63166
Ok
```

FIGURE A.17.
Use of Tab statement.

scores, sum, and average. Figure A.18(c) shows the flowchart for this non-iterative processing.

Figure A.18(a) shows the complete BASIC program. The heading prints as one line on the output. In the BASIC program, two lines (lines 390 and 400) are needed to set up one printed line. Since the TAB is used, semicolons are also

FIGURE A.18.   **BASIC program for calculation of average grades on a test.**

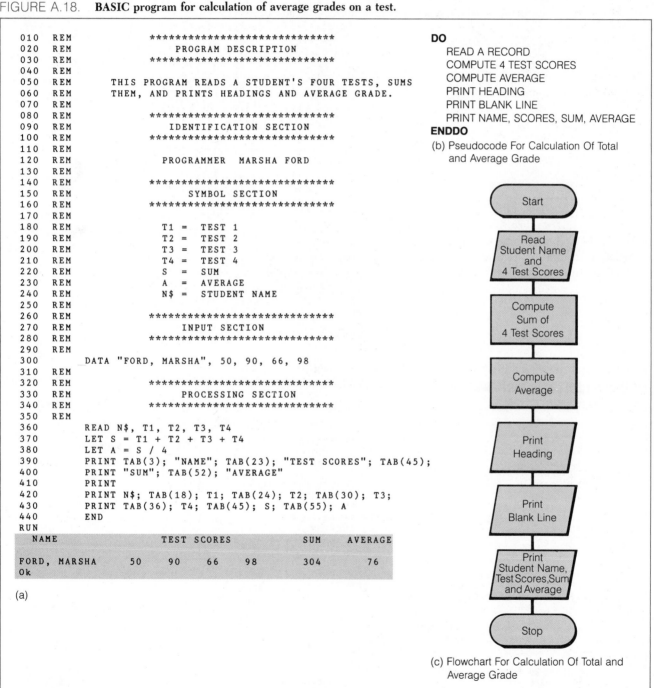

```
010    REM                  ***************************
020    REM                        PROGRAM DESCRIPTION
030    REM                  ***************************
040    REM
050    REM         THIS PROGRAM READS A STUDENT'S FOUR TESTS, SUMS
060    REM         THEM, AND PRINTS HEADINGS AND AVERAGE GRADE.
070    REM
080    REM                  ***************************
090    REM                      IDENTIFICATION SECTION
100    REM                  ***************************
110    REM
120    REM                    PROGRAMMER   MARSHA FORD
130    REM
140    REM                  ***************************
150    REM                         SYMBOL SECTION
160    REM                  ***************************
170    REM
180    REM                    T1  =   TEST 1
190    REM                    T2  =   TEST 2
200    REM                    T3  =   TEST 3
210    REM                    T4  =   TEST 4
220    REM                    S   =   SUM
230    REM                    A   =   AVERAGE
240    REM                    N$  =   STUDENT NAME
250    REM
260    REM                  ***************************
270    REM                         INPUT SECTION
280    REM                  ***************************
290    REM
300           DATA "FORD, MARSHA", 50, 90, 66, 98
310    REM
320    REM                  ***************************
330    REM                      PROCESSING SECTION
340    REM                  ***************************
350    REM
360           READ N$, T1, T2, T3, T4
370           LET S = T1 + T2 + T3 + T4
380           LET A = S / 4
390           PRINT TAB(3); "NAME"; TAB(23); "TEST SCORES"; TAB(45);
400           PRINT "SUM"; TAB(52); "AVERAGE"
410           PRINT
420           PRINT N$; TAB(18); T1; TAB(24); T2; TAB(30); T3;
430           PRINT TAB(36); T4; TAB(45); S; TAB(55); A
440           END
RUN
  NAME                    TEST SCORES              SUM      AVERAGE

FORD, MARSHA      50      90      66      98       304         76
Ok
```

(a)

DO
  READ A RECORD
  COMPUTE 4 TEST SCORES
  COMPUTE AVERAGE
  PRINT HEADING
  PRINT BLANK LINE
  PRINT NAME, SCORES, SUM, AVERAGE
ENDDO

(b) Pseudocode For Calculation Of Total
   and Average Grade

Start

Read
Student Name
and
4 Test Scores

Compute
Sum of
4 Test Scores

Compute
Average

Print
Heading

Print
Blank Line

Print
Student Name,
Test Scores, Sum
and Average

Stop

(c) Flowchart For Calculation Of Total and
   Average Grade

used along with various literals for the headings. Line 410 gives a blank printed line which separates the heading from the data. There is an exception to the shaded area that shows the output. Some Apple computers accommodate 40 characters on a screen rather than 80; this can be changed by purchasing a 80 position card. If the Apple II Plus or Apple IIe does not have this feature, the heading and data output will each exceed one line. This is a small point, but it is important, if the program is run on this brand of microcomputer.

Figure A.18(a) shows one possible way of creating headings. There is another way that headings can be prepared; this way incorporates the use of the PRINT USING statement which is available on some versions of BASIC.

PRINT USING STATEMENT

The PRINT USING statement's purpose is to allow the user to prepare headings and to edit data; otherwise, business reports would be very difficult to read. Most reports do not include the leading zeros because the zeros are suppressed by the PRINT USING statement; for example, 00002 would be printed as 2, with the appropriate number of spaces before the significant character. The PRINT USING instruction also allows the user to include punctuation such as the $ and the period in a numeric field. Not all computer systems have a PRINT USING statement; Apple and Pet/Commodore 64 do not.

The way we communicate the type of editing desired is through the use of **control characters** which refer to the way that the printed line is laid out. There are times where we will need to center a message within an area of a printed line; the control character of C is used. Other times we might wish a message to begin printing for the extreme left position in a field; the L control character is used in this case. Other times the message is to print from the extreme right position; the R control character is used. When numbers are to be printed, the control character of a # is used.

The PRINT USING statement is not standardized; hence, it differs drastically. Notice in Figures A.19 and 20 how two instructions are used; the line number following the PRINT USING statement points to the instruction that lays out the format of the printed line.

When numeric fields are to be edited, a # is placed wherever data is to be printed to establish the format of the output data. If leading zeros appear in the data to be edited for printing, the leading zeros are suppressed and only the significant character or characters printed. This does not mean, however, that any zeros to the right of significant characters are suppressed. Dollar signs can also be included; according to most BASIC programs, these remain fixed in a position, however. Some BASIC programs allow the dollar sign to float, which means that it moves and prints next to the first significant character.

The following discussion centers on the Microsoft BASIC's PRINT USING statement. As Table A.2 indicates, there are quite a few ways to edit data. The secret to successfully using the table is to realize that each time a # sign is used, there is a possibility of data to be printed there. Examining the line of the table used for the # control character, any positions that are not significant characters would print as blanks. For example, the PRINT USING format could be entered as follows:

FIGURE A.19.
Justifying alphanumeric data.

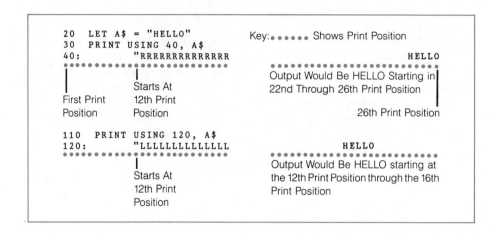

Example 1: **30   PRINT USING "###.##"; N**

Example 2: **40   PRINT USING "$#######.##"; A**

Using Example 1 if the data was 145.02 all three whole numbers would print along with the decimal point and the two numbers following the decimal point. If, however, the data was 008.92, only the 8.92 would print; the decimal points would be aligned on output.

Using Example 2 for the $ control character, the $ prints with all insignificant positions printed as blanks. If the data to be printed was all zeros, however, the $ and 0.00 will print. If, however, the $$ control characters are used, the $ floats which means it positions itself directly to the left of the first significant digit. Examine the column headed "Possible Data" to contrast the output.

Examples 1 and 2 above generate two printed lines. If only one printed line was desired, a semicolon would follow the variable on the first PRINT USING instruction.

If alphanumeric data is to be printed, a pair of slashes are used. The number of spaces left between the slashes indicates the maximum length of the display characters.

Example: **50   PRINT "\   \"; N$**

FIGURE A.20.
Suppressing zeros and using headings.

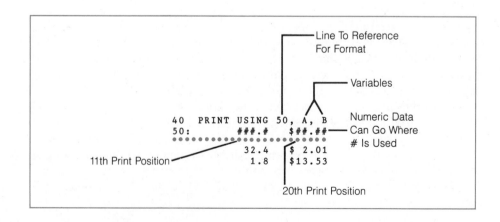

TABLE A.2. **Print Using Statement Additional Options.**

CONTROL CHARACTER	PURPOSE	UNUSED POSITIONS PRINT AS	AVAILABLE ON			PRINT USING EXAMPLE	POSSIBLE DATA
			IBM	TRS 80	DEC		
#	Allows numbers to print where used	blank	×	×	×	###.##	145.02 8.92
$	Prints $ where positioned	zero	×	×	×	$###.##	$145.02 $008.92
$$	$ floats; prints next to first significant character	blank	×	×	×	$$###.##	$145.02 $8.92
**$	* floats; $ prints next to first significant character	blank	×	×		**$###.##	**$145.02 ****$8.92
+	+ used before # prints + if data is positive; prints − if data is negative	blank	×	×		+##.##	+65.00 −8.92
∧∧∧∧	Prints exponential form	zero	×			###.##∧∧∧∧	6.50E+01
[[[[	Prints exponential form	zero		×		###.##[[[[	6.50E+01

List the various ways that print spacing can be accomplished?

Explain when commas are used? Semicolons? The PRINT USING statement?

READ, DATA, AND INPUT STATEMENTS

The READ with the DATA statement or the INPUT statement provides a means to input data. The READ and DATA statements are used for inputting large volumes of data. When the INPUT statement is used, a type of conversation exists between computer system and user.

READ and DATA Statements

READ and DATA statements work together to combine the inputting of data as well as the actual values assigned to each variable. In Figure A.18(a) one line of input data is used in the program, appearing on line 300. The READ instruction appears on line 360. If other data was to be inputted with this same program, the user could re-key line 300 followed by RUN. Two other ways are available for inputting many records into the program. These two methods use the INPUT statement and multiple DATA statements.

FIGURE A.21.
Use of the INPUT statement.

```
010   REM               *****************************
020   REM                    PROGRAM DESCRIPTION
030   REM               *****************************
040   REM
050   REM          THIS PROGRAM USES THE INPUT STATEMENT RATHER THAN
060   REM          THE READ AND DATA STATEMENT SO THAT INTERACTIVE
070   REM          PROCESSING CAN EXIST BETWEEN COMPUTER AND USER.
080   REM
090   REM               *****************************
100   REM                    PROCESSING SECTION
110   REM               *****************************
120   REM
130        INPUT "WHAT IS YOUR NAME"; N$
140        INPUT "IN WHICH CITY WERE YOU BORN"; C$
150        INPUT "IN WHICH STATE WERE YOU BORN"; S$
160        END
RUN
WHAT IS YOUR NAME? MOIRA MAYNARD
IN WHICH CITY WERE YOU BORN? HOUSTON
IN WHICH STATE WERE YOU BORN? TEXAS
Ok
RUN
WHAT IS YOUR NAME? BROWN, JOHN
?REDO FROM START
WHAT IS YOUR NAME? BROWN JOHN
IN WHICH CITY WERE YOU BORN? CINCINNATI
IN WHICH STATE WERE YOU BORN? OHIO
Ok
```

INPUT Statement

Another alternative for inputting data is to use the INPUT statement. This statement is very helpful for drill work for mathematics. It provides interactive processing capability, meaning the computer and user communicate as each instruction is executed.

An INPUT statement is used (see Figure A.21) where the user keys in the data as it is asked for by the computer. The reserved word INPUT is used for supplying new data to the computer for execution. Notice when the INPUT statement is used, literals are included on that instruction. This makes it easy for the user to know what he or she is to key. Also notice that the semicolon is used after the literal. The user keys in the value and then executes the instruction. When the instruction executes, the question and the response appear on the same line as the prompt generated from the computer (see Figure A.21). A response cannot contain a comma; a diagnostic results.

Multiple DATA Statements

Another alternative for processing many data records is to group DATA statements at the beginning of the program as shown in Figure A.22(a). The instruction to READ is then executed several times; each time it does, new data is used for the values. This involves the looping concept discussed in Chapter 11. The pseudocode and flowchart for this type of processing are shown in parts b and c of Figure A.22 respectively. Most versions of BASIC do not include a DO WHILE statement, although the BASIC version for the IBM Personal Computer does. (This is discussed in Appendix B.) The use of the IF and GO TO instructions are written by the programmer to accomplish the DO WHILE processing. The line number following the GO TO statement supplies the necessary looping concept.

Examining the output (the shaded area in the BASIC program), notice how the headings print once, since they are not set up within the loop. If the headings were placed within the loop, they would print each time that a line of data printed.

 **Can you:**

Identify the various ways that data can be inputted?

IF THEN and IF THEN ELSE STATEMENTS

Much processing requires selection which is done by IF statements. IF instructions are used for selecting data and for testing for the end-of-data condition. The format of the IF instruction is shown in Figure A.23. When the condition is met, the computer will transfer to the line number listed after the THEN. If the condition that is stated on the IF is not met, the computer will ignore the line number after the THEN and execute the next instruction after the IF instruction.

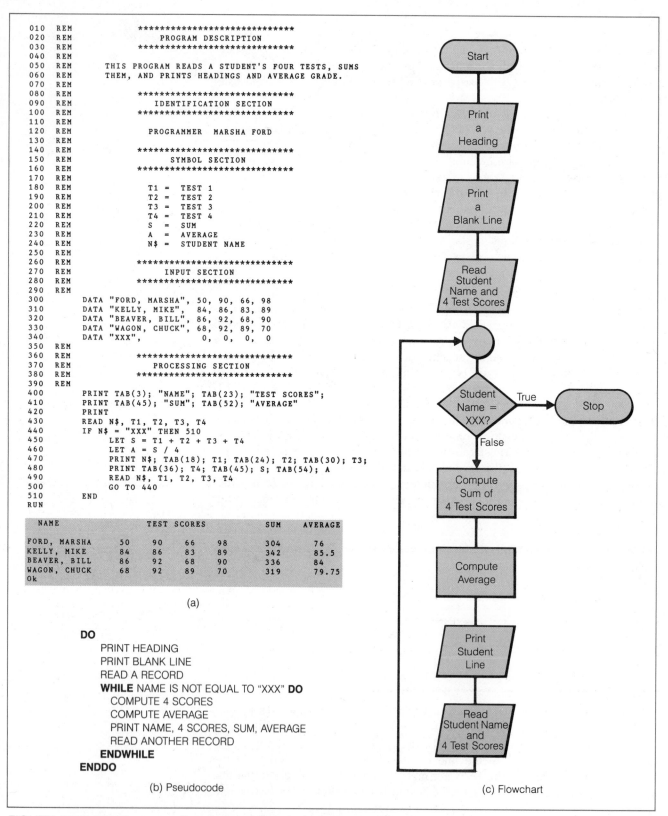

```
010  REM              ****************************
020  REM                  PROGRAM DESCRIPTION
030  REM              ****************************
040  REM
050  REM       THIS PROGRAM READS A STUDENT'S FOUR TESTS, SUMS
060  REM       THEM, AND PRINTS HEADINGS AND AVERAGE GRADE.
070  REM
080  REM              ****************************
090  REM                  IDENTIFICATION SECTION
100  REM              ****************************
110  REM
120  REM                  PROGRAMMER  MARSHA FORD
130  REM
140  REM              ****************************
150  REM                     SYMBOL SECTION
160  REM              ****************************
170  REM
180  REM                  T1  =   TEST 1
190  REM                  T2  =   TEST 2
200  REM                  T3  =   TEST 3
210  REM                  T4  =   TEST 4
220  REM                  S   =   SUM
230  REM                  A   =   AVERAGE
240  REM                  N$  =   STUDENT NAME
250  REM
260  REM              ****************************
270  REM                     INPUT SECTION
280  REM              ****************************
290  REM
300        DATA "FORD, MARSHA",  50, 90, 66, 98
310        DATA "KELLY, MIKE",   84, 86, 83, 89
320        DATA "BEAVER, BILL",  86, 92, 68, 90
330        DATA "WAGON, CHUCK",  68, 92, 89, 70
340        DATA "XXX",            0,  0,  0,  0
350  REM
360  REM              ****************************
370  REM                  PROCESSING SECTION
380  REM              ****************************
390  REM
400        PRINT TAB(3); "NAME"; TAB(23); "TEST SCORES";
410        PRINT TAB(45); "SUM"; TAB(52); "AVERAGE"
420        PRINT
430        READ N$, T1, T2, T3, T4
440        IF N$ = "XXX" THEN 510
450             LET S = T1 + T2 + T3 + T4
460             LET A = S / 4
470             PRINT N$; TAB(18); T1; TAB(24); T2; TAB(30); T3;
480             PRINT TAB(36); T4; TAB(45); S; TAB(54); A
490             READ N$, T1, T2, T3, T4
500             GO TO 440
510        END
RUN
```

```
 NAME                TEST SCORES            SUM    AVERAGE

FORD, MARSHA     50    90    66    98       304      76
KELLY, MIKE      84    86    83    89       342     85.5
BEAVER, BILL     86    92    68    90       336      84
WAGON, CHUCK     68    92    89    70       319     79.75
Ok
```

(a)

```
DO
    PRINT HEADING
    PRINT BLANK LINE
    READ A RECORD
    WHILE NAME IS NOT EQUAL TO "XXX" DO
        COMPUTE 4 SCORES
        COMPUTE AVERAGE
        PRINT NAME, 4 SCORES, SUM, AVERAGE
        READ ANOTHER RECORD
    ENDWHILE
ENDDO
```

(b) Pseudocode

(c) Flowchart

FIGURE A.22. **BASIC** program for calculating the average of four tests.

FIGURE A.23.
Format of the IF Statement.

FORMAT 1

What is Being Tested

```
IF      Relation     THEN   Execute This Statement When Condition Is TRUE

Takes These Statements When FALSE

        GO TO   Takes This Statement When the IF Statement Ends
```

FORMAT 2

What Is Being Tested

```
IF      Relation     THEN   Execute This Statement When TRUE
```

FIRST EXAMPLE Testing For Trailer Value

```
200  IF C$ = "XXX" THEN 240          (Goes to 240)
210      LET T3 = A + B
220      PRINT T3, A                 Does This When Condition Is FALSE
230      GO TO 300
240  PRINT "DOES THIS WHEN TRUE"
250  GO TO 310
 :
300  PRINT "ALSO DOES THIS WHEN FALSE"
310  END                             Goes To Here When End Of File
```

SECOND EXAMPLE

```
400  IF T > 16.4 THEN 480
410      LET T2 = Z / B
420      PRINT "DOES THIS WHEN T < = 16.4"
 :
480  PRINT "EXECUTES WHEN T > 16.4"
```

Executes This Instruction When T Is Equal to or Less Than 16.4

Executes This Instruction When T > 16.4

THIRD EXAMPLE

```
500  IF A$ = "OK" THEN PRINT "ALL RIGHT"
510  PRINT "ALWAYS EXECUTES THIS INSTRUCTION"
```

Only Prints When A$ Contains "OK"

Always Does This Instruction

FOURTH EXAMPLE

```
600  IF X < 7 THEN LET A = A + 1
610  PRINT "ALWAYS EXECUTES THIS INSTRUCTION"
```

Adds 1 To A When Condition Is True

Always Executes Statement 610

When the condition is testing alphanumeric data, the alphanumeric data is included within quotation marks, as shown in Figure A.23 since the computer cannot differentiate between data and variables.

Testing for End of Data

As was discussed in Chapter 11, the programmer often uses a dummy set of data, called a **trailer value,** to tell when the end-of-data or end-of-file condition is met. The IF instruction shown on line 440 in Figure A.22(a) is used for testing the end-of-data condition. When the end-of-data condition is true, the program either finishes processing or does other processing required to arrive at the desired solution. The user knows what designates the end-of-data condition by setting up some data to signal the end-of-data condition. In Figure A.22(a) the end-of-data condition is true when a person's name is made up of three consecutive X's.

For ease in reading, in Figure A.22(a) the false portion of the condition tested on the IF instruction is indented. It makes no difference if the instructions are indented, but it helps the reader in following the logic. The program is directed to line number 510, in this case, when the condition is true.

Selecting Data

IF instructions are also used for selection. The Holden & Miller Department Store pays its employees an hourly wage based upon a rate code that is established by the company. When the rate code is a 1, the employee's salary is $5 per hour. When the rate code is a 2, the hourly salary is $5.20. The management of the department store wishes to pay only those employees who have a rate code of a 1 or a 2; any others are incorrect codes.

The program, output, and flowchart for calculating employees' gross pay are shown in Figure A.24. The IF instruction is used for determining which rate code is inputted, with only rate codes 1 and 2 being acceptable. Any incorrect codes would require a message stating the error; a user wants to know which data was not processed. Follow the flowchart and the appropriate IF instructions to determine how the logic flows. The end-of-data condition is true in this program when a trailer value of 9999 is found in the employee number.

IF instructions can be **nested,** meaning that two or more instructions can be joined together to isolate a range of values. Suppose, for example, that the counselors at your college wish a printout of all those students aged eighteen through twenty-five. In addition, they wish to have the average age calculated for all records read. Figure A.25(b) shows the flowchart. Examine Figure A.25(a), and notice how the IF instruction testing the age is only processed when the end-of-data condition is false. Also, the IF instruction on line 400 is only processed when the IF instruction on line 390 is false. The age data only prints when the age is between the ages of eighteen and twenty-five. After all records are read and processed, line number 470 is executed for calculation of the average age for all records read, other than the dummy record.

IF THEN ELSE Statement

Some versions of BASIC, used primarily on the IBM Personal Computer and TRS-80 (Tandy's Radio Shack computers), provide the IF THEN ELSE statement.

There are two alternatives to this selection, one being true, which follows the THEN part of the instruction, and the other being false, which follows the ELSE. This statement differs from the previously discussed IF THEN statement, which provided only one alternative.

The format of the instruction is shown in Figure A.26(a). Notice how the IF's can also be nested as previously discussed. Two partial flowcharts are shown in Figure A.26(b) for Examples 1 and 5 shown in Figure A.26(a). Using Example 2 in Figure A.26(a), the instruction numbered 500 begins the true alternative; the

```
010   REM                 ****************************
020   REM                     PROGRAM DESCRIPTION
030   REM                 ****************************
040   REM
050   REM        THIS PROGRAM CALCULATES GROSS PAY BY MULTIPLYING
060   REM                 RATE OF PAY BY HOURS WORKED.
070   REM
080   REM                 ****************************
090   REM                       SYMBOL SECTION
100   REM                 ****************************
110   REM                     R = RATE CODE OF PAY
120   REM                     N = EMPLOYEE NUMBER
130   REM                     H = HOURS WORKED
140   REM                     G = GROSS SALARY
150   REM
160   REM                 ****************************
170   REM                       INPUT SECTION
180   REM                 ****************************
190   REM
200         DATA  3, 6666, 10
210         DATA  1, 1234, 40
220         DATA  2, 2727, 42
230         DATA  0, 1414, 40
240         DATA  4, 1489, 45
250         DATA  2, 3333, 38
260         DATA  0, 9999, 00
270   REM
280   REM                 ****************************
290   REM                     PROCESSING SECTION
300   REM                 ****************************
310   REM
320         READ R, N, H
330         LET M$ = " RATE CODE NOT 1 OR 2 BUT IS A "
340         LET S$ = " EMPLOYEE NUMBER IS "
350         LET G$ = " GROSS PAY IS $"
360         IF N = 9999 THEN 500
370               LET G = 0
380         IF R > 0 THEN 410
390               PRINT M$; R; S$; N
400               GO TO 480
410         IF R > 1 THEN 450
420               LET G = H * 5.00
430               PRINT S$; N; G$; G
440               GO TO 480
450         IF R > 2 THEN 390
460               LET G = H * 5.20
470               PRINT S$; N; G$; G
480         READ R, N, H
490         GO TO 360
500   END
RUN
RATE CODE NOT 1 OR 2 BUT IS A  3  EMPLOYEE NUMBER IS  6666
EMPLOYEE NUMBER IS  1234  GROSS PAY IS $ 200
EMPLOYEE NUMBER IS  2727  GROSS PAY IS $ 218.4
RATE CODE NOT 1 OR 2 BUT IS A  0  EMPLOYEE NUMBER IS  1414
RATE CODE NOT 1 OR 2 BUT IS A  4  EMPLOYEE NUMBER IS  1489
EMPLOYEE NUMBER IS  3333  GROSS PAY IS $ 197.6
Ok
```

(a) Program

FIGURE A.24.
BASIC program for calculating gross pay.

FIGURE A.24. (*Continued*)

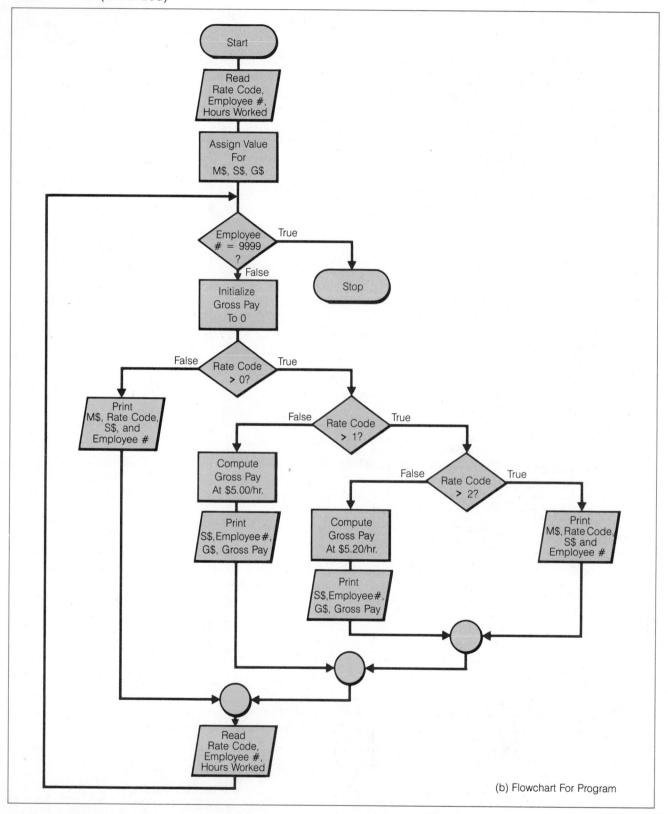

(b) Flowchart For Program

```
010    REM            *****************************
020    REM                 PROGRAM DESCRIPTION
030    REM            *****************************
040    REM
050    REM            THIS PROGRAM PRINTS ONLY THOSE STUDENT RECORDS
060    REM            WHEN THE AGE IS BETWEEN 18 AND 25 INCLUSIVE.  THE
070    REM            AVERAGE AGE IS CALCULATED AND PRINTED FOR ALL
080    REM            RECORDS READ AND IS PRINTED AFTER ALL
090    REM            RECORDS ARE PROCESSED.
100    REM
110    REM            *****************************
120    REM                  SYMBOL SECTION
130    REM            *****************************
140    REM
150    REM              N$  =   NAME OF STUDENT
160    REM              D$  =   ADDRESS OF STUDENT
170    REM              A   =   AGE OF STUDENT
180    REM              T   =   TOTAL AGES OF ALL STUDENTS
190    REM              C   =   COUNT OF RECORDS INPUTTED
200    REM              V   =   AVERAGE AGE OF ALL STUDENTS
210    REM
220    REM            *****************************
230    REM                  INPUT SECTION
240    REM            *****************************
250    REM
260        DATA   "JOYCE SON",    "10 CLAY STREET",    25
270        DATA   "HOMER PAYNE","5 MILLER DRIVE",      23
280        DATA   "LEO ALLEN",    "48 CELLA AVENUE",   17
290        DATA   "MARY CANN",    "100 A STREET",      39
300        DATA   "XXX",          "YYY",               00
310    REM
320    REM            *****************************
330    REM                  PROCESSING SECTION
340    REM            *****************************
350    REM
360        READ N$, D$, A
370        LET T = 0
380        LET C = 0
390        IF N$ = "XXX" THEN 470
400            IF A < 18  THEN 430
410                IF A > 25  THEN 430
420                    PRINT N$; TAB(24); D$; TAB(56)
430            LET T = T + A
440            LET C = C + 1
450            READ N$, D$, A
460            GO TO 390
470        LET V = T / C
480        PRINT TAB(42); "AVERAGE"; TAB(56); V
490        END
RUN
JOYCE SON                10 CLAY STREET                     25
HOMER PAYNE              5 MILLER STREET                    23
                                               AVERAGE      26
Ok
```

(a) Program for Printing Those Records For Ages 18 Through 25

FIGURE A.25.
BASIC program for calculating student records when the age is between 18 and 25.

FIGURE A.25. (*Continued*)

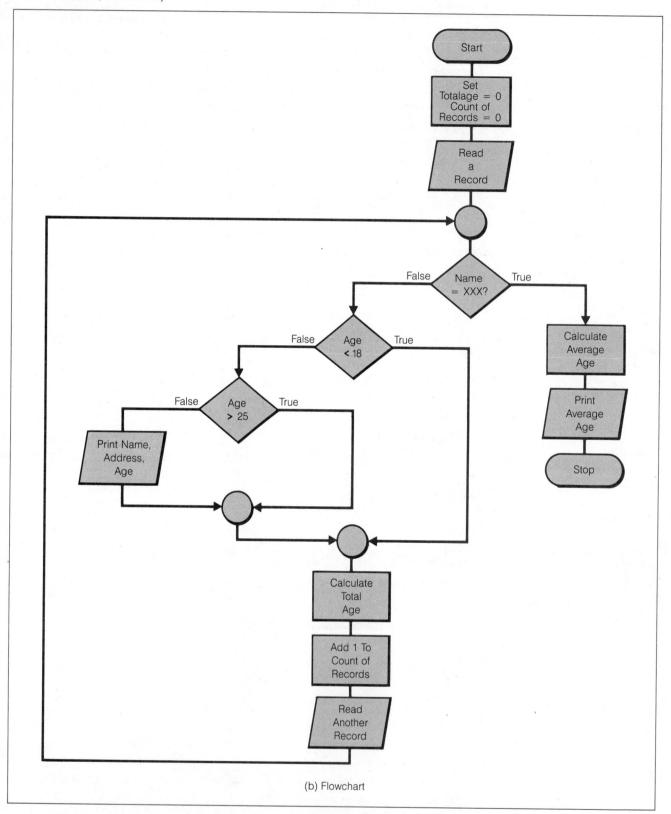

(b) Flowchart

FIGURE A.26.   **IF-THEN-ELSE instructions.**

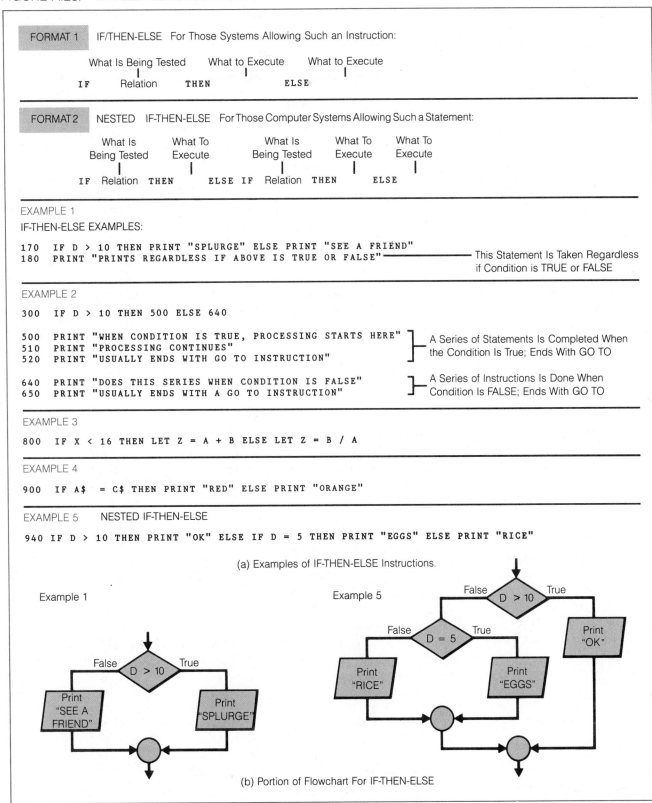

FORMAT 1   IF/THEN-ELSE For Those Systems Allowing Such an Instruction:

```
         What Is Being Tested    What to Execute    What to Execute
                  |                    |                  |
      IF        Relation    THEN                ELSE
```

FORMAT 2   NESTED   IF-THEN-ELSE For Those Computer Systems Allowing Such a Statement:

```
        What Is      What To           What Is      What To    What To
     Being Tested    Execute        Being Tested    Execute    Execute
          |             |                |             |           |
      IF  Relation  THEN      ELSE  IF  Relation  THEN       ELSE
```

EXAMPLE 1

IF-THEN-ELSE EXAMPLES:

```
170   IF D > 10 THEN PRINT "SPLURGE" ELSE PRINT "SEE A FRIEND"
180   PRINT "PRINTS REGARDLESS IF ABOVE IS TRUE OR FALSE"
```
— This Statement Is Taken Regardless if Condition is TRUE or FALSE

EXAMPLE 2

```
300   IF D > 10 THEN 500 ELSE 640

500   PRINT "WHEN CONDITION IS TRUE, PROCESSING STARTS HERE"
510   PRINT "PROCESSING CONTINUES"
520   PRINT "USUALLY ENDS WITH GO TO INSTRUCTION"
```
A Series of Statements Is Completed When the Condition Is True; Ends With GO TO

```
640   PRINT "DOES THIS SERIES WHEN CONDITION IS FALSE"
650   PRINT "USUALLY ENDS WITH A GO TO INSTRUCTION"
```
A Series of Instructions Is Done When Condition Is FALSE; Ends With GO TO

EXAMPLE 3

```
800   IF X < 16 THEN LET Z = A + B ELSE LET Z = B / A
```

EXAMPLE 4

```
900   IF A$ = C$ THEN PRINT "RED" ELSE PRINT "ORANGE"
```

EXAMPLE 5   NESTED IF-THEN-ELSE

```
940 IF D > 10 THEN PRINT "OK" ELSE IF D = 5 THEN PRINT "EGGS" ELSE PRINT "RICE"
```

(a) Examples of IF-THEN-ELSE Instructions.

Example 1

Example 5

(b) Portion of Flowchart For IF-THEN-ELSE

series of instructions ends with a GO TO statement. Line 640 begins the false alternative; the series of instructions ends with a GO TO statement.

CHECKPOINT **Can you:**

Describe when an **IF THEN** statement is used?

Describe when an **IF THEN ELSE** statement is used?

Explain what is a nested **IF** statement?

CALCULATIONS

As was discussed previously in the chapter, calculations can be done by using the appropriate arithmetic operator (* for multiplying, / for dividing, + for adding, and − for subtracting). Calculations are performed not only for arriving at answers in a program but also for looping, which involves counters.

Use of Counters

Counters are used in programming for counting the number of times that something happens. In this way looping can take place. Counting is also used for totalling the number of input records read. Counters, like all other calculation instructions, use the LET statement. The major differences between counters and regular calculation areas are that counters are initialized at the beginning of the program, usually to zero, and are usually incremented by 1 by the programmer's instructions.

How can looping be accomplished? We can use an addition method, in which we start from zero and add a 1 each time we execute the loop. There has to be a way to stop the loop; otherwise, we would be in an infinite loop. It would be just like getting into a circular door and never providing a way to stop. To give an exit from the loop we check to see if we have done the loop the desired number of times.

Another means of looping involves a subtraction method. Here we begin with the maximum number of times we wish to do the loop. Each time we pass through the loop, a 1 is subtracted. In this method, we test to see if the counter has reached zero. When it has, we exit the loop.

Figure A.27 uses the concept of interactive processing and the counter called I in the program. Figure A.27(b) shows the flowchart for the program appearing in Figure A.27(a). The programmer, in this instance, has determined that the user can only execute the program three times.

It must be pointed out that some versions of BASIC generate a question mark after the prompt; others do not. Notice in Figure A.27(b) how a loop exists when

```
010   REM                 ****************************
020   REM                    PROGRAM DESCRIPTION
030   REM                 ****************************
040   REM
050   REM          THIS PROGRAM USES THE INPUT STATEMENT RATHER THAN
060   REM          THE READ AND DATA STATEMENT SO THAT INTERACTIVE
070   REM          PROCESSING CAN EXIST BETWEEN COMPUTER AND USER.
080   REM
090   REM                 ****************************
100   REM                       SYMBOL SECTION
110   REM                 ****************************
120   REM
130   REM                    I  = COUNTER
140   REM                    B$ = ADDRESS
150   REM                    A$ = CONTINUE OR NOT
160   REM                    D$ = CAREER
170   REM                    H$ = HOBBY
180   REM                    N$ = NAME
190   REM
200   REM                 ****************************
210   REM                     PROCESSING SECTION
220   REM                 ****************************
230   REM
240         LET I = 0
250         INPUT "WHAT IS YOUR NAME"; N$
260         INPUT "WHAT IS YOUR ADDRESS"; B$
270         LET I = I + 1
280         PRINT "DETERMINE IF YOU WANT TO CONTINUE."
290         INPUT "TYPE Y FOR YES OR N FOR NO.  Y/N"; A$
300         IF A$ = "Y" THEN 340
310         IF A$ = "N" THEN 400
320             PRINT "PLEASE USE EITHER Y OR N.  TRY AGAIN!"
330             GO TO 280
340         IF I = 2 THEN 380
350             INPUT "WHAT IS YOUR FAVORITE HOBBY"; H$
360             LET I = I + 1
370             GO TO 280
380         PRINT "THIS IS YOUR LAST QUESTION!"
390         INPUT "WHAT IS YOUR CAREER GOAL"; D$
400         PRINT "BYE BYE"; N$
410         END
RUN
WHAT IS YOUR NAME? JIM ANDREWS
WHAT IS YOUR ADDRESS? 50 PHELAN AVENUE
DETERMINE IF YOU WANT TO CONTINUE.
TYPE Y FOR YES OR N FOR NO.  Y/N? Y
WHAT IS YOUR FAVORITE HOBBY?  OIL PAINTING
DETERMINE IF YOU WANT TO CONTINUE.
TYPE Y FOR YES OR N FOR NO.  Y/N? Y
THIS IS YOUR LAST QUESTION!
WHAT IS YOUR CAREER GOAL? PSYCHOLOGIST
BYE BYE JIM ANDREWS
Ok
RUN
WHAT IS YOUR NAME? SALLY MOORE
WHAT IS YOUR ADDRESS? 35 BEACON STREET
DETERMINE IF YOU WANT TO CONTINUE.
TYPE Y FOR YES OR N FOR NO.  Y/N? N
BYE BYE SALLY MOORE
Ok
RUN
WHAT IS YOUR NAME? JOHN MORGAN
WHAT IS YOUR ADDRESS? 1310 CLAY STREET
DETERMINE IF YOU WANT TO CONTINUE.
TYPE Y FOR YES OR N FOR NO.  Y/N? Y
WHAT IS YOUR HOBBY? BOWLING
DETERMINE IF YOU WANT TO CONTINUE.
TYPE Y FOR YES OR N FOR NO.  Y/N? N
BYE BYE JOHN MORGAN
Ok
```

(a) Interactive Processing

FIGURE A.27.
BASIC program using the INPUT statement.

FIGURE A.27. (*Continued*)

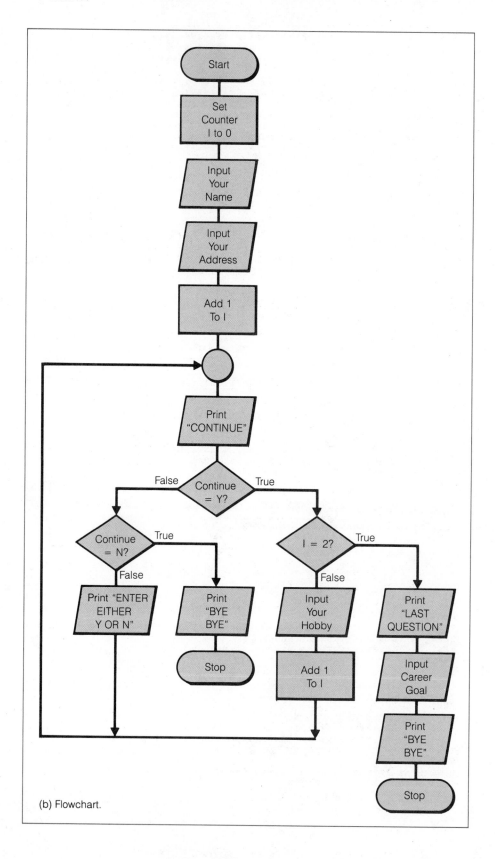

(b) Flowchart.

the answer to the question is other than Y (yes) or N (no). If the user continually answers the prompt by depressing other than the Y or N, there will never be an end to the processing. To prevent a loop like this from happening, a count and a decision could be placed in the program to give only a certain number of times for this loop to continue.

CHECKPOINT **Can you:**

Explain how looping is accomplished in BASIC?
Identify the methods used for looping?

Use of Functions

Manipulations other than adding, subtracting, dividing, and multiplying are available. BASIC has functions that are already written in machine language and are available for use on the computer. A **function** is a series of instructions that are included in the library so the user can invoke those instructions by using a reserved word. Think of a **library** as being those programs and routines that are already set up for anyone's use at the company or computer site. The user must only learn how to call these functions into his or her program. These functions and their purposes are listed below; the (X) indicates the appropriate location for the programmer to include the variable in the function statement:

ABS(X)   Used for obtaining the absolute value of an integer without regard to its sign.

COS(X)   Used for calculation of the cosine.

TAN(X)   Used for calculation of the tangent.

SQR(X)   Used to obtain the square root of a number.

RND(X)   Used for generating random numbers between the values of 0 to 1.

INT(X) Used for changing a variable from a real number to an integer.

Table A.3 illustrates the use of these functions.

Figure A.28 shows the BASIC program which deals with the calculating of the square root, of squaring the variable, and raising it to the third power. Notice in Figure A.28 how the −5976 data when squared and raised to the third power exceeds the size of the zone; the result is stated in exponential form. The program was adjusted and re-run.

A slight variation exists on many computers as to the squaring and raising of a number to a power. Some BASIC versions use the **, some use ^, others use [, and still others use an arrow pointing upwards. You must experiment to de-

TABLE A.3. **Functions.**

ABS For Absolute		
EXAMPLES		
X	ABS(X)	STATEMENT
−4	4	140 LET X = ABS(−4)
4	4	150 LET X = ABS(4)
−4.3	4.3	160 LET X = ABS(−4.3)
COS For Cosine		
EXAMPLE		STATEMENT
		162 LET K = COS(X)
X = 2.3		165 LET T = COS(2.3)
TAN For Tangent		
EXAMPLE		STATEMENT
		168 LET A = TAN(X)
X = .78		170 LET Z = TAN(.78)
SQR For Square Root		
EXAMPLE		STATEMENT
X = 17.6		175 LET B = SQR(X)
		180 LET D = SQR(17.6)
		STATEMENT
		190 LET E = SIN(R)
SIN For Sine		192 LET F = SIN(X/8)
INT For Largest Integer		
X		
EXAMPLE	INT(X)	STATEMENT
26.3	26	193 LET Y = INT(X)
−22.7	−23	
−3.0	−3	
−3.1	−4	
25.7	25	

termine which is acceptable if you choose to run this type of program and a reference manual for your computer is not available.

Let us discuss another function, namely the INT statement. In Figure A.9, the quotient resulted with a value of 2.4. Assuming that the user only wishes integers, the quotient is changed to an integer by the use of the INT statement as shown in Table A.3. The instruction for converting the quotient to the nearest integer could be 100 LET X = INT(Q) assuming that the quotient was stored in Q.

The RND function selects random numbers from the computer. This function is used in most computer games. With this in mind, let us see how the function works.

The values that are randomized from the computer have the values between 0 and 1. This means that numbers such as .892345, .778927, or .016479 could be generated. To make the numbers more useful, a multiplication of the randomized number takes on more meaning and is usable in computer games. If an instruction in a program was keyed as 200 LET X = INT(RND * 10), the integers would be

```
010    REM               ***************************
020    REM                   PROGRAM DESCRIPTION
030    REM               ***************************
040    REM
050    REM               PROGRAM PRINTS SQUARES AND CUBES
060    REM
070    REM               ***************************
080    REM                    PROCESSING SECTION
090    REM               ***************************
100    REM
110           LET X = 5
120           LET Y = 10
130           PRINT "NUMBER", "SQUARE", "CUBE"
140           PRINT X, X∧2, X∧3
150           PRINT Y, Y∧2, Y∧3
160           PRINT Z, Z∧2, Z∧3
170           END
RUN
NUMBER           SQUARE           CUBE
  5               25              125
  10              100             1000
 -5976          3.571258E+07                      -2.13418E+11
Ok
130           PRINT "NUMBER"; TAB(20);"SQUARE"; TAB(44);"CUBE"
140           PRINT X; TAB(21); X∧2; TAB(44); X∧3
150           PRINT Y; TAB(21); Y∧2; TAB(44); Y∧3
160           PRINT Z; TAB(21); Z∧2; TAB(44); Z∧3
RUN
NUMBER               SQUARE                CUBE
  5                   25                   125
  10                  100                  1000
 -5976             3.571258E+07           -2.13418E+11
Ok
```

FIGURE A.28.
Number raised to a power.

generated. For the .778927, the generated random number would be 7. If we wished to round the number, the following instructions would work successfully on many of the microcomputers:

```
15   RANDOMIZE
20   LET R = INT(RND * 10 + 0.5)
```

In this case if the random number was .778927, the variable R would be holding an 8 after execution.

SUMMARY

• BASIC is a language that was developed for users who have no or little programming experience. It is used, however, by experienced programmers for solving business, math, and physics problems.

• Each instruction is made up of three parts: a line number, a statement, and a variable. The PRINT of a blank line and the END instructions are exceptions, however, as variables are not used.

● Reserved words—the statements that are acceptable in the language—include REM, READ, DATA, INPUT, PRINT, LET, GO TO, IF THEN, END, among others.

● Variables are used for naming data. The length of the variable varies depending upon the BASIC variation used for that computer. Generally, the variables are limited to an alphabetic and a number. Variables that represent alphanumeric data are identified as a string and always end with a $.

● Calculations are performed by having a single variable that will receive the result positioned to the left of the equal sign.

● Calculations are performed by using the arithmetic operators of + for addition, − for subtraction, * for multiplication, and / for division. When numbers are to be squared or raised to a power, the ** is used followed by the power to which the number is to be raised.

● Printing is done by the use of the PRINT statement.

● Spacing on hard copy is determined by the use of commas which causes the standardized zones to be used or by semicolons which allow the programmer to specify the spacing.

● TAB can be included in the PRINT instruction to skip over print positions. Following the word TAB is a number that appears in parentheses; this number identifies the print position or positions that are to be skipped depending upon the BASIC used.

● Headings are generated by using a PRINT USING or a PRINT instruction.

● The PRINT USING instruction allows the user to edit data by suppressing unnecessary zeros and to include a $ sign in data.

● A READ instruction is used to input large volumes of data. It lists the variables created by the programmer.

● A DATA instruction is used along with the READ instruction. The DATA instruction specifies the data associated with each variable.

● An INPUT instruction is used for interactive processing, during which the user keys in the data after the computer prompts what data is needed.

● IF instructions are used for selecting data and for testing certain conditions specified by the user. Following the IF is the relation; following the THEN is a line number. The computer will transfer to the line number listed after the THEN when the condition that is tested is true.

● When a condition that is tested on an IF THEN instruction is false, the computer automatically executes the instruction following the IF instruction.

● The IF instruction is used for testing when there is no more data. The programmer can specify dummy data in the DATA instruction, called a trailer value. When this trailer value is read, the program exits to the end of the program or to whatever sequence is programmed next.

● IF instructions can be nested; that is, two or more instructions can be joined to isolate a range of values. Nested IFs contain one or more IFs within the original

IF. The original IF is tested. If that is true, the second IF, the nested one, is then tested.

● IF THEN ELSE statements are available on some versions of BASIC. After the IF statement, the relation is written, followed by the THEN (the true alternative), followed by the ELSE (the false alternative).

● Counters are used for keeping track of the number of records read and the number of occurrences of some happening.

● Looping can be accomplished by using counters to determine the number of times a loop has been executed. Addition or subtraction can be used for counting the times a program passes through the loop. Another method used for looping involves a trailer value where certain data is tested to see if it contains a predetermined value; if it does, the looping is terminated.

● Functions pertain to those series of instructions that are already programmed for your use with calculated data. Function examples are ABS for absolute value, COS for cosine, TAN for tangent, SQR for square root, RND for random numbers from 0 to 1, and INT for integer. The user need only use these statements and the appropriate results are generated.

STUDY GUIDE

REVIEW OF TERMINOLOGY

The following terminology was discussed in this chapter:

constant	numeric constant
control characters	PRINT USING
counters	REM
function	reserved words
IF THEN	statement number
IF THEN ELSE	string
library	TAB
line number	trailer value
literals	variable
nested	zones

MULTIPLE CHOICE

Circle the letter of the item that correctly completes each statement.

1. This is written to show the desired data manipulation:
   a. a string instruction
   b. a statement
   c. a systems command
   d. a string
   e. a variable

2. Values assigned within a program that do not change are called:
   a. an instruction
   b. a statement
   c. a systems command
   d. a constant
   e. a variable

3. We must name data. The name given to data is called:
   a. a string
   b. a literal
   c. a reserved word
   d. a statement
   e. a variable

4. DATA, READ, LET, and PRINT are examples of:
   a. variables
   b. constants
   c. reserved words
   d. strings
   e. literals

5. Any kind of data can be set up as a continuous set of characters called a:
   a. string   d. zone
   b. reserved word   e. function
   c. constant

6. Which arithmetic operator is used for dividing:
   a. ;   d. /
   b. =   e. **
   c. *

7. Each instruction must contain:
   a. a function   c. a counter
   b. an arithmetic   d. a constant
      operator   e. a line number

8. This is used when numbers are multiplied:
   a. ;   d. *
   b. ,   e. %
   c. /

9. This is used for positioning a message at a certain print position:
   a. TAB   d. "
   b. *   e. ,
   c. %

10. If we wish to have the spacing set up in five different columns, we use the:
    a. (d. TAB
    b. ;   e. #
    c. ,

11. When an IF instruction is contained within another one, the IF's are:
    a. functions   d. counters
    b. strings   e. reserved
    c. nested

12. By the rules of hierarchy of arithmetic, which is done first in an equation:
    a. addition   d. exponentiation
    b. division   e. parentheses are
    c. multiplication   cleared

13. When calculating, on the left-hand side of the equal sign there is allowed only one:
    a. arithmetic   c. /
       operator   d. semicolon
    b. variable   e. zone

14. ABS, SIN, and COS are examples of:
    a. strings   d. variables
    b. commands   e. zones
    c. functions

TRUE/FALSE QUESTIONS

Cricle T if the statement is true; F if it is false.

1. **T/F** The ABS function is used for finding the value of the number without any regard for its sign.

2. **T/F** If part of an instruction such as TAB(15); X is used, this instruction means that the data stored in the variable X uses 15 print positions.

3. **T/F** Not every line in the source program requires a line number.

4. **T/F** When an IF instruction is tested, the computer follows the line number after the THEN when the answer to the question is true.

5. **T/F** A variable called A$4 is a legal variable name on all versions of BASIC.

6. **T/F** A variable representing a person's name could be named on all versions of BASIC as AS4$.

7. **T/F** A variable named 5X is a legal variable name.

8. **T/F** The purpose of the END statement is to stop the processing of the program.

9. **T/F** The instruction 30 PRINT tells the printer to print out some data that was calculated in the program.

10. **T/F** A user can omit the line numbers on the statement LET.

11. **T/F** A line number of 9999999999 is a legal line number.

12. **T/F** The instruction
    ```
    20  LET R% = .05
    ```
    initializes the variable called R% to a value of .05.

13. **T/F** All programs must begin with line number of 010 and increment by 10.

14. **T/F** If you wished to initialize a rate of 2.5%, you could write the instruction as:
    ```
    20  LET R% = 2.5%
    ```

15. **T/F** If the following three instructions were executed, the value held in the variable A would be 9.
    ```
    10  LET B = 0.8
    20  LET C = 1.2
    30  LET A = C * B
    ```

16. **T/F** If the following three instructions were written, the result held in the variable F would be 4.4.
    ```
    10  LET D = 8.4
    20  LET E = 4.0
    30  LET F = E - D
    ```

17. **T/F** The value for the variable named X is 24.48 after the following instruction is executed:
```
40   LET X = (4.20 + 6.0
/ 2.0) * (4.1 - 0.7)
```

18. **T/F** The instruction 40 PRINT " ", X causes the data at variable called X to be printed in the second zone.

19. **T/F** If the data of the variable called K was −2.3, the negative sign would print in position 17 if the instruction was written as
```
100   PRINT " ", K
```

20. **T/F** If the data for the variable named M was +78.8 and the instruction was written as:
```
110   PRINT " ", " ", "
", M
```
the + sign would begin printing at position 31.

21. **T/F** If the following instruction was written:
```
10   PRINT A; B; C, D
```
assuming that the value of A was 4.32, B was −4.6, C was 7.1234, and D was −5.4, the value of C would begin printing in print position 32.

22. **T/F** Using data from question 21 above, the value for B would begin printing in print position 15.

23. **T/F** If two PRINT instructions were written as follows:
```
200   PRINT "50"
210   PRINT 50 * -10
```
the first printed line's beginning character would start at print position 2, while the second printed line would begin at print position 1.

24. **T/F** Some instructions appear as follows:
```
300   LET K = 0
310   LET K = K + 1
320   IF K = 25 THEN 400
```
K is being used as a counter.

25. **T/F** If the following instructions appeared:
```
70   PRINT USING X, Y
```
the above instruction would be improperly written.

26. **T/F** Control characters such as #, $, *, -, and + can be used on a PRINT USING instruction.

27. **T/F** A PRINT USING statement must always be used for printing headings.

ANSWERS

Multiple Choice: 1. **b** 2. **d** 3. **e** 4. **c** 5. **a** 6. **d** 7. **e** 8. **d** 9. **a** 10. **c** 11. **c** 12. **e** 13. **b** 14. **c** *True/ False:* 1. **T** 2. **F** 3. **F** 4. **T** 5. **F** 6. **F** 7. **F** 8. **T** 9. **F** 10. **F** 11. **F** 12. **F** 13. **F** 14. **F** 15. **F** 16. **F** 17. **T** 18. **T** 19. **F** 20. **F** 21. **F** 22. **F** 23. **F** 24. **T** 25. **T** 26. **T** 27. **F**

REVIEW QUESTIONS

1. What does BASIC stand for?
2. Why is BASIC such a popular, and widely-used language?
3. What are the three parts of an instruction?
4. Explain how line numbers are used.
5. When is the statement REM used? Why is it used?
6. Identify the three different ways available for inputting data. How do they differ from each other?
7. When is a PRINT USING statement used? Give an example of how the instruction is used.
8. If a variable ends with a $ or a %, it identifies certain data. What type of data is identified in each case? When is each symbol used appropriately?
9. Strings appear only in alphanumeric data. Explain why.
10. What are zones? How big are they? How do you use them?
11. When are semicolons used? What word is popularly used with semicolons for ease in printing data?
12. The DO WHILE construct does not exist in most versions of BASIC. Which instructions are used by a user to include this form of repetition in a program?
13. When is dummy data set up by the programmer? Why is it used?
14. What is meant by nested IFs? Give two examples.
15. Is the use of a % in a variable the same as using the INT function? Explain your answer.
16. Identify the purpose of each function: ABS, SQR, TAN, COS, INT, SIN.

DISCUSSION QUESTIONS

1. Explain why, although BASIC is a standardized language, it is different on most computers.
2. When you look at a READ instruction, you can identify the type of data used in the program. Explain.
3. What are the major differences between PRINT and PRINT USING instructions?
4. Explain the required formats of each of the following instructions: LET, PRINT, END, IF, INPUT.

PROJECTS

1. This program deals with printing your name, social security number, telephone number, and class number. The project extends through several parts. Complete each part and then proceed to the next part, where a modification to the already existing program is requested.

   a. Prepare a program that prints your name on the first line, your social security number on the second line, your telephone number on the third line, and your class number for this class at your school. Use literals. Run the program. Upon successful completion, clear storage (NEW) and clear the monitor (CLS).

   b. Using the concepts in program a, this time using strings for setting up the data. Print one additional line; print your name in zone 1 and your social security number in zone 3. Run the program. After successful completion, clear storage and clear the monitor.

   c. Print your name, followed by 15 spaces; your social security number, followed by 10 spaces; and your telephone number. on one line. Use the TAB option. A printer spacing chart is provided for your convenience. Run the program successfully. Do not clear storage or the monitor.

   d. Using project c, prepare headings that are centered over the three fields of data. Have one blank line between the headings and your data. Run the program successfully. Clear storage and the monitor.

   e. Use the same data as worked with throughout project 1. Provide interactive processing

capability by asking the user his or her name, social security number, and telephone number. Run the program, clear storage, and clear the monitor.

2. This project deals with the number of miles you walked or jogged in each of the last five days.

   a. Use a DATA statement to input these five examples. Print out the data so that it prints in zones.

   b. Change the program so that the printing begins on print position 5 and that there are 10 spaces between each of the five days' data. To accomplish this, move the cursor to the correct line and change the instruction; depress the RETURN key to have the source program changed. Move the cursor to one line past the last instruction; enter RUN.

   c. Adjust the program and possibly the data so that any leading zeros are suppressed and the data prints in columns that are lined up at the low-order position. Also print only two days' data at the most on one line. This assumes a PRINT USING statement is available.

3. This project deals with spelling. Use this project only if your BASIC version is microsoft BASIC. Choose any eight letters of the alphabet. Set these up on a DATA instruction. Read the data as strings.

   a. Print out any three-letter words that are composed from any of the eight letters used as input. Print two words per line, having 15 spaces between words on output. Assume that the data C, A, and B were named C$, A$, and B$, respectively. To spell CAB, 100 PRINT C$ + A$ + B$ will work.

   b. Change the program so that the user is allowed to print only three lines of two words each. When this condition is met, print out a self-explanatory message to the user that the program is to be terminated.

4. This problem deals with data about five of your friends and the money that each has on his or her person for two consecutive days.

   a. Set up five DATA instructions, each that represents a friend's name, amount of money that friend had as of yesterday, and the amount as of today. Since multiple records are used for this program, set up the trailer value. Use the READ instruction that inputs the data for each friend and calculate the difference in money amount as of yesterday versus today. Print out this difference in money and state which day

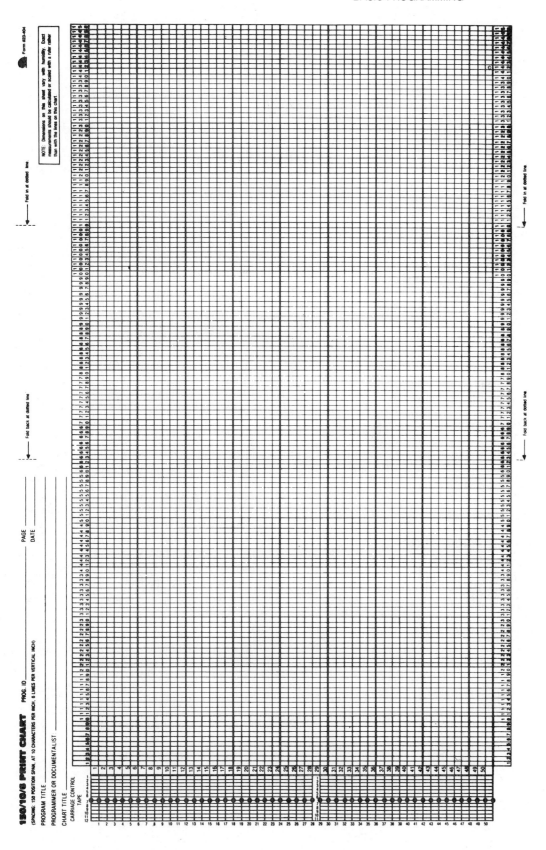

the largest amount was found. An example of possible output is shown; note that the $ is used on only output. Prepare pseudocode and the flowchart for the problem.

NAME	SUNDAY	MONDAY	DIFFERENCE	LARGEST
Joe	$4.20	$3.30	$0.90	Sunday
May	$2.71	$9.46	$7.75	Monday
Toby	$5.01	$0.95	$4.06	Sunday
Sam	$7.16	$7.16	$0	Equal

b. Using the program in *4a*, include another calculation. Calculate the average difference amount for each of the two days. Print out these two difference amounts at the end of the program, using English to identify the respective figures. Using the above data, for example, Sunday's average difference would be $2.48. Prepare pseudocode and the flowchart for the problem.

5. Assume that today you put a penny into your piggy bank. Tomorrow you will put in two pennies. The third day you will put in four pennies, and so on, so that each day you double the amount. At the end of the first month, what will be the amount in your piggy bank? At the end of the first year? At the end of five years? Prepare an edited report to show the amount, using English to identify each of the three amounts shown. Prepare pseudocode and the flowchart for the problem.

6. This project deals with a gas and electric company billing.

   a. The Short & Tall Gas & Electric Company has its data for each customer set up to record an account number, name, and the amount of the readings of the gas and electric meters for January and February. The readings for gas are stated in therms; the readings for electricity are stated in kilowatts. Let us assume that the cost per therm is $0.02231 and that the cost per kilowatt is $0.00054. Calculate the amount of the bill for February for each of six customer records that you will set up. Print out the bill for each customer, identifying the total cost for gas, the total cost for electricity, and the grand total cost for the month.

7. Set up a guessing game to guess numbers between 1 and 10. Give the game player four chances to guess the number. You may help the game player along by giving some hints as to whether the guess is close to the number you have chosen. Remember the types of hints you have given in the past, such as "You are getting warm," and the like.

8. Test the computer's capability to generate random numbers. Keep a count of the number of times certain whole numbers (of your choosing) are generated. Perhaps you wish to determine how many times the numbers 3 or 4 are generated at random in perhaps 10 tries. After you have generated 10 random numbers, print out the various findings, using headings to identify the random number generated, the times it was generated, and its percentage of the total.

9. This problem deals with a checking account's beginning and ending balance, a variable service charge, and a service fee for checks not honored because of insufficient funds.

   a. Assume you have a checking account that has a beginning balance of $400.00. Set up 5 DATA instructions, each of which contains the check number, the dollar amount of the check, and the person to whom you wrote the check. Let us assume that if you keep a $25.00 minimum balance, the service charge for each check is 15 cents. However, if that minimum balance goes below $25 but not lower than $6.50, the service charge is 20 cents per check. Any check written and honored with a minimum balance of less than $6.50 is charged a 25-cent service charge. Make certain for this problem that the balance of the account is always positive. Print out a heading along with the beginning balance. Prepare an instruction that shows the following information for each check that is written:

AMOUNT OF CHECK	PAYEE	SERVICE CHARGE	BALANCE

   b. After you have accurately checked your data from project *a* above, consider the situation that if the balance ever goes negative, you are charged a $7.00 service fee. Enter the amount of your deposit, realizing that $7 of it is to cover the service fee. Calculate the balance accordingly, including the $7 in the service fee on output as well.

Use some of the data used above in project *a,* but this time make certain that the balance goes negative. Print out a message when the check cannot be honored, possibly giving the name of the payee and the amount of the check, and the amount that is needed to cover the check amount. See if your program works. Test it many times on various combinations of data.

10. If you are math-oriented, write a program to solve the quadratic equation. Test all alternative data to make certain your program operates as intended.

B

Intermediate BASIC Programming

OUTLINE

PROLOGUE

"Today, class, we will take some shortcuts in BASIC. Let's use subs and FORs."

Paul Hewitt speaks out. "Sure sounds like war games and golf to me!"

"Mrs. Finley, does it really use such things?" asks Tonya.

HOW DOES IT DO THAT?

READ ON.

OBJECTIVES

After studying the following chapter, you should be able to:

1. Differentiate looping accomplished using counters, switches, FOR/NEXT, and WHILE/WEND statements.

2. Differentiate between lists and arrays.

3. Explain how arrays are used to store, calculate, retrieve, and print data.

4. Explain how subroutines operate.

INTRODUCTION

In Appendix A we discussed many of the elementary instructions written in BASIC. In this chapter, we will expand upon some of these concepts and incorporate different ways for looping. The concept of performing work in small modules is also discussed.

WAYS OF LOOPING

There are several ways a programmer uses repetition, or looping. The methods that are user-defined involve the use of counters or switches. It is also possible to use the FOR/NEXT statements, which is designed specifically for looping. WHILE/WEND statements may be used with some computers. All four means are discussed.

USE OF COUNTERS

In Chapter 11, repetition was accomplished through the use of the DO WHILE or DO UNTIL. As you will recall, a counter was set to determine how many times the loop was to be processed. In the case of the DO WHILE, the counter was tested first before the program executed the loop. As the program passed through the loop, a count was calculated, with a test being made to determine if the desired number of loops had been completed. If all processing was finished in the loop, the processing exited the loop; if it was not, the program again repeated the instructions. Most BASIC language versions do not have a DO WHILE or DO UNTIL statement used for looping. We will improvise.

Figure B.1(a) shows the skeleton of instructions used for looping with a counter. Figure B.1(b) shows the loop done three times. Figure B.2(a) shows three different ways to accomplish looping. The counter is called I in the example. Notice how the program was run three times with different decisions and values for the count. Printing is generated in Figure B.2(a) for your ease in tracking the values of the variables. Notice how the variable S is used for a running total and how the variable I is used for a count. "Play computer" by stepping the program through just as the computer would do, noting how the contents in the variables change. Refer to Figure B.2(b) for the flowchart. Figure B.2(c) shows a different version of looping.

To summarize, a variable is assigned by the programmer for holding the calculated amount. It is initialized to a zero or a certain other value, depending upon how the programmer wishes to use the counter. If the programmer wishes to set up the upper limit in the counter, then a 1 is subtracted each time the program passes through the loop. Looping is completed when the counter turns to zero. Or, the programmer can set the counter to zero and add a 1 each time the program passes through the loop. The test in this example is based upon the program passing through the loop the desired number of times.

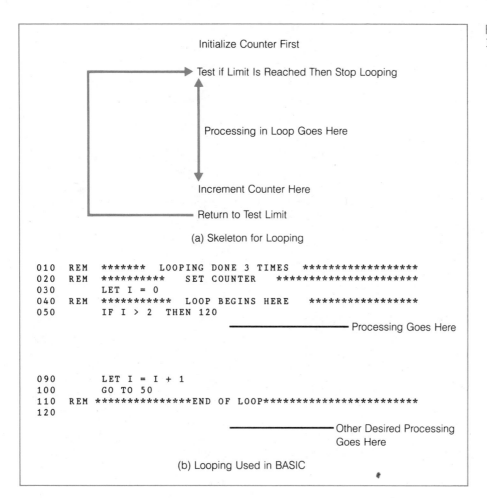

Initialize Counter First

Test if Limit Is Reached Then Stop Looping

Processing in Loop Goes Here

Increment Counter Here

Return to Test Limit

(a) Skeleton for Looping

```
010   REM   *******  LOOPING DONE 3 TIMES   ******************
020   REM   **********  SET COUNTER   *********************
030         LET I = 0
040   REM   **********  LOOP BEGINS HERE   *****************
050         IF I > 2  THEN 120
```
———————————————— Processing Goes Here
```
090         LET I = I + 1
100         GO TO 50
110   REM ***************END OF LOOP************************
120
```
———————————————— Other Desired Processing
Goes Here

(b) Looping Used in BASIC

USE OF SWITCHES

There are times when processing requires that looping be performed on data, but the programmer has no way of knowing how many input records are to be used. Refer to Figure B.3, where N is used for the counter and is increased by 1 each time the loop is executed. Also note that a switch is used for determining when the end-of-data condition is true. The variable A in this case acts as a switch that can be set to any value that the programmer wishes. Activating the switch is like turning a light bulb from off to on. As long as the light bulb is off, you keep doing certain processing. As soon as the light bulb is turned on, you stop processing that set of instructions. In this example, as long as the user wishes to input data, the switch is set to any value other than a zero. Once, however, the user sets A to a zero, the sum and average are calculated.

The switch is also used with the READ and DATA instructions. The programmer is not certain at the time the program is written how many records are to be set up by DATA statements. Rather than adjust the source program each time for setting the upper limit of the counter, it is far easier to set the maximum

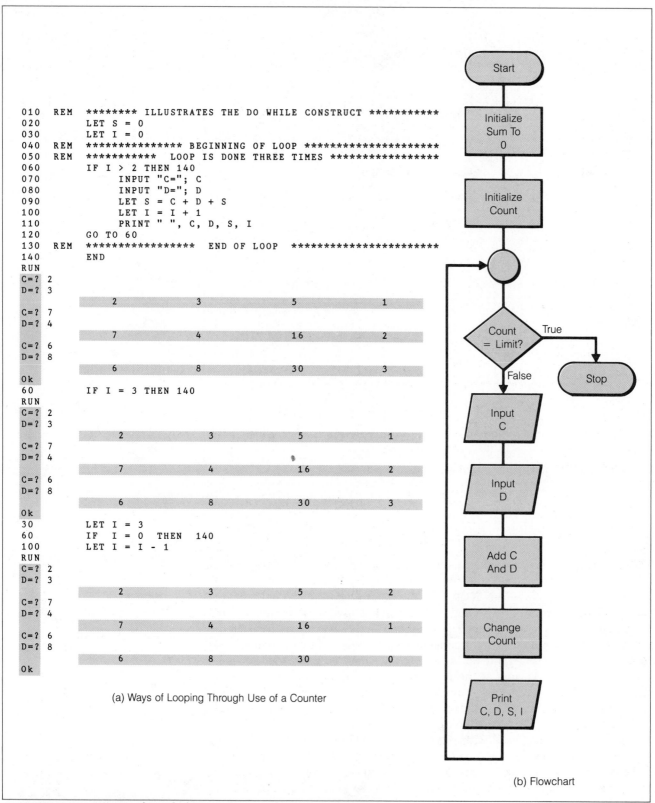

```
010   REM   ******* ILLUSTRATES THE DO WHILE CONSTRUCT ***********
020         LET S = 0
030         LET I = 0
040   REM   ************** BEGINNING OF LOOP *********************
050   REM   **********  LOOP IS DONE THREE TIMES ****************
060         IF I > 2 THEN 140
070             INPUT "C="; C
080             INPUT "D="; D
090             LET S = C + D + S
100             LET I = I + 1
110             PRINT " ", C, D, S, I
120         GO TO 60
130   REM   ****************  END OF LOOP  ********************
140         END
RUN
C=? 2
D=? 3
            2              3              5              1

C=? 7
D=? 4
            7              4              16             2

C=? 6
D=? 8
            6              8              30             3

Ok
60      IF I = 3 THEN 140
RUN
C=? 2
D=? 3
            2              3              5              1

C=? 7
D=? 4
            7              4              16             2

C=? 6
D=? 8
            6              8              30             3

Ok
30      LET I = 3
60      IF I = 0  THEN  140
100     LET I = I - 1
RUN
C=? 2
D=? 3
            2              3              5              2

C=? 7
D=? 4
            7              4              16             1

C=? 6
D=? 8
            6              8              30             0

Ok
```

(a) Ways of Looping Through Use of a Counter

(b) Flowchart

FIGURE B.2.   **Looping through the use of a counter.**

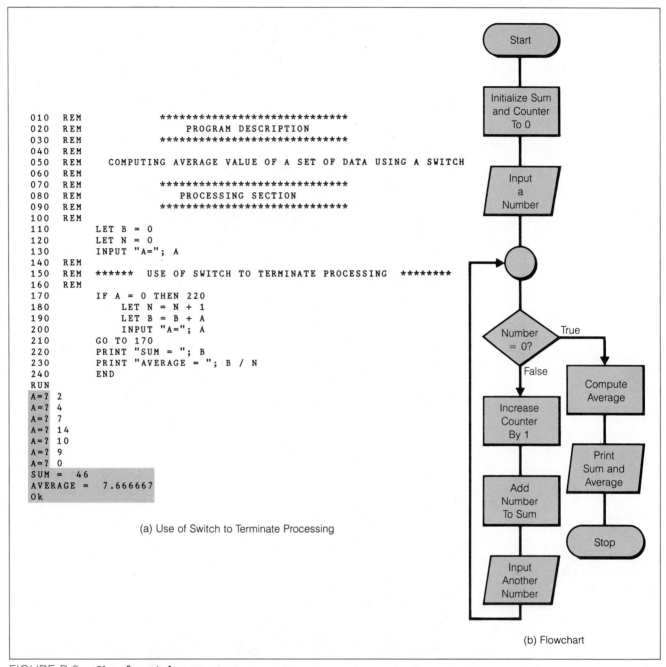

```
010   REM                 ****************************
020   REM                      PROGRAM DESCRIPTION
030   REM                 ****************************
040   REM
050   REM      COMPUTING AVERAGE VALUE OF A SET OF DATA USING A SWITCH
060   REM
070   REM                 ****************************
080   REM                     PROCESSING SECTION
090   REM                 ****************************
100   REM
110         LET  B = 0
120         LET  N = 0
130         INPUT "A="; A
140   REM
150   REM   ******  USE OF SWITCH TO TERMINATE PROCESSING   ********
160   REM
170         IF  A = 0 THEN 220
180             LET N = N + 1
190             LET B = B + A
200             INPUT "A="; A
210         GO TO 170
220         PRINT "SUM = "; B
230         PRINT "AVERAGE = "; B / N
240         END
RUN
A=?  2
A=?  4
A=?  7
A=?  14
A=?  10
A=?  9
A=?  0
SUM =   46
AVERAGE =   7.666667
Ok
```

(a) Use of Switch to Terminate Processing

(b) Flowchart

FIGURE B.3.   **Use of a switch to terminate processing.**

number of times that DATA statements could be used and then test on the end-of-data switch.

In Figure B.4 the loop is tested first and then the end-of-data switch is tested within the loop so that either IF instruction can trigger the program to exit the loop. A program to find the largest and smallest numbers in a series of numbers is shown in Figure B.4. Referring to the figure, follow the logic as the computer

FIGURE B.4.
Looping controlled by programmer.

```
010   REM               ****************************
020   REM                    PROGRAM DESCRIPTION
030   REM               ****************************
040   REM
050   REM           FIND THE LARGEST AND SMALLEST NUMBER
060   REM
070   REM               ****************************
080   REM                    PROGRAMMER   ANH
090   REM               ****************************
100   REM
110   REM               ****************************
120   REM                    SYMBOL SECTION
130   REM               ****************************
140   REM                    S = SMALLEST
150   REM                    L = LARGEST
160   REM                    A = AMOUNT READ
170   REM
180   REM               ****************************
190   REM                    INPUT SECTION
200   REM               ****************************
210   REM
220        DATA 5, 6, 4, 58, 67, 1, 89, 45, 999
230   REM
240   REM               ****************************
250   REM                    PROCESSING SECTION
260   REM               ****************************
270        LET I = 1
280        READ A
290   REM  ****  SET FIRST DATA TO SMALLEST AND LARGEST VALUE  ***
300        LET S = A
310        LET L = A
320   REM  ***************  LOOP BEGINS HERE   ********************
330        IF I >= 50 THEN 430
340          READ A
350          IF A = 999  THEN 430
360          IF L  >= A  THEN 390
370              LET L = A
380              GO TO 410
390          IF S  <= A  THEN 410
400              LET S = A
410        LET I = I + 1
420        GO TO 330
430        PRINT "LARGEST  # IS "; L
440        PRINT "SMALLEST # IS "; S
450        END
RUN
LARGEST  # IS   89
SMALLEST # IS   1
Ok
311        PRINT " I", " A", " S", " L"
312        PRINT I, A, S, L, "PRIMING READ"
411        PRINT I, A, S, L
RUN
```

I	A	S	L	
1	5	5	5	PRIMING READ
2	6	5	6	
3	4	4	6	
4	58	4	58	
5	67	4	67	
6	1	1	67	
7	89	1	89	
8	45	1	89	

```
LARGEST  # IS   89
SMALLEST # IS   1
Ok
```

(a) Program Looping Controlled by Programmer.

FIGURE B.4. (*Continued*)

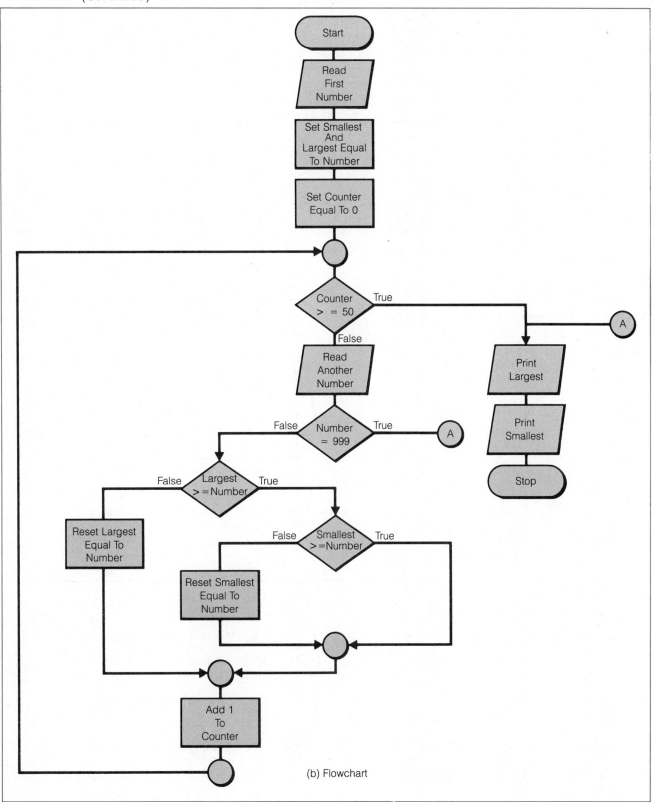

(b) Flowchart

TABLE B.1.   **Data Remembered At Partial Execution Of Program.**

	MEMORY ADDRESSES CALLED			
	A	S	L	I
After first data execution	5	5	5	1
After second data execution	6	5	6	2
After third data execution	4	4	6	3

would. Table B.1 shows some of the data contents stored at the addresses of A, S, L, and I. The values of these variables are shown for each time the loop is executed. Use also Figure B.4(b) for the flowchart of this problem.

FIGURE B.5.
FOR and NEXT statements.

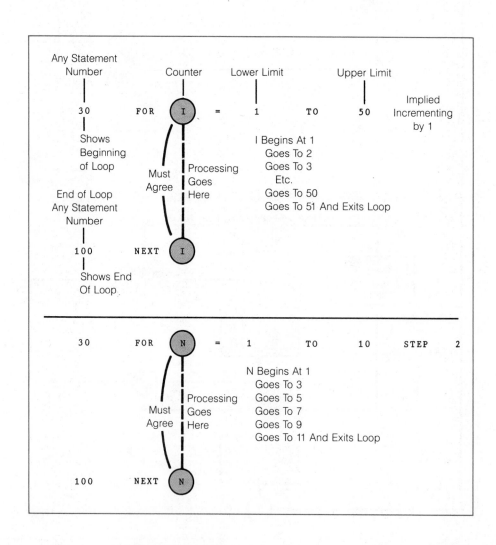

USE OF FOR/NEXT STATEMENTS

When looping is done, does it not seem rather foolish that a programmer must deal with initializing the counter, incrementing the counter as the program passes through the loop, and then testing to determine if the upper limit for the looping is reached? There has to be an easier way.

The FOR and the NEXT instructions that are written by the programmer handle this type of processing. The FOR instruction specifies the counter, the upper limit, and the increment that is to be used shown by the reserved word STEP. If STEP is not used on the FOR instruction, the increment is automatically assumed to be 1. The NEXT instruction tells the computer when to increment the counter. Figure B.5 shows the format of the instructions with two examples.

The programmer must determine where the loop begins. The FOR instruction, placed at the beginning of the loop, identifies the counter. The programmer must determine where the last instruction of the loop is; the NEXT instruction is placed there with the same counter as used on the FOR instruction. Refer to Figure B.6 where the smallest and largest numbers in an array are printed; contrast this figure with Figure B.4. Make certain that you grasp the concept that the programmer does not initialize the counter, or increment it, or test for the upper limit; these instructions are built into the FOR and NEXT instructions.

Refer to Figure B.7 for a problem that deals with calculation of interest. The principal and interest are inputted on lines 230 and 250, respectively. Since the user would input the interest as 0.05 for 5 percent, for example, the printing of the interest on line 270 is multiplied by 100 so the interest prints as 5, not 0.05. Notice how the FOR instruction uses the counter as N but sets the lower limit as a 0, the upper limit as 30, and the increment as 5 since the user wants to print five-year intervals. When line 340 is executed the first time, the gross (G) is equal to the calculation of the principal and the interest that is squared. The first time through the loop, the value of N on line 340 is equal to N raised to the zero power, which is 1. The second time through the loop, the value of N increases to a 5 since the interest is to be shown in five-year periods.

Figure B.7 uses PRINT USING statements. If your version of BASIC is other than Microsoft BASIC, use the PRINT TAB statements instead if you wish to run this program.

CHECKPOINT Can you:

Tell how looping is done with counters?

State when switches are used?

Tell how switches are used?

Tell how the FOR/NEXT instructions are used?

In programming, related values are thought of as being grouped together into an array, sometimes called a list or a table. An **array** represents many data records which are grouped together; this also is referred to as a **table.** An array is known as a **list** when it represents the same data field repeated several times.

When arrays are used, the common data are referenced by the same variable. To identify which data is to be referenced in the array requires the use of a pointer called a **subscript**.

Since we are dealing with arrays, it is important that we tell the computer how much storage area is needed to store an array. To do this, we use the DIM (dimension) statement. This instruction is placed near the beginning of the program so the area can be set up by the computer before we ever reference it. The format for the DIM instruction is as follows:

FIGURE B.6.

BASIC program for calculating the largest and smallest number using FOR/NEXT statements.

```
010   REM                 *****************************
020   REM                     PROGRAM DESCRIPTION
030   REM                 *****************************
040   REM
050   REM          FIND THE LARGEST AND SMALLEST NUMBER
060   REM            USING THE FOR/NEXT STATEMENTS
070   REM                 *****************************
080   REM                     PROGRAMMER   ANH
090   REM                 *****************************
100   REM
110   REM                 *****************************
120   REM                      SYMBOL SECTION
130   REM                 *****************************
140   REM                      S = SMALLEST
150   REM                      L = LARGEST
160   REM                      A = AMOUNT READ
170   REM
180   REM                 *****************************
190   REM                      INPUT SECTION
200   REM                 *****************************
210   REM
220           DATA 5, 6, 4, 58, 67, 1, 89, 45, 999
230   REM
240   REM                 *****************************
250   REM                    PROCESSING SECTION
260   REM                 *****************************
270   REM
280           READ A
290   REM  ****  SET FIRST DATA TO SMALLEST AND LARGEST VALUE ****
300           LET S = A
310           LET L = A
320   REM  ***************  LOOP BEGINS HERE   *******************
330           FOR I = 1 TO 50
340              READ A
350              IF A = 999   THEN 430
360              IF L  >= A   THEN 390
370                 LET L = A
380                 GO TO 410
390              IF S  <= A   THEN 410
400                 LET S = A
410           NEXT I
420   REM  ******************LOOP ENDS HERE********************
430           PRINT "LARGEST  # IS "; L
440           PRINT "SMALLEST # IS "; S
450           END
RUN
LARGEST  # IS  89
SMALLEST # IS  1
Ok
220           DATA  8, 7, 6, 0, 99, 13, 444, 82, 99, 3, 999
RUN
LARGEST  # IS  444
SMALLEST # IS  0
Ok
                                (a) Program
```

FIGURE B.6. (*Continued*)

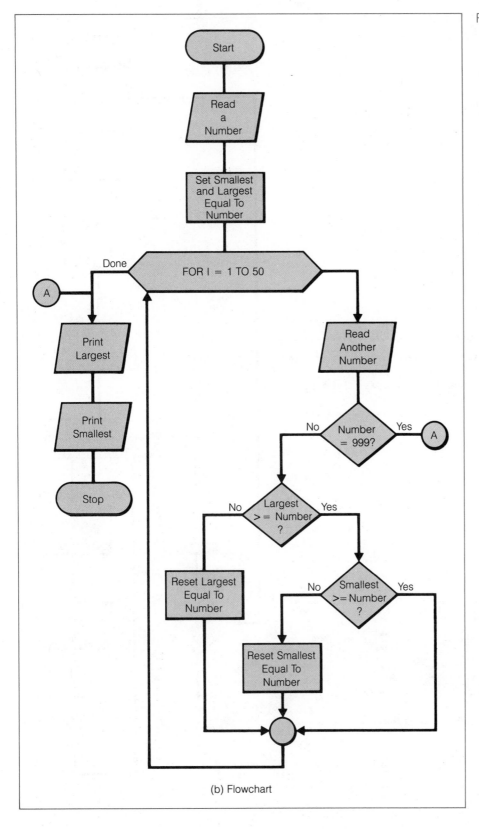

(b) Flowchart

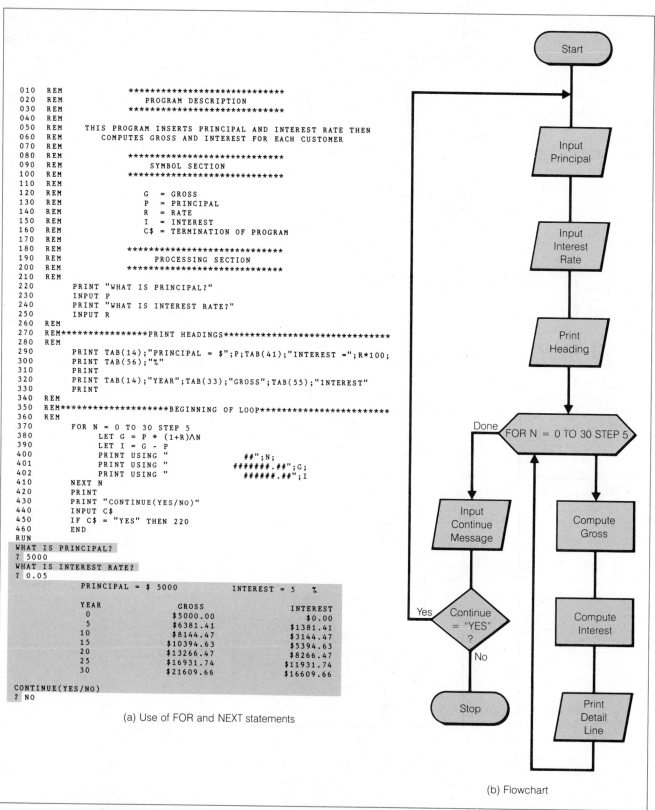

```
010    REM              ****************************
020    REM                   PROGRAM DESCRIPTION
030    REM              ****************************
040    REM
050    REM      THIS PROGRAM INSERTS PRINCIPAL AND INTEREST RATE THEN
060    REM          COMPUTES GROSS AND INTEREST FOR EACH CUSTOMER
070    REM
080    REM              ****************************
090    REM                    SYMBOL SECTION
100    REM              ****************************
110    REM
120    REM                 G  = GROSS
130    REM                 P  = PRINCIPAL
140    REM                 R  = RATE
150    REM                 I  = INTEREST
160    REM                 C$ = TERMINATION OF PROGRAM
170    REM
180    REM              ****************************
190    REM                  PROCESSING SECTION
200    REM              ****************************
210    REM
220         PRINT "WHAT IS PRINCIPAL?"
230         INPUT P
240         PRINT "WHAT IS INTEREST RATE?"
250         INPUT R
260    REM
270    REM****************PRINT HEADINGS****************************************
280    REM
290         PRINT TAB(14);"PRINCIPAL = $";P;TAB(41);"INTEREST =";R*100;
300         PRINT TAB(56);"%"
310         PRINT
320         PRINT TAB(14);"YEAR";TAB(33);"GROSS";TAB(55);"INTEREST"
330         PRINT
340    REM
350    REM*******************BEGINNING OF LOOP************************
360    REM
370         FOR N = 0 TO 30 STEP 5
380             LET G = P * (1+R)^N
390             LET I = G - P
400             PRINT USING "                    ##";N;
401             PRINT USING "             #######.##";G;
402             PRINT USING "             #######.##";I
410         NEXT N
420         PRINT
430         PRINT "CONTINUE(YES/NO)"
440         INPUT C$
450         IF C$ = "YES" THEN 220
460         END
RUN
WHAT IS PRINCIPAL?
? 5000
WHAT IS INTEREST RATE?
? 0.05
          PRINCIPAL = $ 5000          INTEREST = 5    %

          YEAR           GROSS               INTEREST
           0            $5000.00               $0.00
           5            $6381.41            $1381.41
          10            $8144.47            $3144.47
          15           $10394.63            $5394.63
          20           $13266.47            $8266.47
          25           $16931.74           $11931.74
          30           $21609.66           $16609.66

CONTINUE(YES/NO)
? NO
```

(a) Use of FOR and NEXT statements

(b) Flowchart

FIGURE B.7. **Use of FOR and NEXT statements.**

Line number DIM variable (limit)

If, for example, a list is made up of eight values called A1, the dimension statement would be written as:

```
50   DIM A1(8)
```

If there are only six values for A1, no problem exists. If, however, there are nine or more values for A1, a problem will arise. Several arrays and lists can be dimensioned on the same statement such as:

```
50   DIM A1(8), B2(32), X(17)
```

Some computer systems do not require that the programmer prepare the DIM instruction as long as the number of elements in the array or in the list is fewer than eleven. It is safer, however, to use the DIM instruction at all times.

Processing Lists

Like data are grouped together. For example, if you were to enter your weight for January through May, these weights could be entered on one data instruction, with each weight identified by a different variable. To make it simpler, however, a list could be used, in which the weights are known by the same variable, say W. Calling the list by the variable W, W(1) would represent January's weight, W(2) February's weight, and W(5) May's weight. The subscript used within the parentheses identifies which data in the list is worked with. Notice how the data must be read to be stored in the array. Consider the following instructions:

```
090   DIM W(5)
100   DATA  140, 132, 134, 142, 158
110   FOR I = 1 TO 5
120       READ W(I)
130   NEXT I
```

After the above instructions are executed, W(1) would be holding 140, W(2) would be holding 132, and W(5) would be holding 158. Far easier, is it not, when lists are used rather than giving each variable a unique name? If you wished to print out the weight for March, the following instruction could be written, and the data 134 printed:

```
140   PRINT W(3)
```

If the entire list were to be printed, rather than just one element or weight, the following instructions could be written, generating five weights on five lines

```
200   FOR I = 1 TO 5
210       PRINT W(I)
220   NEXT I
```

The output would be generated as:

```
140
132
134
142
158
```

If the average weight was to be calculated, it too would use the FOR/NEXT instructions such as:

```
290   LET  S  =  0
300   FOR  J  =  1  TO  5
310       LET  S  =  S  +  W(J)
320   NEXT  J
330   LET  A  =  S  /  J
340   PRINT  "AVERAGE ";  A
```

Processing Arrays

Often a programmer needs to reference data stored in an array, in which there may be many fields of data containing related information. To accomplish this processing, we think of data records as being placed in an array (table) with each record being considered as a row.

Consider the data that lists the metropolitan area population stated in thousands for five states as of the 1970 census and the 1980 census. In this example, if all fifty states' data were recorded, there would then be fifty rows of data. On each row is the state name, the metropolitan area populations as reported in each census. Refer to Figure B.8, assuming that only five states' data are recorded.

As a second example, dealing with inventory items, suppose a company has 400 stock items; there would be 400 rows of data. On each row of data would be the various fields of data that pertain to the stock item such as stock item number, description, quantity on hand, quantity ordered, cost price, and so on.

To be able to set up data in an array and reference it as we wish, the array's area must be reserved by the use of the DIM statement. Recall, however, that the DIM statement need be used only when the area requires more than ten elements; otherwise, no DIM statement is necessary, for the array area is automatically reserved by most systems programs. To be able to use the same READ, IF, LET, PRINT statements for all elements in the array, requires the use of the subscript so looping can be accomplished.

Let us use Figure B.8 for a reference point in the following discussion regarding arrays. Using the state data illustrated in Figure B.8, how many state names are stored in the array? How many 1970 census population figures are there? How many 1980 census population figures are there? Five is the correct answer in each case. If the programmer used the instruction:

```
20   READ  S$
```

where S$ refers to the state name, the computer would not know which of the state names it was to reference. Rather, if the instruction was written as:

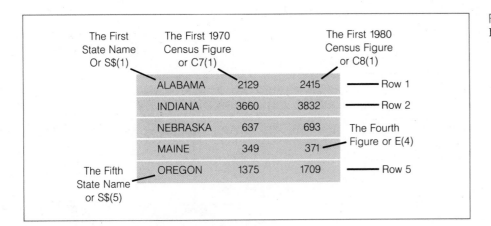

Data for a census.

```
20    READ S$(1)
```

the first state's name would be referenced. The (1) becomes a subscript since it points to whatever data is stored at that area. An instruction:

```
20    READ S$(4), C7(4)
```

would point to the fourth row of the array and the fourth state name and fourth 1970 census figure. Forming the instruction this way allows only one element of the array to be referenced. For flexibility, a variable is used as the subscript. The instruction of:

```
20    READ S$(I)
```

allows access to all elements of the table, with the only restriction being that the value of I, the subscript, must be identified as a 1, a 2, a 3, and so on.

If the programmer needed to enter all fifty states' data, there would be fifty string areas set aside for the state names, fifty 1970 census population figures, and fifty 1980 census population figures. The DIM instruction is an non-executable instruction since it only declares or reserves a working area for the programmer to reference. Refer to Figure B.9. The DATA statements can be placed in any sequence or in random order, but as the DATA statements have been ordered in the example, ALABAMA's data is on row 1 of the array, INDIANA's data is on row 2, and so on.

Notice how the FOR/NEXT instructions are used for storing the data in the array and how a different set of FOR/NEXT instructions are used for later printing the data. Both could have been written using the same FOR/NEXT instructions.

 **Can you:**

Differentiate between lists and arrays?

Explain why subscripts are needed?

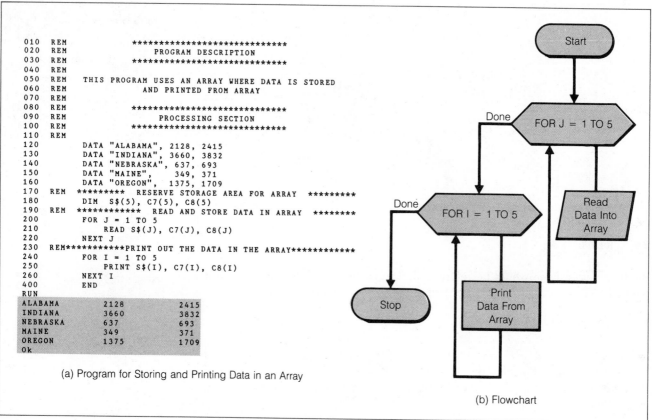

```
010   REM              ****************************
020   REM                  PROGRAM DESCRIPTION
030   REM              ****************************
040   REM
050   REM     THIS PROGRAM USES AN ARRAY WHERE DATA IS STORED
060   REM                 AND PRINTED FROM ARRAY
070   REM
080   REM              ****************************
090   REM                  PROCESSING SECTION
100   REM              ****************************
110   REM
120           DATA "ALABAMA", 2128, 2415
130           DATA "INDIANA", 3660, 3832
140           DATA "NEBRASKA", 637, 693
150           DATA "MAINE",     349, 371
160           DATA "OREGON",   1375, 1709
170   REM  ********   RESERVE STORAGE AREA FOR ARRAY   ********
180           DIM  S$(5), C7(5), C8(5)
190   REM  ************  READ AND STORE DATA IN ARRAY  ********
200           FOR J = 1 TO 5
210                READ S$(J), C7(J), C8(J)
220           NEXT J
230   REM************PRINT OUT THE DATA IN THE ARRAY************
240           FOR I = 1 TO 5
250                PRINT S$(I), C7(I), C8(I)
260           NEXT I
400           END
RUN
ALABAMA           2128            2415
INDIANA           3660            3832
NEBRASKA          637             693
MAINE             349             371
OREGON            1375            1709
Ok
```

(a) Program for Storing and Printing Data in an Array

(b) Flowchart

FIGURE B.9. **Storing and printing data in an array.**

Looking Up Data in an Array

When the user wishes to reference data in an array, the IF statement is used; it compares the desired data with each element in the array until the matching data is found. The programmer must supply an alternative as to what is to be done if the desired data is not found. This could occur if a keying mistake were made or the data had not been entered.

Let us assume that OREGON's 1980 census population data is to be printed. Since it is not known in which row of the array OREGON's data is stored, the user inputs the state name and, when it is found, asks for the 1980 census population figure, as shown in Figure B.10.

Notice in Figure B.9 how the PRINT instruction is contained within the loop since all states' data are to be examined. In the previous example when only OREGON's data was to be referenced, the loop was discontinued when the data were found because OREGON's data appears on only one row of the table. The little problems you can encounter in using loops are beginning to surface!

CHECKPOINT **Can you:**

Explain how arrays are used to store data?

To calculate data?

To retrieve data?

To print data?

FIGURE B.10.
Looking up data in an array.

```
010   REM            ****************************
020   REM                 PROGRAM DESCRIPTION
030   REM            ****************************
040   REM
050   REM      THIS PROGRAM USES AN ARRAY WHERE DATA IS STORED
060   REM                 AND PRINTED FROM ARRAY
070   REM
080   REM            ****************************
090   REM                 PROCESSING SECTION
100   REM            ****************************
110   REM
120         DATA "ALABAMA", 2128, 2415
130         DATA "INDIANA", 3660, 3832
140         DATA "NEBRASKA", 637, 693
150         DATA "MAINE",    349, 371
160         DATA "OREGON",  1375, 1709
170         DATA "XXX",       0,    0
180   REM  ********  RESERVE STORAGE AREA FOR ARRAY  ************
190         DIM  S$(6), C7(6), C8(6)
200   REM  ***********  READ AND STORE DATA IN ARRAY  **********
210   REM  *** COUNTS NUMBER OF STATE RECORDS FOR LATER INQUIRY **
220         N = 0
230   REM  *************  DATA MUST BE STORED IN ARRAY  ***********
240         FOR J = 1 TO 6
250            READ S$(J), C7(J), C8(J)
260            LET N = N + 1
270            IF S$(J) = "XXX" THEN 300
280         NEXT J
290   REM  *****  ARRAY SEARCHED FOR AS MANY STATES AS COUNTED  ****
300         INPUT "STATE DATA DESIRED"; N$
310         FOR I = 1 TO N
320            IF N$ = S$(I) THEN 390
330               IF N$ = "XXX" THEN 360
340         NEXT I
350   REM  *********  DROPS OUT OF LOOP WHEN NOT FOUND  ***********
360         PRINT N$; " NOT FOUND IN ARRAY"
370         GO TO 410
380   REM  **************  PRINTS DATA WHEN FOUND  ***************
390         PRINT S$(I); "  1970 CENSUS = "; C7(I),
400         PRINT "1980 CENSUS =  "; C8(I)
410         END
RUN
STATE DATA DESIRED? OREGON
OREGON  1970 CENSUS =      1375              1980 CENSUS =    1709
Ok
RUN
STATE DATA DESIRED? INDIANA
INDIANA  1970 CENSUS =      3660             1980 CENSUS =    3832
Ok
RUN
STATE DATA DESIRED? MISSOURI
MISSOURI NOT FOUND IN TABLE
Ok
```

WHILE/WEND STATEMENTS

The FOR/NEXT statements, as was just discussed, are supported in all the versions of BASIC, allowing an easy method for looping. The Microsoft BASIC version has, however, included a DO WHILE in its language. The formats of the statements are as shown in Figure B.11. The beginning instruction starts with WHILE; the last instruction uses the WEND statement. Before the WEND statement, however, the programmer must increment the variable, determining if the data stored at the variable I has reached its limit.

All the programmer needs to write is the first instruction (WHILE), the increasing of the counter, and the last instruction (WEND). Notice how the first instruction begins with WHILE and is followed by the variable that acts as a counter and the condition. Notice there is no variable on the WEND instruction. What is basically happening is that the loop is to be done three times, so the computer is testing to see if the counter has turned to three.

Another version of these statements is a WHILE/NEXT. The only difference is that the WEND is changed to NEXT. The NEXT instruction only uses a line number and never a variable.

SUBROUTINES

FIGURE B.11.
**WHILE/WEND or WHILE/
NEXT statements.**

The subprogram, or **subroutine,** allows a program to be divided into smaller parts of logic. This practice is followed in high-level languages and assembly language.

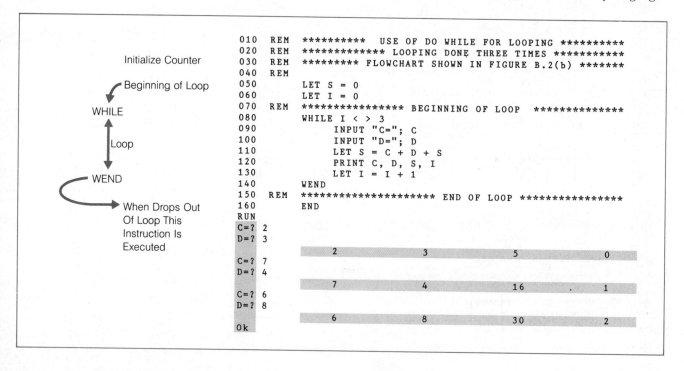

```
010   REM    *********  USE OF DO WHILE FOR LOOPING *********
020   REM    ************ LOOPING DONE THREE TIMES ***********
030   REM    ********* FLOWCHART SHOWN IN FIGURE B.2(b) *******
040   REM
050          LET S = 0
060          LET I = 0
070   REM    *************** BEGINNING OF LOOP   **************
080          WHILE I < > 3
090              INPUT "C="; C
100              INPUT "D="; D
110              LET S = C + D + S
120              PRINT C, D, S, I
130              LET I = I + 1
140          WEND
150   REM    ******************** END OF LOOP ****************
160          END
RUN
C=? 2
D=? 3

          2              3              5              0

C=? 7
D=? 4

          7              4              16      .      1

C=? 6
D=? 8

          6              8              30             2

Ok
```

Initialize Counter

Beginning of Loop

WHILE

Loop

WEND

When Drops Out
Of Loop This
Instruction Is
Executed

The advantage of using subroutines is that, if the subroutine is catalogued in the system library, users at that installation can then call the instructions into their programs by the use of a simple instruction rather than having to re-write the entire subroutine.

In BASIC two subroutine statements are used, namely the GOSUB and the RETURN. The GOSUB appears as the calling statement to tell the computer to execute the series of instructions which begin with the line number that follows the GOSUB. The computer then goes to the subroutine and executes the instructions. The RETURN is used as a vehicle to tell the computer that the subroutine is finished and to return to the instruction directly following the GOSUB instruction, as shown in Figure B.12(a).

Refer to Figure B.12(b) for an example. On line 400, for example, the subroutine is called. The computer executes the instructions on lines 500 through 520, finds the RETURN, and then goes back to line 410 for execution. The same subroutine can be used many times in the same program.

 **Can you:**

Explain how subroutines are written in BASIC?

Tell why the RETURN statement is needed?

SUMMARY

- Looping is done by use of counters, switches, or FOR/NEXT statements. Microsoft BASIC also uses a WHILE/WEND.

- When counters are used, the programmer sets the counter before beginning the loop, to either the upper or lower limit depending upon whether the DO WHILE or DO UNTIL construct is used.

- For looping, the counter is set to zero before the loop is encountered. In this case the counter is added and the test is made if the maximum limit is reached.

- Another way for looping uses the counter being set to 1 before the loop is encountered. The counter is incremented but the test is made if the limit is greater than the desired amount or value.

- Another way for looping sets the counter to its maximum value before the loop is encountered. The counter is decreased by 1; the test is determined if the counter is unequal to zero for the loop to be continued.

- Use of a switch for looping can be compared in concept to throwing a railroad switch so the program can proceed either one way or the other. A variable is set up to hold some initial value that is tested in the program to determine if the contents at that variable have changed.

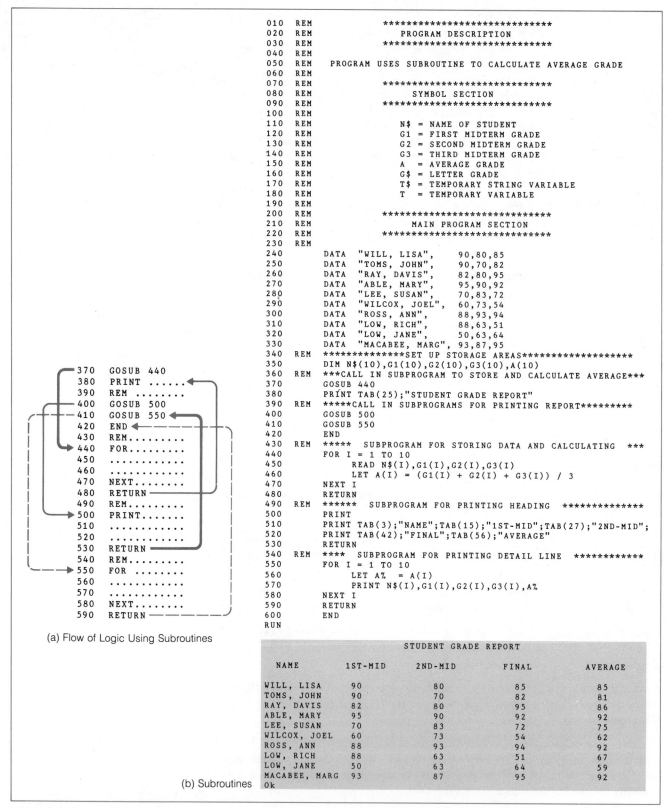

```
010   REM                  *****************************
020   REM                      PROGRAM DESCRIPTION
030   REM                  *****************************
040   REM
050   REM     PROGRAM USES SUBROUTINE TO CALCULATE AVERAGE GRADE
060   REM
070   REM                  *****************************
080   REM                        SYMBOL SECTION
090   REM                  *****************************
100   REM
110   REM                 N$ = NAME OF STUDENT
120   REM                 G1 = FIRST MIDTERM GRADE
130   REM                 G2 = SECOND MIDTERM GRADE
140   REM                 G3 = THIRD MIDTERM GRADE
150   REM                 A  = AVERAGE GRADE
160   REM                 G$ = LETTER GRADE
170   REM                 T$ = TEMPORARY STRING VARIABLE
180   REM                 T  = TEMPORARY VARIABLE
190   REM
200   REM                  *****************************
210   REM                       MAIN PROGRAM SECTION
220   REM                  *****************************
230   REM
240         DATA   "WILL, LISA",      90,80,85
250         DATA   "TOMS, JOHN",      90,70,82
260         DATA   "RAY, DAVIS",      82,80,95
270         DATA   "ABLE, MARY",      95,90,92
280         DATA   "LEE, SUSAN",      70,83,72
290         DATA   "WILCOX, JOEL",    60,73,54
300         DATA   "ROSS, ANN",       88,93,94
310         DATA   "LOW, RICH",       88,63,51
320         DATA   "LOW, JANE",       50,63,64
330         DATA   "MACABEE, MARG",   93,87,95
340   REM   ***************SET UP STORAGE AREAS******************
350         DIM N$(10),G1(10),G2(10),G3(10),A(10)
360   REM   ***CALL IN SUBPROGRAM TO STORE AND CALCULATE AVERAGE***
370         GOSUB 440
380         PRINT TAB(25);"STUDENT GRADE REPORT"
390   REM   *****CALL IN SUBPROGRAMS FOR PRINTING REPORT*********
400         GOSUB 500
410         GOSUB 550
420         END
430   REM   *****  SUBPROGRAM FOR STORING DATA AND CALCULATING  ***
440         FOR I = 1 TO 10
450             READ N$(I),G1(I),G2(I),G3(I)
460             LET A(I) = (G1(I) + G2(I) + G3(I)) / 3
470         NEXT I
480         RETURN
490   REM   ****** SUBPROGRAM FOR PRINTING HEADING *************
500         PRINT
510         PRINT TAB(3);"NAME";TAB(15);"1ST-MID";TAB(27);"2ND-MID";
520         PRINT TAB(42);"FINAL";TAB(56);"AVERAGE"
530         RETURN
540   REM   **** SUBPROGRAM FOR PRINTING DETAIL LINE ************
550         FOR I = 1 TO 10
560             LET A%  = A(I)
570             PRINT N$(I),G1(I),G2(I),G3(I),A%
580         NEXT I
590         RETURN
600         END
RUN
```

Flow of logic (left diagram):
```
370   GOSUB 440
380   PRINT ......
390   REM .......
400   GOSUB 500
410   GOSUB 550
420   END
430   REM.........
440   FOR.........
450   .............
460   .............
470   NEXT.........
480   RETURN
490   REM.........
500   PRINT.......
510   .............
520   .............
530   RETURN
540   REM.........
550   FOR ........
560   .............
570   .............
580   NEXT........
590   RETURN
```

(a) Flow of Logic Using Subroutines

STUDENT GRADE REPORT				
NAME	1ST-MID	2ND-MID	FINAL	AVERAGE
WILL, LISA	90	80	85	85
TOMS, JOHN	90	70	82	81
RAY, DAVIS	82	80	95	86
ABLE, MARY	95	90	92	92
LEE, SUSAN	70	83	72	75
WILCOX, JOEL	60	73	54	62
ROSS, ANN	88	93	94	92
LOW, RICH	88	63	51	67
LOW, JANE	50	63	64	59
MACABEE, MARG	93	87	95	92

(b) Subroutines   Ok

FIGURE B.12. **BASIC program using a subroutine to calculate average grades.**

- A switch is frequently used for determining when the end-of-data signal is reached. This method allows the user to input as many or as few records as desired for processing.

- The FOR statement is used for looping. The FOR instruction provides an easy way for the programmer to specify the counter, the upper limit, and the increment.

- The NEXT instruction, used in conjunction with the FOR instruction, increments the counter specified on the FOR instruction.

- The FOR instruction is placed at the beginning of the loop, while the NEXT instruction is placed as the last instruction of the loop.

- The programmer can identify each value by a unique variable, or a variable can be used to identify and name a grouping of related data. In the latter case, this is called an array.

- An array can represent the same data field repeated several times, which is also known as a list.

- An array can represent several data fields that are related to a subject. This is often referred to as a table.

- Whether a list or table is used, a subscript must accompany the variable that represents more than one set of data. The subscript is contained within parentheses and follows the variable on all instructions.

- The purpose of the subscript is to distinguish one set of similarly named data from another.

- The programmer either prepares the code for assigning the value of the subscript or uses the FOR/NEXT statements.

- When data is stored in the array, the subscript is used to identify which element of the array is being stored.

- When data is being referenced from the array, the subscript identifies which element of the array is to be used.

- To break a program into smaller parts, a subroutine or subprogram is used. If processing so dictates, the subroutine can be used over and over again in the program.

- The subroutine is called in for processing by the statement GOSUB. The computer branches to the statement number following the GOSUB statement. Processing continues until the RETURN statement is encountered. The control returns to the instruction directly following the GOSUB instruction.

STUDY GUIDE

REVIEW OF TERMINOLOGY

The following terminology was discussed in this chapter:

array
list
subroutine
subscript
table

MULTIPLE CHOICE

Circle the letter of the item that correctly completes each statement.

1. The program logic, divided into smaller parts so it can be usable by others, is called:
   a. an array   *d*. a subroutine
   b. a list   *e*. a subscript
   c. a table

2. A grouping of significant records is called:
   a. an array   *d*. an array–table
   b. a list–table   *e*. none of these
   c. a subscript

3. This acts as a pointer so items can be distinguished:
   a. array   *d*. list
   b. subroutine   *e*. return statement
   c. subscript

4. Fields of data that are repeated and grouped together are called a:
   a. table   *d*. subscript
   b. list   *e*. DIM statement
   c. subroutine

TRUE/FALSE QUESTIONS

Circle T if the statement is true, F if it is false.

1. **T/F** When a DO UNTIL construct is used, testing is done after processing occurs once.

2. **T/F** When looping is done using the DO UNTIL, the counter is never initialized to other than zero.

3. **T/F** A switch is like a railroad track switch that can be changed easily by setting an initial value in the switch and then testing to see if that value has changed.

4. **T/F** A switch is rarely used when data is read since the programmer always knows how many input records are to be used anyway.

5. **T/F** An end-of-data switch is never tested in a program.

6. **T/F** There is really no need for a FOR/NEXT and an end-of-data switch to be used in the same program.

7. **T/F** The FOR statement never needs a NEXT statement.

8. **T/F** The word STEP can never be set to zero.

9. **T/F** All FOR/NEXT statements must use a STEP reserved word.

10. **T/F** The STEP statement tells the computer how much to increment the counter.

11. **T/F** When a counter is used on the FOR instruction, the same counter must be used on the NEXT instruction.

12. **T/F** The FOR instruction is placed one instruction after the beginning of the loop.

13. **T/F** A NEXT statement is not needed when the counter is automatically to increment by 1.

14. **T/F** An array represents records perhaps about different people's data.

15. **T/F** A subscript is needed only when the user wishes to reference data other than in row 1 of the array.

16. **T/F** A list never needs a subscript.

17. **T/F** The only names that can be used for a subscript are I or J.

18. **T/F** If in a program you wished to print out the eighth number in a list called S, the instruction
    `310 PRINT S(8)`
    will accomplish this.

19. **T/F** If a list is called M and there are seventeen elements in the list, a programmer never needs to set up a dimension instruction since the computer automatically generates the space.

20. **T/F** The following FOR statement is written correctly:
    `300 FOR I = 1 TO 6 STEP 1.5`

21. **T/F** The following FOR/NEXT statements are written correctly:
```
400 FOR H = 1 TO 10
410 PRINT "HELLO"
420 NEXT H
```

22. **T/F** Using #21 above, HELLO will print nine times.

23. **T/F** Using #21 above, line 420 could be omitted.

24. **T/F** Using #21 above, H does not need to appear on a DIM statement for all BASIC versions.

25. **T/F** If there was a list called X containing five variables, the DIM statement would have to be written as the first instruction on all versions of BASIC.

26. **T/F** If we wished to initialize X to 0, the instructions could be written as:
```
100 DIM X(10)
110 FOR I = 1 TO 5
120 LET X(I) = 0
130 NEXT I
```

27. **T/F** Examine the following instructions and determine if they are written correctly:
```
200 DATA 3, 5, 6, 2, 0
210 DIM X(5)
220 FOR K = 1 TO 50
230 READ X(K)
240 NEXT K
```

28. **T/F** Examine the following instructions.
```
300 RANDOMIZE
310 LET S = 0
320 FOR I = 1 TO 6
330 LET S = S + RND(X)*100
340 NEXT I
350 PRINT S
360 PRINT S / 6
370 END
```
It is impossible to know what the value of S is until the program is run on the computer.

29. **T/F** When a subroutine is used, the programmer must use both the GOSUB and RETURN.

30. **T/F** The GOSUB statement must never appear in a subroutine.

31. **T/F** After the subroutine is executed, the computer returns to the instruction after the RETURN.

32. **T/F** The WHILE/WEND statements work as a pair to accomplish looping.

33. **T/F** Instead of writing FOR/NEXT statements, it is possible to use the WHILE/WEND if your BASIC supports the statements.

ANSWERS

Multiple Choice: 1. **d** 2. **a** 3. **c** 4. **b** *True/False:*
1. **T** 2. **F** 3. **T** 4. **F** 5. **F** 6. **F** 7. **F** 8. **F** 9. **F**
10. **T** 11. **T** 12. **F** 13. **F** 14. **T** 15. **F** 16. **F** 17. **F**
18. **F** 19. **F** 20. **F** 21. **T** 22. **F** 23. **F** 24. **T** 25. **F**
26. **T** 27. **F** 28. **T** 29. **T** 30. **F** 31. **F** 32. **T** 33. **T**

REVIEW QUESTIONS

1. When are counters used? How do they differ when using a DO WHILE instead of a DO UNTIL?
2. When does a programmer test for 0 in the counter?
3. When are switches used? Give two examples of possible uses.
4. The FOR and NEXT statements serve what purpose?
5. When are arrays used? How do they differ from lists?
6. Which instructions are used for processing arrays?
7. Can a subscript ever be an integer? A real number?
8. When is the DIM statement used? Is it needed in all computer systems?

DISCUSSION QUESTIONS

1. Describe the statements and processing needed when arrays are used. Describe any differences when lists are used.
2. Describe how a programmer can input data into an array, retrieve data from an array, and update an array.
3. When are subroutines used? Describe the necessary steps that are followed so the subroutines can process data.

PROJECTS

1. Use project *1d* from Appendix A's projects to set up a subroutine.

2. Use project *1e* from Appendix A's projects to set up FOR/NEXT instructions. Assume that the interactive processing is to be done three times.

3. Use projects numbered *2*, *4*, *6*, and *9* from Appendix A. Change these to incorporate subroutines and FOR/NEXT statements where appropriate.

4. If your version of BASIC supports WHILE/WEND, use projects *2*, *4*, *6*, and *9* for calculations using the WHILE/WEND.

APPENDIX C

C

The Central Processing Unit

OUTLINE

PROLOGUE

"But, Mr. Cerruti, I expect my salary in dollars and cents based upon our decimal numbering system. I will not work for FEF hexadecimal salary a month. Give me $4,000 a month and I will be happy." Mr. Cerruti smiled.

HOW DOES IT DO THAT?

READ ON.

OBJECTIVES

After studying this appendix, you should be able to:

1. Differentiate among the coding used for EBCDIC, ASCII, and BCDIC.

2. Explain when hexadecimal and octal are used.

3. Convert a decimal number to binary, octal, and hexadecimal bases, then convert that base back to decimal.

4. Explain why parity is used.

INTRODUCTION

As was discussed in Chapter 7, an internal code is used for storing data that is to be inputted or outputted. Characters can be used for either display (input and output) or for computation (calculation). Recalling an example from that chapter, to input the data 75 required two bytes of storage, one byte holding the 7 and the other byte holding the 5. But when the 75 was to be used in calculation, it was stored in binary. The binary representation did not use 8 bits for storing the data but rather 32 bits since the data was stored in a register. The question becomes, how can a computer recognize what value is stored in binary? How can it convert data (a number) that is inputted in a different base (base 10) and change the number to a binary number? It is now time to discuss bases.

BASES

In any number system, whether it be decimal (base 10), binary (base 2), hexadecimal (base 16), or octal (base 8), a certain value has a representation. The only difference is, however, that a value is represented differently depending upon the base that is used. For example, a 29 in our regular decimal system is not represented that way in octal, hexadecimal, or binary. For ease in talking about bases, think of a number as having the base stated at the bottom of the line such as 29_{10} which represents a 29 in decimal or a 17_{16} which represents a 17 in hexadecimal.

Table C.1 and Figure C.1 sum up the different bases used in a computer.

TABLE C.1.   **Comparison of The Structure Of Various Bases.**

BASE NAME	BASE	PURPOSE	IN ANY ONE POSITION		
			NUMBER OF POSSIBILITIES	LOWEST POSSIBLE DIGIT	HIGHEST POSSIBLE DIGIT
Decimal	10	Calculation	10	0	9
Binary	2	Calculation Comparison of data Numbering of storage addresses Storing of program	2	0	1
Octal	8	Shorthand for BCD Shorthand for binary	8	0	7
Hexadecimal	16	Shorthand for EBCDIC Shorthand for ASCII Shorthand for binary Calculation	16	0	F

Let us now look into each of these bases to see how each is used and the purpose of each.

FIGURE C.1.

DECIMAL

An analysis of the decimal system is helpful, for it shows the same pattern followed in all other bases. The base is 10, meaning that in any one position there can be 10 possibilities, namely 0 through 9. The highest number in any one position is a 9 which always represents one less than the base. If a 10 or 11 or a 37 or the like is needed for representation, two characters are used.

In all numbering systems, there has to be a value set aside for each position in the number. If a decimal number of 29 was used, the 2 has a **place value** or worth of 10 and the 9 has a place value of 1. In the decimal number 625 the 6 has a place value of 100, the 2 a place value of 10 and the 5 a place value of 1. Please remember: coding is arbitrarily set, and it is only a means of representing data. In all number systems, there is a place value that is assigned to each position in the number. Without place values, the number could mean different amounts.

A place value represents some predetermined value that is always stated in the power of the base. Using Figure C.2 notice how the low-order position (the extreme right position) is always 10 raised to the 0 power, which stands for 1. Maybe an easier way to state this is that the extreme rightmost position is a 1, the next left position is a 10, then 100, then 1,000, then 10,000, and so on.

BINARY

Binary is a base 2 numbering system that is used in all computers for calculation and for numbering storage addresses. Since its base is 2, there are two possibilities in any one position, namely 0 and 1. The highest possible number is then a 1 since it is one less than the base. Its place values are stated in powers of 2, with the low-order position being 2 raised to the 0 power, or 1. Refer to Figure C.3(a) for a binary number that represents a 29 in decimal. Figure C.3(b) also shows other binary numbers with the decimal equivalent written with a subscript 10, as in 29_{10}.

Can you imagine how trying a programmer's task would become if all that programmer did was check 0s and 1s in binary to determine what data is stored

FIGURE C.2.

Place values used in a decimal number.

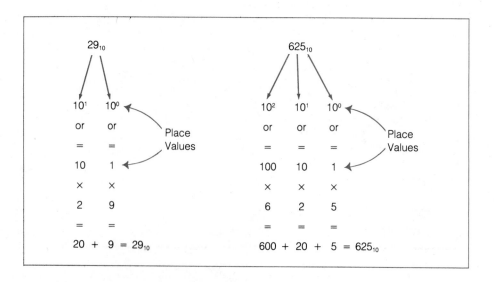

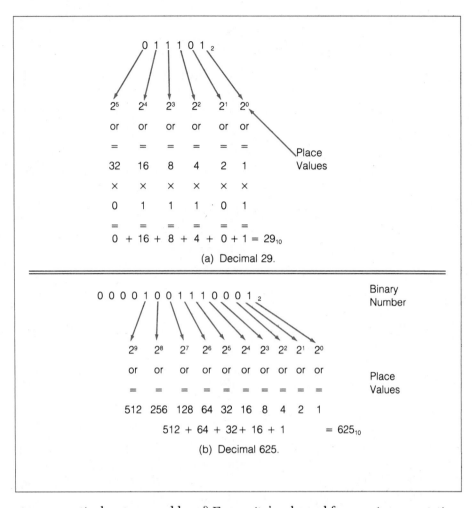

FIGURE C.3.
Binary numbers have place values in power of 2.

at some particular storage address? For sanity's sake and for ease in presentation, two other bases are used: octal and hexadecimal. The systems software determines if octal or hexadecimal is used.

OCTAL

If an internal code used to differentiate display characters is BCDIC (Binary Coded Decimal Interchange Code), or BCD (Binary Coded Decimal), the shorthand used for the internal code and binary is in octal. Octal is a base 8 system, which means there are eight possibilities in one position—0 through 7. The highest possible number in any one position is a 7. Octal, like decimal and binary, has its own place values, which are stated in powers of 8. The low-order position is 8 raised to the 0 power, or 1. Refer to Figure C.4. It is far easier for the programmer to work with the 35 that is base 8 than to work with the binary representation of 011101.

Let us refer to Figures C.3 and C.4 and contrast the 29 in decimal with its representation in binary and octal. Would it make any difference if you were paid 29_{10} or 35_8 or 011101_2? Absolutely not.

FIGURE C.4.
Octal numbers and their place values.

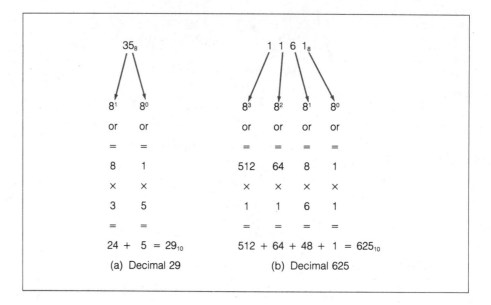

(a) Decimal 29　　　　(b) Decimal 625

HEXADECIMAL

If the internal code of the computer uses EBCDIC or ASCII, hexadecimal is used for the internal code's shorthand. Hexadecimal (hex) represents base 16 with the word *hex* meaning six and the *deci* meaning ten. The number of possibilities must then be 16 in one position. The 0 through 9 give only ten possibilities, so A through F were randomly chosen to represent the eleventh through the sixteenth possibilities. The highest value in any one position is an F. Examining Figure C.5(a), notice that the hex character of A means 10, B means 11, C means 12, D means 13, E means 14, and F means 15.

We just proved in Figure C.4(a) and C.4(b) that a 29 in decimal could be shown as follows in any of the other bases:

$$29_{10} = 011101_2 \text{ or } = 35_8 \text{ or } = 1D_{16}$$

Let us try another number, say, a 625_{10}. Notice in Figure C.6 that the place values for each of the four bases are shown and the value for 625 is shown differently for each base.

CHECKPOINT **Can you:**

Tell when hexadecimal code is used?

Tell when octal code is used?

Tell what the base of each is?

CONVERSIONS FROM
ONE BASE TO ANOTHER

Let us now investigate how these various numbers were arrived at in their respective bases. Certainly if a programmer receives a memory dump, whether it

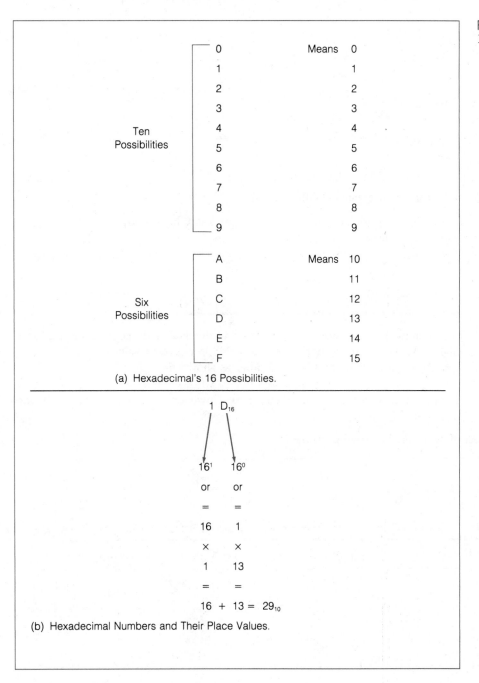

(a) Hexadecimal's 16 Possibilities.

(b) Hexadecimal Numbers and Their Place Values.

FIGURE C.5.
Hexadecimal.

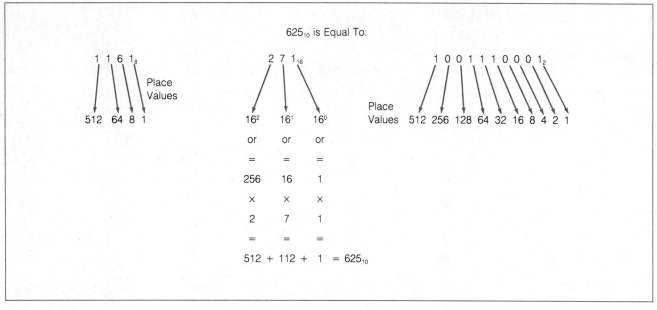

FIGURE C.6.   **The Decimal Value of 625 can be represented in different bases.**

be in octal or hexadecimal, he or she must know how to do the conversions to check the accuracy of the processing.

CONVERSION FROM DECIMAL TO BINARY

Let us show how a positive number of 29 in decimal is stored in a register. You might ask, what combinations make up a 29? Using place values $16 + 8 + 4 + 1 = 29$, we can show the binary number as shown in Figure C.7.

Since 29_{10} was a fairly easy number to work with, we obtained the binary number quickly without special techniques. However, there is a way for converting

FIGURE C.7.   **The decimal number of 29 is stored in a 32-bit register.**

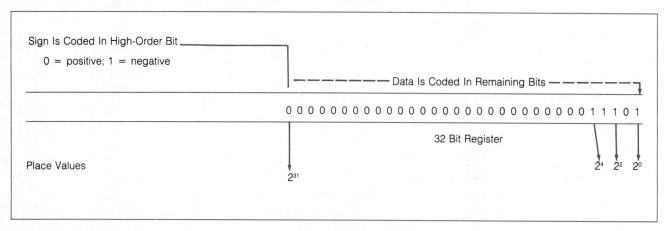

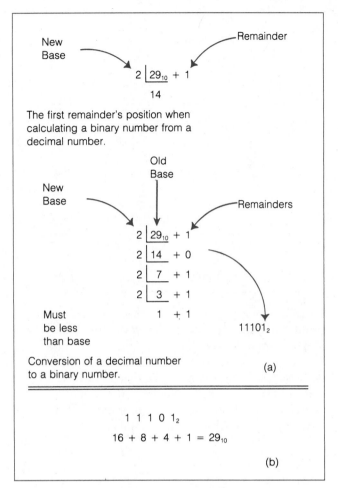

FIGURE C.8.
Conversion of a decimal number to binary using division.

New Base — ... — Remainder

$2 \underline{\smash{)}\, 29_{10}} + 1$
14

The first remainder's position when calculating a binary number from a decimal number.

Old Base

New Base — ... — Remainders

$2 \underline{\smash{)}\, 29_{10}} + 1$
$2 \underline{\smash{)}\, 14} + 0$
$2 \underline{\smash{)}\, 7} + 1$
$2 \underline{\smash{)}\, 3} + 1$
$1 + 1$

Must be less than base

11101_2

Conversion of a decimal number to a binary number.   (a)

$1\ 1\ 1\ 0\ 1_2$
$16 + 8 + 4 + 1 = 29_{10}$

(b)

to a decimal number by doing division. Figure C.8(a) shows a way of converting a decimal number of 29 to a binary number by doing division. The following rules apply:

1. A decimal number is divided by the new base of 2 until the dividend is less than 2.

2. The remainders (0 or 1) are the binary number. The remainder is written directly next to the dividend.

3. Don't forget that last dividend of a 1 since it must be included in the remainder.

Now let us prove the binary number calculated in Figure C.8(a) correct by converting it back to decimal, as shown in Figure C.8(b).

Doing our second number as an example, Figure C.9(a) shows the 625_{10} converted to the binary number.

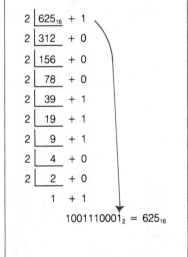

$2 \underline{\smash{)}\, 625_{16}} + 1$
$2 \underline{\smash{)}\, 312} + 0$
$2 \underline{\smash{)}\, 156} + 0$
$2 \underline{\smash{)}\, 78} + 0$
$2 \underline{\smash{)}\, 39} + 1$
$2 \underline{\smash{)}\, 19} + 1$
$2 \underline{\smash{)}\, 9} + 1$
$2 \underline{\smash{)}\, 4} + 0$
$2 \underline{\smash{)}\, 2} + 0$
$1 + 1$

$1001110001_2 = 625_{16}$

FIGURE C.9(a).   **Conversion of a decimal number of 625 to a binary number.**

FIGURE C.9(b).
625_{10} stored in a 32-bit register.

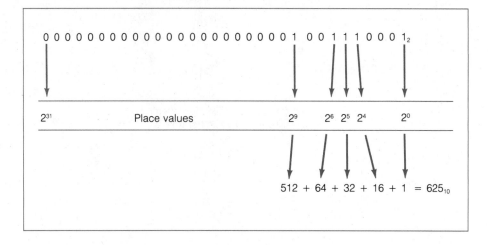

FIGURE C.9(c).
Conversion of a binary number to a decimal number by a series of multiplications and additions.

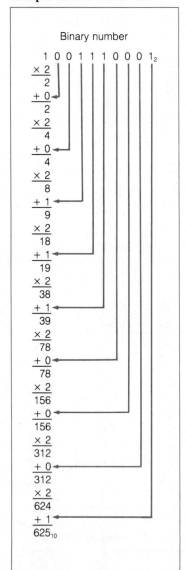

CONVERSION FROM BINARY TO DECIMAL

Also notice in Figure C.9(b) how that same 625_{10} would appear in a 32-bit register. In this same figure, proof is shown that the binary number does equal the value of 625. Figure C.9(c) shows how the binary number can be converted to the decimal equivalent. First the bits are multiplied by 2, with the next bit added stepwise. Each sum is multiplied and added again, with the calculation always ending with an addition. Notice how the multiplication and adding in a series begins at the left and works to the right. This provides you with two different ways of checking what a binary number is worth.

OCTAL CONVERSIONS

Conversions from decimal to octal can also be made in a straightforward way. The method involves division once again; the decimal number is divided by the new base, with the remainders being the octal number. Octal is base 8, thus the divisor for converting a decimal number to an octal number is 8. The remainders have to be 0 through 7. We keep dividing by 8 until the dividend becomes less than 8. The last dividend also becomes a remainder. Refer to Figure C.10.

HEXADECIMAL CONVERSIONS

The same principles are followed for conversion to a hexadecimal numbering system as for binary and octal. The difference, however, lies in handling of the remainders. Recalling that a hexadecimal number must have 16 possibilities in any one position, a remainder of 10 is not 10 but becomes an A. A remainder of 14 becomes a D.

When conversions are performed from hexadecimal back to decimal, the hexadecimal character of an A, for example, is treated as a 10. A hexadecimal character of a B is used in the calculation as an 11. Refer to Figure C.11.

FIGURE C.10.
Octal conversions.

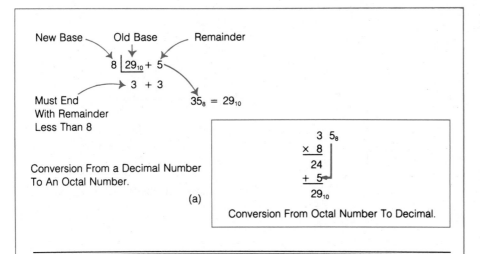

New Base   Old Base   Remainder

$8 \lfloor 29_{10} + 5$

$\rightarrow 3 + 3$

Must End $35_8 = 29_{10}$
With Remainder
Less Than 8

Conversion From a Decimal Number
To An Octal Number.

(a)

$$3 \; 5_8$$
$$\times \; 8$$
$$24$$
$$+ \; 5$$
$$29_{10}$$

Conversion From Octal Number To Decimal.

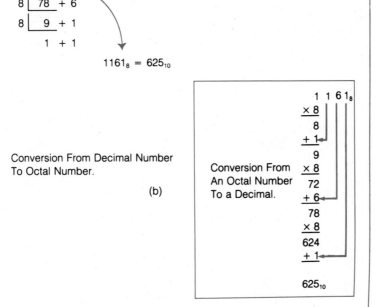

$8 \lfloor 625_{10} + 1$

$8 \lfloor 78 + 6$

$8 \lfloor 9 + 1$

$1 + 1$

$1161_8 = 625_{10}$

Conversion From Decimal Number
To Octal Number.

(b)

$$1 \; 1 \; 6 \; 1_8$$
$$\times 8$$
$$8$$
$$+ 1$$
$$9$$
$$\times 8$$
$$72$$
$$+ 6$$
$$78$$
$$\times 8$$
$$624$$
$$+ 1$$
$$625_{10}$$

Conversion From
An Octal Number
To a Decimal.

CHECKPOINT **Can you:**

Write the rules for converting a decimal number to another base?
Write the rules for converting an octal or hexadecimal base back to decimal?

FIGURE C.11.
Hexadecimal conversions.

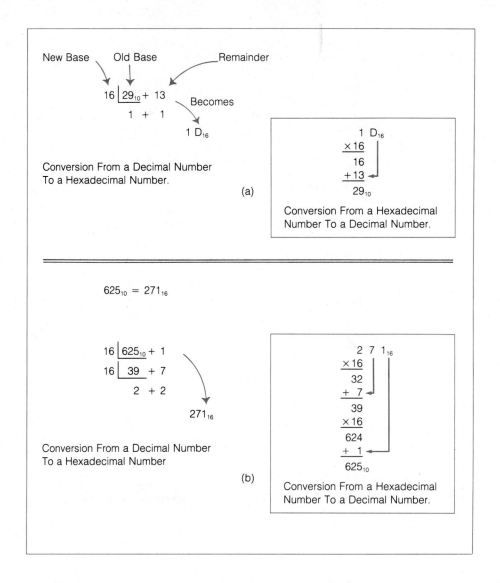

New Base   Old Base   Remainder

$16 \underline{| 29_{10}} + 13$ Becomes

$1 + 1$

$1 \; D_{16}$

Conversion From a Decimal Number
To a Hexadecimal Number.

(a)

$1 \; D_{16}$
$\times 16$
16
$+ 13$
29_{10}

Conversion From a Hexadecimal
Number To a Decimal Number.

$625_{10} = 271_{16}$

$16 \underline{| 625_{10}} + 1$
$16 \underline{| 39} + 7$
$2 + 2$

271_{16}

Conversion From a Decimal Number
To a Hexadecimal Number

(b)

$2 \; 7 \; 1_{16}$
$\times 16$
32
$+ 7$
39
$\times 16$
624
$+ 1$
625_{10}

Conversion From a Hexadecimal
Number To a Decimal Number.

BINARY CODED DECIMAL

As we try to communicate with a computer, we use various symbols (0, 1, 2, 3, A, B, C, −, *), each of which takes on meaning. But the computer, because of its circuitry, understands only two possibilities, which are 0s and 1s. Obviously there must be many 0s and 1s used together to then be able to code any of these symbols or characters.

Let us start first of all with coding some numbers. To do this we will use a code called **Binary Coded Decimal (BCD).** Let us use 4 bits in a pattern to code the numbers 0 through 9. This is just an extension of binary that we previously discussed with the exception that only 0 through 9 can be coded.

The binary coding systems also assign place values, doing so in groups of 4 bits. The place values are 8 4 2 1 for 4 bits grouped together. Refer to Figure C.12(a). Since all internal binary coding systems use a 1 and 0 for coding, let's set up some rules for determining how the numbers 0 through 9 are coded:

1   is used in the place value when it represents the number that is to be coded, or when it represents the sum of the place values to code the number.

0   is used in all other positions.

Let us begin with the easiest first. The data 0 uses all 0s in the place values. For the data 1, use a 1 in place value 1 and all the rest are 0s. In other words, use a 0 in place value 8, a 0 in place value 4, a 0 in place value 2, and a 1 in place value 1. Using the rules above, the data 2 uses a 1 in place value 2, with the remaining place values being 0. For a 3, it is necessary to use the sum of the place values—2 + 1—to code the data. In the table shown in Figure C.12(b), notice how the codings are set up for the numbers 0 through 9. Figure C.12(c) shows that a 29 requires two 4-bit groupings.

We, however, use other symbols other than 0 through 9. To be able to code 10 numbers, 26 alphabetics, and 28 special characters, two additional bits must

FIGURE C.12.

PLACE VALUES

Lowest DATA	8	4	2	1
0	0	0	0	0
1	0	0	0	1
2	0	0	1	0
3	0	0	1	1
4	0	1	0	0
5	0	1	0	1
6	0	1	1	0
7	0	1	1	1
8	1	0	0	0
9	1	0	0	1

Highest

(b) Four-Bit BCD.

4-Bits With Place Values Of

	8	4	2	1
Data 0 is Coded	0	0	0	0

(a) Four Bits Are Grouped For Coding.

Data Coded As:	2	9
	0 0 1 0	1 0 0 1

(c) The Four-Bit BCD Code For A 29 In Decimal.

FIGURE C.13.   **Six-bit BCD.**
(a) Five codes are shown.

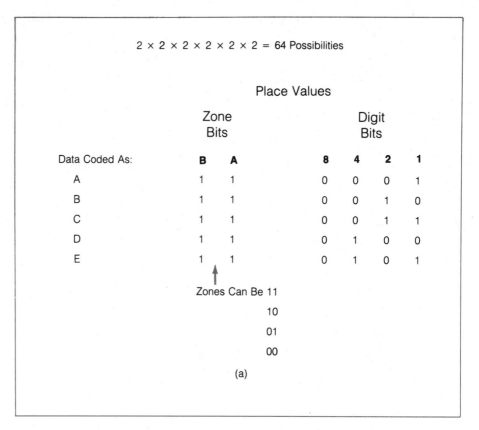

2 × 2 × 2 × 2 × 2 × 2 = 64 Possibilities

Place Values

Data Coded As:	Zone Bits		Digit Bits			
	B	**A**	**8**	**4**	**2**	**1**
A	1	1	0	0	0	1
B	1	1	0	0	1	0
C	1	1	0	0	1	1
D	1	1	0	1	0	0
E	1	1	0	1	0	1

Zones Can Be 11
10
01
00

(a)

FIGURE C.13.
(b) Entire alphabet is shown.

ZONES			
11	**10**	**01**	**DIGIT**
A	J		**0001**
B	K	S	**0010**
C	L	T	**0011**
D	M	U	**0100**
E	N	V	**0101**
F	O	W	**0110**
G	P	X	**0111**
H	Q	Y	**1000**
I	R	Z	**1001**

Data Coded As

A	B A	8 4 2 1
	1 1	0 0 0 1

(b)

be in the code, allowing a **Six-bit Binary Coded Decimal (BCD)** representation. Through the use of 6 bits there can be sixty-four different representations since 2 multiplied six times is equal to 64. In a Six-bit BCD coding system, there are then 6 bits used; the first two are called the **zone bits** and the last four are called the **digit bits.** Simply switching the two zone bits and the digit bits makes sixty-four different codings available. Refer to Figure C.13 for some example characters.

Far more than sixty-four different combinations are often needed in data processing, however. For that reason, the Six-bit BCD code has been replaced, in most cases, with codes using more bits.

EBCDIC CODE

EBCDIC (Extended Binary Coded Decimal Interchange Code) is a coding system developed by IBM Corporation and used by some other computer manufacturers. It offers an advantage over Six-bit BCD because it uses 8 bits, yielding 256 different possible combinations of characters that can be coded (2 multiplied eight times is equal to 256).

EBCDIC code is divided into two parts, the zone and the digit portions, as

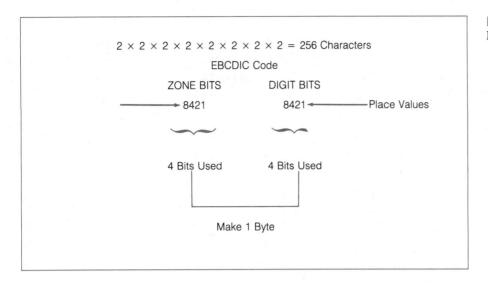

FIGURE C.14.
EBCDIC code.

shown in Figure C.14. In EBCDIC code, the highest number that can be recorded in a storage address is a 9. This follows the same rules as are used in our decimal system since 10 or any number greater uses two positions. In EBCDIC code, a data of 10 would use two bytes.

NUMERIC DATA

As was previously stated, 8 bits make up 1 byte with the value of the numeric data coded in the digit portion. The zone portion of EBCDIC code is used to show the sign of the numeric data (numbers can be either signed or unsigned). When numbers are **signed numbers,** the data is considered to be either positive or negative. Data that is stored as a signed number can reflect some change from a predicted amount (this is discussed shortly) or can represent a payment that was overpaid, underpaid, or prepaid. All data that are calculated by the computer become signed numbers.

Unsigned numbers represent most data that is inputted and then stored in primary storage. Unsigned numbers can also represent data that is never calculated, such as the house numbers in an address data field.

There has to be a coding used to represent each of these three signs. Do not lose sight of the fact that coding is merely a representation and has no inherent significance. For the zone portion of the EBCDIC code, the unsigned is coded as 1111, the positive sign as 1100, and the negative sign as 1101 in the place values 8 4 2 1, respectively. Figure C.15 shows the three types of codings used for the various signs. Notice also that Figure C.15 deals just with a one-position field— a +2, a −9, an unsigned 3.

Let us develop the concept for a field that contains more than one position. For a field that exceeds one position, all numbers in that field other than the low-order position (extreme right) are always considered as unsigned. Refer to Figure C.16. The low-order position records the sign for the entire field—unsigned,

FIGURE C.15.
EBCDIC coding used for numbers.

	UNSIGNED PLACE VALUES			POSITIVE PLACE VALUES			NEGATIVE PLACE VALUES	
	8 4 2 1	8 4 2 1		8 4 2 1	8 4 2 1		8 4 2 1	8 4 2 1
0	1 1 1 1	0 0 0 0	+0	1 1 0 0	0 0 0 0	−0	1 1 0 1	0 0 0 0
1	1 1 1 1	0 0 0 1	+1	1 1 0 0	0 0 0 1	−1	1 1 0 1	0 0 0 1
2	1 1 1 1	0 0 1 0	+2	1 1 0 0	0 0 1 0	−2	1 1 0 1	0 0 1 0
3	1 1 1 1	0 0 1 1	+3	1 1 0 0	0 0 1 1	−3	1 1 0 1	0 0 1 1
8	1 1 1 1	1 0 0 0	+8	1 1 0 0	1 0 0 0	−8	1 1 0 1	1 0 0 0
9	1 1 1 1	1 0 0 1	+9	1 1 0 0	1 0 0 1	−9	1 1 0 1	1 0 0 1

positive, or negative. The computer examines only the low-order position (extreme right) of each field to determine the sign for that entire field.

An inventory example is used to illustrate the three possible types of codings. The inventory number is an unsigned field. The average size of weekly shipments

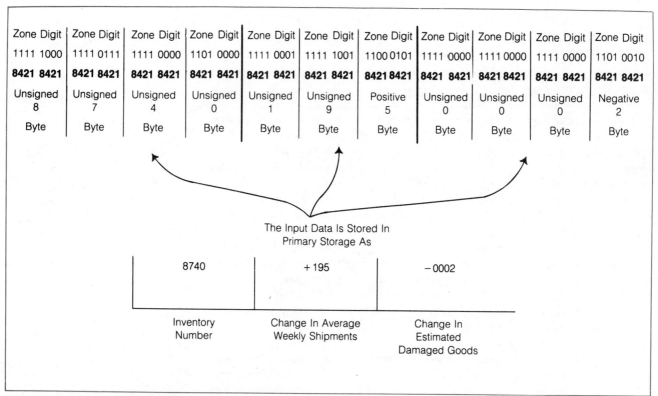

Zone Digit	Zone Digit	Zone Digit	Zone Digit	Zone Digit	Zone Digit	Zone Digit	Zone Digit	Zone Digit	Zone Digit	Zone Digit
1111 1000	1111 0111	1111 0000	1101 0000	1111 0001	1111 1001	1100 0101	1111 0000	1111 0000	1111 0000	1101 0010
8421 8421	**8421 8421**	**8421 8421**	**8421 8421**	**8421 8421**	**8421 8421**	**8421 8421**	**8421 8421**	**8421 8421**	**8421 8421**	**8421 8421**
Unsigned 8	Unsigned 7	Unsigned 4	Unsigned 0	Unsigned 1	Unsigned 9	Positive 5	Unsigned 0	Unsigned 0	Unsigned 0	Negative 2
Byte	Byte	Byte	Byte	Byte	Byte	Byte	Byte	Byte	Byte	Byte

The Input Data Is Stored In Primary Storage As

8740	+195	−0002
Inventory Number	Change In Average Weekly Shipments	Change In Estimated Damaged Goods

FIGURE C.16.　**Examples of numeric data using EBCDIC coding.**

are forecast for the entire year as well as the quantity of damaged goods that will be returned to the plant. A change from projected averages is then reported by using a positive or negative figure. Although a sign is keyed at the high-order position (leftmost position in the field), the sign is recorded in only the extreme right byte of the field. If the average weekly shipments are projected as being 500 cases, and the weekly shipment is 695 cases, the average weekly shipments would be recorded as a +195. If, however, only 497 cases were shipped, the data would be recorded as a −003.

If 29 were inputted, the data would appear as an unsigned 2 and an unsigned 9. The EBCDIC code would then be 1111 0010 1111 1001. If the data 625 were inputted, the EBCDIC code would be

1111 0110   1111 0010   1111 0101

Before we go any further, make certain you understand that a 29 and 625 is coded in EBCDIC code as just stated. The coding is different, however, for a binary representation. If you have any doubt, refer again to Figures C.7 and C.9.

ALPHABETIC DATA

The alphabetic characters are coded using the zone and the digit portions. The alphabet is divided into three parts: the first part is for characters A through I, the second part for characters J through R, and the third part for characters S through Z. Each part has a specific zone portion as shown in Figure C.17. Notice in Figure C.17 how the digit portion of the code uses the digits 1 through 9 for the alphabetics A through R. The alphabetics S through Z use the digits 2 through 9 so that the alphabet ends with 9.

You might ask, is not the A coded exactly the same as a +1? This is correct; the positive numbers use the same coding as the alphabetic characters A through I, while the negative numbers use the same alphabetic coding as J through R. In your program you must identify the data as numeric or alphabetic. It is the computer's responsibility to remember which type of data is stored.

PARITY

A computer has many checking systems. One of these systems is known as **parity.** Some of the newest computer systems and secondary storage devices no longer use parity as a checking system; rather, the accuracy of the bits is checked by a semiconductor chip.

Parity provides a means to check whether a computer has lost a 1-bit in the data transmission. Two types of parity are used: odd bit parity and even bit parity, with the former being the most common. Without checking systems, a user of a computer could never feel certain that data is correct. A parity bit is assigned by a computer when the input data is read into primary storage. Each time the data is used, the computer checks to make sure that the correct parity is present.

For those computers using parity and EBCDIC code, there are really 9 bits

FIGURE C.17.
Alphabetic codes using EBCDIC coding.

ZONE PORTION			DIGIT PORTION
1100	**1101**	**1110**	
A	J		**0001**
B	K	S	**0010**
C	L	T	**0011**
D	M	U	**0100**
E	N	V	**0101**
F	O	W	**0110**
G	P	X	**0111**
H	Q	Y	**1000**
I	R	Z	**1001**

DATA	ZONE	DIGIT
A	1100	0001
B	1100	0010
C	1100	'0011
D	1100	0100
E	1100	0101
I	1100	1001
J	1101	0001
K	1101	0010
L	1101	0011
R	1101	1001
S	1110	0010
T	1110	0011
U	1110	0100
V	1110	0101
Z	1110	1001

that are used—8 bits for differentiating a character and another bit, called the **parity bit,** for checking the validity of the bit configuration. If a computer uses **odd parity** with EBCDIC code, all 9 bits must contain an odd number of 1-bits (1 1-bit, 3 1-bits, 5 1-bits, or 7 1-bits). When **even parity** is used with EBCDIC code, there must be an even number of 1-bits used in the 9 bits. The parity bit is set as a 1 or a 0 depending upon the number of 1-bits used in the bits that code a character. If a byte contains 5 1s within the 8 bits, and even parity is used, then a 1 bit is set as the parity bit. If odd parity is to be used, then the parity bit is set to 0. There is one parity bit for each byte. The parity bit is never used to distinguish one character from another; that is the role of the internal coding system. The same concept is used for ASCII and 6-bit BCD, as one additional bit is needed for the parity bit.

Figure C.18 shows parity for an odd parity and an even parity computer. P stands for parity bit in the place values for each byte. The systems software determines if odd or even parity is to be used in primary storage.

Parity is automatically done by the computer and is of little concern to most users. It is important to the computer operator, however. If an error exists in parity, a light will appear on the console signaling an invalid character. A validity error may occur, for example, on an odd parity checking computer when an even number of 1-bits in a bit configuration is detected in storage. The computer will stop processing on that program until the operator intervenes.

FIGURE C.18.   **Types of parity.**

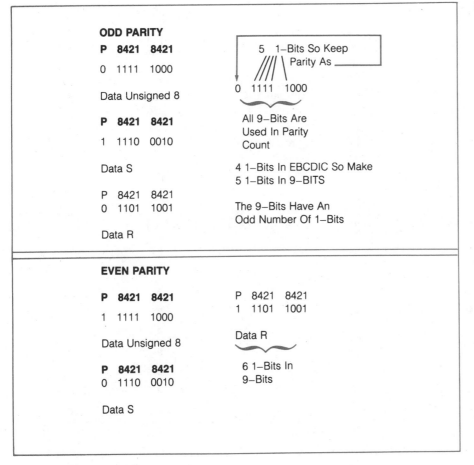

CHECKPOINT Can you:

Tell why parity is used?

Tell what types of parity are used?

MEMORY DUMP

A memory dump is a printout of the contents of storage, which can be data and instructions along with the respective addresses. A shorthand code called hexadecimal is used for representing the 0s and 1s used in primary storage. This was discussed in Chapter 7, although no reason was given for the grouping of 4 bits that were represented by one hexadecimal character. The reason is that since hexadecimal is base 16 and binary digits are base 2, 4 bits are needed to represent one hexadecimal character ($2 \times 2 \times 2 \times 2$ is equal to 16).

ASCII CODE

ASCII (American Standard Code for Information Interchange) is the most popular of all the coding systems used since it is used by microcomputers, many mainframes, and in data communications. (The reason that EBCDIC code was discussed first is because it has a more obvious coding pattern. To a user, however, this is of no importance.) Referring to Figure C.19(a), we find that ASCII uses 7 bits to code its 128 possible characters.

FIGURE C.19(a).   **ASCII code.**

CHAR	ZONE	DIGIT	HEX	CHAR	ZONE	DIGIT	HEX	CHAR	ZONE	DIGIT	HEX	CHAR	ZONE	DIGIT	HEX
A	100	0001	41	J	100	1010	4A					0	011	0000	30
B	100	0010	42	K	100	1011	4B	S	101	0011	53	1	011	0001	31
C	100	0011	43	L	100	1100	4C	T	101	0100	54	2	011	0010	32
D	100	0100	44	M	100	1101	4D	U	101	0101	55	3	011	0011	33
E	100	0101	45	N	100	1110	4E	V	101	0110	56	4	011	0100	34
F	100	0110	46	O	100	1111	4F	W	101	0111	57	5	011	0101	35
G	100	0111	47	P	101	0000	50	X	101	1000	58	6	011	0110	36
H	100	1000	48	Q	101	0001	51	Y	101	1001	59	7	011	0111	37
I	100	1001	49	R	101	0010	52	Z	101	1010	5A	8	011	1000	38
												9	011	1001	39

CHAR	ZONE	DIGIT	HEX	CHAR	ZONE	DIGIT	HEX	CHAR	ZONE	DIGIT	HEX	CHAR	ZONE	DIGIT	HEX
A	1100	0001	C1	J	1101	0001	D1					0	1111	0000	F0
B	1100	0010	C2	K	1101	0010	D2	S	1110	0010	E2	1	1111	0001	F1
C	1100	0011	C3	L	1101	0011	D3	T	1110	0011	E3	2	1111	0010	F2
D	1100	0100	C4	M	1101	0100	D4	U	1110	0100	E4	3	1111	0011	F3
E	1100	0101	C5	N	1101	0101	D5	V	1110	0101	E5	4	1111	0100	F4
F	1100	0110	C6	O	1101	0110	D6	W	1110	0110	E6	5	1111	0101	F5
G	1100	0111	C7	P	1101	0111	D7	X	1110	0111	E7	6	1111	0110	F6
H	1100	1000	C8	Q	1101	1000	D8	Y	1110	1000	E8	7	1111	0111	F7
I	1100	1001	C9	R	1101	1001	D9	Z	1110	1001	E9	8	1111	1000	F8
												9	1111	1001	F9

EBCDIC and ASCII both use hexadecimal as the shorthand on a memory dump, but they have a different coding pattern in the zone and digit.

Let's begin by looking at an unsigned 8 in ASCII code. Its code is 011 1000 as shown in Figure C.19(a). Refer to Table C.2 and find a 0011, inserting an additional 0 in the high-order bit position. Its hex notation is a 3. Again using

FIGURE C.19(b).
EBCDIC code.

TABLE C.2. **Hexadecimal Characters Use 4 bits.**

PLACE VALUES 8421	HEX NOTATION
0000	0
0001	1
0010	2
0011	3
0100	4
0101	5
0110	6
0111	7
1000	8
1001	9
1010	A
1011	B
1100	C
1101	D
1110	E
1111	F

Table C.2 find the 1000 code; its hex notation is an 8. The hex shorthand for the ASCII code of 011 1000 is then 38. Two hex characters represent the bits. If an F was stored instead of an unsigned 8, the ASCII code would be 100 0110. Refer to Table C.2 again, find the 100 and the 0110. You will see that 100 is a 4 in hex, while the 0110 is a 6 in hex. This shorthand in hex is 46.

BCDIC CODE (OR SIX-BIT BINARY CODED DECIMAL) AND OCTAL NOTATION

The BCDIC (Binary Coded Decimal Interchange Code) system, also called Six-bit Binary Coded Decimal by many, is used on a word-addressable computer. Its memory dumps are, however, in octal.

Octal notation, or octal, is a base 8 number system with 8 possibilities—7 being the highest number in any one position. The place values of BA8421 used in BCDIC are changed to fit an octal number. The BA8 are changed for the shorthand notation to 421 since 4 + 2 + 1 = 7. The octal shorthand is based upon 421 421. For the data A, the BCDIC code would be 11 0001; its octal shorthand is 61 as shown in Figure C.20.

TABLE C.3. **Comparison of Number Systems and Internal Codes.**

CODING SYSTEM USED	PURPOSE	BASE	HIGHEST DIGIT	PLACE VALUES	SHORTHAND NOTATION
ASCII	Internal code for storing input and output data.	10	9 in 7 bits.	421 8421	Hexadecimal
Binary	Calculations.	2	+2,147,483,648 in a 32-bit register	2^{63} to 2^0	Hexadecimal
				2^{35} to 2^0	Octal
				2^{31} to 2^0	Hexadecimal
				2^{15} to 2^0	Hexadecimal
Four-bit BCD	Internal code for storing input and output data.	10	9 in four-bits.	8421	Hexadecimal
Six-bit BCD (BCDIC)	Internal code for storing input and output data.	10	9 in six-bits.	BA 8421	Octal
EBCDIC	Input and output.	10	9 in eight bits.	8421 8421	Hexadecimal
Octal	Shorthand for internal code.	8	7 in three bits.	421	Not applicable.
Hexadecimal	Shorthand for internal code.	16	F in four bits.	8421	Not applicable.

Character Coded	ZONE BA	DIGIT 8421	OCTAL Place Values	Character Coded	ZONE BA	DIGIT 8421	OCTAL
A	11	0001	61	1	00	0001	01
B	11	0010	62	2	00	0010	02
C	11	0011	63	3	00	0011	03
D	11	0100	64	4	00	0100	04
E	11	0101	65	5	00	0101	05
F	11	0110	66	6	00	0110	06
G	11	0111	67	7	00	0111	07
H	11	1000	70	8	00	1000	10
I	11	1001	71	9	00	1001	11
J	10	0001	41	0	00	1010	12
K	10	0010	42				
L	10	0011	43				
M	10	0100	44				
N	10	0101	45				
O	10	0110	46				
P	10	0111	47				
Q	10	1000	50				
R	10	1001	51				
S	01	0010	22				
T	01	0011	23				
U	01	0100	24				
V	01	0101	25				
W	01	0110	26				
X	01	0111	27				
Y	01	1000	30				
Z	01	1001	31				

Data **STATE** Octal Shorthand

22 23 61 23 65

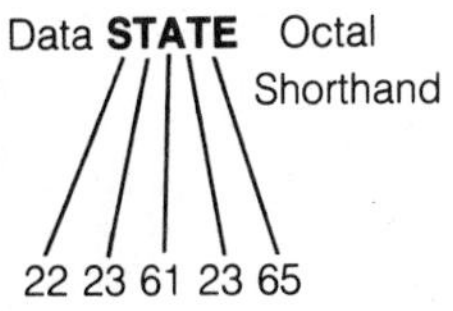

FIGURE C.20. **BCDIC (six-bit BCD) With Octal Notation.**

CHECKPOINT **Can you:**

Name the various types of coding systems used?

Tell how each one is coded for a certain character, such as an A? 5? X? 3? T?

SUMMARY

- The following are different bases for number systems: decimal (base 10), binary (base 2), hexadecimal (base 16), and octal (base 8).

- In any given base, each digit has a place value which represents an amount that is assigned to each position.

- The place values for a decimal are read from left to right, but their values are from right to left—1, 10, 100, 1,000, 10,000, etc. The low-order position (extreme right) is 10 raised to the zero power, which equals 1.

- The place values for an octal number are, reading left to right, 4096, 512, 64, 8, 1. The 1 represents 8 raised to the zero power, or 1; the 4096 represents 8 raised to the fourth power.

- The place values for a binary number are reading, left to right, 128, 64, 32, 16, 8, 4, 2, 1; these values are 2 raised to the seventh power down through 2 raised to the zero power.

- The place values for a hexadecimal number are, reading left to right, 4096 (16 raised to the third power), 256, 16, and 1.

- Regardless of the base used, there are as many possible digits in any one position as the base value. For example, if the base is octal, there are 8 possible digits (0 through 7). The highest possible digit is one less than the maximum number of possibilities.

- In hexadecimal, because its base is 16, there must be 16 possibilities in any one digit position. Because 0 through 9 represents 10 possible digits, A through F are arbitrarily chosen to represent the remaining six possibilities.

- Conversion from one base to another is done in a systematic way. If a decimal value is available and you wish to convert that value to a value in another base, divide the decimal number by the new base. The remainders will be the new base amount.

- When converting from decimal to a new base—say binary, for example—remember to write the remainder next to the dividend that was just used in the division.

- When conversion is done from the new base (say binary) to the decimal base, multiply the left digit by the new base of 2 and add the next binary digit. Continue this series of multiplications and additions until the calculation ends with an addition.

- An internal code is used for storing data used for input and output. Data that is inputted for later calculation must be changed from internal code to binary for calculation.

- There are several internal coding systems used: Four-bit Binary Coded Decimal (BCD), Six-bit Binary Coded Decimal, EBCDIC (Extended Binary Coded Decimal Interchange Code), and ASCII (American Standard Code for Information Interchange).

- Four-bit BCD uses 4 bits to store the numbers 0 through 9. Ten possible numbers can be coded.

- Six-bit BCD uses 6 bits for storing input and output data. Because there are two additional bits used for storing the zone, alphabetic data and special characters can also be coded, a characteristic setting Six-bit BCD apart from the Four-bit BCD code.

- Zone bits are used to designate which part of the alphabet is used. Two more bits are used along with the digit bits, and two raised to the sixth power is 64. There are then sixty-four possible characters that can be coded in Six-bit Binary Coded Decimal.

- ASCII uses 7 bits for its data transmission.

STUDY GUIDE

REVIEW OF TERMINOLOGY

The following terminology was discussed in this appendix:

American Standard Code for Information Interchange (ASCII)
Four-bit Binary Coded Decimal (BCD)
digit bits
even parity
Extended Binary Coded Decimal Interchange Code (EBCDIC)
octal

octal notation
odd parity
parity
parity bit
place value
signed numbers
Six-bit Binary Coded Decimal
unsigned numbers
zone bits

MULTIPLE CHOICE

Circle the letter of the item that correctly completes each item.

1. In all the internal coding systems discussed, this uses four place values in an internal code:
   a. parity
   b. digit bits
   c. zone bits
   d. parity bit
   e. odd parity

2. This is used as a way of protecting data to make certain that no 1-bit was lost in data transmission:
   a. parity
   b. zone bits
   c. signed numbers
   d. unsigned numbers
   e. octal notation

3. How many bits does ASCII internal code use for coding a character:
   a. 6 bits
   b. 7 bits
   c. 8 bits
   d. 9 bits
   e. 16 bits

4. How many bits does EBCDIC code use for coding a one-position signed number:
   a. 1 bit
   b. 6 bits
   c. 7 bits
   d. 8 bits
   e. 16 bits

5. An additional bit is used with the internal code; this is called a:
   a. zone-digit bit
   b. zone bit
   c. digit bit
   d. parity bit
   e. signed bit

6. When a computer must have 3 1-bits, 5 1-bits, or 7 1-bits in its total of 9 bits, this computer uses:
   a. even parity
   b. a parity byte
   c. an odd number of place values
   d. odd parity
   e. a zone bit

7. In ASCII code, there are three place values set aside for:
   a. odd parity
   b. even parity
   c. parity bit
   d. zone bits
   e. digit bits

8. ASCII code can differentiate among:
   a. 64 different characters
   b. 128 different characters
   c. octal notation
   d. 256 different characters
   e. hexadecimal notation

9. The place values can be B A, 4 2 1, or 8 4 2 1. These place values represent the:

a. Six-bit BCD code
b. digit bits
c. octal notation
d. zone bits
e. hexadecimal notation

10. A number that is inputted that contains no sign is considered to be:
a. an invalid character
b. a signed number
c. having odd parity
d. having even parity
e. an unsigned number

TRUE/FALSE QUESTIONS

Circle T if a statement is true; F if it is false.

1. **T/F** All internal codes use 8 bits for each character.
2. **T/F** EBCDIC, ASCII, and BCDIC use the same digit codes for numbers.
3. **T/F** A zone is used for coding a sign of a number.
4. **T/F** An unsigned number has a positive or negative value.
5. **T/F** An unsigned 7 has the same digit positions in all codes.
6. **T/F** Whatever internal code is used in a computer is really of no importance to most users.
7. **T/F** A user knows what type of internal code is used by looking at the 0s and 1s on a memory dump.
8. **T/F** Using hexadecimal code, one hexadecimal character always represents 3 bits.
9. **T/F** If an internal code is 111 1010, you know that this internal code cannot be EBCDIC.
10. **T/F** An internal code of 100 1010 represents an ASCII code for the character J.
11. **T/F** An ASCII internal code of 100 1111 would appear on a memory dump as an O.
12. **T/F** BCDIC code uses octal as its shorthand since there are only 6 bits used in the code.
13. **T/F** If an internal code using BCDIC were 010100, the octal shorthand would be 24.
14. **T/F** Using the BCDIC code of 010100, the character stored there would be a 24.
15. **T/F** If on a memory dump the hexadecimal code was E5, the internal code would be 11010101.
16. **T/F** $115_{16} = 73_{10}$
17. **T/F** $73_8 = 59_{10}$
18. **T/F** $78_{10} = 4E_{16}$
19. **T/F** $00000000000000000000000001100011_2 = 99_{10}$
20. **T/F** $63_{16} = 99_{10}$
21. **T/F** $00000000000000000000000000111111_2 = 63_{10}$
22. **T/F** If a number is 1010101101 its base could be decimal, octal, hexadecimal, or binary.
23. **T/F** If a number is 7777, its base could be decimal, octal, or hexadecimal.
24. **T/F** If a number is 7F, its base could only be hexadecimal.
25. **T/F** A number of 80 could never be an octal number.

ANSWERS

Multiple Choice: 1. **b** 2. **a** 3. **b** 4. **d** 5. **d** 6. **d** 7. **d** 8. **b** 9. **d** 10. **e** *True/False:* 1. **F** 2. **T** 3. **T** 4. **F** 5. **T** 6. **T** 7. **F** 8. **F** 9. **T** 10. **T** 11. **F** 12. **T** 13. **T** 14. **F** 15. **F** 16. **F** 17. **T** 18. **T** 19. **T** 20. **T** 21. **T** 22. **T** 23. **T** 24. **T** 25. **T**

REVIEW QUESTIONS

1. Identify the various bases. What is the number of possibilities used in each? What is the highest value in any digit?
2. When is binary used? Six-bit BCD? Octal? EBCDIC? ASCII? Hexadecimal?
3. Explain how it is possible to convert from a decimal number to another base.
4. What is a place value? What is it worth in binary? In Six-bit BCD? In ASCII?
5. Name the two parts of EBCDIC code. Why is each part used?
6. Why can ASCII differentiate among 128 characters?
7. How many alphabetic characters can be stored in a byte?
8. What is parity? Why is it used? How does odd parity differ from even parity?

DISCUSSION QUESTIONS

1. ASCII and EBCDIC are two of the most popular coding systems used. Explain how they differ.
2. When there are signed numbers used for input, the internal code can be the same as some alphabetic data. Explain how this can be true.
3. Assume that the initials of your name are stored in various computers' primary storage. These initials could very possibly be stored differently. Explain why this is true.
4. Using the information in question 3 above, the memory dumps could also be different. Why? Give an example of what each memory dump would print for the initials of your name.
5. Explain when signed data is used. How does it differ from unsigned data?

D

Evolution of Computers: How It All Began

OUTLINE

PROLOGUE

A man in the Navy began working at the Pentagon in 1961. He began his work on machines that required manual insertion of wires much like that done on the old-time telephone switchboards. Next, he was promoted to working with a computer that was so large it took up the size of a small auditorium.

Today he sits, not at a thirty-ton machine, but at one that weighs about 30 pounds. The amazing thing is he is doing processing at speeds much faster than the thirty-ton machine did. What also is interesting is that he is currently developing a program for his grandchild to learn to count.

HOW DOES IT DO THAT?

READ ON.

OBJECTIVES

After studying this chapter, you should be able to:

1. Explain how punched cards played an important role in the early days of data processing.

2. Identify the first types of computers.

3. Differentiate among generations of computers.

4. Explain why integrated circuits are important.

5. Identify some of the people and companies responsible for the development of computers.

6. Identify various professional computing organizations along with the accomplishments or goals of each.

INTRODUCTION

Following the historical development of computers is a fascinating study. It is a history that blends the imagination of designers, the courage of pioneers who believed that machinery could be used for fast calculation, the dedication of those people to technological advancement, and much hard work. Along with the historical facts are presented views of record-keeping before and after computers were developed.

The appendix gives a brief history of the computer industry. Hardware and software developments are discussed separately in order to recognize the contributions of people involved in each area to the advancement of the computing industry. Also included is explanation of the important goals that some professional organizations of the computer industry have pursued and will continue to follow.

HISTORICAL DEVELOPMENT OF HARDWARE

Let us arbitrarily divide the historical periods into timeframes, each of which produced a significant improvement in data processing equipment. The first two timeframes—before the 1880s and the 1880s through the 1930s—were not associated with a generation of computers. Each of the remaining timeframes, however, represents a generation of computers.

Each generation introduced a revolutionary equipment change which resulted in better equipment performance that gave a user greater reliability, faster operating speeds, and lower costs for each job. Generations are marked by improvements in the design of the logic circuitry.

Let us now examine each of these timeframes, noting the major achievements in each.

FIGURE D.1.
Pascal's counting machine.

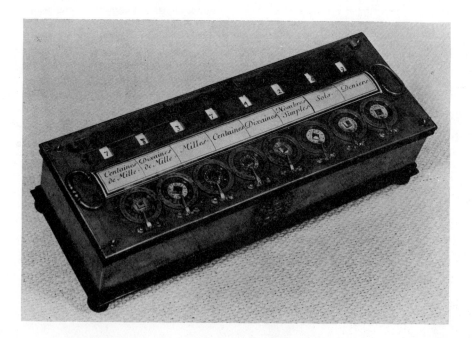

BEFORE THE 1880s

Certainly prehistoric man kept records. The Chinese developed the abacus which consisted of pebbles or stones for doing arithmetic. But specifically, three men in this pre-1880s era gave ideas to others for developing machines that we know today.

In 1642, **Blaise Pascal** developed the first arithmetic machine that was capable of carrying a one to the next leftmost position in a number (9 to 10, 99 to 100, and so on). The concepts set forth by Pascal were used in calculators until the electronic calculator was introduced in the mid-1960s. A popularly used computer language is named after this Frenchman. Refer to Figure D.1.

In 1801 **Joseph Jacquard** used punched cards to determine the pattern when cloth was woven on a loom. The cards were used to give such instructions to the machine as telling it when to use different threads so that a pattern could be woven accordingly. This was a new approach; punched cards ran a machine. Refer to Figure D.2.

FIGURE D.2.
Jacquad's loom.

FIGURE D.3.
Babbage's diffidence machine.

     The first type of data processing machine whose method of calculation resembled the computer's goes all the way back to **Charles Babbage,** who is recognized as being the father of computers. In 1823, Charles Babbage designed the **Difference Machine,** which was to be used for calculating mathematical tables. The gears and levers used provided the electrical path. Refer to Figure D.3. Babbage was truly a genius, far ahead of his time. His ideas could not be implemented, however, because the science of metallurgy had not progressed substantially. Because of this metallurgy problem, his machine gave inaccurate results.

     Charles Babbage was not a man to give up easily. In 1833 he devoted his time to the development of the **Analytical Engine,** the ideas of which are used in computers today. This machine was to perform addition, subtraction, multiplication, and division. Totals were to be calculated and stored in a memory for later recall. Instructions were supplied to the Analytical Engine through the use of punched cards. His model of the Analytical Engine consisted of an input device (used for sending data), a processor which was the calculator, the control unit (a coordinator of the machine), storage (for filing data for later use), and output devices (for accepting results).

     When Charles Babbage was developing the Analytical Engine, he met **Ada Byron, Countess of Lovelace.** Ada Byron's father was the well-known poet Lord Byron, although she never knew him. Ada Byron was an accomplished mathe matician. At age fifteen she had mastered geometry. It was felt, however, that because she was a woman, her career as a mathematician was limited. Charles Babbage and Ada Byron worked on the development of the mathematical tables to be used in the Analytical Engine. When a paper was prepared to explain how the Analytical Engine worked, Byron prepared some comments about the machine. Although the paper was recognized as being of excellent quality and used computer terminology still in use today, Byron was not fully recognized. Only her initials were allowed on the paper because she was a woman. Ada's contribution is indeed remembered in the history of computing, however, as she is recognized as the first programmer. One of the latest computer languages, developed by the Department of Defense, bears her name (Ada).

THE 1880s TO THE LATE 1930s

The U.S. government felt the impact that data would have on society when it prepared the census every ten years. The totals for the 1870 census were not finalized until 1878. By this time, the data had little meaning, being out of date almost before being published. To make the data useful and meaningful, **Herman Hollerith** began work on the punched card. He got the idea from watching a ticket taker on a train. Herman Hollerith is also known for founding the Tabulating Machine Company, which later became IBM Corporation.

Punched Cards

In 1882, Herman Hollerith designed the equipment that could record (punch) data into cards. He also designed the equipment that could read (look at) the holes in the cards and know what it had read (which characters were punched in the card). This equipment could also calculate such totals as: total men, total women, total children, total state population, and so on. About 700 cards were punched per day; about eighty cards were counted per minute.

The concept of punched cards, although it originated in the 1880s, is still being used today. Two types of punched cards are being used; the eighty- and ninety-six-character cards, shown in Figure D.4. This figure also shows the Hollerith code which used a unique set of holes to code a character.

The equipment which used punched cards as input was known as **punched-card data processing (PCDP)** equipment. PCDP equipment was also referred to as **electromechanical** equipment since it consisted of a series of wheels, levers, gears, pulleys, buttons, toggle switches, and control panels that were used to direct the equipment as to what manipulation was to be done. There were many PCDP machines; each had basically one or two manipulations it could perform. None had any memory in the sense that computers today do. Each worked on one punched card at a time.

An operator plugged wires into a **control panel** that specifically completed the instructions to the machine as to what it was to do. Equate a control panel to a telephone switchboard which lit up with incoming calls. A control panel, as shown in Figure D.5, had to be completely rewired for each job that was run.

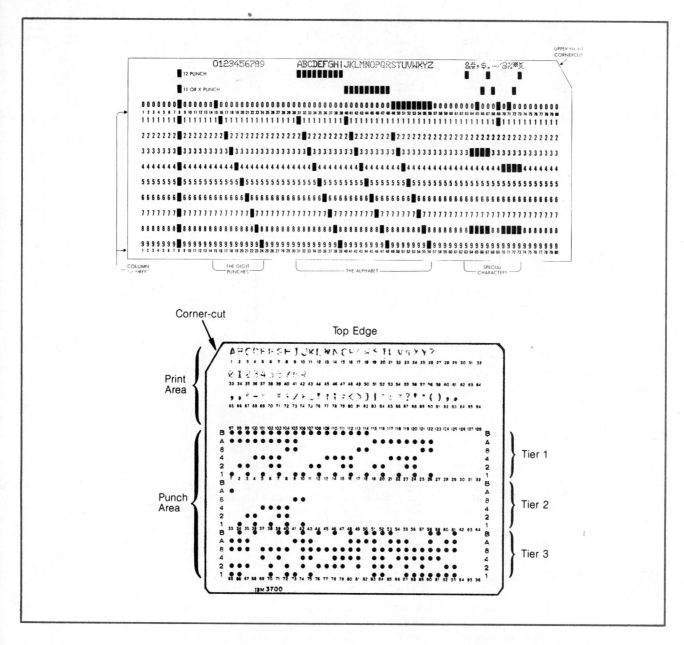

FIGURE D.4.

An 80-column and 96-column card.

The wired control panel and the punched cards were inserted into the machine. Since each machine could only do one or two functions, an operator had to walk the deck of punched cards from machine to machine before any report was prepared, for example.

There are installations that still use punched cards, but their number decreases each year. Other types of input and output are faster, easier to handle, and require less storage space. A key punch (shown in Figure D.6(a)) is used for capturing data on punched cards. Punched cards are fed into the card reader, as shown in Figure D.6(b). An accounting machine, as shown in Figure D.7, did calculations and printed reports.

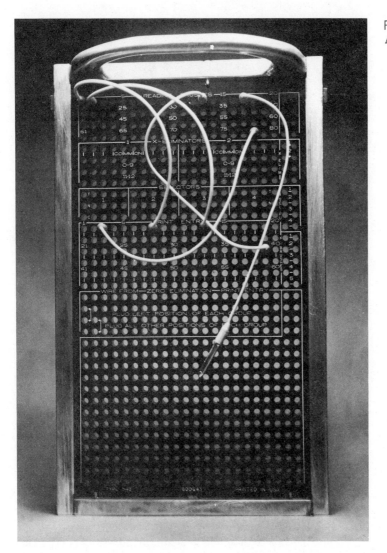

FIGURE D.5.
A control panel.

Large companies used PCDP equipment for processing their payroll, billing, inventory, and accounting records. The military also used PCDP equipment in World War II at Pearl Harbor for helping to break the Japanese coded messages before the Battle of Midway. But companies began to drown in punched cards as their volume became overwhelming. Still, they did not want to destroy cards, for once the cards were discarded, the data was completely gone. A need for better machinery was obvious.

CHECKPOINT **Can you:**

Tell how punched cards played an important role in early data processing?

FIGURE D.6(a).
A key punch machine.

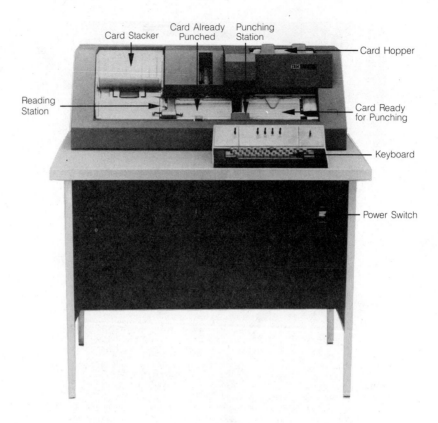

THE 1940s THROUGH 1958

The stage was set for a transition from these electromechanical machines to those that operated electronically.

In the late 1930s, **Thomas Watson, Sr.,** president of the Tabulating Company, donated $500,000 to Harvard for the development of the Mark I. In 1939 Professor **Howard Aiken** of Harvard University began work in developing the **Mark I** to provide faster results than were being accomplished on the PCDP machines. In 1944 the Mark I was introduced with the ability to add, subtract, multiply, divide, and work with previously calculated data that was stored in the memory of the machine. Although it was electromechanical rather than electronic, it was very different from the electromechanical machines that worked on the principle of one card at a time. The Mark I was known for computing mathematical tables. Refer to Figure D.8.

In 1942, **Dr. John V. Atanasoff** along with his assistant, Clifford Berry, built a prototype of a computer called the **Atanasoff-Berry Computer (ABC).** Although this computer was not assembled until 1942, its concepts were developed in the early 1930s.

In 1941 **John Mauchly** and **J. Presper Eckert** teamed together to produce an all-electronic calculator; they are recognized for inventing the electronic digital computer. This machine was called the **ENIAC (Electronic Numerical Integrator**

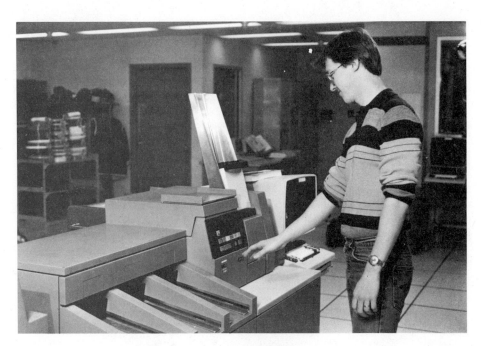

FIGURE D.6(b).
A card reader.

FIGURE D.7.
An IBM 402.

FIGURE D.8.
The Mark I.

and **Calculator**). It was superior to the Mark I in that it could do additions 500 times faster.

Figure D.9(a) shows the ENIAC. It was the first general-purpose electronic computer ever produced and is known for its work in the ballistic laboratory at the Aberdeen Proving Grounds in Maryland. Several technicians hand-wired the plug boards. Some 6,000 switches had to be set before the program was run. The plug boards and the switches gave instructions to the computer on what to do. Over 18,000 vacuum tubes were used in this computer. Incredible though it may sound, the processing done by this thirty-ton ENIAC can be duplicated today on a printed circuit board that can be hand-held. Refer to Figure D.9(a).

First-generation computers used the **vacuum tube,** shown in Figure D.9(b). It required a heated cathode, an electrical heater that made the tube glow and operate. The disadvantages were that this heater required a tremendous amount of energy and it gave off great amounts of heat.

Another first-generation computer, introduced in 1949 shortly after the ENIAC, was called the **BINAC (Binary Automatic Computer).** Its exclusive air conditioning is shown in Figure D.10. Today hundreds of thousands of dollars are sometimes spent on air conditioning the computer site.

In 1946 **Dr. Herman Goldstine** developed the theory of using binary digits (bits), which could be either one of two states—"on" or "off" (or as we think of them today 0s or 1s). Thus began the binary coding used in electronic computers. **John von Neumann,** a noted mathematician, advanced this binary theory, and from that concept developed a stored program computer concept. John von Neumann's ideas of processing one instruction after the other, known as **serial processing,** have been followed in all computers produced to date. Think of this

FIGURE D.9(a).
The ENIAC.

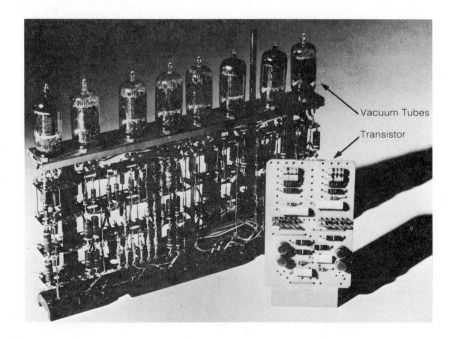

FIGURE D.9(b).
Vacuum Tubes.

FIGURE D.10.
The BINAC.

processing as analogous to passengers boarding a bus, one passenger at a time. The first stored program computer developed was called the **EDSAC (Electronic Delay Storage Automatic Computer)**; it was followed by the **EDVAC (Electronic Discrete Variable Automatic Computer).** Instead of using hand-plugged wires for their instructions like the ENIAC, the EDSAC and EDVAC were programmed by an internally stored set of instructions.

In 1951 Eckert and Mauchly produced the first commercially available computer; its name was the **UNIVAC I.** It was used at the Bureau of Census where it proved to be very successful. In Figure D.11 the console of the UNIVAC I is shown. It is from the **console** that the operator gave the computer special instructions. By depressing certain buttons and flipping certain levers, the computer functions accordingly. The same concept is used today in mainframes; an operator depresses buttons and keys to communicate with the operating system.

The technological advancement of the first-generation computer was a giant step forward, yielding calculation speeds several hundreds of times faster than the punched card data processing machines. This was a beginning.

CHECKPOINT **Can you:**

Identify some of the first computers ever built?
Tell what the distinguishable characteristic is for each?
Identify the people responsible for the development?

FIGURE D.11.
The UNIVAC.

Development of Secondary Storage Devices

In 1946 magnetic tape was developed for computer equipment, although its concepts were developed earlier in 1898 by **Valdema Paulsen** in Denmark. Until this time, all input was on punched cards. Now data could be stored on and processed from magnetic tape by a computer. Magnetic tape was fifty to seventy-five times faster than using punched cards.

In 1952, magnetic disk was developed, allowing a large volume of data to be stored. Data was retrieved in about one second. This breakthrough gave direct access processing rather than the sequential processing. With **direct access processing** there is the capability of going directly to the desired record without having to read all previous records associated with the application. All types of processing needs could be met. **Sequential processing,** you recall, requires the reading of each record, one record after the other. Equate sequential processing to your examining a deck of playing cards. If the cards are to be examined sequentially, the first card is looked at, then the second card is looked at, then the third, and so on, until you have finally found the card you wanted or have examined all 52 cards.

1959 THROUGH 1963

In a **second-generation computer** (shown in Figure D.12) the vacuum tubes were replaced by discrete components, each capable of performing a single (or discrete)

function. These were the transistors which were developed by the Bell Laboratories about 1948. William Shockley and the coinventors, John Bardeen and Walter Brattain, received the Nobel prize for the invention of the transistor. The transistor was a tremendous breakthrough in technology. A number of them put together are smaller than your little toenail; by contrast, the vacuum tubes were four inches high. Refer to Figure D.12.

The central processing unit uses thousands of transistors as switches that are either in an "on" or "off" state. Transistors do not generate much heat and require a small amount of electrical power to operate. The size of the transistor drastically reduced the size of the computer system while greatly increasing operating speed. Generally, most second-generation computers' speed was stated in microseconds.

In 1959, minicomputers made their debut, as was noted in Chapter 3. Some of the processing work done on mainframes (large computers) was at that point being done on minicomputers (larger than personal computers.) Applications that could not be scheduled on mainframes were often run on minicomputers.

1964 TO THE 1980s

Third-generation computers were introduced in 1964. Figure D.13 shows a popularly used third-generation computer. The concept of a family of computers was introduced in this generation, with the IBM 360 and IBM 370 being the most popularly used.

Solid-logic technology was introduced in this generation, drastically reducing the size of circuits. **Solid-state** uses metals or crystals in a very special way to conduct the flow of current. Third-generation computers used no tubes of any kind. The need for warm-up time was eliminated because no heating filaments were used; thus, less energy was used compared to previous generation computers. The speed of these computers is stated in nanoseconds. This technology is capable of switching a current from "on" to "off" in 30 billionths of a second.

In the third generation of computer technology, the **integrated circuit,** often

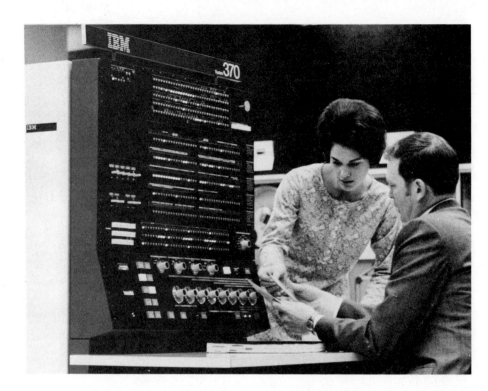

FIGURE D.13.
The IBM 370.

called IC, was introduced in 1971 for computer usage, although the IC concepts were introduced by Jack S. Kilby in 1958. The integrated circuit was so named because it combines (or integrates) a number of discrete components which are single-function devices into a system or a series to accomplish a number of functions. Anything that can be done with an integrated circuit can be done with a large number of discrete components. The purposes of integrated circuits are many. They achieve mass production yielding extremely low costs and provide the smallest possible size. They also keep complex functions as simple as possible. Refer to Figure D.14.

When third-generation computers were introduced, the density with which the components were grouped was called medium-scale integration (MSI). A transition to **large-scale integration (LSI)** soon followed. In large-scale integration about 150,000 components were fabricated on an integrated circuit that is about one-tenth the size of a postage stamp. Thousands of integrated circuits were batch produced on a chip along with the necessary wiring to make a circuit. The third-generation computers were introduced with the development of the integrated circuit; the intermediate third-generation computers used the large-scale integrated circuit.

Manufacture of Integrated Circuits

If our country had not sent a man to the moon, question arises as to how sophisticated the computer technology would be today. There had to be a way to make computers light-weight, very fast, and extremely reliable. It was through these efforts that integrated circuits were developed.

The manufacturing of these chips must be handled in an extremely detailed and closely monitored atmosphere. When the design of the circuit is completed, the measurements stated in the design are expressed in microns (millionths of a meter).

The area that is world renowned for the manufacture of these integrated circuits is called **Silicon Valley,** an area located about sixty miles south of San Francisco, California, that is concentrated in the communities of Palo Alto, Mountain View, Sunnyvale, Santa Clara, and Cupertino. Silicon Valley gets its name from the silicon substrate that is used in the manufacture of the integrated circuit chips. The chips are used in digital watches and electronic calculators as well as in most computer equipment.

CHECKPOINT **Can you:**

Tell why integrated circuits are so important to the use of computer equipment?

1980s TO DATE

The **fourth-generation computers** have come into existence with the technological advancement known as **microelectronics,** which uses micro-scale circuitry, resulting in higher densities and higher performance. The compactness with which the components are fabricated on a chip is referred to as **very large-scale integration (VLSI).** Hewlett-Packard Corporation has developed an integrated circuit chip that places 450,000 transistors on a single square chip measuring one-sixteenth of an inch. The chip is capable of processing all the information that is contained in 1,000 books in one second. This breakthrough continues the trend in the industry, which is to get more and more transistors (and therefore, data) on one chip. As design, testing, and use of very large-scale integration chips continues, many more components will be located in a still smaller area. The smaller the chip, the faster the computer operates since there is a smaller distance for an impulse to travel.

Lawrence Livermore National Laboratories and Scientific Research Institute (SRI) among others, are working jointly to develop a network of super-computers that will operate at processing speeds 1,000 times faster than third-generation computers.

FIGURE D.15.
Commandor Grace Hopper.

CHECKPOINT **Can you:**

Identify the four generations of computers?

Tell what technological advancement marked each generation?

HISTORICAL DEVELOPMENT OF SOFTWARE

Rarely do you see a computer textbook without the picture of Commodore **Grace Murray Hopper,** recognized as the genius of programming. (See Figure D.15). Remember the Mark I discussed previously in this chapter? Commodore Hopper learned how to program the electromechanical machine while at Harvard. Later she joined the Eckert-Mauchly Computer Corporation to work as a mathematician for the UNIVAC I computer.

In 1952, she began publishing the first of fifty papers of interest dealing with software in the operating system, how computers should perform work associated with programming, and how standards should be set within the computer industry. She estimates, according to periodicals, that the federal government spends $450 million unnecessarily each year because of its lack of standards for use when programs are written.

In 1959 Commodore Hopper participated in the **Committee on Data Systems Languages (Codasyl)** which developed the language designed for solving business problems, called COBOL. This language was not tied to any specific hardware as most other languages were. Later she served on the **American National Standards Institute (ANSI),** which sets the standards for many of the problem-solving languages developed today.

This remarkable woman still tours the country giving speeches on things that she feels deeply. Some of these are that the use of computers has just begun and the areas dealing with weather forecasting, managing energy, and improving agricultural output need attention. She has earned almost every professional organization's top award.

PROFESSIONAL ORGANIZATIONS

While people were busy developing hardware and software, professional organizations also played their part in the history of computing. Many professional organizations have emerged for the advancement of the art of computing. The **American Federation of Information Processing Societies (AFIPS),** formed in 1961, is a national federation of the many professional societies that exist today. Some of the societies in AFIPS are briefly discussed.

Data Processing Management Association (DPMA) began its operations in 1951; it was then composed of professionals using punched-card data processing equipment. DPMA, representing the largest world-wide organization serving the information processing and management personnel, has probably done more for the encouragement of high standards of education than most other organizations. The organization's latest extensive efforts have been directed at seeking a standardized introductory course material, soliciting needs of data processing professionals and educators across the United States. The organization finalized its curriculum plans in 1982. DPMA also gives recognition to an outstanding person in the field as a yearly award is granted.

The **Association for Computing Machinery (ACM)** was founded in 1947. The thrust of this organization is towards exchanges of scientific, educational, and technical ideas between specialists and the public. ACM stresses the advancement of information processing through special interest groups for the study of specific problems, techniques, and advancements.

The **Institute of Electrical and Electronic Engineers (IEEE)** has greatly contributed to the efforts to standardize some of the hardware. On the back of most computer equipment, you will see the IEEE standardized number or the RS number. This organization has also directed extensive efforts towards the development of an accurate and systematic software development. The organization is currently generating software engineering standards, or guidelines. The **software engineering** concept is the setting up of scientific principles as to how computer programs are to be developed. IEEE presents an excellent magazine highlighting the newest technology.

The **Association for Systems Management (ASM)** was founded in 1947. Its purpose is aiding individuals in keeping current in the rapidly changing technological areas. ASM holds many conferences for the purpose of educating professionals and publishes the *Journal of Systems Management* for the same reason.

The **Institute for Certification of Computer Professionals (ICCP)** was established in 1973 for the purpose of testing an individual's knowledge and skills. An examination is given only to those individuals who have, at the minimum, five years work experience in a computer information system environment. If the five-part examination is passed, a certificate called the **Certificate of Data Processing**

(CDP) is earned. Another five-part examination tests programming knowledge and skills and is called a **Certificate of Computer Programming (CCP)**.

The **Data Entry Management Association (DEMA)** in 1983 gave its first examination to those individuals claiming expertise in data entry. The material in the examination was covered in a 181-page manual prepared by the association. After successful completion of the examination, the person is given a certificate of achievement, the recognition of which will prove helpful in employment.

 **Can you:**

Identify some of the professional organizations in the computing field?

SUMMARY

- Blaise Pascal in 1642 developed the first arithmetic machine that was capable of carrying a one to the next left position.

- In 1801 Joseph Jacquard used punched cards to determine the pattern when cloth was woven on a loom.

- Beginning in 1823 Charles Babbage developed the Difference Machine. In 1833 he developed the concepts for the Analytical Engine, which are similar to modern-day computers. Ada Byron, Countess of Lovelace, assisted Charles Babbage in the mathematical work for the Analytical Engine and is recognized as the first programmer.

- In 1882 Herman Hollerith developed the idea of using punched cards for recording of data.

- Punched card data processing (PCDP) machines were used for data manipulation in large companies.

- Each piece of PCDP equipment was limited to one or two jobs that it could perform. An operator had to manually wire a control panel and had to walk the deck of punched cards from machine to machine before any report was prepared.

- There are four generations of computers. Each generation is notable for some revolutionary equipment change that usually gave greater reliability, faster operating speeds, and lower costs per job.

- The first generation of computers was introduced in about 1941.

- The Mark I was designed by Howard Aiken of Harvard. It could multiply, divide, add, and subtract, and work with the previously calculated data stored in its memory.

- John Mauchly and J. Presper Eckert invented the electronic digital computer called the ENIAC. It did calculations 500 times faster than the Mark I.

- For the ENIAC to process data, technicians had to wire the plug boards so the machine would receive its instructions.

- The EDSAC was the first computer to store a program internally; the EDVAC followed shortly after.

- The first-generation computers used vacuum tubes for operation. Generation of excessive heat was a problem.

- In 1946 magnetic tape was developed for use on computers.

- In 1952 magnetic disk was developed, allowing records to be accessed randomly rather than sequentially.

- The second generation of computers began about 1959. This generation was marked with the use of the transistor.

- The transistor was developed by William Shockley at the Bell Laboratories in 1948. Transistors required that very little heat be dissipated and allowed the size of computers to be drastically reduced. In 1958 Jack S. Kilby introduced the integrated circuit concept.

- In 1959 minicomputers were introduced.

- In about 1964 third-generation computers were introduced. These used solid-state technology. The family of computers were introduced in this generation.

- The integrated circuit was the marked technological improvement in the third generation, which began with medium-scale integration and then progressed through large-scale integration (LSI). Large-scale integration meant about 150,000 components were fabricated on an integrated circuit that is about one-tenth the size of a postage stamp.

- Integrated circuits are produced in many areas of the United States, but Silicon Valley outside of San Francisco, California, is the best known single area of their manufacture.

- Fourth-generation computers involve microelectronics; these machines are currently being designed, tested, and produced. These computers use very large-scale integration (VLSI) technology. About 450,000 transistors can be fabricated onto a single chip measuring one-sixteenth of an inch across. The smaller the distance the electrical impulse has to travel, the faster the operation is of the computer. Fourth-generation computers will be the fastest yet.

- The American Federation of Information Processing Societies (AFIPS) represents a national federation of many professional societies in computer usage.

- The Data Processing Management Association (DPMA), Association for Computing Machinery (ACM), Institute of Electrical and Electronic Engineers (IEEE), Institute for Certification of Computer Professionals (ICCP), and Data Entry Management Association (DEMA) are some of the professional organizations.

STUDY GUIDE

REVIEW OF TERMINOLOGY

The following terminology and individuals were discussed in the appendix:

Howard Aiken
American Federation of
 Information Processing
 Societies (AFIPS)
American National
 Standards Institute
 (ANSI)
Analytical Engine
Association for
 Computing Machinery
 (ACM)
Association for Systems
 Management (ASM)
John V. Atanasoff
Atanasoff-Berry
 Computer (ABC)
Charles Babbage
BINAC (Binary
 Automatic Computer)
Ada Byron, Countess of
 Lovelace
Certificate of Computer
 Programming (CCP)
Certificate of Data
 Processing (CDP)
Committee on Data
 Systems Languages
 (Codasyl)
console
control panel
Data Entry Management
 Association (DEMA)
Data Processing
 Management
 Association (DPMA)
direct access processing
J. Presper Eckert
EDSAC (Electronic
 Delay Storage
 Automatic Computer)
EDVAC (Electronic
 Discrete Variable
 Automatic Computer)
ENIAC (Electronic

Numerical Integrator
 and Calculator)
electromechanical
first-generation computer
fourth-generation
 computer
Herman Goldstine
Herman Hollerith
Grace Murray Hopper
Institute of Electrical and
 Electronic Engineers
 (IEEE)
Institute of Certification
 of Computer
 Professionals (ICCP)
integrated circuit
Joseph Jacquard
Jack S. Kilby
large-scale integration
 (LSI)
Mark I
John Mauchly
microelectronics
Blaise Pascal
Valdema Paulsen
punched-card data
 processing (PCDP)
second-generation
 computer
sequential processing
serial processing
William Shockley
Silicon Valley
software engineering
solid-state
third-generation
 computer
transistor
UNIVAC I
vacuum tube
very large-scale
 integration (VLSI)
John von Neumann
Thomas Watson, Sr.

MULTIPLE CHOICE

Circle the letter of the item that correctly completes each statement.

1. The inventor of the Analytical Engine, which developed in crude form computer concepts used today, was developed by:
 a. Pascal   d. Babbage
 b. Watson   e. Aiken
 c. Jacquard

2. Use of punched cards to determine the pattern when cloth was woven on a loom was originated by:
 a. Pascal   d. Babbage
 b. Watson   e. Aiken
 c. Jacquard

3. The use of punched cards for recording data was developed by:
 a. Pascal   d. Aiken
 b. Watson   e. Ada Byron
 c. Hollerith

4. The equipment that used punched cards as the input and did its data manipulation through the use of a control panel was called:
 a. PCDP   d. magnetic tape
 b. punched card   e. magnetic disk
 c. computers

5. The man who donated $500,000 for the development of the Mark I was:
 a. Aiken   d. Watson
 b. Mauchly   e. Paulsen
 c. Eckert

6. Technicians used plug boards and set some 6,000 switches for this computer to operate:
 a. Mark I   d. ABC
 b. ENIAC   e. PCDP
 c. BINAC

7. This computer stored its program internally:
 a. MARK I   d. BINAC
 b. ENIAC   e. PCDP
 c. EDVAC

8. Magnetic tape was developed in this year for use with computers:
 a. 1898   d. 1958
 b. 1946   e. 1965
 c. 1952

9. The first-generation computer got its power source from:
   - *a.* transistors
   - *b.* integrated circuits
   - *c.* vacuum tubes
   - *d.* control panels
   - *e.* switches

10. This computer's concepts were developed in the 1930s by:
    - *a.* Herman Hollerith
    - *b.* Thomas Watson
    - *c.* John Atanasoff
    - *d.* Charles Babbage
    - *e.* J. Presper Eckert

11. The person very actively involved with software development is:
    - *a.* Joseph Jacquard
    - *b.* Grace Murray Hopper
    - *c.* Blaise Pascal
    - *d.* Herman Hollerith
    - *e.* Thomas Watson, Sr.

12. The second-generation computers introduced the use of:
    - *a.* transistors
    - *b.* integrated circuits
    - *c.* vacuum tubes
    - *d.* control panels
    - *e.* family of computers

13. Large-scale integration and medium-scale integration are associated with:
    - *a.* first-generation computers
    - *b.* second-generation computers
    - *c.* third-generation computers
    - *d.* fourth-generation computers
    - *e.* all of these

14. Bell Laboratories developed this in 1948:
    - *a.* vacuum tube
    - *b.* transistor
    - *c.* integrated circuit
    - *d.* magnetic tape
    - *e.* magnetic disk

15. The fourth-generation computers use:
    - *a.* LSI and MSI
    - *b.* VLSI
    - *c.* solid-state technology
    - *d.* transistors
    - *e.* vacuum tubes

16. That area of the United States known for the development and fabrication of integrated circuits is called:
    - *a.* IC Town
    - *b.* New York
    - *c.* Silicon Valley
    - *d.* San Francisco
    - *e.* Chicago

TRUE/FALSE QUESTIONS

Circle T if a statement is true; F if it is false.

1. **T/F** Most first-generation computers' speed is stated in microseconds.
2. **T/F** Most second-generation computers' speed is stated in nanoseconds.
3. **T/F** There were many punched-card data processing machines because each one was capable of doing a limited amount of data manipulation.
4. **T/F** The inventors of electronic computers are J. Presper Eckert and John Mauchly.
5. **T/F** The Mark I computer was an electromechanical machine.
6. **T/F** The smaller the area of computer components, the faster the computer is able to operate.
7. **T/F** Since the integrated circuit was developed, there has been only a gradual improvement in computer speed.
8. **T/F** Only the vacuum tubes had trouble with dissipation of heat.
9. **T/F** The size of the computer was greatly reduced with the introduction of transistors.
10. **T/F** DPMA and DEMA are the largest professional computer societies.
11. **T/F** The newest professional computer organization is ICCP.
12. **T/F** Certificates for proficiency in programming and data processing are awarded after successful completion of examinations and required work experience.
13. **T/F** Software engineering refers to the scientific development of computer programs.

ANSWERS

Multiple Choice: 1. **d** 2. **c** 3. **c** 4. **a** 5. **d** 6. **b** 7. **c** 8. **b** 9. **c** 10. **c** 11. **b** 12. **a** 13. **c** 14. **b** 15. **b** 16. **c**
True/False: 1. **F** 2. **F** 3. **T** 4. **T** 5. **T** 6. **T** 7. **F** 8. **F** 9. **T** 10. **F** 11. **F** 12. **T** 13. **T**

REVIEW QUESTIONS

1. What are the three factors that usually indicate a computer generation has evolved?

2. Who was the father of modern-day computers? Why did his efforts fail?

3. Who developed an important arithmetic operation in machines?

4. What was Joseph Jacquard's contribution?

5. How did Herman Hollerith get his ideas for processing data? What is he best known for?

6. What does PCDP stand for? How did PCDP equipment get instructions as to what to do?

7. What role did Thomas Watson, Sr., play in the development of computers?

8. Who was Howard Aiken? What were his accomplishments?

9. What was the ENIAC? Who developed it? How did it operate?

10. What was the EDVAC known for?

11. When was magnetic tape developed? Who did it?

12. Why was the transistor such an important technological advancement? Who developed it?

13. In what computer generation was the integrated circuit introduced?

14. What does LSI stand for? VLSI?

15. What role did Ada Byron play in the development of computers?

DISCUSSION QUESTIONS

1. The efforts of many people were required to make computer technology a success. Explain this statement.

2. There are several generations of computers. Trace the history of each, noting the particular highlights of each generation.

3. VLSI is an important breakthrough in computer technological advancements. How does this affect a user when compared to MSI or LSI?

GLOSSARY

Absolute address A location used in primary storage that cannot be changed once it has been assigned by the loader or linkage editor.

Access time The time from the request for the data to the delivery of the data to primary storage.

Acoustic coupler Sends data by sounds and puts the sounds on speakers, permitting then the use of a regular telephone line for computer transmission.

Action Used with a decision table; shows path for required processing when condition is true.

Actuator The arm that swings in and out over the magnetic disk platter so that reading and writing of data can be accomplished.

Ada A high-level transportable, portable, fully structured programming language recently developed under the specifications of the Department of Defense for use by the military.

Address An area of primary or secondary storage that identifies it and distinguishes it from all other storage; similar in concept to house numbers on a street.

Address register A register that holds the address of the data that is called for by the instruction.

Ad hoc application An application that is designed for a single user.

AI Refer to *Artificial intelligence*.

Algorithm The details that are worked out as to how a problem is to be solved; step-by-step approach which must be carefully planned so that the program that is later coded executes correctly.

Alphabetic character Any of the letters A through Z.

Alphabetic field A group of alphabetic characters that collectively represent a person's data, a thing, a happening; spaces are also permitted in this type of field.

Alphanumeric character One of a set of characters that includes numbers, alphabetic characters, and special characters.

Alphanumeric field A group of related characters composed of numbers, special characters, and/or alphabetic characters; represents at least two kinds of characters recorded in a field.

ALU Refer to *Arithmetic-logic unit*.

Analog computer A computer that measures continually; used in scientific applications and in manufacturing to control an operation by translating physical conditions into electrical quantities; contrast *Digital computer*.

Analysis The study of a problem before any action is taken.

ANSI (American National Standards Institute) An organization that analyzes and then provides standards for many fields of computer use.

ANSI COBOL A business-oriented language that has several standards established as of 1968 and 1974; the 1980 version is currently pending lawsuit clarification.

APL (A Programming Language) A programming language designed to be used on terminals because of its design for interactive problem solving.

Application The job or kind of job that is run on the computer.

Application software The program written to solve a specific, everyday problem such as billing, accounts payable, checking accounts, or grade point averages.

Architecture The internal design of the computer system.

Arithmetic-logic unit (ALU) That part of the central processing unit where calculations and decision making are performed.

Array A grouping of many data records; contrast with *List*.

Artificial intelligence (AI) An experimental field involving use of computer technology in the study of automatic decision making; computer performs reasoning usually associated with the human intelligence.

Ascending order A sequence that has the smallest value first and the largest value last.

ASCII (American Standard Code for Information Interchange); An internal code that uses 7 bits plus a parity bit.

Assembler A program that converts a source program (assembly language) into an object program; part of the operating system.

Assembly language A programming language containing an operation code and an operand; one step removed from machine language.

Asynchronous terminal A slow speed terminal that has no clocking mechanism and no protocol other than a start/stop protocol; contrast *Synchronous terminal*.

Asynchronous transmission Start/stop transmission; contrast *Synchronous transmission*.

ATM Refer to *Automated teller machine*.

Audit trail A check that is used to make certain that a new system is working correctly and efficiently.

Automated office A concept involving integrated use of data processing, word processing, expert systems, data base processing, and other electronics in the office environment.

Automated teller machines (ATM) Terminals that appear outside a bank and in lobbies, providing a twenty-four-hour banking service electronically.

Auxiliary storage Refer to *Secondary storage*.

Back-end processor (BEP) A computer that handles the accessing of data in a data base for a larger central processing unit.

Bandwidth The maximum number of bits that are transmitted over a communications facility in data communications.

Bar code A grouping of parallel, dark lines on a product which identify the product; most common on grocery store products; often referred to as Universal Product Code (UPC).

Bar-code reader A device used to read a bar code or Universal Product Code (UPC) by altering the physical code to digital signals.

Base The number of possible numbers in any one position in a numbering system such as decimal, octal, binary, and hexadecimal.

Base address The beginning position of a stored program; used in an operating system for allocating memory in a multiprogramming environment.

BASIC (Beginners' All-Purpose Symbolic Instruction Code) The most popular of all high-level computer languages; a language that is used on terminals.

BASIC interpreter That translator program used with BASIC which translates a line of code and then executes it; the translated instruction is not saved after it executes the instruction.

Batching Refer to *Batch processing*.

Batch processing A technique that is used where data to be processed is collected into one group prior to processing and run through the computer in a continuous flow at one time.

Batch total A total derived through the calculation of significant data such as total salaries of all employees or the number of gallons of gasoline sold.

Baud The number of bits transmitted per second in data communications.

BCDIC (Binary Coded Decimal Interchange Code) A coding system used by some computers for internal storage; also called six-bit BCD.

Bench mark Involves the use of typical problems for comparisons of hardware performance.

BEP Refer to *Back-end processor*.

Binary Stems from the word bi meaning two; two possibilities are used in this number system—a 1 and a 0.

Binary digit (bit) The smallest or most basic unit (either a 1 or a 0) for coding data in primary storage and secondary storage.

Bit Refer to *Binary digit*.

Bit configuration A grouping of bits that together code a character.

Bits per second (bps) The speed with which bits are transmitted between the central processing unit and the peripheral devices.

Blocked records Records grouped (laid out) on secondary storage devices to use storage space more efficiently.

Blocking factor The number of logical records that are included in a physical block of records.

Bottom-up design The beginning programming technique used in the 1950s, through which details of a problem's solution are investigated first; contrast *Top-down design*.

bps Refer to *Bits per second*.

Broadband Refer to *Wideband*.

Bubble memory A memory device which uses a bubble (magnetized spot) to represent a 1-bit and no bubble to represent a 0-bit; bubbles float in a looped pattern on a piece of garnet; a non-volatile memory.

Buffer A high-speed temporary storage area into which data is transmitted from the peripheral device; its purpose is to smooth out time differences for inputting or outputting data as contrasted with calculation or other data manipulation done by a computer.

Buffer Storage Refer to *Buffer*.

Bug An error that exists in a program.

Bulletin Board Service (BSS) The supplying of public domain software either for free or for a copying charge.

Bundled Hardware, software, or a combination of both that are sold as a package for a single price.

Bus A cable used in smaller computers, generally, to connect peripherals with the processor.

Business data processing Data processing that deals with the financial transactions of companies.

Byte A group of 6, 7, or 8 bits that are used for coding a character in BCDIC, ASCII, EBCDIC, or ASCII-8 internal codes.

Byte-addressable Refer to character-addressable computers.

CAD Refer to Computer-Aided Design.

Cache memory An extremely fast semiconductor storage; can be used with magnetic disk storage.

CAI Refer to *Computer-assisted instruction*.

Canned program A program that is already-written and tested; requires no computer operator or programmer; more recently referred to as packaged software.

Capacity Number of characters that can be stored in a primary storage or secondary storage.

Capturing data Process of recording data on some medium, such as floppy disk, magnetic tape, or the like.

Card reader An input device used for sensing the patterns of holes in punched cards.

Carrier (1) The name of the housing that holds an integrated circuit chip; (2) in data communications, a company that supplies a service.

Cathode ray tube (CRT) Television-like screen that displays input and output.

Central memory Refer to *primary storage*.

Central processing unit (CPU) Synonymous with mainframe and central processor; contains primary storage, arithmetic-logic unit, and a control section.

Central processor Refer to *Central processing unit*.

Centralized computer system A computer system that uses a large-scale computer to service many workstations at various locations.

Chain printer An output device whose characters to be printed are positioned on a chain that revolves.

Channel The communication link that is used for interconnecting peripheral devices with the central processing unit.

Character Information that can be the letter A through Z (alphabetic character), 0 through 9 (numeric character), or a special character (symbols used in punctuation).

Character-addressable computer A computer that looks up or stores one byte at a time; synonymous with byte-addressable.

Character printer Prints one character at a time; also known as a serial printer.

Check bit Refer to *Parity bit*.

Circuit An electrical path used in a telephone line for data transmission.

Classifying data Process used in logical operations so that data can be sorted, grouped, extracted, and searched.

Clustered terminals Those terminals that share the same telephone line for transmitting data to the host computer.

Coaxial cable A communication facility using strands of copper for transmission, much like cable TV.

COBOL (Common Business-Oriented Language) A high-level programming language that uses English sentences and phrases for business data processing applications.

Code (1) A symbol for a set of rules on how data is to be entered in a shortened version, such as M for male, F for female; (2) to write instructions into a computer language.

COM Refer to *Computer output microfilm*.

Compiler A translator program used for high-level languages; replaces source instructions (macro instructions) written by a programmer with a series of machine language instructions.

CompuServe A network used for microcomputers.

Computer The combination of peripheral devices, an arithmetic-logic unit, a control section, and primary storage that work as one entity to provide humans with enormous processing and manipulative capability.

Computer-aided design (CAD) A process used by engineers for laying out circuit boards or for designing some product by a computer-generated picture.

Computer-aided manufacturing (CAM) A process by which manufacturing is accomplished by computerized control.

Computer-assisted instruction (CAI) Deals with drill work that is done for such subjects as history, English, arithmetic.

Computer operator The person who makes certain that the flow of jobs passes through the computer for processing and also is responsible for mounting proper equipment for a given job.

Computer output microfilm (COM) Output data from the printer or magnetic tape that is microfilmed.

Computer system Combination of hardware and software that is used for a purpose; hardware includes central processing unit, input and output devices, and storage.

Concentrators Microcomputers that are used in a pair for intelligently sending many transmissions of data to the host computer over the same telephone line.

Concurrent processing Processing that allows two or more users to be served by the computer at basically the same time; user is unaware of another user; a form of multitasking.

Condition Used on flowcharts and decision tables for asking questions about data; there are always at least two alternatives as to the direction the logic flows.

Console That portion of the computer which contains lights, switches, and buttons that can be manipulated by an operator or engineer to correct errors, to examine contents of storage, to manually revise contents of storage, and to insert data or instructions into storage.

Constraint A restriction enforced by management upon the systems analyst, the users, and employees of a given system.

Construct A technique used in structured programming which can be that of sequence, selection, or repetition.

Contention A data communications process for controlling the traffic over a telephone line; each terminal competes for time.

Contents Whatever is stored in memory: data, storage addresses, or a program.

Continuous form A sheet of paper that is used on printers.

Control key A device used on terminals and small computer systems to communicate with the operating system.

Control Program for Microcomputers (CP/M) An operating system name used for a large number of microcomputers.

Control section That section of the central processing unit that enables a computer to carry out instructions for processing.

Control unit Intermediary hardware between peripheral devices and a channel.

Controller Provides the interface between the central processing unit and a device such as magnetic disk, magnetic tape, floppy disk (diskette), or terminals.

Conversion The change-over from an old system to a new one. Refer to *Parallel conversion* and *Direct conversion*.

Core storage A small doughnut-shaped, magnetic-coated storage device that is used to remember a 1 or a 0; coating of the core allows the molecules on the outside to be polarized either clockwise or counterclockwise, as a 1 or a 0, respectively.

CP/M Refer to *Control Program for Microcomputers*.

CPU Refer to *Central processing unit*.

CRT Refer to *Cathode ray tube*.

CRTL A control key used on terminals and microcomputers for giving instructions as to what is to be done by the computer.

Cursor A small dot or bar on a cathode ray tube that blinks to tell the user the next position that is to be keyed.

Cylinder Relates to the method of storage arrangement used on many secondary storage devices for reading and storing data; many read-write heads that while remaining in one position can read many storage locations.

Daisy-wheel printer A printer that prepares letter quality printing by using a wheel which has the characters printed on the end of the spokes.

DASD Refer to *Direct-access storage device*.

Data Facts about some subject matter such as a banking account, a student's records, an athletic performance.

Data base A community-type of logically related files of data that are stored on disk storage for use in retrieval of data and for associating data for decision making.

Data base administrator (DBA) The person responsible for creating and maintaining the data base.

Data base management system (DBMS) The software package that creates, updates, and maintains a data base so data can be accessed and used.

Data communications The transmitting of data or programs between processing sites using a communications facility such as telephone, telegraph, microwave, coaxial cable, fiber optics, or satellite.

Data elements The different fields of data that are chained or grouped together when using a data base.

Data entry operator The worker in the operations group who enters data into the computer.

Data independence The data is separate from hardware.

Data integrity The accuracy of the data.

Dataphone Digital Service (DDS) The direct digital service that is available from AT&T; no voice transmission is used.

Data processing The procedures for preparation of source data; handling of data; classifying, sorting, calculating, and outputting of data in meaningful reports.

Data relatability The way that data is associated and related in a data base.

Data structure The logical linking of data relationships. Refer to *Network data structure*, *Hierarchical data structure* and *Relational data structure*.

DBA Refer to *Data base administrator*.

DBMS Refer to *Data base management system*.

DDD Refer to *Direct distance dialing*.

DDP Refer to *Distributed data processing*.

DDS Refer to *Dataphone Digital Service*.

Debug To check the logic of a program to correct errors in writing instructions or in problem-solving logic and assure correct program execution.

Decentralized computer system An organizational plan for a system in which computers are placed at various geographic locations and each site works independent of the others.

Decision Question is asked of the computer about data or a certain condition that is present.

Decision support system (DSS) A system which concentrates on quick solutions of modeling and analysis service for problems using computers; this group works with end-users, and the solutions are considered user-friendly.

Decision table A table including conditions, actions, and rules in a logical organization; used in place of the flowchart for problem solving.

Dedicated general-purpose computer A computer whose instructions are built directly into the hardware.

Dedicated line A private telephone line used for data transmission, providing a twenty-four-hour connection; often called leased lines.

Demodulation An activity associated with a modem in the transmission of data; the changing of digital signals to analog signals.

Density The number of bits that can be coded in a given area on secondary storage devices.

Detail printing A type of output which represents one printed line for each record that is read; totals can also be included in the output.

Device Mechanical, electronic, or electrical equipment that is used for a purpose such as data input or data recording.

Diagnostic A message that is outputted from the compiler, interpreter, or assembler indicating possible errors in the source instruction.

Dial-up line A regular telephone line used for data transmission; often called switched lines.

Digital computer A computer that can do a variety of processes in any order (calculate, make decisions, store data, follow a stored program); contrast *Analog computer*.

Digital line A line used solely for transmitting data in the Dataphone Digital Service by AT&T; some digital lines in local-area networks transmit voice and data, since a telephone is used.

Direct access A processing capability to read or write a record in any order without reading or rewriting the entire file.

Direct-access processing A method of handling the processing of data in random order; the data is stored on direct-access storage devices.

Direct-access storage device (DASD) A device, usually associated with magnetic disk; that can handle the processing of data in a batch or can operate in on-line processing or in real time.

Direct conversion A method of implementing a system in which the old system is stopped and the new one begins immediately.

Direct distance dialing (DDD) Use of regular telephone lines that can be used to connect to any number by dialing the desired number.

Direct file organization One of three file organization types used for secondary storage devices; the file organization for storing data is based upon randomizing or hashing.

Directory Used in secondary storage for showing a file's name and beginning address.

Disk drive Hardware used with magnetic disk or diskettes (floppy disk) for holding medium so read-write head can read or store the contents.

Disk operating system Name of an operating system that is stored (resides) on magnetic disk or a diskette (floppy disk).

Disk pack Many disks platters are mounted together to form a unit.

Distributed data processing (DDP) Data processing carried out via computers placed at the location where the data is collected and worked with by the users.

DO A sequence of instructions that are to be done, one instruction after the other; represents a module in pseudocode.

Documentation The written report that spells out in detail how a system is to operate.

Dot-matrix printer An impact printer that prints characters in little dots resembling scoreboards.

Double-sided Capable of recording data or programs on both sides (said of a diskette).

DO UNTIL An instruction setting up the repetitive processing used for looping; does processing and then asks the question if the loop is to be again executed; continues looping while condition is false.

DO WHILE An instruction setting up the repetitive processing used for looping; asks the question first before the remainder of the instructions in the loop are executed; continues looping while condition is true.

Down-line loading Transferring of data or programs from a host computer to terminals.

Downloading The transferring of programs from a host computer (usually a microcomputer) to another microcomputer; process used with bulletin board services that supply public domain software.

DSS Refer to *Decision support system*.

Dumb terminal A terminal with no intelligence; its only work can be capturing data and making inquiries.

Dump The reading out of storage and outputting on a printer or another device the contents of a computer's memory; also called a memory dump, a tape dump, or a disk dump.

Duplex circuit A communication line allowing data transmission in two different directions at the same time; often called a full-duplex circuit.

EBCDIC (Extended Binary Coded Decimal Interchange Code) An 8-bit plus parity coding system used primarily on IBM computers.

Edit mode Programs or data are entered in this timeframe.

EEPROM Refer to *Electrically erasable programmable read-only memory*.

EFT Refer to *Electronic funds transfer*.

Electrically erasable programmable read-only memory (EEPROM) A type of semiconductor memory which allows a user to change a program by electrically erasing the previous program and storing the new program through the use of a peripheral device.

Electronic cottage The concept of employees working at home rather than at the office, using computers and telecommunication facilities for the transmittal of work between the home and office.

Electronic data processing Processing data by use of analog, digital, and hybrid computers.

Electronic funds transfer (EFT) A method of transferring funds electronically around the world, making payments without use of cash possible.

Electronic messaging The electronic transmission of messages that are stored and forwarded from one site to another; an alternative to use of the U. S. Post Office's services.

Electronic spreadsheet A program that allows the user to store, then set data up in rows and columns, hence providing the capability to do budget and financial analysis by calculating columns and rows of data.

Electrostatic printer/plotter Used for the printout of the design generated by CAD.

End-user Anyone who uses the computer as an adjunct to his or her job; includes such people as clerks, sports announcers, and television and radio broadcasters.

EPROM Refer to *Erasable programmable read-only memory*.

Erasable programmable read-only memory (EPROM) A non-volatile memory used for storing a program in an integrated circuit chip; the chip has a little window that allows an ultraviolet light to erase the already stored program.

Even parity A checking system used by the computer to make certain a 1-bit was not lost in data transmission.

Exception report A report that prints out only data that is the exception, or unusual.

Extracting data The choosing of certain data from a file by comparing data.

Facsimile (fax) A means of electronic transferral of data and images; uses paper at both sending and receiving site.

Family of computers Several computers belonging to the same processor group, for example, the VAX 111/780, IBM 370, and IBM 3081; different processing capabilities are offered in various models of a family, but they possess some degree of compatibility.

Feasibility study The detailed analysis undertaken to provide the objectives, constraints, capabilities, audit trails, and the like for a system.

Feedback The process of modifying, correcting, and improving a result by exchanging ideas.

Fiber optics Strands of glass thinner than a hair that are used in place of coaxial cable for data transmission.

Field A group of characters that collectively mean something—a customer number, a telephone number, your height.

FIFO Refer to *First-in first-out*.

File An organized collection of data for some application; can also represent a program that is used for processing some application.

First-generation computers Those computers using vacuum tubes.

First-in First-out (FIFO) Method used by a sequential scheduler for determining which program is given time on the computer.

Fixed block architecture (FBA) Latest developed method for accessing data in secondary storage; each track is divided into sectors; addressability is based upon using a sector and a record number.

Fixed word length Number of characters recorded on secondary storage that is consistent for each logical record in a file.

Flat file File that has no repeating fields of data.

Flowchart Use of symbols and phrases to designate the logic of how a problem is solved.

Format Design of input and output; a data layout.

Formatter Sets up the track and sector arrangement so that data or programs can be stored on a diskette.

FORTH A high-level, structured, portable language designed for writing applications and systems software.

FORTRAN (FORmula TRANslator) A high-level language that is used for scientific data processing; the language uses formulas to solve problems.

Fourth-generation computers Those computers using microelectronics technology.

Front-end processor (FEP) The processing unit that handles all communication existing between the host central processing unit and the terminals.

Full duplex circuit Refer to *Duplex circuit*.

Function Series of instructions that are included in the library so the user can invoke these statements by using a reserved word; examples of SQR, meaning square root, and ABS, meaning the absolute value.

G Refer to *Giga*.

Gap An interval of space or time that is used to signal an end of a record, a block, or a file; also refer to *Interrecord gap (IRG)* and *Interblock gap (IBG)*.

Garbage Meaningless data.

General-purpose computer Most commonly used digital computer; usable by most commercial installations.

Geosynchronous satellite Satellite positioned 22,300 miles up in the atmosphere; needs no tracking; used for relaying electronic messages.

Giga (G) Refers to the number of characters that are stored in a computer's storage; 10 raised to the ninth power.

Gigabytes A billion bytes (characters) of data.

Graphics computer A computer which tests the accuracy of the design of an integrated circuit chip; provides a user with three-dimensional images projected on the monitor.

Grouping data A way of classifying data by placing it into categories or groups.

Group printing Represents one line of printing for a group of data that may be classified by major (most important), intermediate (second most important), and minor (the detail).

Half duplex circuit A communication carrier that is used to transmit data one way at a time; used in teleprocessing.

Handshaking The connection and disconnection of a line for transmitting data over dial-up lines.

Hard copy Printed copy from a printer that is generated on paper.

Hard-sectored An electronic division of the diskette into theoretical pieces of pie which is used for accessing data in a limited area of the diskette.

Hardware The physical equipment or devices that make up the computer complex—peripheral devices, central processing unit, storage devices.

Hardwired Pertains to instructions that cannot be changed or deleted.

Hashing An algorithm method used to locate a logical record stored in a direct file organization.

Header label Used for identifying a file specifically; includes the name of the file assigned by the programmer, the date of creation, and the number of days the file is to be retained without change.

Hex Refer to *Hexadecimal*.

Hexadecimal Shorthand used in many computers for showing the contents of storage; its base is 16 with values used as 0 through F in any one position.

Hierarchical data structure A type of structure for a data base, in which the logical file is always entered at the root (the most basic data).

Hierarchy chart A problem-solving methodology used for determining the overview of how a problem is to be solved by setting up levels of importance which are shown by rectangles; resembles an organization chart of a company.

Hierarchy plus Input-Process-Output (HIPO) Set of diagrams used to document the details of input, processing, and output for some problem solution.

High-end processor The processor in a family of computers which has the greatest capability and speed.

High-level language The type of language that uses English for the source program; examples are Pascal, FORTRAN, BASIC, COBOL.

High-order position Leftmost position in a field.

HIPO Refer to *Hierarchy plus Input-Process-Output*.

Hit The matching (finding equal) of a desired record in secondary storage.

Hollerith code Coding system used for punched cards; named for Herman Hollerith.

Host computer The main central processing unit in a network of distributed terminals or smaller computers.

Hybrid computer A combination of both digital and analog computers that work together; used in manufacturing and for doing simulation.

IBG Refer to *Interblock gap*.

IF-THEN Selection technique used for decision making that provides what to do only when the condition is true.

IF-THEN-ELSE Selection technique used for asking questions of the computer that provides two alternatives as to what processing is to be done when the condition is true (THEN) or false (ELSE).

Image processing Scientific data processing in which pictures and images are generated by a series of numbers; data can be manipulated into a picture and analyzed statistically; an example is Landsat.

Impact printer A printer which strikes a ribbon against paper, similar in operation to a typewriter.

Index Pointer used by the operating system for an indexed sequential file organization to locate a desired record.

Indexed sequential file Used on direct-access storage devices; uses the sequential and random-access concepts, by which sequentially created records can be accessed in any order without the entire file being read; accomplished by use of indexes.

Indexed sequential file organization Uses indexes that point to a particular cylinder and a particular recording surface; allows a record to be accessed directly without having to read the entire file up to that record.

Information Data that has been processed on the computer; meaningful facts.

Information center Group of data processing professionals who train, teach, and help users; they do not do the work for users.

Information processing Formerly synonymous with data processing but now gradually changing to mean record-keeping, predicting future trends, and making intelligent decisions.

Information resource management (IRM) A management viewpoint which considers a company's data and information as important as financial resources; an information executive manages the data.

Information system All the finished data that aids management in making decisions on a day-to-day basis as well as for forecasting.

Initialization Setting of areas to zeros, blanks, or any other value.

Input Data that is transferred from peripheral devices to the internal storage of the computer.

Input device Equipment used for transmitting data to the central processing unit.

Input job stream Used on large computer systems; includes job control language, program, and data that is to be executed for batch processing.

Input/output control system (IOCS) Set of programs used in an operating system for handling all input and output work such as opening files, closing files, backspacing tape, and moving tape forward when a bad spot is encountered.

Inquiry The asking for information that is stored in computer storage.

Instruction An order to a computer to tell it what to do, for example, to read a record and write a line on the printer.

Instruction register That register used by the control section for determining the next executable machine language instruction.

Integer A field that is composed of only whole numbers.

Integrated circuit chip Invented by Ted Hoff in 1971; the complex circuitry of a computer is etched on a silicon wafer; it represents the entire circuit board of transistors needed to store data, calculate data, or do some other particular function.

Intelligent terminal Has an internal processor which means that the terminal can be programmed by the user; can be a microcomputer.

Interactive mode Conversation type of environment that is used on terminals; computer asks questions of the user to which user responds.

Interface Type of connection used between control units of peripheral devices and a channel; how the user and the computer use something to form a common boundary.

Internal code The coding system used for storing data in work-areas for input and output data; possibilities are ASCII, EBCDIC, and BCDIC.

Internal memory Refer to *Primary storage*.

Internal storage Refer to *Primary storage*.

Interpreter A translator program giving immediate response for each line of code written by a user as to the correctness of the syntax.

Interrecord gap (IRG) Space or time that is allocated in secondary storage devices for spacing between blocks of data.

IOCS Refer to *Input/output control system*.

I/O device Any device that is used for input as well as output, for example, a visual display terminal.

IPL (Initial Program Loader) Initializes the system at the beginning of the day and may also bring in the scheduler program which is part of the operating system.

IRG Refer to *Interrecord gap*.

Item A record.

Item number A field that identifies a record, distinguishing it from another record, for example, a customer number, a telephone number.

Iterative processing The repeating of instructions for many different records that are to be processed in the same manner.

JCL (Job control language) Used to tell the computer the various steps it is to do—compile, link edit, execute, and so on.

Job management Function performed by the supervisor program for determining and assigning priority.

Joystick An input device used on a microcomputer for game playing; user pushes a lever.

JOVIAL A programming language similar to ALGOL.

Justification Positioning of data to create straight margins according to the left or right boundaries of the field; also refer to *Left justification* and *Right justification*.

K (kilobyte) A measurement of the capacity of a computer's storage; 1K refers to 1,024 bytes.

Key Used in secondary storage processing to identify the desired record.

Key-entry device Used to enter data directly onto a medium that can later be used by a computer; examples are key-to-tape, key-to-disk, and key-to-cartridge.

Key-to-cartridge Uses a small magnetic cartridge of tape to hold its data; also refer to *Key-entry device*.

Key-to-disk Uses a floppy disk or a magnetic disk for its data recording; also refer to *Key-entry device*.

Key-to-tape Uses a magnetic tape for the recording of its data; also refer to *Key-entry device*.

Kilobyte Refer to *K*.

Label A part of the assembly language used to identify a certain instruction; also refers to a location for storing file information, such as a header label or trailer label.

Large-scale computer Type of computer used in industry for many years; has great computing power, speed, and flexibility.

Leased line Refer to *Dedicated line*.

Left justification The alignment of alphabetic and/or alphanumeric data within the field at the left margin; all unused positions in the field are blank.

Librarian Person in the operations group who is responsible for maintaining the accuracy of all the magnetic tapes and magnetic disks used at the computer installation.

Library The collection of files that are maintained by the operating system for recall; application programs, data, and operating system programs are contained in the library.

Life cycle The many changes that exist from the beginning to the end of a series.

Line number Identifies an instruction and differentiates it from all others in the source program; used with BASIC.

Line printer A printer that prints one line at a time.

Linkage editor Program in the operating system that is used for bringing in subroutines and assigning addresses to already translated programs.

Linked list Used in data base processing for maintaining the relationships of records by giving a path to locate desired record.

List To print data; also refers to one field of data that is grouped together.

Load module Executable program that is in machine language; has all necessary subroutines included.

Local–area network That collection of computers that operate as a network at one site or within a building.

Local loop That area from the user's telephone to the central office (telephone company's office) of that user; also known as subscriber loop.

Local site That location where the user runs his or her programs needed for processing.

Local terminal Those terminals that are positioned anywhere from 50 feet up to about 10,000 feet from the computer.

Logical The way we perceive how a record is laid out or how equipment is designed.

Logical operation Deals with comparisons of data.

Logical record Record composed of information about one subject matter; concept is used on secondary storage devices.

Loop or **Looping** A means of accomplishing repetitive processing work on input data, on calculations work, or on printing.

Low-end processor A computer in a family of computers that has slower processing capability than other computers in the family.

Lower-level management That group of supervisors whose work deals with solving everyday problems.

Low-order position Rightmost position of a field; contrast *High-order position*.

Machine language A series of 0s and 1s used to direct the computer what it is to do; gives instructions to the microprogram from which electrical signals are generated.

Macroinstruction Most elemental set of instructions in a computer; not written by a programmer but included in the micro-program which is called firmware.

Magnetic disk A platter used for storing data or programs by 0s and 1s; platters form a disk pack.

Magnetic ink character recognition (MICR) Device which reads the magnetic ink characters recorded on a check to a central processing unit for processing.

Magnetic tape Data is stored on a plastic tape that is coated with a ferromagnetic substance.

Mainframe Large computer system that has greater flexibility and processing speed than most minicomputers and microcomputers.

Main storage Refer to *Primary storage*.

Management Information System (MIS) Provides valuable information to a company about its previous, current, and future environments.

Mass storage Secondary storage device that combines the use of magnetic tape and magnetic disk; operates similar to a juke box.

Match A comparison of data which shows the same item on one source of data as on another source.

Megabyte One million characters or bytes.

Memory Refer to *Primary storage*.

Memory dump A printout that shows the contents of primary storage at some point in time; like a snapshot.

Menu Listing that appears on the screen of a terminal which gives the names of the different programs and functions that can be used.

Merge To combine data from one file with another file.

Message switching Capability of receiving and forwarding messages to their correct destination; this function is accomplished by a communications processor or front-end processor.

MICR Refer to *Magnetic ink character recognition*.

Micro Refer to *Microcomputer*.

Microcomputer (micro) A personal computer that is used widely both in the home and in the business world.

Microelectronics Technological advancement associated with fourth-generation computers which uses a micro-scale circuitry, resulting in higher densities and better performance.

Microfiche Small pieces of film used with computer output microfilm.

Microprocessor Composed of arithmetic-logic unit and control section.

Microprogram Program of many instructions wired in read-only memory that set electrical paths within the computer.

Microsecond A millionth of a second.

Middle-level management Represents that group of district managers or regional managers whose work deals with forecasting in a one-year timeframe.

Millisecond A thousandth of a second.

Mini Refer to *Minicomputer*.

Minicomputer (mini) That classification of digital computers that has more processing speed and flexibility than microcomputers but generally less than mainframes.

Mips Stands for millions of instructions executed per second by a computer; super-computers execute over 50 mips.

MIS Refer to *Management information system*.

Mnemonics Use of symbols in assembly language to represent operation codes such as L (load), MVC (move characters) and CVB (convert to binary).

Modem Short for modulator-demodulator; a device that modules and demodulates signals as they pass over the communication facilities.

Modulation Converts digital signals to analog signals, suitable for transmission on communication facilities.

Module In structured programming, a segment of a program that solves some particular type of processing; examples of a module might be the inputting of a record, the editing of the data, and the calculating of the data.

Monitor Television-like screen used on microcomputers and terminals.

Mouse Small device that is slid to position cursor.

Multidropped line A telephone line that is shared among many terminals.

Multiplexor Hardware used for combining many telephone line transmissions into one telephone line transmission.

Multiprocessing Two or more central processing units used as a computer system; can be doing the same functions or different functions.

Multiprogramming A programming technique in which more than one program is sharing the time of the central processing unit; by shifting from one program to another, the illusion of simultaneous processing is created.

Multitasking Computer's capability to do several tasks at one time, for example, reading tape, writing to disk, and calculating.

Nanosecond A billionth of a second.

Narrowband type of bandwidth used by Western Union; maximum transmission is 45 to 300 bps.

Nested IFs Represent the selection technique used for asking questions; two or more IF statements that are used jointly to test for a series of values or conditions.

Network Series of interconnected central processing units and peripheral devices to allow processing of programs.

Network data structure A structure for a data base that allows a user to enter the data base at different points.

Node Point where hardware is connected in a network.

Nonimpact printer Printer uses heat, chemicals, electrical, or optical techniques for printing.

Non-iterative processing The processing of just one record; no looping is involved.

Non-volatile memory Type of storage device that retains the stored information if power is shut off; examples are magnetic disk, magnetic tape, floppy disk, mass storage.

Numeric character Represents the data 0 through 9; no blanks are allowed in this type of data.

Numeric field Characters that are only 0 through 9.

Object module Refer to *Object program*.

Object program The machine language of computers that results from the translation of a source program.

Odd parity Checking technique used by computers in primary storage for which an odd number (1, 3, 5, etc.) of 1-bits is used in the bit configuration for the character coding to be valid.

OEM Refer to *Original equipment manufacturer*.

Office of the future A 1990s office approach which represents full automation.

Off-line Describes a computer system or a peripheral device that is not under control of a central processing unit.

On-line Describes a peripheral device under the control of a central processing unit; can send or receive data.

On-line processing Type of processing involving the direct connection to a computer for asking questions, doing calculations, and receiving responses.

Op-code (operation code) Used in assembly language to tell the computer what operation to perform.

Operand Used in assembly language along with an op-code; completes the instruction to the computer, telling it what to add, what to input, where to get the data to print.

Operating system A group of programs that manage the source programs for the successful use of a computer; for example, utility programs, compilers, assemblers, linkage editor, IPL, loader, supervisor, sort-merge.

Operation code Refer to *Op-code*.

Operations group Includes the supervisors and the personnel who operate the computers, key in data, and maintain the libraries of secondary storage media.

Optical character recognition (OCR) Uses optical scanning equipment to read (sense) handwriting, and printed characters appearing in different typefaces.

Optical disk A disk storage that is similar to the laser-optical video disks used in the home; information is stored in a digital form.

Optical mark recognition (OMR) Reads score sheets for which the user has filled in the area within dotted lines; referred to as mark sensing.

Optical wand Reads the labels on clothing or other merchandise tags.

Original equipment manufacturer (OEM) Refers to the second manufacturer of a product where value is added on a product purchased from the original manufacturer.

Output Information that is transferred from primary storage of a computer to peripheral devices; the results.

Output device Hardware that receives processed information from the computer for example, a printer.

Packet Data that is to be transmitted using a value-added network (VAN).

Packet switching network Those series of computers and hardware supplied by a value-added network (VAN) for transmittal of data over dedicated carrier lines.

Page printer Printer which prints one page at a time and usually uses laser technology.

Paper tape Resembles ticker tape; holes are made, making the tape usable only once for recording data; reusable many times for reading, however.

Parallel conversion That change-over to a new system that is done in stages, usually by applications; the old system runs with the new system for a time.

Parallel printer Printer prints one line at a time.

Parity bit Synonymous with check bit; a checking device used for primary storage and secondary storage data to make certain that a 1-bit was not lost in transmission.

Pascal Programming language that is truly structured and is used for teaching structured programming techniques.

Password A secret word or series of numbers that identifies a user as a legitimate to a computer system.

Pen plotter A small plotter that works on a 8½ × 11-inch paper.

Peripheral device Any input, output, or secondary storage device that is used with the central processing unit; refers to all hardware other than the central processing unit, console, and primary storage.

Personal computer Synonymous with microcomputer; that classification of digital computers that is used in the home, in the school, in businesses, in fact almost anywhere.

Physical block Logical records are grouped in a block; is used on secondary storage devices.

Physical record How the record is actually formatted.

Picosecond A trillionth of a second.

Pixel Short for picture element, which refers to the various dot positions on a cathode ray tube used to create images.

Place value The position of a digit in data or a coding structure; uses the base of the number.

PL/I A high-level, structured programming language that is considered general-purpose; combines advantages of FORTRAN, COBOL, and ALGOL.

Plotter An output device used for creating drawings and graphs.

Plug compatible A device that is manufactured so that it can operate with several manufacturers' products.

Point of sale (POS) On-line terminals which usually appear in grocery stores or retail outlets for assigning a price to an item.

Point to point A line configuration in which a terminal uses a port to the computer.

Polling A method of managing the traffic on a telephone line; a round-robin technique in which the host computer polls the terminals.

Port The entry place of the computer.

POS Refer to *Point of sale*.

ppm (pages per minute) Usually associated with page printers.

Preliminary analysis The first step in solving a problem; involves the conducting of interviews, the evaluating of the cost justification for changing an existing system, and the studying of the constraints of management and users.

Primary storage Synonymous with main storage, memory, central storage, internal storage; the area where instructions and data are stored and worked on by the central processing unit.

Priming read The reading of the first record outside of a loop; after the priming read, the loop is entered and is executed for as long as there is data.

Printer Busiest of all the peripherals; prepares printed reports.

Printout Output generated by a printer.

Priority scheduler A program that is part of the supervisor program and establishes execution of programs by a priority method.

Private line Refer to *Leased line*.

Processing How data is worked with to become information.

Processor Refer to *Central processing unit*.

Program Set of instructions that solves a problem or handles some routine or procedure; classified as systems software or applications software.

Programmable read-only memory (PROM) Type of memory which is a read-only memory that is programmable; used for storing programs or prompts often used by the computer.

Program maintenance The upgrading and updating of existing programs as changes are needed by a company or individual user.

Programmer Person who instructs the computer in what to do by the use of a computer language.

Programmer trainee Person who works directly with a programmer to learn the skill of programming.

Programming group Composed of those people who are actively involved in writing computer programs.

Program status word (PSW) A series of bits that are used by the operating system in determining the next executable instruction's address; also used for determining if data is negative and if the results of comparisons are equal to, less than, or greater than.

PROM Refer to *Programmable read-only memory*.

Prompt Appears on the screen of the user's terminal, giving hints as to what is wrong, how the user can ask for help, and how the problem might be solved.

Proof inscriber Used for encoding (coding) the dollar amount on the check; also takes batch totals.

Protocol The rules designating the way bits are to be transmitted in a teleprocessing system.

Pseudocode Type of English statements that are written to represent the logic patterns when developing an algorithm.

Query language English-type language used to access data from a data base; designed for end-users rather than most programmers.

Random access Refer to *Direct access*.

Random-access memory (RAM) Volatile semiconductor memory which is used as primary storage.

Randomizing Procedure for calculating a storage address for a secondary storage device.

RAM Refer to *Random access memory*.

Read The looking up of data that is already stored in secondary storage.

Read-only memory (ROM) Non-volatile memory that has instructions permanently written into the circuitry; a chip that is programmed once by the manufacturer; stores systems software or applications software that are read from only.

Read-write head Hardware used to code data into a machine-readable form or to play the contents back used on secondary storage devices.

Reader-sorter Used in banking installations for transmitting the account number and dollar amount of a check to a central processing unit and for sorting the checks physically.

Real-time data processing Gives immediate answers to questions; is used in time-sharing environment and multiprogramming.

Redundant data The repeating of the same data over and over again; is reduced to a minimum in a data base.

Record The related data for one person, thing, or happening.

Register An internal temporary storage used by the control section for holding instructions, data, and storage addresses.

Relational data structure Newest type of data base technology; data is set up in tables for easy access and understanding of user.

Remote job entry (RJE) Formerly thought of as a printer and a card reader that is located away from the central processing unit; all types of transactions are batched. Now thought of as those terminals that are removed from the host computer site that are used for transmitting data to the headquarters of the company.

Remote site Site of terminals that are located away from the host computer site.

Remote terminals Those terminals that are positioned 10,000 or more feet from the computer (an arbitrary number of feet depending upon manufacturer's specifications).

Repetition A construct of structured programming that performs looping.

Report generators Software that prepares output according to a user's specifications.

Report program generator (RPG) Language written by the programmer that tells the computer what processing is needed; the program is then prepared by the computer to accomplish this processing.

Reserved word A certain operation and word used in a computer program which the computer understands without further clarification by the user.

Response time The time required from a user's request for data until the desired data is received.

Resource sharing Sharing of the source programs, communication facilities, printers, and other peripherals among the users at a company; operates in a distributed data processing environment.

RJE Refer to *Remote job entry*.

Right justification Aligning numeric fields at the rightmost position so that the data is correctly positioned in the field; unused positions are filled with leading zeros.

Ring network A configuration of computers that has no host computer.

ROM Refer to *Read-only memory*.

Rotational delay Lapse of time when the record that is being looked up on magnetic disk must rotate in order to come under the read-write heads; also referred to as latency.

RPG Refer to *Report program generator*.

Rule Column on the decision table that represents a path of logic.

Run mode A type of operation when a program is being executed as opposed to the operation that the program is being keyed.

Satellite Used for broadcasting and data transmission; positioned in the air for handling large volume of data transmission; acts as a relay station.

Schema The physical records used for creating a data base.

Scientific data processing Deals with the sciences such as chemistry, astrology, physics, research, and space exploration.

Scratch pad memory A fast storage area where the control section finds out what it is to do; is composed of registers.

Scrolling A user moves lines up and down on the monitor to see the contents of a program or text.

Searching data Looking for a desired record or a characteristic of data.

Secondary storage Those type of devices, such as magnetic disk, floppy disk (diskette), mass storage, and magnetic tape, that are used for storing programs and data for later recall and updating.

Sector An electronic division of a magnetic disk which has been cut into theoretical pieces of pie; addressing is done electronically.

Seek Positioning of the access arms for locating a record on magnetic disk.

Selection Process which tests for a certain condition or asks a question about data in order to decide which of two paths to select.

Sequence The instructions or series of instructions that are executed one after the other.

Sequential file A type of file whose data in secondary storage are arranged in ascending or descending order usually by key; type of storage is usually associated with magnetic tape, although magnetic disk can be processed sequentially as well.

Serial printer Printer prints one character at a time.

Signed numbers Those numbers that have either a positive or a negative sign.

Simplex circuit One-way communication line; can either send data or receive data; never both.

Simultaneous peripheral operation off-line (SPOOL) Object program or output data are often stored on disk for later callout and then printed when the printer is available; synonymous with SPOOLing.

Smart terminal Terminal with an internal processor that has been programmed by the manufacturer.

Soft copy The output shown on a cathode ray tube; contrast *Hard copy*.

Software A program that solves systems or applications work.

Software engineering Method of design for computer programs using scientific principles.

Solid-character printer Prints characters much as a typewriter does.

Sorting Placing of data in some order or sequence—alphabetical order, ascending numerical order, or descending numerical order—to make processing more rapid or logical.

Sort-merge program A utility program that places fields of data in an order and then combines the files into a single updated file.

Source document Document on which data were originally recorded on an application form, an invoice, or a purchase order, for example.

Source program Program written by the programmer to solve a problem by using a high-level or assembly language.

Special characters Group of characters that are symbols, such as − + = # $ % ' * & ( ) [ ] ; and :, oriented to computer usage.

Special-purpose computer One of a group of specially designed computers for installations that cannot efficiently use general-purpose computers; monitoring of a patient's vital signs is done by a special-purpose computer.

Speech synthesizer 1. An input device used to recognize and to change speech to a machine-readable form; 2. An output device that changes machine-read data to a human voice message.

SPOOL program Refer to Simultaneous peripheral operation *off-line*.

Standalone A self-contained device or computer system.

Statement Tells the computer what operation is to be done.

Storage Synonymous with memory; refers to primary or secondary storage.

Storage address That location in primary storage that has a number that can then be accessed directly by the computer.

Stored program Machine language of a source program placed in primary storage for execution.

String A group of alphabetic or alphanumeric characters that are used together; an example is the words "End of job".

Structure chart One of the first tools used by the programmer in developing an algorithm; control module is considered level 0, the next level, containing more detail, is level 1.

Structured programming Set of techniques designed to improve the organization of the program, to facilitate the solving of a problem, and to make the code easier to read and write.

Structured walk-throughs A programming methodology that uses peer review to evaluate whether an algorithm will work correctly.

Subprogram Refer to *Subroutine*.

Subroutine Synonymous with subprogram; a program or a small part of a program that is usable by others for calculation or inputting or outputting data.

Subschema Logical records in a data base.

Subscriber loop Refer to Local loop.

Subscript Represents a letter that acts as a pointer to identify which data is to be referenced in an array or list.

Subsystem Represents a smaller part of a larger system.

Summarized data Represents data that has been condensed into some kind of meaningful form.

Super-computers Most powerful of all computer types.

Switched line Refer to *Dial-up line*.

Synchronous terminal Terminal that sends many characters at one time; contrast *Asynchronous terminal*.

Synchronous transmission Where two pieces of hardware transmit to each other, with their transmissions being controlled by a clocking mechanism; contrast *Asynchronous transmission*.

Syntax How an instruction is to be punctuated or formed in coding; rules, comparable to grammar rules for language.

System Group of related procedures that are used to produce a common goal.

Systems analysis A step by step investigation as to how a problem can be solved in the best way.

Systems analyst Person who sets up procedures that are laid down for establishing a system or for developing it; has the responsibilities of interviewing and of evaluating responses before further analysis is undertaken.

Systems command The type of instruction used for communicating with the operating system as to what the computer is to do.

Systems design Problems uncovered in the systems analysis are then evaluated and alternative plans presented for their solution.

Systems flowchart A graphic representation of an overview of how a system is to be organized; focuses on input and output rather than on processing details.

Systems group Includes those specialized personnel whose responsibilities deal with setting up and modifying systems by providing the interface between the user and the computer.

Systems implementation The last phase in revising or creating a new system.

Systems programming Programs devoted to the development and maintenance of the operating system.

Systems software Those programs that comprise the operating system; used for managing application programs.

Tape drive Hardware used for mounting a magnetic tape; contains a tape read–write head for reading and writing data onto the tape.

Task A unit of work to be executed.

Technical support and repair group Those people who repair computers or alter the processing of them so they perform according to the user's specifications.

Telecommunications Refer to *Teleprocessing*.

Teleconferencing Involves the transmitting of voice and images between people at two or more locations, allowing the immediacy required for a conference.

Teleprinter An input/output device which acts as a terminal but can also prepare hard copy.

Teleprocessing Synonymous with telecommunications; uses telephone, telegraph lines, microwave, or satellite for transmitting data, voice, or images to a computer center and/or a remote terminal.

Template Plastic guide that is used when drawing symbols on a flowchart.

Terminal Represents an input and/or output device that can be used for transmitting data; can be a remote terminal—one that uses teleprocessing.

Throughput The amount of work that is accomplished by a computer in a given day.

Time sharing An arrangement whereby two or more users can be using the same central processing unit without being aware that the computer is shared.

Top-down design The solving of a problem by beginning with the main ideas first and then working out the details; breaks processing done in a program into modules, each of which handles a certain type of work; contrast *Bottom-up design*.

Top-level management Group of managers including president and possibly vice-presidents, who deal with long-range forecasting and planning.

Track Area on magnetic tape used for storing bits which runs the length of the tape; on magnetic disk or diskette, the concentric circle used for holding data or programs.

Trackball An input device used by rotating a ball; used for game playing on microcomputers.

Trailer label Information that is written at the end of a file; retains such information as how many logical records make up the file or what the batch total is.

Trailer value A dummy data set up to signal end of data and cause a computer to stop repeating a loop.

Transfer rate Rate that data is read from magnetic tape; density of the tape and the speed at which it moves determine the transfer rate.

Turnkey system Implies that once the computer is set up, it is able to be plugged in, being ready to operate.

Unbundled Software and hardware sold separately rather than using one unit price; contrast *Bundled*.

UNIX An operating system developed by Bell Laboratories.

Unpacked Synonymous with zoned decimal or EBCDIC; a coding system that is used for character-addressable computers.

Up-line dumping Transferring of data or program from a node to a computer.

Uploading The transferring of a program from a microcomputer to a host computer; used with bulletin board services where a user supplies public domain software.

Unsigned number Numeric data that contains no positive or negative sign.

User-friendly Hardware and software that is easy to learn to use.

Users Those people who require the use of some computer service.

Utility program A program that performs specialized functions such as sorting, copying contents from one peripheral device to another, or merging.

Value added network (VAN) A company, such as Telenet and Tymnet, which provides to the user a communication line, an interface for terminals, and a method of transmitting data.

VAN Refer to *Value added network*.

Variable A name prepared by a programmer for identifying data or storage locations.

Variable word length A record which contains a varying number of characters.

VDT Refer to *Visual display terminal*.

VDU Refer to *Visual display unit*.

Videotex system Used for a personal computing network.

Videotext system Same as videotex system.

Virtual storage Also called virtual memory; used as an extension of multiprogramming where a program is divided into smaller parts enabling a small part of many programs to be in primary storage at one time; a swapping exists between primary and secondary storage.

VisiCalc VisiCalc is the best known spreadsheet program, although there are many on the market.

Visual display terminal (VDT) The most popular of all input/output devices; consists of a keyboard, possibly a mouse, and a monitor; used for capturing data or keying programs.

Voiceband The bandwidth used on regular telephone lines; maximum is 9,600 bps.

Voice-grade line Regular telephone line that can be used for transmitting voice and data; the data is transmitted in pulse trains.

Volatile memory Type of storage that loses its data once the electrical power is removed.

WATS (Widearea Telephone Service) The 800 number exchange that is frequently used in the business world.

Widearea Telephone Service Refer to *WATS*.

Wideband Bandwidth used by coaxial cable, fiber optics, satellites, microwave, and telephone transmissions extending over long distances.

Winchester drive Hard disk drive used for secondary storage.

Window That area where a monitor is sectioned to show how each program is processing.

Word Smallest number of characters that can be read or stored at one time.

Word-addressable computer Type of computer that can look up or store many characters at a time; contrast *Character-addressable computer*.

Word processing Refers to the use of microcomputers or minicomputers for the preparation of text.

Workarea Synonymous with scratch area, temporary area; the area in primary storage where data is manipulated by the programmer for producing results and output; consecutive storage addresses that basically can be located anywhere in primary storage.

Zone bit Used in different combinations along with digit bits to code a character.

Zoned decimal Refer to *Unpacked* and EBCDIC.

INDEX

Packet switching network, 318
Page printer, 246
Pages per minute, (ppm), 246
Pages, 435
Parallel conversion, 509
Parallel printer, 244
Parity:
    bit, C-17–19
    even, C-18–19
    odd, C-18–19
Pascal, 423–425, 429
Pascal, Blaise, D-3
Password, 83
Paulsen, Valdema, D-13
PDP/1, 74
PBX, 335
Pen plotter, 256–257
Peripheral devices, 45
Personal computer, 132–187
Personal computing, 10
Physical, 52
Physical record, 272–278, 478, 485
Picosecond, 13
PILOT, 520
PIN, 243
Pixel, 237, 559
Plotter, 50, 256–258
PL/I, 422–423, 429, 531
Plug compatible, 196, 249
Point of sale (POS), 251
Point to point, 322, 327
Polling, 325
Port, 322
Portable terminal, 252, 254
Portability, 424, 578
POS, 251
Ppm, 246
Pre-defined process symbol, 364
Preliminary analysis, 505
Presentation languages, 578
Priming read, 363
Primary storage:
    addressability, 203–212
    bubble memory, 199–200
    definition, 54
    magnetic core, 198–199
    semiconductor memory, 201–202
    switches and gates, 201–202
    types of, 149–151
Printer:
    character, 244, 248
    daisywheel, 244, 248
    definition, 49
    jet-ink, 247–248
    line, 244
    page, 246
    solid-character, 246
    types, 244–248
Printing, types, 106, 108–110
Printer spacing charts, 171–173

PRINT statement, A-5–23, A-12
Printout, 50
Priority scheduler, 430–431
Privacy, 561
Private lines, 319
Problem defintion phase, 504
Problem solving steps, 170
Processing:
    batch, 21
    business data, 8
    concurrent, 79, 136, 168
    data, definition, 6
    distributed, 86–91, 338–340
    information, 7
    network, 86–91, 329–340
    on-line, 18
    program, 430–431
    real-time, 20
    word, 11
Processor:
    back-end, 329
    front-end, 329
    high-end, 78
    low-end, 78
Production department, 457
Program:
    applications, 162–165, 354, 356, 408–427
    control, 430
    compiler, 432
    definition, 15
    design language (PDL), 427
    maintenance, 357
    processing, 430
    stored, 57, 408–410
    utility, 166–167, 432–434
Programmable read-only memory (PROM), 150
Programmer: 7
    definition, 7
    skill levels, 29
Programmed Inquiry Learning or Teaching (PILOT), 520
Programmer trainee, 29
Programming group, 28
PROM, 150
Prompt, 176, 178
Proof inscriber, 239–240
Protocol, 319
Pseudocode, 380
Pulse train, 314
Punched card data processing (PCDP), D-5-7
Purpose classification, 70

Quad density, 148
Query languages, 482

RAM, 141, 149–150
Random access memory (RAM), 141, 149–150

RANDOMIZE, A-39
Randomizing, 294
Read only memory (ROM), 150
READ statement, A-8, A-12, A-24
Read-write head, 144, 279, 281–284
Reader-sorter, 49, 239, 241
Real-time processing, 20
Real storage, 435
Record:
    definition, 41
    blocked, 274, 278
    unblocked, 273–274
Redundant data, 478
Reference manual, 26
Register, 213–217
Relatability of data, 479
Relational data structure, 486
REM statement, A-11
Remote cluster controller, 325
Remote job entry (RJE), 238
Remote sites, 329
Repeaters, 312
Repetition, flowchart, 369
Report generators, 482, 526
Report Program Generator, 417–419
Reserved words, A-3
Resource management facility (RMF), 539
Resource sharing, 86
Response time, 83
RETURN key, 175
RETURN, B-19
Right justification, 105
Ring network, 336
RJE, 237–238
RMF, 539
RND in BASIC, A-34–35
Robot, 72, 190–191, 557–558, 575
Roberts, Ed, 132
ROM, 150
Root, 485
Rotational delay, 280
RPG, 417–419
Rule in decision table, 392
Run mode, 61
Running in parallel, 82

Sales department, 455
Satellites in data communication, 309–311, 313
Satellite Business Systems (SBS), 310
SAVE, 179
SBS, 310
Scheduler:
    priority, 431
    sequential, 431
Schema, 481
Scientific data processing, 9
Scrolling, 138

Computers, Inc.; (d) Courtesy of Hewlett-Packard; (e) Courtesy of Apple Computers, Inc. **Fig. 2.7** Courtesy of Texas Instruments. **Fig. 2.9** Courtesy of NCR Corporation. **Fig. 2.10** (a) Courtesy of Epson America, Inc.; (b) and (c) Courtesy of Hewlett-Packard. **Fig. 2.11** (a) Courtesy of Versatec; (b) Courtesy of NCR Corporation. **Fig. 2.12** Courtesy of the Amdahl Corporation. **Fig. 2.14** Courtesy of NCR Corporation. **Chapter 3** Courtesy of Xerox Corporation. **Fig. 3.2** Ford Motor Company Photo. **Fig. 3.3** Photos courtesy of Apple Computers, Inc. **Fig. 3.5** Courtesy of Zilog Corporation. **Fig. 3.6** Courtesy of Honeywell. **Fig. 3.7** Courtesy of Digital Equipment Corporation. **Fig. 3.8** Reprinted with the permission of International Business Machines Corporation. **Fig. 3.9** Courtesy of Cray Research, Inc. **Fig. 3.10** Courtesy of Cray Research, Inc. **Fig. A-1 and A-2** Courtesy of Bechtel, Inc. **Chapter 4** Courtesy of Hewlett-Packard. **Chapter 5** Woodfin Camp and Associates. Photographer John Blaustein. **Fig. 5.1** (a) Courtesy of Atari; (b) Courtesy of Hewlett-Packard. **Fig. 5.2** Courtesy of Rolm, Inc. **Fig. 5.3** Courtesy of Digital Equipment Corporation. **Fig. 5.4** Courtesy of Dataproducts Corporation. **Fig. 5.5** (a) Photo by Jerry Bushey; (b) Courtesy of Morrow, Inc.; (c) Courtesy of Memorex. **Fig. 5.6** Courtesy of Interphase Corporation. **Fig. 5.9** Courtesy of Zilog. **Chapter 6** Courtesy of Hewlett-Packard. **Fig. 6.1** Courtesy of Noumenon Corporation. **Fig. 6.2** Courtesy of Borland International. **Fig. 6.6** Courtesy of Commodore. **Fig. 6.7** Courtesy of Apple Computers, Inc. **Chapter 7** Courtesy of Sperry Univac Corporation. **Fig. 7.1** (a) and (b) Courtesy of the NCR Corporation. **Fig. 7.4** Courtesy of AT&T. **Fig. 7.18** Courtesy of The Amdahl Corporation. **Fig. 7.20** Courtesy of Cray Research, Inc. **Chapter 8** Courtesy of Firestone. **Fig. 8.1** Courtesy of NCR Corporation. **Fig. 8.5** (a)and (b) Courtesy of NCR Corporation. **Fig. 8.6** Courtesy of Infortex, Inc. **Fig. 8.7** Courtesy of NCR Corporation. **Fig. 8.8** Courtesy of Durango Systems, Inc. **Fig. 8.9** Courtesy of DTC. **Fig. 8.10** Courtesy of Ramteck. **Fig. 8.11** Reprinted with the permission of International Business Machines Corporation. **Fig. 8.13** Courtesy of NCR Corporation. **Fig. 8.14** Courtesy of NCR Corporation. **Fig. 8.16** Courtesy of NCR Corporation. **Fig. 8.18** Courtesy of Xerox, Inc. **Fig. 8.19** (b) Courtesy of Epson America, Inc. **Fig. 8.21** Courtesy of NCR Corporation. **Fig. 8.22** (a) Courtesy of Epson America, Inc. (b) Courtesy of MSI. **Fig. 8.23** Courtesy of Digital Equipment Corporation. **Fig. 8.24** Courtesy of G.E. Calma Corporation. **Fig. 8.25** (a) Courtesy of Hewlett-Packard. **Fig. 8.26** (a) and (b) Courtesy of Versatec. **Chapter 9** Courtesy of Optical Storage International. **Fig. 9.1** (a) Courtesy of Memorex; (b) Courtesy of Vertex Peripherals. **Fig. 9.2** (a) Reprinted with the permission of International Business Machines Corporation. **Fig. 9.8** Courtesy of Braegen Corporation. **Fig. 9.9** Courtesy of Armco, Inc. **Fig. 9.12** (a) Courtesy of Memorex. **Fig. 9.13** Courtesy of Memorex. **Fig. 9.14** Courtesy of Memorex. **Fig. 9.15** Courtesy of Eastman Kodak Company. **Fig. 9.16** Reprinted with the permission of International Business Machines Corporation. **Chapter 10** Courtesy of Rolm. **Fig. 10.1** (a) and (b) Courtesy of MSI Corporation; (c) Courtesy of Xerox Corporation. **Fig. 10.2** Taurus Photos. Photo by W. Wright. **Fig. 10.3** Taurus Photos. Photo by Duncan. **Fig. 10.4** Courtesy of AT&T. **Fig. 10.5** Courtesy of the San Francisco Examiner. **Fig. 10.7** (a) Courtesy of Versatec, Inc.; (b) Courtesy of Rolm. **Fig. 10.14** Courtesy of Memorex. **Fig. 10.17** Courtesy of Rolm. **Fig. 10.18** Courtesy of the Amdahl Corporation. **Fig. 10.21** Courtesy of Xerox Corporation. **Fig. 10.22** Courtesy of Xerox Corporation. **Fig. 10.23** (a) and (b) Courtesy of Rolm. **Fig. 10.27** Courtesy of Versatec. **Chapter 11** Courtesy of Amdahl Corporation. **Chapter 12** Courtesy of Wang. **Chapter 13** Woodfin Camp and Associates. Photographer David Burnett. **Chapter 14** Courtesy of the NCR Corporation. **Chapter 15** Taurus Photos. Photographer Mikki Ansin. **Chapter 16** Courtesy of Honeywell Inc. **Fig. 16.1** Courtesy of AT&T. **Fig. 16.2** Courtesy of AT&T. **Fig. 16.3** Courtesy of AT&T. **Fig. 16.4** Courtesy of Jerry Bushey. **Fig. 16.5** Courtesy of Intel Corporation. **Fig. 16.6** Courtesy of Sperry Univac Corporation. **Chapter 17** Taurus Photos.

Photographer Laima Druskis. **Fig. 17.1** Fran Heyl Associates. Photo by Dan McCoy. **Fig. 17.2** Stock, Boston. **Fig. 17.3** Courtesy of Quotron. **Fig. 17.4** Fran Heyl Associates. Photo by Dan McCoy. **Fig. 17.5** Reprinted with the permission of International Business Machines Corporation. **Chapter 18** Black Star. Photographer Robert Knowles. **Fig. 18.1** Courtesy of Hewlett-Packard. **Fig. 18.2** Courtesy of Hewlett-Packard. **Fig. 18.3** Courtesy of AT&T. **Appendix D. Fig. D.1** Reprinted with the permission of International Business Machines Corporation. **Fig. D.2** Reprinted with the permission of International Business Machines Corporation. **Fig. D.3** Reprinted with the permission of International Business Machines Corporation. **Fig. D.5** Reprinted with the permission of International Business Machines Corporation. **Fig. D.6** (a) Reprinted with the permission of International Business Machines Corporation; (b) Photo by Jerry Bushey. **Fig. D.7** Reprinted with the permission of International Business Machines Corporation. **Fig. D.8** Reprinted with the permission of International Business Machines Corporation. **Fig. D.9** (a) Courtesy of Sperry Univac Corporation; (b) Reprinted with the permission of International Business Machines Corporation. **Fig. D.10** Courtesy of Sperry Univac Corporation. **Fig. D.11** (a) Courtesy of Sperry Univac Corporation. **Fig. D.12** Courtesy of International Business Machines Corporation. **Fig. D.13** Courtesy of International Business Machines Corporation. **Fig. D.14** Courtesy of International Business Machines Corporation. **Fig. D.15** Courtesy of The Department of Navy.

Color Galleries Credits

Frontmatter Photos: p. i. Fran Heyl Associates. Photo by Dan McCoy. **p. ii.** *Top:* Courtesy of Atari. *Bottom:* Fran Heyl Associates. Photo by Dan McCoy. **p. iv.** *Top:* Reprinted with the permission of International Business Machines Corporation. *Bottom Left:* Courtesy of AT&T. *Bottom Right:* Courtesy of Perkin-Elmer. **p. v.** *Top Left:* Courtesy of AT&T. *Top Right:* Courtesy of Honeywell Inc. *Bottom:* Courtesy of AT&T. **p. vi.** *Top Left:* Courtesy of Chromatics, Inc. *Top Right:* Courtesy of Atari. *Bottom Right:* Courtesy of Perkin-Elmer. **p. vii.** Courtesy of Hewlett-Packard. **p. viii.** *Top Left:* Fran Heyl Associates. Photo by Dan McCoy. *Top Right:* Courtesy of Hewlett-Packard. **p. ix.** Fran Heyl Associates. Photo by Dan McCoy. **p. x.** *Top Left:* Courtesy of Commodore. **p. xi.** *Top Left:* Courtesy of National Semiconductor. *Top Right:* Courtesy of Optical Storage International. **p. xii.** NASA photo. **p. xiii.** Courtesy of Paradyne Corporation. **p. xiv.** *Top Left:* Peter Arnold, Inc. Photographer John Zoiner. *Top Right:* Woodfin Camp and Associates. Photographer Sepp Seitz. **p. xv.** Courtesy of the Braegen Corporation. **p. xvi.** *Top Left:* Fran Heyl Associates. Photo by Dan McCoy. *Top Right:* Reprinted with the permission of International Business Machines Corporation. **Galley 1: Computers In Everyday Life. 1.** Woodfin Camp and Associates. Photo by David Burnett. **2.** Photo by Jerry Bushey. **3.** Woodfin Camp and Associates. Photo by Chuck O'Rear. **4.** Peter Arnold, Inc. Photo by John Zoiner. **5.** Black Star. Photo by Mathew Naythons. **6.** Black Star. Photo by Dennis Brack. **7.** Taurus Photos. **8.** Photo by Jerry Bushey. **9.** Taurus Photos. Photo by L.L.T. Rhodes. **10 and 11.** Courtesy of National Cash Register. **12 and 13.** Courtesy of Apple Computers, Inc. **14 and 15.** Fran Heyl Associates. Photos by Dan McCoy. **16 and 17.** Courtesy of Texas Instruments. **18, 19, and 20.** Courtesy of Apple Computers, Inc. **21.** Courtesy of Radio Shack—A division of Tandy Corporation. **22.** Courtesy of Apple Computers, Inc. **23.** Woodfin Camp and Associates. Photo by John Blaustein. **Galley 2: Primary Storage. 1.** Courtesy of Hewlett-Packard. **2.** Courtesy of Intel. **3.** Courtesy of Hewlett-Packard. **4.** Courtesy of National Semiconductor. **5.** Courtesy of Intel. **6-9.** Courtesy of Hewlett-Packard. **10.** Courtesy of Intel. **11.** Courtesy of National Semiconductor. **12.** Courtesy of Hewlett-Packard. **13.** Courtesy of National Cash Register. **14.** Courtesy of National Semiconductor. **15.** Courtesy of Intel. **16.** Courtesy